THE ECONOMY OF
BRITISH AMERICA,
1607–1789

NEEDS AND OPPORTUNITIES
FOR STUDY

The Omohundro Institute of
Early American History and Culture
is sponsored jointly by
The College of William and Mary
and The Colonial Williamsburg Foundation.

NEEDS AND OPPORTUNITIES FOR STUDY SERIES

Whitfield J. Bell, Jr.
Early American Science

William N. Fenton
American Indian and White Relations to 1830
with a bibliography by L. H. Butterfield, Wilcomb E. Washburn,
and William N. Fenton

Bernard Bailyn
Education in the Forming of American Society

Walter Muir Whitehill
The Arts in Early American History
with a bibliography by Wendell D. Garrett
and Jane N. Garrett

Brooke Hindle
Technology in Early American History
with a directory by Lucius F. Ellsworth

John J. McCusker and Russell R. Menard
The Economy of British America, 1607–1789

The Mother Country, or Mercantilism Personified:
"Europe Supported by Africa & America."

Engraved by William Blake, ca. 1796, this picture appeared as Plate LXXX in J[ohn] G. Stedman, *Narrative of a Five Years' Expedition, against the Revolted Negroes of Surinam in Guiana, on the Wild Coast of South America, from the Year 1772, to 1777* (London, 1796). While Africa and America may be supporting the rather more demure and languorous Europe, she is clearly wealthier (witness the necklace) and more powerful (witness her grasp of the rope that links the three together and the servile armbands on her sister continents). Compare the frontispiece to volume I of Malachy Postlethwayt, ed., *The Universal Dictionary of Trade and Commerce* (London, 1751–1755). Engraved by Charles Mosley, it shows a female Britannia being courted by four other women representing Africa, America, Asia, and Europe. Courtesy the British Library.

The Economy of
British America,
1607–1789

With Supplementary Bibliography

John J. McCusker & Russell R. Menard

Published for the Omohundro
Institute of Early American History and Culture
by the University of North Carolina Press
Chapel Hill and London

© 1985, 1991 The University of North Carolina Press

Manufactured in the United States of America

02 01   6 5 4 3

Library of Congress Cataloging-in-Publication Data

McCusker, John J.
The economy of British America, 1607–1789,
with supplementary bibliography
John J. McCusker, Russell R. Menard.
(Needs and opportunities for study series)
Essay first presented at a conference held in Williams-
burg at the Cascades Conference Center on Oct. 9–10, 1980.
p.   cm.
Includes index.
ISBN 0-8078-4351-2 (pbk. : alk. paper)
1. United States—Economic conditions—To 1865.
2. Great Britain—Colonies—America—
Economic conditions.
I. Menard, Russell R.   II. Institute of Early American
History and Culture (Williamsburg, Va.)
III. Title.
HC104.M38   1991

For our parents, in gratitude—

John J. McCusker and Helen Esse McCusker
Russell R. Menard and Marjorie F. Menard

FOREWORD

This present volume marks the revival of the Needs and Opportunities for Study series of the Institute of Early American History and Culture. From the early 1950s through the mid-1960s the Institute conducted a series of conferences, attended by a small number of invited scholars, designed to explore subjects within the early American period that seemed neglected in current scholarship or exhibited clear signs of arousing renewed interest. At each conference discussion centered on an essay prepared in advance by one or more of the participants and devoted to an examination of the state of the subject and the prospects for future work. One of the principal results of the earlier conferences was the publication of a series of volumes that included a revised version of the conference essay and an accompanying bibliography. Over a ten-year period five such publications appeared under Institute auspices, embracing the subjects of the natural sciences, Indian-white relations, the arts, education, and technology. They quickly established themselves as some of the most influential titles published by the Institute, and indeed still enjoy, as much as twenty-five years after publication, continuing utility for students of early American history.

The long hiatus in the publication of additional Needs and Opportunities volumes was by no means the consequence of a decision to abandon the series. On the contrary, on several occasions members of the staff explored with other early American scholars the prospects for organizing other conferences and publishing additional volumes in the series. We found ourselves in every instance concluding that the time was not right for pursuing any of the themes that we had considered. In retrospect I think we came to see that the early American field had expanded so rapidly and attracted so much more attention from scholars that it was increasingly difficult to identify neglected aspects of the subject. Consequently the Institute's major conference activities turned in other directions, more often toward conferences that explored the "state of the art" of a given subject on which major new work had already begun to appear, for example, a 1974 conference on the seventeenth-century Chesapeake.

Nevertheless, the possibility of reviving the Needs and Opportunities series continued to be an attractive one. A suggestion in 1973 from Professor Simeon J. Crowther of the Department of Economics, California State University, Long Beach, that early American economic history might offer a particularly inviting field set us upon a fairly lengthy period of planning and organizing the conference that has produced this volume. At the time those discussions began, we were fortunate to have both a former and a current Institute Fellow who were actively interested in economic history, John J. McCusker, then as now at the University of Maryland, College Park, and Russell R. Menard, then soon to leave the Institute for his present post at the University of Minnesota.

On the basis of our early discussions with them and with Professor Jacob Price of the University of Michigan we agreed to undertake the organization of a conference for which Professors McCusker and Menard would prepare the essay and bibliography. We held our first informal discussions at the annual meeting of the American Historical Association in Atlanta in December 1975, and continued them at a second meeting with the conference essayists in Williamsburg in the spring of 1976.

As our planning progressed, we were fortunate to find that Liberty Fund, Inc., of Indianapolis, Indiana, had a strong interest in contracting with the Institute to conduct the conference with its support. A final meeting, held in Washington in February 1979, attended by Kenneth Templeton, then executive director of Liberty Fund, Messrs. Menard, McCusker, Price, and myself, resulted in the completion of arrangements.

We agreed at that time on the format and scope of the conference. It seemed preferable to restrict the chronological limits of the conference to the period before 1790, focusing on the colonial economy and the immediate impact of the American Revolution. The national economy that began to develop under the umbrella of the federal Constitution seemed another large subject in its own right. Our decision, in keeping with past Needs and Opportunities conferences, was to invite a group of no more than twenty-five scholars, including the authors of the conference essay. We also wished to include scholars from history, economics, and related disciplines in order to represent as wide a variety of fields of interest and methodological approaches within early American economic history as possible.

Given the large number of qualified scholars whom we would have liked to include in the conference, the size of the invitation list posed a difficult problem of selection. Ultimately we completed our list and were pleased that all but one of our original invitees were able to accept. Of the final group, Professor E. James Ferguson of Queens College of the City University of New York subsequently found it necessary to withdraw because of illness, and we were sorry to lose the benefit of his expertise. The persons who attended the conference as invited participants are listed in Appendix 1, below.

The conference sessions took place in the Cascades Conference Center in Williamsburg on October 9–10, 1980, with the invited participants and a small group of local observers from the Institute, the Colonial Williamsburg Foundation, and the College of William and Mary in attendance. Mr. Templeton was also present representing Liberty Fund. All those who attended ˙generally seemed to agree that the discussions had achieved the desired degree of informality and that they had been unusually lively, wide-ranging, and productive. Professors McCusker and Menard subsequently undertook a revision and expansion of their essay and bibliography in the light of the discussion and comment that had occurred during the conference sessions. The final result is the present volume.

The outcome of the conference and the publication of this volume in my judgment fully justify our sense that economic history was a particularly apt subject for the employment of the format of our earlier Needs and Opportunities conferences. Certainly, as the distinguished list of conference participants would suggest, important work was already being done in the field. Nevertheless, vital areas of early American economic history were then and still remain relatively unexplored in current scholarship, including some of the regional colonial economies, particularly that of New England, the whole subject of domestic and household economy, and aspects of colonial finance and money supply. Moreover, the impact of recent demographic and social history on all historical study had clearly raised important questions about the larger organizing themes for economic history, in particular the relative weight to be assigned to the roles of the transatlantic market and internal growth in the development of the colonial economy. A growing emphasis on cliometric approaches to the study of economic history also had strongly influenced early American economic history, perhaps even leaving open the question of the extent to which future work would be accomplished by economists more than historians, or by a fuller collaboration between the two. To say too much here regarding some of these major interpretative or methodological questions or about specific areas most in need of further study would be needlessly to anticipate much of what Professors McCusker and Menard discuss in the text of the volume. It is sufficient to observe that I believe that they, as a consequence both of their own extensive work and also of the suggestions and advice they received from the conference participants, have achieved an admirable survey of the subject and have effectively opened up numerous questions for future research. The result is a volume that should not only prove helpful to scholars especially interested in early American history but also make some relatively complex aspects of the subject much clearer to a wider group of readers.

By now it must be rather apparent that the contributions of John Mc-

Cusker and Russell Menard have been indispensable to this undertaking from its very inception to its successful outcome in the publication of this volume. Some special acknowledgment is certainly also due Jacob Price, who not only made a strong contribution as a participant in the conference but whose advice and counsel was also extremely valuable in the planning stages. Particular thanks are due, too, to Liberty Fund for its generous sponsorship and for the free hand that the Institute enjoyed in organizing and holding the conference. That the conference itself proceeded so smoothly owes a great deal to the efforts of Patricia C. Blatt and Conrad E. Wright of the Institute staff for their hard work on local arrangements and the preparation of advance copies of the conference essay. Ruth Vaughan, also of the Institute staff, prepared a working transcript of conference discussions that greatly facilitated the authors' revisions. Finally, the other critical ingredient in the successful outcome of the conference was the contribution of all of the invited participants and of many of the local observers as well, whose suggestions and comments are incorporated throughout the volume.

Thad W. Tate, *Director*

CONTENTS

TABLES

FIGURES

PREFACE

The readers of any work deserve to have the authors make explicit what they think it is about. This is especially appropriate for a study that is neither of the two "usual" kinds of history book. It is not a monograph; it is not a grand synthesis. It is, instead, a simple summary of the known, designed both to provoke the exploration of the unknown and to offer the explorer guidance along the way.

We presume that the traveler has a general familiarity with the lay of the land. Our summary will add an economic dimension to his or her understanding of the political, social, or military history of the British colonies during the seventeenth and eighteenth centuries. As these comments suggest, this is not a complete economic history of Great Britain or its colonies. That remains to be written. When it is written, we will be delighted if our efforts helped a bit.

This book is very much a corporate enterprise. Not only is it jointly authored, the result of discussions, writings, and rewritings to which both authors contributed equally, but it is also directly dependent upon the work of many others. While each of us is willing to take the blame for the mistakes that he has made, neither is able to claim credit for the parts that turn out well. Where we stand tall, it is only because we stand on the shoulders of earlier scholars whose works we have used. Gigantes autem erant super terram in diebus illis (Genesis 6:4). Where we stumble, it is our own fault, but we ask for understanding, recalling the words of Robert Recorde, the author of the first popular English treatise on geometry, *The Pathway to Knowledg* ([London, 1551]): "Excuse me, Gentle Reader if oughte be amise, straung paths ar not troden al truly at the first: the way muste needes be comberous, wher none hathe gone before."

To help keep us on the right track, we have been fortunate in our friends. The director of the Institute of Early American History and Culture, Thad W. Tate, and the former editor of publications, Norman Fiering, have lent us support and encouragement at every stage in the planning and execution of this book. Dr. Tate in his Foreword has thanked all those who read and commented on a preliminary version of this text. We warmly second his sentiments and suggest that two of those whom he mentions did extra duty for which we are particularly thankful. Prof. Jacob M. Price joined us early in the planning for the volume and the conference and has read and commented upon more than one draft of the book, as has Prof. Stanley L. Engerman. Dante would surely have found a special place in his paradise for these four if he had been as lucky as we in having them to call upon for advice and assistance in the composition of his *Commedia*.

There are others to thank. Liberty Fund, Inc., of Indianapolis, Indiana, sponsored the writing of the first draft of the book and the conference at which we discussed it. The National Endowment for the Humanities through the American Enterprise Institute, the American Historical Association by means of an Albert J. Beveridge Grant for Research in American History, the American Antiquarian Society with a Fred Harris Daniels Fellowship, the American Philosophical Society, the University of Maryland, and the University of Minnesota have all supported our efforts. Gary J. Hoag, Nancy Goddin Miller, Linda M. Abrams, Craig Donegan, and Linda E. and Lisa E. Emmerich checked bibliographical references for us. Diana B. McCusker, Janet H. Aron, Carol Kaltenbaugh, Sue Caves, Margaret Beegle, and Wordstar faithfully and accurately produced draft after draft of text and notes. The staff at the Institute of Early American History and Culture, especially Conrad E. Wright, Patricia C. Blatt, Cynthia Carter Ayres, Ruth Vaughan, and Doris Leisch, prepared the version presented at the 1980 conference. Thomas Doerflinger and David L. Ammerman as visiting editors of publications and Cynthia Carter Ayres as project editor helped to see the book through its final stages. Numerous friends and colleagues have offered advice and encouragement. Our wives and our children—Kathleen, Elizabeth, and Michael Menard; Diana, John III, Patrick, and Margaret McCusker—have all borne well, even lovingly, the trials known only to those who have a writer in residence. We dedicate the book to our parents. We are grateful to them all.

ABBREVIATIONS

Works are only cited in full the first time they are mentioned. Readers are referred to the Bibliography for complete citations.

Agric. Hist.	*Agricultural History*
AHR	*American Historical Review*
Am. Acad. Pol. and Soc. Sci., *Annals*	American Academy of Political and Social Science, *Annals*
Am. Antiq. Soc., *Procs.*	American Antiquarian Society, *Proceedings*
Am. Econ. Rev.	*American Economic Review*
Am. Neptune	*American Neptune*
Am. Phil. Soc., *Procs.*	American Philosophical Society, *Proceedings*
Assoc. Am. Geographers, *Annals*	Association of American Geographers, *Annals*
Bus. Hist. Rev.	*Business History Review*
Can. Jour. Econ. and Pol. Sci.	*Canadian Journal of Economics and Political Science*
Can. Rev. Am. Studies	*Canadian Review of American Studies*
Col. Soc. Mass., *Pubs.: Trans.*	Colonial Society of Massachusetts, *Publications: Transactions*
Econ. Devel. and Cult. Change	*Economic Development and Cultural Change*
Econ. Hist. Rev.	*Economic History Review*
Econ. Inquiry	*Economic Inquiry*
Eng. Hist. Rev.	*English Historical Review*
Essex Inst., *Hist. Colls.*	Essex Institute, *Historical Collections*

Explorations Econ. Hist.	*Explorations in Economic History*
Explorations Entrep. Hist.	*Explorations in Entrepreneurial History*
Ga. Hist. Qtly.	*Georgia Historical Quarterly*
Geographical Rev.	*Geographical Review*
Hist. Jour.	*Historical Journal*
Hist. Methods	*Historical Methods*
Hist. Reflections	*Historical Reflections/Reflections Historique*
Hist. Soc.	*Histoire Sociale/Social History*
JAH	*Journal of American History*
Jam. Hist. Rev.	*Jamaican Historical Review*
JIH	*Journal of Interdisciplinary History*
Jour. Am. Studies	*Journal of American Studies*
Jour. Barbados Museum and Hist. Soc.	*Journal of the Barbados Museum and Historical Society*
Jour. Carib. Hist.	*Journal of Caribbean History*
Jour. Econ. and Bus. Hist.	*Journal of Economic and Business History*
Jour. Econ. Hist.	*Journal of Economic History*
Jour. Family Hist.	*Journal of Family History*
Jour. Hist. Geography	*Journal of Historical Geography*
Jour. Imperial and Commonwealth Hist.	*Journal of Imperial and Commonwealth History*
Jour. Marriage and Family	*Journal of Marriage and the Family*
Jour. Pol. Econ.	*Journal of Political Economy*
Jour. Soc. Hist.	*Journal of Social History*
Jour. So. Hist.	*Journal of Southern History*

Manchester School Econ. and Soc. Studies	*Manchester School of Economic and Social Studies*
Md. Hist. Mag.	*Maryland Historical Magazine*
N. Am. Soc. Oceanic Hist., Procs.	North American Society for Oceanic History, Proceedings
N.C. Hist. Rev.	*North Carolina Historical Review*
NEHGR	*New England Historical and Genealogical Register*
NEQ	*New England Quarterly*
N.Y. Hist.	*New York History*
N.-Y. Hist. Soc. Qtly.	*New-York Historical Society Quarterly*
Pa. Hist.	*Pennsylvania History*
Perspectives Am. Hist.	*Perspectives in American History*
PMHB	*Pennsylvania Magazine of History and Biography*
Pol. Sci. Qtly.	*Political Science Quarterly*
Qtly. Jour. Econ.	*Quarterly Journal of Economics*
Regional Econ. Hist. Research Center, *Working Papers*	Regional Economic History Research Center, Working Papers
Research Econ. Hist.	*Research in Economic History*
Revs. Am. Hist.	*Reviews in American History*
S.C. Hist. Assoc., *Procs.*	South Carolina Historical Association, *Proceedings*
S.C. Hist. Mag.	*South Carolina Historical Magazine*
Sci. Am.	*Scientific American*
So. Atlantic Qtly.	*South Atlantic Quarterly*
Soc. and Econ. Studies	*Social and Economic Studies*
Soc. Sci. Hist.	*Social Science History*
So. Econ. Jour.	*Southern Economic Journal*

So. Studies	*Southern Studies*
VMHB	*Virginia Magazine of History and Biography*
WMQ	*William and Mary Quarterly*

THE ECONOMY OF

BRITISH AMERICA,

1607–1789

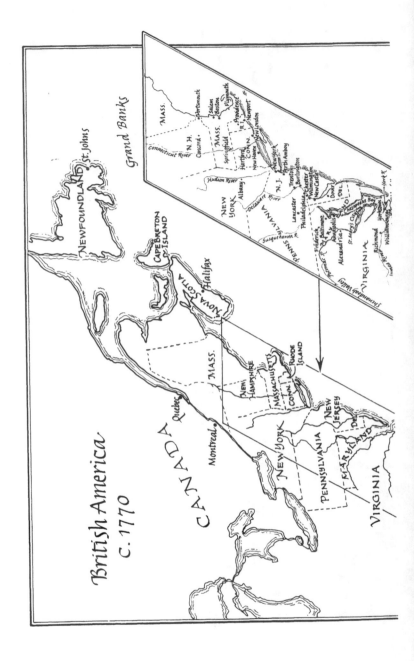

Map by Richard J. Stinely. (Adapted from maps in Lester J. Cappon *et al.*, eds., *Atlas of Early American History: The Revolutionary Era, 1760–1790* [Princeton, N.J., 1976], 7, 74.)

British America c. 1770

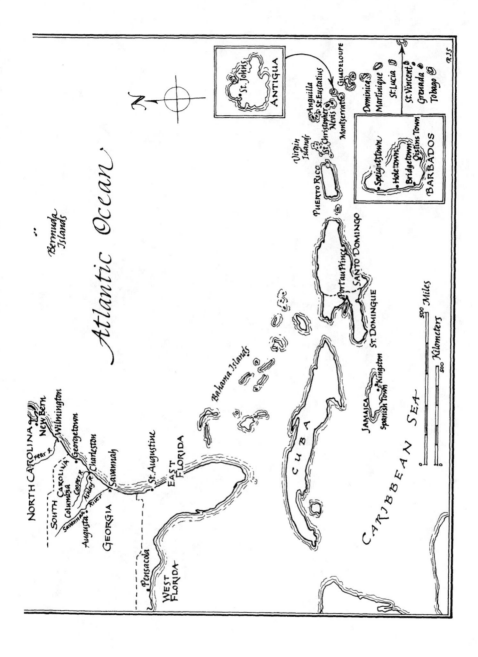

INTRODUCTION

THE PLAN OF

THE ARGUMENT

"The colony of a civilized nation," Adam Smith observed on the eve of the American Revolution, "which takes possession, either of a waste country, or of one so thinly inhabited, that the natives easily give place to new settlers, advances more rapidly to wealth and greatness than any other human society."[1] Smith's casual dismissal of the destruction of native American culture necessary to that "advance" and the implied pejorative contrast between "civilized" Europeans and "natives" is now jarring, but he did capture the essence of colonial economic history during the seventeenth and eighteenth centuries. And, as Smith knew, nowhere was that rise to "wealth and greatness" more rapid than in the colonies of British America.

Our concern is to examine that rise, not through a narrative account or an analytical history, but through a survey of the state of the art, an assessment of where we stand, where we would like to be, and how we can get there from here. By focusing on the literature, we hope to convey the vitality of the field, the liveliness of debate among practitioners, the rapid pace with which new evidence and new methods are challenging (and occasionally confirming) conventional wisdom, and the substantial opportunities that await scholars. Understanding of the economic history of British America seems on the verge of a transformation; this book intends to nudge it along and to suggest directions.

As even a passing familiarity with the historiography of the American economy in the nineteenth century indicates, the engine of change is the "new economic history," the post-1950s emphasis on quantitative and behavioral methods. The new approach goes far beyond simple counting. New or old, economic history demands numbers. Despite the label "cliometrics," the distinguishing characteristics of the new economic history

1. Adam Smith, *An Inquiry into the Nature and Causes of the Wealth of Nations* (1776), ed. R. H. Campbell, A. S. Skinner, and W. B. Todd (Oxford, 1976), II, 564.

are the explicit application of theory to the past and the testing of hypotheses through statistical analysis.

So far, cliometrics has not penetrated very deeply into the history of early British America. Almost all the work in the field now completed and most of that currently under way is descriptive, aimed at measurement and narration, at getting the facts right, rather than at econometric analysis. In part, this is as it should be: careful, detailed empirical work demanding patient grubbing among reluctant documents is essential to good economic history, and an enormous amount of data on the colonies of British America awaits collecting and compiling. And there are limits to theory, as even the most committed cliometricians now admit. Still, one of the principal opportunities in the field is the application of the methods of the new economic history. Cliometricians are just now turning their attention to the colonies of British America; once they arrive in force the terrain will take on a different look.[2]

Following the path laid out by cliometrics can be dangerous, of course. The chief danger is a tendency toward "pure economy," toward the study of those aspects of colonial life most amenable to statistical analysis in isolation from their broader context. We advocate the systematic, quantitative study of market behavior, but we recognize that many questions—some would argue the pivotal questions—do not lend themselves to such a method, or at least not yet. Further, one of the strengths of early

2. If the health of a field is inversely related to the proportion of articles concerned to define its distinguishing features and catalog its accomplishments, cliometrics is now recovering nicely from a very rough childhood. For a recent assessment, see Donald N. McCloskey, "The Achievements of the Cliometric School," *Journal of Economic History*, XXXVIII (1978), 13–28. Classic articles on the field include John R. Meyer and Alfred H. Conrad, "Economic Theory, Statistical Inference, and Economic History," *ibid.*, XVII (1957), 524–544; Robert William Fogel, "The Specification Problem in Economic History," *ibid.*, XXVII (1967), 283–308; and Lance E. Davis, "'And It Will Never Be Literature'—The New Economic History: A Critique," *Explorations in Entrepreneurial History*, 2d Ser., VI (1968), 75–92. Peter D. McClelland, *Causal Explanation and Model Building in History, Economics, and the New Economic History* (Ithaca, N.Y., 1975), provides a rigorous introduction to the logic of historical inquiry from the perspective of a social scientist. Robert William Fogel and Stanley L. Engerman, eds., *The Reinterpretation of American Economic History* (New York, 1971), although somewhat dated, remains a useful anthology of essays, most of them cliometric. Two textbooks also deserve mention. The essays in Lance E. Davis, Richard A. Easterlin, and William N. Parker, eds., *American Economic Growth: An Economist's History of the United States* (New York, 1972), provide often masterly overviews of the growth of the U.S. economy, while Susan Previant Lee and Peter Passell, *A New Economic View of American History* (New York, 1979), is an able summary of recent cliometric contributions.

American history, a main source of its liveliness and creativity, has been its ability to avoid the fragmentation into subdisciplines that has accompanied the arrival of cliometrics in other fields. Early American historians using different methods, sources, and rules of evidence still try to keep in touch with the field as a whole, to explore implications beyond their immediate concerns, to consider points of intersection between various lines of investigation, in short, to talk to each other.

We hope to contribute to the conversation. Thus we have tried to remain sensitive to issues in economic history that are difficult to quantify, to questions of "political economy" and the creative role of entrepreneurs as well as to interactions between the "economic," "social," and "cultural" dimensions of colonial life. It is a truism that human behavior is a "seamless web," that people do not segregate their activities into compartments that conform to the division of labor within the academy. It is no less a truism that abstraction and segregation are essential to understanding that behavior. We hope to have struck the proper balance between these realities, between the fact of interconnectedness and the necessity for discrimination. Whether that balance is a proper one is for the reader to judge.

The issue of boundaries must trouble anyone who attempts a general essay in economic history. What are the proper concerns of the discipline? These could be identified in a practical, empirical fashion as including whatever subjects or issues currently interest economic historians. This definition, though, seems almost whimsical, both too restrictive and too broad. A second definition focuses on method: the domain of economic history encompasses any past process, event, or issue that can be illuminated by economic theory. But this characterization, in addition to being highly controversial, is so open-ended that it fails to set any limits. We have adopted a third approach, which is to focus on the production and distribution of wealth. "Getting and spending" is, after all, the central interest of most economic historians. Moreover, this substantive definition provides guidelines and sets priorities. At the same time, the production and distribution of wealth can be understood more fully when placed in their broad social and political context, thus creating opportunities to study areas too often neglected by economics.

A further problem of boundaries plagues students of British America, especially those persuaded, as we are, that external trade was critical to the process of economic development. Clearly, historians of the British colonies in America cannot work effectively without some knowledge— and the deeper the better—of Europe, Africa, and the American possessions of other European nations. The British colonies grew up within an emerging Atlantic economy as Europeans burst their own boundaries and brought together once isolated regions and peoples to form a New World. British America cannot be understood apart from this larger process: developments in Europe, in Africa, and elsewhere in the Americas formed the arena within which colonists lived, constantly creating, restricting, and channeling their opportunities. Indeed, it could be maintained, following John Stuart Mill, that the economy of British America should not be studied as an entity in itself, but only as part of the British economy to which it belonged. Colonies, Mill argued,

> are hardly to be looked upon as countries, carrying on an exchange of commodities with other countries, but more properly as outlying agricultural or manufacturing establishments belonging to a larger community. Our West India colonies, for example, cannot be regarded as countries, with a productive capital of their own. . . . All the capital employed is English capital; almost all the industry is carried on for English uses. . . . The trade with the West Indies is therefore hardly to be considered as external trade, but more resembles the traffic between town and country, and is amenable to the principles of the home trade.[3]

In a sense, therefore, the concept of a colonial economy is anachronistic, the use of which goes unquestioned largely because of the postcolonial development of the United States. Nevertheless, we are persuaded that British America can be studied as an entity if the international setting is given an important part in the story. Limitations of space and of our competence prohibit comprehensive treatment of the larger Atlantic world, but we have tried to remain sensitive to developments there that shaped the colonial experience.[4]

A final comment on boundaries is necessary. In a sense, all the literature of early American history is relevant to our concern, for all aspects of human activity are affected by "getting and spending." A comprehensive bibliography of all works that, if only indirectly, bear on the economic history of British America would be long indeed and, by its lack of selectivity, not especially helpful. We have tried, in the bibliographic notes that accompany the text, to be selective but at the same time to err on the

3. John Stuart Mill, *Principles of Political Economy with Some of Their Applications to Social Philosophy* (1848), ed. W. J. Ashley (London, [1940]), 685–686.

4. Many useful points of comparison and contrast to the history of the British colonies can be found in the experiences of the rest of "America." See W. T. Easterbrook and Hugh G. T. Aitken, *Canadian Economic History* (Toronto, 1956); William L. Marr and Donald G. Paterson, *Canada: An Economic History* (Toronto, 1980); and Ciro Flamairon S. Cardoso and Héctor Pérez Brignoli, *Historia económica de América Latina* (Barcelona, 1979).

side of inclusiveness. The discussion, however, will take care to distinguish work that is central to the field and directly concerned with matters economic from that which is peripheral to the colonial economy.[5]

Several themes lend coherence and unity to this book. We are concerned first to describe the growth of the American economy, both as an extensive process (increased output flowing from gains in population and settled territory) and as an intensive development (those gains in output resulting from greater productivity). At least by a crude quantitative measure, the former was more important than the latter in colonial America. The economy of British America grew impressively in the century and a half before 1775, if only because population grew so fast. Some argue that that is the whole story, that the principal task of early American economic history is to account for the rapid growth of population and settled area, gains achieved without major changes in the organization of the economy, in per capita income, or in the distribution of wealth. We think there was more to it, however. There were important structural changes in the economy, and income per capita increased sizably. Those seem minor only if the standards of comparison are the massive changes in economic organization and the rapid gains in income associated with industrialization.

The pattern of economic change in British America varied widely by region and over time. We are additionally concerned to account for this variety. Obviously, an adequate description of differences in the pattern of growth, in the organization of the economy, and in the distribution of benefits by time and place is a prime task of economic history. Such variation also provides an analytic opportunity, a way of testing hypotheses and constructing generalizations that are at once both comprehensive and precise. An interest in such differences constitutes a second major theme of this book.

---

5. George Rogers Taylor, comp., *American Economic History before 1860*, Goldentree Bibliographies in American History (New York, 1969), remains useful but needs updating, a task we hope to fulfill. Several other bibliographies in the Goldentree series cover the same periods as our book: Alden T. Vaughan, comp., *The American Colonies in the Seventeenth Century* (New York, 1971); Jack P. Greene, comp., *The American Colonies in the Eighteenth Century, 1689–1763* (New York, 1969); John Shy, comp., *The American Revolution* (Northbrook, Ill., 1973); and E. James Ferguson, comp., *Confederation, Constitution, and Early National Period, 1781–1815* (Northbrook, Ill., 1975). Of particular use are Henrietta M. Larson, *Guide to Business History: Materials for the Study of American Business History and Suggestions for Their Use* (Cambridge, Mass., 1948), and Robert W. Lovett, *American Economic and Business History Information Sources* (Detroit, Mich., 1971). For a more general guide, see Frank Freidel, ed., *Harvard Guide to American History*, rev. ed. (Cambridge, Mass., 1974). Bibliographies of specific topics and regions are listed below, in appropriate sections.

Historians involved with the early American economy can be classified into two categories, sometimes (unfortunately) into two opposing camps. The staples approach focuses on the foreign sector of the economy, takes economic growth as its key problem, and uses as its major explanatory device the analysis of markets. The Malthusian, or frontier, tradition focuses on internal demographic processes, takes as its central problem the process of expansion of settled areas and the absence of structural change, and employs as its major dynamic the pressure of population on resources. We are convinced that both approaches are helpful, although in certain places, at certain times, and for certain questions one is often more useful than the other. Further, we are persuaded that they are not incompatible, not necessarily contending interpretations. Indeed, it is often the interaction between the pull of external markets and the push of internal population pressures that best clarifies the chief processes. This is a third major theme of our book.[6]

We believe that, for organizational purposes if for nothing else, the best discussion of the economic history of British America begins with a recognition of the overriding importance of overseas trade. Almost the entirety of colonial life was linked with overseas trade. The colonists wanted goods imported from abroad; to buy them they had to produce goods for which an export market existed abroad. In the earliest years this was almost on a one-to-one basis; only with some growth and development in the economy and with the production of individual surpluses of exportable goods did it become possible for local domestic exchanges to occur. And even then overseas trade still dominated, for domestic exchanges were linked, though indirectly, with overseas sources and markets. The fully self-sufficient yeoman farmer of colonial America is largely mythical: almost all colonists were tied to overseas trade. The staples approach is thus an excellent way to organize the economic history of British America through 1790, and it is often a powerful explanatory device.

The economy of British America was not made up of overseas trade alone. The greater part of the output of most farms (although perhaps not of most plantations) was consumed on the spot. Further, the home market steadily grew, both within individual colonies and between the several colonies, which were gradually linked through coastwise trade and migration. While such activities were shaped in important ways by the export sector, they responded also to their own internal logic.

Of special importance to production for home use, to the rise of the domestic market, and to the integration of the several colonial economies were the expansion of the population and the spread of settlement. At

6. These historiographic traditions are discussed in more detail in chap. 1, below.

first, these too were tied to the foreign sector. Colonies were established by immigration, and new arrivals accounted for a large share of total population increase in the early years. Over time, however, but sooner in some regions than in others, reproduction dominated the advance of population and territorial expansion. This did not mean that the connection between foreign trade and population increase was thereby severed. Quite the contrary. Reproductive growth supplied workers to produce for overseas customers; opportunities in market agriculture provided capital to finance migration and farm building and offered incentives to move to the edge of European settlement. But reproductive population growth also provided a new and largely internal dynamic that joined with overseas trade to shape the early American economy.

Our purpose, then, is first to set down what we think is the best current understanding of the colonial economy. We will arrange our discussion along lines suggested by the staples approach. Where the state of the art is, in our estimation, somehow deficient—whether due to inadequate investigation or to mistaken conclusions—we will indicate what we perceive to be an opportunity for further work. Moreover, at that point we will often venture a guess about what we expect such further work will reveal. It is here especially that the staples theory and the dynamics of population expansion will inform our guesses. We not only will speculate about what these investigations might reveal, but also will indicate how such opportunities can best be exploited. Our suggestions will be to both primary and secondary sources.

We think that focusing on exports, on population growth, and on settlement helps to explain more than just the narrowly economic aspects of the British Americas in the seventeenth and eighteenth centuries—and we will not be shy in hinting where economics and politics or the economy and society are closely intertwined. Nevertheless, as in all historical investigations we must limit ourselves, so we are forced to divide up for purposes of discussion a process that was highly integrated. We cannot talk about it all at once, so we make what are for us some uncomfortable decisions. Thus a circle of relationships that found the colonists engaged in production for export, that resulted in certain levels of income and wealth, that provided for the acquisition of imported commodities, and that had to be paid for by production for export must be arbitrarily divided.

We begin with what we believe are appropriate points of departure for an exploration of the early American economy. Chapter 1 considers the two interpretive frameworks—the staples approach and the frontier tradition—that organize the field and our book. In chapter 2 we discuss England as a colonizing nation, both to address "mercantilism," a summary phrase for the strategies the English pursued in the Americas, and to discuss the impact of those strategies on the development of the English economy. Chapter 3 sketches the pattern of growth in the colonial economy as a whole over the short and long haul, employing several rough quantitative indicators to suggest the dimensions, the pace, and the patterns of change. Chapter 4 offers a description of colonial trade, assesses its contribution to colonial incomes, estimates the colonial balance of payments, and stresses the centrality of commerce to the colonial economy.

One clear implication of the staples theory is that, early on at least, British America was not a single economy. Rather, there were several distinct regional economies, most of them tied more closely to Great Britain than to each other, and each distinguished from the rest by the goods it produced for export and by the ways it earned credits in the balance of payments. In the second section of this book, chapters 5 through 9, we explore that implication through studies of the major colonial regions. All of those chapters describe regional export sectors, asking how the colonists paid for the goods they imported from abroad. Attention is not confined to overseas commerce, however. We also probe relationships between foreign trade, the advance of population, the domestic sector of the economy, and the structure of society in order to suggest how production for export shaped other aspects of colonial life.

Regional differences among the colonies were so sharp and ties between them so weak that it is misleading to speak of an "American economy" or an "American population" early in the colonial period. However, the variations were patterned rather than random, the colonies were part of the same metropolitan system, and the ties between the several regions grew over time. Such considerations justify the topical organization adopted in Part III. Successive chapters treat population growth, the labor force and the pattern of settlement, wealth and welfare, imports, agriculture, manufacturing, and the role of government in the economy. This leads to some repetition of material from earlier chapters, a repetition warranted by the chance to look at basic processes from another angle.

The chapters just outlined deal with the colonial period, but the needs and opportunities for the study of the economy of early America do not stop with the American Revolution. Indeed, the movement for independence, the war, and its aftermath provide a crucial test of another claim in this book: that the export-led process of development was highly successful over the colonial period and that it promoted an economy increasingly integrated, strong, and flexible, able to function well enough independently of its metropolitan mistress. Thus we will conclude our analysis by extending chronologically our treatment of the topics and regions examined in the earlier sections. We are, of course, interested in how the economy affected and was affected by the separation from Great Britain. Perhaps nowhere in the seventeenth- and eighteenth-century history of British America are those needs and opportunities for the study of the economy greater than in the period 1775 to 1790.[7]

7. There is no easy solution to the problems of nomenclature created for the historian of early British America by the Act of Union of 1707 (Act of 6 Anne c. 40). We have tried to use "England" where we mean England and "Britain" where Britain is meant. We have confined the word "England" to the nation before 1707 unless we mean only the land of the English. Nevertheless, we have frequently, if anachronistically, used "Britain"—as in the title of the book—to refer to the entire period 1607–1790. And custom allows us to use "England" where precision would have us write "England and Wales" (pace, Cymry). Perhaps our readers will accept this explanation in the place of otherwise cumbersome circumlocutions.

Note, too, that our reference in an economic study to the period in the history of the United States from 1776 to 1790 under the title "British America" is done with malice aforethought.

PART I

POINTS OF

DEPARTURE

CHAPTER I

MALTHUS AND

THE MARKET

APPROACHES TO

THE ECONOMY OF

BRITISH AMERICA

For most economic historians of colonial America the pressing issues in the field revolve around growth and development. How can we best explain the successes of the colonial economy, the rapid expansion of population, settled area, and output, and the high per capita incomes attained by the 1770s? How do we account for regional variations in the process? Why, that is, were there such striking differences in economic organization between the several regions of British America, the North and the South, New England and the Chesapeake, the Middle Atlantic area and the Carolinas, the mainland and the island colonies? And why was the postcolonial history of each so different? Why did the northern United States develop but the South only grow?

These concerns lead, naturally, to an interest in the literature of development economics. Upon inspection, however, much of that literature seems inappropriate to the field. It is too concerned with strategy and planning, with the problems of overpopulation and scarce resources, and with the difficulties of competing in a highly industrialized and integrated world economy to serve as a useful guide to the history of colonial America. The colonies grew up with the world economy before the industrial age; they were sparsely populated and had an abundance of natural resources; at the same time, they lacked governments sufficiently powerful to control the economy. The point is not that colonial historians can safely ignore the literature of economic development, but only that those who turn to it in search of a model that will fit the empirical reality of British America are likely to be disappointed.[1]

Within the literature of development economics and early American history, however, are two traditions that have their origins in efforts to write the history of North America and that are concerned with growth in a context of abundant resources and scarce labor and capital. Both can contribute to our purpose. The Malthusian, or frontier, approach locates the central dynamic of early American history in internal demographic processes that account for the principal characteristics of the colonial economy: the rapid, extensive growth of population, of settled area, and of aggregate output combined with an absence of major structural change. The second tradition, usually described as the staples approach or, more generally, as an export-led, or "vent for surplus," growth model, attaches fundamental importance to the export of primary, resource-intensive products. It argues that the export sector played a leading role in the economy of British America and maintains that the specific character of those exports shaped the process of colonial development.

Both traditions have informed the work of many leading historians of colonial America, sometimes explicitly, more often not. We have not attempted in this chapter to make a formal statement of either thesis, but rather to comment on their histories, outline their central terms and assumptions, extract some of their implications, and suggest their utility for historians. Much of the remainder of this book follows the organization described here, tests the models against the available evidence, uses both to identify pressing research needs, and maintains that a focus on the pull of foreign markets and the push of internal population pressures can illuminate the economic history of British America.

We have emphasized in this chapter the staples approach rather than the Malthusian tradition. This is not because we are persuaded that it is the more promising of the two (although for certain issues it clearly is), but rather because the staples thesis has been defined more precisely in the literature. It thus lends itself to a more elaborate and more elegant description than does the Malthusian model. Further, an initial focus on exports provides a compelling organizational scheme, which we have followed in this book. However, we do not intend to slight the power of the

---

1. Historians of colonial America will find especially useful introductions to the issues in development economics in Albert O. Hirschman, *The Strategy of Economic Development* (New Haven, Conn., 1958); Simon Kuznets, *Toward a Theory of Economic Growth* (New York, 1968); Theodore W. Schultz, *Transforming Traditional Agriculture* (New Haven, Conn., 1964); and Stanley L. Engerman and Robert E. Gallman, "U.S. Economic Growth, 1783–1860," *Research in Economic History*, VIII (1983), 1–46. Gerald M. Meier, *Leading Issues in Economic Development*, 3d ed. (New York, 1976), is an excellent anthology.

frontier tradition in early American history. Both approaches are essential to understanding the colonial economy, and often it is in the relationships between population growth and external demand that answers to the most interesting questions will be found.

Although one could, as is often the case with current economic theory, locate the origins of the staples approach in the *Wealth of Nations*,[2] the tradition begins with the work of Harold Innis, a Canadian economic historian. Innis did little in the way of explicit theorizing. He used the staples approach not as a precise analytical tool with specific, limited purposes, but rather as a unifying theme that would permit an integrated interpretation of Canadian development. His work has been justly characterized as more technological history than economic theory. Nonetheless, he did conduct a series of case studies of various commodities that served as an important empirical base on which more-theoretical accounts could rest. Further, Innis demonstrated the power of a focus on staples for the economic history of regions invaded by Europeans (called "new countries") where the aboriginal population proved small or easily displaced, and he showed how, within similar social contexts, different export products had different effects upon growth.[3]

Recent work, especially by Robert Baldwin, Melville Watkins, and Richard Caves, has extracted the major implications of the staples tradition and provided an explicit theoretical framework.[4] At the same time,

2. See especially Smith's summary comments in the *Wealth of Nations* on the impact of foreign trade on growth (I, 376–427). Smith, of course, opposed the encouragement of exports, especially manufactures, at the expense of the domestic and agricultural sectors of the economy. Exports played a central role in mercantilist theory. See chap. 2, below, and Joseph J. Spengler, "Mercantilist and Physiocratic Growth Theory," in Bert F. Hoselitz *et al.*, *Theories of Economic Growth* (Glencoe, Ill., 1960), 3–64.

3. Innis's principal works on the impact of staples on Canadian economic development include *The Fur Trade in Canada: An Introduction to Canadian Economic History* (New Haven, Conn., 1930; rev. ed., Toronto, 1956); *The Cod Fisheries: The History of an International Economy* (Toronto, 1940; rev. ed., 1954); and *Essays in Canadian Economic History* (Toronto, 1956). For a bibliography of his writings, see Jane Ward, comp., "The Published Works of H. A. Innis," *Canadian Journal of Economics and Political Science*, XIX (1953), 233–244. For assessments of his work, see Richard E. Caves and Richard H. Holton, *The Canadian Economy: Prospect and Retrospect* (Cambridge, Mass., 1959), and the special issue of the *Journal of Canadian Studies*, XII (Winter 1977), entitled "Harold Innis, 1894–1952: Twenty-five Years On." John McCallum's *Unequal Beginnings: Agricultural and Economic Development in Quebec and Ontario until 1870* (Toronto, 1980), demonstrates the continuing attraction of a staples approach for economic historians of Canada.

4. Baldwin, "Patterns of Development in Newly Settled Regions," *Manchester School of Economic and Social Studies*, XXIV (1956), 161–179; Watkins, "A Staple Theory of Eco-

empirical studies in the Innis tradition, though often with much greater technical and theoretical sophistication, have built a strong case for the utility of the model in a variety of situations.[5] Staples theory has not gone uncriticized, a matter for discussion later in this chapter, but it is a useful approach to the colonies of British America. And, because those colonies shared an initially similar social context but later developed in sharply divergent ways, the promise goes beyond a deepened understanding of purely historical issues to some theoretical benefits in the form of more-precise hypotheses relating the characteristics of exports to the process of economic growth.

The central assertion of the staples thesis is that expansion of a staple export determines the rate of economic growth in "new countries" or "regions of recent settlement." A small (at first virtually nonexistent) domestic market, abundant resources, and shortages of labor and capital give the colony a strong comparative advantage in the production of resource-intensive commodities, or staples, for export. In such a region, the process of economic growth is twofold: expansion of the export sector and diversification around the export base. The first part of the process is largely a function of increased external demand, although im-

nomic Growth," *Can. Jour. Econ. and Pol. Sci.*, XXIX (1963), 141–158; and Richard E. Caves, "'Vent for Surplus' Models of Trade and Growth," in Robert E. Baldwin *et al.*, *Trade, Growth, and the Balance of Payments: Essays in Honor of Gottfried Haberler* (Chicago, 1965), 95–115.

5. Useful surveys of the literature are provided by Richard E. Caves, "Export-Led Growth and the New Economic History," in *Trade, Balance of Payments, and Growth: Papers in International Economics in Honor of Charles P. Kindleberger*, ed. Jagdish N. Bhagwati *et al.* (Amsterdam, 1971), 403–442; Michael Roemer, *Fishing for Growth: Export-Led Development in Peru, 1950–1967* (Cambridge, Mass., 1970), 5–23; and, especially, John T. Thoburn, *Primary Commodity Exports and Economic Development: Theory, Evidence, and a Study of Malaysia* (London, 1977), 29–54, 234–247. Historians of the United States are most likely to be familiar with the staples approach through the work of Guy S. Callender and of Douglass C. North. See, especially, Callender, "The Early Transportation and Banking Enterprises of the States in Relation to the Growth of Corporations," *Quarterly Journal of Economics*, XVII (1902), 111–162; Callender, *Selections from the Economic History of the United States, 1765–1860* (Boston, 1909); North, "Location Theory and Regional Economic Growth," *Journal of Political Economy*, LXIII (1955), 243–258; and North, *The Economic Growth of the United States, 1790–1860* (Englewood Cliffs, N.J., 1961). North's work is assessed in Stanley L. Engerman, "Douglass C. North's *The Economic Growth of the United States, 1790–1860* Revisited," *Social Science History*, I (1977), 248–257; Callender's in Saul Engelbourg, "Guy Stevens Callender: A Founding Father of American Economic History," *Explorations in Economic History*, IX (1972), 255–267. Work on early America informed by the staples approach is surveyed in David W. Galenson and Russell R. Menard, "Approaches to the Analysis of Economic Growth in Colonial British America," *Historical Methods*, XIII (1980), 3–18.

proved productivity also played a role as planters and merchants learned to make and market colonial staples more efficiently. This stage has been ably described by Richard Caves and others.[6]

The theory assumes a two-region world and an economy combining labor, capital, management, and natural resources to produce staples, services, and manufactured goods. The first region, the metropolis, is a mature, developed, initially self-contained economy that produces all the goods and services consumed by its inhabitants. Despite the limitation on its stock of natural resources, supplies of labor and capital are ample. Further, the level of income and the density of population provide a market for manufactures wide enough to permit firms to take advantage of economies of scale—the "cheaper-by-the-dozen effect"—and to operate under conditions of constant costs. Labor and capital thus have highly elastic supply curves; substantial increases in the demand for workers or in the consumption of manufactures raise wages and prices only slightly. By contrast, products that are natural-resource intensive—agricultural commodities, timber, and metals—have less-elastic supply curves because arable land, appropriate climes, forests, and mineral deposits are available in limited quantities. As a result, given a general increase in demand for the products of the metropolitan economy, the price of staples will rise relative to wages, capital, and manufactured goods.

The second region, the colony, is initially unpopulated and therefore without capital, management, or labor, but it possesses abundant natural resources. Colonization can be understood as the movement of labor, management, and capital from the metropolis to the colony in order to exploit the untapped resources. The incentive to colonize, the probability that colonial ventures will succeed, and the volume and rate of the transfer of labor and capital to the colony vary directly with anticipated profits. Expected profits will reflect the relative costs of staples production in the two regions, transportation costs, and metropolitan prices. At first, however, the high costs of discovery, exploration, and transportation, the severe risks involved, and the uncertainties of enterprise in an unfamiliar environment serve as effective barriers to colonization.

Colonization begins with an increase in demand for staples in the metropolis, although it could be initiated as well by a fall in transport costs or by a discovery that improves knowledge and thus reduces risk and uncertainty. Given the limited metropolitan supply of natural resources,

---

6. Caves, "'Vent for Surplus' Models"; James F. Shepherd and Gary M. Walton, *Shipping, Maritime Trade, and the Economic Development of Colonial North America* (Cambridge, 1972), 13–23.

burgeoning demand produces a sharp jump in staple prices. Those higher prices absorb the high costs of colonial enterprise, raise the rate of return, overcome fears, and increase the incentive to colonize. Capital and labor migrate to the new region, the staple commodity is produced, and trade begins. The metropolis imports the staple and exports manufactures to satisfy the needs of emigrants. It also exports still more capital and labor to further increase supplies of the commodity.

Early on, staple producers earn bonanza profits, but the price of the commodity soon falls as trade expands and moves into regular channels. As production of the staple increases, discovery costs are absorbed, risks decline, and colonists and merchants reduce costs by capturing economies of scale and through various innovations and increases in efficiency. If the staple is raised in the metropolis, marginal producers there will be forced out of business and the labor and capital they employ will be shifted to more-productive uses, either at home or in the colony. Eventually, in the absence of further growth in metropolitan demand, the price will reach a long-run equilibrium and the returns to the factors of production will be the same in both regions. Migration of labor and capital to the colony will stop, trade with the metropolis will level off, and staple exports will stabilize. Further increases in demand will begin another cycle of investment, migration, expansion of staple exports, and movement to a new equilibrium. Each growth wave increases the size of the colonial economy and the real incomes of consumers. Colonial economies may also advance by adding other staples to the export base in response to changing metropolitan demand or as new resources and methods of production are discovered. This becomes more probable once experience leads entrepreneurs to rationalize the process of experimentation.

Staples theory intends more than a description of the expansion of colonial exports. It also attempts to relate the trade in staples to the growth of the domestic economy by analyzing the process of diversification around the export base, the so-called "spread effects of the export sector."[7] A few observations can be drawn directly from the characteristics of metropolis and colony already outlined. Some services, for example, will be provided in the colonial economy from the start of settlement because of the high transportation costs that would otherwise be incurred. Food production is often undertaken immediately, especially if colonization began as a search for farmland. Foodstuffs are resource intensive and very bulky relative to value, making them expensive to transport. This gives the colony a strong comparative advantage in the production of its

7. Watkins, "Staple Theory," 144.

own food. Most colonies specializing in the export of an agricultural staple quickly achieve self-sufficiency in foodstuffs.

Manufactures, by contrast, will develop only slowly in the colony, for several reasons: labor and capital will be scarce, making colonial manufactures expensive; the domestic market will be too small to permit the achievement of scale economies; and the cost of transport for imported manufactures will be relatively low, in effect subsidized by the staples trade, which will call out to the colonies many more vessels than are needed to carry the manufactured imports. (This last phenomenon worked later to lower the costs of travel for immigrants—the steerage trade.) In the production of manufactures, the advantage belongs to the metropolis; colonists can maximize income by concentrating on staples and importing processed goods from the metropolis. Some manufacturing may cluster around the export sector, however, as the staple trade creates opportunities to supply tools to producers and to process and transport commodities. And some entrepreneurs will take advantage of the unique resource endowment of the colony, using the edge provided by cheap primary products to overcome the constraints imposed by small local markets and short supplies of labor and capital. Others will find opportunities in tailoring semimanufactured imports to the tastes of the colonial populace. Moreover, as population densities in the colony rise, increasing numbers of imports will be replaced by colonial products, especially widely consumed items for which only minor scale economies are possible.

The distinguishing feature of the staples approach is the contention that the size and the structure of the domestic sector in an export-led economy are shaped by the particular characteristics of the dominant staple. Some staples have powerful "spread effects" and encourage development in the domestic economy. Others do not. Despite an extensive literature, the precise characteristics separating staples that promote growth from those that inhibit it remain elusive because the context is critical: any given staple export may have a positive effect on the domestic economy in one time and place but not in another. Clearly, historians must avoid the naive horticultural determinism that pervades some work, the assumption that some staples are intrinsically good for development, others bad.[8] Still, it is generally agreed that two interrelated aspects are critical in determining the extent of an export's effects: the production function,

---

8. See Albert O. Hirschman's warning in "A Generalized Linkage Approach to Development, with Special Reference to Staples," *Economic Development and Cultural Change,* XXV (Supplement, 1977), 94–96.

that is, the proportions of land, labor, capital, and entrepreneurial skill required to produce a staple; and the propensity of the product to create "linkages" by inducing investment in other parts of the economy.

Robert Baldwin has highlighted the importance of the production function by contrasting the growth process in two newly settled regions that produce different types of staples for export.[9] The first region (the "plantation colony") produces a labor-intensive crop subject to substantial scale economies that employs large numbers of low-skilled workers in routine tasks. The second region (the "farm colony") produces a crop that requires smaller proportions of labor and is most efficiently produced on a family farm. The differences between the two systems in the pattern of demand, the skills of the work force, the level of investment, and the supply of entrepreneurial talent have important consequences for economic development.

On the one hand, in plantation colonies the production of staple crops results in a highly uneven distribution of income. Plantation workers, the vast majority of the population, will devote their meager incomes to food and simple necessities, much of which may be acquired through self-sufficient production. Plantation owners, in contrast, will spend a large part of their incomes on luxuries, thus exporting much that they have earned from producing the staple. The consumption patterns of workers and owners fail to create a lively local demand attractive to investors. The low skill level of the labor force further hinders diversification, while the absence of attractive alternatives together with the opportunities for large-scale operations channel investment and entrepreneurial talent into the staple. Expanding the export sector thus has little impact on the size of the domestic market and few spread effects.

In farm colonies, on the other hand, the distribution of income is more equal, and a wide range of goods and services that can be produced locally are in demand. The labor force is more skilled, attractive investment alternatives exist, and the opportunities for accumulation in staples production are too limited to command the energies of entrepreneurs. Expansion of the export sector therefore enlarges the domestic market and encourages a variety of local economic activities.

The linkage network generated by staples is as important as the production function in explaining the extent of spread effects in an export-led economy. Some staples induce investment in three related areas: in the domestic production of goods for the use of the export sector (for ex-

9. Baldwin, "Patterns of Development." For an early version of this same distinction, see Herman Merivale, *Lectures on Colonization and Colonies Delivered before the University of Oxford in 1839, 1840, 1841* (London, 1841–1842).

ample, specialized casks for packaging); in processing, transport, and storage; and in the supply of commercial services necessary to assembling cargoes for shipment. All promote development around the export base. Other staples either have few of these requirements or their needs can be met most efficiently by importing the product or service or by having them provided by the metropolis. Either way, in this second case, export gain has only a minor impact on the domestic sector of the economy and does little to encourage development.

In his initial formulation of the idea of linkages, A. O. Hirschman distinguished between backward linkages, production of the goods that are used in producing the staple, and forward linkages, use of the staple in other industries. He thus applied the concept only to inducements to invest in the domestic economy that flowed directly from the export sector.[10] More recently, the concept has been extended to incorporate a general multiplier-accelerator mechanism—the "snowball effect," in which the income generated by investment during one period is subsequently used for investment at a later period. This mechanism is called a final demand, or consumption, linkage. The concept has been amplified further to include government activities, through the notion of fiscal linkages, as when exports are taxed and the revenues used to build roads or to improve port facilities.[11] While such generalization is useful in describing all the spread effects of export expansion, it also makes the concept less precise. With forward and backward linkages, the inducement to invest is focused on a narrow range of activities closely tied to the staple. With consumption and fiscal linkages, in contrast, the inducement is more diffuse and less clearly connected to a specific export. Such stretching has generated considerable criticism of the linkage concept, suggesting that it is best to sacrifice comprehensiveness for precision, especially when the concern is to trace the impact of a staple on the economy.[12]

The issue of linkages, it could be argued, ought to be approached as an aspect of location theory. The problem then becomes not merely to identify the characteristics of staples that encourage linkages: all crops demand some products for their fabrication, processing, transport, and storage. Rather, the question is where those demands will be met, whether in the colony, in the metropolis, or in a third region. In part the issue will be decided by simple considerations of efficiency. If, on the one hand, a colony's technological and factor endowments are appropriate to providing the good or service, or if processing a staple near the point of

---

10. Hirschman, *Strategy of Economic Development*, 98–119.

11. Watkins, "Staple Theory," 145; Hirschman, "Generalized Linkage Approach," 73–90.

12. Thoburn, *Primary Commodity Exports*, 40–41.

production leads to substantial savings, then the export sector will be serviced locally. If, on the other hand, the endowments are inappropriate or local processing only slightly reduces the costs of transport, the colonial economy will derive little benefit from the linkages generated by the staple.[13]

Jacob M. Price has stressed a slightly different point, the place where "the entrepreneurial decision-making center of a trade" was located. When that center was located in a colony, "it necessitated the presence there of a population of sailors, shipwrights, sailmakers, ship chandlers, and the like, as well as specialist brokers, insurance underwriters, and often a manufacturing population to process goods in transit." The location of such a center was determined in part by the availability of capital and entrepreneurial skill, but it reflected as well the impact of restrictive mercantilist legislation and the marketing patterns of certain staple commodities.[14]

The staples approach can be briefly summarized. Initially, colonies are characterized by small domestic markets, limited supplies of labor and capital, and abundant natural resources. Given this combination, colonists can maximize income by producing resource-intensive goods for an external market. The result is a simple exchange system in which colonists ship staples to a metropolis in exchange for manufactured goods and additional supplies of labor and capital with which to further exploit colonial resources. Such a strategy leads to regional specialization within colonies, with the particulars determined by the interaction of local resources and metropolitan demand. Specialization in turn leads to gains in productivity and income.

If the staple is a farm crop that generates an elaborate linkage network, the colonial economy is likely both to grow and to develop. The advance of the export sector will reverberate throughout the entire economy and will foster a swelling domestic market. Local provision of capital and commercial services will increase, import-replacing manufactures will be encouraged, and eventually, an economy capable of operating on its own will develop, free of metropolitan domination. If, in contrast, the staple is a plantation crop offering few opportunities for domestic linkages, the economy will only grow. The advance of the export sector will have only a minor impact on local industry or the size of the market. The region will remain a colonial economy, still export led and dependent on an external metropolis for essential goods and services.

13. Hirschman, "Generalized Linkage Approach," 80–89.

14. Price, "Economic Function and the Growth of American Port Towns in the Eighteenth Century," *Perspectives in American History,* VIII (1974), 121–186 (quotation on p. 173).

The staples approach is a compelling model, with the apparent power to organize much of early American economic, social, and political history, but it has not gone uncriticized. One frequent charge is that it directs attention away from domestic processes, a danger perhaps heightened for British America by the ready availability and superior quality of statistical evidence concerning foreign trade. Further, it allegedly ignores possible alternative uses for resources employed in the production of exports. While it is true that the colonial foreign sector has been studied more intensively than purely local economic activities, the criticism seems off the mark. The principal concern of the staples theory is the relationship between exports and domestic developments; although it argues that foreign trade is the proper starting point for analysis, it need not lead to an emphasis on one sector to the exclusion of others.[15]

A more serious challenge to the staples approach stems from the difficulty of separating the impact of a given staple from that of the organization of labor. Many of the consequences that staples theory attributes to plantation crops—a small domestic market, a poorly skilled work force, a blunting of entrepreneurial talent, the absence of towns, and the inequality of wealth distribution—can also be attributed to slavery. This criticism takes added force when it is realized that some staples—tobacco, for instance—were efficiently produced on small farms before slavery transformed them into plantation crops. While it can be argued that exports shaped regional demand for slaves in British America, and even that different physical properties made some crops more suitable than others to cultivation by slaves, this is not a fully satisfying response. Clearly, disentangling the impact of crop from that of labor system is an important (and difficult) task, but it does not seem incompatible with a research strategy rooted in the staples model.[16]

A third criticism of the staples approach is that it ignores the role of native Americans. Europeans in British America did not discover an empty land. The food supplies, technology, and knowledge of the environment

15. Advocates of the staples approach have sometimes ignored the domestic sector, but it is also true that, in the absence of external demand, the colonists of early British America had few alternative uses for the resources employed in the export sector. The opportunity costs of staple production were therefore low, often consisting mainly of forgone leisure, as is suggested by the frequently observed short-run inelastic supply in ("overproduction" of) the major exports.

16. For recent summary discussions of the effects of slavery on growth written from sharply different perspectives, see Robert E. Gallman, "Slavery and Southern Economic Growth," *Southern Economic Journal*, XLV (1979), 1007–1022, and Eugene D. Genovese and Elizabeth Fox-Genovese, "The Slave Economies in Political Perspective," *Journal of American History*, LXVI (1979), 7–23.

provided by the Indians, the income generated by the furs they caught, and the hope that their labor could be harnessed to the metropolitan market were often essential to the survival and eventual success of initial efforts at colonization. Any theory that ignores this European-Indian encounter, it can be argued, is seriously flawed because it omits a process of fundamental importance to the history of British America.

Two responses are possible. First, even though native Americans were necessary to English success at the beginning of the invasion, they soon became superfluous. They were forced to the periphery of British-American society, victims of overwhelming metropolitan diseases, a powerful metropolitan drive for space, and the seductiveness of metropolitan products. In short, the staples approach simply acknowledges the grisly reality of the British conquest of North America and builds from there.[17]

Second, the staples model can illuminate the central economic interaction between Europeans and Indians, the trade in furs. The staples thesis resembles a theory used to describe regions with large indigenous populations living in a subsistence economy as the people begin to participate in an international market system. Both models "share an essential . . . characteristic in that they depict the effects of trade on growth as involving the exploitation of resources lacking . . . any alternative uses of significant economic value." The principal difference between them lies in what factor is in surplus: in the staples thesis, natural resources are central, while in the other model, the surplus is of labor not fully utilized by the subsistence economy. The fur trade combined elements of both, involving the use of a natural resource by workers whose productive capabilities were underemployed. An analysis of the North American fur trade as a specific case of the interaction between a metropolitan and a subsistence economy in terms of a "vent for surplus" model promises ample rewards.[18]

17. For a recent provocative interpretation of English-Indian relations, see Francis Jennings, *The Invasion of America: Indians, Colonialism, and the Cant of Conquest* (Chapel Hill, N.C., 1975).

18. Caves, "'Vent for Surplus' Models" (quotation on p. 96); W. Arthur Lewis, "Economic Development with Unlimited Supplies of Labour," *Manchester School Econ. and Soc. Studies*, XXII (1954), 139–191; and H. Myint, "The 'Classical Theory' of International Trade and the Underdeveloped Countries," *Economic Journal*, LXVIII (1958), 317–337. The literature on Indians and the fur trade is large, but see especially E. E. Rich, "Trade Habits and Economic Motivation among the Indians of North America," *Can. Jour. Econ. and Pol. Sci.*, XXVI (1960), 35–53; Abraham Rotstein, "Fur Trade and Empire: An Institutional Analysis" (Ph.D. diss., University of Toronto, 1967); Conrad Heidenreich, *Huronia: A History and Geography of the Huron Indians, 1600–1650* (Toronto, 1971); Charles A. Bishop, *The Northern Ojibwa and the Fur Trade: An Historical and Ecological Study*

Despite these criticisms, casual observation suggests the utility of a staples approach to the economic history of British America. Resource-intensive exports—furs, fish, forest products, wheat and corn, tobacco, rice, indigo, and sugar—were important to the growth process and left distinctive imprints on colonies that specialized in one or another of them. Further, reflection on regional differences in British America argues for the power of the plantation-farm dichotomy as an organizational framework. Roughly, and with some obvious exceptions, the colonies described a spectrum ranging from north to south, from New England to the West Indies, marking a fairly steady progression from farm colony to plantation colony. And it is a simple task to construct a list of linkages, instances in which the requirements of a staple export led directly to domestic production of a good or a service.

Unfortunately, the list of studies that, even implicitly, test the propositions of staples theory against evidence for British America is short. We do have important work on urbanization in the mainland South and on regional differences in the prevalence of slavery, several case studies that trace the impact of shifts from one staple to another on social structure and economic organization, some attempts to assess the impact of the export sector on changes in per capita income, and a few general surveys informed by the staples theory.[19] But much work remains before we can

---

(Toronto, 1974); Arthur J. Ray, *Indians in the Fur Trade: Their Role as Trappers, Hunters, and Middlemen in the Lands Southwest of Hudson Bay, 1660–1870* (Toronto, 1974); Arthur J. Ray and Donald B. Freeman, *"Give Us Good Measure": An Economic Analysis of Relations between the Indians and the Hudson's Bay Company before 1763* (Toronto, 1978); and Calvin Martin, *Keepers of the Game: Indian-Animal Relationships and the Fur Trade* (Berkeley and Los Angeles, Calif., 1978).

19. On urbanization and exports, see Price, "Economic Function," and Carville Earle and Ronald Hoffman, "Staple Crops and Urban Development in the Eighteenth-Century South," *Perspectives Am. Hist.*, X (1976), 5–78. On slavery, see Carville V. Earle, "A Staple Interpretation of Slavery and Free Labor," *Geographical Review*, LXVIII (1978), 51–65. For some case studies, see Richard S. Dunn, *Sugar and Slaves: The Rise of the Planter Class in the English West Indies, 1624–1713* (Chapel Hill, N.C., 1972); Peter H. Wood, *Black Majority: Negroes in Colonial South Carolina from 1670 through the Stono Rebellion* (New York, 1974); Lewis Cecil Gray, *History of Agriculture in the Southern United States to 1860* (Washington, D.C., 1933), II, 683–687; Paul G. E. Clemens, *The Atlantic Economy and Colonial Maryland's Eastern Shore: From Tobacco to Grain* (Ithaca, N.Y., 1980); and Richard L. Bushman, *From Puritan to Yankee: Character and the Social Order in Connecticut, 1690–1765* (Cambridge, Mass., 1967). On exports and per capita wealth, see Marc Egnal, "The Economic Development of the Thirteen Continental Colonies, 1720 to 1775," *William and Mary Quarterly*, 3d Ser., XXXII (1975), 191–222, and Allan Kulikoff, "The Economic Growth of the Eighteenth-Century Chesapeake Colonies," *Jour. Econ. Hist.*, XXXIX (1979), 275–288. For recent surveys of early American history that stress the importance of the export sector, see D. A. Farnie, "The Commercial Empire of the Atlantic,

fully assess the value of a staples approach to the colonies of British America.

Perhaps the first priority is to determine the degree to which the economies of British America were export led. Given the data available for the seventeenth and eighteenth centuries, this will prove difficult. Extensive lists of contemporary assertions that this or that staple was central to a regional economy could be compiled, but such unsupported observations are neither precise nor fully persuasive. Alternatively, one could estimate an export's contribution to regional income, remembering, of course, that the resources employed in the export sector may have had alternative uses in the absence of foreign demand. This contribution will probably be quite large for the plantation colonies, especially early in the colonial period and particularly if earnings from subsistence production are excluded.[20]

But that is not the main point: a discovery that the major staple of a region contributed only a small and declining share to total income would not in itself dictate abandonment of an export-led growth model. Indeed, successful development around the export base would progressively reduce the proportion of income earned by staple production. The staples approach contends that colonial economies are especially sensitive to the fortunes of the export sector and that the effects of staple production echo throughout the entire economy. The impact of specific staples should be found, for example, in the character of immigration, the growth of population, the pattern of settlement, the distribution of wealth, the rise of manufacturing, the size of the domestic market, and the standard of living. These are ambitious claims, and some are more fully explored elsewhere in this book. If demonstrable, they enhance the power of a thesis that directs attention toward exports. But we should not be too sanguine about the prospects for demonstration: even with relatively full data for the twentieth century, precise measurement of the effects of the export sector on other parts of an economy has proved elusive, and for the colonial period we shall have to make do with much less.[21]

1607–1783," *Economic History Review*, 2d Ser., XV (1962), 205–218; K. G. Davies, *The North Atlantic World in the Seventeenth Century* (Minneapolis, Minn., 1974); Ralph Davis, *The Rise of the Atlantic Economies* (London, 1973); James A. Henretta, *The Evolution of American Society, 1700–1815: An Interdisciplinary Analysis* (Lexington, Mass., 1973); and Gary M. Walton and James F. Shepherd, *The Economic Rise of Early America* (Cambridge, 1979).

20. For some preliminary estimates, see Shepherd and Walton, *Shipping*, 43–44.

21. See the debate over the impact of the Canadian wheat boom as summarized in Caves, "Export-Led Growth," 405–419.

One promising approach emerges from the analysis of the growth process in the colonial export sector. Since colonial staples production depends on metropolitan demand, colonization is reversible. Demand for the staple could decline and the labor and capital that had migrated to the colony could be drawn back to the metropolis. Such a process is more likely in the early stages of a colony's progress than later in its history, when the economy may have become more diverse and less dependent upon a single staple. There was no long-term decline in world demand for the major exports of British America, but the principle of reversibility underscores the sensitivity of staple economies to short-term disturbances in the export sector. Close attention to that sensitivity—a tracing of the impact of booms and busts in export earnings on the economy as a whole insofar as the evidence allows—is a way of testing some of the claims of the staples thesis. Analysis of business cycles that exploits all the available indicators can provide a powerful tool, one that permits at least a rough assessment of the degree to which a particular region was export led and promises insight into the structure of the early American economy.[22]

The staples theory contains obvious promise for understanding regional differences in British America; in turn, a focus on regional variations is a fruitful way of extracting further implications from the approach. Clearly, the analysis should center on the characteristics of staple exports, on how crops were produced, transported, stored, and marketed. Since the model contains hypotheses concerning, for example, urbanization, domestic industry, education, commercial development, the extent of opportunity, and the degree of inequality, a variety of tests are possible despite the paucity and intractability of the evidence.

Such tests can be conducted in at least three ways: by studying the impact of an individual staple on a regional economy; by comparing regions producing different staple exports; and by examining the impact of a change in staple exports within a specific region. Further, focusing on the colonies of British America should help keep constant several largely exogenous variables—attitudes toward entrepreneurship and accumulation, technology, the terms of trade, and world demand for resource-intensive products—that frequently cloud efforts to test growth models through comparison. Although the data leave much to be desired, early American economic history resembles a laboratory, containing sufficient diversity to encourage analysis but enough similarity to allow control of at least some variables. These conditions offer abundant opportunities to

22. Caves, "'Vent for Surplus' Models," 101. Colonial business cycles are discussed in chap. 3, below.

test the model and hold out the possibility of some theoretical benefits, as empirical studies clarify relationships between specific staples and economic development.

The staples approach can be questioned also for its focus on development, a criticism that has resulted in the elaboration of an alternative model, one stressing the absence of structural change in the colonial economy. Recent research, this argument contends, suggests that an emphasis on development is inappropriate to the economic history of British America; rather, what demands explanation is the absence of development, the pattern of extensive growth achieved without major changes in economic organization or social structure. Studies of wealth per person and per household have uncovered only a slow improvement during the colonial period, a finding confirmed by studies of productivity gains in agriculture. Some studies of wealth distribution show little trend toward greater inequality if the colonies as a whole are considered, while growing inequalities within regions often reflect demographic and inheritance patterns rather than the market. In addition, there was little urban growth in British America, despite the spectacular rise of a few seaboard cities. In 1775, the colonies were overwhelmingly rural, even in the most urbanized regions, and in all likelihood, the proportion of the population living in large cities had declined since 1700. The colonial occupational structure also exhibited little change: throughout the period the vast majority of working people labored in agriculture and the proportion with non-farm jobs increased slowly if at all. Further, the export sector contributed only a small share of total income throughout the colonial period, and the value of exports may have declined during the eighteenth century if measured in per capita terms. In British America farmers consumed most of what they produced and produced most of what they consumed. Moreover, some moved out of market agriculture as settlement spread inland, away from easy access to foreign markets. Finally, studies of farmers in the northern colonies have recently revived an older interpretation, which denies that most farmers were income-maximizing commercial agriculturalists. Instead, they placed feeding their families from the produce of their farms and protecting the long-term security of the enterprise ahead of earning the highest possible income in the short run. Such attitudes, it has been argued, constrained farmers' ability to respond to market opportunities.[23]

While one could (and we will) question the accuracy of many of them,

23. These findings are discussed in more detail below, especially in chaps. 12 and 14.

these new findings emphasize the lack of a major structural transformation in the colonial economy, especially by comparison with the United
States in the nineteenth century or with Great Britain in the eighteenth.
Moreover, such findings have begun a reassessment of early American
economic history and a move away from market-oriented, export-led
approaches. This new model—rather, this revival of an old tradition—
offers an essentially demographic interpretation of the colonies, demographic in the sense that internal population processes rather than external market opportunities provide the central dynamic. Indeed, Daniel
Scott Smith has labeled the years before 1815 the "Malthusian era" of
United States history. While admitting the necessity for some qualifica-
tion, Smith argues that a Malthusian framework—a high and relatively
constant rate of population growth accompanied by an extensive spreading of agriculture within an economic "steady state"—captures the distinguishing features of American history before circa 1815.[24]

This demographic interpretation overcomes the difficulties that recent
findings pose for the staples approach. A Malthusian explanation is consistent with constant per capita incomes, a stable wealth distribution and
occupational structure, the absence of urbanization, and subsistence agriculture. Yet this theory has troubles of its own with the facts of early
American history. One would be hard pressed to make a case for a Malthusian interpretation of the West Indies, nor is it much help, for example, with the movement of population from Old World to New or with
the widespread differences among the several regions of British America.
External-market models seem much more helpful in accounting for transatlantic migration and for regional differences than do internal demographic ones. Further, although it seems compatible with some findings
reported in recent literature, the Malthusian model is largely untested.
The principal task would seem to be the identification of a homeostatic
mechanism that kept income constant and wealth distribution stable,
with migration ensuring a regular extension of the agricultural frontier,
thus permitting a rapid growth of population without producing a crisis
of subsistence.[25] Finally, a Malthusian interpretation of early American

24. Smith, "A Malthusian-Frontier Interpretation of United States Demographic History
before c. 1815," in *Urbanization in the Americas: The Background in Comparative Per-
spective*, ed. Woodrow Borah, Jorge Hardoy, and Gilbert A. Stelter (Ottawa, 1980), 15–24.
The tradition, of course, has its origins partly in the work of Frederick Jackson Turner. See
"The Significance of the Frontier in American History," in *Frontier and Section: Selected
Essays of Frederick Jackson Turner* (Englewood Cliffs, N.J., 1961), 37–62.

25. Darrett B. Rutman offers a persuasive argument for the operation of such a mechanism
in "People in Process: The New Hampshire Towns of the Eighteenth Century," *Journal of
Urban History*, I (1975), 268–292.

history is difficult to integrate with rapid commercial and industrial development during the nineteenth century: it implies a much more radical break with the past than most scholars now advocate.[26]

While the Malthusian approach has often led to an emphasis on continuity in early American economic history, population growth was also a source of change. Migration was part of a complex of responses as people tried to maintain acceptable standards of living when a growing population pushed against the local supply of land. Most noticeably in the oldest settlements, farmers adopted new methods of agriculture, specialized in a narrower range of products for the market, reduced the size of their families, took up by-employments, and abandoned farming altogether when new opportunities appeared. Even though high rates of out-migration did much to relieve the pressure of rapid population increase and thus blunted incentives for change among those who stayed behind, those rates were not so high that all structural change could be avoided. Thus, the steady extension of the agricultural frontier was part of a larger process that gradually transformed rural America. Sorting this out, examining the interactions between population growth, migration, and shifts in other types of economic behavior, is a major challenge for those who view the economy of British America through a focus on the local demographic process.[27]

Properly understood, a Malthusian and a staples approach to the colonial economy are not incompatible. Both have a role to play in the economic history of British America, even though, given time and place, one may seem more promising than the other. A focus on exports, for example, is more useful in the plantation districts of the South than in the more isolated regions of rural New England; a Malthusian explanation is more appropriate in the small-farm regions of the North than in the sugar islands. Still, the interactions between internal demographic processes and external demand for staples are often critical to understanding the development of the colonial economy. Clearly, no economic history of British America can ignore the local population process; it is equally clear that such histories cannot ignore the central role played by exports.[28]

26. See chap. 12, n. 4, below.

27. These issues are discussed more thoroughly below in the several regional chapters in Part II, as well as in chaps. 12 and 14.

28. Daniel Scott Smith discusses relationships between Malthusian and staples approaches to British America in "Early American Historiography and Social Science History," *Soc. Sci. Hist.*, VI (1982), 267–291.

CHAPTER 2

THE STRATEGY OF

ECONOMIC DEVELOPMENT

MERCANTILISM,

COLONIZATION, AND

THE NAVIGATION SYSTEM

To say, as we just have, that governments during the colonial period were insufficiently powerful to orchestrate the economy is not to say that they did not try. There was a strategy to colonial development. Later generations called it mercantilism, but by naming it, they implied a more formal, consistent body of theory and law than in fact existed. We would do well to remember that mercantilism was little more than a shared perception among those who controlled northern and western Europe from the sixteenth to the eighteenth century that foreign trade could be made to serve the interests of government—and vice versa.[1]

Political leaders pursued power and prestige. The rulers of the rising

1. The earliest formulation of mercantile thought—Smith defined it the better to fault it—was, of course, the *Wealth of Nations*, I, 428–543, II, 545–662. The two modern classics on the subject are Gustav F. Schmoller, "Das Merkantilsystem in seiner historischen Bedeutung: Städtische, territoriale und staatliche Wirtschafts-politik," pt. 2 of his "Studien über die wirtschaftliche Politik Friedrichs der Großen und Preußens überhaupt von 1680–1786," *Jahrbuch für Gesetzgebung, Verwaltung und Volkswirtschaft im deutschen Reich*, VIII (1884), 15–61, and Eli F. Heckscher, *Merkantilismen: [ett led i den ekonomiska politikens historia]*, 2d ed., rev. (Stockholm, [1953] [orig. publ. 1931]). Schmoller identified mercantilism as one stage in a conscious process of state building, while Heckscher argued that mercantilism was not the result of such a process. Both of these studies have been translated into English, the first in a variety of editions, the other in an authorized version of the revised second edition, rendered by Mendel Shapiro and edited by E. F. Söderlund (London, 1955). Much has been written on the debate that Schmoller and Heckscher engendered. A

nation-states of Atlantic Europe strove to secure their own thrones and to extend their scepters' sway. They needed money to accomplish these goals. They could raise a continuing revenue by taxing overseas trade through import and export duties; they could raise money in emergencies by borrowing from a group of rich merchants. Maximization of such revenues required the protection and the promotion of the interests of resident merchants. And the merchants were more than happy to consult with and advise governments on how they could best increase trade. More trade meant more money not only in the king's treasury but also in the merchants' treasure chests. We are hard put to determine how plotted and planned, how accidental or fortuitous, the results may have been, but these ideas describe accurately, if simplistically, contemporary perceptions of the way the world did and should work.

Government intervention in the economy to serve the national interest produced not only financial but also strategic advantages. By promoting trade a nation could both enrich itself and beggar its neighbor. By diminishing imports from a trading partner, increasing exports to that partner, and seeing to it that the goods were carried in domestic vessels, the balance of trade could be improved and the inflow of gold and silver increased. Strength not only replaced weakness but also did so at the expense of one's enemies. It was a wise government that followed the dictates of mercantilism—according to the conventional wisdom.

It is helpful to define the mercantilist paradigm in modern terms. Balance-of-payments accounting establishes three categories within which international exchanges take place: the current account; the capital account; and the bullion account. The first of these, the current account, measures the value of goods and services exchanged in a year. While we can picture the importation and exportation of commodities, we have a harder time visualizing a parallel "trade" in the services attendant on the movement of such commodities. As a result, the economist refers to the latter as the "invisibles" in the current account. Among them are included freight charges, insurance premiums, and the costs of short-term

---

short but valuable summary of the discussion appears in Charles Wilson, *Mercantilism* ([London], 1958). See also Herbert Heaton, "Heckscher on Mercantilism," *Jour. Pol. Econ.*, XLV (1937), 370–393, and Philip W. Buck, *The Politics of Mercantilism* (New York, 1942). Several pertinent articles and a useful introduction to the subject appear in D. C. Coleman, ed., *Revisions in Mercantilism* (London, 1969). Added insight has been offered by Joyce Oldham Appleby, *Economic Thought and Ideology in Seventeenth-Century England* (Princeton, N.J., 1978). Coleman has summed up recent work in "Mercantilism Revisited," *Historical Journal*, XXIII (1980), 773–791, concluding "that mercantilism is one of those non-existent entities that had to be invented in order to prevent the study of history from falling into the abyss of antiquarianism" (p. 791).

credit. When they spoke of the balance of trade, writers in the seventeenth and eighteenth centuries not only ignored the invisibles but also focused on merely one class of "visibles," the commodities. Even then, they overlooked some of them, most notably ships and slaves.[2]

Contemporary discussions occasionally dealt with the capital and bullion accounts, though not in those terms. Investments abroad that would have been measured in the capital account were, for example, the buying of shares in the East India Company or in the Bank of England by colonists or the purchase of an interest in a colonial ironworks by a London merchant. The bullion account would have measured the movement of gold and silver in bars or in coin.

In balance-of-payments accounting, imports on the current account create debits and exports earn credits. The same is true of the bullion account. In contrast, exported capital is accounted a debit, while the dividends such investments earn are credits. In theory during a specific accounting period and in practice over the long haul, a nation's credits and debits must balance: both must total to the same sum. Any imbalance in one account—an excess of debits over credits—has to be made up by transfers registered in one or both of the other two accounts. Thus, as early seventeenth-century English mercantilists appreciated, a debit in the balance of trade might well require the export of gold and silver to even things out. Ideally, according to the mercantilists, a nation should so order its international trade as to ensure a net gain in the bullion account. The national treasury would then fill to overflowing, thereby guaranteeing a nation's military and political power.[3]

Colonies fitted neatly the purposes of mercantilism, in theory at least.

2. As one might imagine, a considerable theoretical literature exists on this subject. For a formal statement of the interrelationships among the various accounts, see Harry G. Johnson, *International Trade and Economic Growth: Studies in Pure Theory* (London, 1938), especially chap. 6. See also Jacob Viner, *Studies in Theory of International Trade* (London, 1937), and James E. Meade, *The Balance of Payments*, rev. ed. (London, [1952]). Compare the standard texts: Charles P. Kindleberger and Peter Lindert, *International Economics*, 6th ed. (Homewood, Ill., 1978); and Richard E. Caves and Ronald W. Jones, *World Trade and Payments: An Introduction*, 3d ed. (Boston, 1981).

3. The basic data for England's balance of payments are the figures compiled by the government, beginning in the 1690s, in order to measure the balance of trade, i.e., the "visibles" in the current account. The original accounts are discussed in some detail in chap. 4, below, but much work has yet to be done before we can say anything definitive about England's balance of payments. The data are in large ledgers classed as CUST 3, Public Record Office. The classic discussion of them is in G. N. Clark, *Guide to English Commercial Statistics, 1696–1782* (London, 1938). See also John J. McCusker, "The Current Value of English Exports, 1697 to 1800," *WMQ*, 3d Ser., XXVIII (1971), 607–628. Ralph Davis made good use of these data in "English Foreign Trade, 1660–1700," *Econ. Hist. Rev.*, 2d Ser.,

As consumers of the goods produced in the metropolis, successful colonists would stimulate British domestic manufacturing and increase that nation's exports, thereby earning it credits in the balance of payments. As producers of goods the colonists would supply the metropolis with commodities that previously had to be purchased abroad, thus diminishing debits Great Britain owed to competitors. For Britain such things as tobacco from Spain, sugar from Portugal, and naval timber and naval stores (tar, pitch, turpentine, and the like) from Scandinavia and the Baltic would be far better supplied from British colonies. Moreover, colonial commodities potentially offered two additional advantages. Insofar as these goods required processing in the metropolis before consumption, the jobs created put people to work. Insofar as the quantity of any commodity supplied from the colonies exceeded domestic demand, the surpluses became available for reexport to other countries and thus earned added credits. Over the space of a few decades in the middle of the seventeenth century, England went from being an importer of tobacco and sugar to being an exporter of both. Employed very profitably in the process were English merchants, English shipowners, English capital, English workers, and English sailors.[4]

VII (1954), 150–166, and "English Foreign Trade, 1700–1774," *ibid.*, XV (1962), 285–303. Davis has written the standard book on the shipping industry, *The Rise of the English Shipping Industry in the Seventeenth and Eighteenth Centuries* (London, 1962). See also his *A Commercial Revolution: English Overseas Trade in the Seventeenth and Eighteenth Centuries* ([London], 1967), and *The Industrial Revolution and British Overseas Trade* (Leicester, 1979). We still need to know much more about the bullion and capital accounts and to have careful estimates of the invisibles in the current account. An important step in the study of the capital account is Jacob M. Price, *Capital and Credit in British Overseas Trade: The View from the Chesapeake, 1700–1776* (Cambridge, Mass., 1980). For the bullion account all we have are a few contemporary estimates and no systematic analysis. See L. F. Horsfall, "The Free Port System in the British West Indies, 1766–1815" (Ph.D. thesis, University of London, 1939), 22–23, and Merrill Jensen, ed., *American Colonial Documents to 1776* (London, 1955), 687. See also the account of imported bullion brought directly to the Bank of England, 1748–1765, in Additional Manuscript 32971, fols. 64–67, British Library. Very useful in pursuing all of these questions is Stanley H. Palmer, *Economic Arithmetic: A Guide to the Statistical Sources of English Commerce, Industry, and Finance, 1700–1850* (New York, 1977). Similarly useful is Bertrand Gille, *Les sources statistiques de l'histoire de France des enquêtes du XVIIᵉ siècle à 1870*, 2d ed. (Geneva, 1980).

4. J. F. Rees, "Mercantilism and the Colonies," in *The Old Empire: From the Beginnings to 1783*, vol. I of *The Cambridge History of the British Empire*, ed. J. Holland Rose, A. P. Newton, and E. A. Benians (Cambridge, 1929), 561–602, treats the whole subject well but needs to be brought up-to-date. See also Charles M. Andrews, "The Acts of Trade," *ibid.*, 268–299. The bibliography to this volume, though also outdated, nonetheless does list most of the classic works (see especially pp. 857–861). There are several pieces of interest in K. R. Andrews, N. P. Canny, and P. E. H. Hair, eds., *The Westward Enterprise: English Activities in Ireland, the Atlantic, and America, 1480–1650* (Detroit, Mich., 1979).

The effect of these policies on the English economy has been the subject of considerable discussion. Ralph Davis has made it quite clear that, over time, an increasing proportion of the country's trade, both imports and exports, depended upon the colonists as producers and consumers. Although the data collected by Davis, which are summarized in table 2.1, were not assembled in precisely the categories that a historian of early British America would prefer, the growing importance of the colonies to Britain's foreign sector is obvious.

Foreign trade grew substantially during the first three-quarters of the eighteenth century, imports and exports at just over 1 percent a year and reexports at about 1.5 percent. Indeed, as Jacob Price has noted, "between 1700 and 1770, the most dynamic sectors of an otherwise not too dynamic British economy were 'export industries' and external commerce." And the Americas, broadly defined, contained Britain's most dynamic trading partners: imports from America grew at roughly twice the rate of total imports, exports to them nearly three times as fast as the total. Only as a destination for reexports does the Americas' performance appear unimpressive, and that is quite understandable since it was mainly American products that were reexported. The dawning realization that North America had become a major market for British manufactures has been supposed by some to have provoked the changes in Britain's attitude toward the American economy that characterized the late colonial period.[5]

That colonies were increasingly important to the economy of Great Britain is clear. The question is: How important? In particular, did the colonies make a major contribution to the development and early industrialization of Britain's economy? One response to this question concerns the importance to the British economy of the slave trade. Eric Williams

5. Price, "Colonial Trade and British Economic Development, 1660–1775," *Lex et Scientia*, XIV (1978), 101–126 (quotation on p. 109). A later version of the article appeared in *La révolution américaine et l'Europe*, [ed. Claude Fohlen and Jacques Godechot] (Paris, 1979), 221–242. Compare Lawrence A. Harper, *The English Navigation Laws: A Seventeenth-Century Experiment in Social Engineering* (New York, 1939), 271–272. Contrast Phyllis Deane and W. A. Cole, *British Economic Growth, 1688–1959: Trends and Structure*, 2d ed. (Cambridge, 1967), speaking of Great Britain in the 18th century: "The chief limiting factor to the growth of her exports was the restricted purchasing power of her colonial customers" (p. 88). See also the essays assembled in W. E. Minchinton, ed., *The Growth of English Overseas Trade in the Seventeenth and Eighteenth Centuries* (London, 1969). The impact upon British colonial policy of the awakening appreciation that North American consumers might be as important to the empire as West Indian producers has been the subject of various treatments. See George Louis Beer, *The Origins of the British Colonial System, 1578–1660* (New York, 1908), 75–77; Beer, *British Colonial Policy, 1754–1765* (New York, 1907), 134–135, 155–156; and Curtis Putnam Nettels, *The Money Supply of the American Colonies before 1720* (Madison, Wis., 1934), 128–161.

TABLE 2.1.
Average Annual Value of English Foreign Trade,
1633–1774 (Thousands of Pounds Sterling)

Years	Europe	Asia	America and Africa	Total
		Sources of Imported Goods		
1633	—	—	£68 (3%)	£2,339
1663/1669	£2,665 (76%)	£409 (12%)	421 (12%)	3,495
1699–1701	3,986 (68%)	756 (13%)	1,107 (19%)	5,849
1752–1754	4,433 (54%)	1,086 (13%)	2,684 (33%)	8,203
1772–1774	6,037 (47%)	1,929 (15%)	4,769 (37%)	12,735
		Destinations of Exported Goods		
1663/1669	1,846 (90%)	30 (1%)	163 (8%)	2,039
1699–1701	3,772 (85%)	122 (3%)	539 (12%)	4,433
1752–1754	6,043 (72%)	667 (8%)	1,707 (20%)	8,417
1772–1774	4,960 (50%)	717 (7%)	4,176 (42%)	9,853
		Destinations of Reexported Goods		
1699–1701	1,660 (84%)	14 (1%)	312 (16%)	1,986
1752–1754	2,784 (80%)	81 (2%)	627 (18%)	3,492
1772–1774	4,783 (82%)	63 (1%)	972 (17%)	5,818

Sources: For 1633, A. M. Millard, "Analyses of Port Books Recording Merchandises Imported into the Port of London by English and Alien and Denizen Merchants for Certain Years between 1588 and 1640" (1960; typescript in Public Record Office), table 28. For the other years, Ralph Davis, "English Foreign Trade, 1660–1700," *Economic History Review*, 2d Ser., VII (1954), 150–166; Davis, "English Foreign Trade, 1700–1774," *ibid.*, XV (1962), 285–303. Compare F. J. Fisher, "London's Export Trade in the Early Seventeenth Century," *ibid.*, III (1950), 153–154.

Notes: Figures are for England and Wales except for 1633 and 1663/1669, which are for London only. (In the middle of the century, imports into London accounted for roughly three-quarters of the value of all imports. See chap. 7, n. 9, below.) The totals for goods exported in 1663/1669 include reexports. For the years 1699–1774, the values are nominal and not actual market values. They represent, in effect, a constant value series, the index base for which was 1700–1702 (see John J. McCusker, "The Current Value of English Exports, 1697 to 1800," *William and Mary Quarterly*, 3d Ser., XXVIII [1971], 607–628, and chap. 4, below). Dashes indicate categories for which we have no data.

has argued that the large profits earned by Britons engaged in all colonial enterprises, but especially in the plantation colonies, provided the investment capital that funded British economic development. The trade in slaves, Williams maintained, was central to colonial commerce.

> It was, in the words of one British mercantilist, "the spring and parent whence the others flow"; "the first principle and foundation of all the rest," echoed another, "the mainspring of the machine which sets every wheel in motion." The slave trade kept the wheels of metropolitan industry turning; it stimulated navigation and shipbuilding and employed seamen; it raised fishing villages into flourishing cities; it gave sustenance to new industries based on the processing of colonial raw materials; it yielded large profits which were ploughed back into metropolitan industry; and, finally, it gave rise to an unprecedented commerce in the West Indies and made the Caribbean territories among the most valuable colonies the world has ever known.[6]

Not so, answer critics of the Williams thesis; at least not directly and certainly not inordinately. And the critics have the better of the argument if one interprets Williams narrowly—more so than he intended—through a test of the proposition that slave-trade profits were a key source of capital accumulation in Great Britain. The slave trade, it turns out, was not unusually profitable, at least not for European traders, and the revenues it generated were not "so large as to bear weight as *the*, or *a*, major contributing factor" in British capital formation. Some men grew rich on the slave trade and, especially in Lancashire, put their profits into factories, but they were at best of only minor importance in financing the Industrial Revolution.[7]

6. Williams, *From Columbus to Castro: The History of the Caribbean, 1492–1969* (London, 1970), 148. For the original statement of his thesis, see *Capitalism and Slavery* (Chapel Hill, N.C., [1944]). For other work in what can be called the "Caribbean School" of economic history, see C. L. R. James, *The Black Jacobins: Toussaint L'Ouverture and the San Domingo Revolution*, 2d ed., rev. (New York, 1963), which applied the argument to France, and Walter Rodney, *How Europe Underdeveloped Africa* (London, 1972), which focused on the impact of the slave trade on West Africa. Williams argued not only that the slave trade was critical to industrialization, but also that industrialization later devoured its parent by providing a major source of abolitionist sentiment. On this, see the already classic study by David Brion Davis, *The Problem of Slavery in the Age of Revolution, 1770–1823* (Ithaca, N.Y., 1975).

7. Stanley L. Engerman, "The Slave Trade and British Capital Formation in the Eighteenth Century: A Comment on the Williams Thesis," *Business History Review*, XLVI (1972), 430–443 (quotation on p. 441). For other commentary, see Roger T. Anstey, "*Capitalism and Slavery:* A Critique," *Econ. Hist. Rev.*, 2d Ser., XXI (1968), 307–320; Anstey, *The Atlantic Slave Trade and British Abolition, 1760–1810* (London, 1975); Robert Paul

While the specific argument that slave-trade profits were crucial to British capital formation now finds few defenders, the more general notion that colonial products and markets made important contributions to metropolitan economic growth has some persuasive advocates. "Development of underdevelopment" scholars such as Samir Amin, Andre Gunder Frank, and Immanuel Wallerstein believe that the creation of a European "world system" in the centuries after 1450 and the subsequent unequal relationships between metropolitan or core regions and peripheral areas were essential to the economic development of western Europe. Patrick O'Brien, a harsh critic of the school, provides a concise summary of its central theme.

> The relative backwardness of Asia, Africa, Latin America, and Eastern Europe . . . originated in the mercantile era when Western Europe turned the terms and conditions for international trade heavily in its favour. Through the deployment of military power and superior forms of state organization, the Europeans either plundered and colonized territories in Asia, Africa, and the Americas or reduced weaker economies to conditions of dependency. They actively promoted or encouraged forms of labour control . . . which maintained the cost of producing exports for Western Europe close to the level of subsistence wages. Patterns of trade evolved in which the mineral wealth and primary products of the periphery were exchanged for the manufactured goods and high quality farm produce of the core on highly unequal terms. Over time, such patterns of specialization pushed the economies of Western Europe towards industrialization and higher standards of living and the economies of the periphery towards primary production, monoculture, and far lower levels of per capita income.[8]

Thomas and Richard Nelson Bean, "The Fishers of Men: The Profits of the Slave Trade," *Jour. Econ. Hist.*, XXXIV (1974), 885–914; Seymour Drescher, "Le 'déclin' du système esclavagiste britannique et l'abolition de la traite," trans. C. Carlier, *Annales: Économies, Sociétés, Civilisations*, XXXI (1976), 414–435; Drescher, *Econocide: British Slavery in the Era of Abolition* (Pittsburgh, Pa., 1977); David Richardson, "Profitability in the Bristol-Liverpool Slave Trade," *Revue Française d'Histoire d'Outre-Mer*, LXII (1975), 301–308; and Pierre H. Boulle, "Marchandises de traite et développement industriel dans la France et l'Angleterre du XVIIIᵉ siècle," *ibid.*, 309–330. For a recent defense of Williams, see William A. Darity, Jr., "A General Equilibrium Model of the Eighteenth-Century Atlantic Slave Trade: A Least-Likely Test for the Caribbean School," *Research Econ. Hist.*, VII (1982), 287–326. A useful summary appears in Michael Craton, *Sinews of Empire: A Short History of British Slavery* (Garden City, N.Y., 1974), 109–156.

8. O'Brien, "European Economic Development: The Contribution of the Periphery," *Econ. Hist. Rev.*, 2d Ser., XXXV (1982), 1–18 (quotation on p. 2). The major works in the school

The grand sweep of such a generalization is compelling, as is the promise of a truly integrated history of the world economy since 1450. However, the basic hypotheses of these authors usually lack a systematic statistical substructure. When statistics are brought to bear on the fundamental issues of the "development of underdevelopment" tradition, it seems weak indeed, at least that part of the analysis that attempts to explain growth in the core. The profits earned in colonial trades were not unusually high, were not sufficient to generate a significant source of capital, and were rarely invested directly in industry. Colonial products, although available to consumers in a wide variety at low prices, did not engender major processing industries in the metropolis and did little to stimulate the economy as a whole. Throughout our period, colonial markets for British manufactures were generally small, seldom accounting for more than 20 percent of the output of any industry, and were greatly overshadowed by the home market. Furthermore, British industries that were directly dependent on colonial trade—shipbuilding, for instance— were relatively minor. Finally, these suggestions gain support from those who argue that it was largely internal processes, especially productivity gains in agriculture, that caused British economic growth. For the development of the core economies, the data suggest that "the periphery was peripheral."[9]

---

include Wallerstein, *The Modern World-System: Capitalist Agriculture and the Origins of the European World-Economy in the Sixteenth Century* (New York, 1974); Wallerstein, *The Modern World-System II: Mercantilism and the Consolidation of the European World-Economy, 1600–1750* (New York, 1980); Frank, *World Accumulation, 1492–1789* (London, 1978); Frank, *Dependent Accumulation and Underdevelopment* (London, 1978); and Amin, *Accumulation on a World Scale: A Critique of the Theory of Underdevelopment*, trans. Brian Pearce (New York, 1974).

9. O'Brien, "European Economic Development" (quotation on p. 18), summarizes the case against the notion that colonies were central to European economic development. See also Paul Bairoch, *Commerce extérieur et développement économique de l'Europe au XIXe siècle* (Paris, 1976), and François Crouzet, "Toward an Export Economy: British Exports during the Industrial Revolution," *Explorations Econ. Hist.*, XVII (1980), 48–93. For work on Great Britain stressing the importance of the home market and productivity gains in agriculture, see A. H. John, "Agricultural Productivity and Economic Growth in England, 1700–1760," *Jour. Econ. Hist.*, XXV (1965), 19–34; Eric Kerridge, *The Agricultural Revolution* (London, 1967); and E. L. Jones, *Agriculture and the Industrial Revolution* (Oxford, 1974). Deane and Cole emphasize domestic development, but still give foreign trade a considerable role (*British Economic Growth*, 82–97). Profits from colonial trade were important, although not decisive, in financing industrialization in Scotland. See T. M. Devine, "The Colonial Trades and Industrial Investment in Scotland, c. 1700–1815," *Econ. Hist. Rev.*, 2d Ser., XXIX (1976), 1–13. For evidence that colonial trades were critical to the growth of some cities, see Paul G. E. Clemens, "The Rise of Liverpool, 1665–1750," *ibid.*, 211–225, and Kenneth Morgan, "Bristol Merchants and the Colonial Trades, 1748–1783" (Ph.D. thesis, Oxford University, forthcoming).

Whatever the problems with such grand generalizations, the case is not so easily decided. Certainly it would be premature to invert the Williams thesis and to argue that the colonies were a net loss, a drain on metropolitan resources.[10] As Jacob Price suggests, there seems to have been "a strategic importance to the external, particularly colonial, trades which their mere quantitative dimensions do not convey." Three areas of special significance merit further investigation. First, processing colonial products and manufacturing for colonial markets provided jobs for British workers and used British resources that otherwise would have been underemployed. This activity had some multiplier effects in the core economy.

Second, as Price notes, in some industries overseas demand put pressure on scarce resources and perhaps provided a major spur toward innovation. For example, "with domestic demand more than fully utilizing available local supplies of iron and linen and cotton yarn, the extra or marginal demand coming from overseas, particularly the colonies, should have been a marked upward pressure on prices and thus significantly increased the incentives to experiment with new cost-reducing technologies. In this sense, colonial demand *was* particularly strategic."[11]

Third, Price suggests, colonial trades may have induced certain key institutional changes that fostered greater financial sophistication and assisted in the mobilization of substantial sums of capital. Long-distance colonial trades, because of the risks involved, the time required to turn a profit, and various scale economies, apparently required merchant firms much larger than those serving just the home market. Larger firms in turn required larger suppliers, more-efficient credit arrangements, larger insurers, and more capital. The foreign sector thus "may well have been the hot-house of the British economy, where progressive institutional innovations were forced decades or generations ahead of the times they 'normally' appeared elsewhere in the economy."[12] The plantation trades, Eric

10. An argument advanced by Adam Smith and recently revived in a debate that can be followed in R. B. Sheridan, "The Wealth of Jamaica in the Eighteenth Century," *Econ. Hist. Rev.*, 2d Ser., XVIII (1965), 292–311; Robert Paul Thomas, "The Sugar Colonies of the Old Empire: Profit or Loss for Great Britain," *ibid.*, XXI (1968), 30–45; Sheridan, "The Wealth of Jamaica in the Eighteenth Century: A Rejoinder," *ibid.*, 46–61; Philip R. P. Coelho, "The Profitability of Imperialism: The British Experience in the West Indies, 1768–1772," *Explorations Econ. Hist.*, X (1973), 253–280; R. Keith Aufhauser, "Profitability of Slavery in the British Caribbean," *Journal of Interdisciplinary History*, V (1974), 45–67; and J. R. Ward, "The Profitability of Sugar Planting in the British West Indies, 1650–1834," *Econ. Hist. Rev.*, 2d Ser., XXXI (1978), 197–213.

11. Price, "Colonial Trade," 122–123. Ralph Davis makes similar points in his *Industrial Revolution and British Overseas Trade*, 62–76.

12. Price, "Colonial Trade," 123. See also Price, *Capital and Credit, passim.* Compare Alfred Marshall, *Industry and Trade: A Study of Industrial Technique and Business Organi-*

Williams argues, "provided one of the main streams of that accumulation of capital in England which financed the Industrial Revolution." Perhaps not directly, but that notion may have more merit than recent critics have allowed.[13]

These positive results would not have been achieved had Great Britain not intervened first to promote and then to protect its interests in colonial development. The notion of public promotion of private enterprise was at the very root of colonial settlement. During the sixteenth century the English government had become increasingly aware of the potential value of colonies in the New World. The successes of Spain and Portugal impressed the rest of Europe mightily. English entrepreneurs found their government ready to help whether they were after gold and silver directly, as was Sir Francis Drake, or after New World commodities that could be exchanged for gold and silver, as Richard Hakluyt counseled.

From the time of Sir Humphrey Gilbert on, English monarchs regularly granted the organizers of colonizing expeditions a range of incentives including monopoly trading rights and large tracts of land in both North America and the West Indies. These rights and grants had great potential value and provided businessmen with a basis for attracting investors for joint-stock companies, which would open trade and establish settlements in the New World. The Virginia Company of London and the Massachusetts Bay Company were but two of the earliest such enterprises. Each was given territorial rights and an exclusive license to carry on trade; both became the founding agencies of the colonies that bear their names. They, in turn, recruited settlers by offering them the best possible inducement: land for farms. By the middle of the seventeenth century England claimed a string of colonies organized on the basis of mixed enterprise—part public, part private—on the coast of North America and in the Caribbean, from Boston to Barbados.[14]

---

zation; and of Their Influences on the Conditions of Various Classes and Nations (London, 1919), 171.

13. Williams, *Capitalism and Slavery*, 52.

14. One can do no better, for a start, than to read the first several essays in Rose, Newton, and Benians, eds., *The Old Empire*: J. A. Williamson, "England and the Opening of the Atlantic," 22–52; A. P. Newton, "The Beginnings of English Colonisation, 1569–1618," 53–92; J. Holland Rose and F. R. Salter, "Sea Power: The Spirit of Adventure," 93–114; Rose, "Sea Power: National Security and Expansion," 114–135; and Newton, "The Great Emigration, 1618–1648," 136–182. Again, they need redoing; the bibliographies, while superb, can now be considered only preliminary, but these essays are still a fine point of departure. They can be supplemented by R. Davis, *Rise of the Atlantic Economies*; Davies, *North Atlantic World*; R. Davis, "The European Background," in *Encyclopedia of American Economic History: Studies of the Principal Movements and Ideas*, ed. Glenn Porter

By 1650 England again had to intervene to protect its interests in the New World in order to continue to benefit from them. The Seven United Provinces of the Free Netherlands was the leading maritime power during the first three-quarters of the seventeenth century. Just as the Dutch controlled much of England's European trade, so they increasingly threatened to divert much of England's colonial trade into their own hands. The English Civil War, which disrupted England's ties with its colonies, offered the Dutch an especially good opportunity to insinuate themselves. England's response was initially statutory but eventually military. Parliament's passage of the major Navigation Acts between 1651 and 1673 had as one purpose the reestablishment of England's control of its colonial trade. It had as one result the three Anglo-Dutch Wars, whose net effect was to confirm England's control of its colonial trade. Later laws merely refined the basic system of English mercantilistic legislation set up during these years.[15]

The Navigation Acts are worth examining in some detail both for what they said and for what they did not say. They were the culmination and the epitome of English mercantilist thought as it had developed over several generations. The first of those laws, passed in 1651 by the Commonwealth Parliament and reenacted in 1660 by the Restoration Parliament, had among its antecedents royal orders-in-council from the 1620s and medieval acts dating from as far back as the great King Alfred. This first

---

(New York, 1980), I, 19–33; G. V. Scammell, *The World Encompassed: The First European Maritime Empire, c. 800-1650* (London, 1981); and Frédéric Mauro, *L'expansion européenne (1600–1870)*, 2d ed. (Paris, 1967). Mauro's book also has a grand bibliography. Very useful, too, is B. E. Supple, *Commercial Crisis and Change in England, 1600–1642: A Study in the Instability of a Mercantile Economy* (Cambridge, 1959). That the economic history of early British America is simply one aspect of the economic history of European expansion is a point worth making if only to remind ourselves of the renewed European interest in "colonial history" from just that perspective. One can turn with considerable reward to the publications of the Centre for the History of European Expansion, University of Leiden, both its bulletin, *Itinerario*, and its monographic series, Comparative Studies in Overseas History.

15. A good starting point is J. A. Williamson, "The Beginnings of an Imperial Policy, 1649–1660," in *The Old Empire*, ed. Rose, Newton, and Benians, 207–238. On the Anglo-Dutch rivalry, see Charles Wilson, *Profit and Power: A Study of England and the Dutch Wars* (London, 1957), and J. E. Farnell, "The Navigation Act of 1651, the First Dutch War, and the London Merchant Community," *Econ. Hist. Rev.*, 2d Ser., XVI (1964), 439–454. This is also the place to mention two classic works: Charles M. Andrews, *The Colonial Period of American History*, 4 vols. (New Haven, Conn., 1934–1938), especially Vol. IV, *England's Commercial and Colonial Policy*; and Lawrence Henry Gipson, *The British Empire before the American Revolution*, 15 vols. (Caldwell, Idaho, and New York, 1936–1970).

act, as it applied to the colonies, commanded that all commodities imported into England be brought only in English ships. The earnings from the carrying trade—the invisibles in the current account—would belong to Englishmen.[16]

Even more important than the carrying trade were the commodities carried, the "visibles" in the current account. The Act of 1660, besides incorporating the provisions of the earlier act, stipulated that certain specified items produced in the colonies could be exported from them only to England or to other English colonies. These commodities, which came to be called the "enumerated commodities," included sugar, tobacco, and certain dyestuffs made from New World flora and fauna. The Act of 1663 required that European goods be imported into the colonies only by way of London, Bristol, or some other English port. The Act of 1673 sought to bolster the Act of 1660 by enforcing, through a system of duties and customs officers in the colonies, the shipment of enumerated commodities only to England or its colonies.

The point in all this was, of course, to ensure that the economic benefits from the colonies accrued exclusively to England. The laws created a closed system within which only the citizens of the empire had the right to trade, but this included all citizens, no matter where they lived. As far as the Navigation Acts were concerned, the colonies were a simple extension of the metropolis, the equivalent of new counties, somewhere west of Cornwall. All the laws explicitly recognized the right of the English colonists to participate on equal terms with the residents of England in the trade of the empire, Philadelphia merchants as well as the merchants of Plymouth, sailors from New York as well as sailors from old York. By closing the empire to the Dutch, the Navigation Acts created as many opportunities in trade and commerce for Bostonians as they did for Bristolers.

Protected and encouraged by the Navigation Acts, the colonists moved quickly to seize the chances open to them. Prior to the middle of the seventeenth century, commercial opportunities for residents of the colonies had been few and were largely restricted to acting as commission agents for metropolitan merchants. Nonetheless, all citizens of the empire had clearly absorbed the spirit of mercantilism. Just as the mother country saw fit to protect and promote its own best interests, the colonists also used their local colonial governments to stimulate economic behavior

16. The definitive work on the origins and early development of the Navigation Acts is still Harper, *English Navigation Laws*, supplemented by Beer, *Origins of the British Colonial System*. John Reeves, *A History of the Law of Shipping and Navigation* (Dublin, 1792), describes the status of the system at the end of the 18th century.

perceived to be in the common interest. From the earliest days of settlement, colonial governments both regulated and promoted individual and group economic activities. In the second quarter of the century they were increasingly concerned with overseas trade and finance, not only in New England but in the Chesapeake and the West Indies as well. Regardless of the reasons people settled colonies, they all quickly realized that the success of their effort depended on how readily they could continue to import necessities. To accomplish this end, in a way that can only be called mercantilistic, colonists demanded local government intervention in order to promote the economic good. As the Massachusetts General Court said in 1646, the colony had to improve its own balance of payments by striving to increase "outgate" (exports) and decrease "ingate" (imports).[17]

It should not be at all surprising that colonial interests, intent on controlling their own economy to benefit themselves, sometimes did things that conflicted with metropolitan interests. The earliest government measures taken by the colonies were in the pre-1650 era, when few if any imperial regulations were in force. The colonists' most intensive period of activity in this regard, from the late 1630s and the mid-1640s, was conditioned by the breakdown of the English government during the Civil War. This was accompanied in the colonies by a severe depression from which only they could and did deliver themselves—or so they thought. Thus the colonists, accustomed to managing on their own, largely ignored the Act of 1651, and they paid scant attention to it when it reappeared in 1660. By then Massachusetts, Virginia, Barbados, and the other colonies could point both to mercantilist theory and to several decades of practice, which they believed entitled them to considerable autonomy in their economic affairs.

Yet the colonists were not, nor did they want to be, economically independent of England. Rather, the Englishmen resident in the colonies were economic realists who sought to diminish the risks in and increase the

---

17. Letter to [the Company of Undertakers of the Iron Works in New England], 4 Nov. 1646, in Nathaniel B. Shurtleff, ed., *Records of the Governor and Company of the Massachusetts Bay in New England* (Boston, 1853–1854), III, 92. On the whole subject, see E. A. J. Johnson, "Some Evidence of Mercantilism in the Massachusetts-Bay," *New England Quarterly*, I (1928), 371–395; Johnson, *American Economic Thought in the Seventeenth Century* (London, 1932); and the first volume of Joseph Dorfman's *The Economic Mind in American Civilization, 1606–1933* (New York, 1946–1959). Little systematic writing has been done on the participation of colonial governments in the protection and promotion of the economy. Numerous examples of such measures are cited in passing in Victor S. Clark, *History of Manufactures in the United States*, rev. ed. (Washington, D.C., 1929). Cf. Elmer Beecher Russell, *The Review of American Colonial Legislation by the King in Council* (New York, 1915). See also chaps. 16 and 17, below.

returns from their enterprises. Before the 1660s, when greater returns could be made by trading with the Dutch at New Amsterdam, for example, the colonists sought them out. The later Navigation Acts, especially that of 1673 and another passed in 1696, strengthened the enforcement machinery of English mercantilism and thereby increased the risks attached to ignoring its strictures.[18]

As the repeated passage of such laws suggests, it took some time to convert the colonists from practices already thirty years old in 1660. The colonists behaved better in the 1680s than they had in the 1660s and they were to learn to behave better still. By the end of the War of the Spanish Succession in 1713 colonial trade conformed in almost every particular to the navigation system; it continued to do so until the American Revolution, with a few exceptions. Especially blatant were the smuggling into North America after 1733 of sugar, molasses, and rum from the non-English Caribbean and the trade with the enemy during the War of the Austrian Succession and the Seven Years' War. In these cases the returns simply outweighed the risks, either because the returns were so great—as London merchants' own participation in the wartime trade with the enemy amply demonstrates—or because the risks had been diminished in some way.[19]

Yet the colonists were not weaned away from trade with the Dutch and nudged into compliance with the Navigation Acts only by strictures and

---

18. See Andrews, *Colonial Period*, IV, *passim*, for the later Navigation Acts and colonial response to them. See also Oliver M. Dickerson, *The Navigation Acts and the American Revolution* (Philadelphia, 1951). Of a more general character, but very useful as an introduction and for its bibliography, is Wesley Frank Craven's *The Colonies in Transition, 1660–1713* (New York, 1968). We need careful studies of the origins and the effects of each of the Navigation Acts. Anyone interested in the Act of 1696 must consult Michael Garibaldi Hall, *Edward Randolph and the American Colonies, 1676–1703* (Chapel Hill, N.C., 1960). The best introduction to this later period is Jacob M. Price, "The Map of Commerce, 1683–1721," in *The Rise of Great Britain and Russia, 1688–1715/25*, ed. J. S. Bromley, vol. VI of *The New Cambridge Modern History* (Cambridge, 1970), 834–874.

19. Careful analysis of the legal and illegal trades awaits detailed comparative studies of merchants' records and the colonial naval officer shipping lists discussed hereinafter. Richard Pares, *War and Trade in the West Indies, 1739–1763* (Oxford, 1936), provides the background for studies of commerce set during the War of the Austrian Succession and the Seven Years' War. It is within the context of wartime that we can best appreciate such accounts as that of John W. Tyler, "The Long Shadow of Benjamin Barons: The Politics of Illicit Trade at Boston, 1760–1762," *American Neptune*, XL (1980), 245–279. Similarly, two articles on the Molasses Act that will allow others to test how well the act was observed are Albert B. Southwick, "The Molasses Act—Source of Precedents," *WMQ*, 3d Ser., VIII (1951), 389–405, and Richard B. Sheridan, "The Molasses Act and the Market Strategy of the British Sugar Planters," *Jour. Econ. Hist.*, XVII (1957), 62–83.

the threat of punishments.[20] Traditional emphasis on the negative aspects of the Navigation Acts has blinded many to something that the colonists themselves quickly appreciated: the elimination of the Dutch from the trade of the empire, especially after the conquest of New Netherland in 1664, created numerous opportunities for colonial merchants, the intercolonial trade being only the most obvious one. Colonial planters and merchants took advantage of every opportunity within the empire to enrich themselves. They were largely successful in doing so.

20. The essential ideas underlying much of this chapter (and this book)—that imperial policies based in trade were consciously planned and implemented, and that this implementation proceeded in fits and starts but grew more efficient during the last third of the 17th century and was in some measure responsible for the successes that created the Old Empire—are adopted (and extended somewhat) from the work of three historians. See Herbert L. Osgood (*The American Colonies in the Seventeenth Century* [New York, 1904–1907]), George Louis Beer (*The Commercial Policy of England toward the American Colonies* [New York, 1893]; *Origins of the British Colonial System; The Old Colonial System, 1660–1754* [New York, 1912]), and Charles M. Andrews ("Acts of Trade"; "The Government of the Empire, 1660–1763," in *The Old Empire*, ed. Rose, Newton, and Benians, 405–436; *Colonial Period*).

These ideas have been challenged recently by two major attempts to reinterpret the impact of the Restoration settlement on colonial America. Stephen Saunders Webb argues strenuously in *The Governors-General: The English Army and the Definition of the Empire, 1569–1681* (Chapel Hill, N.C., 1979), that military matters, not commercial considerations, were the important ingredient in the policies of the period. This first book takes him only through the last years of Charles II; he has promised to extend—and refine—his argument for the reigns of James II and William III. J. M. Sosin, in complete contrast, discerns no purpose or planning at all in the relations between the crown and the colonies during the era. See his *English America and the Restoration Monarchy of Charles II: Transatlantic Politics, Commerce, and Kinship* (Lincoln, Nebr., 1980), and *English America and the Revolution of 1688: Royal Administration and the Structure of Provincial Government* (Lincoln, Nebr., 1982). It is not apparent that either of these postulates does much damage to our premises or our conclusions since the laws, their implementation, and their effects worked as we have said. That the crown behaved in these ways within the context of primarily military pursuits—if Webb is right—or within the context of confusion or distraction by domestic or European considerations or both—if Sosin is right—lessens only the centrality of the role that commercial considerations played. Indeed, as the opening discussion in this chapter suggests, the events of the time leave room for all three ideas. The crown sought, perhaps fitfully (Sosin), to protect and to strengthen the nation. To accomplish this it needed a strong military (Webb). To pay the costs, it promoted trade and colonies (Andrews). In terms of emphasis, for the years after 1660, we will, however, stick by Andrews, at least for the moment. As Richard Dunn has written, in a balanced judgment on both Webb's and Sosin's work, the former overstates his case and the latter has to ignore much the most important part of early British America—the West Indies—in order to make his. See Dunn's review of Sosin, *English America and the Restoration*, in *American Historical Review*, LXXXVII (1982), 1150–1151.

CHAPTER 3

THE COURSE OF

ECONOMIC GROWTH

AN OVERVIEW

Between 1607 and 1775 the economy of British America became increasingly successful according to the modern measures of such things. Led by a growing demand for colonial exports, linked to an expanding commercial empire, protected and promoted by a strong imperial system, and endowed with an abundance of natural resources, the British colonies prospered. Moreover, that prosperity was widely shared by the colonists—with the obvious and crucial exceptions of black slaves and native Americans, groups whose members paid a frightful price for white society's well-being. For European Americans in British North America and the British West Indies, the years just before the American Revolution were a "golden age"; they were better off not only than their predecessors in the colonies or than most of their contemporaries elsewhere in the world but also than their descendants were to be again for some time to come. It is not surprising, therefore, that perceived threats to that prosperity, in the shape of "administrative reforms" from London in the 1760s, combined with a growing confidence in the promise of the American economy, should have provoked colonial protests that quickly developed into armed rebellion.[1]

The economy of each British colony was harnessed to its foreign sector. Originally, of course, everything the colonists consumed came by ship from England, although the first settlers often found these supplies inadequate and were forced to depend upon the goodwill of local natives. Only

1. Several good books survey the economic history of early British America, with varying degrees of success from our point of view. R. Davis, *Rise of the Atlantic Economies*, is the most useful, covering all of Western Europe and America over the four centuries prior to 1776. Davies, *North Atlantic World*, is narrower in focus but more detailed. Stuart

slowly did the colonists establish a balance between what they could produce for themselves and what they needed or wanted to import. The
colonists were both fortunate and clever enough to be able to exploit
their environment so as to offset imported goods and services (debits)
with exported goods and services (credits). Their good fortune included
being able to produce a range of commodities for which there was a consistent demand in the rest of the world. Their skill lay in their ability to
exploit a variety of commercial opportunities left open to them within
the British mercantile system. The domestic sector of the colonial economy, led by the foreign sector, organized itself to distribute imports, to
produce goods for the export sector, to supply the mercantile services
necessary to the movement of both, and to provide through subsistence
production goods that could not be obtained on the market. These activities became more and more profitable for the colonists.

The progress of an economy can be measured in several ways. The
most commonly used measure of the growth of an economy is per capita
gross national product (or income). To arrive at this figure for any given
year economists divide the total value of goods and services produced by
the total population. To compare these data over time the yearly values
are deflated to constant values, using a price index. Obvious alternatives
to this measure of economic growth are to use the annual, undeflated figures, thereby retaining the impact of any inflationary or deflationary tendencies in the economy, or to use the aggregate figures not reduced to a
per capita basis. Economists prefer the deflated, or "real," per capita

---

Bruchey, *The Roots of American Economic Growth, 1607–1861: An Essay in Social
Causation* (New York, 1965), though dated, is still the best of the one-volume surveys of the
sweep of colonial and early national economic history. It can be paired nicely with Henretta,
Evolution of American Society. A recent effort that focuses on foreign trade, although with
too little attention to the domestic sector, is Walton and Shepherd, *Economic Rise of Early
America*. Edwin J. Perkins, *The Economy of Colonial America* (New York, 1980), stresses
the contrast between the rapid growth of population, the expansion of settled areas, and the
absence of structural change in the colonial economy. Robert E. Gallman, *Developing the
American Colonies, 1607–1783* (Chicago, 1964), despite its age, is full of useful insights.
Marc Egnal provides a concise, stimulating survey of major trends in the 18th century in
"Economic Development." Compare Kenkichi Omi and Yasuo Sakakibara, "Economic
Development of the American Colonies in the Eighteenth Century," *American Review*
(Tokyo), XV (1981), 108–123, 169–170. The first several articles in Porter, ed., *Encyclo-
pedia of American Economic History*, survey various aspects of the colonial economy. At
least one reviewer has lamented the inadequate coverage therein offered "the 170-year span
of colonialism" (Margaret Walsh, "Another New Look? The Encyclopedia of American
Economic History—A Review Article," *Bus. Hist. Rev.*, LV [1981], 413–414). Richard B.
Sheridan, *Sugar and Slavery: An Economic History of the British West Indies, 1623–1775*
(St. Lawrence, Barbados, 1974), describes Caribbean developments.

gross national product because it more easily allows for comparisons over time and space.[2]

Someday we hope to have a satisfactory set of estimates of the gross national product for the colonies. Until then we must use surrogate measures of the colonial economy in our efforts to trace its performance. One way to view what happened is to look at the rise of population in British America (see table 3.1). Since these people, black and white, were both producers and consumers, changes in the size of the population shaped levels of production and consumption and, therefore, affected both the domestic and the foreign sector of the economy. The effect on the economy depended on whether the colonists produced and consumed per capita more, the same, or less over time.[3]

To begin let us assume that the colonists produced goods and services at the same level per person in 1770 as they had in 1650. By that measure the colonies increased their output (gross national product, or GNP) at the same rate as the increase in total population. The colonial economy then multiplied about twenty-five times over the 120 years. The implied average annual rate of growth is 2.7 percent for British America as a whole and 3.2 percent in British North America. In contrast to a colonial

2. For historians of early British America, among the most useful discussions of this approach to the measurement of economic performance are Simon Kuznets, *National Income: A Summary of Findings* (New York, 1946), 111–139, and Engerman and Gallman, "U.S. Economic Growth." The argument that measures other than GNP might be more appropriate is moot for the colonial period since we have so little of the necessary data. Nonetheless, it is worth noting that a long-term shift of some productive activity from the home to the marketplace has accompanied modern economic growth. As a result, unless household production somehow entered the market, traditionally it has not been measured as part of gross national product. Thus estimates of GNP over time or comparisons between societies at different levels of development may overestimate differences in income unless those estimates account for the share of total output produced in the home and consumed on the spot. Women, especially farmwives, were responsible for a good deal of such household production. On this subject, see Ester Boserup, *Woman's Role in Economic Development* (London, 1970). As an indication of the importance of household production, even as late as the second decade of the 20th century, about 60% of the food and fuel consumed on farms in the United States was also produced there. See W. C. Funk, *Value to Farm Families of Food, Fuel, and Use of House* (Washington, D.C., 1916). Another potential distortion exists. To be valid, comparative GNP figures derived on a per capita basis would seem to require that the two populations involved have roughly the same ratio of men, women, and children. During the early years of colonial settlement, white adult males comprised a significantly higher proportion of the total population than they did later (see table 6.3).

3. Changes in colonial population are discussed more fully in chap. 10, below. Obviously, one of the things this book hopes to accomplish is to induce more work measuring the performance of the early American economy. Those who wish to try might take the example of Deane and Cole, *British Economic Growth*, a useful model because of the imaginative mix of rich theory and poor data.

TABLE 3.1.
Estimated Population of the British Colonies
in the Western Hemisphere, 1650–1770
(in Thousands)

	1650	1700	1750	1770
North American Colonies				
White	53	234	964	1,816
Black	2	31	242	467
Total	55	265	1,206	2,283
West Indian Colonies				
White	44	32	35	45
Black	15	115	295	434
Total	59	147	330	479
Subtotals				
White	97	266	999	1,861
Black	17	146	537	901
Grand Total	114	412	1,536	2,762

Source: John J. McCusker, "The Rum Trade and the Balance of Payments of the Thirteen Continental Colonies, 1650–1775" (Ph.D. diss., University of Pittsburgh, 1970), 584, 586, 703, 704, 712 (and appendix B, *passim*).

Notes: Bermuda and the Bahamas are included in the figures for the North American colonies. Native American Indian residents of the region who lived outside the areas settled by the British are not included in these population figures. For a crude, preliminary attempt to estimate the tribal populations within the territories contiguous to British settlement and with whom, therefore, the British maintained commercial contact, see McCusker, "Rum Trade," 713–716.

growth rate of more than 2,400 percent, during the same sixscore years the population of the British Isles grew by only 50 percent. Clearly, the colonies were a locus of considerable economic opportunity within the British Empire.[4]

4. A summary of the traditional estimates of the population of Britain can be found in John J. McCusker, "The Rum Trade and the Balance of Payments of the Thirteen Continental Colonies, 1650–1775" (Ph.D. diss., University of Pittsburgh, 1970), appendix B, 548–552. These estimates need to be refined, and some work on this is currently under way. See R. D. Lee and R. S. Schofield, "British Population in the Eighteenth Century," in *The Economic History of Britain since 1700*, ed. Roderick Floud and Donald McCloskey (Cambridge, 1981), I, 17–35, and E. A. Wrigley and R. S. Schofield, *The Population History of*

This rather crude measure, based on population, of the improvement in the economic performance of the British colonies is the best one that we can generate for the long term. However, though estimates of the growth rate are on the most tenuous of grounds, little more than guesses, it is clear that the colonial economy must have expanded at a faster rate than the population. Both productivity and the standard of living in the colonies got better during the colonial era, which argues quite forcefully for real per capita growth in the economy.

One way to estimate the rate of real per capita growth for the colonial economy is simply to assume that it equaled the rate of increase in the mother country. Britain's economy grew in real terms at an annual average compound rate of 0.3 percent per capita between 1690 and 1785. Since such an assumption seems unsatisfactory, if only because the colonies started out so far behind, we postulate that the colonial economy grew faster, at perhaps 0.6 percent. Nevertheless, that rate is low by modern standards and even by those of the early national period in United States history. One estimate, thought by some to be too high, puts the rate of growth of GNP at 1.9 percent during the 1790s alone and at 1.3 percent for the years 1789–1825 overall. Still, even so low a yearly rate as 0.6 percent would have been sufficient to double income over 120 years and rapid enough, as Alice Hanson Jones has argued, to produce a standard of living in British North America by about 1774 that was "probably the highest achieved for the great bulk of the population in any country up to that time." Further, those modest growth rates occurred in the face of an extraordinarily rapid expansion of population and settled area, no mean accomplishment given the usual European experience with much slower rates of population gain. In the colonies it was necessary to run very fast merely to stay in place.[5]

England, 1541–1871: A Reconstruction (Cambridge, Mass., 1981). The impact of the colonies on the British economy, as suppliers and as customers, is discussed in chap. 2, above.

5. The quotation is from Jones, "Wealth Estimates for the American Middle Colonies, 1774," *Econ. Devel. and Cult. Change*, XVIII, no. 4, pt. 2 (1970), 130. See chap. 12, below, for a more detailed review of the discussion of increases in colonial prosperity. For the growth of England's economy, see chap. 2, above, and Deane and Cole, *British Economic Growth*, 75–82, 280. The rates of growth for the United States in the early national period are from Thomas Senior Berry, *Revised Annual Estimates of American Gross National Product, Preliminary Annual Estimates of Four Major Components of Demand, 1789–1889* ([Richmond, Va.], 1978), 6–7. Cf. the extended commentary on his work in Engerman and Gallman, "U.S. Economic Growth," 15–16, 18. See also Alice Hanson Jones, "La fortune privée en Pennsylvanie, New Jersey, Delaware (1774)," *Annales: Économies, Sociétés, Civilisations*, XXIV (1969), 235–249. For a discussion of 18th-century rates of growth on the European continent, particularly in France, see James C. Riley and John J. McCusker, "Money Supply, Economic Growth, and the Quantity Theory of Money:

We can explore the implications of these assumed growth rates by projecting them backward through time to construct provisional estimates for aggregate and per capita gross national product. Jones's rough estimates for the thirteen continental colonies in 1774 provide a point of departure. In terms of 1980 dollars, she concluded that income per capita ranged between $742 and $866 on the eve of the Revolution. If we take the midpoint of that range ($804) and assume an average annual growth rate of 0.6 percent, the constant dollar or real per capita value of the gross national product in the continental colonies would have been about $384 in 1650 and $579 in 1720 (see table 3.2). At the lower growth rate of 0.3 percent per year, Jones's estimate yields per capita figures of $550 in 1650 and $681 in 1720 (1980 dollars).

Estimates like these are very crude—indeed, they are best considered informed guesses—but they do allow for comparisons and contrasts. In 1978, for example, gross national product per capita equaled $12,240 in the United States, $397 in Kenya, and $220 in India (1980 dollars). Such figures should not be read strictly. One cannot argue that people in the United States were seventeen to twenty-one times richer in 1978 than the colonists had been in 1720 or that incomes among British Americans in the 1770s were twice those of Kenyans in the 1970s. The economies of these places differ too sharply and the measures of performance are too imperfect to support so exact a calculation. But such figures do indicate orders of magnitude, suggesting both how well the colonial economy performed for its time and how far the United States has come since then.[6]

Combining these per capita income estimates with our data on population size, we can approximate the gross national product for the continental colonies by some "backwards projections" (see table 3.2). While we would again emphasize the conjectural character of the results and

France, 1650–1788," *Explorations Econ. Hist.*, XX (1983), 274–293. After reviewing the literature on the subject, the authors conclude that the annual average compound rate of growth for the French economy between 1650 and 1788 was between 0.3% and 0.5%. For the rest of Europe the rate is presumed to have been somewhat lower.

6. All of the figures in this and the preceding paragraph, except those for the 1978 GNP and those inferred by the procedure described in the text, are from Alice Hanson Jones, *Wealth of a Nation to Be: The American Colonies on the Eve of the Revolution* (New York, 1980), 63, 71. The GNP data are from U.S. Bureau of the Census, *Statistical Abstract of the United States, 1981*, 102d ed. (Washington, D.C., 1981), 878. Compare United Nations, Statistical Office, *Statistical Yearbook/Annuaire statistique, 1978*, 30th ed. (New York, 1979), 751–753. All figures have been reduced to 1980 dollars using the tables in John J. McCusker, "Historical Price Indexes for Use as Deflators of Money Values in Great Britain and the United States, 1600 to the Present," forthcoming. For similar comparisons, see Paul Bairoch, "Europe's Gross National Product, 1800–1975," *Journal of European Economic History*, V (Fall 1976), 277–278.

TABLE 3.2.
Conjectural Estimates of Income in the
Thirteen Continental Colonies, 1650–1774
(1980 Dollars)

Year	Per Capita GNP Growth Rate at:		Aggregate GNP (Millions) Growth Rate at:	
	0.3%	0.6%	0.3%	0.6%
1650	$550	$384	$30	$22
1720	681	579	327	278
1774	804	804	1,892	1,892

Sources: For per capita gross national product, see text, and Alice Hanson Jones, *Wealth of a Nation to Be: The American Colonies on the Eve of the Revolution* (New York, 1980), 54, 63. To derive the figures for aggregate GNP, we multiplied the per capita figures by our estimates of total population. See table 3.1 and n. 3, above.

Note: To allow for easier comparisons with other data in this book, these figures have been reduced to 1980 dollars using the tables in John J. McCusker, "Historical Price Indexes for Use as Deflators of Money Values in Great Britain and the United States, 1600 to the Present," forthcoming.

admit that the notion of a "national" product for the colonies before 1776 is somewhat anachronistic, the exercise is worth pursuing. At least it will make clear the implications of our several guesses and provide a rough index to the size of the colonial economy. Assuming a real annual growth rate of 0.6 percent per capita throughout the period, the gross national product of that part of British America that became the United States equaled $22 million in 1650, $278 million in 1720, and $1,892 million in 1774 (1980 dollars). At the lower real yearly rate of 0.3 percent per capita, the figures are $30 million in 1650 and $327 million in 1720. In other words, the total product of the continental colonies advanced at an annual rate of roughly 3.5 percent over the 120 years following 1650, a truly remarkable performance by any standard. Just how remarkable it was is suggested by a contrast with Great Britain: there, the gross national product grew at a rate of something less than 0.5 percent per year during the same period.[7]

7. The estimate of the growth rate in the English economy is based on Deane and Cole, *British Economic Growth*, 75–82. On the issue of projecting national product estimates for the continental colonies back into the 17th century, see the criteria set out by Simon Kuznets, "The State as a Unit in Study of Economic Growth," *Jour. Econ. Hist.*, XI (1951), 27. Cf. Bairoch, "Europe's Gross National Product," 277, and Riley and McCusker,

The increasing prosperity implied by this economic growth was not shared evenly across society. Indeed, that one-third of the population of British America in 1770 was enslaved suggests that the use of income per head as a central measure of colonial economic performance may be inappropriate. The index implies some measure of choice. It assumes that people had more freedom to determine how they earned and spent their income and how they allocated their time than slaves were allowed. Since slavery, the forceful denial of such choice, was crucial to the high levels of prosperity achieved by several of the regions of British America, one could argue that conventional measures are misleading when applied to the colonial economy. Further, even if it is agreed that income or wealth per head is the best index possible given the evidence and the tools available, the real income of slaves, their material living standard, probably grew little if at all during the period. Perhaps for some purposes slaves should not be included as part of the population when a per capita calculation is made.[8]

If we distribute the income estimates of table 3.2 among just the free

---

"Money Supply," 290–291. For the rate of growth in the economy of one colony, see James A. Bernard, Jr., "An Analysis of British Mercantilism as It Related to Patterns of South Carolina Trade from 1717 to 1767" (Ph.D. diss., University of Notre Dame, 1973).

8. Slaves are excluded, for instance, from some of the calculations of per capita wealth presented in A. Jones, *Wealth of a Nation to Be, passim*. Obviously, we would like to know how the living standards of slaves changed over time, if they did. Evidence on reproduction and life expectancy, discussed in chap. 10, below, suggests some important improvements in welfare, but historians have not devoted sufficient attention to questions of temporal change in the economic aspects of slavery. See Ira Berlin, "Time, Space, and the Evolution of Afro-American Society on British Mainland North America," *AHR*, LXXXV (1980), 44–78. Clearly, since life span increased, standards of living must have risen somewhat, but their nature and significance are unknown to us. Moreover, these improvements may have been a function more of "seasoning" than of living conditions and, therefore, may have characterized only the first few years of settlement. The increasing restrictions on the opportunities for slaves to market the produce of their garden plots (an outgrowth of slaveowners' fears that market meetings promoted thievery and conspiracy) suggest that living standards may actually have declined some in the 18th century. More of these restrictions appear to have been enacted in the mainland colonies than in the West Indies, where instead, a movement was generated to encourage the slaves to provide more of their own food. We are left with the potentially very anomalous suggestion that in the 18th century the standard of living was increasing for West Indian slaves while declining for mainland slaves. Other factors, however, may have served to offset these tendencies. On this subject, see William M. Wiecek, "The Statutory Law of Slavery and Race in the Thirteen Mainland Colonies of British America," *WMQ*, 3d Ser., XXXIV (1977), 258–280, and Elsa V. Goveia, "The West Indian Slave Laws of the Eighteenth Century," *Revista de Ciencias Sociales*, IV (1960), 75–105. See also Neville Hall, "Slaves Use of Their 'Free' Time in the Danish Virgin Islands in the Later Eighteenth and Early Nineteenth Century," *Journal of Caribbean History*, XII (1980), 21–43.

inhabitants of the colonies (using the more conservative 0.3 percent per capita yearly growth rate), three things happen. First, the per capita figures become higher, as should be obvious: $572 for 1650; $826 for 1720; and $1,043 for 1774 (1980 dollars). Second, the long-term average annual per capita rate of growth rises to 0.49 percent, reflecting the more rapid expansion of the slave population than the free population after 1650. Third, the short-term averages are a bit different, again a function of the relative rates of increase for blacks and for whites. During the first seventy years the rate, at 0.52 percent, was higher than that during the subsequent fifty years, 0.43 percent. The year 1720 is not necessarily significant in this context; it was chosen merely to divide the long period in two at a time of peace. What could well be of importance, however, is the suggestion that the colonial economy expanded at a slightly faster rate in the seventeenth century than in the eighteenth, a suggestion that is supported by other evidence on the pattern of growth.[9]

Even among just the white population of the British colonies, income and wealth were unevenly distributed both by region and by rank in society. On the eve of the American Revolution, residents in the southern colonies had, on average, higher levels of income and wealth than those farther north. Free whites in the Caribbean colonies were considerably wealthier than their southern continental cousins and much richer than those in the Middle Atlantic and New England colonies (see table 3.3). And, of course, within each of those areas there were differences among the white population. Those differences appear to have grown over time as increasingly larger percentages of both income and wealth went to families and individuals in the upper ranks. Yet this does not mean that those at the bottom failed completely to benefit from the advancing economy. The colonies experienced little if any of the abject poverty found in contemporary Europe or in the United States during the nineteenth century. Among the white colonists it seems that while the rich got richer the poor prospered as well, but at a slower rate.[10]

9. With regard to the first point, it must be said that these figures are higher than they should be. Before dividing the aggregate GNP by the population we should have reduced the total by some estimate of the proportion consumed by slaves, however small and however unvarying on a per capita basis we believe that to have been (see n. 8, above). Since there are as yet no such estimates, we are unable to make the appropriate adjustments. With regard to the last point, we should note that Alice Hanson Jones suggests that the colonial economy grew more rapidly in the 18th century than in the 17th (*Wealth of a Nation to Be,* 72–79).

10. Trends in wealth distribution are discussed more thoroughly in chap. 12, below. Other questions concern the rate of return individuals earned on various enterprises, how this varied over time, how it differed among regions and societal groups. Almost nothing has been written on the subject. Interest rates for money loaned are sometimes taken as a lower

Just as the growth of the colonial economy did not benefit everyone equally, neither did it occur evenly over time. The trend line in income per capita was not unfailingly upward. While the yearly growth rate for British America as a whole during the entire period was between 0.3 percent and 0.6 percent, those figures summarize the diverse regional and temporal patterns that developed as internal processes joined the pull of foreign markets to shape the performance of the colonial economy. The evidence is still far too thin to permit confident generalization, but there is reason to believe that the economy of British America grew in two fairly rapid spurts sandwiching a much longer period of relative stagnation. The first (and more rapid) of those spurts occurred in each colonial region during the time of settlement as new inhabitants established working farms. This process lies behind our suspicion that colonial income advanced more rapidly in the seventeenth century than in the eighteenth. The second spurt, less pronounced and perhaps less uniform in the several major regions, began during the 1740s and lasted to the Revolution, even though the rate of increase may have slowed somewhat after 1760. This second period of growth can be attributed to a burgeoning metropolitan demand for American products, although more-strictly internal processes that reflected a widening domestic market also played a role. The era of stagnation, or at least slower growth, in each region spanned the years between initial settlement and the 1740s.[11]

The identification, however tentative, of the general trend in the incomes of British Americans does not exhaust the subject of temporal fluctuations. There were also much shorter periods of expansion and contraction in the level of economic activity (see table 3.4). Again, the data are inadequate to support definitive statements about the precise timing

---

bound for rates of return. For colonial interest rates, see n. 18, below. Charles Carroll of Annapolis, the founder of what in 1774 John Adams called "the first Fortune in America," seems to have been satisfied with a rate of return considerably lower than the prevailing interest rates. In 1764 he calculated the value of his estate, his investments, and money owed him at over £70,000 sterling, yet he reckoned his annual income at £1,800, a return of only 2.5%. See the letter from Carroll to his son, Charles Carroll of Carrollton, 9 Jan. 1764, Carroll Papers, Maryland Historical Society, Baltimore, and as printed in Ronald Hoffman, ed., *Dear Papa, Dear Charley: The Letters of Charles Carroll of Carrollton and His Father, 1749–1782* (Chapel Hill, N.C., forthcoming). The Adams reference is from his diary, 14 Sept. 1774, *Diary and Autobiography of John Adams*, ed. L. H. Butterfield *et al.* (Cambridge, Mass., 1961), II, 134. Compare H. J. Habakkuk, "The Long-Term Rate of Interest and the Price of Land in the Seventeenth Century," *Econ. Hist. Rev.*, 2d Ser., V (1952), 26–45, and Richard Grassby, "The Rate of Profit in Seventeenth-Century England," *English Historical Review*, LXXXIV (1969), 721–751.

11. Again, see chap. 12, below.

TABLE 3.3.
Wealth per Free White Person in British America,
ca. 1770–1775 (Pounds Sterling)

Region	Net Worth per Free White Person	Total
Continental colonies (1774)	£74.00	
New England	33.00	£19,000,000
Middle Colonies	51.00	30,000,000
Upper and Lower South	132.00	86,100,000
West Indies (1771–1775)		
Jamaica	1,200.00	18,000,000

Sources: For the continental colonies, U.S. Bureau of the Census, *Historical Statistics of the United States, Colonial Times to 1970* (Washington, D.C., 1975), II, 1175 (Ser. Z 169, prepared by Alice Hanson Jones). For Jamaica, Richard B. Sheridan, *Sugar and Slavery: An Economic History of the British West Indies, 1623–1775* (St. Lawrence, Barbados, 1974), 229–232. Estimates of Jamaica's population (in this instance 15,000 whites) are to be found in John J. McCusker, "The Rum Trade and the Balance of Payments of the Thirteen Continental Colonies, 1650–1775" (Ph.D. diss., University of Pittsburgh, 1970), 692.

Notes: For Jones, wealth (net worth) includes the value of servants and slaves. Total wealth is a multiple of the figures for net worth and Jones's estimates of the total free population in 1774 (New England, 582,285; Middle Colonies, 585,149; Upper and Lower South, 652,585). One may, for purposes of comparison, reduce these figures to 1980 dollars by multiplying each number by 44—taking the pound sterling as having been equal to $4.44 in 1770–1775 and using the tables in John J. McCusker, "Historical Price Indexes for Use as Deflators of Money Values in Great Britain and the United States, 1600 to the Present," forthcoming.

or the duration of these cycles in the colonial economy, but some broad inferences are possible.

The basic data for this discussion are indexes of changing price levels. They can be supplemented by other materials, the best of which are the contemporary statements of informed observers. While increasing prices do not always mean good times nor decreasing prices bad times, the rise and fall of indexes of commodity prices have usually paralleled periods of economic expansion and contraction. Thomas S. Ashton has worked out the cycles in the English economy in the eighteenth century, and table 3.4 shows the results of his efforts. They are presented here for comparison with the trends described by an English price index and a colonial price index. Since the English price index moved in parallel with Ashton's series for the eighteenth century, it is reasonable to assume that the price

TABLE 3.4.
*Periods of Economic Expansion and Contraction
in England and British America,
1614–1796*

England		British America
Phelps Brown and Hopkins	Ashton	
1614–1621 (−)		
1621–1623 (+)		
1623–1628 (−)		late 1620s (−)
1628–1631 (+)		
1633–1638 (+)		mid-1630s (+)
1638–1644 (−)		late 1630s and mid-1640s (−)
1644–1650 (+)		
1650–1655 (−)		mid-1650s (−)
1655–1662 (+)		late 1650s (+)
1662–1672 (−)		late 1660s (−)
1672–1675 (+)		mid-1670s (+)
1675–1681 (−)		
1681–1685 (+)		mid-1680s (+)
1685–1691 (−)		circa 1690 (−)
1691–1699 (+)		
1699–1703 (−)	1701–1702 (−)	
1703–1704 (+)	1702–1704 (+)	?–1701 (+)
1704–1705 (−)	1704–1706 (−)	1701–1705 (−)
1705–1706 (+)	1706–1708 (+)	1705–1708 (+)
1706–1707 (−)		
1707–1711 (+)		
1711–1713 (−)	1708–1712 (−)	1708–1710 (−)
1713–1715 (+)	1712–1714 (+)	1710–1714 (+)
1715–1718 (−)	1714–1716 (−)	1714–1716 (−)
1718–1720 (+)	1716–1718 (+)	1716–1719 (+)
1720–1723 (−)	1718–1722 (−)	1719–1721 (−)
1723–1726 (+)	1722–1725 (+)	1721–1726 (+)
1726–1727 (−)	1725–1727 (−)	1726–1729 (−)
1727–1729 (+)	1727–1728 (+)	
1729–1731 (−)	1728–1730 (−)	1729–1730 (+)
1731–1732 (+)	1730–1733 (+)	1730–1731 (−)
1732–1734 (−)	1733–1734 (−)	1732–1734 (+)

Table 3.4 continued

England		British America
Phelps Brown and Hopkins	Ashton	
1734–1737 (+)	1734–1738 (+)	1734–1736 (−)
		1736–1738 (+)
1737–1739 (−)	1738–1742 (−)	1738–1740 (−)
1739–1741 (+)	1742–1743 (+)	1740–1741 (+)
1741–1744 (−)	1743–1745 (−)	1741–1745 (−)
1744–1746 (+)	1745–1746 (+)	1745–1749 (+)
1746–1747 (−)	1746–1748 (−)	
1747–1749 (+)	1748–1751 (+)	
1749–1751 (−)		1749–1751 (−)
1751–1752 (+)		1751–1753 (+)
1752–1755 (−)	1751–1755 (−)	1752–1756 (−)
1755–1757 (+)	1755–1761 (+)	1756–1759 (+)
1757–1761 (−)		1759–1761 (−)
1761–1767 (+)	1761–1763 (−)	1761–1763 (+)
	1763–1764 (+)	1763–1765 (−)
		1765–1767 (+)
1767–1770 (−)	1764–1769 (−)	1767–1770 (−)
1770–1774 (+)	1769–1772 (+)	1770–1773 (+)
1774–1777 (−)	1772–1775 (−)	1773–1775 (−)
1777–1778 (+)	1775–1777 (+)	1775–1778 (+)
1778–1780 (−)	1777–1781 (−)	1778–1779 (−)
		1779–1780 (+)
		1780–1781 (−)
1780–1784 (+)	1781–1784 (+)	1781–1782 (+)
1784–1787 (−)	1783–1784 (−)	1782–1789 (−)
	1784–1787 (+)	
1787–1788 (+)		
1788–1789 (−)	1787–1789 (−)	
1789–1790 (+)	1789–1792 (+)	1789–1796 (+)
1790–1791 (−)		
	1792–1794 (−)	
1791–1796 (+)	1794–1796 (+)	

Sources: For England, E. H. Phelps Brown and Sheila V. Hopkins, "Seven Centuries of the Prices of Consumables, Compared with Builders' Wage-Rates," *Economica*, N.S., XXIII (1956), 296–314; T. S. Ashton, *Economic Fluctuations in England, 1700–1800* (Oxford,

Table 3.4 continued

1959), *passim*, but especially pp. 172–173. One may compare the inferences drawn here
from these data with the periods of "good trade," "bad trade," and "crises," 1558–1720, in
William Robert Scott, *The Constitution and Finance of English, Scottish, and Irish Joint-
Stock Companies to 1720* (Cambridge, 1911), I, 465–467. For British America, see John J.
McCusker, "Historical Price Indexes for Use as Deflators of Money Values in Great Britain
and the United States, 1600 to the Present," forthcoming.

Note: A period of expansion, designated by a plus sign, defines the time from a trough to
the next peak in the cycle; a period of contraction, designated by a minus sign, is the period
between a peak and the subsequent trough.

index can also be used as an indicator of the fluctuations in the economy
during the seventeenth century. Moreover, several not unexpected similarities appear in the movements of English and colonial price indexes
after 1700. No colonial price index exists for the era before 1700, but
we think that colonial prices again moved in general conformity with
English prices. Contemporary discussions of the economy support this
suggestion.[12]

Periods of economic rise and decline affected almost all the colonies in
one way or another. Moreover, these periods seem, by their coincidence

12. Compare "Condition of Trade," 1650–1710, as graphed in J. Keith Horsefield, *British
Monetary Experiments, 1650–1710* (London, 1960), 4, chart 1, based on William Robert
Scott, *The Constitution and Finance of English, Scottish, and Irish Joint-Stock Companies
to 1720* (Cambridge, 1911), I, 465–467, q.v. See also Joseph A. Schumpeter, *Business
Cycles: A Theoretical, Historical, and Statistical Analysis of the Capitalist Process* (New
York, 1939), I, 132–252; Raymond S. Hartman and David R. Wheeler, "Schumpeterian
Waves of Innovation and Infrastructure Development in Great Britain and the United
States: The Kondratieff Cycle Revisited," *Research Econ. Hist.*, IV (1979), 37–85, who
found "considerable cyclical uniformity" in the parallel data series that they ran (p. 57);
and Charles P. Kindleberger, *Manias, Panics, and Crashes: A History of Financial Crises*
(New York, 1978). Compare Philip Edward Mirowski, "The Birth of the Business Cycle"
(Ph.D. diss., University of Michigan, 1979). The data for the colonies have their origin in
the several price histories done in the 1930s and summed up in Arthur Harrison Cole,
Wholesale Commodity Prices in the United States, 1700–1861 (Cambridge, Mass., 1938).
Those who criticize the use of relatively few commodity prices to compile an index might
note Irving Fisher's comment that "a small number may be nearly as good as a large number
provided they be equally well selected or assorted" (*The Making of Index Numbers: A
Study of Their Varieties, Tests, and Reliability*, 3d ed., rev. [Boston, 1927], 338). See also
Wesley C. Mitchell, *The Making and Using of Index Numbers* (Washington, D.C., 1938),
39, and Earl J. Hamilton, "Use and Misuse of Price History," in *The Tasks of Economic
History: Papers Presented at the Fourth Annual Meeting of the Economic History Association (Jour. Econ. Hist.*, Supplement 4 [New York, 1945]), 50n. The need for carefully done
price histories is apparent from the considerable use made of the few available. We need
them for New England, for the pre-1720 era in all the mainland colonies, for all the West

with periods of contraction and expansion in the metropolis, to have been influenced by more than purely local causes and to have affected more than just one commodity. For instance, the contraction of 1638–1644, long recognized as the "first depression in American history," extended not only well beyond the limits of New England but also seems to have been international in scope. Postwar contractions, beginning with those subsequent to the three Anglo-Dutch wars of the seventeenth century, were a regular feature (1650–1655, 1662–1672, 1714–1716, 1751–1755, 1764–1769, 1783–1784). The longest and most severe was that of 1662–1672, which in England was compounded by plague and fire and climaxed by the "Stop of the Exchequer," when King Charles II suspended payment on outstanding government obligations. The contraction following the War of the Spanish Succession, 1714–1716, had far-reaching consequences in all of the colonies as they tried to adjust to peacetime after more than twenty years of nearly uninterrupted warfare. Probably no contraction had more-severe results politically than that of 1764–1769, which coincided with a series of British attempts to reform the colonial economy and to tighten the imperial administrative system.[13]

To have been influenced by any of these periods of upswing or downswing, colonists had somehow to be tied to changes in the international

---

Indian islands, and for regions and subregions within the colonies. Winifred B. Rothenberg has prepared one for Massachusetts, "A Price Index for Rural Massachusetts, 1750–1855," *Jour. Econ. Hist.*, XXXIX (1979), 975–1001; James Bernard has compiled one for Charleston, 1733–1769, in his "Analysis of British Mercantilism," 97–125; and Donald R. Adams, Jr., has done one for Maryland, "One Hundred Years of Prices and Wages: Maryland, 1750–1850," Regional Economic History Research Center, *Working Papers*, V (1982), 90–129. Russell R. Menard has prepared a commodity price index for southern Maryland for the years 1658 to 1776 based on data from probate inventories gathered by the St. Mary's City Commission. The index is described in Lois Green Carr and Lorena S. Walsh, "Inventories and the Analysis of Wealth and Consumption Patterns in St. Mary's County, Maryland, 1658–1777," *Hist. Methods*, XIII (1980), 81–104.

13. See Marion H. Gottfried, "The First Depression in Massachusetts," *NEQ*, IX (1936), 655–678. Compare Charles William Sorensen, "Responses to Crisis: An Analysis of New Haven, 1638–1665" (Ph.D. diss., Michigan State University, 1973), and Lynn Ceci, "The First Fiscal Crisis in New York," *Econ. Devel. and Cult. Change*, XXVIII (1980), 839–847. The use of a single grand commodity price index for the entire colonial economy raises the question of whether such cycles of expansion and contraction occurred at the same time and to the same degree in all the colonies. While we expect that they did, the close study of prices for the several colonial regions is perhaps the best approach to the issue because it provides a means of assessing the degree of integration in the colonial economy, the extent to which markets in the colonies were tied to each other and to those in the metropolis. Most studies of colonial business cycles have had a local focus, but some more-general work has been done (see n. 12, above). See Egnal, "Economic Development"; Joseph Albert

economy. The usual argument is that since most colonists were self-sufficient farmers and therefore were insulated against cyclical patterns, these changes had little impact on the colonial economy. Some support can be found for this argument. The urban population in the colonies in 1770 was probably no more than two hundred thousand, about 7 percent of the total. But how much of the rural population was truly not market oriented and therefore unaffected by booms and busts? Surely the sugar planters of the West Indies with their several hundred thousand slaves were closely tied to the market. So too were the planters of the tobacco coast and those of the southern continental colonies, who produced rice and indigo. And so were the larger producers of grains and foodstuffs in New England and the Middle Colonies. In fact, any farmer who produced more than he and his family needed and sold the surplus, even just a hogshead of tobacco or a barrel of flaxseed, was not fully insulated from market fluctuations. And all colonists, of course, felt the influence of the market when they purchased something produced outside their immediate region. Farming provided a cushion to buffer people in times of recession—even large planters could increase the subsistence component of their operation and wait out a bad patch—but most colonists, to a greater or lesser extent, bought and sold in the marketplace and thus felt the impact of the cycles of expansion and contraction.[14]

The chief variable of the market economy to which people responded was, of course, the price of goods. The long-term trend in general price levels in England and in the colonies was upward during the colonial era. Comparing four peacetime periods, which each incorporated a full cycle of expansion and contraction, we find that prices in England rose steadily at a ratio of 100 in 1614–1623, to 106 in 1681–1691, to 111 in 1727–1734, and to 150 in 1767–1774. We have colonial price data for only the

---

Ernst, *Money and Politics in America, 1755–1775: A Study in the Currency Act of 1764 and the Political Economy of Revolution* (Chapel Hill, N.C., 1973); and P. M. G. Harris, "The Social Origins of American Leaders: The Demographic Foundations," *Perspectives Am. Hist.*, III (1969), 159–344. Brinley Thomas, "The Rhythm of Growth in the Atlantic Economy of the Eighteenth Century," *Research Econ. Hist.*, III (1978), 1–46, attempts to integrate material on trade cycles in England and in the colonies.

14. Winifred Rothenberg compiled a price index from Massachusetts farmers' account books; compared it with price indexes for New York and Philadelphia; found "how strikingly the cyclical movement of Massachusetts farm produce prices mirrors the cyclical movement of general wholesale prices in the big-city markets"; and concluded with the suggestion "that Massachusetts farmers were not isolated from markets even in the eighteenth century, and that the constraints imposed by high transport costs and long distances to urban markets have been greatly exaggerated" ("Price Index," 980, 985). We consider these questions in more detail in chap. 14, below.

last two of these periods, but they show the same pattern to almost precisely the same degree. Between about 1730 and about 1770 English
prices rose by 35 percent and colonial prices by 33 percent, which works
out to an annual average rate of increase of 0.75 percent. English and,
presumably, colonial prices during the earlier period, between about
1620 and about 1730, rose at an average annual rate of 0.09 percent.
These general price levels followed a five-phase trend line that saw prices
rising until the 1660s, declining until the 1690s, rising again over the following twenty-five years, falling afterward to the early 1740s, and thereafter rising steadily and more quickly.[15]

The prices of individual commodities, though they contributed to the
broad pattern, did not always follow these trends. The prices of colonial
staple commodities in particular marched to their own drummer. But
even they, at different times, fell into a characteristic pattern. The price of
tobacco early in the period, sugar later on, then rice, furs, and other colonial staples all seem to have undergone a similar transformation. Initially
scarce, each of these commodities commanded luxury prices. High prices
induced many to enter the market as producers. As supplies increased
faster than demand and as producers captured various efficiencies in processing and marketing a staple, its price fell sharply. Eventually the price
reached a stable plateau, and then began conforming more closely to the
movement of prices as a whole. This behavior of staple commodity prices
helps to explain many of the peculiarities in the economic history of the
staple-producing colonies.[16]

Although the general levels of American and British prices tended to
move in tandem, the terms of trade between metropolis and colony were

15. Over the long haul these price increases could not be seen to constitute a significant
inflation in colonial prices. Moreover, we find appropriate the suggestion of E. James Ferguson, "Currency Finance: An Interpretation of Colonial Monetary Practices," *WMQ*, 3d
Ser., X (1953): "It is possible that a steady and continuing inflation was not wholly inju-
rious to an expanding country whose people seldom had fixed incomes or large stores of
liquid capital" (p. 162). Prices rose much more quickly and sharply in some colonies than in
others, however, which needs to be studied in terms of both causes and effects. Blaming it all
on paper money will no longer work. See Robert Craig West, "Money in the Colonial American Economy," *Economic Inquiry*, XVI (1978), 1–15. Moreover, we need to determine
whether the supposed relationship between steep inflation and political destabilization has
any support in the colonial experience. For a contemporary view, see Benjamin Franklin
to Richard Jackson, 8 Mar. 1763, in *The Papers of Benjamin Franklin*, ed. Leonard W.
Labaree *et al.* (New Haven, Conn., 1959–), X, 209. Also of interest is David Hackett
Fischer, "Chronic Inflation: The Long View," *Journal of the Institute for Socioeconomic
Studies*, V (1980), 82–103.

16. The price histories of the major staple exports of early British America are discussed
below, in Part II.

not constant. The data needed for a fully adequate index are not now available, and the subject would repay further work. Nevertheless, a rough comparison of prices for British manufactured goods imported by the colonists with prices for some of the principal commodity exports provides a guide to the pattern and suggests hypotheses. Such a comparison indicates a sharp deterioration in the terms of trade early in the colonial period, or at least early in the history of each major staple-producing region, followed by a long era of relative stability (punctuated by sharp, short-term fluctuations) lasting to the 1740s. The final thirty years of the colonial era were marked by a major improvement in the terms of trade as prices for American staples rose more rapidly than those for British manufactures.

Caution is required in interpreting these changes. The early deterioration in the terms of trade, while it clearly benefited European consumers of American products, was not entirely harmful to colonial producers. It was fueled in large part by gains in productivity and lower staple prices, which permitted the capture of larger markets. Nor did British manufacturers necessarily suffer from the post-1740 shift in favor of the colonies, which in part reflected improvements in technology and business organization that allowed industrialists to expand output while maintaining low prices. For colonists, however, as Marc Egnal has noted, "these price movements produced a significant increase in the standard of living. For example, where the 100 bushels of wheat produced by a small farm in the mid-1740s could command 150 yards of woolen cloth, the same 100 bushels could be traded for over 250 yards of cloth in the early 1760s."[17]

While a good deal of information is available concerning commodity prices in the colonies, much less is known about the relative costs of the basic factors of production—land (i.e., raw materials), labor, capital, and managerial skills. Nor will it do to refer to English prices for guidance, as we could with commodity prices, for colony and metropolis differed sharply in factor prices. Indeed, it was precisely these differences that made exchange between them often so beneficial. But if the specifics of

17. Egnal, "Economic Development," 205. The notion of the "terms of trade" has many definitions. See Viner, *Studies in Theory of International Trade*, 558ff., and W. W. Rostow, "The Terms of Trade in Theory and Practice," *Econ. Hist. Rev.*, 2d Ser., III (1950), 1–20. What Viner called the "commodity terms of trade"—the relation between changes in export and import prices—are those most commonly discussed because they are the most easily calculated from historical data. In principle, however, the "double factorial terms of trade"—the commodity terms of trade adjusted for changes in productivity—are the most useful construct. But, as Ralph Davis pointed out, "these are not normally calculable; indeed, their calculation would be, in effect, the writing of the economic history of the countries of the world" (*Industrial Revolution*, 70n). Our discussion of the terms of trade rests on the price data described in n. 12, above.

colonial factor prices remain obscure, the broader pattern of their behavior seems clear enough. In comparison with the metropolis, land was relatively cheap in the colonies, while labor, capital, and management were dear. Although this remained true throughout the period, the colonial economy witnessed a rise in the price of land relative to the costs of other factors. One finds, as a result, a turning away from a land-extensive agricultural system of production to one that used land more carefully (land-intensive), and indeed, a shift out of simple agriculture altogether into processing, manufacturing, and service activities. Although these changes had not proceeded very far by 1775 and the comparative advantage of the colonies remained decisively in agriculture until well after the Revolution, the process had begun in British America on the second day of settlement.[18]

These broad measures of the colonial economy are intended to portray the overall shape of colonial economic history. Of course, not every economic activity or every price conformed completely to the prevailing practice. Indeed, one of the purposes of compiling general indexes is to accentuate discontinuity. Besides describing the wide sweep of change, these measures provide the backdrop against which apparently aberrant behavior can appear all the sharper, all the more worthy of examination and analysis. To deflate a price series using a commodity price index is

18. When discussing the relative costs of the factors of production we give special meaning to our terms. Land, for instance, means all natural resources or raw materials. Thus the factor cost of land is something different from the price per acre of farmlands and, similarly, the factor cost of labor is something different from wage rates. Nevertheless, given the data constraints of the colonial period, which permit us only minimal data on even the price of farm acreage and wages, we are forced to consider *changes* in land prices and wages as reasonable surrogates for *changes* in the factor costs of land and labor. For labor prices in the colonies, see chap. 11, nn. 29, 30, and 31, below. The best work on land prices has been done for the Chesapeake colonies, but the available series are plagued by the difficulty of controlling for soil quality and the extent of improvements (see chap. 6, n. 7, below). Changes in the factor cost of capital probably paralleled the changes in interest rates. So far as we know, there are no studies of the movement over time of colonial interest rates. This quite obvious need could initially be addressed simply by consulting the statutes to determine legal rates of interest; see, moreover, Sidney Homer, *A History of Interest Rates* (New Brunswick, N.J., 1963), chap. 16. One area of law that called for the setting of interest rates concerned protested bills of exchange; for a partial bibliography of such laws, see John J. McCusker, *Money and Exchange in Europe and America, 1600–1775: A Handbook* (Chapel Hill, N.C., 1978), *passim*. One has a general impression that colonial interest rates declined over the period, but that they still remained higher than those in Europe. For the latter subject, see Charles Wilson, *Anglo-Dutch Commerce and Finance in the Eighteenth Century* (Cambridge, 1941); Grassby, "Rate of Profit"; Price, *Capital and Credit*; and James C. Riley, *International Government Finance and the Amsterdam Capital Market, 1740–1815* (Cambridge, 1980). Finally, we presume that the costs of management went down as the opportunities for education—formal and informal—increased.

to point up specifically the ways in which the price of any commodity bucked the trend and to provoke the question "Why?" A careful portrayal of what was usual in economic behavior allows us all the more precisely to identify unusual, even unique, patterns.

Further, by focusing on a few numerical indexes—the level of population, the trend of income, and the movement of prices—we can only sketch an outline of colonial economic history. Indeed, it can be argued that a focus on growth, on the dynamic elements of the colonial economy, is misleading because it directs attention away from a central characteristic of early American economic history: rapid expansion of population and settled area occurred without major structural changes in economic organization. Relatively little change in occupational structure or in the degree of urbanization took place in the colonial period, and British America was as much (or nearly so) a preindustrial society in 1775 as it had been in 1650. However, to acknowledge an absence of major structural change and the persistence of preindustrial forms of social organization is not to argue for a static portrait or to deny that some important changes did occur. But such changes were sometimes subtle. They occurred within a context of persistent continuity in certain basic features of economic structure and in the rhythms of daily life, and the pace and pattern of change varied sharply by region. For these reasons issues of change and continuity in early American economic history are often most successfully approached at the local level, through a study of external commerce in the several major regions of British America that focuses on the interactions between exports and other aspects of the colonial economy. Before examining those regions, however, it is useful to look at patterns of trade and the balance of payments for the colonies as a whole.

CHAPTER 4

THE CENTRALITY

OF TRADE

The notion that commerce was central to colonial economic life is firmly grounded in the literature of colonial American history. The idea that the export sector provides a useful point of departure for understanding the economy of early British America is not new to these pages. That the staples thesis fits neatly with many facts of the case and that it is valuable as an organizational device have long been recognized. But the role of trade transcended even the suggestions of that model.

Overseas commerce did not merely make colonial life comfortable; it made it possible. Without foreign trade, the colonists would have been unable to earn sufficient credits in their balance of payments to buy imported goods. Many of the immigrants would not have come in the first place, and only a few of those who did come would have stayed. Even those who emigrated largely for religious reasons planned carefully to ensure their economic well-being at levels considerably above mere subsistence. Moreover, the vast majority of settlers came to improve their economic condition; they sought far more than simple survival in a "wilderness." The promise of a prosperous America is what attracted settlers, and that prosperity rested in good measure on their ability to buy what they needed. When what they needed had to be imported, the colonists found diverse ways of paying for it, only a few of which involved the direct export of goods back to England.[1]

The colonists adopted a wide range of strategies to earn the needed credits in their balance of payments, strategies that can most easily be identified in regional terms. The chapters of the next section describe the specific trade patterns of the various regions of British America. While the regional patterns were distinct, the colonists shared at least one characteristic: even though they gained some credits on the capital and bul-

1. Migration is treated in chap. 10, below. The role of planning in the early colonial economies is discussed in chap. 16, below.

lion accounts, they earned the greatest amount of credits on the current account. That much is obvious.

What has been less clear is that the invisibles in the current account were considerable for the colonies as a whole and for certain of them were actually more important than the "visibles." Historians have long written about the export trade in goods; what we have to learn more about now is the "export trade" in commercial services. The carrying trade as an earner of credits in the balance of payments was an important alternative strategy to the export of commodities. Some historians believe it will prove on further investigation to have been important enough not only to offset imbalances in the commodity trade but also, perhaps, to create a surplus.[2] Thomas Willing, the foremost merchant of pre-

2. The occasional historical works on the subject of the colonial balance of payments have usually been seriously flawed. One historian compared the average annual difference in constant pounds sterling between the exports and imports of a particular colony with the current value in pounds currency of one man's estate. He concluded that one or more wealthy colonists could have paid the difference out of their own pockets. With travesties such as this being perpetrated by the unsophisticated, it might seem ungrateful to fault more-careful attempts to estimate the colonial balance of payments. Their mistakes, however, reveal needs and opportunities for further work. Curtis P. Nettels offered an extended and insightful description of the balance of payments of the southern and northern mainland colonies between 1698 and 1717 (*Money Supply*, 45–98). James A. Henretta then tried to give Nettels's ideas a tabular form (*Evolution of American Society*, 46). Nettels made a variety of minor and some major errors, however, chief of which was his failure to take full account of shipping earnings. Henretta's table repeated those errors and added a few new ones. The most glaring is the omission of any imports into the mainland colonies from other "colonial regions," i.e., the West Indies. Shepherd and Walton are considerably more thorough and more consistent than Nettels in their estimate of the colonial balance of payments between 1768 and 1772 (*Shipping*, 91–155). Their work, derived substantially from CUST 16/1, PRO, is based on James Floyd Shepherd, Jr., "A Balance of Payments for the Thirteen Colonies, 1768–1772" (Ph.D. diss., University of Washington, 1966). Still, there are numerous minor difficulties and at least three major problems with Shepherd and Walton's estimates. Their use of the CUST 16/1 data in totaling the commodity exports from the mainland colonies and the commodity imports from everywhere but Great Britain and Ireland fails to take into account any smuggling. Considerable quantities of sugar, molasses, and rum were imported but not entered into the official importation accounts (the naval officer shipping lists) from which the CUST 16/1 ledger was compiled. Shepherd and Walton's estimate of shipping costs, both as debits and credits, is based not on full-cargo tonnage but on discounted ship-tonnage figures. Finally, their procedure for allocating these costs as earnings among colonial and metropolitan shipowners seriously distorts reality. Despite these problems, their work will serve as the starting point for future efforts, and we have drawn on it in that way often in this chapter and elsewhere. Jacob M. Price, "A Note on the Value of Colonial Exports of Shipping," *Jour. Econ. Hist.*, XXXVI (1976), 704–724, is the kind of careful corrective to Shepherd and Walton needed for their other figures to give us a more accurate estimate of the colonial balance of payments.

Revolutionary Philadelphia, summed it up precisely: "Carriage is an amazing Revenue."[3]

The traditional emphasis on the commodity trades by both contemporaries and historians is largely a function of the available data. The English government, reflecting seventeenth-century mercantilistic concerns, began in the 1690s the systematic collection and compilation of commercial statistics. Annual accounts, kept in large ledgers in the Custom House, totaled the quantities and the values of goods entering and leaving English and Welsh ports. These data were the basis for all contemporary discussions of England's imports and exports and of its balance of trade with all areas of the world. The Custom House ledgers continue to be the premier source of information on English commerce. Nevertheless, several difficulties must be resolved before these statistics can be used to analyze the economy of the colonial period.[4]

For the modern historian of the economy of British America, the ledgers

---

3. As chairman of a committee of the Second Continental Congress, Willing made the comment on 4 October 1775 in a debate over whether foreign vessels should be permitted to carry colonial produce. He went on to draw a historical lesson in order to emphasize his opposition to such a suggestion: "Holland and England have derived their maritime Power from their Carriage." See John Adams's notes on the debate in *Diary and Autobiography of John Adams*, II, 188–192 (quotation on p. 190). See also Eugene R. Slaski, "Thomas Willing: A Study in Moderation, 1774–1778," *Pennsylvania Magazine of History and Biography*, C (1976), 491–506.

4. The basic introduction to these ledgers—designated CUST 3 in the PRO—is G. Clark, *Guide to English Commercial Statistics*. See also McCusker, "Current Value of English Exports." The ledgers are available commercially on microfilm from EP Microform Limited; there is an introductory booklet by W. E. Minchinton and C. J. French, *Customs 3 (1696–1780) in the Public Record Office, London* ([Wakefield, Yorkshire], 1974). Data were compiled from the ledgers and published by Charles Whitworth, *State of the Trade of Great Britain in Its Imports and Exports Progressively from the Year 1697 [to 1773] . . .* (London, 1776). Despite the title, his data are only for England and Wales. The ledgers were themselves compiled in the office of the Inspector General of Imports and Exports from information that was collected in the custom houses of the kingdom and sent to London. The ledgers, and the raw data from which they were made up, were the basis of almost all contemporary accounts of English trade. See John J. McCusker, *European Marine Lists and Bills of Entry: Early Commercial Publications and the Origins of the Business Press* (Cambridge, Mass., forthcoming). Elizabeth Boody Schumpeter, *English Overseas Trade Statistics, 1697–1808* (Oxford, 1960), is based on the ledgers, but unfortunately her data must be used with caution. See McCusker, "Rum Trade," 991, n. 24. T. S. Ashton presents a useful discussion of the data in his introduction to Schumpeter's book. Despite efforts like Schumpeter's, the ledgers have yet to be fully exploited either for English or colonial economic history. An English scholar, D. W. Jones of the University of York, has recently discovered earlier ledgers giving data for 1693–1695 in the Parchment Records, c. 35–42, House of Lords Record Office, London.

of imports and exports have three major defects. The first problem, long recognized but not always dealt with properly, concerns the prices used to value the commodities. The prices for each product were chosen in the late 1690s and, essentially, never changed; in most cases they remained unaltered into the nineteenth century. Since the market prices of goods did change, the annual totals became, in the words of Thomas Irving, "false data" for studying the balance of trade. Individuals used them for this purpose, government officials based policy decisions on them, but they quickly became inaccurate for such calculations. This means that contemporary statements about the balance of trade between Great Britain and British America (or anywhere else) did not reflect the reality of the commercial situation. In addition it means that statements about the balance of trade by modern historians based either on these figures or on contemporary analyses drawn from them are also inaccurate.[5]

Nevertheless, the data in the English customs ledgers are very valuable sources and can be turned to several uses. The annual totals, compiled at constant values, are de facto an index of English imports and exports with the base period of 1697–1701. They constitute, as a result, a comparative measure of the volume of English commerce. The data for the quantities of each item imported and exported provide a foundation for discussions of the various commodity trades. In turn, studies of commodity trades have the potential for assigning actual market prices to the quantities bought and sold. A combination of many similar studies of separate products may eventually allow us to reconstitute England's actual balance of trade.

As far as British America is concerned, the annual ledgers of imports to and exports from England and Wales pose another problem. Because they recorded just the trade of England and Wales, the only British American trade reported was that with the metropolis. Since the colonists did business with places besides England and Wales, any analysis of

5. From 1786 to 1800 Irving was in charge of the office that compiled the figures. The quote is from CUST 17/12, p. 4, as in John J. McCusker, "Colonial Civil Servant and Counter-revolutionary: Thomas Irving (1738?–1800) in Boston, Charleston, and London," *Perspectives Am. Hist.*, XII (1979), 345. Note that while a few woolen goods were revalued in 1709 (the prices of 49 out of 52 items were set by 1702), and while some further, but very minor changes were made in 1724, we can say for indexing purposes that 1699–1701 was effectively the base period (McCusker, "Rum Trade," 1071 and 1177, n. 197; E. Schumpeter, *English Overseas Trade Statistics*, 70; Minchinton and French, *Customs 3*, 14–16). Mc-Cusker, "Current Value of English Exports," discusses the difficulty in more detail and offers a means to correct the figures. Despite all this, there are still those willing to compare actual money figures with the uncorrected nominal trade figures. See Julian Gwyn, "British Government Spending and the North American Colonies, 1740–1775," *Journal of Imperial and Commonwealth History*, VIII (1980), 74–84 (especially p. 84n).

a colony's commerce drawn solely from the ledgers is, necessarily, incomplete.[6] Although these observations might seem to belabor the obvious, too many historians have drawn conclusions about a colony's balance of trade based on these data alone. It would have been quite possible for a colony to settle a debit in its trade with England by means of a credit in its traffic elsewhere and, moreover, to come out ahead in such three-sided transactions. Or vice versa. The English figures tell only part of the British American story.[7]

The third problem with the English trade figures is that they include only the "visibles" in the current account and thus are an incomplete measure of the national balance of payments. Even certain "visible" items are omitted, such as ships. The ledgers contain a partial tabulation of bullion flows, but what proportion that was of the whole we do not yet know. Nor do we know from the ledgers the dimensions of the capital account. But the omission of the invisibles in the current account is the most destructive of our understanding of either Britain's or the colonies' balance of payments. Contemporaries were aware of the importance of the costs of commercial services and the rest of the invisibles to international trade and finance, and a few authors attempted estimates. Unfortunately, these data were never formally entered into any balance-of-trade calculation. For some of the colonies, credits earned from shipping made the difference in their ability to maintain equilibrium in their overseas

6. The data drawn from the ledgers have sometimes been assumed to describe the trade between the colonies and all of Great Britain. This assumption has misled many historians, particularly those of the tobacco coast, a region where Scots traders were increasingly active in the 18th century. The Scots imported large quantities of Chesapeake tobacco, which does not appear in the CUST 3 ledgers, and returned to the Chesapeake via London large quantities of various goods, which do appear. Data drawn solely from the CUST 3 ledgers show a substantial deficit in the balance of trade for Maryland and Virginia; when Scottish trade figures are added in, the colonies register a small surplus. Cf. Ernst, *Money and Politics*, 13, 65, and Jacob M. Price, "New Time Series for Scotland's and Britain's Trade with the Thirteen Colonies and States, 1740 to 1791," *WMQ*, 3d Ser., XXII (1975), 307–325. This problem is compounded by a mistake in the published series of Scottish import and export values that lists each under the opposite heading. The columns labeled imports should be labeled exports, and vice versa (U.S. Bureau of the Census, *Historical Statistics of the United States, Colonial Times to 1970* [Washington, D.C., 1975], II, 1177–1178 [Ser. Z 227–244]). The correction sheet announcing this mistake that accompanied the original volume apparently failed to impress the publishers of the commercial edition. They neither corrected the mistake nor indicated that it existed. See Ben J. Wattenberg, ed., *The Statistical History of the United States, from Colonial Times to the Present* (New York, 1976).

7. As is the case with many mistaken attitudes and notions about the colonial economy, the roots of these erroneous observations can be traced back to the colonial period. Usually they are based on statements (such as in memorials designed to plead a case before a legislative body) that leave in some doubt the impartiality of the evidence adduced.

commerce. None of this is addressed by the data in the English ledgers of imports and exports.[8]

The distortions wrought by unadjusted commodity prices, the partial picture presented of colonial trade, and the omission of all but the "visibles" in the current account are three major obstacles to using the English ledgers in studying British American economic history. This does not mean that we must discard them, but only that there is a need to repair the distortions and make up for the omissions.

Just as British customs officials kept records of the goods imported and exported through British ports of entry, "naval officers" in British American ports of entry assembled "shipping lists," which recorded all vessels that came and went and the cargoes they carried. Unfortunately, these records—the naval officer shipping lists, sometimes abbreviated NOSL—vary considerably in their consistency and completeness, they make no attempt to place a value on the goods, and they have yet to be compiled adequately. Even though there are NOSL available for a number of ports of entry from as early as the 1670s (and some similar records from still earlier), no complete run exists for even one of the more than sixty ports of entry in British America. Nor is there a complete set of lists for all ports for any single year. A contemporary compilation for the five years 1768–1772 is based on the NOSL for the North American ports of entry, but nothing comparable is available for the Caribbean. Most modern attempts to create similar compilations, either from one port's lists for several years or from the lists from one period for several ports, have run into serious difficulties. Nevertheless, the records do exist from which to establish the current account in many colonies' balance of payments for at least a short period of time.[9]

8. See, for example, Shepherd and Walton's suggestion that the provision of shipping services was second only to the exportation of tobacco as an earner of credits in the colonists' balance of payments (*Shipping*, 135). Similarly, in Price's estimate of the credits earned by the colonies, the exporting of ships ranks sixth, just after fish, in that same ranking ("Note on Colonial Exports," 722). For bullion flows, see chap. 3, above.

9. For these records, see John J. McCusker, *An Introduction to the Naval Officer Shipping Lists* (in progress). The compilation referred to is CUST 16/1. In regard to this volume, see McCusker, "Colonial Civil Servant," 321–325. Many historians have introduced distortions into their work by their crude attempts to reduce the contents of various-sized containers to standard units of weights and measures. Imported and exported goods traveled in a myriad of packages, most of which varied in size by time, by point of origin, and by commodity and had many different names and different capacities. Commercial practice was fairly consistent, but it cannot be discovered by looking at statutory regulations: one has to examine merchants' record books. Most historians have looked at the former rather than the latter, creating considerable confusion. Among them are Shepherd and Walton, *Shipping*, 206, and James F. Shepherd, "Commodity Exports from the British North American Colonies to Overseas Areas, 1768–1772: Magnitude and Patterns of Trade," *Explorations*

For most uses of either the English customs ledgers or the colonial naval officer shipping lists smuggling is less of a problem than might be imagined. The ledgers of imports and exports do not suffer conspicuously from inaccuracies due to smuggling of the major colonial staples into or out of the metropolis. Smugglers preferred low-volume, high-value commodities such as tea and brandy. Even the smuggling of those products was not regularly pursued and was not as important to the total trade as traditional narratives have led us to believe.[10] Nearly all goods said in the ledgers to have been exported from England to British America went there; the records of imports from the colonies neither understate nor overstate greatly the quantities of goods actually landed in British ports.

Smuggling was of considerably greater significance in the trade to and from British American ports. How fully and accurately the colonial naval officer shipping lists reflect what entered and cleared colonial ports is open to question. Not all of the staple goods exported from British America that were supposed to go only to Great Britain (or to other British colonies) ended up there. This was especially true of sugar, tobacco, and the other enumerated commodities. But these activities were illegal only after the passage of the Navigation Acts, they diminished in importance considerably between 1660 and 1700, and by the eighteenth century smuggled goods accounted for a tiny fraction of all quantities handled. In addition, some European goods that were supposed to enter the colonies only by way of British ports found their way to Boston, New York, Bridgetown, and elsewhere either directly from Amsterdam and Bordeaux or by

---

Econ. Hist., VIII (1970), 72–73. To find out how much merchants packed in firkins and hogsheads historians can turn best to their accounts and papers, as was done, most successfully, by Helen Louise Klopfer, "Statistics of the Foreign Trade of Philadelphia, 1700–1860" (typescript, 1936; copies in the University of Pennsylvania Library, Philadelphia, and Hagley Museum and Library, Greenville, Delaware). Cf. McCusker, "Rum Trade," 768–878, and "Weights and Measures in the Colonial Sugar Trade: The Gallon and the Pound and Their International Equivalents," *WMQ*, 3d Ser., XXX (1973), 599–624, with a correction, *ibid.*, XXXI (1974), 164.

10. We are convinced on this point by the reasoning of Harper, *English Navigation Laws*, 246–274, and *passim*. See also T. C. Barker, "Smuggling in the Eighteenth Century: The Evidence of the Scottish Tobacco Trade," *Virginia Magazine of History and Biography*, LXII (1954), 387–399; Jacob M. Price, "The Tobacco Trade and the Treasury, 1685–1733: British Mercantilism in Its Fiscal Aspects" (Ph.D. diss., Harvard University, 1954); W. A. Cole, "Trends in Eighteenth-Century Smuggling," *Econ. Hist. Rev.*, 2d Ser., X (1958), 395–409; Hoh-Cheung Mui and Lorna H. Mui, "Smuggling and the British Tea Trade before 1784," *AHR*, LXXIV (1968), 44–73; Mui and Mui, "'Trends in Eighteenth-Century Smuggling' Reconsidered," *Econ. Hist. Rev.*, 2d Ser., XXVIII (1975), 28–43; W. A. Cole, "The Arithmetic of Eighteenth-Century Smuggling," *ibid.*, 44–49; and Robert C. Nash, "The English and Scottish Tobacco Trades in the Seventeenth and Eighteenth Centuries: Legal and Illegal Trade," *ibid.*, XXXV (1982), 354–372.

way of the Dutch and the French colonists in the New World. It is difficult to estimate the extent of these illegal imports, but they seem mainly to have been luxury wares like brandy, or special items such as Russia duck used for sailcloth, neither of which amounted to any considerable value in a given year.[11]

The major trade that went unrecorded in the colonial naval officer shipping lists was in sugar, molasses, and rum produced in the foreign West Indies and imported into the continental colonies without paying the duties required under the Molasses Act of 1733. This "smuggling" was tolerated, even encouraged, by lax customs enforcement. Tolerated or not, it is noteworthy for the present discussion because of the effect it had on colonial trade records and on our ability to use those records to analyze the colonial balance of payments.[12] Once the English customs ledgers and the colonial NOSL have been fully and carefully analyzed, we will know much more about the overseas business of British America.

In broad outline at least, we can already sketch something of the changing dimensions of colonial overseas trade. Coastwise trades, with small vessels exchanging surplus for surplus, sprang up almost immediately, linking neighboring coastal towns with one another. The natural extension of the coastwise commerce to towns farther away developed eventually into a network of intercolonial trades that stretched from Newfoundland to Barbados—and beyond. Equally natural was the increase in the volume and in the value of the goods exchanged. Vessels that in the first years merely exchanged small quantities of local produce expanded their activity considerably. By the end of the colonial period coastwise trade included everything from West Indian products to the full range of European wares, and for certain colonies at least, exports coastwise rivaled transoceanic commerce in importance.[13]

---

11. Harper makes specific mention of sugar and tobacco and, without denying the existence of smuggling in those commodities, discounts the extent of the illegal trade in both (*English Navigation Laws*, 246–274). There is perhaps more potential for a systematic attempt to assess illegal trade in the colonies than Harper allowed. One could compare the private records of individual merchants with what they entered in the official records. Enough such comparisons, carefully drawn, could provide a basis for cautious conclusions about the whole situation.

12. *Ibid.*, 242, and *passim*. For a limited attempt to estimate the extent of the smuggling of these commodities into North America, see McCusker, "Rum Trade," *passim*.

13. The development of colonial trade is discussed more fully in Part II, below. Cf. Charles M. Andrews, "Colonial Commerce," *AHR*, XX (1914), 43–63, and Kenkichi Omi, "Juhasseiki Amerika shokuminchi no boeki kozo ni tsuite" (On the structure of trade in the eighteenth-century American colonies), *Doshisha Amerika Kenkyu (Doshisha [University] American Studies)*, XVIII (1982), 51–59. For the coastwise trade more narrowly

Oceanic trades also changed during the colonial period, but less so in character than in volume. Imports into British America came mostly from the major British ports, with some exceptions, notably slaves, who were brought directly from Africa. Exports from the colonies went, again, mostly to the mother country. In addition some trade was carried on with "southern Europe" (the Iberian Peninsula and the Mediterranean) and with the Spanish and Portuguese Wine Islands (Madeira, the Azores, and the Canary Islands), largely an exchange of American fish for European wine and salt.

Only late in the colonial period did the character of colonial oceanic commerce begin to alter meaningfully. In the second third of the eighteenth century, as Europe in general became less and less able to feed itself, southern Europe began to import large quantities of colonial rice and wheat directly from the British colonies. By the 1760s this demand for food had expanded the colonists' transatlantic trade considerably, both in volume and in diversity.[14]

One other important change occurred in British American overseas trade between the time of first settlement and the Revolutionary era, a change that was in itself somewhat revolutionary. Initially, the ships that carried colonial imports and exports were owned and managed by Englishmen—the merchants of London, Bristol, and other ports. The element of control over colonial commerce inherent in this arrangement was equaled in importance by the money these merchants earned for themselves and their country from freights charged, interest accrued, and insurance sold.

Slowly but steadily, perhaps even at an increasing rate in the eighteenth century, British American trade came to be controlled by merchants resident in colonial ports. Over time colonial merchants expanded their activities, beginning as commission agents and later becoming both independent exporters and the owners and operators of their own ships.

---

defined, see especially James Floyd Shepherd and Samuel H. Williamson, "The Coastal Trade of the British North American Colonies, 1768–1772," *Jour. Econ. Hist.*, XXXII (1972), 783–810, and the valuable older study by T. W. Van Metre, "American Coastwise Trade before 1789," in Emory R. Johnson *et al.*, *History of Domestic and Foreign Commerce of the United States* (Washington, D.C., 1915), I, 162–174. Despite some useful recent work, Arthur L. Jensen's judgment that "trade among the continental colonies has been treated as something of a poor relation" by historians of early American commerce still stands (*The Maritime Commerce of Colonial Philadelphia* [Madison, Wis., 1963], 70).

14. See Part II, below, for more detail. A useful collection of data on trade, much of it first compiled under the direction of Lawrence A. Harper from the naval officer shipping lists, has been assembled in U.S. Bureau of the Census, *Historical Statistics*, II, 1168–1200 *passim.*

While this development occurred first in colonies that lacked a staple export, eventually indigenous merchants and shipowners were active everywhere. By the second third of the eighteenth century colonial merchants
were not only fully in command of the coastwise commerce, but also had
begun to extend their operations into the transatlantic trades. At first this
expansion involved just the export of codfish, rice, and wheat flour to
southern Europe and the Wine Islands. Around mid-century, however, a
few colonial merchants began to dabble in the export of tobacco and
sugar to Britain itself. They started to compete directly in the business
that merchants of the mother country traditionally thought of as entirely
their own.[15]

Let us attempt to sum up all of these impressions. Despite the inadequacies of the evidence, it is occasionally justifiable to estimate from imperfect data and sometimes simply to guess. Thanks to the efforts of
James F. Shepherd and Gary M. Walton, there is a useful description of
the colonial balance of payments for the years 1768 to 1772. Their estimates for the thirteen continental colonies are summarized in table 4.1.

Clearly the colonies, especially New England and the Middle Colonies,
suffered considerable deficits in the commodity trade with Great Britain,

15. We should be careful, as Richard Pares and others have warned, not to overestimate the
independence of colonial merchants involved in trading with places other than Britain, because English capital, in the form of short-term credit, was often essential. Pares's comment
on the trade between the northern colonies and the West Indies during the 1760s perhaps
applied to other trades as well: "The English capitalist was less directly useful to the trade
between the continent and the sugar islands, and above all he had less control over it, than
in the early days; but the North American entrepreneur would have been hard put to it to
do without him" (*Yankees and Creoles: The Trade between North America and the West
Indies before the American Revolution* [Cambridge, Mass., 1956], 163). See also Price,
"Economic Function," 159–160. For the importance of short-term credit in the colonial
economy, see Price, *Capital and Credit*. Short-term loans connected with the shipment of
goods are accounted for as part of the invisibles in the balance of payments. Clearly, a detailed study of the sources of capital employed by the more independent colonial merchants—those who traded on their own account rather than as factors for British firms—is
a major need in early American economic history. Cf. chap. 16, below. For the activities of a
colonial firm in the export of tobacco to Britain, see Jacob M. Price, "Joshua Johnson in
London, 1771–1775: Credit and Commercial Organization in the British Chesapeake
Trade," in *Statesmen, Scholars, and Merchants: Essays in Eighteenth-Century History Presented to Dame Lucy Sutherland*, ed. Anne Whiteman, J. S. Bromley, and P. G. M. Dickson
(Oxford, 1973), 153–180, and *Joshua Johnson's Letterbook, 1771–1774: Letters from a
Merchant in London to His Partners in Maryland*, ed. Price (London, 1979). For some insights into the way in which colonial businessmen operated, see Harry D. Berg, "The Organization of Business in Colonial Philadelphia," *Pennsylvania History*, X (1943), 157–177,
and Stuart Bruchey, "Success and Failure Factors: American Merchants in Foreign Trade
in the Eighteenth and Early Nineteenth Centuries," *Bus. Hist. Rev.*, XXXIII (1958),
272–292.

TABLE 4.1.
*Estimated Average Annual Debits and Credits
in the Balance of Payments of
the Thirteen Continental Colonies, 1768–1772
(Thousands of Pounds Sterling)*

	Debits	Credits
Current account ("visibles")		
Commodities		
Exports to Great Britain and Ireland		£1,615
Imports from Great Britain and Ireland	£3,082	
Exports to the West Indies		759
Imports from the West Indies	770	
Exports to southern Europe and Wine Islands		426
Imports from southern Europe and Wine Islands	68	
Ship sales		140
Payments for servants	80	
Payments for slaves	200	
Current account (invisibles)		
Trade related		
Earnings from freighting goods		600
Earnings from commissions, interest, insurance		220
Money transfers by immigrants		—
British government collections/expenditures in continental colonies		
Taxes and duties	40	
Military expenditures		400
Salaries of civil servants		40
Capital and bullion accounts		
Specie and indebtedness	—	40
Totals	£4,240	£4,240
Subtotals		
Total exports		2,800
Total imports	3,920	
Balance of commodity trade	1,120	

Table 4.1 continued

Sources: James F. Shepherd and Gary M. Walton, *Shipping, Maritime Trade, and the Economic Development of Colonial North America* (Cambridge, 1972), 115; Walton and Shepherd, *The Economic Rise of Early America* (Cambridge, 1979), 101; and Jacob M. Price, "A Note on the Value of Colonial Exports of Shipping," *Journal of Economic History*, XXXVI (1976), 704–724.

Notes: Southern Europe and the Wine Islands includes Africa. Exports are valued F.O.B. (that is, "freight on board"), exclusive of ocean freight charges, mercantile commissions, interest, and insurance; imports, valued C.I.F. (that is, "cost, insurance, freight"), include such charges. The dashes indicate categories for which we have no estimates; thus they have no impact on the data in the table, though obviously they had some impact in reality. For other problems with these estimates, see n. 2, above.

amounting to nearly £1.5 million sterling over the period. Despite frequent assertions to the contrary, the commodity trade with the West Indies did little to make up the difference. Indeed, with the exception of the Lower South, all of the major colonial regions registered slight deficits in that trade. Due largely to exports from Pennsylvania and New York, the colonies did earn substantial credits in the commodity trade with southern Europe, the Wine Islands, and Africa. Such earnings helped, but the colonies were still left with a large deficit—more than £1.1 million annually—in the current account by the exchange of goods. That deficit was borne entirely by the northern colonies, for the great staple-producing regions of the South actually earned a small surplus through the commodity trade.

Most of the deficit was made up through the provision of shipping and other commercial services and through the sale of ships. Jacob Price has recently estimated, conservatively he believes, that the continental colonies on the eve of the Revolution earned £140,000 sterling per year from the sale of ships built for export. Contemporaries did not include ships sold abroad as part of the "visibles" in the current account. The invisibles in the current account were a still greater earner of credits. Shepherd and Walton estimate that the colonists, most of them New Englanders, New Yorkers, and Pennsylvanians, earned £600,000 annually through freights and an additional £220,000 from various commercial services. Taken together, these several sources of credits were sufficient to reduce the large deficit from the commodity trade to a very modest £160,000 annually.[16]

16. Price, "Note on Colonial Exports," 722–724. Cf. Lord Sheffield's estimate that the continental colonists earned £245,000 annually carrying freight from their ports to the British West Indies in the years just before the Revolution (John, Lord Sheffield, *Observations on the Commerce of the American States*, 6th ed. [London, 1784], 184–185).

Colonists also incurred large deficits in their balance of payments from the purchase of servants and slaves, £280,000 annually by Shepherd and Walton's figures. Part of that deficit was made up by the arrival of free immigrants with some capital. We know so little about this subject that we dare not attempt an estimate, but it was clearly of major importance for certain times and places.[17] The remainder of that deficit was more than covered by the credits earned through British expenditures required to maintain a military presence and a civilian administration; together they produced a net gain to the colonies in the neighborhood of £400,000.[18] All totaled, the colonists on the continent incurred a deficit in their current account of only £40,000 annually. This could have been made up easily through the shipment of specie. As historians have gradually come to appreciate the importance of all these elements, the traditional notion of a severe, chronic deficit for the colonies has been discarded.[19]

17. In New England, during the 1630s and early 1640s, for example. See chap. 5, below.

18. Julian Gwyn has recently offered some revisions to Shepherd and Walton's estimates of imperial expenditures in the colonies. See "British Government Spending," 74–84, and "The Impact of British Military Spending on Colonial American Money Markets, 1760–1783," Canadian Historical Association, *Historical Papers/Communications historiques,* LVIII (1980), 77–99.

19. Recall that any British investments in the colonies are accounted as credits in the colonial balance of payments, and vice versa, any colonial investments in British stocks, as debits. We know almost nothing about long-term investments either by British investors in the colonies or by colonists in British enterprises. One colony, Maryland, invested monies collected from tobacco export duties in shares of the Bank of England. See Jacob M. Price, "The Maryland Bank Stock Case: British-American Financial and Political Relations before and after the American Revolution," in *Law, Society, and Politics in Early Maryland,* ed. Aubrey C. Land, Lois Green Carr, and Edward C. Papenfuse (Baltimore, 1977), 3–40, and Price, *Capital and Credit, passim.* The source of specie for export from the continental colonies was their trade with the West Indies. There are no regular records of the importation (or reexportation) of gold and silver, and estimates are few. Concerning the years just before the War of Independence, Shepherd and Walton considered such imports unlikely to have been "of any large magnitude" (*Shipping,* 153). In contrast, speaking of the first two decades of the 18th century, a contemporary regarded it as "the Opinion of many, that within these Twenty Years, near a Million [pounds sterling] of Gold or Silver hath been exported hence, and I believe they are not much out in their Computation" ([John Colman], *The Distressed State of the Town of Boston, etc. Considered* [Boston, 1720], 4). Thomas Banister, writing of the first half of the period to which Colman referred, thought that "in that Time also we had our Spanish Gold and Silver, and New-England Coin, to make the Balance; of which we sent Home yearly, 30, 40, 50, or 60000*l.* [sterling] 'till all was gone" (*A Letter to the Right Honourable the Lords Commissioners of Trade and Plantations: or, A Short Essay on the Principal Branches of the Trade of New-England . . .* [London, 1715], 9). A draft of Banister's pamphlet is in CO 5/866, fols.

These data on the colonial balance of payments describe a strong, flexible, and diverse economy, one able to operate without a considerable metropolitan subsidy—with the important exception of British defense spending—and to earn credits by several means in a variety of markets. Colonists relied heavily on British markets for the sale of their products, on short-term commercial credit extended by British merchants to finance trade, and on British manufactures to maintain their standard of living. However, they did not depend on large inflows of British capital to finance development and expansion over the long haul. Colonists accumulated most of their capital on their own, through savings and, especially, through the hard work of farm building.

How long had that been the case? We cannot answer the question with any precision until someone replicates Shepherd and Walton's efforts for the more distant colonial past. While the changing pattern of trade suggests that growing demand for food in the West Indies and in southern Europe in the mid-eighteenth century did much to diversify and strengthen the British American economy, it is clear that New Englanders had long since been providing a wide range of goods and services to a variety of customers. There was probably much validity to the complaint of London merchants in 1676 that, based on its extensive trade with European and colonial ports, "New England is now become the greate Martt and Staple." Further, evidence suggests that most colonies registered only small deficits in their balance of payments even early after settlement, and that while most relied on heavy metropolitan subsidies at first, they quickly, within a few decades, outgrew their dependence. Much remains to be learned about the development of British American economies; constructing estimates of the balance of payments by colony or re-

---

221–230v, PRO. Banister thought also that the amount exported had declined by 1715 to £2,500 annually. According to a contemporary calculation by Charles Knowles, the governor of Jamaica, over the years 1735–1752 ships from North America exported an annual average of about £71,000 sterling in specie. Echoing the West Indians' traditional lament, he complained that all of it was taken to French islands to buy French West Indian sugar and molasses (Knowles to Board of Trade, 18 Nov. 1752, CO 137/25, fol. 274v). Had this level of specie exports by the Yankee merchants remained the same until 1768–1772, and had the colonists chosen to use it for another purpose, only a little more than half the sum would have been enough to satisfy the demands of the specie account in their balance of payments. It was reported of Philadelphia in the mid-1760s that "the silversmiths apply for an assay office, in consequence of the large quantities of precious metals which came into the province for manufacture and export" (J. Thomas Scharf and Thompson Westcott, *History of Philadelphia, 1609–1884* [Philadelphia, 1884], I, 260). For an estimate of the balance of payments of the British West Indian colonies, see Sheridan, *Sugar and Slavery*, 467–470.

gion when and where the evidence permits will provide a most useful analytical tool.[20]

Not all British American trade was overseas trade. Colonial merchants, like the Roman god Janus, faced two directions—inland as well as toward the sea. The products that they exported and imported had to be collected from or sold to other colonists, and this involved merchants in a wide variety of activities. More than a simple conduit between producers and consumers, they were often interested in the production or processing of commodities, in shipbuilding, and in finance. And they were immediately concerned with furthering all of these activities by mobilizing, insofar as possible, local, colonial, and imperial authorities to defend and expand the activities in which they were involved. The colonial merchant as entrepreneur served to link the overseas and the domestic economies of British America and thereby to establish and confirm the centrality of trade.[21]

How large was the contribution of external trade to British American colonial income? What was its share of total colonial economic activity? Obviously a precise answer to these questions is impossible, but some estimates have been offered. Shepherd and Walton place the average annual per capita value of commodity exports from the thirteen continental colonies to all overseas areas (including the West Indies) between 1768 and 1772 at £1.40 sterling. Assuming total incomes per capita to have been between £11.00 and £12.50, exports contributed from 11 to 13 percent of the whole. If we include the value of ships sold abroad (£140,000) and an estimate of invisible earnings (£820,000), per capita income from foreign trade rises to £1.75 and exports contributed 14 to

20. Again, see Part II, below, and Shepherd and Walton, *Shipping*, 154–155. The quotation is from a petition signed by 28 merchants and endorsed as having been received 19 Jan. 1675/6, CO 1/36, fol. 16r.

21. Very little work has been done on this subject. Despite the numerous studies published on colonial merchants, one still gets the feeling that, as Arthur H. Cole once wrote, "apparently, the staves and the salt fish, the flour and the pig iron walked themselves to the ports" ("The Tempo of Mercantile Life in Colonial America," *Bus. Hist. Rev.*, XXXIII [1959], 288). We were led to this quotation by the work of one person who has attempted to clarify how internal trade worked in the colonial period. See David E. Dauer, "Colonial Philadelphia's Intraregional Transportation System: An Overview," Regional Econ. Hist. Research Center, *Working Papers*, II, no. 3 (1979), 1–16. Even the best studies of colonial merchants fail to give much attention to their involvement in internal trade. See, for example, W. T. Baxter, *The House of Hancock: Business in Boston, 1724–1775* (Cambridge, Mass., 1945); James B. Hedges, *The Browns of Providence Plantations*, I: *Colonial Years* (Cambridge, Mass., 1952); and Philip L. White, *The Beekmans of New York in Politics and Commerce, 1647–1877* (New York, 1956). But cf. Margaret E. Martin, *Merchants and Trade of the Connecticut River Valley, 1750–1820* (Northampton, Mass., 1939).

16 percent of total income. If we further add the value of commodity exports in the coastal trades (£715,000), the per capita figure reaches £2.10, 17 to 19 percent of the total. This seems a substantial share of colonial income. It would be slightly higher were a reliable estimate of invisible earnings in the coastal trade available, substantially higher if attention was confined to market transactions and production for home use excluded.[22]

Did the contribution of commerce to total income change during the colonial period? A few historians have suggested that its share fell over the eighteenth century, and that is certainly the conclusion indicated by the course of commodity exports to Great Britain. It is clear, however, that other trades grew more rapidly than that with Britain, perhaps fast enough to offset the per capita fall in that trade. When we consider products shipped to places other than Great Britain, earnings from the coastal trade, ship sales, and income from shipping and commercial services, the case for a declining contribution to total output from external commerce is less compelling. At any rate, with external trade accounting for nearly 20 percent of total income at the end of the colonial era and perhaps for a larger share earlier, an approach to the economy of British America through its export sector seems amply justified, even if that sector experienced a slight relative decline over the eighteenth century.[23]

While it is possible to discuss the pattern of *colonial* commerce, the *colonial* balance of payments, and the contribution of exports to *colonial* income, it is clear that the resulting broad generalizations obscure significant differences among the several colonies. In fact, it can be argued that no such thing as a "colonial economy" developed until nearly the end of the era, after the coastwise trade had performed its work of integration, and then only involving British North America. Rather, there were sets of "colonial economies" linked more closely with London than with each

22. Shepherd and Walton, *Shipping*, 44. We have followed their lead in accepting Robert E. Gallman's estimate of per capita income and Stella Sutherland's estimate of total population for purposes of this calculation. See *ibid.*, 29–30; [Gallman], "The Pace and Pattern of American Economic Growth," in *American Economic Growth*, ed. Davis, Easterlin, and Parker, 15–23; and U.S. Bureau of the Census, *Historical Statistics*, II, 1168 (Ser. Z 1). For the value of ship sales and invisible earnings, see table 4.1, above. For the coastal trade, see Shepherd and Williamson, "Coastal Trade," 798.

23. [Robert E. Lipsey], "Foreign Trade," in *American Economic Growth*, ed. Davis, Easterlin, and Parker, 548–581 (especially p. 554), describes a substantial decline in the share of total output contributed by exports after the 18th century. He also makes it clear that exports were a much larger part of the whole at the end of the colonial period than they were by the middle of the 19th century, when they accounted for about 6% of the GNP.

other or, alternatively, one grand "Atlantic economy." Thus a focus on regional patterns often provides the key to a better understanding of the workings of the economy as a whole. Moreover, much of the best literature in early American economic history is regional and local in character. For these reasons, we approach a fuller discussion of the British American economy through an analysis of its major regions.

The groupings that we employ are conventional and firmly rooted in the historiography of the field. They have stood up well over the years and have provided many historians with a useful set of organizational categories. The following section treats each of five areas in successive chapters: New England (composed of Massachusetts, New Hampshire, Connecticut, and Rhode Island—and, for a time, Nova Scotia, Quebec, and even Newfoundland); the Upper South, or Chesapeake (Maryland and Virginia); the British West Indies; the Lower South (North Carolina, South Carolina, Georgia, and Florida); and the Middle Colonies (New York, New Jersey, Pennsylvania, and Delaware). The groupings include colonies with many similarities, and we will often discuss in detail something that happened in one colony and argue that it resembled trends or events in other colonies in the same region. We should stress the tentative, exploratory nature of these statements.

This caution is appropriate for several reasons, not the least of which is that the regions given are static, implying that they have equal analytic validity over the entire period 1607–1790. That was not always the case. Newfoundland only gradually entered Boston's sphere of influence. Nova Scotia, which emerged slowly as New England's outpost, became a separate colony in 1749 and began an equally slow detachment from Yankee influence. Quebec and Connecticut were drawn by degrees into New York's sphere. Another distortion arises from our designation of whole colonies as being entirely in one region when the opposite was frequently true. Economically speaking, East Jersey belonged to New York and West Jersey to Pennsylvania, for instance, while North Carolina can be grouped with both the Upper South and the Lower South. Parts of Maryland were oriented toward the Chesapeake Bay and parts toward the Delaware River. The problem stems from the collection and organization of data by political unit, which is often misleading for the purposes of economic analysis. One is far better off for the colonial era in thinking of economic regions as focused on the major waterways (for example, the Delaware River valley or Albemarle Sound), as organized around the production of a particular staple export, or as comprising the hinterland of a major seaport. Real opportunities exist in analyzing the economy of British America in these terms—with trade at the center of that focus, or as the organizer of that production, or as the magnet drawing people and goods to that seaport.[24]

24. The point here is underscored by an awareness that the colonists in their trade did not always fully observe such things as the limits of the colonial naval officer shipping districts. Anyone who has wondered why almost no slaves were imported into northern Virginia, as the returns from the officers of the port of South Potomac would seem to show, need only read a letter from the firm of Buchanan & Simson to that of Halliday & Dunbar in late 1759: "There are many Negroes imported this Year And as the duty is vastly higher in Virg[ini]a than Maryland all the Vessells have sold on the North side of Potowmack not less than 2000 Slaves" (quoted in Jacob M. Price, "Buchanan & Simson, 1759–1763: A Different Kind of Glasgow Firm Trading to the Chesapeake," *WMQ*, 3d Ser., XL [1983], 29). Cf. Allan Kulikoff, "The Origins of Afro-American Society in Tidewater Maryland and Virginia, 1700–1790," *ibid.*, XXXV (1978), 226–259.

PART II

THE COLONIAL ECONOMY—
A REGIONAL APPROACH

CHAPTER 5

NEW ENGLAND AND

ATLANTIC CANADA

New England long dominated the attention of early American historians and still remains a central concern of current scholarship. Nevertheless, we know surprisingly little about New England's economy. This is not entirely the result of an absence of effort; indeed, a rich monographic literature exists and historians have dealt with many of the major economic topics. Part of the difficulty lies in the structure of the New England economy. From the start it was diverse and complex by colonial standards, less highly specialized and thus less easily summarized than that of the staple-producing plantation regions. But our lack of knowledge also reflects where scholars have put their effort.

Economic issues have seldom commanded center stage in New England studies, and monographic work in economic history has had too little impact on more-general accounts. Historians of New England have focused instead on religious and intellectual issues and on the search for the origins of an elusive "national character," for the transformation of "Puritan" into "Yankee." Recently, these concerns have been supplemented by an interest in social and demographic history, by an effort to understand how families functioned in their community setting. This new focus has made New England central to early American social history, but despite promising beginnings, recent work has as yet failed to yield much insight into the operation of the economy.[1]

1. William B. Weeden's *Economic and Social History of New England, 1620–1789* (Boston, 1891), remains the only comprehensive survey. It is a still-useful compendium, but it is weak on analysis, does not deal with much that is currently of interest, and is obviously dated. Bernard Bailyn's now classic study, *The New England Merchants in the Seventeenth Century* (Cambridge, Mass., 1955), covers more than the title suggests, but even so tells only part of the story since it emphasizes Massachusetts and Boston over other regions and stresses the commercial sector of the economy. A brief survey by Douglas R. McManis, *Colonial New England: A Historical Geography* (New York, 1975), although occasionally superficial, is a good introduction to many topics. On the whole, however, we must rely on

This neglect is unfortunate, because a thorough understanding of New England's economy is necessary for an appreciation of Britain's empire in the Americas. The settlers of New England, earlier and more persistently than those in other regions, tested the limits of a colonial economy. They lacked a major staple commodity to export to the metropolis, yet they needed to import countless things from abroad. To resolve the dilemma they developed a variety of strategies to employ more fully the land, labor, capital, and skills at their disposal and to earn adequate credits in their balance of payments.

Three of the strategies that New Englanders adopted early on were especially effective and set a pattern not only for New Englanders themselves but also for other, like-minded colonists. First, the New Englanders attempted to manufacture some of the things they otherwise would have had to import. Second, they quickly learned that, however little demand existed in England for the goods they could export, there was a considerable demand for them elsewhere in the world, particularly in the West Indies. Yankee merchants pushed the export of those commodities, often sending them to third parties who paid the New Englanders in goods or credits that had currency in London. Finally, they learned that the shipping business itself could generate considerable credits, and merchants soon accepted both the risks and the benefits of the "carrying trade." The New Englanders became the Dutch of England's empire. The earnings from these endeavors joined with a successful subsistence agriculture and a growing domestic market to create a flourishing economy, though one less prosperous than the plantation economies to the south.

The New Englanders created a well-integrated commercial economy based on the carrying trade. As a result, New England resembled nothing so much as old England itself. And that, of course, was the problem. Each of these pursuits, no matter how innocently begun or how small its initial extent, had critical implications for the British Empire. Yet none of the activities ran counter to the letter of the Navigation Acts. New England's early pretensions that acts of Parliament had no meaning unless somehow confirmed or approved by colonial legislatures had already started to crumble well before the events of the 1680s established royal control of

studies specific to time, place, and subject matter, most of which are cited below. A recent article by Bruce C. Daniels, "Economic Development in Colonial and Revolutionary Connecticut: An Overview," *WMQ*, 3d Ser., XXXVII (1980), 429–450, categorizes the major topics and provides a bibliography. Perry Miller was often hostile and occasionally contemptuous of economic history, but we ought not ignore his work, because it remains profoundly influential in New England studies and because it is a compelling interpretation of economic and social developments. See especially *The New England Mind: From Colony to Province* (Cambridge, Mass., 1953).

Massachusetts. New England's own merchants recognized that the opportunities for trade within the empire were ample compensation for concessions on mere matters of form. Simple expansion of New England's trade along the lines set down in the colonies' earliest days gave them more than enough chances to increase their prosperity. But it was in the expansion of domestic processing and manufacturing, of a far-reaching export business, and especially, of an efficient and profitable carrying trade, again, all quite "legal," that New Englanders—and all colonists engaged in similar schemes—mounted a growing challenge to the hegemony of the metropolis. When, after the middle of the eighteenth century, Parliament tried to redress the balance by changing some of the rules of the Old Empire, the colonists cried "foul." In the discovery that they had no constitutional way to protect their economic rights as they saw them, the colonists found the need for political independence; in the prior growth of an autonomous economy, they found the means.

All of this developed steadily over the century and a half following the founding of the several colonies that made up New England. Plans for settlement had included elaborate arrangements to develop the staples that the organizers of the colonies expected to find there. Furs, fish, timber and timber products, and other commodities were assumed both to be abundantly available in the colonies and to be consistently in demand in England. The first few years after the initial settlement at Massachusetts Bay in 1630 seemed to fulfill those expectations. Yet within a decade the colonies' economy suffered a sharp, severe contraction. While not limited to New England, or even to the colonies, that depression caused the leaders of Massachusetts to rethink their entire situation.[2]

The fields of New England produced grain and stones, the latter more easily and abundantly than the former. It was only with some difficulty that the colonists were able to feed themselves; even the small surplus of grains they eventually began to produce would never become a valuable staple export to the metropolis because England grew its own grains. It also caught its own fish. The fishermen of New England, however successful, could not expect to export their catch to England. There was an English market for timber, particularly pine-tree masts for ships, and for timber products, especially tar and turpentine, but the English market was regularly and cheaply supplied from the Scandinavian countries. The New England farmers who cut and fashioned shingles and staves and

2. For the Puritans' early expectations and initial planning, see John Winthrop's "Arguments for the Plantation of New England," and related documents, in *Winthrop Papers, 1498–1649* (Boston, 1929–1947), II, 138–149, and *passim*.

headings for casks in the off season found no market for them in the home country. Even these unfinished wooden products were normally and cheaply supplied to England from other places. New Englanders were able to export some furs, and for a time these produced significant credits in the metropolis. But local supplies proved small and were quickly exhausted, while the French and the Dutch blocked efforts to tap new, more-remote sources. New England's fur trade was in sharp decline by 1660, dead by 1675.[3]

None of this was clear initially, chiefly because the early years of Massachusetts witnessed a prosperity induced, somewhat artificially, by the constant arrival of additional settlers. The early Puritan organizers of the colony were followed across the Atlantic by large numbers of other settlers, all of whom had just liquidated their assets in the mother country. They spent their money in the colony buying food to eat, land to farm, timber to build houses, and all the other things they needed in the New World in order to establish lives as similar as possible to what they had left behind in the Old. They organized an economy with the same priorities in mind and within a decade had come close to duplicating, at least in rough outline, the life of the English towns after which they named those they created in New England: Cambridge, Plymouth, Boston, and the rest.[4]

Except for the very basics of life, New England relied on old England. Even in the 1630s the merchants of Boston were doing a considerable business importing goods from home. In part, they paid for them by exporting local goods, but these were an insufficient source of credits. Boston merchants had even begun in a very small way to trade with their neighbors on the continent and in the Caribbean, notably the English at Barbados and Virginia and the Dutch at New Amsterdam. Some Barbadian sugar, Virginian tobacco, and Dutch furs arrived at London via

3. On New England's fur trade, which clearly merits a new study focusing on prices, quantities, organization, and especially, the role of Indians, see Bailyn, *New England Merchants*, 23–32, 49–60; Arthur H. Buffinton, "New England and the Western Fur Trade, 1629–1675," Colonial Society of Massachusetts, *Publications*, XVIII: *Transactions, 1915–1916* (1917), 160–192; Francis Xavier Moloney, *The Fur Trade in New England, 1620–1676* (Cambridge, Mass., 1931); Ronald Oliver MacFarlane, "The Massachusetts Bay Truck-Houses in Diplomacy with the Indians," *NEQ*, XI (1938), 48–65; and William I. Roberts III, "The Fur Trade of New England in the Seventeenth Century" (Ph.D. diss., University of Pennsylvania, 1958). See also chap. 15, below.

4. For the critical role of migration in the prosperity of the 1630s, see Bailyn, *New England Merchants*, 32–39; Darrett B. Rutman, "Governor Winthrop's Garden Crop: The Significance of Agriculture in the Early Commerce of Massachusetts Bay," *WMQ*, 3d Ser., XX (1963), 396–415; Rutman, *Winthrop's Boston: Portrait of a Puritan Town, 1630–1649* (Chapel Hill, N.C., 1965), 177–183; and Rutman, *Husbandmen of Plymouth: Farms and Villages in the Old Colony, 1620–1692* (Boston, 1967), 13–16.

Boston as early as the mid-1630s. Neither exports nor reexports met the entire cost of New England's imports, however. Their chief remittance of the 1630s was through the bullion and capital accounts. They shipped home either the cash that arriving immigrants had brought with them or the bills of exchange those immigrants drew on funds they had left behind in the hands of merchants. Still, such resources would not last long. As immigration waned other sources of remittances for English goods would be needed.[5]

Whatever the definitive causes of the empire-wide contraction of the late 1630s and early 1640s, the depression was intensified for New England by the ending of immigration. The changed political situation in England, culminating in the calling of the Long Parliament in the fall of 1640, signaled better times for the Puritans and "caused all men to stay in England in expectation of a new world." The resulting depression in New England was profound. Contemporary descriptions tell of disastrous declines in the market prices for corn and cattle and the stopping of all trade: "No man could pay his debts, nor the merchants make return into England for their commodities." Well beyond the abilities of individual farmers or merchants to deal with, the economic crisis required the immediate intervention of the colonial government if the "Citty upon a Hill" was to survive.[6]

The nature and the extent of the Massachusetts government's intervention in the economy during the depression had considerable precedent. From the start, the government had played a central role in the colonial economy: it organized the initial migration, tried to regulate wages and prices, supervised the establishment of towns, and provided incentives to build bridges and roads, construct mills, set up ferries, erect and maintain wharves and cranes, and the like. When hard times threatened, the colony's officials were expected to deal with the crisis. The government's function, after all, was to preserve the Puritan commonwealth.

In order to do just that, to preserve the colony, the governor and the

5. The evidence of Boston's early trade is from the London port books—specifically E 190/41/1, E 190/42/1, E 190/41/5, and E 351/907, PRO—as compiled by A. M. Millard, "The Import Trade of London, 1600–1640" (Ph.D. thesis, University of London, 1956). See also the works by Bailyn and Rutman cited in n. 4, above.

6. [John Winthrop], *Winthrop's Journal: "History of New England," 1630–1649*, ed. James Kendall Hosmer (New York, 1908), II, 31 (2 June 1641). Those inclined to stress the unique motivations of migrants to New England should note that other colonies experienced equally sharp declines in migration around 1640. For the depression and its consequences, see the items cited in n. 4, above, and Gottfried, "First Depression in Massachusetts," 655–678. The reference is, of course, John Winthrop's, borrowing from the Sermon on the Mount, Matthew 5:14 ("A Modell of Christian Charity," on board the *Arabella*, 1630, *Winthrop Papers*, II, 295).

General Court undertook a variety of measures to restore prosperity. These measures took several forms, but they focused on the inherent weaknesses in overseas trade that the depression so starkly revealed. While some of the major successes had more to do with private than public initiative, the result over the years 1640 to 1660 was not only a revival of agriculture and trade but also the establishment of New England's economy on the path it would follow until the end of the colonial period.[7]

The Massachusetts General Court perceived the colony's economic difficulties as a result of its adverse balance of payments. "So long as our ingate exceeds our outgate," the court observed in 1646, "the ballance must needs be made [up] by much within such a proportion as it is with us"; this "cann leave us but litle mony." Their programs called for an increase in exports ("outgate") and a decrease in imports ("ingate"). To accomplish these objectives they would employ promotive measures similar to those used in the colony's first decade. Imports could be cut back if the General Court could induce more colonists to make domestically items that were currently being imported; exports could be expanded if the court encouraged the development of new markets and the production of new exports. A concomitant of the latter goal would be an increase in the colonial-based shipping industry, which would convey such goods abroad to market. While the results differed somewhat from expectations, the general improvement in the economic picture between 1639 and the mid-1650s was most satisfying.[8]

The major thrust of the General Court's program was to cut down on imports, the bulk of which were English manufactured goods. This was to be accomplished by promoting the manufacture of a variety of items that could be produced in the colony. Clothing, shoes and boots, glass, and ironware all seemed likely candidates both because they made up a large share of the total value of imports and because New England possessed the necessary raw materials to produce them. The government's role then became one of promoting the organization of the productive enterprises through a range of devices that included grants of land and money, bounties, monopolies of local markets, tax incentives, freedom from military obligations for workers, and even a relaxation of religious regulations.[9]

7. Bailyn, *New England Merchants*, chaps. 2–4, is the best analysis of the promotive efforts of the government. See also chap. 16, below.

8. Letter to [the Company of Undertakers of the Iron Works in New England], 4 Nov. 1646, in Shurtleff, ed., *Records of Massachusetts Bay*, III, 92.

9. See, for example, E. N. Hartley, *Ironworks on the Saugus: The Lynn and Braintree Ventures of the Company of Undertakers of the Ironworks in New England* (Norman, Okla., 1957).

Although its accomplishments are easily underestimated, the effort to industrialize early New England was not successful. Manufacturing enterprises were plagued by the central characteristics of a colonial economy: scarce and expensive labor, shortages of capital, a lack of entrepreneurial talent, and a small domestic market. These obstacles might have been overcome had New England's export trade remained small. The opening of additional markets for New England produce injured local industry because the colonists were again able to import better-quality English goods in the same way that they had in the 1630s. Edward Johnson's contemporary explanation of the failure of the cloth industry could be generalized to cover the entire range of manufacturing enterprises: "The Farmers deem it better for their profit to put away their cattel and corn for cloathing, then to set upon making of cloth." [10]

Just as the government sought to discourage imports, so also did it encourage exports. Both were means to the same end: the improvement of the region's balance of payments. While domestic industry would later prove important to the New England economy, the mid-century recovery and, indeed, the prosperity of the entire colonial period rested on the foreign sector, on exporting the produce of farm, forest, and sea. Moreover, the industrial base that did develop during the colonial era was closely tied to exports. Overseas trade supplied capital for industrialists, put money in the pockets of local consumers, generated a variety of processing opportunities, and created a demand for manufactures, mainly in shipbuilding and related industries. But that occurred only over the long haul.

In the short run, foreign trade provided markets for New England produce, earned the credits needed to purchase imports, and returned prosperity to a troubled economy. The government could do little to promote commerce, although it tried, and the importance of its contribution should not be underestimated. By and large, however, the growth of overseas trade reflected the initiative of New England merchants attempting to earn credits in England. Their first and in some ways most enduring success was in the fishery. [11]

Fish played a central role in the European colonization of North America and in European expansion generally. We will not offer a detailed history, but several points are worth noting. The European demand for fish grew steadily during the sixteenth century as population growth pushed up meat prices and people searched for other, cheaper sources of protein.

10. [Edward Johnson], *Johnson's Wonder-Working Providence, 1628–1651*, ed. J. Franklin Jameson (New York, 1910), 211.

11. Bailyn, *New England Merchants*, 75–111, is an excellent analysis of the beginnings of foreign trade.

This process not only encouraged growth in Europe's fishing industry, but fostered its geographic expansion as well. As early as the 1540s the Grand Banks fisheries were thoroughly integrated into Europe's Atlantic economy, and cod had emerged as North America's first staple export. In 1578, Anthony Parkhurst counted 350 ships at the Banks, the vast majority French and Spanish but 50 of them English. England's American fishery and its share of the total grew rapidly thereafter, especially following the defeat of the Armada: in 1618 it employed roughly 250 ships and 2,000 men and earned gross receipts of £135,000 sterling.[12]

We need to know much more about the expansion of England's fishery, but numbers will not by themselves provide an adequate index of the industry's importance to English expansion and to the early history of British North America. Fishing aided economic development and underwrote colonization in a variety of ways. It led to more-sophisticated financial markets and fostered the rise of marine insurance. The fishery promoted the growth of a merchant community with skills essential to colonization—able, that is, to finance, organize, and direct large-scale, long-distance activities that yielded returns slowly, often only after several exchanges of commodities. It concentrated capital in shipping, stimulated improvements in ship design and navigational techniques, and served as a "nursery of seamen," of masters and mariners competent in transatlantic voyages. The fishing industry was a major source of information about the geography, resources, inhabitants, and potential of North America, and it contributed directly to the establishment of the fur trade, at first largely a by-product of the fishery. Finally, it supplied a goodly share of the incentives, capital, and settlers for the most successful English efforts at colonization in the late sixteenth and early seventeenth centuries.[13]

12. Innis, *Cod Fisheries*, is the classic study of the North American fishing industry. It is placed in a larger context by A. R. Michell, "The European Fisheries in Early Modern History," in *The Economic Organization of Early Modern Europe*, ed. E. E. Rich and C. H. Wilson, vol. V of *The Cambridge Economic History of Europe* (Cambridge, 1977), 133–184. For England's fishery at the Grand Banks, see Ralph Greenlee Lounsbury, *The British Fishery at Newfoundland, 1634–1763* (New Haven, Conn., 1934); Charles Burnet Judah, Jr., *The North American Fisheries and British Policy to 1713* (Urbana, Ill., [1933]); and Gillian T. Cell, *English Enterprise in Newfoundland, 1577–1660* (Toronto, 1969). For the North American fisheries of other nations, see Charles de La Morandière, *Histoire de la pêche française de la morue dans l'Amérique septentrionale* (Paris, 1962–1966), and H. A. Innis, "The Rise and Fall of the Spanish Fishery in Newfoundland," Royal Society of Canada, *Proceedings and Transactions*, 3d Ser., XXV (1931), sec. 2, 51–70. See also chap. 15, below.

13. On the relationship of fishing to colonization, see David B. Quinn, *North America from Earliest Discovery to First Settlements: The Norse Voyages to 1612* (New York, 1977), 511–532.

The possibility that New England would become a major fishery had attracted entrepreneurs and colonizers since the beginning of the seventeenth century and played no small role in the plans of the Massachusetts Bay Company. England's Newfoundland fishery had been most successful, and the more southerly grounds off the New England coastline were fertile, yielding larger fish over a longer season. Being close to shore, they were also more easily worked. Yet in the 1630s the fishery contributed little to New England's economy beyond a supplementary food supply in the form of fish caught off the New England coast by English West Country and foreign ships and purchased from them whenever they called at Boston. In the late 1630s and early 1640s, however, the number of English fishermen who frequented the banks of the North Atlantic fell. The decline grew starkly worse in the era of the Civil War because the fighting involved both the territory and the men and ships of the fishing regions of England. In the consequent disruption the New Englanders found opportunities to both decrease their "ingate" and increase their "outgate." Fewer fishing ships called at Boston since fewer were on the banks, but their old customers remained, both in New England and in Catholic Europe. New Englanders, properly mobilized, could cater to that demand.[14]

Their efforts met with immediate success. As early as 1641, Gov. John Winthrop reported a catch of 300,000 cod worth £6,750; four years later the value of exported fish alone was £10,000. The value of both domestic sales and overseas exports was to increase manyfold over the next decades, although the pattern of growth in New England's fishery lacks precise definition. That expansion had a major, lasting impact on the local economy, just as it had earlier encouraged England's economy. It fostered the New England shipbuilding industry, which was substantial as early as the mid-seventeenth century. The fishery was the employer of many part-time fishermen who worked at other jobs the rest of the year; as late as 1770 more than 10 percent of the region's adult males found work in the fishery, and the proportion was far higher among those living along the coast. And the industry was a nursery both for the sailors of New England's trading ships and, perhaps more important, for the Yankee merchants who orchestrated the economy's far-reaching and increasingly complex commercial networks.[15]

14. The best account of the beginnings of New England's fishing industry is Bailyn, *New England Merchants*, 76–82.

15. On the New England fishery, in addition to work already cited see Raymond McFarland, *A History of the New England Fisheries* ([Philadelphia], 1911); Stanley D. Dodge, "The Geography of the Codfishing Industry in Colonial New England," Geographical Society of Philadelphia, *Bulletin*, XXV (1927), 43–50; William Hammond Bowden, "The

Such benefits were realized in the long run. For the short term the expansion of New England's fishing industry made its greatest impact on the colonial balance of payments. It cut down on "ingate" and increased "outgate" in the obvious ways, but it did still more. Debits were decreased because New Englanders ate fish caught in their own boats; credits were created because increasingly larger quantities of fish were exported. Those exports came initially at the expense of the West Country fishermen, whose effective monopoly London merchants helped New Englanders break in the 1640s. The Londoners exchanged English manufactured goods for New England's fish; they then traded the fish to Spain, to Portugal, and to the Wine Islands; the wine was taken back to London.

At first, London merchants controlled all three legs of this triangular trade. They supplied most of the capital and shipping, and they had contacts in established foreign markets. New England merchants were confined to organizing the annual catch and to curing, sorting, and packing the fish for shipment abroad. Nevertheless, colonial merchants were quick to expand their role. They were unable to control the entire circuit, for the outward voyage from London in which manufactures were delivered to the colonies remained the preserve of English merchants. But they did succeed, by joining together among themselves or forming partnerships with Londoners, in capturing a substantial share of the other two legs of the trade, the export of fish to the Wine Islands and the shipment of wine to England and the colonies.

Once involved in such a trade, the New Englanders began to serve the other demands of these markets. The residents of the Wine Islands needed foods besides fish; they needed barrels for their wine; they needed other timber products as well. Operating on a smaller scale than the Londoners and loading their ships with mixed cargoes, the New Englanders were engaged in trade with the Portuguese and Spanish islands by the mid-1640s. According to Bernard Bailyn, "By the Restoration the New Englanders not only were in complete command of their own fishery but

Commerce of Marblehead, 1665–1775," Essex Institute, *Historical Collections*, LXVIII (1932), 117–146; and H. E. S. Fisher, *The Portugal Trade: A Study of Anglo-Portuguese Commerce, 1700–1770* (London, 1971). For shipbuilding, see Bernard Bailyn and Lotte Bailyn, *Massachusetts Shipping, 1697–1714: A Statistical Study* (Cambridge, Mass., 1959), and chap. 15, below. On employment in the fishing industry, see Timothy Pitkin, *A Statistical View of the Commerce of the United States of America* (Hartford, Conn., 1816), 74, 78–79; U.S. Bureau of the Census, *Historical Statistics*, II, 1195 (Ser. Z 536); and Daniel F. Vickers, "Maritime Labor in Colonial Massachusetts: A Case Study of the Essex County Cod Fishery and the Whaling Industry of Nantucket, 1630–1775" (Ph.D. diss., Princeton University, 1981).

also had a fleet of locally owned and operated vessels plying steadily between their home ports and the southeastern Atlantic markets." [16]

New England's trade to the Wine Islands grew up at the same time and in the same ways as did its trade to the West Indies. Both areas bought the provisions and the timber products of North America; North Americans consumed the wine, fruit, and salt of the Wine Islands and the sugar, molasses, rum, cotton, dyes, and other exotic goods of the sugar islands. All the lessons of the former commerce were also evident in the latter. The trade was most profitably accomplished in small ships with mixed cargoes, with their New England owners close on the scene and thus able to respond quickly to changing conditions. The sale of goods was matched as an earner of credits in the colonial balance of payments by the sale of the invisibles in the current account—freighting, insurance, short-term credit, and other commercial services. To obtain the right mix of goods in a cargo, New Englanders traveled the coast of North America exchanging what they had for what they wanted: manufactures for wheat in Philadelphia; foodstuffs for tar and turpentine in North Carolina; fish for rice in South Carolina or for tobacco in Virginia; New England rum everywhere for anything with a market. The Yankee merchant, born of necessity, quickly became the master of the New World's commerce. [17]

Despite the heroic efforts of New England's government officials and resident merchants and their often considerable success in discovering new ways of earning credits in the balance of payments during the seventeenth and early eighteenth centuries, they ultimately were not successful in harnessing the full productive capacity of the region's farmers to the export sector. A major source of difficulty was the rapid increase in population. Although there was relatively little immigration after 1640, New

16. Bailyn, *New England Merchants*, 82. New England's trade with the Wine Islands is a field of considerable opportunity, with sources available in the United States, Great Britain, and Portugal. See, for example, the Amory Family Papers in the Library of Congress, the Amory Family Manuscripts in the Massachusetts Historical Society, and the materials used by H. E. S. Fisher, *Portugal Trade.* Compare T. Bentley Duncan, *Atlantic Islands: Madeira, the Azores, and the Cape Verdes in Seventeenth-Century Commerce and Navigation* (Chicago, 1972).

17. For the trade of New England (and of other North American colonies) to the West Indies, see chap. 7, below, and, especially, Pares, *Yankees and Creoles*, the notes to which provide a guide to manuscript material. For the activities of "Yankee merchants," there are some valuable studies of individuals and firms: Baxter, *House of Hancock*; Hedges, *Browns of Providence Plantations*; Byron Fairchild, *Messrs. William Pepperrell: Merchants at Piscataqua* (Ithaca, N.Y., 1954); and Glenn Weaver, *Jonathan Trumbull, Connecticut's Merchant Magistrate (1710–1785)* (Hartford, Conn., 1956).

England registered high rates of population growth throughout the colonial period. The number of inhabitants, exclusive of Indians, had reached 50,000 by 1670, 90,000 by 1700, 210,000 by the 1730s, and nearly 700,000 by 1774 (see table 5.1).[18] By contrast, the population of the British West Indies grew only fivefold over the same century (see table 7.2). The markets for New England products were simply too small and grew too slowly to employ the growing population of colonists in production for export.

The inability of New Englanders to take full advantage of the burgeoning Atlantic economy had profound consequences for New England's history—for the pattern of population growth, the persistence of utopian communalism, the organization of families, the level and distribution of wealth, and the extent of opportunity. It also led to some pronounced differences in economic organization within the region. Yet its significance has not been fully appreciated, which perhaps accounts for some of the puzzling characteristics of recent scholarship on New England.

For the past two decades New England social history has been the most exciting and creative field in early American studies, but it now seems in danger of defaulting on its initial promise. In part this failure is the result of insufficient attention to economic history: too often the social historian has ignored the economic pursuits of townspeople or, at best, presented such activities as background information rather than as one of the fundamental dynamic agencies in New England society. This deficiency also reflects the characteristic unit of analysis in recent scholarship. Much of the best work has approached the field through the study of particular small communities. That the intensive, detailed study such a method permits has enhanced our understanding is clear, but the approach also encourages the assumption that the major processes were internal to the community under study and that relations with the wider world were unimportant. Recently, the community study has floundered on the issue of typicality. We have been overwhelmed with detailed empirical work at the local level, but are unable yet to make full use of that data for lack of broad, organizing generalizations. Herein lies a major opportunity for synthesis. Analysis of the pull of the market and the push of population growth within a framework that locates the changing position of particular towns in the larger Atlantic economy should provide the required generalizations.[19]

18. New England's population history is discussed in greater detail in chap. 10, below.

19. The literature on New England social history focusing on particular communities is large, and we discuss it at several places in this book, especially in chaps. 10, 11, 12, and 14. Here it is sufficient to list the major recent books: Charles S. Grant, *Democracy in the Connecticut Frontier Town of Kent* (New York, 1961); Sumner Chilton Powell, *Puritan Village:*

TABLE 5.1.
Estimated Population of New England, 1620–1780
(in Thousands)

Year	Whites	Blacks	Total
1620	0.1	0.0	0.1
1630	1.8	0.0	1.8
1640	13.5	0.2	13.7
1650	22.5	0.4	22.9
1660	32.6	0.6	33.2
1670	51.5	0.4	51.9
1680	68.0	0.5	68.5
1690	86.0	1.0	87.0
1700	90.7	1.7	92.4
1710	112.5	2.6	115.1
1720	166.9	4.0	170.9
1730	211.2	6.1	217.3
1740	281.2	8.5	289.7
1750	349.0	11.0	360.0
1760	436.9	12.7	449.6
1770	565.7	15.4	581.1
1780	698.4	14.4	712.8

Source: U.S. Bureau of the Census, *Historical Statistics of the United States, Colonial Times to 1970* (Washington, D.C., 1975), II, 1168 (Ser. Z 2–8, compiled by Stella H. Sutherland).

Note: Native American Indian residents of the region who lived outside the areas settled by the British are not included in these population figures. For a crude, preliminary attempt to estimate the tribal populations within the territories contiguous to British settlement and with whom, therefore, the British maintained commercial contact, see John J. McCusker, "The Rum Trade and the Balance of Payments of the Thirteen Continental Colonies, 1650–1775" (Ph.D. diss., University of Pittsburgh, 1970), 713–716.

The Formation of a New England Town (Middletown, Conn., 1963); John J. Waters, Jr., *The Otis Family in Provincial and Revolutionary Massachusetts* (Chapel Hill, N.C., 1968); John Demos, *A Little Commonwealth: Family Life in Plymouth Colony* (New York, 1970); Philip J. Greven, Jr., *Four Generations: Population, Land, and Family in Colonial Andover, Massachusetts* (Ithaca, N.Y., 1970); Kenneth A. Lockridge, *A New England Town, the First Hundred Years: Dedham, Massachusetts, 1636–1736* (New York, 1970); Robert A. Gross, *The Minutemen and Their World* (New York, 1976); Christopher M. Jedrey, *The World of John Cleaveland: Family and Community in Eighteenth-Century New England* (New York, 1979); Patricia J. Tracy, *Jonathan Edwards, Pastor: Religion and Society in Eighteenth-Century Northampton* (New York, 1980); and David Grayson Allen, *In English Ways: The Movement of Societies and the Transferal of English Local Law and Custom to Massa-*

Although our knowledge remains incomplete and the argument is not entirely persuasive, recent work offers a precise description of the internal demographic dynamic of New England's rural towns. Early migrants to New England, because their new environment offered material abundance and because they lived in relative isolation from the larger Atlantic community, escaped the major constraints that had severely curtailed population growth back home. Mortality rates, especially among infants and children, fell dramatically, reflecting improved diets and the barriers against disease provided by sparse settlement and the isolation of largely self-sufficient agricultural communities. Among women, age at marriage was low and the proportion of those marrying was high, reflecting the preponderance of males and the ease with which young couples could acquire land and set up farms. Marital fertility rates were high, and families consequently were large by British or European standards. Since the towns were initially able to supply land and thus offer a chance to young adults, rates of out-migration were low and families remarkably stable. Village life was not without tension and conflict, but the relative homogeneity of a social structure rooted in subsistence agriculture and the stability of a population provided with a still-ample resource base permitted the persistence of the utopian communalism brought by the Puritans during the Great Migration. By all but perhaps their own high standards, many of New England's country towns remained "peaceable kingdoms" throughout the early colonial period.[20]

Those peaceable kingdoms could not last, however. The conditions that made them possible—rapid population growth with low out-migration, material abundance, ample opportunities, and a largely self-sufficient farm economy—were incompatible in the long run. Kenneth Lockridge summarizes the process succinctly.

> Clearly there were evolutionary patterns present within the society of early New England, patterns which reflect most significantly on the direction in which that society was heading. . . . A finite supply

chusetts Bay in the Seventeenth Century (Chapel Hill, N.C., 1981). More sensitive to the issues we mention is Stephen Innes, *Labor in a New Land: Economy and Society in Seventeenth-Century Springfield* (Princeton, N.J., 1983).

20. Helpful reviews of this recent synthesis include John M. Murrin, "Review Essay," *History and Theory*, XI (1972), 226–275; James A. Henretta, "The Morphology of New England Society in the Colonial Period," *JIH*, II (1971), 379–398; and Jack P. Greene, "Autonomy and Stability: New England and the British Colonial Experience in Early Modern America," *Journal of Social History*, VII (1974), 171–194. The phrase is from Michael Zuckerman, *Peaceable Kingdoms: New England Towns in the Eighteenth Century* (New York, 1970).

of land and a growing population, a population notably reluctant to emigrate, were combining to fragment and reduce landholdings, bringing marginal lands increasingly into cultivation and raising land prices. Ultimately, the collision of land and population may have been polarizing the structure of society, creating an agricultural "proletariat" and perhaps even a corresponding rural "gentry."

A sharp change in New England's demographic regime accompanied the process. Expectation of life declined, age at marriage rose, birthrates fell, emigration increased, and town populations stagnated. Conflict appeared in community and family as members competed for scarce resources; diversity replaced the old homogeneity of structure and values as non-farm occupations proliferated and as wealth became less equally distributed; nuclear villages fragmented as settlers moved to peripheral family farms. The peaceable kingdom, once a reasonably accurate description of social relationships in New England towns, became a past fondly remembered and an ideal to be pursued.[21]

This emerging scholarly consensus is both compelling and comprehensive, full of dramatic tension and irony, able to integrate a variety of themes into a coherent whole. Yet it can be challenged at several points. One could, for example, question the typicality of the account. Not all New Englanders lived in country towns during the seventeenth century and not all country towns were so thoroughly isolated from the transatlantic economy or so completely trapped in subsistence agriculture. Clearly, quite different sets of social relationships and patterns of development prevailed in places such as Boston, Salem, New Haven, and Springfield.

Even for relatively isolated rural areas the account seems overly pessimistic. It can be argued that people were less reluctant to migrate than Lockridge suggests, or at least that they became less so over time, and that migration both relieved the pressure on resources in older settlements and permitted some colonists to re-create peaceable kingdoms on the frontier. It is also possible that by-employments among farm families, a growing diversity of occupations, increasing opportunities to market farm products, and a more intensive agriculture helped maintain incomes in long-settled regions despite the decreasing size of farms, so that the dismal Malthusian outcome was at least mitigated if not avoided altogether.

Finally, the process described by Lockridge and others is difficult to relate to the subsequent industrial and commercial development of New

21. Kenneth Lockridge, "Land, Population, and the Evolution of New England Society, 1630–1790," *Past and Present*, XXXIX (1968), 62–80 (quotation on p. 74).

England's economy. It does account for the rise of an inexpensive work force (although it is not clear that cheap labor was critical to New England's industrialization), but it is of less help in explaining where the needed capital came from. How consumers paid for manufactures in the face of steadily eroding incomes is also a puzzle.[22]

Much of the difficulty stems from the tendency to study particular towns in isolation from their larger regional and international contexts. Doubtless there were towns where economic activities were organized around subsistence agriculture and where production for markets played little role. And in such towns, the internal dynamic driven by the changing ratio of people to land explains major developments. The method of the community study, which directs attention inward and assumes that the town is the appropriate unit of analysis, works well in such places. But not all towns were so insulated from the outside world, and their proportion declined over the course of the eighteenth century. The community study, while successful in reconstructing the internal demographic dynamic, has too often neglected commercial developments and the role of New England's export sector. Yet commerce and exports played an important role in the rural economy; good prospects in market agriculture, the growth of non-farm jobs, and capital provided by merchants to finance migration were crucial in permitting residents of New England's interior towns to avoid a severe Malthusian crisis. To repeat a refrain of this book, it is in the interactions between the push of population growth and the pull of market opportunities that answers to the central questions in New England social and economic history are likely to be found.

22. For recent studies of more-commercial towns, see Rutman, *Winthrop's Boston*; Richard P. Gildrie, *Salem, Massachusetts, 1626–1683: A Covenant Community* (Charlottesville, Va., 1975); Stephen Innes, "Land Tenancy and Social Order in Springfield, Massachusetts, 1652 to 1702," *WMQ*, 3d Ser., XXXV (1978), 33–56; Lynne Elizabeth Withey, "Population Change, Economic Development, and the Revolution: Newport, Rhode Island, as a Case Study, 1760–1800" (Ph.D. diss., University of California, Berkeley, 1976); and Robert Owen Decker, "The New London Merchants, 1645–1909: The Rise and Decline of a Connecticut Port" (Ph.D. diss., University of Connecticut, 1970). By contrast, see Gary B. Kulik, "The Beginnings of the Industrial Revolution in America: Pawtucket, Rhode Island, 1672–1829" (Ph.D. diss., Brown University, 1980). For studies of migration in colonial New England, see Lois Kimball Mathews, *The Expansion of New England: The Spread of New England Settlement and Institutions to the Mississippi River, 1620–1865* (Boston, 1909); Rutman, "People in Process"; Douglas Lamar Jones, *Village and Seaport: Migration and Society in Eighteenth-Century Massachusetts* (Hanover, N.H., 1981); and chap. 11, n. 51, below. While we often disagree with his conclusions (see chap. 14, below), James A. Henretta provides a compelling interpretation and a useful review of recent work on New England agriculture in "Families and Farms: *Mentalité* in Pre-industrial America," *WMQ*, 3d Ser., XXXV (1978), 3–32. On by-employment and early industrial activities, see chap. 15, below.

The task will demand much additional work in New England's economic history traditionally defined. We know a good deal about the economy in the middle decades of the seventeenth century and in the final years of the colonial period, but the years in between, from the 1660s to the 1750s, have been neglected. In part this neglect stems from the perception that the basic structure of commerce was quickly defined and then changed little. As Bailyn has put it, "Despite acts of navigation, large increases in population, and changes in both the quantity and types of supply and demand, the character of the economic system as it emerged" between 1640 and 1660 "remained essentially the same until just before the American Revolution."[23] While the perception seems accurate, it is still necessary to describe the pattern of expansion in the export sector with precise data on prices and quantities. That part of the task will be relatively simple, for the essential evidence can be assembled from the records of merchants and the returns of the colonial naval officers. It will be much harder to describe regional patterns and to assess the degree of integration in the economy, that is, the ability of merchants to tie producers and consumers of interior towns into the larger world economy. However difficult, the effort is necessary, for without a more precise understanding of regional patterns and interrelationships the dynamics of New England's economic and social history will remain obscure.[24]

Table 5.2, which describes New England's commodity exports at the end of the colonial period, supplies a useful summary of one aspect of the foreign sector on the eve of revolution and thus offers a way of assessing continuity and change since the mid-seventeenth century. Perhaps the most striking characteristic of the export sector is its diversity: no single commodity and no single market dominated, in sharp contrast to other regions of early British America. Almost as striking is that all the major commodities (except potash and rum) and all the major destinations (except Africa) had been central to New England's foreign trade for more than a century.[25]

23. Bailyn, *New England Merchants*, 45.

24. Recent work on regional patterns in the New England economy includes Jackson Turner Main, *The Social Structure of Revolutionary America* (Princeton, N.J., 1965); Edward M. Cook, Jr., *The Fathers of the Towns: Leadership and Community Structure in Eighteenth-Century New England* (Baltimore, 1976); Bushman, *From Puritan to Yankee*; Bruce C. Daniels, *The Connecticut Town: Growth and Development, 1635–1790* (Middletown, Conn., 1979); Van Beck Hall, *Politics without Parties: Massachusetts, 1780–1791* (Pittsburgh, Pa., 1972); and Bettye Hobbs Pruitt, "Agriculture and Society in the Towns of Massachusetts, 1771: A Statistical Analysis" (Ph.D. diss., Boston University, 1981).

25. On New England's rum trade, see McCusker, "Rum Trade," chaps. 7 and 8. For the African trade, see Virginia Bever Platt, "'And Don't Forget the Guinea Voyage': The Slave Trade of Aaron Lopez of Newport," *WMQ*, 3d Ser., XXXII (1975), 601–618, and Jay

TABLE 5.2.
Average Annual Value and Destinations of
Commodity Exports from New England, 1768–1772
(Pounds Sterling)

Commodity	Great Britain	Ireland	Southern Europe	West Indies	Africa	Total
Fish	£206		£57,195	£94,754		£152,155
Livestock, beef, pork	374		461	89,118		89,953
Wood products	5,983	£167	1,352	57,769		65,271
Whale products	40,443		804	20,416	£440	62,103
Potash	22,390	9				22,399
Grains, grain products	117	23	3,998	15,764		19,902
Rum	471	44	1,497		16,754	18,766
Other	6,991	1,018	296	247		8,552
Total	£76,975	£1,261	£65,603	£278,068	£17,194	£439,101

Source: James F. Shepherd and Gary M. Walton, *Shipping, Maritime Trade, and the Economic Development of Colonial North America* (Cambridge, 1972), 211–212, 217, 220, 223–224, 227. For a discussion of this compilation of the data in CUST 16/1, Public Record Office, see chap. 4, above.

Notes: "Southern Europe" here includes all of the continent south of Cape Finisterre, plus the Wine Islands off the west coast of Africa. Wood products here include hoops; whale products combine whale oil and spermaceti candles. "Other" commodities are defined as any that were individually less by value than 2 percent of the total average annual exports.

This is not to deny that there were important changes. Clearly, an enormous expansion took place (although not necessarily much growth on a per capita basis) and some notable shifts occurred in the relative importance of products and markets. Furs dwindled to insignificance and grains played a lesser role than they once had, while whale products accounted for a much larger share of the total than in the mid-seventeenth century and British and West Indian markets probably gained relative to those in southern Europe. Furthermore, Boston, which had held a near

Coughtry, *The Notorious Triangle: Rhode Island and the African Slave Trade, 1700–1807* (Philadelphia, 1981).

monopoly of New England's trade a century earlier, lost ground to lesser ports on the North Shore and in Rhode Island and Connecticut.[26]

Yet the dominant impression is one of continuity. Fish, livestock, and wood products were still the principal commodity exports, southern Europe, the Wine Islands, and the sugar islands still important markets. And, as in the early colonial period, earnings from those trades helped make up the large deficit in the balance of payments with Great Britain.[27]

Although it provides a useful description of New England's export sector, table 5.2 is almost as revealing in what it omits as in what it shows. One thing missing is the coastal trade, which has yet to receive the attention it merits but which was clearly of major importance to the New England economy. Shepherd and Williamson estimate that the coastal trade was worth at least £304,000 sterling, nearly 70 percent of the total value of overseas exports. Innis suggests a much higher total, between £300,000 and £400,000 to Newfoundland alone in 1774, a figure that includes smuggled goods and reexports of British manufactures, neither of which appear in the customs records Shepherd and Williamson used. Whatever the true value, New England's coastal trade reinforces the impression of diversity in products and markets and of continuity with the early colonial period that emerges from examination of longer-distance commerce.[28]

Also missing from table 5.2 are the invisibles in the current account.

26. For the New England whaling industry, see Alexander Starbuck, *History of the American Whale Fishery from Its Earliest Inception to the Year 1876* (Washington, D.C., 1878), and chap. 15, n. 3, below. For the relative decline of Boston, see Price, "Economic Function," 140–149. On the North Shore ports, see William I. Davisson and Dennis J. Dugan, "Commerce in Seventeenth-Century Essex County, Massachusetts," Essex Inst., *Hist. Colls.*, CVII (1971), 113–142; James Duncan Phillips, *Salem in the Seventeenth Century* (Boston, 1933); and Phillips, *Salem in the Eighteenth Century* (Boston, 1937).

27. On New England's trade in fish during the 18th century, see four recent essays by James G. Lydon: "The Salem and Bilbao Fish Trade: Symbiosis in the Eighteenth Century," North American Society for Oceanic History, *Proceedings*, I (1977); "Fish and Flour for Gold: Southern Europe and the Colonial American Balance of Payments," *Bus. Hist. Rev.*, XXXIX (1965), 171–183; "North Shore Trade in the Early Eighteenth Century," *Am. Neptune*, XXVIII (1968), 261–274; and "Fish for Gold: The Massachusetts Fish Trade with Iberia, 1700–1773," *NEQ*, LIV (1981), 539–582. For wood, wood products, and naval stores, see Joseph J. Malone, *Pine Trees and Politics: The Naval Stores and Forest Policy in Colonial New England, 1691–1775* (Seattle, Wash., 1964); Charles F. Carroll, *The Timber Economy of Puritan New England* (Providence, R.I., 1973); and David E. Van Deventer, *The Emergence of Provincial New Hampshire, 1623–1741* (Baltimore, 1976).

28. Shepherd and Williamson, "Coastal Trade"; Innis, *Cod Fisheries*, 195. For more on New England's coastal trade, see Walter Freeman Crawford, "The Commerce of Rhode Island with the Southern Continental Colonies in the Eighteenth Century," Rhode Island Historical Society, *Collections*, XIV (1921), 99–110, 124–130; Curtis Nettels, "The Economic Relations of Boston, Philadelphia, and New York, 1680–1715," *Journal of Economic and Business History*, III (1931), 185–215; Virginia Bever Platt, "Tar, Staves, and

Again, these are difficult to estimate, but they were clearly of major importance to New England's economy. Shepherd and Walton conservatively estimate that New Englanders earned £427,000 sterling from the sale of freight and commercial services in overseas trade during an average year between 1768 and 1772. When the sale of ships and earnings in the coastal trade are added to that figure, the centrality of commerce to the New England economy, the diversity of the export sector, and the persistence of patterns first established in the middle of the seventeenth century are striking indeed.[29]

Early in the colonial era, New England developed a diverse and tightly integrated commercial economy. Farming, fishing, and trade employed the bulk of the population in an interdependent and profitable round of economic activity. Each called upon and served the other and was in turn served by related endeavors. Farmers counted on millers to grind their grain; fishermen needed shipbuilders to keep them afloat; and the importer of molasses supplied the rum distiller with raw materials. All of them relied on a shipping industry to disperse their products to market and to bring back again those things that they consumed. A similar pattern existed in most of the other colonies to a greater or lesser degree, even, as will be seen, in Maryland and Virginia.

In the 1760s and 1770s the economy of New England resembled on a larger scale the state it was in a hundred years earlier. Much depended on the foreign sector. Roughly half of all exports by value were produced by the fishing and whaling industries. Animal products and timber products equaled in value the export of fish. Also contributing to the economy were several important industrial processing businesses such as sugar refining, rum distilling, and flour milling, as well as some manufacturing. Most of the latter was of the household variety and designed for home consumption, although such activities as shoe production and shipbuilding were organized on a larger scale for export. Of these only exported ships added significantly to the credit column of the balance of payments. The domestic consumption of New England's rum, sugar, flour, and shoes was more important than their exportation.[30]

New England Rum: The Trade of Aaron Lopez of Newport, Rhode Island, with Colonial North Carolina," *North Carolina Historical Review*, XLVIII (1971), 1–22; and David C. Klingaman, "The Coastwise Trade of Colonial Massachusetts," Essex Inst., *Hist. Colls.*, CVIII (1972), 217–234.

29. Shepherd and Walton, *Shipping*, 128, 134. Jacob Price estimates the annual value of New England built shipping sold abroad during the late colonial period at £60,000 to £90,000 sterling ("Note on Colonial Exports," 721).

30. For processing and manufacturing industries in New England, see chaps. 13 and 15, below. For agriculture, see chap. 14, below.

The greatest source of credits for the New Englanders was not an exported commodity at all, however. The invisibles earned in New England's carrying trade, when we are finally able to estimate them adequately, will probably prove to have been worth more than the value of exported goods. If that judgment is accurate, then fully half of the colonies' credits were earned by their merchant fleets. It was this development that led the English mercantilist Sir Josiah Child, writing as early as 1668, to assert "that New-England" was "the most prejudical Plantation to this Kingdom." Why that seemed so to Child and why many commentators and policymakers near the end of the colonial period were similarly persuaded is revealed in part by a brief examination of the settlements "down east," in Atlantic Canada.[31]

The British colonies that can be grouped under the heading "Atlantic Canada"—Newfoundland, Nova Scotia, and after 1763, Quebec—have seldom gained the notice of historians concerned with the part of early British America that later became the United States. The reasons for this lack of interest are not difficult to fathom. The region was but sparsely settled (see table 5.3). In 1700, Nova Scotia, then the French colony of Acadia, had only 2,000 inhabitants. Quebec was much larger, with some 14,000 inhabitants in 1700, most of them strung out along a narrow strip on either side of the St. Lawrence, but with large clusters at Montreal and Quebec City, and a much smaller one at Trois-Rivières. Newfoundland had just under 4,000 permanent residents at the turn of the century, but the population swelled to nearly three times that size with the arrival of the fishing fleet in March or April, only to fall again when the fleet departed in October. Population grew rapidly over the eighteenth century, but the inhabitants remained few in number by comparison with colonies to the south. As late as 1770, Newfoundland contained only 11,000 European Americans, Nova Scotia about 26,000 (mostly English and some living in what would become New Brunswick and Prince Edward Island), and Quebec just over 80,000, the majority of them French. The region, in short, seems a poorly settled backwater, disconnected from the main lines of colonial development, with little to interest historians of the more obviously important colonies. Further, the inhabitants did not declare for independence in 1776, so their subsequent history belongs to the Second British Empire and to Canada. There seem few compelling reasons for

31. Sir Josiah Child, *A New Discourse of Trade* (London, 1693), 204. In his preface Child asserts that he wrote his tract "long before" the 1669 session of Parliament but "deferred the printing of it"; other internal evidence shows it to have been composed after 1667. See William Letwin, *Sir Josiah Child, Merchant Economist, with a Reprint of "Brief Observations Concerning Trade, and Interest of Money"* (1668) (Boston, 1959), 32.

TABLE 5.3.
Estimated Population of Atlantic Canada
and Quebec, 1650–1780 (in Thousands)

Year	Quebec	Nova Scotia	Newfoundland
1650	0.7	0.2	1.7
1660	4.0	0.3	1.8
1670	6.6	0.4	2.0
1680	9.7	0.6	2.2
1690	10.8	0.9	2.3
1700	14.1	2.0	3.8
1710	18.3	3.4	3.3
1720	24.5	5.5	3.7
1730	34.1	8.0	4.8
1740	44.2	10.5	5.9
1750	51.9	17.1	6.9
1760	63.1	22.0	13.1
1770	82.2	26.4	11.4
1780	106.9	38.1	10.7

Sources: John J. McCusker, "The Rum Trade and the Balance of Payments of the Thirteen Continental Colonies, 1650–1775" (Ph.D. diss., University of Pittsburgh, 1970), 586, based on material listed in [Canada, Bureau of Statistics, Division of Demography], "Chronological List of Canadian Censuses" (mimeograph; Ottawa, [1934?]); for Newfoundland, contemporary summaries of the yearly reports of the commanders of the Newfoundland squadron, now in CO 389/17, pp. 264–266, and T 70/1205, nos. 45, 46, Public Record Office. See also J. N. Biraben, "Le peuplement du Canada français," Annales de Demographie Historique, III (1966), 105–138, and A. J. Pelletier, "Canadian Censuses of the Seventeenth Century," Canadian Political Science Association, Papers and Proceedings, II (1930), 20–34.

Note: Native American Indian residents of the region who lived outside the areas settled by the British are not included in these population figures. For a crude, preliminary attempt to estimate the tribal populations within the territories contiguous to British settlement and with whom, therefore, the British maintained commercial contact, see McCusker, "Rum Trade," 713–716.

those concerned with the colonial past of the United States to pay them much attention.[32]

This neglect is unfortunate. The region deserves study in its own right, for it was both a significant part of Britain's Atlantic empire and a fre-

32. The estimates for Nova Scotia and Newfoundland may be too high. See Robert V. Wells, The Population of the British Colonies in America before 1776: A Survey of Census

quent focus of conflict in the rivalry between Great Britain and France. In addition, the region illustrates some of the range of possibilities in the process of colonial development and provides occasions to test a variety of hypotheses that emerge from the economic history of other colonies against new evidence in another context. Moreover, Atlantic Canada, especially Nova Scotia and Newfoundland, played an important, if unrecognized, role in the New England economy. A large portion of the region became, in John Bartlet Brebner's phrase, "New England's outpost," a string of settlements extending from present-day Maine in the south to Newfoundland in the north. The area was gradually integrated into New England's economy through two processes, each illustrative of the central themes of this book.[33]

On the one hand, and this was particularly the case with Nova Scotia, the area was tied to New England through migration. This was slow to develop, for Acadia had first to be won from the French (1713) and the Acadians themselves expelled from the settlement (1755). Once the region was secured, however, and cleared of "turbulent Gallicks," it was quickly repeopled, in Edmund Burke's phrase, "by overflowings from the exuberant population of New England." The process is a familiar one, although historians have seldom recognized that its impact was felt so far to the north and east. Attracted by market opportunities in fish, timber, and farm produce and pushed by the pressure of population on the land in more-densely settled regions, New Englanders flocked to Nova Scotia during the 1760s as part of the same migration that had earlier led them to New York, New Hampshire, Vermont, and Maine and that would later lead them to the Midwest. We know very little about the particulars of this migration or of the numbers involved, but they were sufficient to

Data (Princeton, N.J., 1975), 47, 61; C. Grant Head, *Eighteenth Century Newfoundland: A Geographer's Perspective* (Toronto, 1976), 255–258; and Andrew Hill Clark, *Acadia: The Geography of Early Nova Scotia to 1760* (Madison, Wis., 1968), 99–100, 121–131, 201–212, 278, 345–351. We know little about the demographic history of Nova Scotia and Newfoundland, although the documentation for the latter is especially rich. New France, by contrast, has been well served by population historians, and there is much literature that merits the attention of students of British America. See chap. 10, n. 1, below, and Richard Colebrook Harris, *The Seigneurial System in Early Canada: A Geographical Study* (Madison, Wis., 1966). R. Cole Harris and Leonard Guelke, "Land and Society in Early Canada and South Africa," *Journal of Historical Geography*, III (1977), 135–153, is suggestive of ways in which French Canada resembled and differed from New England.

33. Brebner, *New England's Outpost: Acadia before the Conquest of Canada* (New York, 1927). See also George A. Rawlyk, *Nova Scotia's Massachusetts: A Study of Massachusetts–Nova Scotia Relations, 1630 to 1784* (Montreal, 1973), and John G. Reid, *Acadia, Maine, and New Scotland: Marginal Colonies in the Seventeenth Century* (Toronto, 1981).

make Nova Scotia a "new New England" and to help bring the region into Boston's expanding commercial orbit.[34]

On the other hand, Atlantic Canada was integrated into New England's economy through "the aggressive commercialism" of its merchants (see table 5.4). The major fishing waters frequented by colonial fishermen stretched in a line from Cape Cod to Newfoundland, linking the whole of what we might call "greater New England" in one grand economic region. Anchoring the eastern end of that chain were the English (and Irish) fishing communities on the southern and eastern shores of Newfoundland, a part of the world that in the eighteenth century had closer ties to Boston than to London or Quebec. The progressive transformation of Newfoundland from the seasonal base of English West Country fishermen into a colony of settled communities involved the forging of an economic linkage with the mainland colonies. In the lives of the fishermen of Newfoundland the trading vessels from Boston came to compete with the sack ships from England as their source of supplies, the market for their fish, and their point of contact with the rest of the world. How and to what degree Newfoundland was weaned from mother Britain and then assimilated into the colonial family we are only beginning to understand. However, it is clear that a similar process occurred in Nova Scotia. There, by 1770, the majority of trade, whether measured by the value of imports or exports, by the number of ships, or by total tonnage, was in the hands of colonial merchants. When the issues are finally unraveled, we suspect that, in this case as in so many others, interactions between demographic and commercial processes, in this instance combined with the "imperial" ambitions of colonial merchants, will prove to have been central to the integration of Atlantic Canada into New England's economy.[35]

34. For the "turbulent Gallicks," see John Adams to Nathan Webb, 12 Oct. 1755, in *Papers of John Adams*, ed. Robert J. Taylor *et al.* (Cambridge, Mass., 1977–), I, 5. Burke is quoted by John Bartlet Brebner, *The Neutral Yankees of Nova Scotia: A Marginal Colony during the Revolutionary Years* (New York, 1937), 24, which remains the best analysis of the migration.

35. See Innis, *Cod Fisheries*; Ralph Greenlee Lounsbury, "Yankee Trade at Newfoundland," *NEQ*, III (1930), 607–626; Head, *Eighteenth Century Newfoundland*; Keith Matthews, "The West Country–Newfoundland Fisheries (Chiefly in the Seventeenth and Eighteenth Centuries)" (Ph.D. thesis, Oxford University, 1968); Andrew H. Clark, "New England's Role in the Underdevelopment of Cape Breton Island during the French Regime, 1713–1758," *Canadian Geographer*, IX (1965), 1–12; and Glanville James Davies, "England and Newfoundland, Policy and Trade, 1660–1783" (Ph.D. thesis, University of Southampton, 1980). Especially useful is the work of Jean Daigle, "Les relations commerciales de l'Acadie avec le Massachusetts: Le cas de Charles de Saint-Étienne de la Tour, 1695–1697," *Revue de l'Université de Moncton*, IX (1976), 53–61, and "'Nos amis les ennemis': Les marchands Acadiens et le Massachusetts à la fin du 17ᵉ siècle," Société Historique Acadienne, *Cahiers*, VII (1976), 161–170. On the imperial ambitions of merchants

TABLE 5.4.
Average Annual Value and Destinations of Commodity Exports from Quebec, Nova Scotia, and Newfoundland, 1768–1772
(Pounds Sterling)

Commodity	Great Britain	Ireland	Southern Europe	West Indies	Total
Fish	£6,524	£2,387	£115,621	£9,400	£133,932
Grains, grain products	309	2,979	13,035	609	16,932
Whale products	12,183	707	2,693	154	15,737
Deerskins	13,832				13,832
Other	2,209	209	93	602	3,113
Total	£35,057	£6,282	£131,442	£10,765	£183,546

Source: James F. Shepherd and Gary M. Walton, *Shipping, Maritime Trade, and the Economic Development of Colonial North America* (Cambridge, 1972), 211, 217, 220, 223. For a discussion of this compilation of the data in CUST 16/1, Public Record Office, see chap. 4, above.

Notes: "Southern Europe" here includes all of the continent south of Cape Finisterre, plus the Wine Islands off the west coast of Africa. Wood products here include hoops; whale products combine whale oil and spermaceti candles. "Other" commodities are defined as any that were individually less by value than 2 percent of the total average annual exports.

As with Nova Scotia and Newfoundland, so with Quebec, although there the prize was furs rather than fish and it was New York rather than New England that captured most of the benefits. While some of this is mentioned below, in our discussion of New York, it is appropriate to observe here that a working relationship between the merchants of French Canada and of British New York long preceded 1763. Rivals though they were in trade with the Indians, each found much advantage in an exchange of goods and services along the wilderness highway formed by Lake Champlain, Lake George, and the Hudson River—and later made famous as the line of march of Gen. John ("Gentleman Johnny") Burgoyne. However much these contacts took root before the Seven Years'

(and others), see G. M. Waller, *Samuel Vetch: Colonial Enterpriser* (Chapel Hill, N.C., 1960); Richard W. Van Alstyne, *Empire and Independence: The International History of the American Revolution* (New York, 1965), 1–20; and chap. 17, below.

War, the following era was clearly the time of their blossoming. Complementary comparative advantages in foreign trade permitted firms with bases in both colonies to gain considerably during the interwar years. Symbolizing much of this is the title given to a New York City newspaper after 1773: *Rivington's New-York Gazetteer; or the Connecticut, New-Jersey, Hudson's-River, and Quebec Weekly Advertiser.* Foreign trade had, once again, served to integrate colonies into a region and a region into the wider imperial economy.[36]

36. For the trade before 1763, see Jean Lunn, "The Illegal Fur Trade out of New France, 1713–1760," Canadian Hist. Assoc., *Report of the Annual Meeting*, [XVIII] (1939), 61–76. For one firm heavily involved in these developments, see R. H. Fleming, "Phyn, Ellice and Company of Schenectady," *Contributions to Canadian Economics*, IV (1932), 7–41, and James M. Colthart, "Robert Ellice," *Dictionary of Canadian Biography*, IV (Toronto, 1979), 261–262. See also chap. 9, below, and Innis, *Fur Trade in Canada*, especially pp. 119–145. The standard work on Quebec after the conquest is, of course, Fernand Ouellet, *Histoire économique et sociale du Québec, 1760–1850: Structures et conjoncture* (Montreal, 1966). For the impact of the conquest on the merchants of Montreal, see José Eduardo Igartua, "The Merchants and *Négociants* of Montréal, 1750–1775: A Study in Socio-Economic History" (Ph.D. diss., Michigan State University, 1974). To lend perspective to what happened in Canada after the conquest, one can turn with profit to such works as Jean Lunn, "Economic Development in New France, 1713–1760" (Ph.D. diss., McGill University, 1943); James Stewart Pritchard, "Ships, Men, and Commerce: A Study of Maritime Activity in New France" (Ph.D. diss., University of Toronto, 1971); and Terence Allan Crowley, "Government and Interests: French Colonial Administration at Louisbourg, 1713–1758" (Ph.D. diss., Duke University, 1975).

CHAPTER 6

THE UPPER SOUTH

After several decades in which studies of New England dominated the field, attention shifted southward during the 1970s and the Chesapeake region emerged as a central interest of historians of British America. That change has done much to right a severe imbalance in our understanding of the colonies. Generalizations applied to all of British America based only on data for Massachusetts or Connecticut, while still encountered, are now rare; interpretive frameworks appropriate to New England are less casually imposed upon other areas. Moreover, much of the recent work on Maryland and Virginia has had a demographic, social, and economic focus; religious, political, and intellectual issues, the major themes in New England studies, have not commanded center stage along the tobacco coast.

In large part because of the work of the last decade, but also because it was possible to build upon an impressive body of earlier scholarship, we perhaps know more about the Chesapeake economy than that of any other part of British America. Much basic research has been completed, and major trends can be described with more precision and confidence than is usually the case. This is not to argue that the needs are few or the opportunities slender. Scholarly progress has opened up new questions as often as it has resolved old ones, several pressing issues remain unexplored, and we must move beyond description and an informal explanatory style to a rigorous statistical testing of competing hypotheses. Opportunities for analysis abound, particularly in the study of the interactions among growth at the local level, regional developments, and the dynamic processes of an emerging Atlantic economy.[1]

Although founded in a burst of enthusiasm and with great expectations of quick success and spectacular profits, Virginia's first decade

1. Thad W. Tate, "The Seventeenth-Century Chesapeake and Its Modern Historians," in *The Chesapeake in the Seventeenth Century: Essays on Anglo-American Society*, ed. Thad W. Tate and David L. Ammerman (Chapel Hill, N.C., 1979), 3–50, presents a thoughtful survey of the recent literature. See also Ian K. Steele, "Another Early America: Getting and Begetting in the Chesapeake," *Canadian Review of American Studies*, XII (1981), 313–322. Compare Allan Kulikoff, "The Colonial Chesapeake: Seedbed of Ante-

proved troublesome and disappointing. The death rate at Jamestown was appalling: about 60 percent in 1607, 45 percent in 1608 and 1609, and over 50 percent in 1610. The colony was severely mismanaged, both at home and on the scene; relations with the Indians were strained, to say the least; food supplies were inadequate; and no profitable staple exports were found. Investor interest quickly waned: roughly five ships and 300 colonists left England for Virginia each year from 1606 to 1611, but from 1612 to 1616 a total of only seven ships and a handful of souls made the voyage. In 1616, a decade following the initial landing and after an investment of well over £50,000 sterling and the migration of more than 1,700 settlers, Virginia counted only 351 European inhabitants. Its survival as an English colony in the Americas was far from certain.[2]

Paradoxically, Virginia became a relatively stable, permanent plantation with a secure future only when it began to build upon smoke. It was not that the colony's troubles disappeared with the beginnings of commercial tobacco cultivation; indeed, most of the problems of the first decade persisted, in some cases exacerbated by the booming export sector. Still, tobacco proved nearly the ideal staple commodity from a mercantilistic perspective: it permitted the English to acquire a commodity from a colony rather than on the international market; it created a processing industry in England and a valuable product for reexport; it attracted capital and labor to profitable employment across the Atlantic; and it provided Virginians the means to purchase manufactures and commercial services in the English market.

With the discovery of tobacco the Virginia boom was on. From 1617 to 1623, when the initially high prices for the crop began to falter, an average of fourteen ships left England for Virginia each year, bringing

bellum Southern Culture?" *Journal of Southern History*, XLV (1979), 513–540. Tate and Ammerman, eds., *Chesapeake in the Seventeenth Century*, and Land, Carr, and Papenfuse, eds., *Law, Society, and Politics*, contain representative selections of recent articles. Gloria L. Main, *Tobacco Colony: Life in Early Maryland, 1650–1720* (Princeton, N.J., 1982), provides an insightful commentary on many of the issues addressed in this chapter and suggests directions for future research.

2. The best introduction to the early years of the Virginia settlement is Edmund S. Morgan, *American Slavery, American Freedom: The Ordeal of Colonial Virginia* (New York, 1975), chap. 4. On mortality, migration, and the growth of population, see Carville V. Earle, "Environment, Disease, and Mortality in Early Virginia," in *Chesapeake in the Seventeenth Century*, ed. Tate and Ammerman, 96–125, and Karen Ordahl Kupperman, "Apathy and Death in Early Jamestown," *JAH*, LXVI (1979), 24–40. On investment, see Irene Winchester Duckworth Hecht, "The Virginia Colony, 1607–1640: A Study in Frontier Growth" (Ph.D. diss., University of Washington, 1969).

with them a total of roughly 5,000 new planters, while English investors pumped at least £100,000 sterling into the venture. Despite annual mortality rates nearing 50 percent, the colony's population tripled, approaching 1,300 in 1623. Difficulties remained, but the English foothold along the Chesapeake Bay was at last secure.[3]

"The trade of this province," the Maryland assembly observed in 1697, "ebbs and flows according to the rise or fall of tobacco in the market of England."[4] The assertion applies as well to Virginia as to Maryland and describes the 1620s and 1770s as accurately as the 1690s. This is not to discount the local differences along the Bay, nor is it to deny the increasing diversity of the economy as different commodities entered the export trade and as the development process erected hedges against the uncertainties of dependence on a single crop in a volatile international market. Indeed, precise specification of local variations and analysis of the process of diversification are among the major opportunities for study in the Chesapeake colonies. But tobacco dominated the economy of Maryland and Virginia throughout the colonial period: the fortunes of the Upper South remained closely tied to those of the crop, and its production demands and marketing requirements left a distinctive imprint on social structure and economic organization in the area. The tobacco industry must stand at the center of any interpretation of the economy of the colonial Chesapeake. Although some important questions persist, the main outlines of the crop's history have been clearly defined by recent scholarship.[5]

3. On Virginia during the initial boom, in addition to the works cited in n. 2, above, see Wesley Frank Craven, *Dissolution of the Virginia Company: The Failure of a Colonial Experiment* (New York, 1932), and Irene W. D. Hecht, "The Virginia Muster of 1624/5 as a Source for Demographic History," *WMQ*, 3d Ser., XXX (1973), 65–92.

4. William Hand Browne *et al.*, eds., *Archives of Maryland* (Baltimore, 1883–), XIX, 540.

5. The best introduction to the Chesapeake tobacco industry is the work of Jacob M. Price. See especially "Tobacco Trade"; "The Rise of Glasgow in the Chesapeake Tobacco Trade, 1707–1775," *WMQ*, 3d Ser., XI (1954), 179–199; *The Tobacco Adventure to Russia: Enterprise, Politics, and Diplomacy in the Quest for a Northern Market for English Colonial Tobacco, 1676–1722* (Philadelphia, 1961); "The Economic Growth of the Chesapeake and the European Market, 1697–1775," *Jour. Econ. Hist.*, XXIV (1964), 496–511; *France and the Chesapeake: A History of the French Tobacco Monopoly, 1674–1791, and of Its Relationship to the British and American Tobacco Trades* (Ann Arbor, Mich., 1973); and "Buchanan & Simson." See also, in addition to items noted elsewhere in this chapter, Arthur Pierce Middleton, *Tobacco Coast: A Maritime History of Chesapeake Bay in the Colonial Era* (Newport News, Va., 1953), and Gray, *History of Agriculture*, 213–276. Clemens, *Atlantic Economy*, 29–40, 111–119, provides a useful brief overview of the growth of the tobacco trade.

There is little direct evidence of the size of the Chesapeake crop, but British imports of American colonial tobacco can serve as a proxy for trends in production (figure 6.1). The Chesapeake tobacco industry, these data indicate, experienced two long periods of growth during the colonial era, one beginning in 1616 with the start of commercial cultivation and extending to the 1680s, the second running from about 1715 to the American Revolution. Sandwiched between these two eras of expansion were thirty years of stagnation during which the quantity of tobacco raised fluctuated around twenty-eight million pounds, notwithstanding a strong surge at the turn of the century.[6]

Tobacco prices at the farm cannot be as firmly established as production figures because of substantial local differences and the difficulties of converting colonial currencies into a constant value series, but the major trends are clear. Farm prices fell sharply and at a steadily decelerating rate from the 1620s to the 1680s and then moved slowly upward until the 1720s. For the next twenty years farm prices showed no long-term increase, indeed they perhaps went down slightly, but they started a sustained rise just before mid-century, a trend that continued to the Revolution.[7] Prices in the major markets of Europe tended to parallel prices at the farm during the seventeenth century, albeit war and changing tax policies occasionally distorted the relationship. Then, as distribution costs fell, farm prices and European market prices tended to converge.

6. Jacob Price compiled the data on British tobacco imports for U.S. Bureau of the Census, *Historical Statistics*, II, 1190–1191 (Ser. Z 441–472), and he discusses their strengths and weaknesses on pp. 1161–1163. Additional data and some useful commentary appear in Stanley Gray and V. J. Wyckoff, "The International Tobacco Trade in the Seventeenth Century," *So. Econ. Jour.*, VII (1940), 1–26; Neville Williams, "England's Tobacco Trade in the Reign of Charles I," *VMHB*, LXV (1957), 403–449; Barker, "Smuggling in the Eighteenth Century"; Clemens, "Rise of Liverpool"; and Nash, "English and Scottish Tobacco Trades." For the regional breakdown of tobacco exports from Maryland and Virginia, see Price, *France and the Chesapeake*, 669–670; E. Morgan, *American Slavery*, 415; Clemens, *Atlantic Economy*, 171; and Robert Polk Thomson, "The Tobacco Export of the Upper James River Naval District, 1773–75," *WMQ*, 3d Ser., XVIII (1961), 393–401.

7. On farm prices for Chesapeake tobacco, see Russell R. Menard, "Farm Prices of Maryland Tobacco, 1659–1710," *Maryland Historical Magazine*, LXVIII (1973), 80–85; Menard, "A Note on Chesapeake Tobacco Prices, 1618–1660," *VMHB*, LXXXIV (1976), 401–410; Allan Lee Kulikoff, "Tobacco and Slaves: Population, Economy, and Society in Eighteenth-Century Prince George's County, Maryland" (Ph.D. diss., Brandeis University, 1976), 501–504; Carville V. Earle, *The Evolution of a Tidewater Settlement System: All Hallow's Parish, Maryland, 1650–1783* (Chicago, 1975), 228–229; Paul Gilbert Eli Clemens, "From Tobacco to Grain: Economic Development on Maryland's Eastern Shore, 1660–1750" (Ph.D. diss., University of Wisconsin, 1974), 163–165; and Harold B. Gill, Jr., "Cereal Grains in Colonial Virginia" (research report, Colonial Williamsburg Foundation, Inc., 1974), appendix. See also Gill, "Wheat Culture in Colonial Virginia," *Agricultural History*, LII (1978), 380–393. Prices for other commodities in the Chesapeake ap-

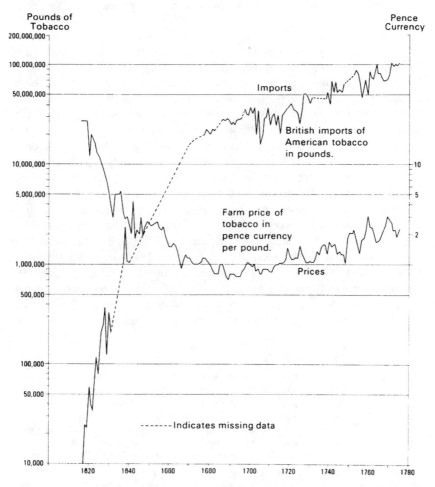

FIGURE 6.I.

Farm Prices and British Imports of Chesapeake Tobacco, 1616–1775

Sources: For 1616 to 1730, the data are drawn from Russell R. Menard, "The Tobacco Industry in the Chesapeake Colonies, 1617–1730: An Interpretation," *Research in Economic
History*, V (1980), 157–161. For 1731 to 1775, they are from U.S. Bureau of the Census,
Historical Statistics of the United States, Colonial Times to 1970 (Washington, D.C.,
1975), II, 1190, 1198 (Ser. Z 449, 579).

Note: This graph uses a semilogarithmic projection. Semilog graphs are used to plot time
series because they permit us both to see the general directions of any trend lines and to
compare the rates of increase (or decrease) of each series. The steeper the slope of a line in a
semilog graph, the sharper the rate of increase (or decrease) it describes.

The trend continued in the eighteenth century as European prices fell, a decline that made Chesapeake leaf ever more competitive with tobacco raised elsewhere. After 1750 European and farm prices again moved in parallel.[8]

Prior to the 1680s, then, the Chesapeake tobacco industry expanded rapidly within a secular context of falling tobacco prices. The pattern of behavior has often been interpreted as a simple consequence of overproduction: planters grew more tobacco than the market would bear, forced the price down, and reduced their profit margins.[9] Overproduction did on occasion drive prices down, particularly in the years immediately following the recurring booms in the trade, but that is only part of the story. More important, productivity gains steadily lowered the costs of making and marketing the staple, permitting planters to earn adequate profits despite falling prices. Smaller risks, cheaper credit, falling prices for manufactured goods and foodstuffs, greater output per worker, savings in distribution costs, and lower customs charges combined to reduce the costs of raising tobacco and to lower its price at the farm and in Europe, thus expanding the market for the staple. It would be difficult to overestimate the importance of this process. Had costs not declined, Chesapeake tobacco would have remained a high-priced luxury item with a limited market, too expensive to compete with poorer-quality European tobaccos for the mass of consumers. Without an expanding market for the staple, the rapid advance of population and settlement that oc-

---

pear in the Kulikoff and Clemens dissertations, cited above, and in Russell Robert Menard, "Economy and Society in Early Colonial Maryland" (Ph.D. diss., University of Iowa, 1975), 486–489; V. J. Wyckoff, "Land Prices in Seventeenth-Century Maryland," *American Economic Review*, XXVIII (1938), 82–88; and Wyckoff, "Seventeenth-Century Maryland Prices," *Agric. Hist.*, XII (1938), 299–310. Data from probate inventories collected by the St. Mary's City Commission promise to add greatly to our understanding of Chesapeake price history. A preliminary commodity price index based on those data and compiled by Menard appears in Carr and Walsh, "Inventories and Analysis of Wealth," 96–97.

8. For European prices of Chesapeake tobacco, see Price, *France and the Chesapeake*, 671–677, 852; N. W. Posthumus, *Inquiry into the History of Prices in Holland* (Leiden, 1946–1964), I, 199–206; Russell R. Menard, "The Tobacco Industry in the Chesapeake Colonies, 1617–1730: An Interpretation," *Research Econ. Hist.*, V (1980), 150; and Warren Martin Billings, "'Virginia's Deploured Condition,' 1660–1676: The Coming of Bacon's Rebellion" (Ph.D. diss., Northern Illinois University, 1968), 156. Additional price data may yet be compiled from the European price currents identified and listed in John J. McCusker and Cora Gravesteijn, *The Commodity Price Currents, Exchange Rate Currents, and Money Currents of Early Modern Europe: The Beginnings of Commercial and Financial Journalism*, forthcoming.

9. For a recent version of this argument, see E. Morgan, *American Slavery*, especially pp. 180–195.

occurred in Maryland and Virginia from the 1620s to the 1680s would have been unlikely if not impossible.[10]

Throughout most of the seventeenth century the price of Chesapeake tobacco fell and the amount produced rose. But the rate of expansion slowed steadily until the 1680s. Output then stayed steady for roughly thirty years. Why the slowdown and eventual stagnation? Contemporaries blamed the industry's troubles on metropolitan colonial policy, particularly on the heavy customs charges that tobacco carried, on the requirement that the crop be shipped first to the mother country no matter where its final market, and on the exclusion of the Dutch from the Chesapeake trade. Historians have often followed this lead. The significance of mercantilism for the tobacco industry was mixed, however; there were benefits as well as costs. While the issue merits more-precise analysis, it is clear that the impact of policy has been exaggerated to the neglect of the more fundamental part played by the shifting costs of production and distribution.

The inability of planters and merchants after 1660 to achieve major cost reductions that could be passed on to consumers was central to the slower growth and eventual stagnation of the Chesapeake tobacco industry. The largest gains in productivity were captured early in the seventeenth century. Further, by the 1670s planters faced mounting prices for land and labor. Distribution costs did fall after 1680, although not as sharply as before, but this no longer resulted in lower market prices. Instead the savings had to be passed on to the planter to absorb the climbing costs of production. Given rising costs and the failure to capture substantial gains in productivity, further expansion would have to rely on increased demand. But conditions in the Atlantic economy in the decades around the turn of the century did not encourage demand-led growth. War closed many of Europe's markets to Chesapeake tobacco and raised the costs of transport. All this heightened the prices of colonial crops in those markets that did remain open, giving European producers a strong competitive edge. Eventually, peace and the growth of population and income in Europe did intensify demand and promoted expansion of the Chesapeake tobacco industry, but in the meantime planters suffered thirty years of hard times marked by only two brief periods of prosperity.[11]

10. The process is discussed in Menard, "Tobacco Industry," 142–155. See also Terry L. Anderson and Robert Paul Thomas, "Economic Growth in the Seventeenth-Century Chesapeake," *Explorations Econ. Hist.*, XV (1978), 368–387.

11. The best account of the Chesapeake economy at the turn of the century remains John Mickle Hemphill II, "Virginia and the English Commercial System, 1689–1733: Studies in the Development and Fluctuations of a Colonial Economy under Imperial Control" (Ph.D. diss., Princeton University, 1964). See also, in addition to work already cited in this chapter,

The blossoming of the Chesapeake tobacco industry after 1715 differed from the seventeenth-century expansion in several respects. Despite
being punctuated by sharp, short-term fluctuations, the pace of growth
was fairly steady in contrast to the gradual deceleration that marked the
years before the 1680s. And it was much slower. British imports of Chesapeake tobacco grew at only 2 percent a year during the eighteenth century, whereas even as late as the 1670s the rate had approached 4 percent.
Further, the industry advanced despite production costs and tobacco
prices that rose steadily, except for roughly twenty years from the mid-
1720s when costs and prices remained fairly constant. This suggests that
stepped-up demand provided the major stimulus, while before the 1680s
improvements in supply had joined with rising demand to expand exports.

These contrasts do not exhaust the major differences. The English domestic market, the principal outlet for Chesapeake tobacco before 1700,
showed little growth after the 1680s and gradually dwindled in importance when compared with the swiftly expanding reexport trade: by the
last decade of the colonial era some 85 to 90 percent of British tobacco
imports found their way to markets in continental Europe. The eighteenth century also witnessed major structural modifications in the organization of Chesapeake markets, particularly the displacement of the
consignment system and of independent local merchants by resident factors who purchased for the reexport trade. In addition, there were changes
in the organization of production. During the seventeenth century most
tobacco was raised on owner-operated farms by small planters with the
help of family members and an occasional servant. Yeomen planters remained important throughout the colonial period, but in the eighteenth
century tenant farms and large plantations worked by slaves dominated
production. The eighteenth century was marked besides by the appearance of sharp local differences within the colonies and by the development of a diversified Chesapeake economy.[12]

Gloria L. Main, "Maryland and the Chesapeake Economy, 1670–1720," in *Law, Society, and Politics*, ed. Land, Carr, and Papenfuse, 134–152; Paul G. E. Clemens, "Economy and Society on Maryland's Eastern Shore, 1689–1733," *ibid.*, 153–170; and Margaret Shove Morriss, *Colonial Trade of Maryland, 1689–1715* (Baltimore, 1914).

12. Besides the several works by Price cited in n. 5, above, see Clarence P. Gould, *Money and Transportation in Maryland, 1720–1765* (Baltimore, 1915); Gould, *The Land System in Maryland, 1720–1765* (Baltimore, 1913); Kathryn L. Behrens, *Paper Money in Maryland, 1727–1789* (Baltimore, 1923); Paul H. Giddens, "Trade and Industry in Colonial Maryland, 1753–1769," *Jour. Econ. and Bus. Hist.*, IV (1932), 512–538; Charles Albro Barker, *The Background of the Revolution in Maryland* (New Haven, Conn., 1940); Calvin Brewster Coulter, Jr., "The Virginia Merchant" (Ph.D. diss., Princeton University, 1944); C. G. Gordon Moss, "The Virginia Plantation System: A Study of Economic Conditions in

Despite these differences, there were important continuities in the colonial tobacco industry, continuities perhaps most evident in the remarkable cyclical pattern of prosperity and depression that buffeted the regional economy. In part such movements were the result of a largely self-contained price and production cycle: planters and merchants regularly responded too robustly to short-term bursts in demand. The lower prices consequent upon overproduction then permitted penetration of new markets. This routine also reflected metropolitan business cycles and the random results of war and weather. Booms and busts in the tobacco trade have been the subject of intense study, particularly in the early colonial period. These studies provide powerful evidence that the Chesapeake economy was export led, for the fluctuating fortunes of the tobacco industry reverberated throughout the entire economy and affected the pace of immigration, the advance of settlement, the extent of opportunity, government policy, experiments with other staple exports, the spread of manufacturing, and the level of material well-being in the colonies.

More work on these short-term movements would be welcome. In particular, the study of the relationships between the ups and downs in tobacco and the other sectors of the economy ought to move beyond casual empiricism to close statistical analysis. In addition, we need assessments of the effects of policy, especially of the various tobacco inspection systems. And we should examine the extent to which the development of other sectors in the Chesapeake economy succeeded in erecting hedges against short-term disturbances in the export sector. However, work on

the Colony for the Years 1700–1750" (Ph.D. diss., Yale University, 1932); Robert Polk Thomson, "The Merchant in Virginia, 1700–1775" (Ph.D. diss., University of Wisconsin, 1955); James H. Soltow, "The Role of Williamsburg in the Virginia Economy, 1750–1775," *WMQ*, 3d Ser., XV (1958), 467–482; Soltow, "Scottish Traders in Virginia, 1750–1775," *Econ. Hist. Rev.*, 2d Ser., XII (1959), 83–98; Soltow, *The Economic Role of Williamsburg* (Williamsburg, Va., 1965); Samuel Michael Rosenblatt, "The House of John Norton and Sons: A Study of the Consignment Method of Marketing Tobacco from Virginia to England" (Ph.D. diss., Rutgers University, 1960); Rosenblatt, "The Significance of Credit in the Tobacco Consignment Trade: A Study of John Norton and Sons, 1768–1775," *WMQ*, 3d Ser., XIX (1962), 383–399; T. M. Devine, *The Tobacco Lords: A Study of the Tobacco Merchants of Glasgow and Their Trading Activities, c. 1740–90* (Edinburgh, 1975); Ronald Hoffman, *A Spirit of Dissension: Economics, Politics, and the Revolution in Maryland* (Baltimore, 1973); John W. Tyler, "Foster Cunliffe and Sons: Liverpool Merchants in the Maryland Tobacco Trade, 1738–1765," *Md. Hist. Mag.*, LXXIII (1978), 246–279; Aubrey C. Land, "Economic Base and Social Structure: The Northern Chesapeake in the Eighteenth Century," *Jour. Econ. Hist.*, XXV (1965), 639–654; Land, "Economic Behavior in a Planting Society: The Eighteenth-Century Chesapeake," *Jour. So. Hist.*, XXXIII (1967), 469–485; and Land, "The Tobacco Staple and the Planter's Problems: Technology, Labor, and Crops," *Agric. Hist.*, XLIII (1969), 69–81.

trade cycles in the tobacco industry has been useful, and the analysis ought to be extended to other sections of British America.[13]

By responding creatively to the periodic depressions in the tobacco industry, Chesapeake planters escaped the most severe consequences of dependence on a single crop in an uncertain international market. Their response was partly public: in the face of falling prices, declining profits, and expensive imported manufactures, colonial officials attempted to control the price, quality, and quantity of tobacco, as well as to promote towns, encourage alternative staples, and support local industry. Despite the creation of viable inspection systems for tobacco in the eighteenth century, such efforts met with little success and were usually abandoned with the recovery of prices for the principal export. Thoughtful officials noted the trap: when times were prosperous colonists possessed the means to diversify but not the will; during depressions the will was there but not the means. These efforts merit close study, both for the insight they yield into contemporary understanding of the economy and for the chance they afford to examine the impact of policy.[14]

But policy was overshadowed, in impact if not visibility, by private responses to shifting incentives. Such responses should not be dismissed as mere efforts to "retreat into subsistence and ride out the storm," for in the long run they led to marked improvements in living standards.[15] Low prices for tobacco, for example, stimulated efforts to improve productivity and may have accounted for some of the sharp increase in output per worker that occurred in the middle decades of the seventeenth century. Relatively higher freight charges during periods of depressed tobacco

13. Much of the work on the tobacco industry already cited in this chapter is concerned with trade cycles, but see especially Hemphill, "Virginia and the English Commercial System"; Menard, "Tobacco Industry," 123–142; and Ernst, *Money and Politics*, 43–88.

14. On the public response, see Vertrees J. Wyckoff, *Tobacco Regulation in Colonial Maryland* (Baltimore, 1936); Philip Alexander Bruce, *Economic History of Virginia in the Seventeenth Century: An Inquiry into the Material Condition of the People* (New York, 1895); Joan de Lourdes Leonard, "Operation Checkmate: The Birth and Death of a Virginia Blueprint for Progress, 1600–1676," *WMQ*, 3d Ser., XXIV (1967), 44–74; John C. Rainbolt, *From Prescription to Persuasion: Manipulation of Seventeenth-Century Virginia Economy* (Port Washington, N.Y., 1974); Rainbolt, "The Absence of Towns in Seventeenth-Century Virginia," *Jour. So. Hist.*, XXXV (1969), 343–360; and Edward M. Riley, "The Town Acts of Colonial Virginia," *ibid.*, XVI (1950), 306–323. Mary McKinney Schweitzer, "Economic Regulation and the Colonial Economy: The Maryland Tobacco Inspection Act of 1747," *Jour. Econ. Hist.*, XL (1980), 551–569, is especially notable for its effort to specify the impact of one such attempt at regulation, but a comparison between Maryland tobacco produced for an expanding reexport trade with the Continent and Virginia sweet-scented sold on a stagnant English market perhaps led to some overestimate of the effect of the Maryland inspection system.

15. The quotation is from Genovese and Fox-Genovese, "Slave Economies," 17.

prices led to tighter and more-careful packaging and to permanent savings in shipping costs.[16] The difficulty of paying for English goods caused by low tobacco prices acted to stimulate domestic industry, as planters discovered the advantages of manufacturing at home the shoes, clothing, and tools that they had previously imported from abroad. Depressions were marked besides by an intensified interest in alternative exports as planters and merchants experimented with new products and new markets in an effort to reduce their dependence on a single staple. Although subsistence production, domestic industry, and alternative staples were often cut back with the recovery of tobacco prices, these depression-induced activities had a cumulative effect that contributed to the greater diversity and improved performance of the Chesapeake economy.[17]

The progress of self-sufficient activities and production for nearby markets are neglected topics in the history of the region: scholarship has focused on exports. These activities cannot be understood as simple responses to short-term disturbances in the export sector, for secular demographic processes also encouraged self-sufficiency. In part this neglect stems from a lack of evidence; self-sufficient production and local exchange are less accessible to our scrutiny than exports, even though they can be approached through probate documents, plantation account books, and county court records. In addition, this neglect reflects the false assumption that such activities were relatively static, unimportant to dynamic processes in Chesapeake society. Over the course of the colonial period plantations were transformed from specialized units producing tobacco and food into more-flexible organizations still chiefly concerned with tobacco and food but capable of supplying a much wider range of goods and services for plantation use.[18]

The advent of plantation self-sufficiency was partly the result of efforts to reduce the risk of dependence on a single crop, but it resulted as well from the need to keep servants and slaves employed during slack times in the tobacco cycle. Moreover, larger numbers of women and children cre-

16. On freight charges in the Chesapeake tobacco trade, see V. J. Wyckoff, "Ships and Shipping of Seventeenth Century Maryland," *Md. Hist. Mag.*, XXXIII (1938), 334–342; John M. Hemphill II, "Freight Rates in the Maryland Tobacco Trade, 1705–1762," *ibid.*, LIV (1959), 36–58, 153–187; Shepherd and Walton, *Shipping*, 49–90; and Menard, "Tobacco Industry," 146–149. On tobacco production per worker, see *ibid.*, 145–146.

17. See nn. 13 and 14, above, and Earle, *Evolution of a Tidewater Settlement System*, 101–142.

18. On the growth of plantation self-sufficiency, see Earle, *Evolution of a Tidewater Settlement System*, 101–142, and Gerald W. Mullin, *Flight and Rebellion: Slave Resistance in Eighteenth-Century Virginia* (New York, 1972), 3–34. Ralph V. Anderson and Robert E. Gallman provide a useful perspective on the process in "Slaves as Fixed Capital: Slave Labor and Southern Economic Development," *JAH*, XLIV (1977), 24–46.

ated additional demands and provided additional labor. Self-sufficiency was achieved with minimal reduction in the resources devoted to to-bacco—either auxiliary production was scheduled when the staple required little attention or it was performed by household members who did not work in the fields. Thus self-sufficiency led to substantial improvements in living standards. Trends in production for local exchange are less clear. Greater population densities deepened the domestic market, but greater self-sufficiency perhaps subverted the related opportunities.[19]

Although better understood than the growth of self-sufficiency or the role of local markets, the substantial diversification of the Chesapeake export sector and the accompanying local differentiation that occurred in the eighteenth century has yet to be studied as fully as the evidence permits.[20] The process had its beginnings in the 1680s. Aggregate data de-

19. There is little information available on the issue, but see the discussion in Lorena See-bach Walsh, "Charles County, Maryland, 1658–1705: A Study of Chesapeake Social and Political Structure" (Ph.D. diss., Michigan State University, 1977), 262–305, which suggests that local exchange increased with growing settlement density.

20. The diversification of the Chesapeake export sector can be followed in the naval officer shipping lists, available for Virginia ports from 1699 to 1706 and 1725 to 1772. These have been effectively analyzed in Peter Victor Bergstrom, "Markets and Merchants: Economic Diversification in Colonial Virginia, 1700–1775" (Ph.D. diss., University of New Hampshire, 1980). The Maryland records are less full, but some ports are covered for the 1690s and from the mid-1740s. On commercial food production in the Chesapeake region, see David C. Klingaman, *Colonial Virginia's Coastwise and Grain Trade* (New York, 1975 [Ph.D. diss., University of Virginia, 1967]); Klingaman, "The Significance of Grain in the Development of the Tobacco Colonies," *Jour. Econ. Hist.*, XXIX (1969), 268–278; Klingaman, "Food Surpluses and Deficits in the American Colonies, 1768–1772," *ibid.*, XXXI (1971), 553–569; Gaspare John Saladino, "The Maryland and Virginia Wheat Trade from Its Beginnings to the American Revolution" (M.A. thesis, University of Wisconsin, 1960); Malcolm Cameron Clark, "The Coastwise and Caribbean Trade of the Chesapeake Bay, 1696–1776" (Ph.D. diss., Georgetown University, 1970); Geoffrey Neal Gilbert, "Baltimore's Flour Trade to the Caribbean, 1750–1815" (Ph.D. diss., Johns Hopkins University, 1975); G. Terry Sharrer, "Flour Milling in the Growth of Baltimore, 1750–1830," *Md. Hist. Mag.*, LXXI (1976), 322–333; and Gill, "Wheat Culture." Iron production also played an important part in the diversification of the Chesapeake economy. See Keach Johnson, "The Genesis of the Baltimore Ironworks," *Jour. So. Hist.*, XIX (1953), 157–179; Johnson, "The Baltimore Company Seeks English Markets: A Study of the Anglo-American Iron Trade, 1731–1755," *WMQ*, 3d Ser., XVI (1959), 37–60; Johnson, "The Baltimore Company Seeks English Subsidies for the Colonial Iron Industry," *Md. Hist. Mag.*, XLVI (1951), 27–43; and Michael Warren Robbins, "The Principio Company: Iron-Making in Colonial Maryland, 1720–1781" (Ph.D. diss., George Washington University, 1972). For other products, see Sinclair Snow, "Naval Stores in Colonial Virginia," *VMHB*, LXXII (1964), 75–93. The best analysis of the process of diversification at the local level is Clemens, *Atlantic Economy*, which focuses on the rise of commercial grain production. Clemens has extended the story in "The Agricultural Transformation of the Northern Chesapeake, 1750–1800" (paper presented at the annual meeting of the Eighteenth-Century Studies Association, Washington, D.C., Apr. 1981).

scribe roughly thirty years of stagnation in tobacco production from the 1680s to the 1710s, but conceal shifting patterns within regions by which some areas expanded output while other areas contracted, moving away from the staple and toward a diverse economy built on the West Indian and coastal trades and a heightened degree of regional self-sufficiency. The decades surrounding 1700 began a sorting-out process in the Chesapeake economy. Marginal producers who made a low grade of tobacco on poor-quality land found that raising the staple was no longer profitable and turned to other tasks. Planters on the better tobacco soils, who made crops of better quality and had access to the best markets, took up the slack and expanded their output of tobacco without raising the amount produced in the colonies as a whole.

There were important differences within the two colonies in the seventeenth century, but planters everywhere had relied on tobacco as the cash crop. This relative homogeneity was disrupted in the 1680s as planters on the lower Eastern Shore, in southeastern Virginia, and in adjacent North Carolina concentrated more and more on grains, meat, and forest products. The pace of differentiation accelerated in the eighteenth century, particularly after 1740, as relative gains in food prices persuaded planters in northern Maryland to abandon tobacco for wheat and as small farmers moved into the Shenandoah Valley. By the 1760s the region resembled a horseshoe, with a plantation district raising tobacco for export to Europe in the center and a farming area yielding foodstuffs, forest products, hemp, and flax for a variety of markets around the periphery.[21]

The extent of diversification in the Chesapeake economy on the eve of the Revolution is suggested by table 6.1, which describes the average annual value of selected commodity exports for the years 1768 to 1772. These data understate the progress of diversification. They do not include

21. Robert D. Mitchell, *Commercialism and Frontier: Perspectives on the Early Shenandoah Valley* (Charlottesville, Va., 1977), is an especially valuable study of a portion of the periphery. Other useful local studies include, in addition to work cited elsewhere in this chapter, Susie M. Ames, *Studies of the Virginia Eastern Shore in the Seventeenth Century* (Richmond, Va., 1940); Robert Wayne Ramsey, *Carolina Cradle: Settlement of the Northwest Carolina Frontier, 1747–1762* (Chapel Hill, N.C., 1964); Kevin Peter Kelly, "Economic and Social Development of Seventeenth-Century Surry County, Virginia" (Ph.D. diss., University of Washington, 1972); Sarah Shaver Hughes, "Elizabeth City County, Virginia, 1782–1810: The Economic and Social Structure of a Tidewater County in the Early National Years" (Ph.D. diss., College of William and Mary, 1975); James Blaine Gouger III, "Agricultural Change in the Northern Neck of Virginia, 1700–1860: An Historical Geography" (Ph.D. diss., University of Florida, 1976); James Russell Perry, "The Formation of a Society on Virginia's Eastern Shore, 1615–1655" (Ph.D. diss., Johns Hopkins University, 1980); and John Thomas Schlotterbeck, "Plantation and Farm: Social and Economic Change in Orange and Greene Counties, Virginia, 1716 to 1860" (Ph.D. diss., Johns Hopkins University, 1980).

TABLE 6.1.
Average Annual Value and Destinations of
Commodity Exports from the Upper South, 1768–1772
(Pounds Sterling)

Commodity	Great Britain	Ireland	Southern Europe	West Indies	Total
Tobacco	£756,128				£756,128
Grains, grain products	10,206	£22,962	£97,523	£68,794	199,485
Iron	28,314	416		461	29,191
Wood products	9,060	2,115	1,114	10,195	22,484
Other	23,344	3,357	526	12,368	39,595
Total	£827,052	£28,850	£99,163	£91,818	£1,046,883

Source: James F. Shepherd and Gary M. Walton, *Shipping, Maritime Trade, and the Economic Development of Colonial North America* (Cambridge, 1972), 213–214, 218, 221, 224–225. For a discussion of this compilation of the data in CUST 16/1, Public Record Office, see chap. 4, above.

Notes: "Southern Europe" here includes all of the continent south of Cape Finisterre, plus the Wine Islands off the west coast of Africa. Wood products here include hoops. "Other" commodities are defined as any that were individually less by value than 2 percent of the total average annual exports. Compare Harry J. Carman, ed., *American Husbandry* (1775) (New York, 1939), 183, which shows Virginia and Maryland with total exports for 1763 valued at £1,040,000, of which £30,000 was for ships sold abroad.

commodities shipped to other mainland colonies in the coastal trade, in this period worth roughly £88,000 sterling annually, nor do they include those goods that were transported overland to Philadelphia. Also excluded are minor products—oats, peas, beans, shingles, and ships, for example—that collectively made a significant contribution to Chesapeake export earnings. Despite these defects the data provide a useful summary of the region's foreign sector at the end of the colonial era. Tobacco remained the dominant commodity and Britain the main destination, but both had slipped considerably since the early eighteenth century, when they contributed more than 95 percent of the totals. Most of the shift reflects the rapid expansion of the grain trade to southern Europe and the West Indies, which accounted for nearly 20 percent of the region's export earnings around 1770. Data assembled by Peter Bergstrom suggest an even more dramatic change (see table 6.2). His work indicates that tobacco accounted for only 61 percent of Virginia's exports in 1773, down sharply from more than 77 percent forty years earlier. Again, grain and wood products, sent chiefly to the Caribbean and Mediterranean Europe, along with iron for Britain, appear as the principal source of the developing diversity of the Chesapeake export sector. These secondary trades had an important impact on the balance of payments in the Upper South, turning a deficit in the "visibles" in the current account of the trade with Great Britain into a small surplus.[22]

Local differences in exports within the Chesapeake colonies offer scope for testing the utility of a staples approach to the economic history of British America, either by comparative analysis of areas producing different exports or by close study of places that shifted from one staple to another. Recent work on the progress of Chesapeake urbanization suggests the promise.

The settlement system along the tobacco coast dismayed contemporaries and has long puzzled historians. A few statistics reveal the paradox: in 1770, Maryland and Virginia accounted for over 30 percent of the population of British North America and their exports were valued at more than £1,000,000 sterling, yet neither was the site of a major colonial city. The two principal towns, Norfolk and Baltimore, had populations of only 6,000 each, while Williamsburg had only 2,000 inhabitants and Annapolis 3,700, all a far cry from Philadelphia's 30,000, New York's 25,000, Boston's 16,000, Charleston's 12,000, or even Newport's 11,000.

Further reflection only deepens the puzzle. All the larger colonial cities served areas whose export trade was far smaller than that of the Chesapeake. Baltimore and Norfolk were situated on the periphery of the region and owed little of their prosperity to tobacco. Williamsburg and Annapolis were capital cities dependent as much on government as on trade. Something about the tobacco coast discouraged the growth of towns.[23]

22. For the coastal trade, see Shepherd and Williamson, "Coastal Trade," 798. According to contemporary estimates, 340,000 bushels of wheat and 100,000 bushels of corn were shipped overland from Maryland to Philadelphia in 1774 (Edward C. Papenfuse, Jr., "Economic Analysis and Loyalist Strategy during the American Revolution: Robert Alexander's Remarks on the Economy of the Peninsula or Eastern Shore of Maryland," *Md. Hist. Mag.*, LXVIII [1973], 173–195). For ships sold abroad, see Price, "Note on Colonial Exports." For other products, see Bergstrom, "Markets and Merchants," *passim*.

23. On urbanization in the Chesapeake colonies, see Price, "Economic Function"; Earle and Hoffman, "Staple Crops"; Carville Earle and Ronald Hoffman, "The Urban South: The First Two Centuries," in *The City in Southern History: The Growth of Urban Civilization in the South*, ed. Blaine A. Brownell and David R. Goldfield (Port Washington, N.Y., 1977), 23–51; Edward C. Papenfuse, *In Pursuit of Profit: The Annapolis Merchants in the Era of the American Revolution, 1763–1805* (Baltimore, 1975); Lois Green Carr, "'The Metrop-

TABLE 6.2.
Value of Commodity Exports from Virginia,
1733 and 1773 (Pounds Sterling)

Commodity	1733	1773
Tobacco	£121,078	£337,391
Grains, grain products	9,447	145,360
Iron	6,411	15,562
Wood products	4,924	31,740
Other	16,133	23,080
Total	£157,993	£553,133

Sources: Peter Victor Bergstrom, "Markets and Merchants: Economic Diversification in Colonial Virginia, 1700–1775" (Ph.D. diss., University of New Hampshire, 1980), 150, table 5.5. The values in the original table were based on quantities extracted from the Virginia naval officer shipping lists and on Philadelphia market prices. To allow for easier comparison with those in table 6.1, Bergstrom's figures have been reduced to their sterling equivalent using rates of exchange from John J. McCusker, *Money and Exchange in Europe and America, 1600–1775: A Handbook* (Chapel Hill, N.C., 1978), 184, 186.

Geography contributed to what happened—the extensive river system made a single large transshipment center unnecessary—but it was clearly of minor importance compared to a complex of economic factors associated with tobacco. The staple generated few forward linkages of the sort that promoted urban development. Tobacco did not require much processing or elaborate storage facilities, and its relatively low bulk did not

---

olis of Maryland': A Comment on Town Development along the Tobacco Coast," *Md. Hist. Mag.*, LXIX (1974), 124–145; John W. Reps, *Tidewater Towns: City Planning in Colonial Virginia and Maryland* (Williamsburg, Va., 1972); Clarence P. Gould, "The Economic Causes of the Rise of Baltimore," in *Essays in Colonial History Presented to Charles McLean Andrews by His Students* (New Haven, Conn., 1931), 225–251; Paul Kent Walker, "Business and Commerce in Baltimore on the Eve of Independence," *Md. Hist. Mag.*, LXXI (1976), 296–309; James J. O'Mara, "Urbanization in Tidewater Virginia during the Eighteenth Century: A Study in Historical Geography" (Ph.D. diss., York University, 1979); Peter V. Bergstrom and Kevin P. Kelly, "'Well Built Towns, Convenient Ports and Markets': The Beginnings of Yorktown, 1690–1720" (paper presented at the annual meeting of the Southern Historical Association, Atlanta, Ga., Nov. 1980); and Thomas M. Preisser, "Alexandria and the Evolution of the Northern Virginia Economy, 1749–1776," *VMHB*, LXXXIX (1981), 282–293.

encourage an extensive internal transport network. Mercantilist restrictions and a marketing system focused on Britain kept the supply of shipping and commercial services firmly in the hands of metropolitan merchants. At best, colonial merchants functioned as factors for British firms, collecting the staple and retailing imports. Slavery also inhibited town growth: it limited consumer demand, encouraged plantation self-sufficiency, and channeled entrepreneurial energies into staple production. These characteristics combined to limit the need for urban services in the Chesapeake. The services that the colonists did require were either concentrated in British ports or dispersed on particular plantations.

In the eighteenth century, however, increases in population density, differences in the marketing of tobacco, the diversification of the export sector, and an intensification of the domestic market joined to promote the advancement of towns. Some evidence of the process is provided by the proliferation of small villages within the plantation district. Yet most had only a few hundred residents employed in servicing the tobacco industry and were unable to centralize other urban functions in their trading areas.

The most striking changes occurred on the periphery of the plantation belt. Foodstuffs and forest products generated more-extensive forward linkages in marketing, processing, transport, and storage than did tobacco, and provincial merchants were better able to control these activities. Further, it can be argued, the production of such goods fostered a more even distribution of income and a livelier consumer demand, while the constraints on unit size attracted ambitious individuals with entrepreneurial skills out of agriculture and into other activities. The results are evident in a thriving Norfolk, the sudden rise of Baltimore, a mere hamlet as late as 1750, and the appearance of an extensive network of small towns in the backcountry. Tobacco dominated the Chesapeake throughout the colonial period, still accounting for three-quarters of all exports on the eve of independence, but the relatively small trade in foodstuffs on the region's periphery had induced a much greater degree of urbanization and an economy more developed and less "colonial" than that of the plantation belt.[24]

Recent scholarship has greatly improved our understanding of demographic processes along the tobacco coast. Estimates of total population describe a rapid but decelerating growth to the 1670s followed by a

24. Price, "Economic Function"; Earle and Hoffman, "Staple Crops"; Joseph A. Ernst and H. Roy Merrens, "'Camden's Turrets Pierce the Skies!' The Urban Process in the Southern Colonies during the Eighteenth Century," *WMQ*, 3d Ser., XXX (1973), 549–574; and Ronald Eugene Grim, "The Absence of Towns in Seventeenth-Century Virginia: The Emergence of Service Centers in York County" (Ph.D. diss., University of Maryland, 1977).

steady expansion at an annual rate of 2.7 percent to the Revolution. This increase was accompanied by dramatic changes in composition. Table 6.3, which contrasts the population of Virginia in 1625 with that of Maryland in 1704 and 1755, shows the principal changes among whites. (Similar shifts occurred among blacks, but at later dates.) In 1625, Virginia was dominated by adult males, who outnumbered women by 7.5 to 1 and children by nearly 5 to 1. By 1704 men were only 37 percent of Maryland's population, the sex ratio (men per hundred women) had fallen to 157, and the proportion of children had registered a dramatic advance, soaring to nearly 40 percent of the total. The 1755 census shows that these trends continued into the eighteenth century, but the major alterations had occurred by 1704. In 1755 men comprised only 27 percent of Maryland's white population, the sex ratio had fallen to 113, and children made up nearly half the total.

The effect of these transformations on the Chesapeake economy needs study. On the one hand, the decline in the proportion of men led to a fall in the percentage of the adult population employed in the export sector, while the larger numbers of children heightened the dependency ratio. Both of these processes reduced incomes per capita. On the other hand, the growing proportion of women and children boosted demand for subsistence production and created incentives for harder work and higher rates of savings and investment. Further, greater population density and bigger domestic markets fostered some scale economies and created occasions for functional specializations. It is not clear that the benefits exceeded the costs, but a simple Malthusian identification of greater dependency ratios and settlement densities with lower incomes may prove misleading in the Chesapeake colonies and, perhaps, in British America generally.[25]

The decades around 1700 witnessed another major change in Chesapeake population history, the spread of slavery. Blacks accounted for only 7 percent of the region's inhabitants as late as 1690, but their proportion thereafter grew quickly, reaching 13 percent by 1700 and nearly 20 percent by 1720 (see table 6.4). By mid-century slaves were 30 percent of Maryland's population and 40 percent of Virginia's, and many counties had substantial black majorities. The progress of slavery in the Chesapeake colonies was a complex process involving developments in Europe, Africa, and British America. It can be approached by assuming that planters chose their work force by comparing costs and output among the alternatives in order to maximize net returns and by focusing on shifts in the supply and demand for labor.

25. Chesapeake demographic patterns are discussed in chap. 10, below.

TABLE 6.3.
The European-American Population in Virginia
and Maryland

	Men	Women	Children	Total
Virginia				
1625	558 (74.4%)	74 (9.9%)	118 (15.7%)	750
Maryland				
1704	11,262 (36.7%)	7,163 (23.3%)	12,248 (39.9%)	30,673
1755	29,141 (27.2%)	25,731 (24.0%)	52,337 (48.8%)	107,209

Sources: Edmund S. Morgan, *American Slavery, American Freedom: The Ordeal of Colonial Virginia* (New York, 1975), 408; Russell R. Menard, "Five Maryland Censuses, 1700 to 1712: A Note on the Quality of the Quantities," *William and Mary Quarterly*, 3d Ser., XXXVII (1980), 620; *Gentlemen's Magazine and Historical Chronicle* (London), XXXIV (1764), 261.

Cheap land kept wage rates high and made it easy for workers to become planters. The widespread availability of cheap land and a lively metropolitan demand for tobacco combined to encourage the use of unfree labor in the Chesapeake colonies. For a long time, indentured servitude supplied tobacco planters with sufficient workers. Through the middle decades of the seventeenth century the number of servants grew more rapidly than the number of households and the price of servants remained constant and possibly fell (despite a sharp, short-term rise in the 1640s). This permitted planters to meet their requirements for labor without resort to slaves. Planters, however, depended on a steady addition to the number of young Englishmen willing to try their luck in tobacco, which in turn depended on the high birthrate and secular decline in real wages that characterized English society before 1650. Just prior to mid-century, the birthrate in England fell, its population began to shrink, and wages went up. The colonies as a whole felt the result immediately—migration from England to America peaked in the 1650s and then fell—but the diminishing attractiveness of the West Indies and the continuing failure of New England to find a staple concentrated the migrant stream on the tobacco coast and kept numbers climbing there for another twenty years.

In the 1670s, despite efforts to recruit more widely in the British Isles, the supply of servants started to diminish and their price rose sharply. Tobacco planters faced a labor shortage, a shortage aggravated by ex-

TABLE 6.4.
Estimated Population of the Chesapeake Colonies,
1610–1780 (in Thousands)

Year	Maryland	Virginia	Total Whites	Total Blacks	Total Population
1610		0.3	0.3	—	0.3
1620		0.9	0.9	—	0.9
1630		2.5	2.4	0.1	2.5
1640	0.6	7.6	8.0	0.1	8.1
1650	0.7	12.0	12.4	0.3	12.7
1660	4.0	20.9	24.0	0.9	24.9
1670	11.4	29.6	38.5	2.5	41.0
1680	20.0	39.9	55.6	4.3	59.9
1690	26.2	49.3	68.2	7.3	75.5
1700	34.1	64.0	85.2	12.9	98.1
1710	43.9	79.7	101.3	22.4	123.7
1720	57.8	100.8	128.0	30.6	158.6
1730	81.8	142.8	171.4	53.2	224.6
1740	116.1	180.4	212.5	84.0	296.5
1750	141.1	236.7	227.2	150.6	377.8
1760	162.3	339.7	312.4	189.6	502.0
1770	202.6	447.0	398.2	251.4	649.6
1780	248.0	538.0	482.4	303.6	786.0

Sources: For 1610–1620, Carville V. Earle, "Environment, Disease, and Mortality in Early Virginia," in *The Chesapeake in the Seventeenth Century: Essays on Anglo-American Society,* ed. Thad W. Tate and David L. Ammerman (Chapel Hill, N.C., 1979), 110–111, 119; for 1630–1730, Russell R. Menard, "The Tobacco Industry in the Chesapeake Colonies, 1617–1730: An Interpretation," *Research in Economic History,* V (1980), 157–166; for 1740–1780, U.S. Bureau of the Census, *Historical Statistics of the United States, Colonial Times to 1970* (Washington, D.C., 1975), II, 1168 (Ser. Z 13–14, compiled by Stella H. Sutherland), and Allan Kulikoff, "A 'Prolifick' People: Black Population Growth in the Chesapeake Colonies, 1700–1790," *Southern Studies,* XVI (1977), 415–417.

Notes: Native American Indian residents of the region who lived outside the areas settled by the British are not included in these population figures. For a crude, preliminary attempt to estimate the tribal populations within the territories contiguous to British settlement and with whom, therefore, the British maintained commercial contact, see John J. McCusker, "The Rum Trade and the Balance of Payments of the Thirteen Continental Colonies, 1650–1775" (Ph.D. diss., University of Pittsburgh, 1970), 713–716. Figures have been rounded off and thus the totals do not always equal the sum of their parts. Dashes indicate categories for which we have no data.

panding demand in the Chesapeake, the newly settled Middle Colonies, and the Carolinas. Dwindling supplies and spiraling prices for servants joined with ample supplies and a steady, perhaps falling, price for slaves to persuade planters to draw on Africa for labor. As they did so, they transformed the region into a slave society, a process well under way by the early eighteenth century.

The impact of slavery on the Chesapeake economy merits close study. It clearly led to some increase in the scale of operations. Tobacco farms remained small in comparison with contemporary rice or sugar plantations, but they were on average bigger in the eighteenth century than in the seventeenth. Since black women usually worked the tobacco crop, the growth of slavery cushioned the diminished proportion in the work force occasioned by the changed composition of the white population. Further, slaves were maintained at the subsistence level, and their increase permitted many whites to keep incomes substantial despite the fall in earnings per capita from the staple that was produced by shifts in the demographic structure of white society.[26]

One additional explanation for the smaller supply of indentured servants rests in declining opportunities for ex-servants in the Chesapeake. Early on, the chances were good that indentured servants who survived their terms would themselves become planters. Although it is unlikely that young English workers were more than vaguely aware of the change, as the century progressed the odds of later establishing a family and acquiring land became very slim. The lure of the Upper South for potential English emigrants lessened accordingly.

26. This discussion follows the argument in Russell Menard, "From Servants to Slaves: The Transformation of the Chesapeake Labor System," *Southern Studies*, XVI (1977), 355–390. Other recent contributions to these issues include G. Main, "Maryland and the Chesapeake Economy"; Richard N. Bean and Robert P. Thomas, "The Adoption of Slave Labor in British America," in *The Uncommon Market: Essays in the Economic History of the Atlantic Slave Trade*, ed. Henry A. Gemery and Jan S. Hogendorn (New York, 1979), 377–398; David W. Galenson, *White Servitude in Colonial America: An Economic Analysis* (Cambridge, 1981), 117–168; and E. Morgan, *American Slavery*, 295–315. On the slave trade to the Chesapeake colonies, see Herbert S. Klein, "Slaves and Shipping in Eighteenth-Century Virginia," *JIH*, V (1975), 383–412; Allan Kulikoff, "A 'Prolifick' People: Black Population Growth in the Chesapeake Colonies, 1700–1790," *So. Studies*, XVI (1977), 391–428; Darold D. Wax, "Black Immigrants: The Slave Trade in Colonial Maryland," *Md. Hist. Mag.*, LXXIII (1978), 30–45; Wax, "Negro Import Duties in Colonial Virginia: A Study in British Commercial Policy and Local Public Policy," *VMHB*, LXXIX (1971), 29–44; Elizabeth Suttell, "The British Slave Trade to Virginia, 1698–1728" (M.A. thesis, College of William and Mary, 1965); Charles L. Killinger III, "The Royal African Company Slave Trade to Virginia, 1689–1713" (M.A. thesis, College of William and Mary, 1969); and Susan Alice Westbury, "Colonial Virginia and the Atlantic Slave Trade" (Ph.D. diss., University of Illinois, 1981).

The likelihood of advancement for servants was directly related to the expansion of the tobacco industry. During the initial period, when the industry was growing vigorously, it created demands for goods, services, and workers and attracted credit that permitted poor men easy access to the planter ranks. The tobacco coast was "a good poor man's country" through the middle decades of the seventeenth century. But as the tobacco industry grew more slowly and finally stagnated the chances of "making good" decreased sharply, first in the older areas, later in the Upper South as a whole. By the end of the century former servants often left the Chesapeake for more-promising regions.[27]

Less is known about the chances for success in the eighteenth century, but the renewed strength of the tobacco trade did not create an economy as open as that of the early colonial period. The costs of starting a plantation were mounting, slaves took many of the jobs, and significantly, it was young native-born men, often backed by substantial family resources, who led the movement to the frontier.[28]

The altered pattern of economic expansion, changes in the way the population grew, the advent of slavery, and the contraction of opportunity for ordinary colonists combined to give birth to one of the central themes in the history of the tobacco coast, the rise of the Chesapeake gentry. The process merits close study, but the outcome is clear: by the early eighteenth century, Maryland and Virginia were thoroughly dominated by a small number of great planter families. Bound together by shared interests, common experience, and ties of kinship, their wealth rested on land, slaves, and commerce. They dominated local politics, grew ever more conscious of their class position, and viewed their futures as intimately tied to the future of the colonies.

The great planters played a central role in the development of the re-

27. On opportunities in the 17th century, see Russell R. Menard, "From Servant to Freeholder: Status Mobility and Property Accumulation in Seventeenth-Century Maryland," *WMQ*, 3d Ser., XXX (1973), 37–64; Lorena S. Walsh, "Servitude and Opportunity in Charles County, Maryland, 1658–1705," in *Law, Society, and Politics*, ed. Land, Carr, and Papenfuse, 111–133; Lois Green Carr and Russell R. Menard, "Immigration and Opportunity: The Freedman in Early Colonial Maryland," in *Chesapeake in the Seventeenth Century*, ed. Tate and Ammerman, 206–242; and Thomas J. Wertenbaker, *The Planters of Colonial Virginia* (Princeton, N.J., 1922), 60–83.

28. On 18th-century opportunities, see Kulikoff, "Tobacco and Slaves," chap. 5; Edward C. Papenfuse and Gregory A. Stiverson, "General Smallwood's Recruits: The Peacetime Career of the Revolutionary War Private," *WMQ*, 3d Ser., XXX (1973), 117–132; Papenfuse, "Planter Behavior and Economic Opportunity in a Staple Economy," *Agric. Hist.*, XLVI (1972), 297–311; Stiverson, *Poverty in a Land of Plenty: Tenancy in Eighteenth-Century Maryland* (Baltimore, 1977); Clemens, "Economy and Society"; and Michael L. Nicholls, "Origins of the Virginia Southside, 1703–1753: A Social and Economic Study" (Ph.D. diss., College of William and Mary, 1972).

gional economy. They provided much of the capital needed to develop productive resources and to extend the Chesapeake frontier, and they contributed entrepreneurial skill to the task of diversifying the economy. They shaped the role of colonial government in economic affairs, and eventually they led the colonies into the independence movement. Their success demands the attention of economic historians, for close study of the origins, behavior, and ideology of the Chesapeake gentry promises a deepened understanding of the political economy of the tobacco coast.[29]

Planters often engaged in trade, and they provided capital to provincial merchants. By the end of the colonial period such activities had begun to have a noticeable impact on the structure of the Chesapeake economy. The magnitude of the transformation remains obscure and could be overstated easily. Chesapeake commerce, after all, was dominated by metropolitan merchants throughout the colonial era, while resident merchants had been active since the seventeenth century. Still, there is mounting evidence that, as Jacob Price has argued, "the growth of the independent indigenous merchant" was the "most dynamic feature of the Chesapeake economy" during the 1760s and 1770s. Earlier in the eighteenth century colonial merchants who were not merely agents for British firms had concentrated in the West Indian and coastal trades, but in the 1760s increased demand for cereals in Europe, higher tobacco prices, and easier British credit provided colonial traders the chance to make money in transatlantic commerce. Most shipped grain and flour to southern Europe, but a few even challenged Britain's hegemony in the tobacco trade. Despite some excellent work, we still know far too little about such men, particularly their sources of capital, their relations with British merchants, and their role in colonial politics and the independence movement.[30]

An exceptional set of probate records survives for the Chesapeake colonies, particularly for Maryland, which permits detailed analysis of

29. The literature on the Chesapeake gentry is extensive. Bernard Bailyn, "Politics and Social Structure in Virginia," in *Seventeenth-Century America: Essays in Colonial History*, ed. James Morton Smith (Chapel Hill, N.C., 1959), 90–115, is still the place to begin, while Aubrey C. Land, *The Dulanys of Maryland: A Biographical Study of Daniel Dulany, the Elder (1685–1753) and Daniel Dulany, the Younger (1722–1797)* (Baltimore, 1955), is a good case study of an important family. Charles S. Sydnor, *Gentlemen Freeholders: Political Practices in Washington's Virginia* (Chapel Hill, N.C., 1952), continues to have value. Economic historians will be challenged by Rhys Isaac, *The Transformation of Virginia, 1740–1790* (Chapel Hill, N.C., 1982).

30. Price, *Capital and Credit*, 128. The firm of Wallace, Davidson & Johnson, which operated out of Annapolis late in the colonial period, has been studied in detail. See *Joshua Johnson's Letterbook* and Papenfuse, *In Pursuit of Profit*. There is much useful material on colonial merchants in Hoffman, *Spirit of Dissension*.

wealth and welfare in the region. Initial estimates for the lower Western Shore of Maryland show wealth per capita rising swiftly, by 2.5 to 3 percent per year until the 1680s, and then declining slightly for two decades. There followed a long period of stability, and then, beginning by the 1750s, a last, pre-Revolutionary growth spurt with rates again near 3 percent. Both the initial and final phases were marked by heightened inequality: during the first, mean wealth grew while median wealth held steady; during the second, median wealth rose but more slowly than mean wealth.

All this seems compatible with a simple export-led explanation. The tobacco industry also expanded quickly to the 1680s, stagnated around the turn of the century, and then grew steadily but not any faster than population after 1710. Rising tobacco prices and the development of other exports would account for the final growth spurt.[31] However, closer inspection quickly demonstrates the inadequacy of this account. The phase at the end of the colonial period probably was export led, but the initial expansion almost certainly was not. The apparent coincidence between movements in wealth and the expansion of the tobacco industry was just that, a coincidence, the result of aggregating a series of discrete, sequential, local gains in wealth per head. Income from tobacco placed a floor under wealth levels in the seventeenth century, but early development was based on farm building, self-sufficient activities, and production for nearby markets.[32]

Perhaps the most promising approach to variations in wealth and welfare in the Chesapeake colonies—one that allows us to relate such movements to shifting vital rates, to the extent of opportunity, and to the pattern of internal migration—is through the intensive study of small areas. We are far from a precise understanding of the local development process, but enough evidence is available to suggest that places within the tobacco coast had broadly similar histories, with the timing of major

31. Russell R. Menard, P. M. G. Harris, and Lois Green Carr, "Opportunity and Inequality: The Distribution of Wealth on the Lower Western Shore of Maryland, 1638–1705," *Md. Hist. Mag.*, LXIX (1974), 169–184; Menard, "Comment on Paper by Ball and Walton," *Jour. Econ. Hist.*, XXXVI (1976), 123–125; Kulikoff, "Economic Growth"; Gloria Lund Main, "Personal Wealth in Colonial America: Explorations in the Use of Probate Records from Maryland and Massachusetts, 1650–1720" (Ph.D. diss., Columbia University, 1972); Carr and Walsh, "Inventories and Analysis of Wealth"; Clemens, *Atlantic Economy*, 206–223, 228–232. On the growth in exports per capita in 18th-century Virginia, see Bergstrom, "Markets and Merchants."

32. P. M. G. Harris, "Integrating Interpretations of Local and Regionwide Change in the Study of Economic Development and Demographic Growth in the Colonial Chesapeake, 1630–1775," Regional Econ. Hist. Research Center, *Working Papers*, I, no. 3 (1978), 35–71.

changes at least roughly related to the date at which Europeans first arrived in substantial numbers. If we set aside the necessary qualifications and usual confessions of uncertainty, it is possible to offer a brief summary of what happened.

Excluding the original outposts along the James and St. Mary's rivers, newly planted parts of Maryland and Virginia during the seventeenth century usually included a considerable proportion of recently freed, recently married, already-seasoned indentured servants, young men and women who struck out for the frontier in search of the opportunities that had attracted them to the Americas. The composition of the population—the predominance of young adults and, by Chesapeake standards, the high proportion of women—led to a high birthrate in the decade or so following first arrival. The rate may not have been high enough to overcome the short life expectancies and unbalanced sex ratios characteristic of immigrants, but it was sufficient to have a major impact on the growth process as the children born in the wake of the initial migration came of age and started to have children of their own. Soon, however, the birthrate declined in response to several changes in the composition of the population: an increase in the proportion of children; the advancing age of the first settlers, which carried them beyond the time when they could become parents; and a rise in the sex ratio as prosperous planters purchased large numbers of young, predominantly male indentured servants. Falling birthrates were accompanied by an increase in the death rate, a function of the same shifts in population structure, and the area began, if it had not done so from the start, to register a net loss.

At first, new communities were characterized by low levels of wealth and by the crude egalitarianism of frontier life. But as Percy Bidwell noted, pioneering was "a process of capital making," and wealth burgeoned as planters cleared the land, erected buildings and fences, built up livestock herds, planted orchards, improved their homes, and the like.[33] Inequality also progressed as a few men, often the earliest arrivals or those who began with more capital and good business connections, pulled ahead of their neighbors. These pioneers served markets created by high rates of in-migration and farm making, and in addition they produced staples for the export trade. Initially, most newly freed servants stayed in the neighborhood, quickly becoming planters on their own land, but dwindling chances to prosper gradually persuaded many to follow their masters' early example and strike out for the frontier. Within roughly twenty

33. Percy Wells Bidwell and John I. Falconer, *History of Agriculture in the Northern United States, 1620–1860* (Washington, D.C., 1925), 82. The process is explored in Russell R. Menard, Lois Green Carr, and Lorena S. Walsh, "A Small Planter's Profits: The Cole Estate and the Growth of the Early Chesapeake Economy," *WMQ*, 3d Ser., XL (1983), 171–196.

years of settlement, emigration started to have a noticeable impact on the local work force.

Coincident with the beginning of significant out-migration, the birthrate began to climb as the native born became a substantial proportion of the adult population. Creoles differed demographically from their immigrant parents in several ways: they possessed an equal proportion of men and women; they lived longer; and they married younger. In consequence, as the number of creole adults grew, the rate of reproduction rose until, perhaps thirty years after first settlement, a surplus of births replaced a surplus of deaths and the local population began to increase steadily through natural means.

Over time, however, as the children and grandchildren of the first generation of natives matured, they also encountered the diminished opportunities that accompanied higher population densities and mounting land prices. Some were able to replace their parents in the social structure and others stayed as tenants or on farms too small to provide more than a meager living, but enough moved on to prevent the dismal Malthusian consequences of rapid population growth within a static economy. Thus, roughly sixty years after beginning, the process came full circle. Former frontiers that had once expanded quickly because of the prosperity they promised arriving planters now started to register a net loss to migration. This loss helped offset gains from natural increase, thereby preventing a drop in incomes or greater inequality.[34]

Each locality did not march in lockstep through this process. Diverse local conditions—exceptionally destructive or mild disease environments, excellent or mediocre soils, the degree of specialization in tobacco or for a single market, for example—generated significant deviations from the norm. Moreover, Chesapeake-wide developments in the economy and the rate and structure of immigration had a profound effect on population growth and kept newly opened territories from repeating earlier patterns. The long period of stagnation in the tobacco trade around the turn of the century, for example, struck marginal producers on the frontier with special severity and caused many newly freed servants to leave even the most recently settled areas. A higher proportion of women among indentured servants brought on gains in the rate of reproduction throughout the colonies, in new neighborhoods as well as old. The waning of European immigration, the replacement of servants by slaves, and the ap-

34. Chesapeake demographic patterns are summarized in Russell R. Menard, "Immigrants and Their Increase: The Process of Population Growth in Early Colonial Maryland," in *Law, Society, and Politics*, ed. Land, Carr, and Papenfuse, 88–110, and Kulikoff, "Colonial Chesapeake."

pearance of a creole majority altered the planting process. Typically, new areas first farmed in the eighteenth century were opened by second- and third-generation natives, who drew on blacks rather than whites for unfree labor. And, without a population marked by the peculiar characteristics of immigrants,.places settled after 1700 did not suffer a long period in which deaths exceeded births. Finally, the booming export sector of the quarter century before independence, since it permitted fuller employment of available resources, temporarily reduced the rates of outmigration from the older locales and contributed to gains in income throughout the Chesapeake.

Despite local and temporal variations, the basic relationships were widespread and persistent. In place after place along the tobacco coast, the demographic differences between immigrants and their offspring, the rapid increase and subsequent stagnation of wealth levels, and the gradual erosion of the chances for success for young adults worked a profound and fundamentally similar effect on the local growth process. Further, this local demographic process—the initially high but later lessening rate of immigration, the gradual replacement of a predominantly immigrant population by a mostly native-born population, and the emergence of reproductive increase as the principal engine of population growth— played a central role in the dynamics of social change. Those dynamics, the interactions between migration, opportunity, population growth, and economic development, should be a focus of future research on the Chesapeake colonies.[35]

35. The best introduction to these issues is P. Harris, "Integrating Interpretations." Much of the work cited in this chapter, but particularly that by Clemens, Earle, Kulikoff, Land, Main, Morgan, Nicholls, Papenfuse, Stiverson, and Walsh, is concerned with the interactions between economic, demographic, and social processes.

CHAPTER 7

THE WEST INDIES

The British West Indies are without the rich historiographical tradition of the mainland colonies. This reflects the subsequent development of the region. The United States became a major industrial nation and a major metropolitan center; its colonial origins have been a central interest of those concerned with its national history. The islands remained political colonies until well into the twentieth century and are impoverished colonial economies still. As a result they have failed to develop the strong national historical traditions that have focused so much attention on the mainland. This neglect testifies as well to a still-lingering sense that the colonists in the British West Indies do not merit study because their settlements were "disastrous social failures," brutal, exploitative places, a "wilderness of mere materialism" without a sense of community responsibility or loyalty to place. Indeed, they were hardly societies at all but rather "monstrous distortion[s] of human society," "amazingly effective sugar-production machines" in which the "all-powerful sugar magnate" drove "his abject army of black bondsmen" with a callous disregard for human life and dignity.[1]

While eighteenth-century commentators often shared the judgment of modern historians that the sugar colonies were social failures, many were persuaded at the same time that the West Indies were the most valuable of

1. The quotations are from Dunn, *Sugar and Slaves*, xiii, 340–341; Frank Wesley Pitman, *The Development of the British West Indies, 1700–1763* (New Haven, Conn., 1917), 2, 41, quoting J. R. Seeley, *The Expansion of England* (London, 1883), 155; and Orlando Patterson, *The Sociology of Slavery: An Analysis of the Origins, Development, and Structure of Negro Slave Society in Jamaica* (London, 1967), 9. For similar judgments, see among others, Lowell Joseph Ragatz, *The Fall of the Planter Class in the British Caribbean, 1763– 1833: A Study in Social and Economic History* (New York, 1928), and Carl and Roberta Bridenbaugh, *No Peace beyond the Line: The English in the Caribbean, 1624–1690* (New York, 1972). The major exception to the assertion that the West Indies lacks a historiographical tradition is the writings of the "Caribbean School" of economic history, chief among which is E. Williams, *Capitalism and Slavery* (see chap. 2, n. 6, above). See also Elsa V. Goveia, *A Study on the Historiography of the British West Indies to the End of the Nineteenth Century* (Mexico City, 1956), and Hilary McD. Beckles, "The Two Hundred Year War: Slave Resistance in the British West Indies—An Overview of the Historiography," *Jamaican Historical Review*, XIII (1982), 1–10.

Great Britain's American possessions. Arthur Young's rough estimates describe a perception of the relative worth of island and mainland settlements to the metropolitan economy that was widely shared by his contemporaries: "The sugar colonies added above three millions a year to the wealth of Britain; the rice colonies near a million, and the tobacco ones almost as much." Clearly, any economic history of early British America must pay close attention to the islands.[2]

The sugar islands were also indispensable to the development of the mainland colonies. The economies of the mainland and the islands were so tightly intertwined that full understanding of developments in one is impossible without an appreciation of developments in the other. The West Indies interacted with the mainland colonies in several ways: they served as a major market for colonial exports, particularly foodstuffs and wood products; they supplied a variety of goods that the continental colonists imported, processed, consumed, and reexported; and they provided an important source of foreign exchange that helped balance colonial accounts and pay for British manufactures.

Yet the significance of the islands for understanding the mainland goes beyond the reality of economic interdependence. The West Indies sat at one end of a spectrum that described the range of possibilities in British America, a spectrum running from north to south, from farm colony to plantation colony, from New England to the sugar islands. As Jack Greene has argued,

> Neither in their materialistic orientation, their disease environment, their number of African inhabitants, their concern to cultivate British values and institutions, nor perhaps even their commitment to the colony was there a sharp break between island and mainland societies. Rather, there was a social continuum that ran from the Caribbean through Georgia and South Carolina to the Chesapeake through Pennsylvania and New York to urban and then rural New England. The social contrast between a sugar plantation in Barbados and a small homogeneous farming community in New England was considerable. But it would no doubt have been less apparent to a contemporary traveler had he proceeded not directly from one to the other, but through a series of intermediate stops along the coast.

If we are to understand Anglophone America—and this applies as well to social and cultural historians as to students of the economy—we must

2. Arthur Young, ["An Inquiry into the Situation of the Kingdom on the Conclusion of the Late Treaty,"] *Annals of Agriculture and Other Useful Arts,* I (1784), 13.

pay attention to all segments of the spectrum, for the parts will become fully comprehensible only if placed in the proper context.[3]

Fortunately, recent work, much of it published in the past twenty years, has begun to fill the gaps. Much remains to be done, but there is now a solid foundation on which to build. Broad patterns of economic and social development in the islands have been described with greater clarity, while the central role of the Caribbean in the Atlantic world and, especially, the critical importance of the West Indies to the mainland colonies have been defined with increased precision. Out of all this have come several new suggestions.

A large part of this recent effort has concerned the black population of the islands. Harsh condemnations of West Indian society have often rested on European standards, on the apparent inability of whites to build the richly textured communities and the lively culture that appeared on the mainland, on the failure of the great planters to develop a sense of social responsibility or deep local commitments. These assessments, however accurate when applied to European Americans, ignore the creativity and the vitality of Afro-Americans who constructed and maintained a lively "underground economy" and an autonomous culture and world view, a viable "little tradition" that lent structure, meaning, and dignity to their lives despite the brutality of their masters, the heavy work demands of the sugarcane, and the destructive demographic regime under which they labored. Changes in interpretation have also risen from a modified view of the great planters and of white society. There are clear limits to the rehabilitation, for the great planters often were harsh, brutal, and self-centered, shocking to modern sensibilities in their calculated willingness to destroy life in pursuit of profit. White society was not totally impoverished, however, and some planters were sufficiently competent, energetic, innovative, and socially responsible, by their standards, to command a grudging respect.[4]

3. Greene, "Society and Economy in the British Caribbean during the Seventeenth and Eighteenth Centuries," *AHR*, LXXIX (1974), 1499–1517 (quotation on p. 1517). See also the recent surveys of the literature by Woodville K. Marshall, "A Review of Historical Writing on the Commonwealth Caribbean since c. 1940," *Social and Economic Studies*, XXIV (1975), 271–307, and William A. Green, "Caribbean Historiography, 1600–1900: The Recent Tide," *JIH*, VII (1977), 509–530.

4. For some of the newer interpretations that have resulted from the greater interest in the black experience, see especially Edward Brathwaite, *The Development of Creole Society in Jamaica, 1770–1820* (Oxford, 1971); Elsa V. Goveia, *Slave Society in the British Leeward Islands at the End of the Eighteenth Century* (New Haven, Conn., 1965); Michael Craton, with the assistance of Garry Greenland, *Searching for the Invisible Man: Slaves and Plantation Life in Jamaica* (Cambridge, Mass., 1978); and Hilary McD. Beckles, "The Economic

Englishmen were first attracted to the Caribbean by the chance to fight Spaniards. Beginning with John Hawkins's three peaceful, if not legitimate, voyages in the 1560s, English activity in the greater Caribbean gradually became more violent and aggressive but remained sporadic through the 1570s and early 1580s. After the outbreak of war with Spain in 1585, however, privateers turned to the Caribbean in force, largely to capture treasure ships, but also, given the chance, to raid and loot Spanish settlements. Privateering was big business in late Elizabethan England, attracting not only wild, shadowy figures as participants but also major London merchants and respectable country gentlemen as investors and supporters. During the nearly twenty years of warfare, the value of prize goods brought to England ranged between £100,000 and £200,000 per year. Nor did it stop with the end of formal fighting. There was "no peace beyond the line," that is, outside the territorial limits of European treaties. Privateering remained the major English activity in the Caribbean until the 1630s.

English privateering in the Caribbean left legacies of two sorts. Most dramatically, privateering led to piracy, which flourished in the Indies, particularly at Port Royal, Jamaica, until the late seventeenth century. Pi-

---

Origins of Black Slavery in the British West Indies, 1640–1680: A Tentative Analysis of the Barbados Model," *Jour. Carib. Hist.*, XVI (1982), 36–56. For the partial rehabilitation of great planters, note the history of the Price family as told by Craton and James Walvin, *A Jamaican Plantation: The History of Worthy Park, 1670–1970* (Toronto, 1970), and the careful distinctions by time and place drawn in Sheridan, *Sugar and Slavery*. Standard bibliographies of the secondary literature are Joseph Lowell Ragatz, *A Guide for the Study of British Caribbean History, 1763–1834, Including the Abolition and Emancipation Movements* (Washington, D.C., 1932); Goveia, *Study on Historiography*; and Lambros Comitas, *The Complete Caribbeana, 1900–1975: A Bibliographic Guide to the Scholarly Literature* (Millwood, N.Y., 1977). Jerome S. Handler, *A Guide to Source Materials for the Study of Barbados History, 1627–1834* (Carbondale, Ill., 1971), discusses both primary and secondary literature. K. E. Ingram, *Sources of Jamaican History, 1655–1838: A Bibliographical Survey with Particular Reference to Manuscript Sources* (Zug, Switzerland, 1976), does something similar for that island. For primary materials, see also Ingram, *Manuscripts Relating to Commonwealth Caribbean Countries in United States and Canadian Repositories* (St. Lawrence, Barbados, 1975); E. C. Baker, *A Guide to Records in the Leeward Islands* (Oxford, 1965); Baker, *A Guide to Records in the Windward Islands* (Oxford, 1968); M. J. Chandler, *A Guide to Records in Barbados* (Oxford, 1965); Herbert C. Bell, David W. Parker, *et al.*, *Guide to British West Indian Archive Materials, in London and in the Islands, for the History of the United States* (Washington, D.C., 1926); and Peter Walne, ed., *A Guide to Manuscript Sources for the History of Latin America and the Caribbean in the British Isles* (London, 1973). McCusker, "Rum Trade," provides a bibliography of source materials and secondary literature (pp. 1219–1377). See also John J. McCusker, "New Guides to Primary Sources on the History of Early British America," *WMQ*, 3d Ser., XLI (1984), 277–295.

racy made the islands the Wild West of the period, "promising far more in the way of glamor, excitement, quick profit, and constant peril" than did colonies on the mainland, and thus attractive to men determined to do "some thinges worthy of ourselves, or dye in the attempt." More prosaically, piracy led to colonization, providing some of the capital, knowledge, and incentives that created the first English settlements in the Caribbean.[5]

Englishmen who settled in the West Indies hoped to produce the same commodities that the Spanish and the Portuguese colonists cultivated. During the century after Columbus, Europeans had learned that a variety of cash crops could be grown in the tropics and shipped home profitably. The two that most attracted the attention of English settlers were tobacco and sugarcane, but others included cacao, fiber crops such as cotton and flax (for linen), and dye plants such as logwood (brown), fustic (yellow), brazilwood (red), and indigo (blue).[6] We can follow their initial experimentation and eventual concentration on sugar through the history of

5. Quotations are from Dunn, *Sugar and Slaves*, 10, 11. Dunn's source for the second passage is the contemporary journal of Sir Henry Colt as printed in V. T. Harlow, ed., *Colonising Expeditions to the West Indies and Guiana, 1623–1667* (London, 1925), 91. There is a large literature on Elizabethan privateering, much of it written to celebrate the sea dogs and of limited use for economic history. Two books by Kenneth R. Andrews are exceptions, however, and provide helpful detail on the privateers, their sources of capital, the extent of their activity, and their profits: *Drake's Voyages: A Re-assessment of Their Place in Elizabethan Maritime Expansion* (New York, 1967), and *Elizabethan Privateering: English Privateering during the Spanish War, 1585–1603* (Cambridge, 1964). Similarly scholarly, but with a broader perspective, is Paul Butel, *Les Caraïbes au temps des flibustiers, XVIᵉ–XVIIᵉ siècles* (Paris, 1982). Theodore K. Rabb, *Enterprise and Empire: Merchant and Gentry Investment in the Expansion of England, 1575–1630* (Cambridge, Mass., 1967), lists investors (pp. 61–66), while Arthur Percival Newton, *The Colonizing Activities of the English Puritans: The Last Phase of the Elizabethan Struggle with Spain* (New Haven, Conn., 1914), describes anti-Spanish activity in the Caribbean after 1603. David Beers Quinn places privateering in context in several works. See especially *England and the Discovery of America, 1481–1620* (New York, 1974), and *North America from Earliest Discovery*. See also chap. 17, below. Pirates are the subject of an even larger literature than privateers, but again there is little of use to economic historians. See, however, Violet Barbour, "Privateers and Pirates of the West Indies," *AHR*, XVI (1911), 529–566; Hugh F. Rankin, *The Golden Age of Piracy* (Williamsburg, Va., 1969); and Marcus Rediker, "'Under the Banner of King Death': The Social World of Anglo-American Pirates," *WMQ*, 3d Ser., XXXVIII (1981), 203–227.

6. There are useful treatments of some of the individual commodities, but we need more of them. See Arthur M. Wilson, "The Logwood Trade in the Seventeenth and Eighteenth Centuries," in *Essays in the History of Modern Europe*, ed. Donald C. McKay (New York, 1936), 1–15, and the very valuable study by Dauril Alden, much wider in breadth and importance than the title would indicate, "The Significance of Cacao Production in the Amazon Region during the Late Colonial Period: An Essay in Comparative Economic History," American Philosophical Society, *Proceedings*, CXX (1976), 103–135.

one colony, Barbados, England's most valuable Caribbean possession in the seventeenth century. The pattern of development there was replicated, at least in broad outline, in all of the British islands in the West Indies.

The colonists of Barbados spent their first years setting up farms to achieve local self-sufficiency in food and trying a variety of cash crops to see which one would yield the greatest return. Cotton and tobacco proved the early winners, but even as early as the 1630s the colonists had some success in making sugar. Of the three, sugar demanded the largest outlays of capital, however. One could grow tobacco or cotton on small plots of land by oneself or with a few workers and harvest and sell it with little processing. Sugar required more land and labor, and it had to be processed with expensive equipment before it could be shipped to market profitably. Sugar manufacture also called for considerable skill. The necessary land, labor, capital, and talent were acquired only slowly in the years before 1640. Some sugar was made on Barbados and shipped to London and other English colonies in the 1630s, but the real boom was delayed until the next decade.

The beginnings of the sugar boom in Barbados are usually attributed to a conjuncture between depression in the Anglo-American economy and the needs of the Dutch. The depression in the late 1630s hit Barbadian tobacco growers with special severity; efforts to substitute cotton for tobacco as the major export quickly failed. The island planters were thus quite interested in finding more-profitable alternative uses for their land, labor, and capital. The Dutch, their control of the Brazilian sugar region at Pernambuco threatened by the Portuguese, provided the answer. They taught the Barbadians how to manufacture sugar, loaned them capital for assembling large plantations and building sugar works, delivered the slaves who would plant, cultivate, cut, grind, and boil the cane, and carried the crystallized sugar to markets in Europe.[7]

While this interpretation is attractive for its simplicity and drama, it seems inconsistent with several bits of evidence. For one thing, the population of Barbados rose sharply in the late 1630s, advancing sevenfold between 1635 and 1639. If the island economy was so troubled, why did it attract so many immigrants? For another, the Dutch remained in control of Pernambuco until 1654, more than a decade after the beginnings

7. For early Barbados, see F. G. Innes, "The Pre-Sugar Era of European Settlement in Barbados," *Jour. Carib. Hist.*, I (1970), 1–22, and Gary A. Puckrein, "The Acquisitive Impulse: Plantation Society, Factions, and the Origins of the Barbadian Civil War (1627–1652)" (Ph.D. diss., Brown University, 1978). For an additional perspective on this and other questions, see Otis Paul Starkey, *The Economic Geography of Barbados: A Study of the Relationships between Environmental Variations and Economic Development* (New York, 1939).

of sugar production at Barbados. Although the evidence is thin, we suspect that additional study will diminish the importance of the role of the Dutch and enlarge the role of English merchants and Barbadian planters in bringing sugar to the island. Indeed, some recent work suggests that it was English planters themselves who went to Brazil in the 1630s and learned firsthand how to plant and process sugarcane.[8]

While the origins of the Barbadian sugar revolution may be unclear, the outcome is not. "There is a greate change on this island of late," a planter rejoiced in 1646, "from the worse to the better, praised be God." With astonishing speed in the late 1630s and early 1640s, Barbados was transformed from a colony of small farmers who grew minor staples for export and provisions for home use into "the most flourishing Island in all those American parts, and I verily beleive in all the world for the producing of sugar[,] Indico [and] Ginger." Hyperbole to be sure, but the enthusiasm is understandable. As early as 1655, London merchants imported 103,067 hundredweight (5,236 metric tons) of sugar from Barbados, worth roughly £130,000 at the island, £180,000 in London.[9]

8. For the shift into sugar, see Robert Carlyle Batie, "Why Sugar? Economic Cycles and the Changing of Staples on the English and French Antilles, 1624–54," *Jour. Carib. Hist.*, VIII (1976), 1–41, and Matthew Edel, "The Brazilian Sugar Cycle of the Seventeenth Century and the Rise of West Indian Competition," *Caribbean Studies*, IX (1969), 24–44. For evidence that the Dutch role in Barbados has been overstated, at least in the early slave trade, see Ernst van den Boogaart and Pieter C. Emmer, "The Dutch Participation in the Atlantic Slave Trade, 1596–1650," in *Uncommon Market*, ed. Gemery and Hogendorn, 353–375. For evidence that the role of London merchants has been underestimated, see Robert Paul Brenner, "Commercial Change and Political Conflict: The Merchant Community in Civil War London" (Ph.D. diss., Princeton University, 1970). Compare McCusker, "Rum Trade," 198–199, citing A. P. Canabrava, "A Influência do Brasil na técnica fabrico de açucar nas Antilhas francesas e inglesas no maedo do século XVII," Faculdade de Ciências, Económicas e Administrativas [de Universidade de São Paulo], *Anuário, 1946–1947*, 63–76. But see also John R. Pagan, "Dutch Maritime and Commercial Activity in Mid-Seventeenth-Century Virginia," *VMHB*, XC (1982), 485–501. The Bridenbaughs, in *No Peace beyond the Line*, provide evidence of the importance of farm building among resident planters to the process of capital formation in the pre-sugar era. See especially their discussion of the cultivation of cotton, "an agricultural accomplishment of the first magnitude" (p. 57).

9. William Hay and William Powrey to Archibald Hay, 8 Oct. 1646, "Papers Relating to the Island of Barbados," in Hay of Haystoun Documents, GD 34, Scottish Record Office, Edinburgh (quoted in Dunn, *Sugar and Slaves*, 59); Thomas Robinson to Thomas Chappell, 24 Sept. 1643, "Papers Relating to . . . Barbados," in Hay of Haystoun Documents (quoted in J. H. Bennett, "The English Caribbees in the Period of the Civil War, 1642–1646," *WMQ*, 3d Ser., XXIV [1967], 372). For the quantity of sugar imported, see CO 1/12, fol. 127a, PRO, and the discussion in McCusker, "Rum Trade," 189, 208, 283, n. 217. In the fiscal year 1652–1653 London merchants paid about 72% of total customs revenues (Exchequer, Declared Accounts, E 351/653, PRO). If a similar proportion applied for imported sugar and London was therefore the port of entry for three-quarters of all sugar that entered the country, then the total English importation amounted to 143,000

Sugarcane transformed the population of the island, reorganized its economy, and restructured its society. Perhaps the truly striking aspect of the change was demographic. Sugar required large numbers of workers, and only Africans were available in quantities sufficient to meet the demand. The small number of blacks living on the island in 1640 exploded to nearly 13,000 by 1650, 27,000 by 1660, when they outnumbered whites on the island, and 50,000 by the end of the century, when they accounted for three-quarters of the population. That is only the most obvious change. Sugar brought an almost unbelievably destructive demographic regime to Barbados, a regime so severe that the slave population proved unable to reproduce itself until the end of the eighteenth century. In addition, it led to a smaller white population, a result of both higher mortality and fewer chances to succeed. The number of whites on the island peaked at about 30,000 in 1650 and then fell off steadily, to 20,000 in 1680, to 13,000 in 1710 (compare table 7.1 and table 7.2).[10]

---

hundredweight. Sugar wastage during shipment is not considered in these estimates; because of wastage during the voyage more sugar left Barbados than arrived in England. Note that 3,042 hundredweight of the sugar imported at London paid duty as white sugar and the rest as brown sugar. The values used here—25 shillings at Barbados and 35 shillings at London—are based on estimates of the price per hundredweight in 1655, but we have no direct evidence of such prices. Writing from his experiences in Barbados between 1647 and 1650, Richard Ligon in *A True and Exact History of the Island of Barbados* (London, 1657), priced Barbados sugar at 28 shillings on the island and 112 shillings at London (pp. 92, 95, 96, 112). By the early 1660s it was down to 15 shillings in Barbados and 21 shillings at London (Vincent T. Harlow, *A History of Barbados, 1625–1685* [Oxford, 1926], 170, 312n). Compare Sheridan, *Sugar and Slavery*, 397. See also A. P. Thornton, "Some Statistics of West Indian Produce, Shipping, and Revenue, 1660–1685," *Caribbean Historical Review*, IV (1954), 251–280, and the references cited in nn. 17–18, below.

10. For changes in indentured servitude accompanying these demographic shifts, see Hilary McD. Beckles, "Sugar and White Servitude: An Analysis of Indentured Labour during the Sugar Revolution of Barbados, 1643–1655," *Journal of the Barbados Museum and Historical Society*, XXXVI (1981), 236–246. For the growth of the black population and the slave trade to the West Indies, see chap. 10, n. 15, below; A. P. Thornton, "The Organization of the Slave Trade in the English West Indies, 1660–1685," *WMQ*, 3d Ser., XII (1955), 399–409; Richard B. Sheridan, "The Commercial and Financial Organization of the British Slave Trade, 1750–1807," *Econ. Hist. Rev.*, 2d Ser., XI (1958), 249–263; Sheridan, "Africa and the Caribbean in the Atlantic Slave Trade," *AHR*, LXXVII (1972), 15–35; and Leslie Imre Rudnyanszky, "The Caribbean Slave Trade: Jamaica and Barbados, 1680–1770" (Ph.D. diss., University of Notre Dame, 1973). For vital rates among West Indian slaves, see the discussion in chap. 10, below; Gabriel Debien, *Plantations et esclaves à Saint-Domingue* (Dakar, Senegal, 1962); and Michael Craton, "Jamaican Slave Mortality: Fresh Light from Worthy Park, Longville, and the Tharp Estates," *Jour. Carib. Hist.*, III (1971), 1–27. The estimates of population assembled in table 7.1 and table 7.2 may be too high for the second half of the 17th century. Compare Henry A. Gemery, "Emigration from the British Isles to the New World, 1630–1700: Inferences from Colonial Populations,"

Sugar demanded capital as well as slaves, capital to purchase the workers, acquire the land and livestock, and buy the processing equipment needed to operate on a competitive scale. Early on, the capital requirements were apparently modest. In 1646 a Barbadian estimated that an investment of only £200 "might quickly gaine an estate by sugar, which thrives wonderfully." Later estimates were much higher, ranging from £3,500 to £12,000. Already in the 1640s, land alone brought £5 an acre on Barbados (ten times its price before the advent of sugar), while fully equipped sugar plantations sold for £1,800 to £4,500 per hundred acres.[11]

With land so expensive and capital requirements so high, little room was left for poor men and newly freed servants who had earlier found it possible to grow tobacco or cotton and provisions on small farms. A few managed to hang on around the fringes of the great plantations: as late as 1680 there were nearly 1,200 small farmers on the island working ten or fewer acres, usually without servants or slaves. Others took jobs in the four island towns—Bridgetown, Speightstown, Holetown, and Oistins Town—or on the great estates. But most poor men left, roughly 30,000 between 1650 and 1680 according to some estimates, moving to islands not yet fully given over to sugarcane or to the mainland. This constituted "the largest population movement within the colonies during the 17th century."[12]

Research Econ. Hist., V (1980), 218; Dunn, *Sugar and Slaves*, 312; and Patricia A. Molen, "Population and Social Patterns in Barbados in the Early Eighteenth Century," *WMQ*, 3d Ser., XXVIII (1971), 289.

11. James Parker to John Winthrop, 24 June 1646, *Winthrop Papers*, V, 84. For land prices and plantation values, see Sheridan, *Sugar and Slavery*, 264–266, and Dunn, *Sugar and Slaves*, 66. How all this was financed has been the subject for some debate and needs further work. We are inclined to agree with Richard Pares, who concluded that "Adam Smith was wrong: the wealth of the British West Indies did not all proceed from the mother country; after some initial loans in the earliest period which merely primed the pump, the wealth of the West Indies was created out of the profits of the West Indies themselves" (*Merchants and Planters* [*Econ. Hist. Rev.*, Supplement, no. 4 (Cambridge, 1960)], 50). See chap. 2, above; Frank W. Pitman, "The Settlement and Financing of British West India Plantations in the Eighteenth Century," in *Essays in Colonial History*, 252–283; K. G. Davies, "The Origins of the Commission System in the West India Trade," Royal Historical Society, *Transactions*, 5th Ser., II (1952), 89–107; and Richard Pares, "The London Sugar Market, 1740–1769," *Econ. Hist. Rev.*, 2d Ser., IX (1956), 254–270.

12. Alfred D. Chandler, "The Expansion of Barbados," *Jour. Barbados Museum and Hist. Soc.*, XIII (1946), 106–136 (quotation on pp. 106–107). David Lowenthal, "The Population of Barbados," *Soc. and Econ. Studies*, VI (1957), 445–501, offers a similar estimate, but Dunn thinks the figures much too high and suggests that 10,000 is closer to the mark (*Sugar and Slaves*, 112–113). The importance to the founding of South Carolina of this emigration is discussed in chap. 8, below.

TABLE 7.I.
Estimated Population of Barbados, 1630–1780
(in Thousands)

Year	Whites	Blacks	Total
1630	1.8	—	1.8
1640	14.0	—	14.0
1650	30.0	12.8	42.8
1660	26.2	27.1	53.3
1670	22.4	40.4	62.8
1680	20.5	44.9	65.4
1690	17.9	47.8	65.7
1700	15.4	50.1	65.5
1710	13.0	52.3	65.3
1720	17.7	58.8	76.5
1730	18.2	65.3	83.5
1740	17.8	72.1	89.9
1750	17.2	78.8	96.0
1760	17.8	86.6	104.4
1770	17.2	92.0	109.2
1780	16.9	82.4	99.3

Sources: For 1630–1640, Henry A. Gemery, "Emigration from the British Isles to the New World, 1630–1700: Inferences from Colonial Populations," *Research in Economic History*, V (1980), 211; for 1650–1780, John J. McCusker, "The Rum Trade and the Balance of Payments of the Thirteen Continental Colonies, 1650–1775" (Ph.D. diss., University of Pittsburgh, 1970), 699. See also n. 10, above.

Sugarcane and slavery increased the wealth of Barbados, promoted major inequalities among the settlers, and sustained the rise of the great planters. A detailed census taken in 1680 and recently analyzed by Richard Dunn permits a description of the extent of their domination of island society at the height of their power. The 175 big planters of Barbados (defined, somewhat arbitrarily, as those with 60 or more slaves) made up only 7 percent of the property holders, but owned more than half the land and labor. And this disguises the degree of concentration, for the census not only underrepresents the great planters' acreage and work force, but also omits other forms of property, especially processing equipment, of which they owned the major share.

The big planters were very big indeed: they owned on average about

TABLE 7.2.
Estimated Population of the British Caribbean, 1650–1780
(in Thousands)

Year	Whites	Blacks	Total
1650	44	15	59
1660	47	34	81
1670	44	52	96
1680	42	76	118
1690	37	98	135
1700	33	115	148
1710	30	148	178
1720	35	176	212
1730	37	221	258
1740	34	250	285
1750	35	295	330
1760	41	365	406
1770	45	434	479
1780	48	489	537

Source: John J. McCusker, "The Rum Trade and the Balance of Payments of the Thirteen Continental Colonies, 1650–1775" (Ph.D. diss., University of Pittsburgh, 1970), 712 (with a correction in addition for 1760). Bermuda and the Bahamas are not included here as part of the British West Indies. See also n. 10, above.

Note: Figures have been rounded off and thus the totals do not always equal the sum of their parts.

250 acres, 115 slaves, and 6 servants. No estimate of total worth is available, but an average of £4,000 sterling seems conservative, a striking figure considering that an estate valued at one-fourth that amount was enough to make a man exceptionally rich along the tobacco coast. The great planters, the majority of whom were second- or third-generation colonists whose families had been on the island since at least mid-century, thoroughly dominated local politics. They controlled nearly all the positions of real power on the council, in the assembly, on the bench, and in the militia.

They were about to realize their "one consuming ambition"—to escape the West Indies for England. Absenteeism was relatively rare in 1680, but the irony in the accomplishments of the sugar magnates was that, in accumulating fortunes, they transformed the island in ways that made it "almost uninhabitable" by their standards. Once they acquired sufficient wealth and discovered that they could protect their interests more effectively at home than on the island, the exodus began. By the early eighteenth century, "absenteeism had become a permanent way of life for many of the Barbados gentry." [13]

Sugar likewise offered some prospects for farmers and merchants in the mainland colonies. As early as 1647, John Winthrop learned that Barbadians were "so intent upon planting sugar that they had rather buy foode at very deare rates than produce it by labour, soe infinite is the profitt of sugar workes after once accomplished." [14] Food was not the only commodity the planters wanted from the mainland. Barbados is small, with less than 100,000 arable acres, and the forests were quickly cut down to make room for cane. The planters still needed wood, however, for fuel, buildings, and fences, and for hogsheads to ship the crop. And they needed livestock to power the mills.

The demands of the sugar planters proved central to the economic development of the mainland colonies. Traders were able to operate independently of the major metropolitan merchants (although sometimes on London capital); farmers had customers for their surplus; the credits earned—"returns via the West Indies"—helped settle unfavorable trade balances with England; and the elaborate linkages generated made the mainland economies more diverse, more flexible, and less "colonial." By 1770 all the continental colonies, but notably those in the North, depended on West Indian markets to a greater or lesser degree. In that year exports to the islands were worth £759,000 sterling, more than one-fourth of the value of all commodity exports and nearly half that of exports to Great Britain. When the considerable earnings in the invisibles on the current account—from the carrying trade and the sale of commercial services—are added to that figure, it becomes even more significant. Lord Sheffield estimated that the value to the mainland merchants of the

---

13. Dunn, *Sugar and Slaves*, is both the best study of the process and the source of the quotations (pp. xv, 116, 103). See also Richard S. Dunn, "The Barbados Census of 1680: Profile of the Richest Colony in English America," *WMQ*, 3d Ser., XXVI (1969), 3–30, and Richard B. Sheridan, "The Rise of a Colonial Gentry: A Case Study of Antigua, 1730–1775," *Econ. Hist. Rev.*, 2d Ser., XIII (1960), 342–357. For absenteeism, see Lowell J. Ragatz, "Absentee Landlordism in the British Caribbean, 1750–1833," *Agric. Hist.*, V (1931), 7–24, and Douglas Hall, "Absentee-Proprietorship in the British West Indies, to about 1850," *Jam. Hist. Rev.*, IV (1964), 15–35. Hall dissents strongly from the traditional view, which focuses on the destructive impact of absenteeism. He argues that absenteeism has been exaggerated and that, to the extent it existed, it created opportunities for creoles, who often proved competent managers.

14. The quotation is from Richard Vines to John Winthrop, 19 July 1647, *Winthrop Papers*, V, 172.

freight alone was £245,000. It is clear that the island trade made a major contribution to mainland incomes.[15]

The concept of a "sugar revolution," a "révolution de la canne," describes the economic, social, and demographic changes that transformed Barbados. Sugar monoculture displaced diversified farming based on tobacco, cotton, and provisions; large estates swallowed up small farms; African slaves replaced European indentured servants; blacks grew in number and whites left; destructive demographic patterns were established that prevented the natural replacement of the black population; the island came to depend on imported food and fuel; and the great planters took control—all within a few decades after 1640. "Here indeed is the 'sugar revolution,'" K. G. Davies notes. "But where else? No other English or French island was so early conquered by sugar, and in few was the victory so swift or complete." Sorting this out, tracing the progress of the cane through the Caribbean, measuring the pace and pattern of the accompanying transformations, explaining the differences among the several islands, and accounting for why it happened first, fastest, and most thoroughly on Barbados are major opportunities in the economic history of the West Indies. The effort is already under way, as the recent work of Richard Dunn and Richard Sheridan demonstrates. When it is finished we will have a much richer history of the economy of early British America.[16]

15. For trade between the West Indian and mainland colonies, see table 4.1, above, and especially Pares, *Yankees and Creoles*, and Herbert C. Bell, "The West India Trade before the American Revolution," *AHR*, XXII (1917), 272–287. See also David H. Makinson, *Barbados: A Study of North-American–West-Indian Relations, 1739–1789* (The Hague, 1964). Work on trade between the islands and particular mainland colonies is cited in the other regional chapters in Part II. For the value of earnings in the current account, see chap. 4, above, the sources cited there, and Lord Sheffield, *Observations on Commerce*, 184–186.

16. Davies, *North Atlantic World*, 180. As the quotation suggests, the international character of the West Indies provides a variety of opportunities in comparative economic history. Richard Sheridan, *The Development of the Plantations to 1750 [and] An Era of West Indian Prosperity, 1750–1775* (Barbados, 1970), moves in that direction. Such comparative work will be facilitated by studies of individual islands (and groups of islands). See Harlow, *History of Barbados*; Starkey, *Economic Geography of Barbados*; C. S. S. Higham, *The Development of the Leeward Islands under the Restoration, 1660–1688: A Study of the Foundations of the Old Colonial System* (Cambridge, 1921); Louis Philippe May, *Histoire économique de la Martinique (1635–1763)* (Paris, 1930); Christian Schnakenbourg, "Les sucreries de la Guadeloupe dans la seconde moitié du XVIIIème siècle (1760–1790): Contribution à l'étude de la crise de l'économie coloniale à la fin de l'Ancien Régime" (Ph.D. thesis, Université de Paris II, 1973); and Schnakenbourg, "Recherches sur l'histoire de l'industrie sucrière à Marie-Galante, 1664–1964," *Bulletin de la Société d'Histoire de la Guadeloupe*, XLVIII–L (1981), 5–144. See also McCusker, "Rum Trade," 302–391. For a

The fundamental characteristics of the history of the British West Indian sugar industry emerge from an examination of the available data on prices and output. We are fortunate in having fairly reliable prices for sugar in several European markets from the mid-1670s, but these need to be extended back in time. Moreover, we lack a good series of plantation prices sensitive to variations in quality. Still, the data we do have are sufficient to permit a description of basic trends (see figure 7.1).

The directions followed by the price of sugar are those of the classic staple commodity. Prices were very high when the Barbadian sugar revolution began, eighty to one hundred shillings per hundredweight for muscovado at London, sixty shillings at the plantation. As with tobacco prices, sugar prices afterward fell off sharply and at a steadily decelerating rate until the 1680s, when sugar brought as little as ten shillings at the islands, sixteen to twenty shillings in London. European prices jumped sharply in the late 1680s and remained high for the next two decades, probably because of war-induced shortages. These high prices brought little benefit to the planters, however, for they faced difficulties getting their crops to the market. Prices fell slowly in the twenty years following the Peace of Utrecht, returning to the level of the 1680s by the early 1730s, and then rose rapidly, more than doubling in the thirty years to 1760. From that time until the outbreak of the American Revolution,

more general but very useful overview of the French colonies, see Michel Devèze, *Antilles, Guyanes, la mer des Caraïbes de 1492 à 1789* (Paris, 1977). Such work will also be aided by studies of individual plantations (and other enterprises). See, for example, Edwin F. Gay, ed., "Letters from a Sugar Plantation in Nevis, 1723–1732," *Jour. Econ. and Bus. Hist.*, I (1928), 149–173; Frank J. Klingberg, ed., *Codrington Chronicle: An Experiment in Anglican Altruism on a Barbados Plantation, 1710–1834* (Berkeley and Los Angeles, Calif., 1949); Richard Pares, *A West-India Fortune* (London, [1950]); J. Harry Bennett, Jr., *Bondsmen and Bishops: Slavery and Apprenticeship on the Codrington Plantations of Barbados, 1710–1838* (Berkeley and Los Angeles, Calif., 1958); Bennett, "Cary Helyar, Merchant and Planter of Seventeenth-Century Jamaica," *WMQ*, 3d Ser., XXI (1964), 53–76; Bennett, "William Whaley, Planter of Seventeenth-Century Jamaica," *Agric. Hist.*, XL (1966), 113–123; Julian P. Marsh, "The Spring Plantation Estate: A Study of Some Aspects of a Jamaican Sugar Plantation, 1747–1801" (B.A. thesis, University of Nottingham, 1969); D. W. Thoms, "The Mills Family: London Sugar Merchants of the Eighteenth Century," *Business History*, XI (1969), 3–10; Richard B. Sheridan, "Planters and Merchants: The Oliver Family of Antigua and London, 1716–1784," *ibid.*, XIII (1971), 104–113; Sheridan, "Simon Taylor, Sugar Tycoon of Jamaica, 1740–1813," *Agric. Hist.*, XLV (1971), 285–296; Jerome S. Handler and Frederick W. Lange, *Plantation Slavery in Barbados: An Archaeological and Historical Investigation* (Cambridge, Mass., 1978); and Roderick Alexander McDonald, "'Goods and Chattels': The Economy of Slaves on Sugar Plantations in Jamaica and Louisiana" (Ph.D. diss., University of Kansas, 1981). See also Carlton Rowe Williams, "Sir Thomas Modyford, 1620–1679: 'That Grand Propagator of English Honour and Power in the West Indies'" (Ph.D. diss., University of Kentucky, 1979).

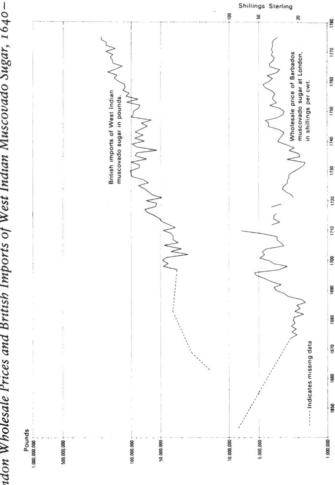

FIGURE 7.1.

London Wholesale Prices and British Imports of West Indian Muscovado Sugar, 1640–1775

Sources: Prices for the years following 1674 and imports for the years following 1697 are drawn from John J. McCusker, "The Rum Trade and the Balance of Payments of the Thirteen Continental Colonies, 1650–1775" (Ph.D. diss., University of Pittsburgh, 1970), appendix D, 896–898, appendix E, 1143. For estimates for the earlier years, see n. 9, above, and n. 16, below.

Note: This graph uses a semilogarithmic projection. Semilog graphs are used to plot time series because they permit us both to see the general directions of any trend lines and to compare the rates of increase (or decrease) of each series. The steeper the slope of a line in a semilog graph, the sharper the rate of increase (or decrease) it describes.

when war again drove them sharply upward, London sugar prices declined gently.[17]

Trends in sugar output are more difficult to summarize than secular movements in prices. Numerous islands exported sugar, and its quality varied considerably. The option was always available to sell more sugar of a lower quality if there was a market for it. During the eighteenth century two new developments made the situation still more complex. Sugar's by-products, molasses and rum, which had always played a certain role in the British islands, became viable as alternatives to crystalline sugar. In addition, secondary markets in North America established themselves as essential to the West Indian export sector (table 7.3).

The impact of these various factors needs to be sorted out by developing annual series describing the total value of West Indian exports by island, product, and export destination. In the meantime, we can gain an introduction to the subject through an examination of data showing the volume of British imports of muscovado sugar (see figure 7.1). These describe a rapid growth to the last decade of the seventeenth century, a fourfold increase in fifty years, followed by stagnation at a level of about 400,000 hundredweight (20,000 metric tons) during the quarter century of war after 1689. British muscovado imports more than doubled from 1710 to 1730, and then declined slightly until the late 1740s. Imports grew again thereafter, in a sustained rise that lasted until the Revolution, doubling once more from the 1750s to the 1770s.[18]

Using data on imports into Great Britain as crude proxies for figures on West Indian production, the evidence suggests that prices and output in the sugar industry were often inversely related, at least over the long run. Until the late 1680s, during the 1710s and 1720s, and from 1760 to 1775, imports rose and prices fell; from 1730 to 1750 prices rose and imports fell. The two variables moved in tandem only around the turn of the century, when prices and imports fluctuated violently but revealed no long-term trend, and briefly during the 1750s, when both went up. Any explanation of this inverse relationship offers the possibility of consider-

17. For prices of sugar and its by-products, see McCusker, "Rum Trade," 988–1188, and Sheridan, *Sugar and Slavery*, 392, 397, and appendix 5.

18. For import data, see the sources cited in n. 17, above, and Lowell J. Ragatz, comp., *Statistics for the Study of British Caribbean Economic History, 1763–1833* (London, [1928]). The standard work on sugar cultivation is still Edmund O. von Lippmann, *Geschichte des Zuckers seit den ältesten Zeiten bis zum Beginn der Rübenzucker-Fabrikation: Ein Beitrag zur Kulturgeschichte*, 2d ed. (Berlin, 1929; reprint, Neiderwalluf bei Wiesbaden, 1970). Noel Deerr relied heavily on Lippmann for his own book, *The History of Sugar* (London, 1949–1950). See also McCusker, "Rum Trade," *passim*. Sheridan, *Sugar and Slavery*, begins the discussion of short-term fluctuations in the sugar industry (pp. 389–486), a topic that needs further work.

TABLE 7.3.

Average Annual Value and Destinations of
Selected Commodities Exported from the
West Indies, 1768–1772 (Pounds Sterling)

Commodity	Great Britain	North America	Total
Sugar			
Muscovado	£2,652,050	£110,200	£2,762,250
White	350,700	73,500	424,200
Rum	380,943	333,337	714,280
Molasses	222	9,648	9,870
Total	£3,383,915	£526,685	£3,910,600

Source: John J. McCusker, "The Rum Trade and the Balance of Payments of the Thirteen Continental Colonies, 1650–1775" (Ph.D. diss., University of Pittsburgh, 1970), 232, 233, 234, 402, 406, 414, n. 25.

Notes: The values used in this calculation are for the commodities as imported into North America (£1.45 per hundredweight sterling for muscovado sugar; £2.10 for white sugar; 22.58d per gallon for rum; and 10.67d per gallon for molasses). They thus overstate the F.O.B. ("freight on board") value in the West Indies (but less so than if we had used British prices). When comparing quantities (and values) of these commodities as exported from the West Indies with figures for them as imported into Great Britain or North America, note the need to account for wastage during transit. The West Indies exported commodities other than these three, of course, but there are few data. Harry J. Carman, ed., *American Husbandry* (1775) (New York, 1939), 429–499 *passim*, prints figures for 1763 in which all commodities other than the above amounted to less than 6 percent of the total. If that same percentage held true for 1768–1772, then total exports for those years would have averaged about £4,100,000.

able insight into the dynamics of the Caribbean economy. At the very least, the data showing rising output in the face of falling prices suggest that some substantial gains in productivity occurred in the West Indian sugar industry. The picture of a backward, unenterprising, conservative class of great planters unable or unwilling to innovate may be seriously misleading.[19]

19. For the traditional view of planters, see especially Ragatz, *Fall of the Planter Class*. For evidence that they did not stubbornly resist change, see R. Keith Aufhauser, "Slavery and Technological Change," *Jour. Econ. Hist.*, XXXIV (1974), 36–50; Richard B. Sheridan, "Samuel Martin, Innovating Sugar Planter of Antigua, 1750–1776," *Agric. Hist.*, XXXIV (1960), 126–139; and chap. 15, below. At least for the 17th century, we expect that the dynamics of price and production in sugar resembled those in tobacco discussed in chap. 6, above.

These data also suggest that planters were often caught in a profit squeeze, particularly during the seventeenth century, from 1710 to 1730, and after 1760. They responded creatively in several ways and were largely successful in maintaining profits at an acceptable level over the long haul, despite occasional setbacks. In their efforts to protect and enhance the profitability of their operations, they sought first to maintain, even to expand, sugar output while at the same time cutting costs. Later, they tried a variety of other schemes: to boost their selling price by widening the circle of customers to whom they could export; to ensure a monopoly in British and British colonial markets for their sugar; to decrease their costs by lowering the prices of the supplies they purchased abroad; and to increase their incomes by diversifying their product line. This last activity is the most interesting of all, and the one that not only brought the greatest success but had the broadest consequences as well.[20]

Everything that the sugar planters attempted in order to deal with their economic problems had to be accomplished within the confines of English mercantilism. The point has been made elsewhere in this book that in the decades immediately after the passage of the Navigation Acts in the 1660s, English businessmen, at home and in the colonies, reacted in two ways. First, since the crown was obviously intent on enforcing the laws, merchants began to obey them. Second, everyone began the search for means to prosper under the laws. For the West Indians that search was rewarded by the discovery that the Navigation Acts offered colonists any number of possibilities. In the century after the Restoration, the sugar planters of the West Indies adopted several devices not only to soften the laws' restrictions but also to take advantage of the openings inherent in them.[21]

The Navigation Acts designated sugar an enumerated commodity, thereby denying to the planters access to any buyers outside England and England's other colonies. Increasingly efficient customs operations made the higher returns once possible from direct sale to foreign consumers no longer a realistic option for sugar planters. Instead of risking their exports in illegal voyages, they directed their attention to making more profitable the markets still open to them. In pursuit of these goals, they made

20. On profits in sugar planting, see chap. 2, above; Douglas Hall, "Incalculability as a Feature of Sugar Production during the Eighteenth Century," *Soc. and Econ. Studies*, X (1961), 340–352; and J. R. Ward, "Profitability of Sugar Planting."

21. For much of what follows, see Pitman, *Development of the British West Indies*; Starkey, *Economic Geography of Barbados*; McCusker, "Rum Trade," *passim*; and Sheridan, *Sugar and Slavery*. Most of this is clear enough in outline, but its precise delineation awaits further work.

allies of the "sugar interest" in the mother country. The "sugar interest" had two components: absentee planters, now members of the landed gentry; and the West Indian merchants in London and the outports. The planters worked through paid agents who represented them and their colonial governments in Whitehall and Westminster. While the concerns of resident planters, absentee planters, and merchants in the West Indian trade were not always the same, they all recognized the value of pursuing together the goals that they did hold in common. One critical area in which they were successful was the import duty on sugar. Noting that these duties jumped by roughly 600 percent between 1660 and 1770, one might question how successful they really were. The answer, quite simply, is that the planters and the sugar interest kept them from going still higher.[22]

Parliament not only responded to the planters' pleas that it not hurt the islands, but it also answered many of their requests for help. The government was particularly sympathetic to proposals that would protect or enlarge the number of customers for island produce. Consequently, the same laws that collected import duties on British sugars set much-higher, prohibitive duties on foreign sugars. As a result, the British West Indians had a monopoly on the supply to the mother country. The crown countenanced other laws and regulations that eased access to British buyers, particularly with regard to customs entry procedures, the payment of duties, and the collection of rebates. In 1739, after almost eighty years of planters' petitions, Parliament even allowed a rare variance from the Navigation Acts and permitted the direct export of sugar from the islands to European ports in Spain, Portugal, and the Mediterranean. All of these measures served to lower costs or enlarge returns and, thus, to ease the squeeze on the planters' profits.

There were so many advantages in having a monopoly on the supply of customers at home that the sugar planters began to argue for the same privileges in the other colonies. By the 1720s they had come to the conclusion that it would be in their best interest if the North Americans were allowed to trade only with the British West Indies. This would accomplish two things. First, it would alter the terms of trade between North America and the West Indies to the great advantage of the British sugar planters. Circumscribing the market in which the Yankee merchants could sell their provisions and timber products would work to lower the prices

---

22. The standard accounts of the "sugar interest" are by Lillian M. Penson: "The London West India Interest in the Eighteenth Century," *Eng. Hist. Rev.*, XXXVI (1921), 373–392; and *The Colonial Agents of the British West Indies: A Study in Colonial Administration, Mainly in the Eighteenth Century* (London, 1924).

planters had to pay for such things; expanding the market in which planters could sell their sugar, molasses, and rum would work to increase the prices they were to be paid. Second, legally limiting North America's commerce with the French, the Dutch, and the others in the West Indies would have just the reverse effects on the terms of trade for these foreign sugar planters. It would raise their costs and lower their prices, squeezing them nicely. The second result of the proposed restrictions was as significant as the first because any damage done to foreign sugar growers in the West Indies would diminish their ability to compete in Europe. This, in turn, would enhance Continental markets for British West Indian goods shipped as reexports from London and the outports. British colonists were right to recognize powerful competitors in the planters of the foreign islands, especially the French on Martinique, Guadeloupe, and St. Domingue.[23]

The Navigation Acts of the seventeenth century hardly touched on the trade between English and foreign colonies. To accomplish their goals the West Indians had to convince Parliament to take additional steps and to outlaw the trade between North America and the foreign West Indies. Bills to this effect were twice submitted to Parliament, once in 1731 and again in 1732. They failed. A new, third bill said nothing about exports to the foreign sugar colonies and did not forbid the importation of sugar, molasses, and rum, but merely set import duties on them. The bill passed and became known as the Molasses Act of 1733.

Had the Molasses Act been enforced and obeyed, without doubt it would have gone quite far toward accomplishing the objectives of the sugar planters, but it was clearly neither enforced nor obeyed. The North Americans discovered numerous ways around and over the compliant customs men stationed in their ports. They found collectors and comptrollers to be willing partners to the continuing importation of mounting quantities of foreign sugar, rum, and, in particular, molasses. Sometimes such partnerships came at a cost but rarely if ever at a cost equivalent to

23. For trade with the foreign West Indies, see Pares, *War and Trade*; Vera Lee Brown, "Anglo-Spanish Relations in America in the Closing Years of the Colonial Era," *Hispanic American Historical Review*, V (1922), 325–483; Brown, "Contraband Trade: A Factor in the Decline of Spain's Empire in America," *ibid.*, VIII (1928), 178–189; Dorothy Burne Goebel, "The 'New England Trade' and the French West Indies, 1763–1774: A Study in Trade Policies," *WMQ*, 3d Ser., XX (1963), 331–372; Francis Carroll Huntley, "Trade of the Thirteen Colonies with the Foreign Caribbean Area" (Ph.D. diss., University of California, Berkeley, 1949); Frances Armytage, *The Free Port System in the British West Indies: A Study in Commercial Policy, 1766–1822* (London, 1953); and Jean Louise Willis, "The Trade between North America and the Danish West Indies, 1756–1807, with Special Reference to St. Croix" (Ph.D. diss., Columbia University, 1963).

the full duty, even on part of the cargo. The Molasses Act was passed again at the end of its initial five-year period and reenacted regularly thereafter until 1764, when, as the Sugar Act of that year, it was revised and made perpetual. The reduction of the duties in 1764 made them no more attractive and the more active enforcement of the laws did little beyond greatly antagonizing the North American colonists. The Revenue Act of 1766 reduced the duty on molasses still further, to a penny a gallon, and collected it on all molasses, British West Indian as well as the rest. By that time the point of the act had been lost as far as the sugar planters of the British islands were concerned.[24]

The attempts by British sugar planters to protect and improve the profitability of their enterprise by guaranteeing themselves monopolies in the markets where they bought their supplies and sold their output were only partially successful. Their attempt to reach the same objective by gaining direct access to new customers was equally mixed, having come, apparently, too late. What they were very successful in doing, however, was developing and diversifying their produce to something more than the basic raw brown muscovado sugar. They began to process and sell other kinds of sugar, chiefly clayed white sugar like that commonly shipped from Brazil in the seventeenth century and from the French West Indies in the eighteenth century. Still more important, they began to exploit fully the by-products of sugar manufacturing: molasses and its distillate, rum. In so doing, they shifted the emphasis of their activities in ways that eventually induced their descendants to produce more rum than sugar.

The planters of Barbados had learned their trade from the planters of Brazil, and they therefore knew about clayed sugar from the beginning. To clay sugar was to leech out more of the liquid molasses, thus converting the raw soft brown muscovado into a more immediately salable, harder white sugar that was not yet refined sugar but was a considerable cut above muscovado. Clayed sugar took longer to process, however, and it required additional expertise and facilities. Nevertheless, over time the Barbadians turned an increasingly greater proportion of their crop into clayed sugar.

The advantages of making clayed sugar at Barbados were several. It sold in the island and at home at a higher price than muscovado sugar. Even though the reprocessing resulted in a total output of lesser weight, this was more than offset by the better return. It saved shipping costs be-

24. For the Molasses Act and its enforcement, see Sheridan, "Molasses Act"; Gilman M. Ostrander, "The Colonial Molasses Trade," *Agric. Hist.*, XXX (1956), 77–84; Thomas C. Barrow, *Trade and Empire: The British Customs Service in Colonial America, 1660–1775* (Cambridge, Mass., 1967); and chap. 2, above.

cause a planter's crop converted into clayed sugar filled fewer hogsheads and thus required less cargo space than it did as muscovado. It saved import duties besides. By long-standing arrangement with British customs, clayed sugar, although it was white and sold as such, paid the same import duty as muscovado. Finally, since the claying process drained away more of the sugar's molasses, it left the planter with additional molasses from which to distill rum.

The other British West Indian islands had not yet followed the example of Barbados by the time of the American Revolution. Production estimates testify to this. Circa 1770 all of the islands together manufactured about 132,000 metric tons (2,591,000 hundredweight) of muscovado sugar, almost all of which was exported, and about 41,800,000 liters (11,050,000 gallons) of molasses. From the molasses—less what was consumed and exported—they distilled about 41,600,000 liters of rum. The ratio of rum to sugar was 315 liters of rum per ton of sugar, apparently a considerable gain over earlier periods.

For Barbados the figures paint a somewhat different picture. Total muscovado sugar production amounted to 18,600 metric tons, of which 3,600 tons were exported without further processing. The island exported another 7,200 tons of clayed sugar. All this activity yielded a good bit more molasses relative to gross sugar output, 7,100,000 liters, which the planters distilled into much more rum, 9,100,000 liters. This was the equivalent of 489 liters of rum per metric ton of sugar, or 50 percent more than the British West Indian average. The result was, of course, proportionately greater returns for the planters of Barbados.

Why, we must ask, were they so far in advance of their neighbors? We can only guess at this stage in our understanding, but it might well be another example of the leading role that Barbadians had always played in the British West Indies. The island had been the first to experience the sugar revolution. For that reason its planters were forced to come to terms sooner with declining prices, expanding output, and lower profits. Barbadians were the first to use slave labor on a large scale. Barbadians led the fight in the 1680s for lower English import duties and, again, in the 1720s, for a British West Indian monopoly in North American markets.

In contrast, the crisis reached sugar planters in the Leeward Islands more slowly. In the late seventeenth century, the planters of St. Christopher, Nevis, Montserrat, and Antigua still had virgin land to cultivate. (It is frequently easier to move to fresh soil—because yields are so much higher—than it is to find some other way to come to terms with decreasing returns from the current acres.) By the early eighteenth century some had retreated to resignation or complacency, others to poorer-quality sugars. Jamaicans seemed always to have new lands to open up and new crops to try. Barbadians, never complacent but without any more land, chose another alternative, to innovate. Their resort to and reliance on sugar's by-products portended nineteenth-century sugar-planting practices.[25]

As the figures in table 7.3 reveal, the islands, to a much larger degree than any of the mainland regions, remained highly specialized plantation colonies committed to monoculture. The planters of the West Indies did not respond to the pressure on their profits by cultivating new crops for export (despite frequent experiments) or by engaging in collateral forms of enterprise (such as entering the carrying trade). Sugar provided ample opportunities for profit, largely because the planters, with those of Barbados in the lead, processed and distilled more and more of it. Molasses and rum became almost as valuable to the West Indians as sugar itself. In the next century they would dominate.

The increasingly significant role played by molasses and rum had other effects on the economy of the British islands. Again, some of this happened first or on a larger scale on Barbados. What economic development did occur in the West Indies can be largely related to the spread effects not so much of sugar as of molasses and rum. Sugar as a commodity in foreign trade had a relatively limited effect on the domestic economy. It passed through directly and rather predictably on its way from the plantation to the overseas consumer. Molasses and rum offered a variety of possibilities to local entrepreneurs. Both entered the island economies when plantation managers used them to pay taxes, secure services, or buy provisions and other necessities. Some was resold for local consumption and quantities were exported, largely to the continental colonies.

The locus of this commercial activity was the port town, and the organizer of the business was the town merchant. The direct export trade in sugar no more required the services of colonial merchants than did the early export trade in tobacco from Maryland and Virginia. Everything could be nicely managed from London, including the importation and sale of slaves from Africa, whose disposition could easily be handled by

---

25. This distinction already operated, and was seen to be operative, in the 1660s, as is evident from a conditional pardon granted by an English court in 1664 to 25 condemned prisoners in the Home Circuit. The court recognized a critical difference between Barbados and Jamaica. The prisoners were ordered "to be transported beyond the seas upon agreement for serving five yeares after their landing and if at Jamaica at 5 yeares end to have 30 acres of land a piece and if at the Barbadoes the value of £10 sterling in Sugar and in the mean time to be maintayned" (C 82/2318, fol. 24, PRO, as quoted in a forthcoming study, *Crime and the Courts in England, 1660–1800*, by John Beattie, to whom we are indebted).

one or two local agents of the Royal African Company. But the profit squeeze revealed the high cost of shipping provisions and wood products from England to the islands. It also showed the comparative advantage of buying them from North America and paying for them with molasses and rum, for which there was a considerable demand in the continental colonies and little or none, at first, in the metropolis. Resident planters and the plantation managers of absentee planters turned to the local merchants, who would arrange these exchanges in the port towns.

With the growth in the importance and number of the local merchants of the British West Indies came the development of the port towns themselves. Places like Kingston (Jamaica), St. Johns (Antigua), and most especially Bridgetown (Barbados), grew as more of the island's activities located there—but not without some difficulties, as the case of Kingston attests. The greater role, economic and otherwise, of these urban places attracted more people who demanded the range of goods and services typical to towns and cities. Eventually they even became collection points for some of the sugar that had previously been shipped directly from the plantations. The presence of part of the sugar crop passing through the port towns helped give rise in the eighteenth century to an urban sugar-refining industry organized by the town merchants. The investments in warehouses (to store sugar until shipment) and in sugar refineries were only two spread effects introduced into the island's economy by changes in the production practices of the sugar plantations themselves, changes that helped to maintain the profitability of the staple and perpetuated the plantation colony in the West Indies.[26]

On the eve of the American Revolution, the planters of Barbados and the other British sugar islands were near the peak of their prosperity. Their efforts to protect and increase their income and wealth by political and economic means had been eminently successful. For the free white population of the islands, with a net worth several times higher than that of the mainland colonies, these were very good times (see table 3.3). The

26. Although many such developments occurred in Port Royal, Jamaica, Michael Pawson and David Buisseret, *Port Royal, Jamaica* (Oxford, 1975)—the only history of a West Indian port town—does not treat them. As early as the 1680s some of the town's mercantile functions had begun to be transferred across the harbor to Kingston. The history of the later attempt to make Kingston the island's capital, and its defeat by the planters, who preferred Spanish Town, is told succinctly in George Metcalf, *Royal Government and Political Conflict in Jamaica, 1729–1783* (London, 1965), 122–136; he emphasizes the political results of the attempted removal rather than its economic causes. See also Stephen Alexander Fortune, "Merchants and Jews: The Economic and Social Relationships between the English Merchants and Jews in the British West Indian Colonies, 1650–1740" (Ph.D. diss., University of California, San Diego, 1976).

period between the Seven Years' War and the American War of Independence was indeed the "silver age" of the British West Indies.[27]

27. The phrase is from Pares, *Merchants and Planters*, 40. For him the "golden age" occurred in the earlier era, more than a century before, when very high prices and much lower costs resulted in even greater profits. Sheridan, *Development of the Plantations*, shares in the distinction (p. 74). The role of the imperial government in promoting the prosperity of the West Indies was characterized by the preferential treatment accorded them. As Jacob M. Price once mused: "The original laws [of trade] too, whatever they said on paper, were never seriously intended to apply to the West Indies where 'international trade' remained the rule rather than the exception. How really serious were the British ministers after 1763 in wishing to alter the trade [between the British and the non-British colonies]? The establishment of free ports, *inter alia*, suggests a greater interest in legitimizing rather than stopping it" (review of Barrow, *Trade and Empire*, in *Jour. Econ. Hist.*, XXVII [1967], 400). For the later period, see Karl Stewart Watson, "The Civilised Island: Barbados, a Social History, 1750–1816" (Ph.D. diss., University of Florida, 1975).

CHAPTER 8

THE LOWER SOUTH

One of the themes of this book is the relative neglect of the southern continental colonies and the West Indies by historians of early British America. Recent work on the Chesapeake has done a great deal to right the balance for that region, but the new interest in the colonial South has just begun to reach the Carolinas and Georgia. This is particularly true in economic history. Rice and indigo have received less attention than tobacco; Charleston has attracted less interest than Philadelphia or Boston; and the demography of the Lower South has been neglected by comparison with the Chesapeake tidewater or the New England town. We simply know less about the economy of the Lower South than about that of any other section of British America.

This gap in our knowledge is not for lack of evidence. Of course the evidence leaves much to be desired, as it nearly always does for colonial history, but the documentation in general is not especially thin by the standards of British America. Indeed, for some classes of material—naval officer shipping lists, plantation records, price data, business letters—it is often superior.[1] Our knowledge is so slim that almost any issue in economic history merits study, while the data are often sufficient to make studies like these profitable. In the Lower South, need and opportunity converge.

The British occupation of the Lower South differed from that of the other major regions of British America because it initially proceeded

1. Although there are frequent breaks in the series, naval officer shipping lists are available for Charleston from 1717 and for Savannah from 1752. Converse D. Clowse provides a useful compilation in *Measuring Charleston's Overseas Commerce, 1717–1767: Statistics from the Port's Naval Lists* (Washington, D.C., 1981). The *South Carolina Gazette* (Charleston), which began publication in 1732, is an invaluable source for trade statistics, prices, and other materials of interest to economic historians. George Rogers Taylor, "Wholesale Commodity Prices at Charleston, South Carolina, 1732–1791," *Jour. Econ. and Bus. Hist.*, IV (1932), 356–377, is largely dependent on this source. Several major collections of business papers survive, the most important being *The Papers of Henry Laurens*, ed. Philip M. Hamer *et al.* (Columbia, S.C., 1968–), and *The Letterbook of Robert Pringle, 1737–1745*, ed. Walter B. Edgar (Columbia, S.C., 1972).

more by migration from other colonies than by direct passage from the British Isles. One observer called the early settlers "the dregs and gleanings of all other English Colonies." The first group arrived in the 1650s in the Albemarle district as a spillover from Virginia; that part of North Carolina is perhaps best approached as an extension of the Upper South.[2] The Lower South proper—South Carolina, Georgia, the Cape Fear district of North Carolina, and at the end of the colonial period, East and West Florida—originated in the sugarcane-induced transformation of Barbados.

Two aspects of that transformation are noteworthy because of their ramifications for the Lower South: the timing and nature of the outmigration from Barbados; and the creation there of markets for foodstuffs and timber products. By 1660, the island was severely overcrowded in comparison with other colonies, then or later. Population density on Barbados had already reached 250 persons per square mile, and within a generation it would surpass 400. Most of the arable land was occupied and cultivated, while the costs of entry into sugar production were so high that only those with substantial capital were capable of joining the planter class. Further, since almost the entire island was suitable for sugarcane, alternative agricultural possibilities—for instance, raising provisions for large plantations or producing an export crop that needed a smaller initial investment—were limited. Servants "out of their time" found their progress blocked. Some took supervisory jobs on large plantations, others worked in Bridgetown, a few became small farmers. But the largest number simply left. During the seventeenth century roughly 10,000 Barbadians, the majority of them recently freed indentured servants but including a sprinkling of wealthy planters, departed from the island for other colonies.

An expanding market for imported foodstuffs, draft animals, and timber products was another result of this exodus from Barbados. As the remaining colonists concentrated the island's productive capacities on sugar, they left not an acre free for planting provisions, for growing trees, or for anything else. This gave settlers in other colonies the chance to supply the island's economy with food to feed its large and increasing

2. The phrase is from John Urmstone, a clergyman in the Albemarle district from 1710 to 1721, as quoted in Harry Roy Merrens, *Colonial North Carolina in the Eighteenth Century: A Study in Historical Geography* (Chapel Hill, N.C., 1964), 33. Regional differences in North Carolina were so striking that contemporaries occasionally suggested dividing the colony and attaching the parts to South Carolina and Virginia (A. Roger Ekirch, *"Poor Carolina": Politics and Society in Colonial North Carolina, 1729–1776* [Chapel Hill, N.C., 1981], 87).

slave labor force, animals to work the grinding mills, and wood to build buildings, fuel the boiling-houses, and pack the finished product. By 1660, entrepreneurs recognized the possibilities inherent in these developments. They could tap the Barbadian migrant stream, colonize the North American coastline between the Chesapeake and Spanish Florida, as yet unoccupied by Europeans, and supply the Barbadian consumer. The scheme had significant imperial implications as well as attractive commercial promise.[3]

After several false starts, in 1670 a permanent settlement was established on the Ashley River in what is now South Carolina. Despite being troubled in the beginning by disease and by food shortages, the colonists found these difficulties to be less severe than at Jamestown or on the islands and the population rose steadily: 200 settlers in 1670 had become 1,000 in 1680, 4,000 by 1690, and roughly 6,000 at the turn of the century (see table 8.1). Initially the economy relied on immigrants, the "Chief subsistence of the first Settlers being by Hoggs, & Cattle they sell to the New-Comers, and with which they purchase Cloathes, and Tooles from them." An export trade was quick to develop, however. The volume and organization of that trade merits further study, but its basic structure is clear. As late as 1687 settlers had failed to find "any Commodityes fit for the market of Europe but a few Skins they purchased from the native Indians and a little Cedar with which they helpe to fill the ship that brings the skins for London." The colonists had to proceed indirectly to earn the foreign exchange necessary to purchase English manufactures. This they did by shipping provisions and timber products to Barbados for slaves, sugar, bills of exchange, and European goods.[4]

3. On the sugar-induced transformation of Barbados and its relationship to the development of South Carolina, see chap. 7, above, and Dunn, *Sugar and Slaves*, 46–116. On the migration, see Richard S. Dunn, "The English Sugar Islands and the Founding of South Carolina," *South Carolina Historical Magazine*, LXXII (1971), 81–93; St. Julien Ravenel Childs, "The First South Carolinians," *ibid.*, LXXI (1970), 101–108; Wood, *Black Majority*, 3–34; Adelaide Berta Helwig, "The Early History of Barbados and Her Influence upon the Development of South Carolina" (Ph.D. diss., University of California, Berkeley, 1930); Richard Waterhouse, "South Carolina's Colonial Elite: A Study in the Social Structure and Political Culture of a Southern Colony, 1670–1760" (Ph.D. diss., Johns Hopkins University, 1973), chap. 1; and Waterhouse, "England, the Caribbean, and the Settlement of Carolina," *Journal of American Studies*, IX (1975), 259–281.

4. CO 5/288, fol. 120, PRO. Converse D. Clowse, *Economic Beginnings in Colonial South Carolina, 1670–1730* (Columbia, S.C., 1971), is a good descriptive introduction to the period. George David Terry's recent dissertation, "'Champaign Country': A Social History of an Eighteenth Century Lowcountry Parish in South Carolina, St. Johns Berkeley County" (Ph.D. diss., University of South Carolina, 1981), provides a detailed account of the operation of the economy at the local level.

TABLE 8.1.
Estimated Population of the Lower South, 1660–1780
(in Thousands)

Year	Georgia	North Carolina	South Carolina	Total Population	Total Whites	Total Blacks
1660		1.0		1.0	1.0	0.0
1670		3.8	0.2	4.0	3.8	0.2
1680		5.4	1.2	6.6	6.2	0.4
1690		7.6	3.9	11.5	9.7	1.8
1700		10.7	5.7	16.4	13.6	2.9
1710		15.1	10.3	25.4	18.8	6.6
1720		21.3	18.3	39.6	24.8	14.8
1730		30.0	30.0	60.0	34.0	26.0
1740	2.0	51.8	54.2	108.0	57.8	50.2
1750	5.2	73.0	64.0	142.2	82.4	59.8
1760	9.6	110.4	94.1	214.1	119.6	94.5
1770	23.4	197.2	124.2	344.8	189.4	155.4
1780	56.1	270.1	180.0	506.2	297.4	208.8

Sources: U.S. Bureau of the Census, *Historical Statistics of the United States, Colonial Times to 1970* (Washington, D.C., 1975), II, 1168 (Ser. Z 15–17, compiled by Stella H. Sutherland). Those for South Carolina, 1710–1740, have been reestimated by the authors. Compare the revised totals for North Carolina for 1730 (31.9), 1750 (73.0), and 1770 (190.0) suggested by Harry Roy Merrens, *Colonial North Carolina in the Eighteenth Century: A Study in Historical Geography* (Chapel Hill, N.C., 1964), 53, 194–201, 218, n. 1, and discussed in John J. McCusker, "The Rum Trade and the Balance of Payments of the Thirteen Continental Colonies, 1650–1775" (Ph.D. diss., University of Pittsburgh, 1970), 720, n. 31.

Notes: Native American Indian residents of the region who lived outside the areas settled by the British are not included in these population figures. For a crude, preliminary attempt to estimate the tribal populations within the territories contiguous to British settlement and with whom, therefore, the British maintained commercial contact, see McCusker, "Rum Trade," 713–716. Figures have been rounded off and thus the totals do not always equal the sum of their parts.

Carolinians had high hopes for the island trade, for it seemed that the proximity of Carolina to the West Indies would provide definite price advantages and permit them to dominate the market. Some thought the island trade alone would prove sufficient to make the young colony "far more considerable than . . . those other places to the North of us."[5] In

5. Quoted in Wood, *Black Majority*, 32.

fact, island markets offered quite limited chances for profit. The period of rapid expansion in sugar production had ended by the 1680s, and the industry was showing signs of stagnation. Carolina faced tough competition from better-established settlements. The West Indian trade served South Carolina well during its infancy, providing an essential source of foreign exchange and the income needed to purchase "Neagroes & Sarvants to rayse a plantacon," but entrepreneurs remained on the lookout for a staple that could be sold in Europe. Such a staple would allow South Carolinians to escape their initial position as "the colony of a colony."[6]

During the seventeenth century it appeared that trade with the native Americans might produce that staple. In their dealings with southern Indians, geography provided Carolinians with an edge over other English colonists; access to superior English manufactures and the lively London market also gave Carolina-based traders a competitive edge over the Spanish and the French. Animals with the most highly prized furs were not native to the area, but deer were available in abundance and deerskins purchased from the Indians quickly emerged as a very valuable export. As early as 1700, exported skins were valued at roughly £20,000 sterling. The trade grew only slowly during the eighteenth century— deerskin exports were worth £35,000 in the late 1740s and £55,000 around 1770. Despite this slow growth, skins commanded a major share of the Lower South's export earnings throughout the colonial period, accounting for 18 percent of the total as late as 1749 and nearly 10 percent on the eve of independence (see table 8.2).[7]

For a time, native American slaves were also an important part of the trade. The size of this local slave trade is unknown, but the presence of 1,400 Indian slaves in South Carolina in 1708 (15 percent of the colony's reported population) suggests that it was extensive, especially since a substantial proportion of the enslaved Indians were exported to other colonies. The trade seems to have been very volatile, rising and falling with war and peace; apparently it peaked in the aftermath of the Yamasee war (over 300 Indians were exported in 1717) and then quickly declined to insignificance.[8]

Although already the subject of an excellent study by Verner Crane, the trade in deerskins with the Indians of the Lower South merits further investigation. Crane was particularly interested in the imperial and politi-

6. *Ibid.*, 33, 34.

7. Verner W. Crane, *The Southern Frontier, 1670–1732* (Durham, N.C., 1928), 110–112; Clowse, *Economic Beginnings*, 121.

8. William Robert Snell, "Indian Slavery in Colonial South Carolina, 1671–1795" (Ph.D. diss., University of Alabama, 1972); John Donald Duncan, "Servitude and Slavery in Colonial South Carolina, 1670–1776" (Ph.D. diss., Emory University, 1972).

TABLE 8.2.
Average Annual Value and Destinations of
Commodity Exports from the Lower South, 1768–1772
(Pounds Sterling)

Commodity	Great Britain	Ireland	Southern Europe	West Indies	Africa	Total
Rice	£198,590		£50,982	£55,961		£305,533
Indigo	111,864					111,864
Deerskins	37,093					37,093
Naval stores	31,709					31,709
Wood products	2,520	£228	1,396	21,620		25,764
Grains, grain products	302	169	1,323	11,358		13,152
Livestock, beef, pork	75	366	103	12,386		12,930
Other	11,877	515	365	785	£362	13,904
Total	£394,030	£1,278	£54,169	£102,110	£362	£551,949

Source: James F. Shepherd and Gary M. Walton, *Shipping, Maritime Trade, and the Economic Development of Colonial North America* (Cambridge, 1972), 215, 218–219, 222, 225, 227. For a discussion of this compilation of the data in CUST 16/1, Public Record Office, see chap. 4, above.

Notes: "Southern Europe" here includes all of the continent south of Cape Finisterre, plus the Wine Islands off the west coast of Africa. Wood products here include hoops. "Other" commodities are defined as any that were individually less by value than 2 percent of the total average annual exports.

cal aspects of the trade to the neglect of more-strictly economic issues. Fairly good data on volume are available, but we know less about organization and little about prices.[9] The impact of the trade on the native American economy is poorly understood: given the relatively high quality of the evidence, close study should prove rewarding. The trade in Indian slaves also needs attention and is of greater than local significance. By understanding the one North American context in which that kind of

9. Crane, *Southern Frontier*.

trade flourished, we may learn why Indian slavery failed to become a major source of labor in the British colonies.[10]

Finally, the staples approach insists on the importance of assessing the impact of the trade with the Indians on other sectors of the Lower South economy. Preliminary indications are that this was limited. The trade did subsidize the costs of exploration and discovery and proved the chief source of foreign exchange before the emergence of rice, naval stores, and indigo, but it provided employment for relatively few people and made merely minimal demands on local producers. Its principal linkage was probably in the encouragement of entrepreneurial talent and the accumulation of capital that could be employed in other endeavors, but the extent of these spread effects remains unknown.[11]

In addition to the establishment of a trade in provisions and timber with Barbados and the development of commerce with the Indians, the seventeenth century witnessed success in the search for an agricultural staple that would command a direct European market. The search was rational and systematic, involving experimentation with the local resource base and tests of overseas demand. A variety of crops and products were tried, among them sugarcane, indigo, tobacco, cotton, silk, naval stores, ginger, wine, and rice.[12] Eventually, the period of experimentation culminated in the 1690s with the successful commercial cultivation of rice, the crop that became in the eighteenth century the "only Commodity of Consequence produced in South Carolina . . . as much their staple Commodity, as Sugar is to Barbadoes and Jamaica, or Tobacco to Virginia and Maryland." Rice branded a distinctive mark on the social structure and the economic organization of the region.[13]

Although the beginnings of commercial rice cultivation in South Carolina are obscure and the subject of some controversy, fairly reliable data on exports are available from 1699, shortly after the start of successful production (see figure 8.1). These describe a pattern of expansion that bears at least a general resemblance to that of the other great colonial

10. The only general study of the topic is Almon Wheeler Lauber, *Indian Slavery in Colonial Times within the Present Limits of the United States* (New York, 1913).

11. The subject is briefly treated in Crane, *Southern Frontier*, especially pp. 108–136; Clowse, *Economic Beginnings*, 162–166; and Earle and Hoffman, "Staple Crops," 16–17. See also Stuart Owen Stumpf, "The Merchants of Colonial Charleston, 1680–1756" (Ph.D. diss., Michigan State University, 1971), and Philip M. Brown, "Early Indian Trade in the Development of South Carolina: Politics, Economics, and Social Mobility during the Proprietary Period, 1670–1719," *S.C. Hist. Mag.*, LXXVI (1975), 118–128.

12. Clowse, *Economic Beginnings*, 58–68; Gray, *History of Agriculture*, 52–55.

13. Quoted in Wood, *Black Majority*, 35.

staples, tobacco and sugar. Rice exports expanded at a rapid but steadily decelerating pace during the first three decades of the eighteenth century, passing 1.5 million pounds by 1710, 6 million in 1720, and nearly 20 million by 1730. Then followed several years of sluggishness in the early to middle 1730s, a sharp upward surge at the end of the decade, virtual stagnation in the 1740s and early 1750s, another sharp surge in the mid-1750s, and a fairly steady expansion from 1760 to the Revolution. This rapid advance quickly made rice the dominant export of the Lower South and one of the principal staples of British America. Rice achieved primacy among exports in the section during the 1720s; by the late 1740s it accounted for nearly 60 percent of total exports by value. Its position slipped over the next twenty years, chiefly because of the growth of indigo production, but around 1770 rice still accounted for more than half the area's commodity export earnings (see table 8.2). At that time it ranked third among exports from the British continental colonies, behind tobacco and wheat products, accounting for 10 percent of the value of all commodities shipped from British North America.[14]

We lack a reliable, consistent series of rice prices at the plantation during the colonial period, a series that probably could be assembled from probate inventories. Scattered observations are available from a variety of sources, however, while annual wholesale prices exist for Philadelphia from 1720 and Charleston from 1732 (see figure 8.1). These describe a fairly steep decline until the 1740s, a pattern typical of the early years of staple production. This was followed, again typically, by a gentle fluctuation around a relatively stable trend.[15] We know little about the sources of

14. On the beginnings of rice cultivation, see A. S. Salley, Jr., *The Introduction of Rice Culture into South Carolina* (Columbia, S.C., 1919); Duncan Clinch Heyward, *Seed from Madagascar* (Chapel Hill, N.C., 1937); Wood, *Black Majority*, 55–62; David Leroy Coon, "The Development of Market Agriculture in South Carolina, 1670–1785" (Ph.D. diss., University of Illinois, Urbana-Champaign, 1972), 164–214; James M. Clifton, "The Rice Industry in Colonial America," *Agric. Hist.*, LV (1981), 266–283; Henry C. Dethloff, "The Colonial Rice Trade," *ibid.*, LVI (1982), 231–243; and Daniel C. Littlefield, *Rice and Slaves: Ethnicity and the Slave Trade in Colonial South Carolina* (Baton Rouge, La., 1981), 74–114. Gray, *History of Agriculture*, 277–290, remains the best introduction to the rice industry in the colonies. Export statistics are assembled in U.S. Bureau of the Census, *Historical Statistics*, II, 1192–1193 (Ser. Z 481–499), with an introduction (pp. 1163–1165) that provides an able discussion of their quality. Rice export figures are not a good proxy for production since substantial quantities—one-third of the total by one estimate—were consumed in the region.

15. Gray, *History of Agriculture*, 287–290; U.S. Bureau of the Census, *Historical Statistics*, II, 1197 (Ser. Z 561); A. Cole, *Wholesale Commodity Prices*. To enhance their comparability these prices can be reduced to sterling units using the exchange rates in McCusker, *Money and Exchange*, 183–186, 222–224. For a general discussion of Charleston prices

FIGURE 8.1.
Charleston and Philadelphia Wholesale Prices and Lower South Exports of Rice, 1698–1774

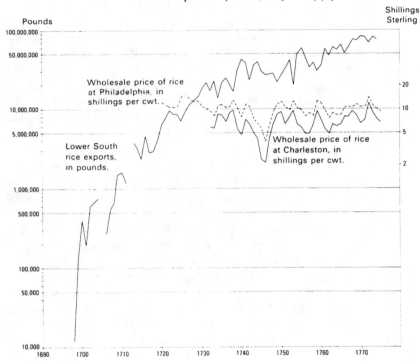

Sources: U.S. Bureau of the Census, *Historical Statistics of the United States, Colonial Times to 1970* (Washington, D.C., 1975), II, 1192, 1197 (Ser. Z 481–561); Arthur Harrison Cole, *Wholesale Commodity Prices in the United States, 1700–1861* (Cambridge, Mass., 1938), II, 15–68. Prices were reduced to sterling using the exchange rates in John J. McCusker, *Money and Exchange in Europe and America, 1600–1775: A Handbook* (Chapel Hill, N.C., 1978), 183–186, 222–224. No allowance was made here for the difference between the hundredweights used to sell rice at Philadelphia (112 lbs.) and at Charleston (100 lbs.). See John J. McCusker, "Weights and Measures in the Colonial Sugar Trade: The Gallon and the Pound and Their International Equivalents," *William and Mary Quarterly*, 3d Ser., XXX (1973), 599–624, and "Correction," *ibid.*, XXXI (1974), 164.

Note: This graph uses a semilogarithmic projection. Semilog graphs are used to plot time series because they permit us both to see the general directions of any trend lines and to compare the rates of increase (or decrease) of each series. The steeper the slope of a line in a semilog graph, the sharper the rate of increase (or decrease) it describes.

these price movements over either the short or the long run. In the short term, the rice planters seem to have weathered cycles of boom and depression similar to those that plagued sugar and tobacco producers. War, weather, and European recession disrupted trade, and the colonists responded too robustly to temporary increases in demand. Moreover, rice growers reacted to adversity in ways characteristic of staple producers, with efforts to support prices, control volume and quality, reduce costs, diversify the export base, and develop domestic sources of manufactured goods. The subject, however, wants study. The evidence is sufficient to reward close investigation, while examination of booms and busts in the rice trade promises important insights into the structure of the regional economy.[16]

In disentangling movements of price and production over the long term, it may prove useful to begin with changes in supply. Techniques of rice cultivation changed dramatically during the colonial period because of the development of irrigation, the movement of production from moist uplands to inland swamps and finally to the tidewater, extensive experimentation with seed to produce varieties well adapted to soil and climate, and innovations in the laborious cleaning process. Unfortunately, little is known about the introduction, diffusion, and impact of these techniques. It is clear, nevertheless, that these innovations played a major role in the development of the industry. They resulted in impressive productivity gains, and they worked in combination with improvements in packaging, shipping, and marketing to permit growers and merchants first to reduce the price of rice to consumers and later to hold it steady in the face of burgeoning costs for land and labor. Close study of the changing techniques of cultivation and processing is a necessity to the history of rice in the Lower South. When completed, a study like this may pose another serious challenge to the conventional wisdom that colonial agriculture achieved little in the way of productivity gains.[17]

---

and the source of the data in the Cole volume, see Taylor, "Wholesale Commodity Prices." See also Peter A. Coclanis, "Rice Prices in the 1720s and the Evolution of the South Carolina Economy," *Jour. So. Hist.*, XLVIII (1982), 531–544.

16. M. Eugene Sirmans, *Colonial South Carolina: A Political History, 1663–1763* (Chapel Hill, N.C., 1966), contains useful information on the public response to trade cycles.

17. Sam B. Hilliard, "Antebellum Tidewater Rice Culture in South Carolina and Georgia," in *European Settlement and Development in North America: Essays on Geographical Change in Honour and Memory of Andrew Hill Clark*, ed. James R. Gibson (Toronto, 1978), 91–115; Gray, *History of Agriculture*, 280–284; David Doar, *Rice and Rice Planting in the South Carolina Low Country* (Charleston, S.C., 1936), 7–41; and Clowse, *Economic Beginnings*, 123ff.

The selling of rice also needs investigation, particularly to assess the impact of English mercantilism on the industry. South Carolinians apparently shipped rice directly to Portugal and the foreign West Indies within a few years of its successful commercial cultivation, thereby avoiding substantial English import duties. In response, in 1705 Parliament added rice to the list of enumerated commodities, thereby requiring that it be brought to England and import duties be paid. While it could thereafter be reexported, the colonists argued that these changes severely restricted foreign sales, for two reasons. Not only did the import duties raise the final price, but the indirect route made it impossible to get the fall crop to Portugal in time for Lent, when demand for rice peaked. After much lobbying by the South Carolinians, Parliament relaxed the requirements in 1731: rice could be shipped directly to the Iberian Peninsula and Mediterranean Europe.

Despite the encouragement that the relaxation of the restrictions offered to planters, its full impact is difficult to gauge. The available data suggest that the effect was small. Between 1712 and 1717, roughly 9 percent of colonial rice exports went directly to southern Europe. That figure doubled in the 1730s, but afterward, except in years of poor European harvests such as 1768 and 1770, the countries south of Cape Finisterre took a declining share of the Lower South's rice crop. Northern Europe, served by reexports from Great Britain, was the principal purchaser of colonial rice throughout the eighteenth century. The markets the colonists shipped to directly that did increase were the British Caribbean, the other continental colonies (though they reexported the bulk of their rice to Great Britain), and after the further relaxation of restrictions in 1763, the foreign West Indies.[18]

The production of naval stores gave the economy of South Carolina an important boost in the early eighteenth century, albeit in the long run of far less significance than rice. The crown provided the incentive for the industry as a reaction to the disruption of its traditional supply from the Baltic and to high prices produced by war and Swedish mercantilist policy. In 1705, Parliament offered substantial bounties for tar, pitch, resin, turpentine, hemp, masts, yards, and bowsprits produced in the colonies. The bounties were designed to subsidize the colonists' exploitation of their immense supplies of standing timber, to offset the high wages and freight charges the colonists had to pay, to reduce English dependence on foreign sources of critical military products, and to promote colonial importation of English manufactures. As a result of Parliament's push, the

18. Gray, *History of Agriculture*, 284–287; Bernard, "Analysis of British Mercantilism."

naval stores industry in South Carolina grew rapidly. Insignificant before 1705, by 1718 Charleston exports of pitch and tar surpassed 50,000 barrels and approached 60,000 by the mid-1720s.

Thereafter, the production of naval stores in South Carolina underwent rapid decline. Colonial tar and pitch were inferior products. In part because of inexperience but largely because of high wages, colonial producers used crude laborsaving techniques that sacrificed quality for quantity. The resulting complaints from the Admiralty, the ending of the war, cheaper prices, and the lobbying of Baltic merchants persuaded the government to alter policy. In 1724, the crown insisted that quality standards be met before bounties were paid, and then, in 1729, it reduced the bounties substantially. These changes in the subsidy at home and the diversion of resources to rice in the colony sharply reduced naval stores production in South Carolina during the 1730s.[19] Nonetheless, along with other forest products such as planks, shingles, and staves, naval stores continued to play an important role in the economy of the Lower South (see table 8.2). They helped finance the first important direct imports of slaves from Africa into the region and, for a time, provided the colonists with productive work for their labor force in the off-season. Naval stores also served as a mainstay of agriculture outside the rice belt, especially in North Carolina but also in Georgia and Florida, where they provided small farmers with a major marketable product.[20]

In the early eighteenth century the South Carolina export sector was diverse by colonial standards, but that was not to last. Settlers and merchants shipped rice and naval stores across the Atlantic, traded with the native Americans on their borders for deerskins and slaves, and sent provisions and timber products to the West Indies. The diversity proved short-lived because rice quickly emerged as the dominant staple. The volume of exports per capita eloquently describes its rise: from a mere 69

19. Gray, *History of Agriculture*, 151–160; Justin Williams, "English Mercantilism and Carolina Naval Stores, 1705–1776," *Jour. So. Hist.*, I (1935), 169–185; Eleanor Louisa Lord, *Industrial Experiments in the British Colonies of North America* (Baltimore, 1898); Nettels, *Money Supply*, 128–161. For exports of naval stores, see U.S. Bureau of the Census, *Historical Statistics*, II, 1194 (Ser. Z 500–509), and Clowse, *Economic Beginnings*, 256–258. Useful price data on Carolina naval stores are available in Sir William Beveridge, *Prices and Wages in England: From the Twelfth to the Nineteenth Century* (London, 1939), 673, 675.

20. Clarence L. Ver Steeg, *Origins of a Southern Mosaic: Studies of Early Carolina and Georgia* (Athens, Ga., 1975), 103–132; G. Melvin Herndon, "Naval Stores in Colonial Georgia," *Georgia Historical Quarterly*, LII (1968), 426–433; Herndon, "Timber Products of Colonial Georgia," *ibid.*, LVII (1973), 56–62; Herndon, "Forest Products of Colonial Georgia," *Journal of Forest History*, XXIII (1979), 130–135; Merrens, *Colonial North Carolina*, 85–107; and Gray, *History of Agriculture*, 151–160.

pounds per capita in 1700, South Carolina rice exports reached 147 pounds per head in 1710, 380 in 1720, 626 in 1730, and peaked at over 900 pounds in 1740. This last is an extraordinary figure. Calculated differently, on the assumption that the colony's labor force—all adult males and adult female slaves—constituted one-half of the total population, it equals 1,800 pounds per laborer. Around mid-century, a prime field hand could produce just 2,000 to 2,500 pounds per year. On a per capita basis, it would appear that rice exports accounted for between 72 and 90 percent of the output of the colony's labor force.

The expansion of rice culture worked a dramatic transformation in South Carolina society. Put simply, rice brought the demographic regime of the sugar islands to South Carolina. The character and dynamics of the change are as yet poorly understood, but its outline resembled the earlier, sugarcane-induced transformation of the British West Indies.[21] Probably the most striking change was in the composition of the population. Fueled by expanding production of rice and naval stores, demand for labor increased greatly in the early eighteenth century, a demand that was met largely by imports of slaves from Africa. Charleston slave imports averaged 275 a year during the 1710s, nearly 900 in the 1720s, and over 2,000 in the 1730s.[22] As early as 1708, blacks outnumbered whites in South Carolina; by 1730 the ratio of blacks to whites stood at 2 to 1, by 1740 at 2.6 to 1.

These aggregate figures obscure significant local differences. In long-settled plantation districts spread along the tidewater in both directions

---

21. Wood, *Black Majority*, provides an excellent, suggestive account of the impact of rice culture on society in the Lower South.

22. On the growth of slavery and the slave trade in the region, see Peter H. Wood, "'More Like a Negro Country': Demographic Patterns in Colonial South Carolina, 1700–1740," in *Race and Slavery in the Western Hemisphere: Quantitative Studies*, ed. Stanley L. Engerman and Eugene D. Genovese (Princeton, N.J., 1975), 131–171; Elizabeth Donnan, "The Slave Trade into South Carolina before the Revolution," *AHR*, XXXIII (1928), 804–828; J. Duncan, "Servitude and Slavery"; W. Robert Higgins, "Charles Town Merchants and Factors Dealing in the External Negro Trade, 1735–1775," *S.C. Hist. Mag.*, LXV (1964), 205–217; Higgins, "The Geographical Origins of Negro Slaves in Colonial South Carolina," *South Atlantic Quarterly*, LXX (1971), 34–47; Higgins, "Charleston: Terminus and Entrepôt of the Colonial Slave Trade," in *The African Diaspora: Interpretive Essays*, ed. Martin L. Kolson and Robert I. Rotberg (Cambridge, Mass., 1976), 114–131; Higgins, "The South Carolina Negro Duty Law, 1703–1775" (M.A. thesis, University of South Carolina, 1967); Littlefield, *Rice and Slaves*; Philip David Morgan, "The Development of Slave Culture in Eighteenth Century Plantation America" (Ph.D. thesis, University College, London, 1977); Ulrich Bonnell Phillips, "The Slave Labor Problem in the Charleston District," *Political Science Quarterly*, XXII (1907), 416–439; and Ralph Gray and Betty Wood, "The Transition from Indentured to Involuntary Servitude in Colonial Georgia," *Explorations Econ. Hist.*, XIII (1976), 353–370.

from Charleston, the black share of the population approached 90 percent by 1740, roughly the proportion in the sugar islands. But slaves were scarce in the recently established small-farm areas around the periphery of the rice belt.[23]

There are more demographic parallels between the Lower South and the West Indies. The white population declined with the advance of slavery, not in the colony as a whole, but within the rice district, largely because of emigration but possibly also because of higher death rates attendant on the introduction of African diseases.[24] The slave population was also transformed as African imports swelled the sex ratio, increased mortality, perhaps depressed fertility, and turned a total population that had been growing rapidly through reproduction into one that registered a net natural decrease.[25]

Shifting racial proportions, a declining white population, and a work force dependent on immigration for continued increase are neither the only changes that accompanied the spread of rice nor the only ways in which South Carolina tended to replicate the history of the West Indies. There are several other parallels. First, the scale economies possible in rice production led to a sharp rise in the size of productive units as small, diversified family farms were "swallowed up" by large, specialized plantations. In St. George Parish, for example, where rice was introduced during the mid-1710s, there were nearly eight slaves per household as early as 1720, twelve by 1726, and twenty-four by 1741.[26] Second, although it remains to be documented, the spread of rice cultivation doubtless brought with it both increased wealth and income and greater inequality in their distribution. Third, this was accompanied by fewer occasions for

23. On the regional distribution of South Carolina's slave population, see Robert L. Meriwether, *The Expansion of South Carolina, 1729–1765* (Kingsport, Tenn., 1940), 160–161.

24. The demography of South Carolina's white population is discussed more fully in chap. 10, below. For reports of an actual decline in the early 18th century, see Clowse, *Economic Beginnings*, 104–105. Cf. U.S. Bureau of the Census, *Historical Statistics*, II, 1168 (Ser. Z 16).

25. Wood, *Black Majority*, 131–136; Philip D. Morgan, "Afro-American Cultural Change: The Case of Colonial South Carolina Slaves" (paper presented at the annual meeting of the Organization of American Historians, New Orleans, La., Apr. 1979). Cheryll Ann Cody, "Slave Demography and Family Formation: A Community Study of the Ball Family Plantations, 1720–1896" (Ph.D. diss., University of Minnesota, 1982), illuminates many of these issues. See also Cody, "A Note on Changing Patterns of Slave Fertility in the South Carolina Rice District, 1735–1865," *So. Studies*, XVI (1977), 457–463.

26. The phrase is quoted in Gray, *History of Agriculture*, 411. The St. George Parish data are from Wood, "'More Like a Negro Country,'" 154–163. See also Philip D. Morgan, ed., "A Profile of a Mid-Eighteenth Century South Carolina Parish: The Tax Return of St. James', Goose Creek," *S.C. Hist. Mag.*, LXXXI (1980), 51–65.

poor men without capital to set up as rice growers and by a substantial migration as alternative economic activities were pushed out to the periphery of the rice district. Fourth, the colony's self-sufficiency in food-stuffs may have ended as resources were concentrated on the staple. Finally, there is evidence of greater owner absenteeism, a decline in the skill level of the work force as the economy became more specialized, a considerable improvement in the balance of trade with Great Britain, and a shift in the orientation of commerce away from the Caribbean and toward Europe. Rice, in short, turned a farm colony into a plantation colony and produced, in the process, a region more similar to the Caribbean islands than to the other continental colonies. That transformation invites further research: tracing the impact of rice culture as it spread in the beginning along the coastal areas of South Carolina and later into Georgia and North Carolina represents a primary opportunity in the history of the Lower South and promises a test of the utility of a staples approach to the economy of early British America.[27]

All this notwithstanding, the transformation was incomplete. Differences between the Lower South and the West Indies persisted and kept the former region from resembling the ideal type of a plantation colony as closely as did the sugar islands. Rice plantations were much smaller than sugar plantations and rice planters less wealthy than sugar planters. Owner absenteeism was consequently more limited in the Lower South than in the West Indies. This was the chief difference between the two regions.

Instead of moving to London, merging with the British gentry, and leaving their estates in the hands of resident overseers, rice growers retained direct managerial control and withdrew for only limited periods during the year, to Charleston for the social season or to Newport, Rhode Island, to escape the heat and disease of late summer. Although Lower South colonists spent a good share of their profits on imported luxury goods, much of their income and their often considerable entrepreneurial talents were employed locally and gave a boost to the domestic economy

27. On the spread of rice culture, see David Rogers Chesnutt, "South Carolina's Expansion into Colonial Georgia, 1720–1765" (Ph.D. diss., University of Georgia, 1973); Chesnutt, "South Carolina's Penetration of Georgia in the 1760's: Henry Laurens as a Case Study," *S.C. Hist. Mag.*, LXXIII (1972), 194–208; Douglas C. Wilms, "The Development of Rice Culture in Eighteenth Century Georgia," *Southeastern Geographer*, XII (1972), 45–57; James M. Clifton, "Golden Grains of White: Rice Planting on the Lower Cape Fear," *N.C. Hist. Rev.*, L (1973), 365–393; and Merrens, *Colonial North Carolina*, 125–133. The unsuccessful effort to extend rice production into East Florida is described in David R. Chesnutt, "South Carolina's Impact upon East Florida, 1763–1776," in *Eighteenth-Century Florida and the Revolutionary South*, ed. Samuel Proctor (Gainesville, Fla., 1978), 5–14. On the distribution of wealth, see A. Jones, *Wealth of a Nation to Be.*

often absent in the Caribbean. The limited, temporary nature of owner absenteeism in the Lower South also had important political implications, for it permitted the establishment of a powerful, self-conscious ruling class capable, however reluctantly, of leading the colonies in rebellion and into a new nation. This indigenous ruling class helped set South Carolina apart from the Caribbean islands.

A second significant difference lay in the continued existence of a diversified economy around the edges of the rice belt. Both the rice belt and the sugar islands created their own colonies, places where poor men in search of their fortunes could migrate and earn modest livings through mixed farming. They supplied the food needs of the plantation work force and produced for export small quantities of grain, meat, and forest products. Whereas the sugarcane (especially on Barbados and the smaller islands) tended to drive alternative economic activities out of the area altogether, rice merely pushed them to the periphery of the plantation sector, to the backcountry, to North Carolina, and to Georgia.

That these "colonies of colonies" remained integral to the region in the Lower South had important consequences. For one thing, the economy of the Lower South remained relatively dynamic and diverse and thus managed to avoid the highly specialized monoculture characteristic of the islands. For another, because rice planters quickly found that they could supply their needs from inland farms, the Lower South was not transformed into an importer of foodstuffs and wood products as a result of the rise of plantation agriculture. Moreover, the rapid expansion of a diversified farming area around the edges of the plantation sector offered an open season to local merchants by providing a lively demand for imported manufactures and a supply of farm products for export.[28]

The differences between the sugar islands and the Lower South are probably most evident in the flourishing of Charleston. Our knowledge of Charleston's size is very rough, but clearly it was unique by the standards of the South and the West Indies. Carl Bridenbaugh estimated a population of 2,000 by 1700—probably exaggerated since it suggests that more than one-third of South Carolina's inhabitants lived in town— 4,500 in 1730, and 8,000 by 1760. In 1775, Charleston numbered

28. For the persistent diversity of the economy of the Lower South, particularly around the periphery of the plantation district, see Merrens, *Colonial North Carolina*; Meriwether, *Expansion of South Carolina*; James C. Bonner, *A History of Georgia Agriculture, 1732– 1860* (Athens, Ga., 1964); Milton L. Ready, *The Castle Builders: Georgia's Economy under the Trustees, 1732–1754* (New York, 1978 [Ph.D. diss., University of Georgia, 1970]); Charles Christopher Crittenden, *The Commerce of North Carolina, 1763–1789* (New Haven, Conn., 1936); and Robert Earle Moody, ed., "Massachusetts Trade with Carolina, 1686–1709," *N.C. Hist. Rev.*, XX (1943), 43–53.

roughly 12,000 residents, sufficient to make it the fourth largest city in British America, far smaller than Philadelphia and New York but not a great deal behind Boston and twice as large as Baltimore and Norfolk, its nearest competitors in the South.

The sources of Charleston's growth are but poorly understood; indeed, it is the least studied of the principal colonial ports, and major opportunities await its historians. Charleston's initial prosperity rested on the trade in deerskins to London and in provisions and timber to the West Indies, as well, perhaps, as on the consumer demands of free immigrants who arrived at the port. While there is some evidence of shipbuilding and an indigenous merchant group, Charleston seems to have been unable to reap the full benefit of its West Indian trade. Shipping and commercial services were already provided by British merchants who controlled such activities as the staple and slave trades and by northern colonial merchants, especially Bostonians, who were established in island markets before Charleston was founded.

In the eighteenth century, Charleston's expansion depended increasingly on the great staples of the region, rice and indigo, and on the trade in slaves. As Peter Wood has noted, Charleston was the Ellis Island of the North American black population. Two features of these trades demand more-precise explanation. First, to a remarkable extent Charleston monopolized the foreign trade of South Carolina and even of North Carolina and Georgia, despite the absence of a strong geographical advantage. Apparently, as Jacob Price suggests, "there were no ultimate economies in a more dispersed pattern." Why this happened remains to be established. Second, Charleston was small relative to the volume of its trade (it was a busier port than New York in the late colonial period) and lacked the substantial shipbuilding industry and large indigenous business community of the northern cities. According to Price, this was a function of the "'colonial' character of Charleston's commercial life." Because South Carolinian commodities found British markets, British merchants dominated the trade, making Charleston a mere "shipping point" rather than a real "commercial center" or a "general entrepôt." "Entrepreneurial decisions were made in Britain, capital was raised there, ships were built or chartered there and outfitted there, insurance was made there—all for the South Carolina trade." On the eve of the American Revolution, residents of the colonies owned fewer than two out of every five vessels clearing Carolina ports (see table 9.1).

Carville Earle and Ronald Hoffman suggest that by the 1760s Charleston had begun to overcome its "colonial" status through its control of backcountry products. Yet the volume of that trade remained small, and much of the commercial activity it generated was probably captured by northern merchants rather than local businessmen. Charleston was also a major "consumer city" in the eighteenth century with a large population of affluent gentry. Many wealthy planters lived in town for part of the year to escape the boredom and health problems of life in the plantation district and to enjoy the social season, a pattern that produced an occupational mix and a social structure more like the port towns of the West Indies than the cities of the northern colonies.[29]

The economy of the Lower South received a further boost in the 1740s with the rise of indigo as a leading export. Despite its importance and the relative abundance of evidence, the indigo industry has received little attention.[30] South Carolinians grew indigo successfully during the seventeenth century, but the crop was soon abandoned. The colonists were clearly unable to compete with superior West Indian dyes and concentrated instead on more-profitable exports. At any rate, English manufacturers soon came to rely on Jamaican indigo and later, as settlers there turned increasingly to sugarcane, on the French West Indies.

"'Twas intirely owing to the last War that we became an Indigo Country," Henry Laurens explained in 1755.[31] King George's War (1739–1748) severely disrupted the rice trade by forcing up freight and insur-

29. Price, "Economic Function," 161–163; Earle and Hoffman, "Staple Crops," 14–19; George C. Rogers, Jr., Charleston in the Age of the Pinckneys (Norman, Okla., 1969). On Charleston merchants, see Leila Sellers, Charleston Business on the Eve of the American Revolution (Chapel Hill, N.C., 1934); Stumpf, "Merchants of Colonial Charleston"; Stuart O. Stumpf, "Implications of King George's War for the Charleston Mercantile Community," S.C. Hist. Mag., LXXVII (1976), 161–188; and Warner Oland Moore, Jr., "Henry Laurens: A Charleston Merchant in the Eighteenth Century, 1747–1771" (Ph.D. diss., University of Alabama, 1974). For exports from Charleston, see Charles Joseph Gayle, "The Nature and Volume of Exports from Charleston, 1724–1774," South Carolina Historical Association, Proceedings, VII (1937), 25–33; James Cleveland Hite, "A Statistical Analysis of Trade in the Charleston Area, 1750–1769" (M.A. thesis, Emory University, 1964); and Clowse, Economic Beginnings, 256–258.

30. Gray, History of Agriculture, 290–297, remains the best introduction to the indigo industry in the Lower South. See also D. D. Wallace, "Indigo Culture in the South," in The South in the Building of the Nation, ed. Julian Alvin Carroll Chandler et al. (Richmond, Va., 1909–1913), V, 178–183; G. Terry Sharrer, "Indigo in Carolina, 1671–1796," S.C. Hist. Mag., LXXII (1971), 94–103; Sharrer, "The Indigo Bonanza in South Carolina, 1740–1790," Technology and Culture, XII (1971), 447–455; John J. Winberry, "Reputation of Carolina Indigo," S.C. Hist. Mag., LXXX (1979), 242–250; and C. Robert Haywood, "Mercantilism and South Carolina Agriculture, 1700–1763," ibid., LX (1959), 15–27. Recent work by David L. Coon is especially helpful. In addition to his dissertation, cited above, see "Eliza Lucas Pinckney and the Reintroduction of Indigo Culture in South Carolina," Jour. So. Hist., XLII (1976), 61–76. For indigo exports, see U.S. Bureau of the Census, Historical Statistics, II, 1189 (Ser. Z 432–435).

31. Laurens to Sarah Nickelson, 1 Aug. 1755, Laurens Papers, I, 309.

ance charges and by closing some chief European markets, thus inducing Carolina colonists to consider other staples. At the same time the war cut off British supplies of French colonial indigo and drove prices sharply upward. Shifting incentives led to intense experimentation with the crop, most prominently by Eliza Lucas Pinckney, with successful commercial cultivation initially achieved in the middle 1740s. Parliament encouraged the infant industry with a substantial bounty at war's end, but the bounty's impact has been exaggerated. Scarce labor and abundant resources seemingly encouraged production techniques that led to an inferior dye, and English manufacturers continued to prefer French colonial indigo despite the subsidy.

Indigo exports from the Lower South fell off sharply in the early 1750s, sinking to 3,800 pounds in 1752. The industry seemed on the verge of extinction, only to recover as war again cut off supplies from the French islands. Indigo production boomed during the Seven Years' War—exports peaked at nearly 900,000 pounds in 1757 and the industry spread to Georgia—and fell off with the return of peace. Any repetition of the postwar collapse of the early 1750s was avoided, however, despite a reduction of the bounty from six pence to four pence per pound, probably because Parliament imposed a stiff duty on foreign indigo in 1764. Lower South indigo exports held steady at around a half-million pounds to the early 1770s when the bounty was returned to six pence. In the years just prior to the Revolution cultivation extended to Florida, where the climate fostered a product superior to that possible in areas to the north, and exports rose sharply, passing one million pounds in 1775. By then, indigo was a principal crop. It ranked second in value to rice among the commodity exports of the Lower South and fifth for all the mainland colonies.

Indigo served the economy of the Lower South well. It was, as the South Carolina assembly noted in 1749, "an excellent colleague Commodity with Rice," providing growers with employment for their slaves during slack periods in producing the staple, providing uses for land otherwise unsuited for commercial agriculture, and providing those who could not produce rice with a profitable export.[32] Indigo contributed substantially to the prosperity of the district during the third quarter of the eighteenth century and clearly merits further study. It offers opportunities to examine the responsiveness of planters to fresh possibilities, the impact of mercantilist policies on a local economy, and the process of experimentation with new products and techniques and their diffusion through a territory.

32. Quoted in Coon, "Eliza Lucas Pinckney," 64.

"Few countries," David Ramsay argued in 1809, "have at any time exhibited so striking an instance of public and private prosperity as appeared in South-Carolina between the years 1725 and 1775." Despite Ramsay's view being colored by his understanding of the independence movement, his observation rings true and can be extended to the Lower South as a whole. The prosperity rested on a brutal, exploitative system of slavery and plantation agriculture thoroughly dominated by a confident and class-conscious local gentry. And it depended on the sale of the major staples of the region, rice and indigo, in European markets (see table 8.2). Commerce with other mainland colonies and earnings in the carrying trade, of critical importance elsewhere on the continent, made just a minor contribution to incomes in the region. In the pre-Revolutionary Lower South, as in the contemporary Caribbean and the antebellum South, the plantation system was so successful that diversification was unnecessary in order to attain economic growth. Economically rational residents of the Lower South who had a choice raised rice. Perhaps the career of Henry Laurens, long Charleston's leading merchant, illustrates the pervasiveness of the staple. He began his career as a merchant, but after accumulating some capital, he bought land and slaves and became a planter. Eventually he gave up the countinghouse and devoted his resources entirely to his crops. In the Lower South, plantation agriculture, not trade or manufacturing, afforded the best chances for success.[33]

33. David Ramsay, *History of South Carolina, from Its First Settlement in 1670, to the Year 1808* (Charleston, S.C., 1809), I, 123. On the coastal trade, see Shepherd and Williamson, "Coastal Trade," 798. Shepherd and Walton report the earnings in the carrying trade for the Upper and Lower South as one total figure (*Shipping*, 128–134). Nevertheless, however those earnings were allocated between the two regions, they had only a minimal impact on the balance of payments.

CHAPTER 9

THE MIDDLE COLONIES

If the settlers of New England set the pattern by which the farm colonies solved their balance-of-payments problems, the Middle Colonies perfected it. The produce of their fields and forests provided the colonists with a rich harvest; they exported the surpluses in their own ships to a steadily spreading market. Farming in the region owed its richness to fertile lands and good water resources as well as to farming practices that drew on British, Dutch, and German traditions. New Yorkers built on a mercantile heritage that combined the trading expertise of the original settlers of New Amsterdam with the skills and connections of the English who supplanted them. The trade of Philadelphia throve upon a business acumen that, by the time of the Revolution, made the name "Quaker" a byword for hard work and good sense. All benefited from the advantages of a protected imperial system that kept potential competitors outside the empire or otherwise preoccupied within it. Well before 1770 Philadelphia and New York had replaced Boston as the colonial mercantile capital, and the general level of income and wealth in the Middle Colonies had advanced beyond the level enjoyed by New Englanders. The two cities continued to grow until each became, successively, the commercial and financial center of the new republic.[1]

Some of these developments provoked considerable tension. By the middle of the eighteenth century, entrepreneurs seeking to enlarge the trade of the colonies started to move in new directions. The one major trade in which the colonists had traditionally taken little part, largely because it had been successfully dominated by British merchants, was the transatlantic carrying trade between the colonies and the metropolis. Some merchants of New York and Philadelphia entered into this trade, doing so all quite legally and well within the letter of the Navigation

---

1. For comparative levels of wealth, see chap. 3, above. For the later development of these cities, see Robert Greenhalgh Albion, *The Rise of New York Port [1815–1860]* (New York, 1939); David T. Gilchrist, ed., *The Growth of the Seaport Cities, 1790–1825: Proceedings of a Conference Sponsored by the Eleutherian Mills–Hagley Foundation, March 17–19, 1966* (Charlottesville, Va., 1967); and Diane Lindstrom, *Economic Development in the Philadelphia Region, 1810–1850* (New York, 1978).

Acts. Nonetheless, many British merchants were annoyed by what they considered to be intrusions into their personal preserve. Their complaints about colonial business practices were part of the impetus behind the series of reforms Parliament enacted in the 1760s. Those reforms, in turn, provoked colonial merchants, and other colonists later, to rethink their place in the empire. The innovative trading activity of the merchants of the Middle Colonies called attention to the more assertive role that the colonists were playing in imperial trade and helped precipitate events that led to the American Revolution.

Strictly speaking, the economic region known as the Middle Colonies incorporated four political jurisdictions: the two principal colonies, Pennsylvania and New York; the satellite settlement of them both, New Jersey; and Delaware, which belonged to Pennsylvania both politically and economically for most of the period. Part of the economic development of the Middle Colonies depended upon the expansion of the region. In the seventeenth century a good portion of northern and eastern Long Island, although politically a part of New York, was oriented economically toward New England. As time went on, the economic region grew to conform to the political boundaries; later it grew beyond them. First the southern shore and then the northern shore of Long Island Sound were drawn into New York's ambit. Much later, after 1750, the whole of Connecticut, until then economically a part of New England, came to be associated increasingly with New York. As a result of the Seven Years' War, the far northerly reaches of the economic region "New York" extended well into the new colony of Quebec. (The process had even begun, in a limited way, while Quebec was still French!) Similar developments occurred to the south as more and more of Maryland's Eastern Shore and northern counties, and part of the Shenandoah Valley, fell under Philadelphia's shadow. The progress of Baltimore after 1750 was largely the result of the economic penetration of Maryland by Philadelphia's merchants and reflected a still-further enlarging of the region we call the Middle Colonies.[2]

From the very beginning of Dutch settlement on the Hudson and Delaware rivers, the emphasis had been on trade. The Dutch West India Company sought to establish trading posts, not colonies like Virginia or Massachusetts. The arrival of the Quakers a half-century later merely confirmed

2. See Gaspare John Saladino, "The Economic Revolution in Late Eighteenth Century Connecticut" (Ph.D. diss., University of Wisconsin, 1964); Ouellet, *Histoire économique*; and Gould, "Economic Causes."

the basic commercial orientation of the area. The Dutch merchants of early New Amsterdam and the Quaker merchants of Philadelphia, a small portion of the population, were not the only participants in the commercial economy. The farmers of the region produced a surplus of agricultural goods for exportation and demanded a range and a quality of goods that were available only through importation. Servicing both requirements created new potentials for profit for resident merchants. Colonies founded for trade grew and prospered as trade itself grew.[3]

The colony of New York, set up as a trading post by the Dutch, developed along the lines that they had set down, lines modified only slightly after 1664 to conform to the English navigation laws. Especially important was New York's continuing trade in provisions to the Dutch West Indies, which served as a conduit to their Caribbean neighbors, particularly the Spanish on the Main. The merchants of New York were well positioned to enjoy the fruits of these early established contacts between North America and the Dutch—and later the Danish—West Indies in the same way that the New Englanders garnered to themselves much of the continental trade with the French West Indies.

New Yorkers also had very good contacts with European commercial and financial centers, notably Amsterdam, which they exploited to their advantage. Their export trade in flaxseed, which was used in the Irish linen industry, also oriented them eastward in the eighteenth century. Nevertheless, New York's trade, transatlantic and otherwise, was relatively small throughout the period, by several measures much smaller than that of any other major colonial port. Yet it was also diverse and complex, able to sustain a range of entrepôt and brokerage services and to maintain a favorable trade balance with Great Britain, which no other northern colony could do. All of these activities were, in large measure, faithful to the Navigation Acts while earning for the colonists considerable credits in their balance of payments, both through the export of goods and through the provision of services. Even though legal, the pattern of trade led to direct competition with London merchants. On the eve of the American Revolution, residents of the colonies owned three out of every five vessels clearing the port of New York for Great Britain (see table 9.1).[4]

3. There is no treatment of the economic history of the region per se, but much can be learned from some of the broader studies, such as William S. Sachs, "The Business Outlook in the Northern Colonies, 1750–1775" (Ph.D. diss., Columbia University, 1957), and Price, "Economic Function." See also Douglas Greenberg, "The Middle Colonies in Recent American Historiography," *WMQ*, 3d Ser., XXXVI (1979), 396–427.

4. The earliest history of New York is tied to the fur trade, which is treated in several recent studies: Van Cleaf Bachman, *Peltries or Plantations: The Economic Policies of the Dutch*

TABLE 9.1.
Ownership of Vessels Trading between British Ports
and Colonial Ports on the North American Continent,
1770

| | Residence of Vessels' Owners | | | |
| | | Continental Colonies | | |
Colony from Which Vessels Cleared	Great Britain	British Merchants Temporarily Resident	Permanent Residents of the Colonies	Total of Continental Colonies
New England	12.5%	12.5%	75.0%	87.5%
New York	37.5%	37.5%	25.0%	62.5%
Pennsylvania	25.0%	37.5%	37.5%	75.0%
Maryland and Virginia	75.0%	12.5%	12.5%	25.0%
North Carolina	62.5%	25.0%	12.5%	37.5%
South Carolina and Georgia	62.5%	25.0%	12.5%	37.5%

Sources: Compiled by Thomas Irving, Inspector General of Imports and Exports and Register General of Shipping for North America, 1768–1774, for presentation before the Board of Trade, 1791, Board of Trade Papers, class 6, vol. 20, fols. 269–273, Public Record Office. See John J. McCusker, "Colonial Civil Servant and Counterrevolutionary: Thomas Irving (1738?–1800) in Boston, Charleston, and London," *Perspectives in American History*, XII (1979), 346–347n.

West India Company in New Netherland, 1623–1639 (Baltimore, 1969); Thomas J. Condon, *New York Beginnings: The Commercial Origins of New Netherland* (New York, 1968); George L. Smith, *Religion and Trade in New Netherland: Dutch Origins and American Development* (Ithaca, N.Y., 1973); Thomas Elliot Norton, *The Fur Trade in Colonial New York, 1686–1776* (Madison, Wis., 1974); Oliver Albert Rink, "Merchants and Magnates: Dutch New York, 1609–1664" (Ph.D. diss., University of Southern California, 1976); Stephen Hosmer Cutcliffe, "Indians, Furs, and Empires: The Changing Policies of New York and Pennsylvania, 1674–1768" (Ph.D. diss., Lehigh University, 1976); and Ceci, "First Fiscal Crisis," based on Lynn Ceci, "The Effect of European Contact and Trade on the Settlement Pattern of Indians in Coastal New York, 1524–1665: The Archeological and Documentary Evidence" (Ph.D. diss., City University of New York, 1977). There is no thorough history of agriculture in New York, but the related and important topic of land policy has received considerable attention. See Sung Bok Kim, *Landlord and Tenant in Colonial New York: Manorial Society, 1664–1775* (Chapel Hill, N.C., 1978); Armand Shelby LaPotin, "The Minisink Patent: A Study in Colonial Landholding and Problems of Settlement in Eighteenth-Century New York" (Ph.D. diss., University of Wisconsin, 1974); and Jack Harold Christenson, "The Administration of Land Policy in Colonial New York" (Ph.D. diss., State University of New York, Albany, 1976). For New York's trade, the best

The great rise of the port of New York was still in the future, nevertheless; during the second half of the eighteenth century Philadelphia was preeminent. Whereas much of New York's success as a port can be attributed to what might be called the "Dutch Connection," Philadelphia's merchants relied on business contacts with their coreligionists, the "Quaker Connection." Even before the city had been settled, English Quaker merchants who were planning to follow William Penn started organizing for the expected commerce between Pennsylvania and ports in the metropolis and the West Indies. The import trade in English manufactured goods was to be funded by an export trade in the agricultural produce of the rich lands of the Delaware River valley. The colonial merchants of Philadelphia were the entrepreneurs par excellence of the British colonies in the second century of colonial development.[5]

---

work is still Virginia D. Harrington, *The New York Merchant on the Eve of the Revolution* (New York, 1935). See also William I. Davisson and Lawrence J. Bradley, "New York Maritime Trade: Ship Voyage Patterns, 1715–1765," *New-York Historical Society Quarterly*, LV (1971), 309–317; Lawrence James Bradley, "The London/Bristol Trade Rivalry: Conventional History, and the Colonial Office 5 Records for the Port of New York" (Ph.D. diss., University of Notre Dame, 1971); and Jan Kupp, "Aspects of New York–Dutch Trade under the English, 1670–1674," *N.-Y. Hist. Soc. Qtly.*, LVIII (1974), 139–147. There are almost no studies of individual New York merchant firms. See White, *Beekmans of New York*, and Clifton James Taylor, "John Watts in Colonial and Revolutionary New York" (Ph.D. diss., University of Tennessee, 1981). For the export of flaxseed, see Thomas M. Truxes, "Connecticut in the Irish-American Flaxseed Trade, 1750–1775," *Eire-Ireland*, XII (Summer 1977), 34–62. For a more general statement, see Samuel McKee, Jr., "The Economic Pattern of Colonial New York," in *History of the State of New York*, ed. Alexander C. Flick (New York, 1933), II, 247–282. See also Bruce Martin Wilkenfeld, "The Social and Economic Structure of the City of New York, 1695–1796" (Ph.D. diss., Columbia University, 1973).

5. Pennsylvania's economy has been somewhat better served by historians than has New York's, except with regard to its very earliest years. For the periods just prior to and just after settlement, see *James Claypoole's Letter Book, London and Philadelphia, 1681–1684*, ed. Marion Balderston (San Marino, Calif., 1967). See also two good articles by Gary B. Nash: "Maryland's Economic War with Pennsylvania," *Md. Hist. Mag.*, LX (1965), 231–244; and "The Quest for the Susquehanna Valley: New York, Pennsylvania, and the Seventeenth-Century Fur Trade," *New York History*, XLVIII (1967), 3–27. The colony's mercantile origins and development are the background for Frederick B. Tolles, *Meeting House and Counting House: The Quaker Merchants of Colonial Philadelphia, 1682–1763* (Chapel Hill, N.C., 1948). Pennsylvania's trade is described in A. Jensen, *Maritime Commerce*; Marc Matthew Egnal, "The Pennsylvania Economy, 1748–1762: An Analysis of Short-Run Changes in the Atlantic Trading Community" (Ph.D. diss., University of Wisconsin, 1974); and Egnal, "The Changing Structure of Philadelphia's Trade with the British West Indies, 1750–1775," *PMHB*, XCIX (1975), 156–179. See also Mary Alice Hanna, *Trade of the Delaware District before the Revolution* (Northampton, Mass., 1917). For studies of particular Pennsylvania industries, see Arthur Cecil Bining, *Pennsylvania Iron*

Those entrepreneurial talents were not much in evidence during the first seventy or so years of the colony's history, however. Before 1750 the principal business of Philadelphia merchants was a "simple bilateral trade" in provisions to the West Indies, "supplemented by occasional shipments of wheat and flour to southern Europe as market conditions there justified." Direct trade with Great Britain was minimal, and the volume of British exports sent directly to the colony remained low. Philadelphia merchants developed little in the way of an entrepôt trade in European manufactures, instead often acquiring such goods indirectly, by way of New England. So simple a pattern of trade, Jacob Price has observed, "encouraged the development of a large community of small merchants in Philadelphia, big enough to trade to the West Indies but not very venturesome outside those familiar waters, all too glad to sell wheat and flour and provisions to New England craft that visited their haven in return for fish and European goods, but not too inclined to send their own craft to New England or Newfoundland and only rarely to England."[6]

Philadelphia's trade patterns and the Philadelphia merchant community changed dramatically after 1750. Army expenditures on supplies were especially heavy in Pennsylvania during the Seven Years' War and provided Philadelphia merchants with a lot of business and a large stock of bills of exchange on London, which were used to finance trade with Great Britain. A more enduring stimulus was provided by the secular upswing in European cereal prices that began about mid-century. Increasing populations and a series of bad harvests joined to swell already existing markets for wheat and flour in Spain and Portugal and to open new markets in Mediterranean Europe, France, and even Great Britain. Philadelphia merchants, situated at the center of the major North American wheat-producing area, were particularly well placed to exploit such changing circumstances. As they did so, the community of merchants became much wealthier, more sophisticated, better connected, and more aggressive. Some of what happened can be followed in shipping records.

During the last twenty-five years of the colonial period, Philadelphia

---

Manufacture in the Eighteenth Century (Harrisburg, Pa., 1938); John Flexer Walzer, "Transportation in the Philadelphia Trading Area, 1740–1775" (Ph.D. diss., University of Wisconsin, 1968); and Simeon J. Crowther, "The Shipbuilding Output of the Delaware Valley, 1722–1776," Am. Phil. Soc., *Procs.*, CXVII (1973), 90–104. See also John J. McCusker, "Sources of Investment Capital in the Colonial Philadelphia Shipping Industry," *Jour. Econ. Hist.*, XXXII (1972), 146–157. There are few, if any, parallel studies for New Jersey or Delaware. See James H. Levitt, *For Want of Trade: Shipping and the New Jersey Ports, 1680–1783* (Newark, N.J., 1981).

6. Price, "Economic Function," 152–153.

showed a more significant shift in the orientation of its trade than any other colonial port. Data on shipping clearances provide the basis for this comparison (see table 9.2). From the mid-1760s to the early 1770s, the total tonnage clearing the ports of New York and Boston increased impressively, but most of the advance came in voyages to other British American colonies and, indeed, to other North American ports. Philadelphia's trade both gained rapidly and shifted to new destinations; the direct trade to southern Europe and to Great Britain grew faster than that to other places. These changes were part of a continuing trend that can be traced back to the 1750s. Whereas only 20 percent of the shipping clearing Philadelphia between 1750 and 1754 went to Europe, by the early 1770s more than 30 percent did so. At Boston and New York, by contrast, the proportion of shipping tonnage clearing for transatlantic destinations actually declined between the early 1750s and the early 1770s. We know that by 1770 three-fourths of the shipping clearing Philadelphia on transatlantic voyages was owned in the colony, which was likewise an increase over earlier proportions. The conjuncture of these two trends suggests that the merchants of colonial Philadelphia were taking greater control of their own trade and were sending their cargoes to places where they had not previously sailed.[7]

The Philadelphia merchant identified the trade between the colonies and Europe as potentially more profitable than the traditional modes of commerce. The chances for a profitable voyage in the West Indian trade, for instance, had lessened over time if only because the population of the continental colonies was growing at a faster rate than in the Caribbean. The coastal trade among the several continental colonies was linked, in part, to the West Indian trade and rose and fell as it did. The most significant of the newer trades that the Philadelphians moved into was the grain export trade to the Iberian Peninsula and Mediterranean Europe. This

7. Given the large quantity of surviving materials, including many records of individual mercantile firms, we have surprisingly few studies of Philadelphia merchants. See, however, William T. Parsons, "Isaac Norris II, The Speaker" (Ph.D. diss., University of Pennsylvania, 1955); Carl Leroy Romanek, "John Reynell, Quaker Merchant of Colonial Philadelphia" (Ph.D. diss., Pennsylvania State University, 1969); Eugene R. Slaski, "Thomas Willing: Moderation during the American Revolution" (Ph.D. diss., Florida State University, 1971); Jerry Grundfest, "George Clymer, Philadelphia Revolutionary, 1739–1813" (Ph.D. diss., Columbia University, 1973); and James Donald Anderson, "Thomas Wharton, 1730/31–1784: Merchant in Philadelphia" (Ph.D. diss., University of Akron, 1977). Still of considerable value is Harry Dahl Berg, "Merchants and Mercantile Life in Colonial Philadelphia: 1748–1763" (Ph.D. diss., University of Iowa, 1941). See also John J. McCusker, "Ships Registered at the Port of Philadelphia before 1776: A Computerized Listing" (unpubl. MS, Historical Society of Pennsylvania, Philadelphia), and Thomas Main Doerflinger, "Enterprise on the Delaware: Merchants and Economic Development in Philadelphia, 1750–1791" (Ph.D. diss., Harvard University, 1980).

TABLE 9.2.
*Destinations of Shipping Clearing Boston, New York,
and Philadelphia Annually for Selected Years,
1750–1772 (in Thousands of Registered Tons)*

	Destination					
	Transatlantic			Coastwise		
Port of Origin	Great Britain	Ireland	Southern Europe	North America	West Indies	Total
Boston						
1753–	3.0	0.2	2.2	11.5	10.3	27.2
1754	(11.0)	(0.7)	(7.9)	(42.3)	(38.0)	
1765–	5.1	0.2	1.6	12.8	8.2	28.0
1766	(18.3)	(0.6)	(5.7)	(46.0)	(29.3)	
1772	6.2	0.2	1.0	24.5	10.7	42.5
	(14.5)	(0.4)	(2.3)	(57.6)	(25.2)	
New York						
1754	2.2	1.5	0.5	2.5	6.0	12.7
	(17.4)	(11.9)	(4.3)	(19.3)	(47.1)	
1765–	2.9	2.0	3.5	3.0	8.4	19.8
1766	(14.5)	(10.3)	(17.6)	(15.3)	(42.3)	
1772	4.3	1.6	2.7	11.9	8.1	28.6
	(15.0)	(5.6)	(9.5)	(41.6)	(28.3)	
Philadelphia						
1750–	1.1	2.5	1.7	12.7	7.2	25.2
1754	(4.5)	(9.9)	(6.9)	(50.2)	(28.5)	
1765–	1.8	4.8	4.8	14.6	13.5	39.5
1766	(4.6)	(12.2)	(12.0)	(36.9)	(34.2)	
1772	3.1	2.5	8.4	15.1	15.7	45.8
	(7.0)	(5.6)	(18.8)	(33.7)	(35.0)	

Sources: For Boston for 1753–1754, Murray G. Lawson, "The Routes of Boston's Trade, 1752–1765," Colonial Society of Massachusetts, *Publications*, XXXVIII: *Transactions*, *1947–1951* (1959), 89, 91. For Philadelphia for 1750–1754, John J. McCusker, "Sources of Investment Capital in the Colonial Philadelphia Shipping Industry," *Journal of Economic History*, XXXII (1972), 151. For all of the other figures, Virginia D. Harrington, *The New York Merchant on the Eve of the Revolution* (New York, 1935), 356, 358, 368. The ultimate source for all of these data is, of course, the colonial naval officer shipping lists.

Notes: Figures in parentheses are the percentages of the total tonnage for each year. Figures have been rounded off and thus the totals do not always equal the sum of their parts. "Southern Europe" as used here includes the Wine Islands and Africa; Bermuda and the Bahamas are included as part of North America.

trade did much to stimulate colonial grain production, not only in Pennsylvania but also in Delaware and Maryland. Intercolonial shipments of grain were brought to Philadelphia overland as well as by water, which made the city the center of an export trade of significant dimensions and great profitability. Some Philadelphia firms, in order to ensure adequate supplies to meet their export commitments, extended their contacts well into the Chesapeake, to Baltimore, Alexandria, and Norfolk. It is a classic example of domestic economic activity—agriculture and local trade—being led by overseas trade. Philadelphia merchants played the pivotal part.[8]

New York merchants similarly expanded their trade to southern Europe during the initial years of the grain-export boom, but they did not continue those efforts after 1760, nor did they even maintain their level of involvement. This was due, in part, to the relatively narrow district on which they could draw, compared with the Philadelphians. After the Seven Years' War, the New Yorkers were distracted besides by the potential profits that newly conquered Canada offered for overland trade, a trade not reflected in shipping clearances.[9]

Yet New Yorkers and Philadelphians both showed marked interest in one other trade new to the colonists, the direct trade with Great Britain. Between mid-century and the eve of the War of Independence, New York's export trade with Great Britain doubled and Philadelphia's trade tripled. Again this coincided with an increase in the ownership by colonists of the vessels involved in the trade (see table 9.1). The merchants of the metropolis could, and some did, see this change as an attempt by the colonists to gain control of the lucrative trade that linked them. From the colonists' perspective, they were simply stepping up their legitimate trad-

8. On the grain trade from the perspective of the colonists, see Clemens, *Atlantic Economy*, 179–183, and *passim*. See also Papenfuse, "Economic Analysis." Compare the documents he cites: "Aggregate of Wheat, Flour, and Indian Corn annually exported from the Eastern Shore of Maryland, on an average, from the year 1770, to 1775," and "Annual Exports of each of the eight Counties on the Eastern Shore of Maryland," both in George Chalmers Papers, 1606–1812, Maryland, vol. I, fol. 52, New York Public Library. For the English perspective, see E. Lipson, *The Economic History of England*, 6th ed. (London, 1956), II, 419–448; T. S. Ashton, *An Economic History of England: The Eighteenth Century* (London, 1961), 48–51; and A. H. John, "English Agricultural Improvement and Grain Exports, 1660–1765," in *Trade, Government, and Economy in Pre-industrial England: Essays Presented to F. J. Fisher*, ed. D. C. Coleman and A. H. John (London, 1976), 45–67.

9. See chap. 5, above, and for economic activities on New York's northern frontier, David Arthur Armour, "The Merchants of Albany, New York: 1686–1760" (Ph.D. diss., Northwestern University, 1965); Charles R. Candey III, "An Entrepreneurial History of the New York Frontier, 1739–1776" (Ph.D. diss., Case Western Reserve University, 1967); and Milton Wheaton Hamilton, *Sir William Johnson, Colonial American, 1715–1763* (Port Washington, N.Y., 1976).

ing activity within the empire, actions which were in no way a breach of the Navigation Acts. Thus, in the volatile 1760s, when rumors began circulating in the Middle Colonies of impending restrictions on colonial commerce, the merchants of New York and Pennsylvania were understandably angered.

In large part because merchants at New York and Philadelphia were quick to turn every occasion to a profit, the Middle Colonies had the best-balanced economies in colonial America. Some of that balance is reflected in table 9.3, which describes overseas exports by commodity and destination. On the one hand, grain and grain products, chiefly wheat, flour, and bread, dominated the list of commodities to roughly the extent that tobacco was dominant in the Chesapeake colonies and rice and indigo in the Lower South. On the other hand, however, there are characteristics that suggest a greater similarity to New England than to the plantation districts. Several minor products—flaxseed, pig iron, beef and pork, potash, staves and shingles, for example—made important contributions to export earnings. Nevertheless, the commerce of the region was evenly divided among the leading markets, more so than that of New England, which depended heavily on the West Indies.

Some aspects of external commerce not reflected in table 9.3 confirm the notion that the economy of the Middle Colonies was both diverse and balanced. Between 1768 and 1772, merchants in the Middle Colonies exported commodities worth £220,000 sterling annually to other mainland areas. Further, they earned more than £250,000 a year through the sale of invisibles in the current account, freight charges and commercial services. The Middle Colonies, it would seem, lived up to their name by combining the best of two colonial worlds. Like the plantation colonies they possessed a staple export much in demand overseas; like New England they supplied customers in a variety of markets, participated heavily in commerce with other mainland colonies, and earned substantial credits through the carrying trade.[10]

Although considerable detail remains to be filled in and major questions are still unanswered, the external commerce of the Middle Colonies, the flow of goods to and from foreign markets, and the activities of merchants in New York and Philadelphia can be described with some precision. The preeminent needs and opportunities for the economic history of the region lie elsewhere, in the agricultural hinterlands of the great port cities. The concerns of the new social history, which have had a

10. For the coastal trade, see Shepherd and Williamson, "Coastal Trade," 798. For an estimate of the value of invisibles, see Shepherd and Walton, *Shipping*, 128, 134.

TABLE 9.3.
Average Annual Value and Destinations of
Commodity Exports from the Middle Colonies, 1768–1772
(Pounds Sterling)

Commodity	Great Britain	Ireland	Southern Europe	West Indies	Africa	Total
Grains, grain products	£15,453	£9,686	£175,280	£178,961		£379,380
Flaxseed	771	35,185				35,956
Wood products	2,635	4,815	3,053	18,845		29,348
Iron	24,053	695		2,921		27,669
Livestock, beef, pork	2,142		1,199	16,692		20,033
Potash	12,233	39				12,272
Other	11,082	1,310	2,227	6,191	£1,077	21,887
Total	£68,369	£51,730	£181,759	£223,610	£1,077	£526,545

Sources: James F. Shepherd and Gary M. Walton, *Shipping, Maritime Trade, and the Economic Development of Colonial North America* (Cambridge, 1972), 212–213, 217–218, 221, 224, 227. For a discussion of this compilation of the data in CUST 16/1, Public Record Office, see chap. 4, above.

Notes: "Southern Europe" here includes all of the continent south of Cape Finisterre, plus the Wine Islands off the west coast of Africa. Wood products here include hoops. "Other" commodities are defined as any that were individually less by value than 2 percent of the total average annual exports. Compare Harry J. Carman, ed., *American Husbandry* (1775) (New York, 1939), 91, 128–129, which shows New York and Pennsylvania with total exports for 1763 valued at £1,231,500, of which £31,500 was for ships sold abroad. According to Robert Proud, *The History of Pennsylvania, in North America, from . . . 1681, till after the Year 1742 . . .* (Philadelphia, 1797–1798), II, 268–271, the average annual value of all goods exported from Pennsylvania for 1771–1773 amounted to £700,000. According to Andrew Elliot, the collector of customs at New York, and his counterpart there, Lambert Moore, the comptroller of customs, the annual value of all exports from the colony "(Hats Excepted) on an average is £400,000 Sterling" (Elliot and Moore to Gov. William Tryon, 26 Dec. 1773, CO 5/1105, fol. 320r, Public Record Office). See also Governor Tryon's report to the Board of Trade, 11 June 1774, CO 5/1105, fols. 266–288, printed (in part) in E. B. O'Callaghan [and Berthold Fernow], eds., *Documents Relative to the Colonial History of the State of New-York . . .* (Albany, N.Y., 1853–1887), II, especially p. 761. The total of the Proud and the Elliot-Moore figures, £1,100,000, is almost the same as the *American Husbandry* figure of a decade earlier and more than twice the Shepherd and Walton estimate.

dominant impact on work on New England and the Upper South, have not been much in evidence in the Middle Colonies outside of the two large urban centers.[11] We need detailed studies at the local level that explore interactions between population growth, the spread of settlement, migration, and market developments; that analyze wealth distribution, patterns of inheritance, and family structure; and that illuminate the dynamics of community life and the growing diversity of the rural economy.

Perhaps the late start will be an advantage, for historians of the small community in the Middle Colonies have a rich tradition on which to draw, a tested stock of hypotheses and methods that should permit them to catch up quickly. They may learn as well from past mistakes. In particular, we hope that they will not take the economy as given and thus ignore the economic concerns of the people they study. Further, we hope that historians of the region will not assume that a particular community responded to its own internal dynamic, insulated from developments in the greater Atlantic world.[12]

Community studies in the Middle Colonies will differ from the New England model in one critical respect: they will have to deal with ethnicity and with ethnic differences. The European population of the Middle Atlantic region was the most diverse in British America. The area was home to substantial numbers of Dutch and German settlers, to many from Britain's Celtic fringe, and to small clusters of French and Swedish colonists, as well as, of course, to people of English descent.

11. Gary B. Nash has led the extension of the new social history into colonial New York and Philadelphia. See especially *The Urban Crucible: Social Change, Political Consciousness, and the Origins of the American Revolution* (Cambridge, Mass., 1979). See also Thomas J. Archdeacon, *New York City, 1664–1710: Conquest and Change* (Ithaca, N.Y., 1976); Joyce Diane Goodfriend, "'Too Great a Mixture of Nations': The Development of New York City Society in the Seventeenth Century" (Ph.D. diss., University of California, Los Angeles, 1975); and Billy G. Smith, "The Material Lives of Laboring Philadelphians, 1750 to 1800," *WMQ*, 3d Ser., XXXVIII (1981), 163–202. For studies of smaller cities, see Stephanie Grauman Wolf, *Urban Village: Population, Community, and Family Structure in Germantown, Pennsylvania, 1683–1800* (Princeton, N.J., 1976), and Jerome H. Wood, Jr., *Conestoga Crossroads: Lancaster, Pennsylvania, 1730–1790* (Harrisburg, Pa., 1979).

12. A good beginning has been made by James T. Lemon, *The Best Poor Man's Country: A Geographical Study of Early Southeastern Pennsylvania* (Baltimore, 1972). Several recent dissertations treat some of these issues: Barry John Levy, "The Light in the Valley: The Chester and Welsh Tract Quaker Communities and the Delaware Valley, 1681–1750" (Ph.D. diss., University of Pennsylvania, 1976); Jessica Kross Ehrlich, "A Town Study in Colonial New York: Newtown, Queens County (1642–1790)" (Ph.D. diss., University of Michigan, 1974); and Dennis P. Ryan, "Six Towns: Continuity and Change in Revolutionary New Jersey, 1770–1792" (Ph.D. diss., New York University, 1974). Henretta, "Families and Farms," attempts to integrate community studies of New England and the Middle Colonies.

The significance of this ethnic diversity for economic history is far from clear. Most work on ethnicity in the region has focused on its impact on political alignments. Those who have explored its consequences for the economy have too often depended on eighteenth-century stereotypes ("feisty and independent" Scots-Irish; "industrious and thrifty" Germans; and so on), that provide only blunt analytical instruments. We suspect that market considerations were more critical than ethnicity in determining land use, crop choice, farming techniques, and the like, and that colonists of different ethnic groups responded similarly to price changes. Nonetheless, it is clear that shared language, background, attitudes, and religious persuasion had a profound impact on behavior in the Middle Colonies. Membership in an ethnic group bound people together, informed decisions about where to live, whom to marry, and which merchants and craftsmen to patronize. It may also have made people more secure by providing networks of acquaintances who could be contacted when disaster struck, when work needed to be done, or when money had to be borrowed to start a farm or finance a business. Assessing the impact of ethnicity on economic behavior and on the ties binding people together is an important task for community studies in the Middle Colonies.[13]

Another difference between community studies of the Middle Colonies and those conducted for other parts of early British America is the unit of analysis. It usually does not matter whether someone is using town records or county records to study such questions as inheritance patterns or gender roles. But the unit of analysis is critical when, for example, the dynamics of community life are the subject of investigation. The New England town and the Chesapeake county have seemed such obvious choices that scholars investigating those areas have not addressed the question. They have taken for granted that the local community and the political unit were coextensive. But this is not so in the Middle Colonies, or at least not in Pennsylvania. Pennsylvania counties are too large for the community approach, and most "colonists settled not in towns but on farms scattered in seemingly random fashion across the landscape." It has been suggested that the township is Pennsylvania's equivalent of the New England town or the southern county. While that may be true, the proposition ought not to be accepted as a given. Instead, students of local his-

13. In addition to works already cited, recent studies of ethnicity and ethnic groups that illuminate the economic history of the region include David Evan Narrett, "Patterns of Inheritance in Colonial New York City, 1664–1775: A Study in the History of the Family" (Ph.D. diss., Cornell University, 1981); Daniel Snydacker, "Kinship and Community in Rural Pennsylvania, 1749–1820," *JIH*, XIII (1982), 41–61; Marianne Wokeck, "The Flow and the Composition of German Immigration to Philadelphia, 1727–1775," *PMHB*, CV (1981), 249–278; and Susan Klepp, "Five Early Pennsylvania Censuses," *ibid.*, CVI (1982), 483–514.

tory in the Middle Colonies ought to approach the issue systematically, perhaps by exploring the network of interactions among inhabitants as a means of identifying the bounds of community.[14]

While the effort is premature and subject to error in many particulars, the evidence in recent scholarship is sufficient to permit a sketch of some of the probable findings of local historians of the Middle Atlantic region. We can focus on Pennsylvania and begin with its population (see table 9.4). The new colony grew rapidly in the 1680s, reaching 11,000 by 1690 and 18,000 by 1700, strong testimony to the commitment and organizational skill of William Penn's Quaker network. But that impressive performance did not continue, and the population increased much more slowly in the initial decades of the eighteenth century. The pace quickened again between 1720 and 1760, a development strikingly revealed in annual average growth rates: 5.3 percent in the 1720s, 5.2 percent in the 1730s, 3.4 percent in the 1740s, and 4.4 percent in the 1750s. The rate fell thereafter, but that perhaps reflects a difficulty with the unit of analysis rather than a real slowing down. Beginning in the late 1740s, Pennsylvanians and Europeans arriving at Philadelphia started to spread down the Shenandoah Valley into Maryland, Virginia, and North and South Carolina. If we thought in terms of a "greater Pennsylvania," the decline in the rate after 1760 would seem much less pronounced. Taking the pattern of population growth as an index of trends in the economy as a whole, the settlement boom of the 1680s was followed by several relatively sluggish decades. Then, commencing in the 1720s, a long, powerful, sustained expansion characterized the remainder of the colonial period, with perhaps some (but not much) tailing off after 1760.[15]

Some evidence indicates that, in fact, Pennsylvania's economy did grow fairly slowly in the early decades of the eighteenth century following the initial settlement boom, and then more rapidly thereafter. The population of Philadelphia, for example, which can serve as a rough proxy for urbanization, reached 2,000 by 1690 and then stayed roughly the same over the next twenty years before starting a sustained, steady increase.

14. Lucy Simler, "The Township: The Community of the Rural Pennsylvanian," PMHB, CVI (1982), 41–68 (quotation on p. 44). Useful methodological perspectives on community studies are provided in Thomas Bender, Community and Social Change in America (New Brunswick, N.J., 1978); Darrett B. Rutman, "Community Study," Hist. Methods, XIII (1980), 29–41; and Richard R. Beeman, "The New Social History and the Search for 'Community' in Colonial America," American Quarterly, XXIX (1977), 422–443.

15. For the expansion of Pennsylvania, see Wayland Fuller Dunaway, "Pennsylvania as an Early Distributing Center of Population," PMHB, LV (1931), 134–169; Ramsey, Carolina Cradle; and R. Mitchell, Commercialism and Frontier. Work on the population history of the Middle Colonies is discussed in chaps. 10 and 11, below.

TABLE 9.4.
Estimated Population of the Middle Colonies,
1630–1780 (in Thousands)

Year	Delaware	New Jersey	New York	Penn-sylvania	Total Whites	Total Blacks	Grand Total
1630			0.4		0.4	—	0.4
1640			1.9		1.7	0.2	1.9
1650	0.2		4.1		3.8	0.5	4.3
1660	0.5		4.9		4.8	0.6	5.5
1670	0.7	1.0	5.8		6.7	0.8	7.4
1680	1.0	3.4	9.8	0.7	13.4	1.5	14.9
1690	1.5	8.0	13.9	11.4	32.4	2.5	34.8
1700	2.5	14.0	19.1	18.0	49.9	3.7	53.5
1710	3.6	19.9	21.6	24.4	63.4	6.2	69.6
1720	5.4	29.8	36.9	31.0	92.3	10.8	103.1
1730	9.2	37.5	48.6	51.7	135.3	11.7	147.0
1740	19.9	51.4	63.7	85.6	204.1	16.5	220.5
1750	28.7	71.4	76.7	119.7	275.7	20.7	296.5
1760	33.2	93.8	117.1	183.7	398.9	29.0	427.9
1770	35.5	117.4	162.9	240.1	521.0	34.9	555.9
1780	45.4	139.6	210.5	327.3	680.5	42.4	722.9

Source: U.S. Bureau of the Census, *Historical Statistics of the United States, Colonial Times to 1970* (Washington, D.C., 1975), 1168 (Ser. Z 9–12, compiled by Stella H. Sutherland).

Notes: Native American Indian residents of the region who lived outside the areas settled by the British are not included in these population figures. For a crude, preliminary attempt to estimate the tribal populations within the territories contiguous to British settlement and with whom, therefore, the British maintained commercial contact, see John J. McCusker, "The Rum Trade and the Balance of Payments of the Thirteen Continental Colonies, 1650–1775" (Ph.D. diss., University of Pittsburgh, 1970), 713–714. Figures have been rounded off and thus the totals do not always equal the sum of their parts. Dashes indicate categories for which we have no data.

The spread of settlement followed a similar path, at least if the number of towns established can serve as an index. Seven new towns were established in Pennsylvania during the last two decades of the seventeenth century, but only one in the first thirty years of the eighteenth century, suggesting that the settled area enlarged slowly after 1700. Progress resumed in the fourth decade, however, for three new towns were founded in the 1730s, eleven in the 1740s, sixteen in the 1750s, twenty-two in the 1760s, and eight in the 1770s. By the Revolution the settled area had long since spread beyond Pennsylvania's boundaries.

Land prices exhibited a similar behavior. Land in southeastern Pennsylvania remained cheap through the early 1720s, but after that it began
to get more expensive, reaching ten shillings per acre in the 1730s, twenty
shillings in the 1740s, and more than forty shillings per acre in the 1760s.
Per capita imports from England, a crude guide to living standards, stayed
constant from 1700 to 1720, but then grew at an annual rate of 1.7 percent to 1750 and at 2.7 percent between 1750 and 1770. Finally, the
average value of farm inventories in Lancaster County went up constantly
after the 1720s, reaching £105 in the 1730s, £153 in 1750, £208 in
1760, and about £400 in 1780, strong evidence that farmers made substantial gains during the eighteenth century despite the leisurely gait of
growth in the initial three decades.[16]

How can we account for this temporal pattern, for the slow increase
early in the eighteenth century and the extraordinary expansion thereafter? It seems a clear case of the export sector regulating the performance
of the economy as a whole. Like the first New Englanders, Pennsylvanians
quickly discovered that they lacked products that could command an English market, despite some early success with tobacco and furs. They
needed to find other means to pay for the manufactures they imported. In
the beginning, again like the New Englanders, the first settlers of Pennsylvania relied on capital brought by new settlers, but that was only a short-
term solution. They also shipped a wide variety of goods, especially timber and grain products, to several markets—Newfoundland, the other
continental colonies, Lisbon and the Wine Islands, and most important,
the West Indies. There, Philadelphia's Quaker merchants, "keeping their
Trade within themselves and maintaining a strict Correspondence and
Intelligence over all parts where they are," used contacts with other
Quakers to capture a substantial share of the market. Yet none of these
trades proved especially expansive. Newfoundland and the Wine Islands
were served by Boston merchants, the continental colonies raised their
own food and cut their own timber, the Lisbon market was temporary,
and the West Indian market was small, unpredictable, and became in-
tensely competitive in the decades following 1700. As a consequence,
Philadelphia's export trade grew hardly at all in the thirty years after
1690. By a per capita measure, it probably declined.[17]

The export sector showed significantly more life after 1720, particu-

16. For the population of Philadelphia, see G. Nash, *Urban Crucible*, 407–408. For town
foundings, land prices, and farm inventories, see Lemon, *Best Poor Man's Country*, 67–69,
87–93, 123. For English imports per capita, see table 13.1, below.

17. George Keith *et al.*, "An Account of the State of the Church in North America," Protestant Episcopal Historical Society, *Collections*, I (1851), xix, quoted in Tolles, *Meeting*

larly toward the end of the decade. Initially, the gains owed little to the West Indian trade, then the largest Philadelphia market, which remained stagnant to the 1740s, showing a sharp relative decline in importance. Rather, they were achieved in the sale of wheat, flour, and bread to southern Europe and to Ireland and through a strengthening of the coastal trade. These advances were considerable, and Philadelphia's external commerce, however measured, nearly tripled in size between 1720 and 1740. Even though still organized around the need to earn credits to pay for British manufactures, the colony's trade became much more diverse than it had been earlier, when the West Indian market dominated. "We make our Remittances a great many different ways," John Reynell explained in 1741,

> sometimes to the West Indies in Bread, flour, Pork, Indian Corn, and hogshead Staves, sometimes to Carrolina and Newfoundland in Bread and Flour sometimes to Portugall in Wheat, Flour and Pipe Staves sometimes to Ireland in Flax Seed Flour, Oak and Walnut Planks and Barrel Staves and to England in Skinns, Tobacco, Beeswax, staves of all Kinds, Oak and Walnut Planks, Boat Boards, Pigg Iron, Tarr, Pitch, Turpentine, Ships, and Bills of Exchange.[18]

Pennsylvania's export sector continued to grow to the end of the colonial period, although there were, of course, short-term reversals. From the 1740s to the 1760s, most of the increase occurred in the coastal and West Indian trades. The rate of growth in those trades began to slow down in the early 1760s, but commerce with southern Europe and Great Britain, fueled in great measure by a burgeoning demand for food, picked up the slack. Philadelphia's foreign trade brought prosperity to farmers in its hinterland in the form of higher prices for farm products, larger, more dependable markets, and a steadier flow of consumer goods. Wheat, the major export at the end of the colonial period, after falling sharply in price before 1720, rose impressively thereafter, slowly at first, more rapidly later. By 1770, it brought twice as much at Philadelphia as it had a half-century earlier.[19]

House and Counting House, 89. Tolles provides a good introduction to the early economy of Pennsylvania, as does Gary B. Nash, *Quakers and Politics: Pennsylvania, 1681–1726* (Princeton, N.J., 1968). See also John McI. Weidman, "The Economic Development of Pennsylvania until 1723" (Ph.D. diss., University of Wisconsin, 1935).

18. Reynell to Thomas Smith, 4 Sept. 1741, Reynell Letter Book, 1738–1741, Hist. Soc. Pa. Philadelphia's foreign commerce during this period is described in James G. Lydon, "Philadelphia's Commercial Expansion, 1720–1739," *PMHB,* XCI (1967), 401–418.

19. For Pennsylvania's external commerce after 1740, in addition to the work cited in n. 5, above, see Egnal, "Economic Development," 208–209, 217–218. We are fortunate in hav-

One remarkable characteristic of the export-led growth process was the diversity it promoted in the rural economy. Farm families pursued a variety of by-employments in slack times when agriculture did not demand their full attention, activities that supplemented income and helped make life more comfortable. Local entrepreneurs seized every occasion for processing products and moving them to market and for supplying farmers, who had money to spend from the sale of their crops, with a wide range of goods and services. While the pace and process of diversification remains obscure, the outcome is clear. By the end of the colonial period rural Pennsylvania was dotted with small towns, processing firms, and manufacturing establishments. Its inhabitants could avail themselves of numerous non-farm employments, most of which were tied, more or less directly, to the export sector.[20]

A second remarkable characteristic of the rural prosperity that accompanied the expansion of the export sector is that it was widely shared and thus did not lead to a sharp increase in inequality. James Lemon and Gary Nash found in a study of Chester County assessments, for example, that the proportion of taxable wealth owned by the richest 10 percent of property owners stayed small and stable between 1730 and 1760. Duane Ball's study of probate records for the same county reached a similar conclusion, while reporting substantial gains in wealth per household and, it appears, per capita. Alice Hanson Jones also found lower levels of wealth inequality (and more wealth per head) in the Middle Colonies than elsewhere on the continent, despite the inclusion in her sample of Philadelphia County, where wealth inequality was high.[21]

Why such low levels of inequality? Part of the answer has to do with scale. The food crops grown for export in the region were efficiently produced on family farms. Slavery made no progress in rural Pennsylvania, although at times it was important in Philadelphia: blacks were less than

---

ing good data on Philadelphia prices. See Anne Bezanson, Robert D. Gray, and Miriam Hussey, *Prices in Colonial Pennsylvania* (Philadelphia, 1935), and Bezanson *et al., Prices and Inflation during the American Revolution: Pennsylvania, 1770–1790* (Philadelphia, 1951).

20. On diversification and backcountry towns, see Lemon, *Best Poor Man's Country,* 131–148, 184–217, and Earle and Hoffman, "Staple Crops," 5–78. On by-employments among farmers, see chap. 15, and for agriculture more generally, chap. 14, below.

21. James T. Lemon and Gary B. Nash, "The Distribution of Wealth in Eighteenth-Century America: A Century of Change in Chester County, Pennsylvania, 1693–1802," *Jour. Soc. Hist.,* II (1968), 1–24; Duane E. Ball, "Dynamics of Population and Wealth in Eighteenth-Century Chester County, Pennsylvania," *JIH,* VI (1976), 621–644; A. Jones, *Wealth of a Nation to Be,* 164.

3 percent of the colony's population in 1770. Servants were more numerous than slaves in the rural economy, but there were not enough of them to permit any one farmer to acquire a labor force much larger than those of his neighbors. Free wageworkers were not available in great numbers either, although we know little about this group. Farmers in Pennsylvania relied, for the most part, on their own labor and that of their families, which severely constrained the size of their operations and prohibited the acquisition of great wealth.[22]

Migration was another limit on the spread of inequality. The reproductive growth rate among rural Pennsylvanians was apparently quite high, although this is another subject about which not enough is known. In contrast to assertions concerning the deleterious impact of rapid population increase in New England, dire Malthusian consequences seem not to have been the result in Pennsylvania. Migration to the frontier, perhaps financed by merchants interested in augmenting the supply of exportable crops and made attractive by the occasions for market agriculture, proved a quick response to declining prospects at home. What is striking from our perspective is that the rapid extension of the settled area in Philadelphia's hinterland cannot be interpreted in strict Malthusian terms as

22. On the importance of slavery in Philadelphia, see Gary B. Nash, "Slaves and Slaveowners in Colonial Philadelphia," *WMQ*, 3d Ser., XXX (1973), 223–256. On the Pennsylvania slave trade, see four articles by Darold D. Wax: "Quaker Merchants and the Slave Trade in Colonial Pennsylvania," *PMHB*, LXXXVI (1962), 143–159; "Robert Ellis, Philadelphia Merchant and Slave Trader," *ibid.*, LXXXVIII (1964), 52–69; "Negro Imports into Pennsylvania, 1720–1766," *Pa. Hist.*, XXXII (1965), 254–287; and "The Demand for Slave Labor in Colonial Pennsylvania," *ibid.*, XXXIV (1967), 331–345. For slaves outside the city, see Alan Tully, "Patterns of Slaveholding in Colonial Pennsylvania: Chester and Lancaster Counties, 1729–1758," *Jour. Soc. Hist.*, VI (1973), 284–305. Edward Raymond Turner, *The Negro in Pennsylvania, Slavery—Servitude—Freedom, 1639–1861* (Washington, D.C., 1911), remains useful. Work on servants and free workers is discussed in chaps. 10 and 11, below. See also Sharon Vineberg Salinger, "Labor and Indentured Servants in Colonial Pennsylvania" (Ph.D. diss., University of California, Los Angeles, 1980). Slaves were more numerous in New York and New Jersey than in Pennsylvania. See Edgar J. McManus, *A History of Negro Slavery in New York* (Syracuse, N.Y., 1966); Thomas Joseph Davis, "Slavery in Colonial New York City" (Ph.D. diss., Columbia University, 1974); Frances D. Pingeon, "'Land of Slavery': Blacks in New Jersey from 1665 to 1846" (Ph.D. diss., Columbia University, 1977); and Joyce Diane Goodfriend, "Burghers and Blacks: The Evolution of a Slave Society at New Amsterdam," *N.Y. Hist.*, LIX (1978), 125–144. For the New York slave trade, see Virginia Bever Platt, "The East India Company and the Madagascar Slave Trade," *WMQ*, 3d Ser., XXVI (1969), 548–577; Jacob Judd, "Frederick Philipse and the Madagascar Trade," *N.-Y. Hist. Soc. Qtly.*, LV (1971), 354–374; and James G. Lydon, "New York and the Slave Trade, 1700 to 1774," *WMQ*, 3d Ser., XXXV (1978), 375–394. For slavery in the region as a whole, see Edgar J. McManus, *Black Bondage in the North* (Syracuse, N.Y., 1973), and Berlin, "Time, Space, and Afro-American Society," 45–54.

simply a response to internal population pressures. The part played by European immigrants seems strong evidence of the key role of the expanding export sector, but so too do the decisions of thousands of native-born men and women to move to the frontier. Again, to repeat the refrain of this book, interactions between the pull of foreign markets and the push of local demographic processes helped keep rural Pennsylvania a good "poor man's country" throughout the colonial period.[23]

23. For evidence that Pennsylvanians were highly mobile and that opportunities on the frontier were an important incentive to migration, see Lemon, *Best Poor Man's Country*, 71–97, and J. Main, *Social Structure*, 180–183, 193–196, 280–281.

It is not clear whether the picture of rural prosperity and relative equality that emerges from the still scanty evidence for Pennsylvania will apply also to New York. There, it could be argued, the land system fostered more-substantial inequalities while the Indian presence contained the spread of settlement. Kim, *Landlord and Tenant*, makes a strong case that the manorial system did not inhibit development in New York and that tenants were often prosperous. However, it is clear that New York's population did not grow as rapidly as Pennsylvania's in the 18th century (see table 9.4), while the frequent unrest after 1750 suggests that some tenants at least were less than fully satisfied with their landlords. For a recent dissent to Kim's defense of landlords and tenancy, see Edward Countryman, "'Out of the Bounds of the Law': Northern Land Rioters in the Eighteenth Century," in *The American Revolution: Explorations in the History of American Radicalism*, ed. Alfred F. Young (DeKalb, Ill., 1976), 37–69.

PART III

THE COLONIAL ECONOMY—

A TOPICAL APPROACH

CHAPTER 10

THE GROWTH OF

POPULATION

Over the past fifteen years, historians of early British America, encouraged by the example of French and British scholarship and excited by the possibilities of family reconstitution, have devoted extraordinary energy to the exploration of demographic issues. Although marred by some serious technical deficiencies, focused disproportionately on New England, and seemingly unaware of the colonial economy and of the potential of economic theory as an explanatory tool, the recent literature has greatly expanded our knowledge of the population of early British America. Our understanding of birth, marriage, and death in all the colonies continues to grow daily. The limitations that plagued the field in its infancy plague us no longer. The technical skills of colonial demographers are improving. Most important, there is a far greater awareness of the dynamic interaction between demographic and economic processes and of the usefulness of economic theory for unraveling the mysteries of marriage, fertility, and migration.[1]

1. Recent reviews of work on early British American population history include Daniel Scott Smith, "The Estimates of Early American Historical Demographers: Two Steps Forward, One Step Back, What Steps in the Future?" *Hist. Methods*, XII (1979), 24–38; Maris A. Vinovskis, "Recent Trends in American Historical Demography: Some Methodological and Conceptual Considerations," *Annual Review of Sociology*, IV (1978), 603–627; and Daniel Blake Smith, "The Study of the Family in Early America: Trends, Problems, and Prospects," *WMQ*, 3d Ser., XXXIX (1982), 3–28. Maris A. Vinovskis, ed., *Studies in American Historical Demography* (New York, 1979), is a representative collection of articles. Efforts to survey major trends include D. S. Smith, "Malthusian-Frontier Interpretation," and the now dated but still useful essay by J. Potter, "The Growth of Population in America, 1700–1860," in *Population in History: Essays in Historical Demography*, ed. D. V. Glass and D. E. C. Eversley (London, 1965), 631–688. See also D. S. Smith, "Early American Historiography." The peculiar parochialism of much early American demographic history is also worth noticing. Historians of population in the British colonies are usually well informed about European demographic history, but—with the exception of students of slavery—they often ignore work on the American colonies of other nations. Of particular importance for its methodological sophistication and for the pattern it reports is recent work on New France by members of the Demography Department at the University of Montreal. See especially Jacques Henripin, *La population canadienne au début du XVIIIe*

Colonial demography is not an entirely new concern, even though professional historians were rarely interested in it before the mid-1960s. Eighteenth-century observers—Benjamin Franklin, Ezra Stiles, Edward Wigglesworth, and Thomas Malthus among them—were fascinated by the population of British America, especially by its "rapidity of increase, probably without parallel in history," an increase that contrasted considerably with the slow and uneven expansion of Europe. Indeed, the demography of the thirteen continental colonies played a central role in the thought of Malthus, serving as the basis of his "rule" that unchecked populations grow geometrically.[2]

Commentators agreed on the sources of this rapid rise in population. "People increase in Proportion to the Number of Marriages," Franklin argued in a typical and well-known analysis,

> and that is greater in Proportion to the Ease and Convenience of supporting a Family. When Families can be easily supported, more Persons marry, and earlier in Life. . . .
>
> Land being thus plenty in America, and so cheap as that a labouring Man, that understands Husbandry, can in a short Time save Money enough to purchase a Piece of new Land sufficient for a Plantation, whereon he may subsist a Family; such are not afraid to marry; for if they even look far enough forward to consider how their Children when grown up are to be provided for, they see that more Land is to be had at Rates equally easy, all Circumstances considered. . . .
>
> Hence Marriages in America are more general, and more generally early, than in Europe.[3]

siècle: Nuptialité, fécondité, mortalité infantile ([Paris], 1954), and Hubert Charbonneau, *Vie et mort de nos ancêtres: Étude démographique* (Montreal, 1975). See also n. 5, below.

2. The quotation is from Thomas Robert Malthus, *An Essay on the Principle of Population, as It Affects the Future Improvement of Society* (London, 1798), 105. James H. Cassedy, *Demography in Early America: Beginnings of the Statistical Mind, 1600–1800* (Cambridge, Mass., 1969), is a good introduction to contemporary opinion on the growth of population in the colonies. Daniel Scott Smith, "A Homeostatic Demographic Regime: Patterns in West European Family Reconstitution Studies," in *Population Patterns in the Past*, ed. Ronald Demos Lee (New York, 1977), 19–51, provides a survey of recent work especially useful in highlighting American-European contrasts. For more-general reviews of work in population history and assessments of prospects for the future, see Lawrence Stone, "Family History in the 1980s," *JIH*, XII (1981), 51–87, and E. A. Wrigley, "Population History in the 1980s," *ibid.*, 207–226.

3. Benjamin Franklin, "Observations Concerning the Increase of Mankind, Peopling of Countries, etc." (1751), in *Franklin Papers*, IV, 227, 228. Franklin's views on population growth and economic change are ably summarized in Drew R. McCoy, *The Elusive Republic: Political Economy in Jeffersonian America* (Chapel Hill, N.C., 1980), 48–75.

This formulation merits close attention. Its essential premise—that the sources of the fast-growing colonial population are to be found in widespread early marriages and in the remarkable fertility associated with material abundance—has been supported by some recent work. Franklin's construction implies two things. First, the colonial economy was an unchanging but steadily expanding one in which there were only minor productivity gains once functioning farms had been carved from the "wilderness." Second, colonial population growth did not reduce incomes, because migration relieved the pressure on resources. This interpretation remains attractive, especially for the areas with small farms in the North and in the southern backcountry. In such places, immigration and minor changes in fertility functioned as a kind of homeostatic mechanism to keep incomes and their distribution fairly stable through the regular extension of the agricultural frontier. This permitted Malthus's "rapidity of increase . . . without parallel in history" while avoiding the usual dismal Malthusian outcome.[4]

Franklin, Malthus, and most twentieth-century historians have looked at the demographic history of only one group, however. From a European point of view, Malthus was correct: the population of the colonies did experience unparalleled advances. But from the viewpoint of native Americans, decline was the central demographic reality. The magnitude of that decline is now impossible to measure—satisfactory estimates of the size of precontact Indian populations are beyond the reach of modern scholarship—but it is clear that European and African diseases decimated the aboriginal inhabitants of North America. This catastrophe played a major role in the subsequent course of colonial economic development, albeit one seldom analyzed or even acknowledged. Assessment of that role will require explicit counterfactual analysis as well as comparison with territories invaded by Europeans where the resident population did not decline so sharply. All that is beyond the scope of this book. Suffice it to note that the destruction of Indian peoples had a fundamental impact on the availability of land, the supply of labor, the costs of establishing colonies, the market for European goods, and the trade in furs. We hope that economic historians will soon turn their attention to these issues.[5]

The first fact for demographers is total population. Recent work in demographic history has done little to improve our knowledge of the size

4. For the persistent attraction of such a model, see Daniel Scott Smith, "The Demographic History of Colonial New England," *Jour. Econ. Hist.*, XXXII (1972), 165–183; Rutman, "People in Process"; and, especially, D. S. Smith, "Malthusian-Frontier Interpretation."

5. Henry F. Dobyns, *Native American Historical Demography: A Critical Bibliography* (Bloomington, Ind., 1976), is a good introduction to the field. See also the essays and bibli-

of colonial populations. For the thirteen British mainland colonies, scholars continue to depend on the estimates of Stella Sutherland and W. A.
Rossiter, despite their often considerable inconsistencies, their failure to
specify the way in which they derived their estimates, and the substantial
amount of evidence uncovered since their work was done.[6] This is not to
suggest that either series is wildly inaccurate or likely to mislead those
interested in rough estimates of the relative size of the colonies or in the
general pattern of growth, even if Sutherland's and Rossiter's guesses are
sometimes off the mark by a factor of two. Both were careful scholars
who used the data at hand with skill. But we can now do much better,
particularly for the Middle Colonies and the Lower South, for the seventeenth century, and for those early years of each region's history when the
evidence available to Sutherland and Rossiter was especially thin and
when reliance on the comments of enthusiastic promoters apparently
produced some significant exaggerations. New estimates of total population by colony are clearly a major need in the economic history of early
British America.

   The task will not be easy. True censuses, the most useful source for
counts of colonial populations, are rare. Those that do survive are frequently not comparable in their categories and of uncertain reliability,
qualities that reflect official indifference and incompetence, popular suspicion of enumeration, errors in counting, in addition, and in transcrip-
tion, and the sheer difficulty of taking an accurate census. Nevertheless,
they are the best source we have and will play a central role in any study

---

ography in William M. Deneven, ed., *The Native Population of the Americas in 1492*
(Madison, Wis., 1976). The prototype for such studies is, of course, the work of Sher-
burne F. Cook and Woodrow Borah, *Essays in Population History*, 3 vols. (Berkeley and
Los Angeles, Calif., 1971–1979).

6. Sutherland's series appears in U.S. Bureau of the Census, *Historical Statistics*, II, 1168
(Ser. Z 1–19). See also Stella H. Sutherland, *Population Distribution in Colonial America*
(New York, 1936), and Sutherland, "Colonial Statistics," *Explorations Entrep. Hist.*, 2d
Ser., V (1967), 58–107. W. A. Rossiter's series is in U.S. Bureau of the Census, *A Century of
Population Growth: From the First Census of the United States to the Twelfth, 1790–1900*
(Washington, D.C., 1909). See also Franklin B. Dexter, "Estimates of Population in the
American Colonies," American Antiquarian Society, *Proceedings*, N.S., V (1887), 22–50.
Sutherland, Rossiter, and Dexter confine their estimates to the mainland colonies that be-
came the United States. Herman R. Friis, *A Series of Population Maps of the Colonies and
the United States, 1625–1790* (New York, 1968), organizes and maps these data. Useful
compilations of census materials appear in Evarts B. Greene and Virginia D. Harrington,
American Population before the Federal Census of 1790 (New York, 1937); U.S. Bureau of
the Census, *Century of Population Growth*, 149–185; and U.S. Bureau of the Census, *Historical Statistics*, II, 1169 (Ser. Z 24–132). For decadal population estimates for other British colonies, see McCusker, "Rum Trade," 548–767.

of colonial populations. But they must be used with caution, with strict attention to what Herbert Heaton once called "the quality of the quantities." If examined closely for internal consistency, checked against independently generated partial counts, and questioned strictly for the plausibility of the characteristics they describe, the censuses can be made to reveal a great deal about the size and structure of the population of British America.[7]

Numerous partial counts of population also survive, especially of taxables, militia, and households. These can be used to estimate totals through the application of multiples. Conversion must be approached gingerly, however, for the ratio of part to whole differed sharply by region and by time and was very sensitive to changing birthrates and to age-, sex-, and race-specific movements in mortality and migration. The vast majority of such data, furthermore, are available only by minor civil division—county, town, and parish—and thus demand additional multiplication to generate colony-wide estimates. Still, these form a rich source that can materially improve existing estimates.[8]

7. Heaton, "Thomas Southcliffe Ashton, 1889–1968: A Memoir," *Jour. Econ. Hist.*, XXIX (1969), 265. The most thorough analysis of colonial censuses is Wells, *Population of the British Colonies*. Wells, however, fails to exploit much of the available information and gives only cursory attention to the quality of the data, failings for which reviewers have rightly taken him to task. See, for example, Darrett B. Rutman, "History Counts: Or, Numbers Have More Than Face Value," *Reviews in American History*, IV (1976), 372–378. For efforts to evaluate the quality of colonial census materials, see Cassedy, *Demography in Early America*, 59–90; Robert V. Wells, "The New York Census of 1731," *N.-Y. Hist. Soc. Qtly.*, LVII (1973), 255–259; Gary B. Nash, "The New York Census of 1737: A Critical Note on the Integration of Statistical and Literary Sources," *WMQ*, 3d Ser., XXXVI (1979), 428–435; Darrett B. and Anita H. Rutman, "'More True and Perfect Lists': The Reconstruction of Censuses for Middlesex County, Virginia, 1668–1704," *VMHB*, LXXXVIII (1980), 37–74; Russell R. Menard, "Five Maryland Censuses, 1700 to 1712: A Note on the Quality of the Quantities," *WMQ*, 3d Ser., XXXVII (1980), 616–626; and Lorena S. Walsh, "The Historian as Census Taker: Individual Reconstitution and the Reconstruction of Censuses for a Colonial Chesapeake County," *ibid.*, XXXVIII (1981), 242–260.

8. Some of the available material is collected in the work of Greene and Harrington and of McCusker, cited in n. 6, above, but this represents only the tip of an iceberg of partial population counts that remain buried in local records. For some indication of the volume of such materials, see the compilations of taxable figures for Maryland and Virginia in Arthur Eli Karinen, "Numerical and Distributional Aspects of Maryland Population, 1631–1840" (Ph.D. diss., University of Maryland, 1958), appendix; Nicholls, "Origins of the Virginia Southside," 44–45; Menard, "Economy and Society," 457–463; and Kulikoff, "Tobacco and Slaves," 421–427. The most frequently used multiples are those presented by Greene and Harrington in *American Population*. They suggest the following ratios: militia, 5 to 1; polls and taxables, 3 to 1 in the South, 4 to 1 elsewhere; families, from a low of 5.7 to 1 to a high of 6 to 1; houses, at least 7 to 1 (p. xxii). However, such ratios varied substantially

Terry Anderson and Robert Thomas have attempted to improve upon estimates of New England's population through the use of a stable-population model, defined as a population closed to migration with constant fertility and mortality schedules. Unfortunately, the rigorous assumptions of such a model severely restrict its usefulness. During the last half of the seventeenth century, New England perhaps came close to that model, but it is unlikely that any other region in British America did so. Further, the model demands precise measurement of at least two critical demographic parameters (birth and death rates, for example), and an accurate count of the population at one date upon which other estimates can be built. These are difficult to come by. Moreover, even for New England the method obscures temporal fluctuations and regional variations in the growth rate, subtleties that may provide important clues to the contours of change in the economy and to the interaction among demographic and economic factors. Anderson and Thomas have applied a modified version of the method to the Chesapeake colonies, but the assumptions they were forced to make about the volume and pattern of migration, rates of seasoning and mortality, and the level of fertility are not sufficiently rooted in evidence to produce reliable results. Nevertheless, their work is an important addition to the literature because it points to the possibility of drawing out more fully the implications of traditionally grounded estimates. The use of mathematical models in combination with detailed empirical work promises to yield much more dependable series of population figures for the British colonies.[9]

---

across time and space, and the application of universal multiples could lead to serious errors. For an informed treatment of the difficulties, see the discussion of the 1699 Virginia census in Rutman and Rutman, "'More True and Perfect Lists,'" 42–48, and the methodological note by Charles Wetherell, "A Note on Hierarchical Clustering," *Hist. Methods Newsletter*, X (1977), 109–116. See also Joseph B. Felt, "Statistics of Population in Massachusetts," American Statistical Association, *Collections*, I (1847), 121–216; Arthur E. Karinen, "Maryland Population, 1631–1730: Numerical and Distributional Aspects," *Md. Hist. Mag.*, LIV (1959), 365–407; Herbert A. Whitney, "Estimating Precensus Populations: A Method Suggested and Applied to the Towns of Rhode Island and Plymouth Colonies in 1689," Association of American Geographers, *Annals*, LV (1965), 179–189; E. Morgan, *American Slavery*, 400–405; John K. Alexander, "The Philadelphia Numbers Game: An Analysis of Philadelphia's Eighteenth-Century Population," *PMHB*, XCVIII (1974), 314–324; and Gary B. Nash and Billy G. Smith, "The Population of Eighteenth-Century Philadelphia," *ibid.*, XCIX (1975), 362–368.

9. Anderson and Thomas, "White Population, Labor Force, and Extensive Growth of the New England Economy in the Seventeenth Century," *Jour. Econ. Hist.*, XXXIII (1973), 634–667; Anderson and Thomas, "The Growth of Population and Labor Force in the Seventeenth-Century Chesapeake," *Explorations Econ. Hist.*, XV (1978), 290–312; Russell R. Menard, "The Growth of Population in the Chesapeake Colonies: A Comment,"

Until that work is done we shall have to rely upon the admittedly crude figures available. Estimates by region, decade, and race appear in figures 10.1, 10.2, and 10.3. The details of their construction are described elsewhere; it is sufficient to note here that they rely heavily on the work of Sutherland for the mainland and on that of John McCusker for the islands, with occasional revisions as suggested by more-recent scholarship. Notwithstanding the figures are crude and provisional—indeed, one of the principal arguments of this section is that they need refinement—they are adequate to support some rough generalizations.[10]

Data on total population size, once assembled, provide the basis for discussions of population growth. Perhaps the most obvious feature of the data for the several regions is the similarity of the growth curves they describe: excepting the colonies of Atlantic Canada, all show a tendency to grow quickly at first, although at a steadily decelerating pace, before settling in to a slower and fairly even advance. For British America as a whole and for the West Indies in particular, a fairly constant average annual growth rate was reached early in the colonial period, approximately 1660, although there were, of course, fluctuations around the trend line. For the mainland colonies as a group and for the two regions of New England and the Upper South, steady growth set in about 1670. In the Middle Colonies and the Lower South, places settled somewhat later, the beginning of stable expansion was delayed to the 1690s.

Equally striking is the variety in the average annual growth rates once relative stability was attained. The total population of the British colonies rose by 2.6 percent a year from 1660 to 1780, just below a Malthusian doubling every quarter century, while the colonies on the continent grew at 3 percent, just above the Malthusian level. The mainland colonies also show considerable diversity, with average annual rates ranging from a low of 2.4 percent in New England to a high of 4.3 percent in the Lower South. However, the sharpest difference was between the islands, where population increased at only 1.5 percent per year, and the continental colonies, where the average annual rate was twice as great (see figure 10.1).

---

ibid., XVIII (1981), 399–410; and Anderson, "From the Parts to the Whole: Modeling Chesapeake Population," *ibid.*, 411–414.

Approaches based on stable-population theory such as "inverse projection" and "back projection" may prove useful in early British American demographic history. For the former, see Ronald Lee, "Estimating Series of Vital Rates and Age Structures from Baptisms and Burials: A New Technique, with Applications to Pre-industrial England," *Population Studies*, XXVIII (1974), 495–512; for the latter, see Wrigley and Schofield, *Population History of England*, appendix 15.

10. We hope to publish a detailed account of these estimates shortly. In the interim, see the discussions in Part II of this book and in this chapter.

FIGURE 10.1.
Population of British America, 1610–1780

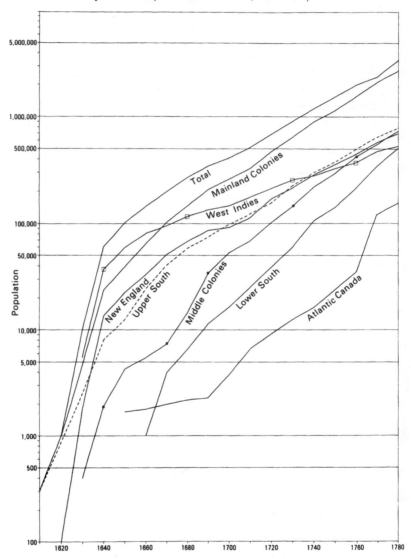

Sources: Tables 5.1, 5.3, 6.3, 7.2, 8.1, and 9.4, above.

Note: This graph uses a semilogarithmic projection. Semilog graphs are used to plot time series because they permit us both to see the general directions of any trend lines and to compare the rates of increase (or decrease) of each series. The steeper the slope of a line in a semilog graph, the sharper the rate of increase (or decrease) it describes.

These distinctions deepen when the data are disaggregated by race. When attention is focused on the Euro-American population, as in figure 10.2, the mainland colonies seem then to break into two groups. In the older regions, New England and the Upper South, which probably suffered a net loss to migration during the eighteenth century, the white population expanded at slightly below the Malthusian rate after about the 1680s, at 2 to 2.5 percent per year. In the more recently settled colonies of the Middle Atlantic and Lower South, important destinations for immigrants throughout the period, white population rose more rapidly than the Malthusian doubling each quarter century, at 3 to 4 percent a year. But the disparities among the mainland colonies pale when conditions there are compared with the West Indies, where the white population was barely larger on the eve of the American Revolution than it had been in 1660.

The great differences among the colonies in the ratio of blacks to whites are especially noteworthy. During the eighteenth century, the number of Afro-Americans grew at about 1.5 percent a year in the West Indies, just over 3 percent in the Middle Atlantic colonies and New England, and roughly 4.5 percent in the South (see figure 10.3). Despite its Malthusian growth rate, the black population in the northern colonies remained small, both absolutely and in relation to the total. They comprised less than 3 percent of New England's population and under 8 percent in the Middle Colonies (see table 10.1). Conversely, blacks became an important part of the population in the South by the early eighteenth century and by 1780 made up roughly 40 percent of the total. Aggregate figures obscure substantial variations within the Upper and Lower South, both of which contained areas where blacks were the majority and areas where their numbers were negligible. The West Indies again present a sharp contrast to the colonies on the North American continent: more than 40 percent of the population was black as early as 1660, and the share had passed 90 percent by the eve of the Revolution. Only the rice-growing districts of the Lower South approached the racial composition of the sugar islands.

Populations grow through natural increase and through immigration. Even given the recent surge of interest in colonial demographic history, immigration remains a neglected topic. Our knowledge of the transatlantic migration of Europeans is poor; at best, it is limited to particular regions and selected years. This is partly a function of the sources. The registers of indentured servants bound for the colonies are perhaps the best evidence for the study of migration from Great Britain to the Ameri-

FIGURE IO.2.
European-American Population of British America, 1610–1780

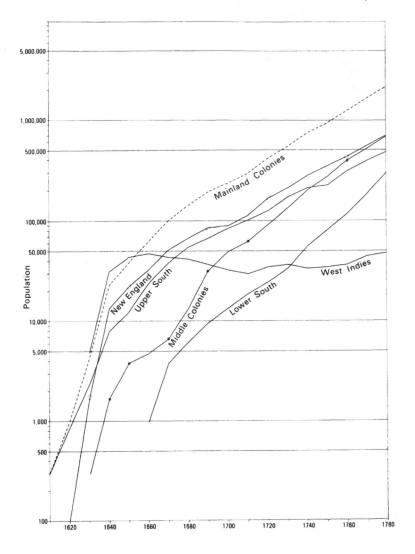

Sources: Tables 5.1, 6.3, 7.2, 8.1, and 9.4, above.

Note: This graph uses a semilogarithmic projection. Semilog graphs are used to plot time series because they permit us both to see the general directions of any trend lines and to compare the rates of increase (or decrease) of each series. The steeper the slope of a line in a semilog graph, the sharper the rate of increase (or decrease) it describes.

FIGURE 10.3.
Afro-American Population of British America, 1780

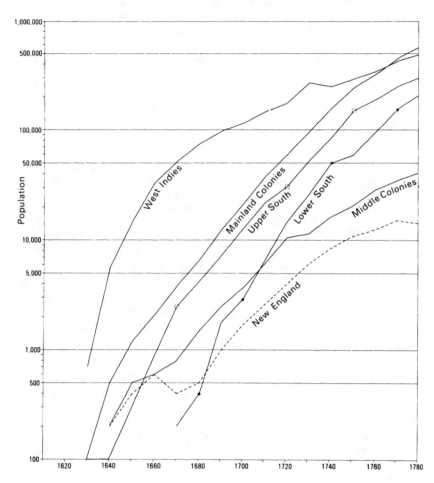

Sources: Tables 5.1, 6.3, 7.2, 8.1, and 9.4, above.

Note: This graph uses a semilogarithmic projection. Semilog graphs are used to plot time series because they permit us both to see the general directions of any trend lines and to compare the rates of increase (or decrease) of each series. The steeper the slope of a line in a semilog graph, the sharper the rate of increase (or decrease) it describes.

TABLE 10.1.

Percentage of Afro-Americans in the Total Population
of the British Colonies, 1660–1780

Year	New England	Middle Colonies	Upper South	Lower South	West Indies
1660	1.7	11.5	3.6	2.0	42.0
1700	1.8	6.8	13.1	17.6	77.7
1740	2.9	7.5	28.3	46.5	88.0
1780	2.0	5.9	38.6	41.2	91.1

Sources: U.S. Bureau of the Census, *Historical Statistics of the United States, Colonial Times to 1970* (Washington, D.C., 1975), II, 1168 (Ser. Z 1–19); John J. McCusker, "The Rum Trade and the Balance of Payments of the Thirteen Continental Colonies, 1650–1775" (Ph.D. diss., University of Pittsburgh, 1970), 712. The data for the continental colonies incorporate some of the corrections suggested in tables 6.4 and 8.1, above.

cas. While they supply much useful biographical material, they were kept only sporadically in a few ports and, of course, never recorded free migrants. The registers also omitted those servants who made the crossing without indenture to serve by the "custom of the country," a large but indeterminate part of the total group who were distinctive in significant, recognizable ways from servants with written contracts.[11]

Estimates of emigrants can be compared with estimates of the numbers at the receiving end of the migrant stream. Some historians have used colonial land records to figure the number of immigrants. Since several colonies distributed land by granting warrants ("headrights") to immigrants, the registers of these transactions would seem a promising source. Yet such records are limited in scope and their relationship to the actual

11. For bibliographic discussion of the surviving registers, see David Walter Galenson, "The Indenture System and the Colonial Labor Market: An Economic History of White Servitude in British America" (Ph.D. diss., Harvard University, 1979), 25–44. Indentured and customary servitude are discussed in chap. 11, below. Studies of particular migrations include, in addition to work cited elsewhere in this chapter, T. H. Breen and Stephen Foster, "Moving to the New World: The Character of Early Massachusetts Immigration," *WMQ*, 3d Ser., XXX (1973), 189–222; R. J. Dickson, *Ulster Emigration to Colonial America, 1718–1775* (London, 1966); Ian Charles Cargill Graham, *Colonists from Scotland: Emigration to North America, 1707–1783* (Ithaca, N.Y., 1956); Audrey Lockhart, *Some Aspects of Emigration from Ireland to the North American Colonies between 1660 and 1775* (New York, 1976); Walter Allen Knittle, *The Early Eighteenth Century Palatine Emigration: A British Government Redemptioner Project to Manufacture Naval Stores* (Philadelphia, 1936); Newton, "Great Emigration"; Clifford K. Shipton, "Immigration to New England, 1680–1740," *Jour. Pol. Econ.*, XLIV (1936), 225–239; N. C. P. Tyack, "Migra-

number of migrants is uncertain, to say the least.[12] Colonial port records may eventually prove helpful, as may newspapers and the comments of contemporaries, but it is clear that the available compiled data are not sufficient to support direct, comprehensive, reliable counts.[13]

Given the paucity of evidence, scholars have proceeded indirectly, attempting to calculate the volume of migration as a residual, that is, as the portion of a population not accounted for by reproduction. In ideal circumstances—if we knew birth and death rates and the size of colonial populations—construction of reliable estimates of net migration would be a simple task. The most systematic effort to use this procedure has been made by H. A. Gemery, who recently compiled a series of decennial estimates of emigration from Great Britain to the several colonial regions during the seventeenth century.

Gemery's work is easily criticized. One could argue that the effort is premature because we still know too little about the size or vital rates of colonial populations, or one could reject the particular figures as inaccurate. But that would miss the point. By following Gemery's lead we are likely to improve our understanding of the size and sequence of migration. Clearly, a grand opportunity awaits the scholar who refines Gem-

---

tion from East Anglia to New England before 1660" (Ph.D. diss., University of London, 1951); George R. Mellor, "Emigration from the British Isles to the New World, 1765–1775," *History*, N.S., XL (1955), 68–83; Anthony Salerno, "The Social Background of Seventeenth-Century Emigration to America," *Journal of British Studies*, XIX (1979), 31–52; and Frank Ried Diffenderffer, *The German Immigration into Pennsylvania through the Port of Philadelphia, 1700 to 1775* (Lancaster, Pa., 1900). Maria Sophia Wokeck, "A Tide of Alien Tongues: The Flow and Ebb of German Immigration to Pennsylvania, 1683–1776" (Ph.D. diss., Temple University, 1983), is an important contribution to our understanding of the movement of Germans into Pennsylvania during the 18th century. See also Sharon V. Salinger, "Colonial Labor in Transition: The Decline of Indentured Servitude in Late Eighteenth-Century Philadelphia," *Labor History*, XXII (1981), 165–191.

12. See, especially, Wesley Frank Craven, *White, Red, and Black: The Seventeenth-Century Virginian* (Charlottesville, Va., 1971), and the comments on Craven's use of headright records both in Edmund S. Morgan, "Headrights and Head Counts: A Review Article," *VMHB*, LXXX (1972), 361–371, and in Russell R. Menard, "Immigration to the Chesapeake Colonies in the Seventeenth Century: A Review Essay," *Md. Hist. Mag.*, LXVIII (1973), 323–329. This is not to argue that headright records cannot be made to yield usable information on migration. Clearly they can, but only if used with great care. George D. Terry discusses headrights as a source for estimating migration to South Carolina ("'Champaign Country,'" 64–70).

13. Abbot Emerson Smith, *Colonists in Bondage: White Servitude and Convict Labor in America, 1607–1776* (Chapel Hill, N.C., 1947), 307–337, surveys much of the available material. Wokeck, "German Immigration to Philadelphia," 249–251, nn. 2–3, provides a listing of guides to ship passenger lists, sources that have yet to be fully utilized.

ery's procedure by constructing a range of net migration figures that allows for the probable discrepancies in existing estimates of population and vital rates and then extends the series through the eighteenth century. Initially, that range of figures will be large, reflecting the uncertain reliability of the available data, but as our knowledge of colonial demography improves, it can be narrowed. Moreover, checks against alternative, direct measures of migration for those times and places where sources prove adequate will permit assessment of the quality of the results.[14]

Ironically, the flow of Africans to the colonies of British America is better documented than the flow of whites. The slave trade was long a monopoly, imported slaves were frequently subject to a tax, slaves were considered a commodity and as such recorded in the colonial naval officer shipping lists, and the arrival of Africans was commonly of greater interest to contemporaries than the coming of Europeans. Because of these distinctive characteristics, the Atlantic slave trade has left a voluminous record, often sufficient to permit the direct measurement of migration. Interpolation, inference from the size of populations, and estimation remain necessary, but scholarship on African migration is much more firmly rooted in an empirical base than are studies of the movement of Europeans. This is not to argue that the work is complete. Our knowledge of African migration is capable of improvement in many particulars. But the outline of the story seems clear, and it is unlikely that additional studies will radically revise our understanding of this aspect of early American demography.[15]

14. Gemery, "Emigration from the British Isles." For a preliminary effort to extend Gemery's procedure into the 18th century, see Galenson, *White Servitude*, 212–218. Potter, "Growth of Population," 644–646, and Marcus Lee Hansen, *The Atlantic Migration, 1607–1860: A History of the Continuing Settlement of the United States* (Cambridge, Mass., 1940), provide useful discussions of the issue. On sex ratios among European immigrants, see Herbert Moller, "Sex Composition and Correlated Culture Patterns of Colonial America," *WMQ*, 3d Ser., II (1945), 113–153, and R. Thompson, "Seventeenth-Century English and Colonial Sex Ratios: A Postscript," *Population Studies*, XXVIII (1974), 153–165. As Gemery points out, we know little about "gateway mortality"—deaths during passage or due to "seasoning"—among European immigrants, a necessity if we are to develop reliable estimates of volume. On the crossing, see John Duffy, "The Passage to the Colonies," *Mississippi Valley Historical Review*, XXXVIII (1951), 21–38. Useful information on seasoning appears in Duffy, *Epidemics in Colonial America* (Baton Rouge, La., 1953), which contains a helpful bibliography, and in several of the works cited in the discussion of the demography of specific colonial regions, below. Useful estimates of migration from England are provided in Wrigley and Schofield, *Population History of England*.

15. The starting point, of course, is Philip D. Curtin's *The Atlantic Slave Trade: A Census* (Madison, Wis., 1969). For other useful general studies, see Kenneth Winslow Stetson, "A Quantitative Approach to Britain's American Slave Trade, 1700–1773" (M.S. thesis, Uni-

Beyond the total numbers involved, satisfying generalizations concerning the pace and pattern of immigration and the shifting composition of the migrant groups have been slow in coming. Unfortunately, historians have focused on particular migrations wrenched out of their international context and have devoted too much attention to the ranking of factors (religious, economic, social, political), in an effort to understand motives. Recently, however, some progress has been made by viewing movement from Great Britain to the Americas within the context of a British migration system and by thinking of the several colonies and the home country as part of a single labor market.[16] This approach may not be of much help with the religiously motivated migration of free persons in family groups during the early, utopian years of New England and Pennsylvania. Yet the vast majority of transatlantic migrants were individuals in bondage; and the decisions that moved them, whether their

---

versity of Wisconsin, 1967); Herbert S. Klein, *The Middle Passage: Comparative Studies in the Atlantic Slave Trade* (Princeton, N.J., 1978); Craton, *Sinews of Empire*, 1–107; K. G. Davies, *The Royal African Company* (London, 1957); James A. Rawley, *The Transatlantic Slave Trade: A History* (New York, 1981); W. E. Minchinton, "The Slave Trade of Bristol with the British Mainland Colonies in North America, 1699–1770," in *Liverpool, the African Slave Trade, and Abolition: Essays to Illustrate Current Knowledge and Research*, ed. Roger Anstey and P. E. H. Hair (Liverpool, 1976), 39–59; Richard Nelson Bean, *The British Trans-Atlantic Slave Trade, 1650–1775* (New York, 1975 [Ph.D. diss., University of Washington, 1971]); George Frederick Zook, *The Company of Royal Adventurers Trading into Africa* (Lancaster, Pa., 1919); R. Thomas and Bean, "Fishers of Men"; and Gemery and Hogendorn, eds., *Uncommon Market*. Elizabeth Donnan, ed., *Documents Illustrative of the History of the Slave Trade to America*, 4 vols. (Washington, D.C., 1930–1935), is a remarkable collection. Philip D. Curtin, "The African Diaspora," *Historical Reflections/ Reflections Historique*, VI (1979), 1–17, surveys the field from an African perspective. Mc-Cusker, "Rum Trade," 548–767, collects much of the available quantitative evidence. Joseph C. Miller, "Mortality in the Atlantic Slave Trade: Statistical Evidence on Causality," *JIH*, XI (1981), 385–423, provides an assessment of the large and growing literature on "gateway mortality" among Africans. See the comment on this essay by Raymond L. Cohn and Richard A. Jensen, "Mortality in the Atlantic Slave Trade," *ibid.*, XII (1982), 317–329, with a reply by Miller, *ibid.*, 331–336. See also James C. Riley, "Mortality on Long-Distance Voyages in the Eighteenth Century," *Jour. Econ. Hist.*, XLI (1981), 651–656, and Cohn and Jensen, "The Determinants of Slave Mortality Rates on the Middle Passage," *Explorations Econ. Hist.*, XIX (1982), 269–282. Studies of the trade to particular colonies and colonial regions are cited in Part II of this book.

16. Galenson, *White Servitude*; Russell R. Menard, "British Migration to the Chesapeake Colonies in the Seventeenth Century" (paper presented at the Economic History Workshop, University of Chicago, Feb. 1980); John Wareing, "Migration to London and Transatlantic Emigration of Indentured Servants, 1683–1775," *Jour. Hist. Geography*, VII (1981), 356–378; and David Souden, "Seventeenth-Century Indentured Servants Seen within a General English Migration System" (paper presented at the annual meeting of the Organi-

own or someone else's, can be analyzed as economic choices. Market models are not the only approach to migration, but they do seem more promising than the alternatives.

The second source of population gain is through natural increase. Historians have made much more progress in recent years in the study of the vital rates of colonial populations than in the study of migration. This is particularly true for New England, where demographic patterns are by far the best documented in British America. New England's population expanded quickly, albeit at a steadily more leisurely gait, to roughly 1670. At that time about 50,000 European Americans, almost all of English extraction, and a handful of blacks lived in the region. Thereafter, the average annual growth rate remained fairly stable at around 2.4 percent per year, slightly below a Malthusian doubling every quarter century.

In New England more than in any other colonial region, a Malthusian description of the population process seems appropriate. After a burst of immigration in the 1630s, advance was achieved almost entirely through reproduction as the region quickly settled into a demographic regime unique by European standards but well understood by eighteenth-century commentators on colonial populations. Early and nearly universal marriage, elevated rates of marital fertility, and a remarkably long expectation of life, all made possible by the abundance of land and a favorable disease environment, joined to produce a high intrinsic growth rate. Although there is evidence from the eighteenth century both that marriage came later and was less widespread and that family size declined and mortality rates advanced, this demographic regime persisted throughout the colonial period. Migration to the agricultural frontier both within New England and to other colonies, especially New York and New Jersey, relieved the pressure of an expanding population on resources and

---

zation of American Historians, New Orleans, La., Apr. 1979). For the literature on migration within England, see John Patten, "Rural-Urban Migration in Pre-industrial England," University of Oxford, School of Geography, *Research Papers*, VI (1973), 1–73, and Peter Clark, "Migration in England during the Late Seventeenth and Early Eighteenth Centuries," *Past and Present*, LXXXIII (1979), 57–90. The usefulness of thinking about movement to the colonies within the context of English migration patterns has been stressed by E. E. Rich: "Between migration and emigration there is but a small difference. The Irish plantations and the mass Puritan emigrations of the next generation became the sensible and commonplace actions of ordinary people—and this lack of distinction is probably the most important thing about the peopling of British North America. The distance across the Atlantic and the virgin soils were for most of the emigrants the only new factors . . . they and their families were already accustomed to migration; emigration held few additional terrors" ("The Population of Elizabethan England," *Econ. Hist. Rev.*, 2d Ser., II [1950], 263–264).

prevented declining yields, deepening poverty, and subsistence crises of the sort that so regularly plagued Europeans. This growth process produced a population conspicuously homogeneous by colonial standards. In the late eighteenth century, when the other regions of British America exhibited a marked ethnic and racial diversity, New England remained overwhelmingly white, its whites almost exclusively of English stock.[17]

The pattern of population growth in the Upper South was generally similar to that in New England. Virginia and Maryland also grew quickly until about 1670 before settling into a 2.7 percent average annual growth rate, slightly above New England's. But this similarity of results obscures

17. Recent work on New England's population history, in addition to that already cited in this chapter, includes Greven, *Four Generations*; Kenneth A. Lockridge, "The Population of Dedham, Massachusetts, 1636–1736," *Econ. Hist. Rev.*, 2d Ser., XIX (1966), 318–344; John Demos, "Families in Colonial Bristol, Rhode Island: An Exercise in Historical Demography," *WMQ*, 3d Ser., XXV (1968), 40–57; Demos, *Little Commonwealth*; Maris A. Vinovskis, "American Historical Demography: A Review Essay," *Hist. Methods Newsletter*, IV (1971), 141–148; Vinovskis, "The 1789 Life Table of Edward Wigglesworth," *Jour. Econ. Hist.*, XXXI (1971), 570–590; Vinovskis, "Mortality Rates and Trends in Massachusetts before 1860," *ibid.*, XXXII (1972), 184–213; Vinovskis, *Fertility in Massachusetts from the Revolution to the Civil War* (New York, 1981); Susan L. Norton, "Population Growth in Colonial America: A Study of Ipswich, Massachusetts," *Population Studies*, XXV (1971), 433–452; Daniel Scott Smith, "Population, Family, and Society in Hingham, Massachusetts, 1635–1880" (Ph.D. diss., University of California, Berkeley, 1973); Smith, "Parental Power and Marriage Patterns: An Analysis of Historical Trends in Hingham, Massachusetts," *Journal of Marriage and the Family*, XXXV (1973), 419–428; Edwin S. Dethlefsen, "Colonial Gravestones and Demography," *American Journal of Physical Anthropology*, N.S., XXXI (1969), 321–333; Robert Higgs and H. Louis Stettler III, "Colonial New England Demography: A Sampling Approach," *WMQ*, 3d Ser., XXVII (1970), 282–294; Stettler, "The New England Throat Distemper and Family Size," in *Empirical Studies in Health Economics: Proceedings of the Second Conference on the Economics of Health*, ed. Herbert E. Klarman (Baltimore, 1970), 17–27; Nancy Osterud and John Fulton, "Family Limitation and Age at Marriage: Fertility Decline in Sturbridge, Massachusetts, 1730–1850," *Population Studies*, XXX (1976), 481–494; Alan Swedlund, Helena Temkin, and Richard Meindl, "Population Studies in the Connecticut Valley: Prospectus," *Journal of Human Evolution*, V (1976), 75–93; H. Temkin-Greener and A. C. Swedlund, "Fertility Transition in the Connecticut Valley: 1740–1850," *Population Studies*, XXXII (1978), 27–41; Linda Auwers Bissell, "Family, Friends, and Neighbors: Social Interaction in Seventeenth-Century Windsor, Connecticut" (Ph.D. diss., Brandeis University, 1973); Russell Walter Mank, Jr., "Family Structure in Northampton, Massachusetts, 1654–1729" (Ph.D. diss., University of Denver, 1975); Edward Byers, "Fertility Transition in a New England Commercial Center: Nantucket, Massachusetts, 1680–1840," *JIH*, XIII (1982), 17–40; and D. Jones, *Village and Seaport*. On the ethnic composition of the population, see American Council of Learned Societies, "Report on Linguistic and National Stocks in the Population of the United States," American Historical Association, *Annual Report . . . for the Year 1931* (Washington, D.C., 1932), I, 103–441, and the recent critique of this report by Forrest McDonald and Ellen Shapiro McDonald, "The Ethnic Origins of the American People, 1790," *WMQ*, 3d Ser., XXXVII (1980), 179–199.

profound dissimilarities in means. Our understanding of the demography of the tobacco coast is not nearly as good as it is of the Puritan colonies, and given the quality of the evidence the gap is likely to persist, especially for the seventeenth century. Still, the outlines of the story are clear and the contrast to New England pointed. The principal distinction, and the one from which many others followed, was the continuing importance of immigration to the Upper South. Those immigrants were predominantly male, lived short lives, and because most arrived as servants bound for a term of years, were relatively old at first marriage. As a consequence, immigrants to the Chesapeake colonies failed to reproduce themselves fully, and the total number of people who had arrived in the region during the seventeenth century outnumbered the total population in 1700 by at least 15,000 and perhaps by as much as 50,000.

Immigrants did have some children, however, and they transformed Chesapeake demography. Life remained short by New England standards, but the native born lived longer than their immigrant forebears and the sex ratio among them approximated equality. Perhaps more important, creole women married in their mid- to late teens, six to ten years younger on average than their immigrant mothers and much earlier than their New England counterparts, who were usually in their early twenties at first marriage. Consequently, in section after section in the Upper South, as creoles became the majority of the inhabitants, populations that had once suffered an excess of deaths over births began to grow quickly through natural increase. Areas that had once been hungry consumers of new settlers became net losers to migration. In the eighteenth century, with mortality rates declining and age at marriage rising, Chesapeake vital rates tended to converge on those of New England. Nevertheless, significant differences in population structure persisted. Since 40 percent of the population was black and more than 30 percent of the whites were not English—they were chiefly Scots and Germans living in the backcountry—there was much greater diversity among the inhabitants of the Upper South than among the New Englanders.[18]

We know less about the population process in the Middle Colonies than in the neighboring colonies to the north or south. Following the tra-

18. On the population history of the Chesapeake region, in addition to work already cited in this chapter, see Hecht, "Virginia Muster"; Lorena S. Walsh and Russell R. Menard, "Death in the Chesapeake: Two Life Tables for Men in Early Colonial Maryland," *Md. Hist. Mag.*, LXIX (1974), 211–227; Menard and Walsh, "The Demography of Somerset County, Maryland: A Progress Report," *Newberry Papers in Family and Community History*, 81-2 (1981); Darrett B. Rutman and Anita H. Rutman, "Of Agues and Fevers: Malaria in the Early Chesapeake," *WMQ*, 3d Ser., XXXIII (1976), 31–60; Rutman and Rut-

dition that earned them the label "Middle Colonies," one is tempted to assume that vital rates there were somewhere between those of New England and the Chesapeake. Despite that temptation, we suspect that they resembled New England more than the tobacco coast, at least the seventeenth-century tobacco coast of short lives and very early marriages. In at least one respect, however, the population history of the Middle Atlantic region diverged from both of its neighbors: while it shared with them an initial period of fast but decelerating growth followed by one of steady expansion, its regular average annual growth rate was notably larger, about 3.4 percent per annum from the 1690s to the end of the colonial period, quite dissimilar to the 2.7 percent in the Upper South and 2.4 percent in New England. This remarkable rate of increase resulted in the region's enlarging its share of the population of British America: by 1780 it had surpassed New England and nearly caught up to the Upper South.

Such spectacular growth is clear evidence of the continued importance of immigration in Middle Atlantic demography. High rates of immigration also produced a diverse population in the region. This was not because of slavery, even though there were large numbers of blacks in New York and New Jersey. It was more because of non-English Europeans, who with their descendants accounted for more than half the total population of the Middle Atlantic region in 1790.[19]

The Lower South still awaits its demographic historians. Death rates were probably greater there than in other mainland colonies, at least in

---

man, "'Now-Wives and Sons-in-Law': Parental Death in a Seventeenth-Century Virginia County," in *Chesapeake in the Seventeenth Century*, ed. Tate and Ammerman, 153–182; Earle, "Environment, Disease, and Mortality"; Menard, "Immigrants and Their Increase"; Daniel Blake Smith, "Mortality and Family in the Colonial Chesapeake," *JIH*, VIII (1978), 403–427; Walsh, "Charles County"; Nancy Lou Oberseider, "A Socio-demographic Study of the Family as a Social Unit in Tidewater Virginia, 1660–1776" (Ph.D. diss., University of Maryland, 1975); and Darrett B. Rutman, Charles Wetherell, and Anita H. Rutman, "Rhythms of Life: Black and White Seasonality in the Early Chesapeake," *JIH*, XI (1980), 29–53.

19. The most thorough student of population processes in the Middle Colonies is Robert V. Wells, whose work focuses on marriage and fertility among Quakers. See "A Demographic Analysis of Some Middle Colony Quaker Families of the Eighteenth Century" (Ph.D. diss., Princeton University, 1969); "Family Size and Fertility Control in Eighteenth-Century America: A Study of Quaker Families," *Population Studies*, XXV (1971), 73–82; and "Quaker Marriage Patterns in a Colonial Perspective," *WMQ*, 3d Ser., XXIX (1972), 415–442. See also Wolf, *Urban Village*, 249–286; Louise Kantrow, "Philadelphia Gentry: Fertility and Family Limitation among an American Aristocracy," *Population Studies*, XXXIV (1980), 21–30; and Ehrlich, "Town Study."

the lowland rice-producing areas, where malaria and yellow fever killed many. But regardless of the heavy mortality, the average annual rate of population growth was much stronger than elsewhere in British America, roughly 4.4 percent annually from the 1690s, when steady expansion replaced an elevated but decelerating rate of growth. Immigration of blacks into the lowlands and of whites into the backcountry, probably in conjunction with a sharp reproductive increase outside the plantation areas, produced the great rate of growth. The Lower South resembled the Chesapeake region in that it had a substantial proportion of blacks; it resembled the Middle Atlantic colonies in the ethnic diversity of its white inhabitants.[20]

The demographic contrasts between the West Indies and the continental colonies are striking. For one thing, after a rapid expansion in the size of the islands' population during the middle third of the seventeenth century, the average annual growth rate fell sharply, to only about 1.5 percent a year from 1660 to 1780, half the mainland average during the same period. Consequently, the West Indian share of the population of British America fell steadily, from about 60 percent in the middle of the seventeenth century to less than 20 percent by the eve of the Revolution. And the difference deepens when the population is analyzed by race, because growth in the West Indies was entirely a function of the expansion of slavery. On the one hand, blacks, who were 40 percent of the total as

20. The best introduction to the demography of the population of the Lower South is P. Wood, *Black Majority*. Julian J. Petty, *The Growth and Distribution of Population in South Carolina* (Charleston, S.C., 1943), pt. 2, 13–58, is a helpful compilation of data. Terry, "'Champaign Country,'" 90–142, contains rough but useful estimates of several demographic parameters. See also St. Julien Ravenel Childs, "Notes on the History of Public Health in South Carolina, 1670–1800," S.C. Hist. Assoc., *Procs.*, II (1932), 13–22; Childs, *Malaria and Colonization in the Carolina Low Country, 1526–1696* (Baltimore, 1940); John Duffy, "Yellow Fever in Colonial Charleston," *S.C. Hist. Mag.*, LII (1951), 189–197; Duffy, "Eighteenth-Century Carolina Health Conditions," *Jour. So. Hist.*, XVIII (1952), 289–302; Joseph I. Waring, *A History of Medicine in South Carolina, 1670–1825* ([Charleston, S.C.], 1964); Alan D. Watson, "Household Size and Composition in Pre-Revolutionary North Carolina," *Mississippi Quarterly*, XXXI (1978), 551–569; Amy Ellen Friedlander, "Carolina Huguenots: A Study in Cultural Pluralism in the Low Country, 1679–1768" (Ph.D. diss., Emory University, 1979); and Gerald L. Cates, "'The Seasoning': Disease and Death among the First Colonists of Georgia," *Ga. Hist. Qtly.*, LXIV (1980), 146–158. Work in progress by Jon Butler (University of Illinois, Chicago Circle), Diana Canala (Johns Hopkins), and Scot M. Wilds (University of Pennsylvania) promises substantial improvements in our understanding of the issues. James M. Gallman's well-executed essays, "Mortality among White Males: Colonial North Carolina," *Soc. Sci. Hist.*, IV (1980), 295–316, and "Determinants of Age at Marriage in Colonial Perquimans County, North Carolina," *WMQ*, 3d Ser., XXXIX (1982), 176–191, concern that part of North Carolina best approached as an extension of the Chesapeake region.

early as 1660, broadened their share to past 90 percent by 1770. The white population, on the other hand, peaked in 1660, declined gently for the next sixty years, and then grew only slowly and erratically, not returning to its mid-seventeenth-century level until the American Revolution. While out-migration had a material impact on the Euro-American population of the islands, it is clear that the intrinsic rate of reproduction was low—indeed, it was often negative—because high mortality kept life short and families small, while the destructive disease environment may have depressed fertility. This is the antithesis of the mainland, where the intrinsic growth rate among whites in the eighteenth century usually approached Malthusian dimensions.[21]

One of the axioms of early American historical demography is the disparity between the reproductive performance of slaves in the British West Indies and those in British North America. During the colonial period, the total number of Africans brought to the British islands outnumbered those brought to the British mainland colonies by roughly five to one, yet in 1770 the black population on the continent was slightly larger than that in the Caribbean. Explaining this incongruity and, especially, accounting for the extraordinary reproductive success of blacks in North America is a central concern of colonial economic history. The task is important, because the quick natural expansion of the slave population transformed the United States from a marginal participant in the African trade into a major slave power. Moreover, the explanation for this growth is intrinsically difficult, demanding the examination of numerous factors affecting natural increase. The critical variables include the age and sex structure of immigrant populations, work routines, the attitudes of both masters and slaves toward reproduction, unit size and population density, the household and familial arrangements of slaves, the material well-being of the work force, and the disease environment. Data are sparse and intractable, especially for the pre-Revolutionary era. Nevertheless, some progress has been made, and given the intensity of work on the issue, more can be expected in the near future.[22]

---

21. Most demographic work on the West Indies has focused on blacks, but see Dunn, *Sugar and Slaves*, 300–334; Dunn, "Barbados Census"; Molen, "Population and Social Patterns"; and Lowenthal, "Population of Barbados." Compare Gary Puckrein, "Climate, Health, and Black Labor in the English Americas," *Jour. Am. Studies*, XIII (1979), 179–193.

22. Useful introductions to the issues are provided by Robert W. Fogel and Stanley L. Engerman, "Recent Findings in the Study of Slave Demography and Family Structure," *Sociology and Social Research*, LXIII (1979), 566–589; Engerman, "The Realities of Slavery: A Review of Recent Evidence," *International Journal of Comparative Sociology*, XX (1979), 46–66; Engerman, "Some Economic and Demographic Comparisons of Slavery in

In a sense the West Indies–mainland divergences are deceptive, however dramatic they might seem. Slave populations in all the chief plantation areas of British America exhibited a similar growth process. "In the sugar colonies," Philip Curtin has noted, "demographic history tended to fall into a regular pattern over time." Although there may have been periods in the early history of many islands when slave populations were small but reproducing, the introduction of sugar cultivation involved a greater dependence on workers from Africa. The consequent high ratio of slave imports to population led to a net natural decline (i.e., more deaths than births). The decline necessitated continued high rates of importation, both to make up the deficit that the decline produced and to serve the demands of an expanding sugar industry for more workers. This, in turn, caused the deficit to persist, because immigrant slaves were predominantly male and suffered grave levels of morbidity and mortality when introduced to a new disease environment. Further, the few women who were imported were on average well advanced into their childbearing years and therefore had too few children to offset the effects on natural increase of sexual imbalance and short lives. Over time, however, as a sugar colony reached full production, the relative need for new workers diminished. Slaves continued to be imported, but only enough to cover the deficit created by high mortality rates. Creoles, who lived longer, married earlier, and possessed a better-balanced sex ratio than had their immigrant parents, grew in proportion to the total population; the surplus of deaths over births decreased and then disappeared; and the black population began to expand through reproduction.[23]

Given the emphasis placed on the Caribbean–North American contrast in recent literature, it is notable that Curtin's account provides as

---

the United States and the British West Indies," *Econ. Hist. Rev.*, 2d Ser., XXIX (1976), 258–275; Magnus Mörner, "'Comprar o Criar': Fuentes Alternativas de Suministro de Esclavos en las Sociedades Plantaciónistas del Nuevo Mundo," *Revista de Historia de América*, XCI (1981), 37–81 (originally titled "'Buy or Breed?': Alternative Sources of Slave Supply in the Plantation Societies of the New World" [paper presented at the 15th International Congress of Historical Sciences, Bucharest, 1980]); and Daniel C. Littlefield, "Plantations, Paternalism, and Profitability: Factors Affecting African Demography in the Old British Empire," *Jour. So. Hist.*, LXVII (1981), 167–182. The literature on the subject is extensive, but see especially—in addition to work cited in nn. 23–28, below—Richard S. Dunn, "A Tale of Two Plantations: Slave Life at Mesopotamia in Jamaica and Mount Airy in Virginia, 1799 to 1828," *WMQ*, 3d Ser., XXXIV (1977), 32–65; Craton, *Searching for the Invisible Man*; and B. W. Higman, *Slave Population and Economy in Jamaica, 1807–1834* (Cambridge, 1976).

23. Curtin, *Atlantic Slave Trade*, 29. See also Philip D. Curtin, "Epidemiology and the Slave Trade," *Pol. Sci. Qtly.*, LXXXIII (1968), 190–216.

accurate a description of the demography of slavery in the Chesapeake region and South Carolina as it does for the sugar islands. The distinction between the continental plantation districts and the West Indies was not a function of the ways that changes occurred, which seems to have been everywhere similar, for whites as well as for blacks. Rather, the differences depended on timing, on how long it took for a reproducing creole majority to emerge and to reverse the net natural decline. In Maryland and Virginia the transition occurred in the 1720s and in South Carolina during the 1770s, but not until 1810 in Barbados and in Jamaica only in 1840, following emancipation. Recognition of this shared experience changes the issues to be resolved: the need is not only to account for the difference between the West Indies and the mainland but also to explain why a similar course took longer to complete in some regions than in others.[24]

More was involved than just timing, however. When adjustment is made for the proportion of Africans in the population and attention is focused on creoles, demographic distinctions between the islands and the continent diminish, but they do not disappear. In spite of evidence of local variations and regardless of our imprecise measures, it seems clear that mortality rates were somewhat higher and fertility much lower in the West Indies than on the continent.

The debate over what caused these differences has generated three explanations.[25] One model stresses the disease environment, arguing that the climate of the islands permitted a wide variety of tropical diseases to flourish and thus kept mortality elevated while depressing fertility, no matter what strategies were adopted by masters and slaves.[26] A second, more traditional argument emphasizes direct planter control, suggesting that masters were able to shape the reproductive performance of their slaves and that calculations of profit and loss were central to their decisions. In this model the supply of slaves from Africa plays a central role. On the one hand, when imports were cheap and plentiful, planters were unconcerned with reproduction, maintained their slaves poorly, worked them hard, and replaced them from abroad. On the other hand, when

24. Russell R. Menard, "The Maryland Slave Population, 1658 to 1730: A Demographic Profile of Blacks in Four Counties," *WMQ*, 3d Ser., XXXII (1975), 29–54; Kulikoff, "'Prolifick' People"; P. Wood, *Black Majority*, 131–166; P. Morgan, "Afro-American Cultural Change"; and Terry, "'Champaign Country,'" 143–175. For evidence of a similar pattern in a major northern city, see Nash, "Slaves and Slaveowners," 232–241.

25. Herbert S. Klein and Stanley L. Engerman, "The Demographic Study of the American Slave Population: With Particular Attention Given the Comparison between the United States and the British West Indies" (unpubl. MS, 1975).

26. Curtin, "Epidemiology and the Slave Trade," stresses the disease environment.

imports were dear and scarce, planters improved the material conditions of the slaves, lessened the work load, and encouraged natural increase in order to expand, or at least stabilize, the size of the labor force. Another version of this argument stresses the importance of the crop, pointing out that the major plantation products demanded different work routines and conditions, hours and intensity of labor, and optimum unit sizes and that these affected reproduction.[27]

A third argument, now gaining currency, stresses the behavior of slaves, particularly their own decisions regarding fertility and the familial and living arrangements they adopted, suggesting that these were crucial to the reproductive performance of the black population.[28] Although emphasis in the debate is shifting away from direct planter control and toward the impact of an autonomous disease environment, crops, and the choices of slaves, the issues are far from settled. And the debate is important, because the demography of slavery has implications extending beyond reproductive performance to the structure of slave society, the dynamics of plantation economics, and relations among slaves and between slaves and masters.

There is hard work to be done before we can fully describe the demographic history of the several regions of early British America. We need detailed local studies in areas other than New England and the Chesapeake that use the techniques of family reconstitution, or some adaptation of those techniques, to overcome the inadequacies of existing records.[29] We also need better estimates of the size and composition of

27. For a version of the planter-intervention argument that contends they encouraged reproduction, see Richard Sutch, "The Breeding of Slaves for Sale and the Westward Expansion of Slavery, 1850–1860," in *Race and Slavery*, ed. Engerman and Genovese, 173–210. For an argument stressing the importance of economic regime, see Michael Craton, "Hobbesian or Panglossian? The Two Extremes of Slave Conditions in the British Caribbean, 1783 to 1834," *WMQ*, 3d Ser., XXXV (1978), 324–356.

28. Herbert S. Klein and Stanley L. Engerman, "Fertility Differentials between Slaves in the United States and the British West Indies: A Note on Lactation Practices and Their Possible Implications," *WMQ*, 3d Ser., XXXV (1978), 357–374; Patterson, *Sociology of Slavery*; Herbert G. Gutman, *The Black Family in Slavery and Freedom, 1750–1925* (New York, 1976).

29. Daniel Scott Smith, "A Perspective on Demographic Methods and Effects in Social History," *WMQ*, 3d Ser., XXXIX (1982), 442–468, is a useful introduction to the logic of demographic analysis. Methodological discussions of particular interest to early British American historians appear in E. A. Wrigley, ed., *An Introduction to English Historical Demography: From the Sixteenth to the Nineteenth Century* (New York, 1966), and in T. H. Hollingsworth, *Historical Demography* (Ithaca, N.Y., 1969). See also Louis Henry, *Population: Analysis and Models*, trans. Étienne van de Walle and Elise F. Jones (London, 1976). A large number of texts introduce the techniques of demographic analysis. Among

colonial populations, additional work on the demography of slavery, and more-precise descriptions of migration patterns. Despite the gaps in our knowledge, it is clear that the British colonies exhibited an extraordinary demographic diversity. The material differences in vital rates among both blacks and whites suggest that it is futile and perhaps misleading to attempt all-inclusive estimates of the sources of growth in British America. The notion of a "colonial" birthrate, death rate, and rate of net migration is very artificial, abstracting so severely from sharp regional variations as to be nearly meaningless. There was no "colonial demographic regime," but rather several regimes, each with a unique combination of vital rates and a unique outcome.

This diversity should not lead those searching for integrating generalizations to despair or to conclude that population characteristics can be accounted for entirely by isolated local processes. While the range of vital rates argues against the notion of a single demographic *regime*, it is not incompatible with the more elastic concept of a population *system* that can be studied profitably as a unit. The diversity was regular rather than random, and it should prove capable of systematic explanation.

Early British America describes a demographic spectrum ranging from the farm colonies of the North to the plantation colonies of the South and the West Indies. This spectrum is most apparent in death rates and racial proportions, but it is perhaps visible as well in the sex ratios of European immigrants, family size, marriage ages, illegitimacy, rates of bridal pregnancy, and the like. Moreover, it may be possible to relate the fluctuations in these elements to the export sector by focusing on the ways in which demand for labor influenced immigration and then on how differences in immigration shaped the overall growth process. Further, despite considerable diversity in vital rates, in the makeup of the population, and in timing, there was a rough similarity in the ways in which population expanded at the local level as rapidly increasing immigrant societies pressed against the available resource base and gave way to native-born communities that grew more slowly and exhibited significant rates of out-migration. Efforts at generalization are now premature; we as yet know too little about actual developments, let alone their sources, to offer plausible, persuasive explanations. But the shape those explanations are likely to assume is becoming clearer, and given the quickening pace at which work is proceeding, we expect they will gain both power and precision in the near future.

---

the most helpful are Henry S. Shryock, Jacob S. Siegel, *et al.*, *The Methods and Materials of Demography*, 2d ed. (Washington, D.C., 1973), and George W. Barclay, *Techniques of Population Analysis* (New York, 1958).

CHAPTER II

THE COLONIAL LABOR

FORCE, THE PATTERN

OF URBANIZATION,

AND THE SPREAD

OF SETTLEMENT

Economic history asks different questions of the population process than does demographic history. At the very least the two lines of approach have different emphases. Economic history is especially concerned with the labor force—its size, organization, occupational structure, and remuneration; with the interactions between population growth and economic development; and with the process of human capital formation. It is also interested in an economic approach to the choices people made that shaped vital rates, especially in illuminating central aspects of family strategy such as marriage, fertility, and migration. In general, the demographic concerns common to economic history have not been in evidence in the study of early British America. Their pursuit represents a major need and a promising opportunity.

Little effort has been made to measure the size of the colonial labor force or to determine its composition, failures that perhaps stem as much from conceptual ambiguity as from the quality of the evidence. The conventional definition of the labor force as "all persons producing marketable goods and services" seems inappropriate to economies in which peoples' productive energies were focused in large part on subsistence rather than on the market.[1] Except in the sugar and rice districts or in the bigger cities, few persons were engaged exclusively in market production.

1. T. Anderson and Thomas, "White Population," 659.

Despite a persistent shortage of labor, both the primitive technology and limited markets severely constrained the ability of the economy to employ fully the available human resources in production for exchange. Even if one recognizes that only a portion of workers' efforts were engaged in production for the market, the problem of determining how they allocated their time between market and subsistence activities would persist. Thus modern notions of the labor force or of the participation rate—the share of the population in the work force—cannot be applied usefully to the colonial economy.

However complicated the issues, the colonial labor force certainly merits study if only because changes in population composition were of considerable consequence to welfare.[2] Indeed, understanding the structure of work is central to understanding the colonial economy. We want to know several things: how tasks were allocated by age, gender, and race, particularly to what extent women and children participated in market-oriented field work; the ages at which children began productive labor; and how work routines changed throughout the year. In addressing these questions, it must be remembered that the composition of the work force varied by region and over time in large part according to the state of the market and the physical requirements of export products.[3] Since technology was simple and capital was hard to find, these variations—more generally, the ability of the economy to engage people in production for markets—may explain a large part of the regional and temporal variations in income per head.[4]

2. The census returns and partial counts of population discussed in chap. 10, nn. 6–8, above, are the best sources for the composition of the population, but the techniques of "mass prosopography" (see the essays by Darrett and Anita Rutman cited in chap. 10, n. 18), can also yield useful information.

3. Useful discussions of the work of women in early British America appear in Lois Green Carr and Lorena S. Walsh, "The Planter's Wife: The Experience of White Women in Seventeenth-Century Maryland," *WMQ*, 3d Ser., XXXIV (1977), 542–571; Laurel Thatcher Ulrich, "'A Friendly Neighbor': Social Dimensions of Daily Work in Northern Colonial New England," *Feminist Studies*, VI (1980), 392–405; Mary Beth Norton, *Liberty's Daughters: The Revolutionary Experience of American Women, 1750–1800* (Boston, 1980); and Julia Cherry Spruill, *Women's Life and Work in the Southern Colonies* (Chapel Hill, N.C., 1938). Although primarily concerned with changes in the early 19th century, Nancy F. Cott provides a useful discussion of the work of women in colonial America in *The Bonds of Womanhood: "Woman's Sphere" in New England, 1780–1835* (New Haven, Conn., 1977), 19–62. See also Boserup, *Woman's Role*.

4. The point is well illustrated by recent discussions of the impact of changes in labor-force participation rates on southern incomes following emancipation. See Roger L. Ransom and Richard Sutch, *One Kind of Freedom: The Economic Consequences of Emancipation* (Cambridge, 1977), and Stanley L. Engerman, "Economic Adjustments to Emancipation in

As an example, agriculture was highly seasonal in its demand for labor. The need for workers was particularly intense during planting and harvest; it was minimal and irregular at other times. Colonial farmers could seldom hire temporary hands, and workers could not shuttle between urban and rural employments. A focus on the strategies that were adopted to cope with seasonal fluctuations in the demand for labor should prove illuminating.[5]

One of the distinguishing features of the economy of early British America was that a substantial proportion of the labor force was not free. Many of its members were bound either as servants for a temporary term or as slaves for life. Explaining precisely why this was true and assessing the impact of bound labor on the colonial economy is an important task for historians. One explanation assumes that because employers wanted to maximize net returns, they chose a labor system on the basis of its relative efficiency; they compared output and costs among the alternatives. Thus, an employer with the option of using slaves, indentured servants, or free workers would be indifferent to the type of labor employed as long as the ratio of their products to their costs was equal. This explanatory

---

the United States and British West Indies," *JIH*, XIII (1982), 191–220. See also Ester Boserup, *Population and Technology* (Oxford, 1981).

5. R. Anderson and Gallman, "Slaves as Fixed Capital," provides a helpful perspective. The importance of regional differences to seasonal fluctuations in the demand for labor is stressed by Carville Earle and Ronald Hoffman, "The Foundation of the Modern Economy: Agriculture and the Costs of Labor in the United States and England, 1800–60," *AHR*, LXXXV (1980), 1055–1094. Several stimulating essays on the pace and intensity of labor in preindustrial societies are concerned to distinguish "task-oriented" from "time-oriented" approaches to work. See Keith Thomas, "Work and Leisure in Pre-industrial Society," *Past and Present*, XXIX (1964), 50–66; E. P. Thompson, "Time, Work-Discipline, and Industrial Capitalism," *ibid.*, XXXVIII (1967), 56–97; and Herbert G. Gutman, "Work, Culture, and Society in Industrializing America, 1815–1919," *AHR*, LXXVIII (1973), 531–588. However, with the exception of A. Cole, "Tempo of Mercantile Life," historians of early British America have had little success in rooting such concerns in a firm empirical base and most studies have relied on "soft," impressionistic evidence. Nonetheless, suggestive material appears in C. Vann Woodward, "The Southern Ethic in a Puritan World," *WMQ*, 3d Ser., XXV (1968), 343–370; Edmund S. Morgan, "The Labor Problem at Jamestown, 1607–18," *AHR*, LXXVI (1971), 595–611; and J. E. Crowley, *This Sheba, Self: The Conceptualization of Economic Life in Eighteenth-Century America* (Baltimore, 1974). Ralph V. Anderson, "Labor Utilization and Productivity, Diversification and Self-sufficiency: Southern Plantations, 1800–1840" (Ph.D. diss., University of North Carolina, 1974), indicates that it may be possible to develop evidence on the pace of work among slaves. However, such information may not be available for other groups in the population, and it is likely that slaves worked longer and harder than free people. Cf. Robert W. Fogel and Stanley L. Engerman, *Time on the Cross: The Economics of American Negro Slavery* (Boston, 1974). On the seasonality of work in the colonial sugar refining and rum distilling industries, see McCusker, "Rum Trade," 54–55, 432–434, and sources cited there.

model then proceeds to identify the factors that weighted the ratios in favor of coercion or freedom for workers.

Until now, the "free-land," or "open resources," hypothesis has dominated the argument about the causes of this dependence on bound labor. Because labor was in short supply in the colonies, wages were high; since land was cheap, the workers who earned these high wages could easily set themselves up as independent farmers, in the process withdrawing from the pool of free workers and making bound labor more attractive to employers.[6] Lately, however, the free-land hypothesis has been criticized severely. While it identifies a powerful incentive to use bound labor, it fails in other ways. It does not specify the conditions under which landlords would be able to act on that incentive; it does not explain why one type of bound labor was preferred in some times and places and why the opposite was true elsewhere; and it does not tell us why servants and slaves dominated the work force in some colonies but not in others.[7] For example, historians of British America wish to know why slavery was central to the economies of the West Indies, the Lower South, and the Chesapeake, but was only peripheral in New England, the Middle Colonies, and the southern backcountry, a regional pattern that the free-land hypothesis fails to illuminate.

As the inadequacy of the free-land model has become apparent, attention has shifted to other explanatory factors. Historians have begun to emphasize the characteristics of plantation agriculture that made it particularly well suited to slavery: its "multiple-day" or "all year" work requirements, which, in effect, lowered the cost of slave labor by increasing productivity; its substantial returns to scale; its high ratio of workers to land, which reduced supervision costs; and its ability to provide employment for women and children. Another factor that historians have emphasized is the strength of the colonial export sector, if only because it both regulated demand for labor in the colonies and determined the colonists' ability to pay for slaves.[8]

6. The clearest statement is provided by Evsey D. Domar, "The Causes of Slavery or Serfdom: A Hypothesis," *Jour. Econ. Hist.*, XXX (1970), 18–32.

7. See, especially, Stanley L. Engerman, "Some Considerations Relating to Property Rights in Man," *ibid.*, XXXIII (1973), 56–59, and Orlando Patterson, "The Structural Origins of Slavery: A Critique of the Nieboer-Domar Hypothesis from a Comparative Perspective," in *Comparative Perspectives on Slavery in New World Plantation Societies*, ed. Vera Rubin and Arthur Tuden (New York, 1977), 12–34, with comments by Engerman and Ira Berlin on pp. 63–71.

8. For recent contributions, see Earle, "Staple Interpretation"; Engerman, "Some Considerations"; and Philip D. Curtin, "Slavery and Empire," in *Comparative Perspectives on Slavery*, ed. Rubin and Tuden, 3–11. These arguments are surveyed in Russell R. Menard, "Why

H. A. Gemery and Jan Hogendorn object to much of this formulation. They suggest that investigations of the growth of slavery in the Americas stressing open resources, plantation agriculture, and the strength of the colonial export sector have focused attention on the demand for unfree workers to the relative neglect of supply.[9] They argue that differences in the comparative elasticity of supply of free workers, indentured servants, and slaves were critical in shaping the composition of the colonial work force. Their model requires certain assumptions. It postulates that the British American colonies can be seen as constituting a single market for labor. It assumes that planters compared costs and prices among different types of unskilled manual workers. And it has to ignore the existing stocks of labor and deal only with the flow of new workers entering the labor force.

According to Gemery and Hogendorn, planters could choose among three kinds of workers, each a possible substitute for the others but available at different prices and in different quantities: free wageworkers, largely from Great Britain; indentured servants, also from Britain; and slaves, from Africa. The supply of free wage laborers was inelastic except at very high wage levels. That was so because it was difficult to attract free workers to the colonies and to keep newly freed servants or young native-born laborers from setting up on their own account. However, the presence of two groups—freedmen and sons who did not yet have sufficient capital to establish farms—created a small pool of free workers available for employment at relatively modest wages.

Indentured servants were available in larger numbers than were free workers because the indenture system permitted recruitment among a pool of laborers in Britain other than those who could afford to pay for passage. Even their supply to any particular colony was far from perfectly elastic, however, because attractive alternative employments were available at home and in other colonial regions. The supply of African slaves was very elastic, but the substantial costs of procurement and transport combined with a rapidly rising demand for labor in European America to keep prices elevated.

The Gemery-Hogendorn model offers useful insights into changes in the composition of the work force in the colonies of British America.

African Slavery? Free Land, Plantation Agriculture, and the Supply of Labor in the Growth of British-American Slave Societies" (paper presented at the Conference on New World Slavery: Comparative Perspectives, Rutgers University, Newark, N.J., May 1980), 2–15.

9. Gemery and Hogendorn, "The Atlantic Slave Trade: A Tentative Economic Model," *Journal of African History*, XV (1974), 223–246.

They concede that if supply was held constant, then variations in demand would dictate the composition of the work force. However, their model argues that such shifts could be triggered as well by changes in supply, for example, by a decrease in the number of servants willing to migrate because of improved conditions at home or by an increase in the available quantity of slaves as that trade gained in efficiency.

However attractive it may be, there are difficulties with what Gemery and Hogendorn propose. No data exist that permit us to measure the actual supply of the various types of labor. All that can be observed are changes over time in the price of labor and in the volume of immigration. While these changes could be interpreted as describing shifts in the supply schedule, they could just as readily describe movement along a fixed curve.[10] Further, the assumption that there was a single labor market and a homogeneous work force is misleading. Local variations in supply were often critical to the composition of the labor force, and differences in the level of skill were also important. Finally, their restriction of the analysis to the flow of new workers is especially limiting.

Still, the Gemery and Hogendorn approach is valuable, for various reasons. As David Galenson has shown, their strict assumptions can be relaxed without compromising the model's utility.[11] Moreover, their effort directs attention to both supply and demand; it points to a research strategy; it isolates diverse variables that potentially influenced the composition of the work force; and it provides a way of studying these transitions as processes rather than as events. It also emphasizes the international character of that process, making clear the necessity of close attention to the interactions between the supply of and the demand for labor in Europe, Africa, and the Americas. Although much research and writing remains to be done, recent empirical investigations imply that the model can illuminate the changing composition of the work force in different regions of British America—the West Indies, the Lower South, the Chesapeake, and the principal northern cities.[12] Finally, it may prove adaptable to other European colonies. The specifics would require modification, but the transition from servants to slaves in the French West Indies, from *negros da terra* to *negros de Guiné* in Brazil, and the inverse relationship between the volume of the African trade and the size of the Indian popu-

10. See, for example, Bean and Thomas, "Adoption of Slave Labor."

11. Galenson, *White Servitude*, 117–168.

12. See chap. 6, n. 26, above, and H. A. Gemery and J. S. Hogendorn, "Elasticity of Slave Labor Supply and the Development of Slave Economies in the British Caribbean: The Seventeenth Century Experience," in *Comparative Perspectives on Slavery*, ed. Rubin and Tuden, 72–83. This evidence is summarized in Menard, "Why African Slavery?" 24–47.

lation in Mexico, are only a few examples we could cite to indicate the model's potential.[13]

Despite a present-day revival of interest, temporary servitude has not attracted the attention it deserves. Scholarship has instead focused on slavery. Yet the various types of short-term bound labor played a leading role in the development of the colonial economy. They were all based on an agreement that contracted a specific period of labor in exchange for passage across the Atlantic, maintenance during service, and certain "freedom dues" payable upon completion of the term. A conservative estimate suggests that half the Europeans who migrated to British America were bound to serve by some form of contract. Two-thirds seems nearer the mark. And for some times and regions—such as the West Indies and the Chesapeake colonies in the seventeenth century—the proportion was as great as 80 to 90 percent.[14] In a time of primitive capital markets, servitude was a primary means of financing migration for people unable to purchase passage. It was also a significant source of workers for labor-starved economies.

While almost every aspect of temporary servitude can benefit from closer study, we understand more about some facets of the system than others. Thanks to the survival of several sets of English registrations, thoroughly exploited by Galenson and others, a good deal is known about the kinds of people who migrated under written contract and about the operation of the indenture market (although additional evidence on the recruitment process would be very welcome).[15] Much less is known

13. Stuart B. Schwartz, "Indian Labor and New World Plantations: European Demands and Indian Responses in Northwestern Brazil," *AHR*, LXXXIII (1978), 43–79; John Tutino, "Slavery in a Peasant Society: Indians and Africans in Colonial Mexico" (unpubl. paper, St. Olaf's College, 1979).

14. A. E. Smith, *Colonists in Bondage*, 3–4; Menard, "Economy and Society," 162.

15. Mildred Campbell, "Social Origins of Some Early Americans," in *Seventeenth-Century America*, ed. J. Smith, 63–89; Campbell, "English Emigration on the Eve of the American Revolution," *AHR*, LXI (1955), 1–20; David Galenson, "British Servants and the Colonial Indenture System in the Eighteenth Century," *Jour. So. Hist.*, XLIV (1978), 41–66; Galenson, "Immigration and the Colonial Labor System: An Analysis of the Length of Indenture," *Explorations Econ. Hist.*, XIV (1977), 360–377; Galenson, "Literacy and the Social Origins of Some Early Americans," *Hist. Jour.*, XXII (1979), 75–91; Galenson, " 'Middling People' or 'Common Sort'? The Social Origins of Some Early Americans Reexamined," *WMQ*, 3d Ser., XXXV (1978), 499–524, with a rebuttal by Campbell, *ibid.*, 525–540, a rejoinder by Galenson, *ibid.*, XXXVI (1979), 264–277, and a reply by Campbell, *ibid.*, 277–286; David Souden, " 'Rogues, whores, and vagabonds': Indentured Servant Emigrants to North America, and the Case of Mid-Seventeenth-Century Bristol," *Social History*, III (1978), 23–41; James Horn, "Servant Emigration to the Chesapeake in the Seventeenth Century," in *Chesapeake in the Seventeenth Century*, ed. Tate and Ammerman,

about the "customary servants" who left seventeenth-century England without signed indentures and served according to "the custom of the country." Penal servitude, a minor institution early in the colonial period but of growing influence in the eighteenth century, also deserves to be more fully studied.[16] Nor are we well informed about the "redemptioners," chiefly German servants who often migrated in family groups and who engaged to arrange payment for their passage upon arrival in the colonies.[17]

Galenson has offered a compelling set of generalizations about the changing role of white servitude in the colonial economy, but more remains to be done. His evidence is drawn principally from only one of the four types of servants, indentured servants with written contracts. It is incomplete and potentially unrepresentative even for that group, and it is far from certain that his hypotheses can properly be extended to include customary servants, convicts, and redemptioners.[18] The literature on the legal aspects of servitude is fairly complete, but we know much less about the actual functioning of master-servant relationships.[19] We would also

---

51–95; Robert O. Heavner, "Indentured Servitude: The Philadelphia Market, 1771–1773," *Jour. Econ. Hist.*, XXXVIII (1978), 701–713; and Salinger, "Colonial Labor in Transition." Students of this subject would benefit from a close reading of Gabriel Debien, "Les engagés pour les Antilles (1634–1715)," *Revue d'Histoire des Colonies*, XXXVIII (1951), 5–274.

16. A. G. L. Shaw, *Convicts and the Colonies: A Study of Penal Transportation from Great Britain and Ireland to Australia and Other Parts of the British Empire* (London, 1966), 21–37, discusses criminal transportation before and after the Act of 1718. Compare J. S. Cockburn, *A History of English Assizes, 1558–1714* (Cambridge, 1972), 130, 248. See also Trevor Oldham, "The Administration of the System of Transportation of British Convicts, 1763–1793" (Ph.D. thesis, University of London, 1933); Abbot Emerson Smith, "The Transportation of Convicts to the American Colonies in the Seventeenth Century," *AHR*, XXXIX (1934), 232–249; Frederick Hall Schmidt, "British Convict Servant Labor in Colonial Virginia" (Ph.D. diss., College of William and Mary, 1976); L. Walsh, "Servitude and Opportunity"; and Kenneth Morgan, "The Organization of the Convict Trade to Maryland: Stevenson, Randolph & Cheston, 1768–1775," *WMQ*, 3d Ser., forthcoming. Compare Gabriel Debien, "Les engagés pour le Canada partis de Nantes (1725–1732)," *Revue d'Histoire de l'Amérique Française*, XXXIII (1980), 583–586.

17. A. E. Smith, *Colonists in Bondage*, remains the best introduction. See also Schmidt, "British Convict Servant Labor," and Cheesman A. Herrick, *White Servitude in Pennsylvania: Indentured and Redemption Labor in Colony and Commonwealth* (Philadelphia, 1926).

18. The argument is summarized in David W. Galenson, "White Servitude and the Growth of Black Slavery in Colonial America," *Jour. Econ. Hist.*, LXI (1981), 39–47.

19. See, especially, Richard B. Morris, *Government and Labor in Early America* (New York, 1946), and Marcus Wilson Jernegan, *Laboring and Dependent Classes in Colonial*

like to know more about what happened to servants "out of their time," an issue so far explored in detail only for the Chesapeake colonies in the seventeenth century.[20] Finally, apprenticeship in the colonies, the practice of binding out children to learn trades or to work as live-in servants in farm households, needs to be studied. Our impression is that it was primarily an urban institution, although variations on apprenticeship were developed to care for orphans in the countryside, but we know too little to be certain. We would like to know how common it was and could benefit from better information about its institutional arrangements and functions.[21]

Although of more persistent interest than white servitude, the economic history of slavery in early British America still invites further research. Modern efforts, despite their impressive bulk, have focused on fairly traditional issues regarding the law, race relations, religion, abolitionism, and slave resistance. This emphasis is beginning to shift as the demography and the economics of slavery in the South and on the islands

---

America, 1607–1783 (Chicago, [1931]). Several older and largely institutional studies are of limited usefulness. See James Curtis Ballagh, *White Servitude in the Colony of Virginia: A Study of the System of Indentured Labor in the American Colonies* (Baltimore, 1895); John Spencer Bassett, *Slavery and Servitude in the Colony of North Carolina* (Baltimore, 1896); Karl Frederick Geiser, *Redemptioners and Indentured Servants in the Colony and Commonwealth of Pennsylvania* (New Haven, Conn., [1901]); Eugene Irving McCormac, *White Servitude in Maryland, 1634–1820* (Baltimore, 1904); and Warren B. Smith, *White Servitude in Colonial South Carolina* (Columbia, S.C., 1961). The decline of the institution needs study, but see William Miller, "The Effects of the American Revolution on Indentured Servitude," *Pa. Hist.*, VII (1940), 131–141, and Salinger, "Labor and Indentured Servants." Oscar and Mary F. Handlin, "Origins of the Southern Labor System," *WMQ*, 3d Ser., VII (1950), 199–222, remains a compelling, if incorrect, account of the changing legal position of servants.

20. Studies of opportunity for ex-servants in the Chesapeake are discussed in chap. 6, above. Hilary McD. Beckles is beginning to report the results of research on former servants in the West Indies. See "Land Distribution and Class Formation in Barbados, 1630–1700: The Rise of a Wage Proletariat," *Jour. Barbados Museum and Hist. Soc.*, XXXVI (1980), 136–143.

21. R. B. Morris, *Government and Labor*, 363–389, is a good introduction to apprenticeship. See also Lawrence William Towner, "A Good Master Well Served: A Social History of Servitude in Massachusetts, 1620–1750" (Ph.D. diss., Northwestern University, 1955). Lois Green Carr, "The Development of the Maryland Orphan's Court, 1654–1715," in *Law, Society, and Politics*, ed. Land, Carr, and Papenfuse, 41–62, describes arrangements developed to care for orphans. On live-in servants in rural New England, see Demos, *Little Commonwealth*, 107–117. The concept of "life-cycle service" suggests a promising approach to the issues. See Peter Laslett, *Family Life and Illicit Love in Earlier Generations: Essays in Historical Sociology* (Cambridge, 1977), 34, and Ann Kussmaul, *Servants in Husbandry in Early Modern England* (Cambridge, 1981).

come to occupy a greater place in the literature, but research and analysis reflecting the change has just gotten under way.[22]

The 1970s witnessed a multitude of efforts to reinterpret the history of slavery in the United States, the principal areas of investigation being the degree of slave autonomy, the structure of black families, and the organization of the plantation community. The latest endeavors have had two thrusts. They have tried to view slaves as active participants in the creation of slave societies, rather than as passive victims of their Euro-American oppressors. And they have attempted to specify the effect of slavery on southern economic development. Yet these studies have often concentrated on the immediate antebellum period and thus have implied that slavery was a relatively static, homogeneous system. Despite their somewhat ahistorical quality, these investigations have been a fruitful source of hypotheses. Perhaps the preeminent opportunity awaiting economic historians of slavery in early British America lies in extending those hypotheses back into the past and testing them against the evidence of the colonial period.[23]

Free wageworkers in early British America have rarely been studied. This is as it should be, one might argue, since there were relatively few of them. Most men and women who worked for wages did so only briefly, when they were young and before they married. High wages, ample occasions for employment, and cheap land guaranteed diligent and frugal workers a quick accumulation of the capital required to set up as independent farmers. In colonial cities, however, wageworkers were a prominent part of the labor force. Since scholarship has focused almost exclusively on their political activities, we know little about their economic position, their incomes and living standards, the regularity of their employment, their working conditions, or their fortunes.

What hard evidence there is suggests that the traditional picture of "comfortable" living standards, steady work at "very high wages," "general prosperity," and "abundance for the common man" is too opti-

22. Recent reviews of the literature include Peter H. Wood, "'I Did the Best I Could for My Day': The Study of Early Black History during the Second Reconstruction, 1960 to 1976," *WMQ*, 3d Ser., XXXV (1978), 185–225, and Berlin, "Time, Space, and Afro-American Society." Joseph C. Miller, *Slavery: A Comparative Teaching Bibliography* (Honolulu, Hawaii, 1977), is comprehensive. A supplement designed to update that listing is now in preparation.

23. A review of recent literature on slavery in the antebellum United States is beyond the scope of this book, but two essays will serve to introduce the issues and literature of particular interest to economic historians: Engerman, "Realities of Slavery," and R. Gallman, "Slavery and Southern Economic Growth." Berlin, "Time, Space, and Afro-American Society," is a strong argument in behalf of testing such hypotheses carefully.

mistic.[24] Billy Smith has argued that the "material position [of wage earners] was extremely vulnerable" and that "they were easily driven below the subsistence level by such ordinary occurrences as business cycles, seasonal unemployment, illness, injury, pregnancy or child-care requirements." Urban wageworkers lived in a "world requiring constant vigilance and struggle to survive," and their position deteriorated sharply just prior to the American Revolution.[25] Moreover, some evidence indicates that there was a growing number of wageworkers in densely settled rural areas by the middle decades of the eighteenth century.[26] Additional study of these issues may force some revision in assessments of the performance of the early American economy.

Most of the labor available in British America, especially in the rural areas of the North, was family labor. The household was the predominant unit of production, and the work was done by family members, often without the assistance of outsiders, bound or free. The consequences of this are not fully apparent from the literature of colonial history, while the literature of economics, despite some valuable new studies, offers only limited guidance. Given the importance of family enterprises in the colonial economy, this subject clearly deserves investigation. We elaborate on some of its implications below, but it is noteworthy here that the success of families in meeting their need for workers through reproduction had some bearing on regional variations in the demand for servants, slaves, and hired workers. The insignificance of servitude and slavery in New England, for example, as well as the low level of immigration after 1640, was partly a function of the considerable rates of reproductive increase in the region. The large size of families and the limited commercial possibilities in agriculture combined to prohibit the profitable employment of bound labor on a large scale and to make the area relatively uninviting to free migrants. Conversely, the frequency with which servants appeared

24. Sam Bass Warner, Jr., *The Private City: Philadelphia in Three Periods of Its Growth* (Philadelphia, 1968), 7, 9; Carl Bridenbaugh, *Cities in Revolt: Urban Life in America, 1743–1776* (New York, 1955), 148–284.

25. B. Smith, "Material Lives" (quotations on pp. 201–202). Gary B. Nash's work is central to this reinterpretation. See especially "Poverty and Poor Relief in Pre-Revolutionary Philadelphia," *WMQ*, 3d Ser., XXXIII (1976), 3–30, and "Up from the Bottom in Franklin's Philadelphia," *Past and Present*, LXXVII (1977), 57–83. See also chap. 12, n. 23, below.

26. J. Main, *Social Structure*, 66; Douglas Lamar Jones, "The Strolling Poor: Transiency in Eighteenth-Century Massachusetts," *Jour. Soc. Hist.*, VIII (Spring 1975), 28–54; and Jones, "Poverty and Vagabondage: The Process of Survival in Eighteenth-Century Massachusetts," *New England Historical and Genealogical Register*, CXXXIII (1979), 243–254.

on even small plantations in the early Chesapeake was a function both of the fortunes to be made in tobacco and of the limits to reproduction imposed by local demographic circumstances.[27]

We have little specific information on the price of labor in British America. Obviously, it was expensive relative both to its cost in Europe and to the cost of land in the colonies. Equally obviously, it became relatively cheaper as time progressed. The high price of labor had a profound impact on the economy of early British America. It is often invoked to account for several distinguishing if contradictory features of colonial society: the plantation societies of the South and the small-farm communities of the North; the slow progress of manufactures and the willingness of Americans to adopt labor-saving technology; the intense regional specialization and the diversity of individual farms; and the marked levels of wealth and the slow growth of per capita incomes.[28]

Given the prominent role they assign to the price of labor, historians must alter their ways. It is vital that they stop simply citing contemporary statements that labor was scarce and expensive; they must start the collection of more-precise quantitative data sensitive to variations by region, time, occupation, gender, and skill. Probate inventories are perhaps the chief source of this information for bound workers, although accounts of slave sales are also useful. The most complete slave price series so far published are for the Chesapeake colonies and some data are available for the West Indies, but we could put to good use evidence for other regions and times.[29] Wage series for mariners in Boston and for laborers, mariners, cordwainers, and tailors in Philadelphia have been published of late. They begin as early as the 1720s but are fairly complete only from 1750; they need to be extended in time and space to reflect other periods, cities, and occupations.[30] Wage rates for agricultural laborers remain obscure.[31]

27. See chaps. 5, 6, and 10 above, and chap. 13, below.

28. The classic study is H. J. Habakkuk, *American and British Technology in the Nineteenth Century: The Search for Labour-saving Inventions* (Cambridge, 1962). But see the arguments in Earle and Hoffman, "Foundation of the Modern Economy."

29. Menard, "From Servants to Slaves," 372; Kulikoff, "Tobacco and Slaves," 485–488; K. Davies, *Royal African Company*, 363–364; David W. Galenson, "The Slave Trade to the English West Indies, 1673–1724," *Econ. Hist. Rev.*, 2d Ser., XXXII (1979), 241–249; Galenson, "The Atlantic Slave Trade and the Barbados Market, 1673–1723," *Jour. Econ. Hist.*, XLII (1982), 491–511; U.S. Bureau of the Census, *Historical Statistics*, II, 1174 (Ser. Z 165–168 [compiled by Richard N. Bean]).

30. B. Smith, "Material Lives," 184, 192, 195, 199; Nash, *Urban Crucible*, appendix.

31. But see Manfred Jonas, "Wages in Early Colonial Maryland," *Md. Hist. Mag.*, LI (1956), 27–38, and D. Adams, "One Hundred Years," 90–124. Again, probate records—

One of the commonplace generalizations of early American economic history is that the overwhelming majority of the work force was employed in agriculture. It was roughly 80 percent on the eve of independence by most estimates, a figure derived by subtracting from the total work force those living in large towns or cities and then making some allowance for rural residents with non-farm jobs. Since so large a proportion of the population worked in agriculture at the end of the colonial period, it seems unlikely that the composition of the work force would have changed dramatically from the preceding decades. Perhaps because this point seems unassailable, little analysis or writing has been done on the subject. Apart from Jacob Price's effort to describe the job structure of the larger cities of the North, recent research on the Chesapeake slave population, a few community studies, and some explorations of the relationship between work and wealth, there have been few detailed empirical investigations of the occupational structure in the colonies. The greatest number labored in agriculture, but there were temporal and regional variations that invite better definition.[32]

It is also a commonplace that improvements in human capital played a minimal role in the development of the colonial economy. Yet, while the evidence prohibits precise assessment, it would be unwise to dismiss too quickly the possibility that changes in the competence of the work force influenced the economic history of early British America. Certainly formal education was of slight significance, and most tasks did not demand deep technical knowledge or even basic literacy. But we must not ignore the effect of colonial schools on the subsequent spread of manufacturing technology.[33] "Learning by doing" also led to some gains in productivity.

---

in this case, accounts of administration that occasionally list wages paid for farm work—should yield the needed data. Winifred Rothenberg of Brandeis University is currently assembling a wage series from account books kept by Massachusetts farmers.

32. Price, "Economic Function," 177–185. For other work on urban occupational structures, see Nash, *Urban Crucible*, appendix; Allan Kulikoff, "The Progress of Inequality in Revolutionary Boston," *WMQ*, 3d Ser., XXVIII (1971), 411–412; Papenfuse, *In Pursuit of Profit*, 136; Wolf, *Urban Village*, 106; Goodfriend, "'Too Great a Mixture of Nations,'" 142–150; and Archdeacon, *New York City*, 52–54. For the Chesapeake slave population, see Menard, "Maryland Slave Population," 35–37, 51–53, and Kulikoff, "Tobacco and Slaves," 237–238. Among several community studies concerned with occupational structure, Earle, *Evolution of a Tidewater Settlement System*, is especially helpful. J. Main, *Social Structure*, contains much useful information.

33. Economic historians have not given much attention to the study of education, but this is changing as education is increasingly recognized as having played a key role in economic development. See Richard A. Easterlin, "Why Isn't the Whole World Developed?" *Jour. Econ. Hist.*, XLI (1981), 1–19. On education in early British America, see especially Ber-

Colonial farmers acquired through experience their knowledge of the techniques and crops suited to their environment. In the same way, substantial improvements in productivity accompanied the growth of a native-born slave population.[34] The economic results of "learning by doing" on the farm were probably more significant in the earliest years of settlement. Perhaps the greatest gains in human capital occurred in the commercial sector of the economy, with the gradual rise of an innovative, knowledgeable group of merchants skilled in the mysteries of overseas commerce.[35]

One promising way to answer questions concerning human capital in a colonial economy is through the study of diet, nutrition, and health, topics as yet little studied in British America. These subjects interact with the concerns of economics and demography in a variety of ways. Nutrition, for example, is an accepted index of welfare. Differences in nutrition are recognized as a primary source of variations in labor productivity, morbidity rates, mortality, and fertility. Precise descriptions of diet in the colonies are difficult to come by, but new research demonstrates that probate records again will prove helpful and that anthropometric data can provide a useful summary index of health and nutrition. One need not insist that people are what they eat to make the point that improved diet was a critical component of both higher living standards and greater productivity in the colonial economy.[36]

nard Bailyn, *Education in the Forming of American Society* (Chapel Hill, N.C., 1960); Lawrence A. Cremin, *American Education: The Colonial Experience, 1607–1783* (New York, 1970); Kenneth A. Lockridge, *Literacy in Colonial New England: An Enquiry into the Social Context of Literacy in the Early Modern West* (New York, 1974); and James Axtell, *The School upon a Hill: Education and Society in Colonial New England* (New Haven, Conn., 1974).

34. Changing methods of farming in early British America have not been studied with the attention they deserve, but there is much useful information in Gray, *History of Agriculture in the Southern United States*, and in Bidwell and Falconer, *History of Agriculture in the Northern United States*. E. L. Jones, "Creative Disruptions in American Agriculture, 1620–1820," *Agric. Hist.*, XLVIII (1974), 510–528, is a suggestive study of one aspect of agricultural innovation. For evidence that the growth of a native-born, and thus more thoroughly acculturated, slave population resulted in greater productivity, see Mullin, *Flight and Rebellion, passim.*

35. The emergence of skilled entrepreneurs is a major theme of Bruchey's lively survey, *Roots of American Economic Growth.* See also chap. 16, below.

36. A recent issue of *Historical Methods*, XIV (1981), is devoted to "The Historical Study of Diet and Nutrition." See especially the essay by Sarah F. McMahon, "Provisions Laid Up for the Family: Toward a History of Diet in New England, 1650–1850," 4–21, for a review of the literature on nutritional history and a demonstration of the usefulness of probate records as a source for the study of diet. Other studies of diet in early British America are cited

Cities, it can be argued, have been courted too ardently by students of early British America. "Urban historians," Daniel Scott Smith has observed, "tend to think not only that cities are important, but that . . . they continuously became even more so." [37] This enthusiasm has led on occasion to the neglect of some central structural facts concerning the role of colonial towns. The colonies, even the most urbanized of them, were overwhelmingly rural and remained so into the early nineteenth century. On the eve of independence only 7 to 8 percent of the population of the continental colonies lived in towns, defined as urban places with 2,500 or more inhabitants. The proportion would be still lower if the island colonies were included. After falling to a nadir of 5.1 percent in 1790, the urban portion of the population did not again reach 7 percent until 1810, and it was still below 10 percent in 1830. Furthermore, the continental colonies apparently experienced a minor de-urbanization during the eighteenth century, despite the spectacular growth of the principal seaports. Carl Bridenbaugh estimated that, in 1690, 9 percent of the continental population lived in the five largest towns, a share that had fallen to about 4 percent by 1775. [38]

This is not to deny that cities had power beyond their size. They played a central, dynamic role in the colonial economy and were crucial flashpoints of Revolutionary political activity. As Gary Nash puts it, the "seaboard commercial cities were the cutting edge of economic, social, and political change." [39] Nor is this a call for a moratorium on urban studies in the colonies, since we are clearly far from an adequate understanding of the urban process in early British America. But we do suggest the desirability of a conceptual reorientation, of an interpretive framework able to comprehend both the presence of rapid *urban growth* and the absence of *urbanization* that characterized the colonial settlement pattern. [40]

---

in chap. 14, n. 1, below. On the use of anthropometric data in the study of health and nutrition, see Robert W. Fogel *et al.*, "The Economics of Mortality in North America, 1650–1910: A Description of a Research Project," *Hist. Methods*, XI (1978), 75–108. On the relationship between diet and fertility, see Jane Menken, James Trussell, and Susan Watkins, "The Nutrition Fertility Link: An Evaluation of the Evidence," *JIH*, XI (1981), 425–441, and Peter T. Marcy, "Factors Affecting the Fecundity and Fertility of Historical Populations: A Review," *Journal of Family History*, VI (1981), 309–326.

37. "Malthusian-Frontier Interpretation," 18.

38. *Cities in the Wilderness: The First Century of Urban Life in America, 1625–1742* (New York, 1938), 6. Figures for 1775 to 1830 are from Price, "Economic Function," 175–177, and U.S. Bureau of the Census, *Historical Statistics*, I, 8, 12 (Ser. A 2, 57).

39. *Urban Crucible*, vii.

40. The distinction between the growth of cities and the process of urbanization is drawn by Kingsley Davis, "The Urbanization of the Human Population," *Scientific American*,

Until lately, urban historians of British America contributed little to the elaboration of this kind of framework, developing instead within two distinct historiographical traditions. On the one hand, historians of commerce have investigated the merchant groups in the seaport cities. These studies, although often very useful, have tended to focus so heavily on the late colonial period and on the role of merchants in the independence movement that they have failed to convey a sense of the urban process in British America.[41] On the other hand, there are Bridenbaugh's monumental studies of the primary colonial cities. While these are invaluable source books and quite successful at integrating a variety of themes into a coherent whole, Bridenbaugh was interested essentially in social and institutional history and unsympathetic toward the behavioral questions his information raised. He thus took the urban economy as a given, a perspective that prevented analysis of the dynamics of town growth or the specification of the changing role of cities in the colonies.[42] The past decade, however, has witnessed the application of more-theoretical and potentially more-fruitful modes of investigation.

Sundry modern attempts have been made to apply central-place theory to the colonial settlement pattern, but so far these efforts have been fairly casual. They have yet to identify the highly articulated, tightly integrated hierarchical network of functions that is the hallmark of central-place systems. Nor does it seem likely that further attempts along these lines will prove any more fruitful, at least if the colonial economy is analyzed as a largely self-contained entity and the network not extended to the empire as a whole. Central-place theory, with its emphasis on retailing, its assumption of a largely closed system, and its inability to account for the spatial impact of foreign trade and the demands of particular exports, seems inappropriate to early British America.[43]

CCXIII (Sept. 1965), 41–53. Davis suggests that urbanization be measured by the ratio of urban to total population. For sharp criticism and alternative measures, see Leo F. Schnore and Eric E. Lampard, "Social Science and the City: A Survey of Research Needs," in *Urban Research and Policy Planning*, ed. Leo F. Schnore and Henry Fagin (Beverly Hills, Calif., 1967), 25–29.

41. Arthur Meier Schlesinger, *The Colonial Merchants and the American Revolution, 1763–1776* (New York, 1918); Harrington, *New York Merchant*; A. Jensen, *Maritime Commerce*; and Sellers, *Charleston Business*. For a recent study in this tradition that overcomes many of its weaknesses, see Papenfuse, *In Pursuit of Profit*.

42. *Cities in the Wilderness*, and *Cities in Revolt*.

43. For a useful discussion of central-place theory and efforts to apply it to early British America, see Edward M. Cook, "Geography and History: Spatial Approaches to Early American History," *Hist. Methods*, XIII (1980), 19–28. Such efforts include James T. Lemon, "Urbanization and the Development of Eighteenth-Century Southeastern Penn-

Particularly propitious are efforts based on the staples hypothesis, most clearly expressed in recent essays by Jacob Price and by Carville Earle and Ronald Hoffman. They emphasize the critical role played by the processing, transportation, and marketing requirements of the export sector. Such an approach seems most likely to provide a compelling account of the unique features of the urban process in the colonies: the rapid rise of the several seaport cities; the general failure of urbanization; and the emergence of distinctive urban patterns, each specific to a particular regional economy.[44]

The task of interpreting the urban process in early America cannot proceed without additional empirical effort. To begin, the demography of the major cities requires more research and analysis. The two principal sets of population figures, Carl Bridenbaugh's and W. A. Rossiter's, differ from each other substantially, and as the latest studies of Philadelphia show, both can be wrong. Gary Nash has provided better estimates for Philadelphia, Boston, and New York, but except for the last, which was enumerated with some regularity, these rest on the application of multiples to partial counts, leaving considerable room for error. We still need new estimates for the other big cities, Charleston and Newport, as well as for nearly all the larger towns.[45]

---

sylvania and Adjacent Delaware," *WMQ*, 3d Ser., XXIV (1967), 501–542; Ernst and Merrens, "'Camden's Turrets Pierce the Skies!'"; Cook, *Fathers of the Towns*, 75–80, 175–177; Daniels, *Connecticut Town*, 140–170; and Bonnie Barton, "The Creation of Centrality," Assoc. Am. Geographers, *Annals*, LXVIII (1978), 34–44. The last, a useful commentary on central-place doctrine, attempts an application to New England. Brian J. L. Berry, *The Geography of Market Centers and Retail Distribution* (Englewood Cliffs, N.J., 1967), is the standard recent account of the model.

44. Price, "Economic Function," 123–186; Earle and Hoffman, "Staple Crops"; and Earle and Hoffman, "Urban South," 23–51. James E. Vance, Jr., *The Merchant's World: The Geography of Wholesaling* (Englewood Cliffs, N.J., 1970), provides a useful perspective. Carville V. Earle, "The First English Towns of North America," *Geographical Rev.*, LXVII (1977), 34–50, is a suggestive account of site selection and urban growth in the early colonial period. A. F. Burghardt, "A Hypothesis about Gateway Cities," Assoc. Am. Geographers, *Annals*, LXI (1971), 269–285; Michael P. Conzen, "A Transport Interpretation of the Growth of Urban Regions: An American Example," *Jour. Hist. Geography*, I (1975), 361–382; and J. Richard Peet, "The Spatial Expansion of Commercial Agriculture in the Nineteenth Century: A Von Thünen Interpretation," *Economic Geography*, XLV (1969), 283–301, describe approaches that should prove useful to historians of urban British America.

45. Bridenbaugh, *Cities in the Wilderness*, 6, 143, 303; Bridenbaugh, *Cities in Revolt*, 5, 216–217. Rossiter's estimates are in U.S. Bureau of the Census, *Century of Population Growth*, 11, 78. For recent work on Philadelphia, see Alexander, "Philadelphia Numbers Game," and G. Nash and Smith, "Population of Eighteenth-Century Philadelphia." Nash's population estimates are in *Urban Crucible*, appendix.

Research on vital rates in urban British America has just begun, but Billy G. Smith's fresh investigation of Philadelphia suggests marked differences between cities and rural areas. Smith reports very considerable (and sharply variable) birth and death rates caused by high levels of in-migration, which resulted in low, sometimes negative, reproductive growth. However, he is forced to rely on aggregate techniques that leave a wide margin for error and are especially sensitive to estimates of total population. Smith is unable fully to segregate natives and long-term residents from newly arrived immigrants, a requirement critical to understanding urban demography, as his excellent exposition makes clear. While additional analysis with aggregated data would be welcome, the techniques of reconstitution—particularly laborious with large and very mobile urban populations—seem necessary in order to estimate more-reliable, group-specific vital rates.[46] Smith further demonstrates that migration was central to the growth process in Philadelphia, but except for some analysis of Boston "warnings out" and some crude measures of persistence, we know relatively little about population movements as they affected urban British America. Greater emphasis on migration is essential to a precise understanding of the demography of colonial cities.[47]

The past decade has also witnessed some powerful advances in the study of urban social structure. Jacob Price has demonstrated that much can be learned from rough descriptions of occupational patterns; they can provide useful clues to economic functions. But, as Price himself warns us, the data are rough and describe only the three largest cities of the North during the late eighteenth century. This kind of investigation must also be refined and extended both back in time and to smaller towns, if Price's attractive hypotheses relating function, size, growth, and marketing networks are to be thoroughly tested.[48]

A good deal of writing has also been done recently on wealth and welfare patterns in Boston, New York, and Philadelphia. These studies are plagued by debilitating, perhaps intractable, evidential problems, and there is considerable disagreement concerning trends in wealth concen-

---

46. "Death and Life in a Colonial Immigrant City: A Demographic Analysis of Philadelphia," *Jour. Econ. Hist.*, XXXVII (1977), 863–889. See also John B. Blake, *Public Health in the Town of Boston, 1630–1822* (Cambridge, Mass., 1959), and Susan Edith Klepp, "Philadelphia in Transition: A Demographic History of the City and Its Occupational Groups, 1720–1830" (Ph.D. diss., University of Pennsylvania, 1980). Allan Sharlin, "Natural Decrease in Early Modern Cities: A Reconsideration," *Past and Present*, LXXIX (1978), 126–138, is a good introduction to the general issues.

47. Kulikoff, "Progress of Inequality."

48. "Economic Function," 123–186. These hypotheses are discussed in chaps. 6, 8, and 9, above.

tration. Nonetheless, a general consensus has already been reached concerning the prospects for success in the cities during the colonial period. In the decades just prior to independence, the working poor in all the larger cities apparently suffered a sharp deterioration in living standards, a deterioration evident in falling real wages, growing unemployment, and swelling poor taxes and relief rolls. The findings present a paradox, for these were also years of rapid commercial expansion and substantial population growth, fueled in large part by high rates of in-migration. If the cities offered so little, it is difficult to understand why they continued to attract so many immigrants from Europe and from their own rural hinterlands.[49]

Although some rural inhabitants moved to cities and towns in search of success, their numbers were dwarfed by the much larger migration to the agricultural frontier. This extension of rural settlement was a central dynamic in the early American economy, because the chance to move to new regions where land was cheap permitted elevated rates of intrinsic reproductive increase without straining the resource base. Indeed, not a few of the distinctive characteristics of British American economic history have been attributed to this process. The persistent importance of small family farms, the combination of high wages and incomes with low levels of inequality, the failure of urbanization and the slow development of industry, and the stubborn refusal of American farmers to adopt the progressive techniques of European agriculture have been traced to the ease of migration.[50]

Given the seeming significance of internal migration and the spread of settlement, it is surprising that they have been so little studied. Basic questions concerning the pace and pattern of internal migration in the colonies await answers. We want to know more about the people who moved—their age and sex composition, their position in the communities they left, and their motivations. Were they predominantly young unattached males or were they drawn from a broader spectrum of the population? Did they come largely from the lower ranks or were more-prosperous individuals well represented? Were most of them pushed by declining prospects at home or pulled by the promise of prosperity at the margin of settlement? We also need to know more about the financing of migration, particularly about the relative roles of family members, public land banks, and private land developers in providing the necessary capital. Questions like these direct attention to the interaction among devel-

49. See n. 25, above, and chap. 12, below.
50. See D. S. Smith, "Malthusian-Frontier Interpretation," 15–23.

opments at the level of the entire Atlantic economy, the several colonial regions, the particular town, and the individual decision to move or stay.[51]

The literature on the economic history of early British America contains two distinct but poorly specified and even contradictory models concerning the relationship between the growth of population and the development of the economy. According to one model, population growth, by expanding the size of the domestic market, permitted specialization, the division of labor, and the capture of various scale economies in the distribution of goods and services and thus promoted development.[52] On the other hand, a classic Malthusian argument is often invoked to describe a process in which population increase pressed against the local resource base and led to diminished yields, falling incomes, declining prospects, and growing inequality, tendencies only partially checked by movement to the frontier.[53]

These differences could be a function of the weight attached to short-term as opposed to long-term considerations. The immediate result of a growing population might have been to depress incomes, but over a longer period that growth could have produced responses leading to a net gain in welfare. The issues, however, are too complex for resolution by a

51. D. Jones, *Village and Seaport*, is the most thorough study of the issues. It provides a review of the literature and a useful discussion of methods and sources. See also chap. 14, below; Rutman, "People in Process"; W. R. Prest, "Stability and Change in Old and New England: Clayworth and Dedham," *JIH*, VI (1976), 359–374; Thomas R. Cole, "Family, Settlement, and Migration in Southeastern Massachusetts, 1650–1805: The Case for Regional Analysis," *NEHGR*, CXXXII (1978), 171–185; and John J. Waters, Jr., "Family, Inheritance, and Migration in Colonial New England: The Evidence from Guilford, Connecticut," *WMQ*, 3d Ser., XXXIX (1982), 64–86. Larry Dale Gragg, *Migration in Early America: The Virginia Quaker Experience* (Ann Arbor, Mich., 1980), provides useful detail on the movement of Pennsylvania Quakers to the south and west. Several recent studies of marital migration in New England deserve mention here: Alan C. Swedlund, "The Genetic Structure of an Historical Population: A Study of Marriage and Fertility in Old Deerfield, Massachusetts," Department of Anthropology, University of Massachusetts, Amherst, *Research Reports*, no. 7 (May 1971); Susan L. Norton, "Marital Migration in Essex County, Massachusetts, in the Colonial and Early Federal Periods," *Jour. Marriage and Family*, XXXV (1973), 406–418; Doris O'Keefe, "Marriage and Migration in Colonial New England: A Study in Historical Population Geography," Department of Geography, Syracuse University, *Discussion Paper Series*, no. 16 (June 1976); Cathy Kelly, "Marriage Migration in Massachusetts, 1765–1790," *ibid.*, no. 30 (Mar. 1977); and John W. Adams and Alice B. Kasakoff, "Migration at Marriage in Colonial New England: A Comparison of Rates Derived from Genealogies with Rates from Vital Records," in *Genealogical Demography*, ed. Bennett Dyke and Warren T. Morrill (New York, 1980), 115–138.

52. Shepherd and Walton, *Shipping*, chap. 2.

53. See chap. 12, below.

simple adjustment of temporal scope. The relationship between population increase (or decrease) and economic growth (or decline) is indeterminate without a thorough specification of the context: the positing of direct, one-way effects is simply inadequate. As Albert O. Hirschman has expressed it, "Population pressure on living standards will lead to counterpressure," to efforts to maintain incomes. If successful, these efforts can result in actual gains, even in the short run. For example, the productive members of a family may respond to a new arrival by working harder. Conversely, in situations in which no such response is possible, a strict Malthusian system would operate. If all productive resources were fully and optimally employed—hardly the case in early British America—a growth in population would inevitably produce a "dilution" of income.[54] However, while the most dismal implications of Malthusian population economics are easily rejected for the colonies, it would be an error to substitute a fully sanguine set of suppositions. Population growth was very rapid in British America, and the oft-quoted phrase from Lewis Carroll seems an appropriate caution: "Now, *here*, it takes all the running *you* can do to keep in the same place" (*Through the Looking Glass and What Alice Found There*). Certainly the issues demand close empirical study.

Studies like these ought to proceed on two fronts. First, they must examine the impact of population growth on the colonial economy as a whole. How substantial were the gains from larger domestic markets? And who benefited from them? Was it merely that scale economies in distribution led to lower consumer prices for foreign goods, or did larger markets provide an opening for local entrepreneurs? How successful were such investments in overcoming "the tyranny of distance" that limited the access of backcountry farmers to international markets? Did the growing number of children lead to improved public education and subsequent gains in human capital? Did the sum of these benefits at least equal the costs imposed by heightened dependency ratios, resource depletion, a denser population, and the extension of settlement to more-marginal locations? And if they did, when did they begin to operate? Certainly a sizable population was necessary to the eventual development of the United States economy, but we wish to know how long it took before some returns were realized.

Second, these studies must examine responses at the household level to growth in the entire population as well as to enlargement in the size of particular families. One frequent assumption—that, other things being equal, each birth tended toward not only an initial reduction in per capita income within families but also a diminished propensity to save—

54. Hirschman, *Strategy of Economic Development*, 176–182 (quotation on p. 177).

clearly needs reexamination. There is evidence that farmers in other times and places often responded to additional children with greater work efforts and higher rates of investment. This last consideration suggests the potential contained in the application of economic theory to the analysis of family strategies, a promise that historians of early British America have yet to pursue.[55]

55. For a thorough critique of Malthusian population economics, see Julian L. Simon, *The Economics of Population Growth* (Princeton, N.J., 1977), and Ester Boserup's minor classic, *The Conditions of Agricultural Growth: The Economics of Agrarian Change under Population Pressure* (London, 1965). Boserup puts the issues as follows: "The first important thing to note about agricultural investment is that a large share of it can be carried out by the cultivators themselves. Furthermore, it is normal for cultivators to have shorter or longer periods of leisure each year when current agricultural work is at a minimum so that working capacity for additional investment is normally available. In other words, the question is not whether the cultivators are able and willing to restrain consumption in order to invest. The question is whether an increasing family provides sufficient incentive to additional work and whether the system of land tenure is such that the cultivators have access to additional cultivable land or sufficient security of tenure to make land improvements a worthwhile investment" (p. 88). See also Boserup, *Population and Technology*.

W E A L T H   A N D   W E L F A R E

Economic and social historians have become more and more concerned with wealth and its distribution in early British America. Did the colonial economy grow in per capita wealth and income? If so, when, where, and why? And at what rates did wealth and income rise? How were the rewards of the economy distributed and how did that distribution vary across region and time? In recent years the literature on these questions has grown rapidly in bulk and sophistication. Some patterns are beginning to emerge, and we can now describe the course of wealth and welfare in several localities and identify the process behind those movements. But much detailed empirical work remains to be done, several major issues are unresolved and subject to debate, and many questions are yet to be explored. This chapter assesses the existing literature, suggests where we might go from here, and surveys the types of sources likely to prove most productive and the methods appropriate to their use. Finally, the chapter offers, with caution and more than the usual trepidation, tentative comments on patterns in the movement of wealth and welfare and some suggestions on the dynamics of change.

Historians of colonial America have been concerned more with the distribution of wealth than with its growth. This is perhaps because distribution seems to have obvious political implications, especially for the Revolutionary War era, and because economic "justice" is central to the democratic, egalitarian ideals of American society. The lack of interest in growth also may reflect the structure of the colonial economy: when measured *extensively* its performance was impressive, but those rapid increases in population, settled area, and total product were accomplished without striking *intensive* changes leading to a substantial rise in income per capita. It was not until the new economic history, characteristically concerned with growth, began to penetrate the colonial era that the issue commanded scholarly attention and direct measurement was attempted. This recent work has not challenged conventional wisdom, but it has improved our knowledge of colonial living standards, changes in wealth levels, and the source of the gains in output achieved in British America.

The new interest in the growth of the colonial economy was born in debate. The origins of the controversy are to be found in the 1959 testimony of Raymond W. Goldsmith before the Joint Economic Committee of the Eighty-sixth Congress. Almost as an afterthought, he made some remarks concerning the annual average rate of economic growth in the colonies that became the United States (i.e., excluding the West Indies). After noting that the growth rate in real national product per head had hovered around 1⅝ percent in the 120 years after 1839, Goldsmith asked rhetorically whether such a rate could have prevailed in the years before 1839. He concluded that it could not have, for two reasons. On the one hand, unless income per head in the mid-eighteenth century had been less than one-half what it was in the mid-nineteenth century, which seems highly unlikely, then the average annual compound growth rate between 1760 and 1839 could have been no higher than 0.6 percent. On the other hand, what if "the measured rate of growth actually had averaged 1⅝ percent before 1839 as it has since"?

> Average real income per head in 1839 may be estimated at about $400 in present [1959] prices. If the trend observed since 1839 had been in force before that date, average income per head in today's prices would have been about $145 in 1776, $80 in 1739, and less than $30 in 1676. It takes only a little consideration of the minimum requirements for keeping body and soul together, even in the simpler conditions prevailing in colonial America, to conclude that at present prices for individual commodities an average level of income below $200 is fairly well ruled out for 1776 or even the early 18th century.

"There seems little doubt, then," Goldsmith concluded, "that the average rate of growth of real income per head was much lower than 1⅝ percent before 1839. If we consider periods of at least 50 years' length, it is questionable that we would find an average rate of growth as high as 1 percent for any of them."[1]

George Rogers Taylor, while agreeing that the period from initial colonization to 1840 as a whole witnessed low rates of growth, identified three distinct eras in the performance of the early American economy.

1. Statement of Raymond W. Goldsmith, in United States Congress, Joint Economic Committee, 86th Congress, 1st sess., *Employment, Growth, and Price Levels: Hearings . . . Part 2—Historical and Comparative Rates of Production, Productivity, and Prices* (Washington, D.C., 1959), 278, and as reprinted (with some mistakes) in Ralph L. Andreano, ed., *New Views on American Economic Development: A Selective Anthology of Recent Work* (Cambridge, Mass., 1965), 355. Goldsmith's choice of dates depended only on the availability of data for those years based on materials in the censuses.

The seventeenth century was characterized by "slow and uneven" growth, and the "level of living remained relatively low . . . as late as about 1710." Similarly, during the Revolutionary and early national periods, from 1775 to 1840, "output per capita improved slowly if at all." Taylor then offered three working assumptions: that "per capita income was relatively low in 1710"; that the United States was a fairly wealthy nation in 1840; and that "per capita income in 1840 was about the same or at least not substantially higher than in the early 1770s." He concluded "that relatively rapid growth must have characterized the years from 1710 to 1775." A casual empiricism persuaded Taylor that per capita income doubled in the 65 years before the Revolution, implying a growth rate of just over 1 percent per year.[2]

More recently, Robert Gallman has offered a substantial revision of Taylor's description of the growth pattern. In the first place, according to Gallman, Taylor probably underestimated per capita income at the beginning of the eighteenth century. His figure of about $45 in 1840 prices implies a total income "about equal in real terms to the per capita level of *food and fuel consumption* of the United States in the mid-nineteenth century." This, Gallman posits, is a "very doubtful proposition," and "it is best to regard Taylor's estimate as a lower limit." As an upper limit, Gallman suggests English per capita income, roughly $60 in 1840 prices. Second, Taylor's view of the Revolutionary and early national growth experience is much "too unfavorable." Instead of stagnation from 1774 to 1840, the best evidence describes a growth rate of at least 0.3 percent per annum. The net result of both a higher level of income in 1710 and a faster rate of growth after 1774 is a substantial reduction of the annual growth rate during the eighteenth century, from the somewhat more than 1 percent suggested by Taylor to between 0.1 percent and 0.6 percent.[3]

---

2. Taylor, "American Economic Growth before 1840: An Exploratory Essay," *Jour. Econ. Hist.*, XXIV (1964), 427, 443–444.

3. [Gallman], "Pace and Pattern of Growth," 17–25 (quotations on pp. 20, 21, 23). Andreano, in *New Views on American Economic Development*, reached similar conclusions on the following grounds: "The trend rate of population growth between 1650 and 1770 was 3.30%, compounded annually. To keep total output growing at the same rate as population therefore implies an annual rate of growth of 3.30%. If an increase of 1% in national output requires that 3½% must be invested (an assumption made for illustrative purposes only), then in the previous example the colonial economy would have to have invested annually 15.05% of its national product. To allow for a 1% increase in income or output per head would require annually investing 18½% of national product. It seems improbable that the colonial economy could have achieved these levels of capital investment or of the implied expansion in total output. This suggests, therefore, that the average per capita per annum increase in national output must have been below 1% and more than likely in the

Despite their different results, the methods of Taylor and Gallman share two characteristics. First, their conclusions about the colonial economy rest heavily on estimates of performance in the postcolonial era. If income per capita grew from 1776 to 1840, it could not have grown rapidly before the Revolution; if it did not grow between 1776 and 1840, high rates of growth in the eighteenth century are needed to explain the living standards that prevailed in the United States in 1840.[4] Second, both

---

range of zero to .5% per annum" (pp. 50–51). We would note, by contrast, our sense that savings rates were very high in early British America, particularly in regions of most recent settlement, and that foreign investors provided some of the needed capital.

4. The performance of the U.S. economy in the early 19th century is beyond the scope of this book, but given its impact on judgments of colonial growth, a brief summary of work on the issue seems necessary. Until the late 1960s, the orthodox position argued for rapid growth during the trade boom of the Napoleonic era, followed by a collapse after the embargo of 1807 and three decades of stagnation in per capita income until a takeoff into sustained growth began in the late 1830s or early 1840s. The main proponents of this position were Robert F. Martin (who argued for an actual decline in incomes from 1809 to 1839 and whose methods have been thoroughly and effectively criticized), Douglass C. North, Barry W. Poulson, Marvin W. Towne and Wayne D. Rasmussen, and W. W. Rostow. See Martin, *National Income in the United States, 1799–1938* (New York, 1939); North, *Economic Growth*; Poulson, *Value Added in Manufacturing, Mining, and Agriculture in the American Economy from 1809 to 1839* (New York, 1975 [Ph.D. diss., Ohio State University, 1965]); Towne and Rasmussen, "Farm Gross Product and Gross Investment in the Nineteenth Century" (with comment by Clarence H. Danhof), in *Trends in the American Economy in the Nineteenth Century*, [ed. William N. Parker] (Princeton, N.J., 1960), 255–315; and Rostow, *The Stages of Economic Growth: A Non-Communist Manifesto* (Cambridge, Mass., 1960). Early reservations against this synthesis were registered by Simon Kuznets, "National Income Estimates for the United States prior to 1870," *Jour. Econ. Hist.*, XII (1952), 115–130, and by William N. Parker and Franklee Whartenby, "The Growth of Output before 1840" (with comment by Samuel Rezneck), in *Trends in the American Economy*, [ed. Parker], 191–216. The orthodox view was challenged in a stimulating essay by Paul A. David, "The Growth of Real Product in the United States before 1840: New Evidence, Controlled Conjectures," *ibid.*, XXVII (1967), 151–195. See also David, "Technical Appendices to U.S. Real Product Growth before 1840: New Evidence, Controlled Conjectures," Research Center in Economic Growth, Stanford University, Memorandum no. 53-A (1966); David, "New Light on a Statistical Dark Age: U.S. Real Product Growth before 1840," *Am. Econ. Rev.*, LVII (1967), 294–306; Moses Abramovitz and Paul David, "Reinterpreting Economic Growth: Parables and Realities," *ibid.*, LXIII (1973), 428–439; and David, "Invention and Accumulation in America's Economic Growth: A Nineteenth-Century Parable," in *International Organization, National Policies, and Economic Development*, ed. Karl Brunner and Allan H. Meltzer (Amsterdam, 1977), 179–228. David argued that modest increases in agricultural productivity and shifts of labor out of agriculture to more-productive activities together produced a growth rate of 1.3% per annum in per capita real gross domestic product between 1790 and 1840. Growth occurred in two upward surges, 1790 to 1806 and 1820 to 1835, followed by periods of retardation, but there was no secular acceleration of the rate during the antebellum era. Thomas Senior Berry reached a simi-

men based their judgments on indirect evidence and deduction rather than on observations of measured growth. In contrast, within the past decade historians have increasingly separated assessments of the colonial economy from those of the early national period and at the same time have developed direct measures of economic progress. Much work remains—indeed, efforts to untangle the difficult methodological issues that surround the measurement of growth in early British America have just begun—but there have been some advances. Given the centrality of the issue to evaluating the performance of the colonial economy, we can expect more progress in the near future.

Progress toward the direct measurement of wealth levels in British America stems from work with probate records that was pioneered by Robert E. Brown, Jackson Turner Main, Richard Sheridan, Aubrey Land, and especially, Alice Hanson Jones.[5] Jones achieved a major breakthrough by demonstrating that per capita wealth estimates could be coaxed out of

---

lar conclusion by a different route. See *Estimated Annual Variations in Gross National Product, 1789 to 1900* (Richmond, Va., 1968), and his *Revised Annual Estimates*. More recently, Robert Gallman has argued for a lower overall growth rate than that reported by David and an acceleration (but not a takeoff) in the rate of growth. See "The Statistical Approach: Fundamental Concepts as Applied to History," in *Approaches to American Economic History*, ed. George Rogers Taylor and Lucius F. Ellsworth (Charlottesville, Va., 1971), 63–86; "Changes in Total U.S. Agricultural Factor Productivity in the Nineteenth Century," *Agric. Hist.*, XLVI (1972), 191–210; "Pace and Pattern of Growth," 17–25; and "The Agricultural Sector and the Pace of Economic Growth: U.S. Experience in the Nineteenth Century," in *Essays in Nineteenth Century Economic History: The Old Northwest*, ed. David C. Klingaman and Richard K. Vedder (Athens, Ohio, 1975), 35–76. See also Claudia D. Goldin and Frank D. Lewis, "The Role of Exports in American Economic Growth during the Napoleonic Wars, 1793 to 1807," *Explorations Econ. Hist.*, XVII (1980), 6–25. For important studies at the regional level, see Lindstrom, *Economic Development*, and Lindstrom, "American Economic Growth before 1840: New Evidence and New Directions," *Jour. Econ. Hist.*, XXXIX (1979), 289–301, with comments by David and R. Gallman, *ibid.*, 303–312. A thoughtful commentary on the debate and the issues, along with suggestions for further research, is provided by Engerman and Gallman, "U.S. Economic Growth."

5. Brown, *Middle-Class Democracy and the Revolution in Massachusetts, 1691–1780* (Ithaca, N.Y., 1955); J. Main, *Social Structure*; Sheridan, "Wealth of Jamaica"; Land, "Economic Base and Social Structure"; Land, "Economic Behavior in a Planting Society." Jones has reported her work on probate inventories in numerous publications, the most important being *Wealth of a Nation to Be*, and *American Colonial Wealth: Documents and Methods*, 2d ed., rev. (New York, 1978). See also Jones, "La fortune privée"; "Wealth Estimates for the Middle Colonies"; and "Wealth Estimates for the New England Colonies about 1770," *Jour. Econ. Hist.*, XXXII (1972), 98–127. Bruce C. Daniels provides a survey of work in early American history based on probate records in "Probate Court Inventories and Colonial American History: Historiography, Problems, and Results," *Histoire Sociale/Social History*, IX (1976), 387–405.

colonial sources. In the process she produced a body of scholarship that, in its explicit discussion of methods and assumptions, imaginative approach to problems of estimation and adjustment, careful consideration of bias, statistical rigor, ease of replication, and presentation of underlying data, provides a model for social science history.

Jones's concern was to estimate private wealth in the thirteen colonies on the eve of the Revolution and to describe its components and distribution. She proceeded by drawing a small, unbiased sample of probate inventories for each of three major regions—New England, the Middle Colonies, and the South. In order to describe fully the property of the decedent population, the inventories were supplemented with other sources and adjusted to comprehend otherwise omitted assets and wealth owners. These estimates for wealth at death were then corrected for age bias and "blown up" to represent the private wealth of the living circa 1774. The results, Jones hopes, are reasonably accurate estimates of the distribution and components of wealth for several categories of inhabitants at the end of the colonial period. If correct within an acceptable margin of error, the figures provide a powerful analytical tool and an important benchmark for the economic history of early British America and the United States.

Probate inventories are certainly the most valuable source available to historians of colonial wealth and welfare, but these records are full of pitfalls and demand careful handling. The major difficulties are four in number and plague all who use the records of the dead to study the wealth of the living. First, inventories do not always report complete assets for decedents who entered probate. Outside of New England, real estate was rarely inventoried, while financial assets and liabilities were reported only irregularly in all the colonies. Furthermore, in some colonies legacies specifically mentioned in wills were not inventoried, nor was the third of the estate due the widow. Second, not all decedent wealth holders entered probate and not all estates that entered probate were inventoried. It seems reasonable to assume, as Jones does, that decedents who entered probate but whose assets were not inventoried possessed on average wealth similar to those whose assets were. However, it is unlikely, as she notes, that decedents who did enter probate form an unbiased sample of all decedent wealth owners. Third, since age and wealth are highly correlated and decedent wealth owners would generally be older than living property owners, inventories must be weighted by age to describe the assets of the population as a whole. Not all will be satisfied with the weighting procedures adopted by Jones, but again, what is important is that she has tried conscientiously to develop methods to deal with the issue. Fourth, inventories were appraised in local currencies that must be transformed into standard values to permit comparison across space or time.

All of these deficiencies demand complex adjustments based on figures of uncertain reliability and, upon occasion, on outright guesses. While Jones demonstrates great skill in identifying and correcting bias, occasions to disagree with, qualify, and improve upon what she has done are plentiful. We expect that Jones's work will provoke a long and fruitful debate as scholars try to assess the quality of her results and tinker with her estimates.[6] Given the centrality of probate records to recent work in colonial economic history, satisfactory resolution of these several difficulties is a high priority.[7]

In addition to the problems inherent in probate records, questions have been raised about the specific procedures that Jones adopted. Although probably necessary, the decision to focus on a single year rather than a cluster of years is troublesome, for the values reported by probate inventories, particularly financial assets and liabilities, fluctuated violently in response to the changing fortunes of the export sector.[8] Her division of the colonies into three regions limits the usefulness of the results, particularly because the sample design prohibits further breakdown. If research costs allowed for only minimal regionalization, perhaps the

6. Extensive reviews of Jones's work include Linda Auwers, "History from the Mean—Up, Down, and Around: A Review Essay," *Hist. Methods*, XII (1979), 39–45; Carville Earle, "A Geographer's Observation of an Economist's Pursuit of 'Exact History,'" *Annals of Scholarship*, I (1980), 107–117; Peter Lindert, "An Algorithm for Probate Sampling," *JIH*, XI (1981), 649–668; David W. Galenson, "Measuring Colonial Wealth," *Revs. Am. Hist.*, IX (1981), 49–54; Maris A. Vinovskis, "Estimating the Wealth of Americans on the Eve of the Revolution," *Jour. Econ. Hist.*, XLI (1981), 415–420; and Allan Kulikoff, "Growth and Welfare in Early America," *WMQ*, 3d Ser., XXXIX (1982), 359–365. Jones has responded to her critics in "Estimating Wealth of the Living from a Probate Sample," *JIH*, XIII (1982), 273–300.

7. Useful discussions of such difficulties and of appropriate strategies for correction are provided by Jones, *American Colonial Wealth*, III; Gloria L. Main, "The Correction of Biases in Colonial American Probate Records," *Hist. Methods Newsletter*, VIII (1974), 10–28; Main, "Probate Records as a Source for Early American History," *WMQ*, 3d Ser., XXXII (1975), 89–99; Daniel Scott Smith, "Underregistration and Bias in Probate Records: An Analysis of Data from Eighteenth-Century Hingham, Massachusetts," *ibid.*, 100–110; Carr and Walsh, "Inventories and Analysis of Wealth"; Carole Shammas, "Constructing a Wealth Distribution from Probate Records," *JIH*, IX (1978), 297–307; Jacob M. Price, "Quantifying Colonial America: A Comment on Nash and Warden," *ibid.*, VI (1976), 701–709; and Harold B. Gill, Jr., and George M. Curtis III, "Virginia's Colonial Probate Policies and the Preconditions for Economic History," *VMHB*, LXXXVII (1979), 68–73. Most of the probate-based work cited in this chapter contains some methodological discussion.

8. Menard, Harris, and Carr, "Opportunity and Inequality."

South rather than the North should have been subdivided, for a case can be made that structural differences in economic organization between New England and the Middle Colonies were smaller than those within the South—between the Chesapeake, the lowland areas of Georgia and the Carolinas, and the backcountry. Finally, questions can be raised about the adequacy of the sample. While designed to generate an unbiased wealth estimate for probated decedents, the sample is small, especially when subdivided by region, and the standard error large; one wonders if the numbers are sufficient to support the elaborate weighting and adjustment needed to generate figures for the living population and still produce reliable results.

Whatever the doubts, Jones's accomplishment is impressive. She has provided usable estimates of wealth and welfare patterns for all the mainland colonies, against which future findings can be tested. Close assessment of the quality of her results, reestimation as new data become available, and extension of the techniques both forward into the nineteenth century and back into the earlier colonial period promise to yield a more precise description of the pattern of economic growth than seemed possible before Jones began her work.

Even though probate inventories are difficult to use, their exploitation along lines suggested by Jones provides the best chance for measuring wealth and describing its components and distribution. Efforts to extend and refine Jones's work are now under way for the Chesapeake colonies and New England, as recent publications by Gloria Main, Terry Anderson, Allan Kulikoff, Paul Clemens, and the several scholars associated with the St. Mary's City Commission testify, but much work remains.[9] Because it becomes progressively more difficult to construct colonial-wide studies as one moves back in time, the immediate future will likely see an emphasis on sharply focused regional studies concerned with change rather than on efforts to measure wealth in all of British America for a particular period. Such an approach permits projects of manageable scale that can fully exploit consistent sets of records and bring intimate knowledge of small units to bear upon the results. The major drawback of this approach, a drawback that Jones's method was designed to over-

9. G. Main, "Personal Wealth in Colonial America"; G. Main, *Tobacco Colony*; Anderson, "Wealth Estimates for the New England Colonies, 1650–1709," *Explorations Econ. Hist.*, XII (1975), 151–176; Anderson, *The Economic Growth of Seventeenth Century New England: A Measurement of Regional Income* (New York, 1975 [Ph.D. diss., University of Washington, 1972]); Kulikoff, "Economic Growth," with comments by David and Gallman; Menard, "Comment," 124–125; Lois Green Carr and Lorena S. Walsh, "Changing Life Styles in Colonial St. Mary's County," Regional Econ. Hist. Research Center, *Working Papers*, I, no. 3 (1978), 72–118; Clemens, *Atlantic Economy*, 228–232.

come, is the difficulty of combining discrete local studies to form unbiased wealth estimates for the colonies as a whole or even for the major
regions. Still, if the data are collected and presented in consistent ways, if
studies of regions outside of New England and the Chesapeake are conducted, and if the work is extended into the early national period, it may
be possible to construct more-comprehensive estimates through weighting. In the meantime, probate-based studies of wealth levels promise a
more precise description and a deeper understanding of the growth process in the several regions of British America.

In addition to efforts to estimate wealth levels through probate records
there have been several attempts to measure growth by studying the productivity of various sectors of the economy. Gary Walton's work on ocean
shipping is the most successful such attempt although it suffers from
some technical problems. He demonstrates that total factor productivity
in shipping along the major colonial routes increased by at least 0.8 percent annually from 1675 to 1775, and he suggests that the gains may
have been even more rapid in the middle decades of the seventeenth century. He also points to a variety of evidence (largely unquantifiable)
indicating improved efficiency in other aspects of distribution. These
findings are important, for distribution costs played a major role in the
expansion of the export sector, and more work along similar lines would
be welcomed. Nevertheless, the results cannot be translated into a measure of growth for the economy as a whole.[10]

More recently, Walton, in collaboration with Duane Ball, has attempted
to estimate total factor productivity in Pennsylvania agriculture by measuring inputs and yields as reported in probate inventories, a technique
extended to New England by Terry Anderson. Given the centrality of
agriculture in the colonies, such a measure could approximate the rate of
productivity advance in the entire economy. Unfortunately, various technical difficulties—the measurement of labor inputs, the treatment of live-

---

10. Walton, "Sources of Productivity Change in American Colonial Shipping, 1675–1775,"
Econ. Hist. Rev., 2d Ser., XX (1967), 67–78; "A Measure of Productivity Change in
American Colonial Shipping," *ibid.*, XXI (1968), 268–282; and (with James F. Shepherd),
Shipping, 49–90. See also Douglass C. North, "Sources of Productivity Change in Ocean
Shipping, 1600–1850," *Jour. Pol. Econ.*, LXXVI (1968), 953–970, and R. Davis, *Rise of
English Shipping*. We suggest that there may have been even greater improvements in the
productivity of shipping—stemming from the adoption of technological improvements—
than Walton (and Shepherd) recognizes. It was not necessary that colonial shipbuilders in-
vent improvements in order for them to have had an impact; it was only necessary that
shipbuilders incorporate such improvements of whatever origin into their designs. They appear to have done so to a greater extent and with more-important results for productivity
than has been credited. On this whole subject, see Nathan Rosenberg, "Factors Affecting
the Diffusion of Technology," *Explorations Econ. Hist.*, X (1972), 29–33.

stock, and the inability to capture the changing importance of by-employments among farmers—make their results questionable.[11] Finally, we must mention Marc Egnal's work, which presents a series of growth rates in per capita income by region for 1720 to 1775 founded on import-export data. The results are not unreasonable, but his basic premise—that the foreign sector contributed a constant percentage to total income—is left implicit and undefended.[12]

Given the sparse and often contradictory approaches to its measurement, generalizations about economic growth in British America are hazardous. Except for the points of reference provided by Jones's figures, little detailed empirical work has been completed outside of New England and the Chesapeake colonies, and most such studies have been less than successful in overcoming the formidable obstacles in the way of reliable wealth estimates. Further, wealth is not income, and the relationship between the two varied by time, region, assets, and occupation.[13] Still, the several bits and pieces now available will support a rough description of the movement of income per capita over time and of variation by region.

We should begin any summary by recognizing that while income grew in early British America, it did not grow rapidly. Curtis Nettels told only part of the tale when he concluded that "the economic history of early America is the story of a rising standard of living." Gallman's suggestion that income per capita rose at between 0.1 percent and 0.6 percent is

11. D. E. Ball and G. M. Walton, "Agricultural Productivity Change in Eighteenth-Century Pennsylvania," *Jour. Econ. Hist.*, XXXVI (1976), 102–117, with comment by Menard, 118–125; T. Anderson, "Economic Growth in Colonial New England: 'Statistical Renaissance,'" *ibid.*, XXXIX (1979), 243–257, with comments by David and Gallman, 303–312. Arguments and evidence reported elsewhere by Ball suggest one of the principal difficulties with this technique: it assumes that a constant share of each farm's resources was devoted to agriculture at a time when rapid diversification of the economy opened many new, alternative opportunities. See Duane Eugene Ball, "The Process of Settlement in Eighteenth-Century Chester County, Pennsylvania: A Social and Economic History" (Ph.D. diss., University of Pennsylvania, 1973), and Ball, "Dynamics of Population and Wealth."

12. Egnal, "Economic Development," 199–200. See John R. Hanson II, "The Economic Development of the Thirteen Continental Colonies, 1720–1775: A Critique," *WMQ*, 3d Ser., XXXVII (1980), 165–172, and Egnal's reply, *ibid.*, 172–175.

13. Obviously, work on the direction and magnitude of such variations would be most welcome. On their possible importance, see Gallman, "Comment," which suggests that the high rates of growth in wealth characteristic of new settlements overstate the growth of income, a suggestion supported by our impression that interest rates (and therefore returns to wealth) tended to fall as new regions became more densely settled. A. Jones, *Wealth of a Nation to Be*, offers an informed discussion of wealth-income ratios in the colonies (pp. 61–64, 369–374). The best introduction to the general conceptual difficulties of measuring economic growth remains Kuznets, *National Income*, 111–134. See also Kuznets, *Theory of Economic Growth*, and Engerman and Gallman, "U.S. Economic Growth."

closer to the truth. We suggest in chapter 3 that the range was more likely to have been 0.3 percent to 0.6 percent and that it was probably closer to the upper end of the range. Although this is slow by modern standards, it is not unimpressive when one remembers that Great Britain and France grew no faster. And it was rapid enough, as Jones argues, to produce a standard of living in 1774 "probably the highest achieved for the great bulk of the population in any country up to that time."[14]

Nor should one conclude that such modest rates were unimportant in shaping the design and structure of the colonial economy. Growth at around 0.3 percent annually would have been all but imperceptible to contemporaries, *if* the rate was doggedly constant. If, however, growth occurred in short bursts alternating with periods of relative stagnation or even decline, the impact on colonial life might have been dramatic. Those well placed to take advantage of the occasions could have accumulated fortunes, outstripped their less successful neighbors, and competed for power and place with other parvenus and with those born to wealth and status. Under such conditions intensive economic growth, although slow and unimpressive when the entire colonial period is considered, could for a time work as a major engine of change.

The evidence suggests that this was the case, that income in early British America grew slowly but unevenly, with short bursts of rapid expansion sandwiching much longer periods of stagnation. We can identify two such bursts, one with some confidence, the other more tentatively. The first and relatively well documented growth spurt occurred in all colonial regions during the generation following the initial settlement of each region. Closer analysis of the composition of estates is necessary before the process can be described with precision. However, it is likely that most of the gains in income and wealth were a result of farm building. Farmers created wealth by clearing and fencing fields, planting orchards, raising barns and other outbuildings, adding to herds of livestock for meat, hides, and dairy products, constructing larger and more-comfortable houses, and the like. The gains also reflect more local buying and selling as growing population densities created occasions to market surplus products from the farm or to supply particular services.

The second growth spurt, about which we are less confident and during which there was probably considerable local variation in growth rates, began during the 1740s and lasted to the Revolution, with perhaps

14. Nettels, *Money Supply*, 278; A. Jones, "Wealth Estimates for the Middle Colonies," 130. For a discussion of comparative rates of growth, see chap. 3, above. For some of the ramifications of the improved standard of living, see Thad W. Tate, "From Survival to Prosperity: The Artistic Greening of Eighteenth-Century America," *Key Reporter*, XLIV (Autumn 1978), 1–3, 8.

a tailing off toward the very end of the period. Its sources were complex, but much of the gain can be attributed to a revitalized export sector, as European demand for American foodstuffs and other products grew. New markets permitted a more complete and efficient use of available resources and augmented the productivity of colonial agriculture. Bracketed by these two growth spurts—of varying duration from region to region depending on the date of initial settlement—was a period of stagnation, perhaps decline.[15]

Within this fluctuating (and far from firmly established) growth pattern is evidence of regional differences in levels of wealth and income. Two explanations of the regionalization process have emerged from the literature. One is Jackson Turner Main's classification of the colonies into four zones: frontier; subsistence farming (or subsistence plus the marketing of surplus products); commercial farm and plantation regions; and urban areas. His scheme suggests that incomes grew as people moved from new settlements to cities. The other theory is based on the plantation/farm spectrum outlined earlier in this book, which argues that income increased as one moved southward through British America, with the exceptions, of course, of northern cities and the southern backcountry. These two patterns, both of which find some confirmation in recent work, are not incompatible. Indeed, they complement each other. Both relate income to the degree of participation in the market, arguing that specialized production for exchange permitted regions to exploit their comparative advantage and to use accessible resources more efficiently. We suspect that these two models can be woven together into a coherent explanation of differences in levels of wealth and income in the several regions of British America.[16]

If generalizations about the pace and pattern of growth are hazardous, identification of its sources may be foolhardy. Nevertheless, a few comments are warranted, at least to suggest the kinds of investigation that appear most promising.[17] We follow convention and divide the sources of

15. P. Harris, "Integrating Interpretations"; Menard, Carr, and Walsh, "Small Planter's Profits"; and the work cited in nn. 8, 9, and 12, above. A. Jones, *Wealth of a Nation to Be*, provides a useful summary of the evidence (pp. 72–79). The growth rates Jones suggests for early British America (0.3%, 1650–1725; 0.4%, 1725–1750; and 0.5%, 1750–1774), are not incompatible with the pattern offered in these pages since we attempt to describe trends at the local level rather than for the colonies as a whole. However, we would argue for somewhat higher rates in the middle years of the 17th century and for somewhat lower rates from ca. 1680 to the 1740s.

16. See chap. 1, above, and J. Main, *Social Structure*.

17. Shepherd and Walton, *Shipping*, 6–48; Bruchey, *Roots of American Economic Growth*; and Engerman and Gallman, "U.S. Economic Growth," are useful introductions to the issues.

economic growth into changes in the supply of resources and changes in their productivity. Changes in the supply of resources, particularly in the form of farm building, played a major role in the period of growth that followed initial settlement, while investment in social overhead capital—roads, bridges, wharves, and the like—probably contributed to rising incomes throughout the colonial period. Capital inflows from Great Britain also assisted the growth of the American economy, although their significance is disputed.[18]

Productivity gains can be attributed to three things: changes in technology; improvements in human capital—that is, in the skills of the work force; and advances in economic organization. Although there were some gains in agriculture, manufacturing, and shipping, improvements in technology had only a minor impact on the colonial economy, although with regard to shipping, probably a greater impact than previously thought. What is clear is that colonists reaped important benefits in the form of lower prices for imports because of technical advances in British industry, benefits apparent in the shift in the terms of trade after 1740.[19] Improvements in human capital also seem to have been of slight importance in the growth process. Nonetheless, the impact of learning by doing, especially as colonists accumulated practical experience with new crops and a new environment, and the impact of declining morbidity and lengthening life expectancy merit close attention.[20] If technology and human capital made relatively minor contributions to gains in income, it follows that improvements in economic organization, specifically shifts away from self-sufficiency and toward production for exchange and the development of more-efficient markets, were the principal sources of growth in the colonies of British America.[21]

The literature on the distribution of wealth in British America is much more extensive than that on growth. Nevertheless, methodological and conceptual problems plague the field, major gaps in knowledge persist, scholars have drawn contradictory conclusions, and confident generalization about trends and patterns remains very difficult. Recent work suggests two competing hypotheses.

18. Egnal, "Economic Development," 214–217; Shepherd and Walton, *Shipping*, 151–154; Price, *Capital and Credit*, 1–19, 124–139; McCusker, "Sources of Investment Capital"; Richard B. Sheridan, "The British Credit Crisis of 1772 and the American Colonies," *Jour. Econ. Hist.*, XX (1960), 161–186.

19. Egnal, "Economic Development," 205.

20. See chap. 11, above.

21. Shepherd and Walton, *Shipping*, 9; John C. H. Fei and Gustav Ranis, "Economic Development in Historical Perspective," *Am. Econ. Rev.*, LIX (1969), 386–426.

The position taken by most historians argues for progressive inequality. While abundant resources, scarce labor, and open markets combined to work as a "leveling principle" that kept the degree of inequality in the colonies below that of Europe, levels were not trends and the difference between New World and Old was gradually diminishing. By the mid-eighteenth century the rapid growth of population fostered by abundance had produced severe overcrowding in older communities. Larger numbers of people living in a static economy with limited resources had obvious consequences—the Malthusian trap: higher rents, smaller yields, lower wages, fewer chances, and greater inequality. Migration to the frontier, specialized production for the market, and non-farm employment permitted some colonists to avoid the consequences of growth, but proved insufficient to check the trend and prevent the "Europeanization" of American society.[22] Work on colonial cities, chiefly Philadelphia, Boston, and New York, supports this argument. These authors have found growing numbers of urban workers trapped in low-paying, seasonal jobs that kept them close to the subsistence margin, swelling relief rolls, rising propertylessness, declining real wages, diminished hopes, and steadily increasing inequality in the distribution of wealth.[23]

Recently, this position has been severely criticized, most forcefully by Peter Lindert and Jeffrey Williamson. They adopt the "romantic" notion of "colonial quiescence," maintaining that "trends were mixed but *in the aggregate* colonial inequality was stable at low levels."[24] Lindert and Wil-

22. Lockridge, "Land, Population, and New England Society"; Kenneth A. Lockridge, "Social Change and the Meaning of the American Revolution," *Jour. Soc. Hist.*, VI (1973), 403–439; Lemon and Nash, "Distribution of Wealth"; Greven, *Four Generations*; Gross, *Minutemen and Their World*; Henretta, "Morphology of New England Society"; Grant, *Democracy in Kent*; Bruce C. Daniels, "Long Range Trends of Wealth Distribution in Eighteenth Century New England," *Explorations Econ. Hist.*, XI (1973), 123–135; Dennis P. Ryan, "Landholding, Opportunity, and Mobility in Revolutionary New Jersey," *WMQ*, 3d Ser., XXXVI (1979), 571–592.

23. James A. Henretta, "Economic Development and Social Structure in Colonial Boston," *WMQ*, 3d Ser., XXII (1965), 75–92; Donald Warner Koch, "Income Distribution and Political Structure in Seventeenth-Century Salem, Massachusetts," Essex Inst., *Hist. Colls.*, CV (1969), 50–71; Kulikoff, "Progress of Inequality"; Gary B. Nash, "Urban Wealth and Poverty in Pre-Revolutionary America," *JIH*, VI (1976), 545–584; Nash, "Poverty and Poor Relief"; Nash, "Up from the Bottom"; Nash, *Urban Crucible*; Richard J. Morris, "Wealth Distribution in Salem, Massachusetts, 1759–1799: The Impact of the Revolution and Independence," Essex Inst., *Hist. Colls.*, CXIV (1978), 87–102; B. Smith, "Material Lives"; William Pencak, "The Social Structure of Revolutionary Boston: Evidence from the Great Fire of 1760," *JIH*, X (1979), 267–278; John K. Alexander, *Render Them Submissive: Responses to Poverty in Philadelphia, 1760–1800* (Amherst, Mass., 1980).

24. Williamson and Lindert, "Long-Term Trends in American Wealth Inequality," Institute for Research on Poverty, *Discussion Papers*, nos. 472–477 (1977), 9. See also Lindert and

liamson make several telling points against proponents of progressive inequality: that they have ignored regions with stable wealth distributions; chosen inappropriate points of comparison from which to measure trends; drawn conclusions from misleading, inconsistent tax assessments; missed the impact of changing age structures on inequality, especially in cities; and most important, fallen victim to the fallacy of composition. Generalizations about the course of inequality in the colonies as a whole can no more be drawn from studies of several communities than from the study of one particular locality—unless the results of the community studies are properly weighted to reflect changes in the shares of wealth and population. Even if all local studies reported progressive inequality (they do not), one may not conclude that the rich captured an ever-larger share of wealth if trends *within* regions were accompanied by a shift *between* regions, from cities and older agricultural areas where inequality was relatively high to newer settlements where inequality was typically low.

The issue is not yet settled. Williamson and Lindert have mounted a persuasive criticism of the argument for growing inequality, but it is not clear that the movement to the frontier was sufficient to overcome trends toward less-equal distribution in older areas. More work is necessary before the question can be closed.[25] Perhaps the most pressing need is to enlarge the geographic scope of the debate to include the South and the West Indies. If it is fallacious to identify a trend toward greater inequality in the North based on the experience of particular communities, it is no less so to conclude "quiescence" for the mainland colonies while ignoring the South. If the distribution of wealth among free householders is at issue, the Lindert and Williamson hypothesis may stand. If, on the other hand, we consider the welfare of the entire population and assess the growth of slavery, the notion of a stable wealth distribution for the colo-

---

Williamson, "Three Centuries of American Inequality," *Research Econ. Hist.*, I (1976), 69–123; Lindert and Williamson, *American Inequality: A Macroeconomic History* (New York, 1980); Jackson Turner Main, "The Distribution of Property in Colonial Connecticut," in *The Human Dimensions of Nation Making: Essays on Colonial and Revolutionary America*, ed. James Kirby Martin (Madison, Wis., 1976), 54–107; Gloria L. Main, "Inequality in Early America: The Evidence from Probate Records of Massachusetts and Maryland," *JIH*, VII (1977), 559–581; G. B. Warden, "Inequality and Instability in Eighteenth-Century Boston: A Reappraisal," *ibid.*, VI (1976), 585–620; and Warden, "The Distribution of Property in Boston, 1692–1775," *Perspectives Am. Hist.*, X (1976), 79–129. A. Jones, *Wealth of a Nation to Be*, provides a convenient summary of recent findings on wealth distribution (pp. 265–268), as do the works by Williamson and Lindert and Gloria Main, cited above.

25. For efforts to specify the relationship between migration and inequality, see D. S. Smith, "Malthusian-Frontier Interpretation," and Rutman, "People in Process."

nies as a whole seems "romantic" indeed. And including the South in the debate will complicate the argument, for slavery underscores the inadequacy of wealth distribution as an index of welfare. Slaves could not own property, but they did command income, if only the barest subsistence (not necessarily a constant), a fact that comprehensive measures of welfare ought to acknowledge. In some situations, the distribution of wealth is an adequate proxy for trends in the distribution of income, but wealth-based indexes of welfare may accentuate contrasts between slave and free societies (and perhaps between cities and rural areas) because the former usually contain larger proportions of persons without property than the latter.[26]

A variety of other methodological difficulties trouble the study of wealth distributions. The principal sources, probate inventories and tax records, yield only imperfect measures. We have discussed the problems of inventories in the context of wealth levels; the same cautions apply here, although incomplete coverage of assets and decedents seems less likely to distort a distribution, at least if the concern is the trend within a region and not comparisons between regions.[27]

Tax records have some advantages over inventories for the study of inequality, chiefly that the data are conveniently assembled in a single document and report the wealth of the living. But their deficiencies are so severe as perhaps to offset these advantages. First, the incomplete coverage of assets often distorts the distribution of wealth because the kinds of property omitted were concentrated in the estates of the rich. Second, the tax base varied across time within communities and between regions. Further, assessors followed convention or law in setting assessments instead of using market values and often assigned fixed rates to similar types of property that in fact varied greatly in quality. Fourth, and perhaps most important, some tax lists were shaped as much by fraud, corruption, and the vagaries of politics as by the actual distribution of prop-

26. Little work has been done on wealth distribution in the Lower South or the West Indies. For South Carolina, see Waterhouse, "South Carolina's Colonial Elite," and Terry, "'Champaign Country,'" 243–297, which report an increase in inequality, and William George Bentley, "Wealth Distribution in Colonial South Carolina" (Ph.D. diss., Georgia State University, 1977), which finds no trend. On the West Indies, see Dunn, *Sugar and Slaves*, especially pp. 264–272, and Sheridan, "Wealth of Jamaica." A. Jones, *Wealth of a Nation to Be*, provides a description of trends in distribution in early British North America consistent with our sense of the pattern of change (pp. 269–272).

27. This is not to imply that studies of wealth and income inequality can ignore bias in probate inventories. Rather, we suggest that such bias seems less likely to produce serious distortion in the movement of inequality over time within jurisdictions than in the movement of mean wealth per head or per property owner.

erty. Boston may represent an extreme case, but G. B. Warden's judgment sounds a caution that historians of other jurisdictions ignore at their peril: "Procedures of assessment and taxation . . . were so chaotic and subject to political manipulation that the surviving tax lists are not a valid indication at all of the actual distributions of wealth and degrees of inequality."

This is not to argue that tax assessments be ignored by students of inequality. They are often the only data available, but where adequate probate records do exist, assessments can also provide assistance in adjusting for bias in inventories. However, tax lists must be used with great care and with particular sensitivity to the shifting politics of taxation, the types of assets covered, the relationship between assessed and market values, and the occasions for fraud. With such precautions it should be possible to construct accurate measures of change across short periods within jurisdictions. However, the prospects seem less promising for comparisons between regions or over the long term, particularly if the task requires comparing results derived from probate records with those from assessments.[28]

Quite apart from problems with sources, students of wealth distribution confront some major technical issues. There are various ways to measure inequality, each one sensitive to a different aspect of wealth distribution. While the question at issue ought to determine which measure is appropriate, presentation of all the common statistical measures in future studies would facilitate comparisons.[29]

Another technical issue concerns the importance of age. All studies of inequality have unearthed a strong relationship between age and wealth. Typically, wealth rose until late middle age as the earning power of men grew and they accumulated savings from past income; it then fell as they retired and distributed assets to heirs. Simple farming communities, where self-sufficient agriculture was the principal economic activity and

28. Useful assessments of tax lists as a source for the measurement of inequality include Warden, "Inequality and Instability," 604–609 (quotation on p. 607); Nash, "Urban Wealth and Poverty," 547–548; Price, "Quantifying Colonial America," 704–706; and J. Main, "Distribution of Property," 54–57. Robert A. Becker's recent *Revolution, Reform, and the Politics of American Taxation, 1763–1783* (Baton Rouge, La., 1980), is an important study of the impact of politics and corruption on the work of assessors that deserves close attention from those who attempt to use tax lists to study inequality.

29. There is a large, growing literature on inequality statistics. For helpful discussions of several of the most commonly used measures, see F. A. Cowell, *Measuring Inequality: Techniques for the Social Sciences* (New York, 1977); Anthony B. Atkinson, "On the Measurement of Inequality," *Journal of Economic Theory*, II (1970), 244–263; and Robert R. Schutz, "On the Measurement of Income Inequality," *Am. Econ. Rev.*, XLI (1951), 107–122.

market production offered few chances for accumulation, were stratified more by age than by wealth. Since the most useful index of economic welfare is lifetime income, distribution studies must pay close attention to life-cycle effects by incorporating the impact of age into inequality statistics or by following the accumulation of property over the careers of individuals and their families.[30]

Further, as Williamson and Lindert have stressed, scholars must take care to avoid fallacies of composition. This pitfall should not discourage studies of distribution within particular communities, for those are likely to yield useful insights into the dynamics of inequality. It should, however, discourage easy generalization from such local studies to an entire region without accounting for shifts in population and resources. Regional or colony-wide samples following the lead of Alice Hanson Jones would attack this problem directly, but approximations could be obtained by an intelligent weighting of local studies. Finally, distribution ought not to be separated from growth since it matters whether (as was often the case) inequality increased in a context of generally rising incomes or because a few gained at the expense of the majority.

This brief survey of the state of the art suggests that generalizations about trends in inequality in British America are perhaps even more perilous than those concerning growth. Existing theory, more concerned with distribution between factors than among people, is not especially helpful, and the empirical base is thin and full of uncertainties.[31] We need more work on the pattern and the sources of inequality—and here analysis of the composition of estates and of inheritance patterns from probate records should prove fruitful—before persuasive explanations will be

30. For the notion of an "age-stratified society," see Henretta, "Families and Farms," 7. See also John J. Waters, "Patrimony, Succession, and Social Stability: Guilford, Connecticut, in the Eighteenth Century," *Perspectives Am. Hist.*, X (1976), 129–160. A. Jones, *Wealth of a Nation to Be*, is perhaps the best introduction to the issues (pp. 166–169, 381–388). Students of colonial inequality will also wish to consult Morton Paglin, "The Measurement and Trend of Inequality: A Basic Revision," *Am. Econ. Rev.*, LXV (1975), 598–609, which introduces an age-adjusted inequality statistic, and the stimulating essay by Simon Kuznets, "Demographic Aspects of the Size Distribution of Income: An Exploratory Essay," *Econ. Devel. and Cult. Change*, XXV (1976), 1–94.

31. Martin Bronfenbrenner, *Income Distribution Theory* (Chicago, 1971), is an able introduction to the economics of inequality that students of wealth distribution in early British America will find helpful. For a review of the literature, see Gian Singh Sahota, "Theories of Personal Income Distribution: A Survey," *Journal of Economic Literature*, XVI (1978), 1–55. A recent essay by Robert E. Gallman, "Influences on the Distribution of Landholdings in Early Colonial North Carolina," *Jour. Econ. Hist.*, XLII (1982), 549–575, analyzes the impact of life cycle processes and family relationships on wealth distribution and describes a promising approach to the study of inequality.

forthcoming. Perhaps the most encouraging result is the apparent congruence between levels of inequality and levels of income: both seem to have been higher in cities than in the countryside, higher on plantations than in farming regions. If that correlation stands the test of further research, it will reinforce the case for integrated studies of wealth and welfare and relieve our present poverty of explanation.

CHAPTER 13

CONSUMPTION,

THE IMPORT TRADE,

AND THE DOMESTIC

ECONOMY

"Getting and spending." The colonial populace participated in the economy by both producing and consuming, by getting *and* spending. Thus far we have paid more attention to the production of goods and services, to the earning and the distribution of income and wealth, than to spending. We have talked about supply, but not as much about demand. This reflects the state of the discipline: colonial economic historians have paid more attention to production than they have to consumption. The time has come to balance the equation.[1]

The most significant aspect of the consumption of goods and services in the colonial economy was probably the increase in demand over time. The size of the colonial market grew tremendously because the population grew. The market grew also because improvements in communication and transportation drew the several, initially separate population centers more closely together. Particularly important in this regard was the spread of coastwise trade. All of this strengthened absolute demand,

1. Perhaps the only colonial historians to address these issues systematically are Gloria Main, *Tobacco Colony*, 140–236, and Carole Shammas, "Consumer Behavior in Colonial America," *Soc. Sci. Hist.*, VI (1982), 67–86, and "How Self-sufficient Was Early America?" *JIH*, XIII (1982), 247–272. Shammas points out the useful perspectives on the subject to be gained from works such as Jan De Vries, "Peasant Demand Patterns and Economic Development: Friesland, 1550–1750," in *European Peasants and Their Markets: Essays in Agrarian Economic History*, ed. William N. Parker and Eric L. Jones (Princeton, N.J., 1975), 205–268, and Joan Thirsk, *Economic Policy and Projects: The Development of a Consumer Society in Early Modern England* (Oxford, 1978). See also [Dorothy S. Brady], "Consumption and the Style of Life," in *American Economic Growth*, ed. Davis, Easterlin, and Parker, 61–89; Carr and Walsh, "Inventories and Analysis of Wealth"; and the work on diet and living standards cited in chap. 11, n. 36, above, and in chap. 14, n. 1, below.

but demand intensified also on a per capita basis as individual levels of income and wealth rose. Per capita demand expanded even further because individuals increasingly tended to specialize as producers and thus to turn to others for goods they had previously supplied themselves. Not all of these things happened everywhere, to everyone, or to the same degree, but their net impact caused a considerable expansion in colonial demand for goods and services over the period 1607–1775.

Perhaps the most important result of the growth in colonial demand involved shifts in the sources of supply. As colonial demand grew, it became more and more possible for local suppliers to take advantage of the consequent scale economies and to begin to produce locally what previously had been imported from overseas. The development of domestic suppliers affected not only these men and their customers but also the overseas suppliers, the carriers of goods in overseas trade, the local producers of other commodities, and local traders and merchants whose livelihoods depended on the exchange of this merchandise. This chapter will examine more closely the changes wrought in the overseas sector. The next two chapters will look at the effects on the domestic economy.

The colonists of early British America consumed a wide variety of commodities imported from many parts of the world. Imports from the Eastern Hemisphere came largely by way of Great Britain as dictated by the Navigation Acts, the most significant exception being immigrant laborers: indentured servants and slaves could be brought directly from their native lands. Western Hemisphere produce came from fellow colonists either in the West Indies or on the continent. Most imports were purchased and consumed as they were. Some, however, offered opportunities for further processing before sale to consumers. The rising colonial standard of living, by creating a demand for greater quantities of refined imports of all types, further stimulated such processing industries. One effect of the changes in colonial imports was the promotion of colonial processing and manufacturing industries.

In 1766, in testimony before the House of Commons, Benjamin Franklin warned the members of the threat to Great Britain's exports should Parliament fail to repeal the Stamp Act. In his statement he made several interesting distinctions and showed clearly how far the colonists had come since the days of Jamestown, when everything had to be imported from the mother country.

> The goods they [the colonists] take from Britain are either necessaries, mere conveniences, or superfluities. The first, as cloth, &c. with a little industry they can make at home; the second they can do without, till they are able to provide them among themselves;

and the last, which are much the greatest part, they will strike off immediately. They are mere articles of fashion, purchased and consumed, because the fashion in a respected country, but will now be detested and rejected.

Franklin's statement was political, but it provides an attractive set of categories within which to distribute colonial imports and it tells us several valuable things about the colonial economy. At least from his perspective, the colonies could do without all of the goods imported from the metropolis. Nevertheless, taste and habit encouraged them to import a great deal. Moreover, the colonies could afford these imports, "much the greatest part" of which were "superfluities . . . [and] mere articles of fashion." Despite the size of the domestic market, the colonists did not attempt to produce enough cloth for it because they were able to import it. Free trade within the empire permitted British cloth to be price competitive in the colonies and allowed the colonists to earn enough to pay the price. Perhaps Franklin spoke simply for effect, but the underlying assumptions in his threat are revealing.[2]

Franklin identified a condition that had long been developing, as the figures in table 13.1 show. These data not only indicate a high level of imports per capita but also testify to a considerable increase in imports during the eighteenth century. Early in the century, between 1700 and 1720, the data show a decline of about 11 percent. The observed decrease may not describe the actual trend at the turn of the century, however. The first period, 1699 to 1704, falls at the end of a long war that disrupted commerce and limited the flow of consumer goods to the colonies. The high level of imports may reflect only the release of pent-up demand, and the reduction between 1700 and 1720 may prove to have been more apparent than real. Whatever the case at the beginning of the century, between 1720 and 1770 per capita imports rose by about 50 percent. The advance was spread out fairly evenly over the period, although the rate of increase was slightly sharper between 1750 and 1770 than in the previous thirty years. Taking into account both the apparent falloff in the early part of the century and the subsequent recovery and reinforcement, per capita colonial imports from the metropolis grew by more than one-third between 1700 and 1770, at an annual compound rate of about 0.4 percent.[3]

2. Great Britain, Parliament, 1766, House of Commons, *The Examination of Doctor Benjamin Franklin Relative to the Repeal of the American Stamp Act, in MDCCLXVI* ([London, 1767]), 23, and as printed in *Franklin Papers*, XIII, 143.

3. Compare Shammas, "How Self-sufficient Was Early America?" 263–265, for an attempt to estimate the retail cost to the colonists of imports from Great Britain.

TABLE 13.1.

Exports from Great Britain to the Continental Colonies,
1700–1770 (Pounds Sterling)

	Annual Average Constant Value per Capita during Selected Periods			
Region	1699–1704 (1700)	1718–1723 (1720)	1747–1751 (1750)	1767–1774 (1770)
Continental colonies	£0.90	£0.80	£1.00	£1.20
New England	0.90	0.80	0.80	1.00
Middle Colonies	0.80	0.70	1.30	1.50
Maryland and Virginia	1.70	1.00	1.00	1.30
North and South Carolina	0.70	0.60	1.00	1.10

Sources: The data are from CUST 3 and CUST 14, Public Record Office, as compiled and printed in U.S. Bureau of the Census, *Historical Statistics of the United States, Colonial Times to 1970* (Washington, D.C., 1975), II, 1176–1178 (Ser. Z 214, 216, 218, 220, 222, 224, 227, 229, 231, 233, 235, 239, 241 [note the incorrect labeling of the column headings of the last seven series]). For the population data, see *ibid.*, 1168 (Ser. Z 1–19).

Notes: The data were originally compiled in ways that make them a constant value series, F.O.B. an English port (that is, freight on board at point of export), just as they stand, with a base 1700–1702 = 100. For the first two periods the data are for exports from England and Wales only; data for Scotland are available only after 1740. See John J. McCusker, "The Current Value of English Exports, 1697 to 1800," *William and Mary Quarterly*, 3d Ser., XXVIII (1971), 607–628. It is thought that there was so little import trade with Scotland before 1740 that the omission of such data makes only a small difference in the table. The periods used are all full cycles in the economy (see table 3.4) and are, essentially, times of peace.

In chapter 3, above, we postulated, as the higher estimate, an annual average compound rate of growth of 0.6 percent for colonial income per capita over the entire period. Let us assume that this rate applied for the years 1700 to 1770 and, further, that consumer demand for goods and services expanded at the same rate as income grew. While both of these assumptions have their faults and the estimated rate of growth itself is only a guess, the postulate nevertheless allows for an interesting comparison and provokes some intriguing speculations.

Consumer demand among the colonists grew more quickly on a real per capita basis than colonial imports from Great Britain. We may safely assume that by 1700 the colonists had long since satisfied their own need for necessities. Thus that larger consumer demand during the eighteenth century meant increased consumption of "mere conveniences" and "superfluities," to borrow Franklin's categories. As we will see below, by 1770 imports from the metropolis were almost entirely such manufactured goods, which had probably been the case since well before 1700. In other words, at the same time that the colonial appetite for "mere conveniences" and "superfluities" was increasing, the colonists were satisfying a progressively greater portion of that demand from places other than the mother country. Some came from the West Indies, which met a colonial demand for greater quantities and better quality of commodities such as sugar and rum as the century progressed. Mostly, however, the demand was met by colonially produced commodities and services, in large measure by goods manufactured in the continental colonies. Increasingly, colonial manufacturers were able to substitute their own products for British imports.

Much of this is simple supposition, of course. The colonial manufacturing that did develop in this way was very small and rather unimpressive, just a beginning. It would be wrong to picture the colonial countryside dotted with factories. But these data do suggest that colonial industry had begun to have an impact on the import trade from Great Britain, an impact that grew during the eighteenth century. If imports from Great Britain had expanded as fast as the economy grew after 1700, the colonists would have consumed about 12 percent more British imports in 1770 than they did, a difference of some £320,000 sterling.

Although imports are an imperfect proxy for the rate of expansion of the entire economy, the data are suggestive concerning the temporal pattern of economic development. On the whole, they support hypotheses offered earlier in this book. The evidence of British imports argues that colonial incomes did not advance and perhaps even receded early in the eighteenth century but then increased impressively after 1720. This is consistent with the conventional wisdom. But insofar as the same conventional wisdom posits a tailing off of the growth rate just prior to the Revolution, these data do not agree. The figures on British imports suggest that colonial incomes grew more rapidly after 1750 than before.[4]

Table 13.1 also shows some substantial differences by region in the value of colonial imports from Great Britain. The absolute differences at any given time are probably not as significant as the comparative patterns of ebb and flow. Since some regions had trading centers that served to

4. See chap. 12, above.

redistribute imports, one cannot infer relative levels of consumption from these data. The changes tell us more. New England, which was importing at the average rate for all of the colonies in 1700, fell to something less than the "national" average by 1770. Since New England had from an early period acted as a transshipper of British imports, this change probably indicates more a diminution in its share of the coastwise trade than a change in consumption levels. In much the same way, the increase in British imports to the Middle Atlantic colonies attests to the enlargement of their coastwise and overland trades, although some of that nearly 80 percent rise in imports must also reflect higher levels of local consumption.[5]

The long-term erosion in Chesapeake imports can probably be explained in two ways. First, we suspect, as mentioned above, that the higher numbers for 1699 to 1704 reflect postwar demand and thus are atypical, which tends to diminish the significance of any subsequent contraction. Second, Maryland and Virginia imports from Great Britain valued on a per capita basis were influenced by the disproportionate gain during these seventy years in the slave portion of the total population. We can safely assume that slave consumption of imports from Great Britain stayed constant or decreased, if indeed slaves consumed any such imports at all. Measured per capita on the basis of the white population only, imports into the tobacco coast were almost the same in 1770 as they had been in 1700.

The most striking change occurred in the Lower South. British imports into North and South Carolina on a per capita basis increased at an annual compound rate of 1.2 percent between 1720 and 1770, from £0.6 to £1.1 sterling. While some of that gain reflects the rise of Charleston as a reexport center, the coastwise trade of the Lower South remained small throughout the eighteenth century. The great majority of imports were consumed locally. Since, just as in the Chesapeake, the slave population of the Lower South expanded faster than the white population, the consumption of imports by whites must have increased at an even greater rate than 1.2 percent. Thus these data provide striking confirmation of the success of the economy of the Lower South during the eighteenth century.

The English customs ledgers, from which the data in table 13.1 were compiled, reveal in great detail what the colonists imported from London and the outports. (The colonial naval officer shipping lists are not useful for this purpose since in general they only recorded the numbers of bales and boxes arriving from the mother country without detailing their con-

5. In this regard see Nettels, "Economic Relations," and *Money Supply*, chap. 3, 99–127.

tents.) Despite their richness, the English ledgers have not yet been thoroughly analyzed for such purposes. Nevertheless, we can say something about the nature of metropolitan exports to British America on the basis of an incomplete and unsystematic look at some of the evidence (see table 13.2).[6]

Nothing impresses one who looks at the customs ledgers so much as the diversity of the commodities that the colonists imported from England. Despite the variety it is possible to draw some useful distinctions and to frame a hypothesis. Colonial imports may be broken down into the same five categories used to analyze imports and exports in more modern times: crude or raw materials (such as coal, wool, or cotton); crude or raw foods (tea, fruits, spices); processed or manufactured foods (wine, butter, flour, sugar); semimanufactured goods (pig iron, lumber, indigo); and manufactured goods (cloth, shoes, wooden casks).[7]

The history of an economy from first settlement to full development can be traced by discussing the relative proportions of imports in terms of these five categories. At first, of course, newly arrived colonists had to import everything, including even food and raw materials. Within a fairly short time, the settlers were able to supply most foods and at least some raw materials, but they began importing more and more manufactured and semimanufactured goods. Yet a place like Barbados might well continue forever to import large amounts of basic foodstuffs. From the mercantilist's perspective, however, the perfect colony imported only finished goods, all the product of the mother country.

The conversion from an agricultural to an industrial economy involved a progress away from that ideal, a reversal of that trend. The change resulted in a slow but steady decrease in the proportion of finished goods imported and a rise in the importation of raw materials, often those required for the domestic production of the finished goods no longer imported. Industrialization in this way shows a return to the ratios that would have applied in the early days of settlement, though the products imported would differ, with raw materials more important than raw foods. Finally, in the most highly developed nations of the modern world, countries like the United States again exhibit somewhat higher proportional levels of imported manufactured goods. In doing so the nation sim-

6. The English customs ledgers (CUST 3) and the colonial naval officer shipping lists are discussed in chap. 2, above. Similar ledgers for Scotland from 1755, CUST 14, and for Ireland from 1698, CUST 15, are also in the PRO. See McCusker, "Current Value of English Exports," 608–610.

7. U.S. Bureau of the Census, *Historical Statistics*, II, 879–880, 889–894 (Ser. U 213–248). Compare North, *Economic Growth, passim.* See chap. 7, above.

TABLE 13.2.
Selected English Exports Sent to British America, 1770

Commodity	Quantities Exported to British America	Percentage of Total Exported from England
Coal	6,085 chaldrons	2.8
Pilchards	160 hogsheads	0.8
White salt	11,024 pounds	23.0
Refined sugar	12,062 hundredweight	31.7
Wrought brass	8,073 hundredweight	25.2
Wrought copper	13,778 hundredweight	55.3
Wrought iron	130,687 hundredweight	59.8
Lead and shot	1,651 fodders	9.3
Tin	216 hundredweight	31.7
Beaver hats	10,790 dozen	69.4
Cordage	11,837 hundredweight	65.6
Glassware and earthenware	2,742,253 pieces	47.9
Iron nails	24,147 hundredweight	76.5
Tanned leather	408 hundredweight	5.2
Fustians	5,116 pieces	15.7
Linen	88,072 pieces	79.2
Wrought silk	30,978 pounds	57.2
Printed cotton and linen	155,789 yards	58.9
Double bays	17,812 pieces	19.9
Single bays	8,702 pieces	12.3
Long cloths	5,176 pieces	15.8
Short cloths	18,249 pieces	36.8
Spanish cloths	1,985 pieces	70.4
Flannel	346,740 yards	42.6
Perpets and serges	76,396 pounds	2.2
Men's worsted stockings	28,806 dozen pairs	34.9
Stuffs	1,225,750 pounds	14.8

Sources: Elizabeth Boody Schumpeter, *English Overseas Trade Statistics, 1697–1808* (Oxford, 1960), 63–69. Her source was the English customs ledgers, CUST 3, Public Record Office. Why she elected to compile the data for these commodities and not for others is not apparent. The best place to turn for descriptions of the various goods listed in the ledgers, especially the textiles, is [Richard] Rolt, *A New Dictionary of Trade and Commerce . . .* (London, 1756). See also Otto Charles Thieme, *By Inch of Candle: A Sale at East-India-House, 21 September 1675* (Minneapolis, Minn., 1982).

ply reflects in its imports the consumption patterns of individuals as levels of income and wealth rise. It spends more and more on manufactured goods, some of which can be supplied more economically as imports.

The proportion of imports into the United States made up by manufactured or processed goods was 79.4 percent in the early 1820s, the first period for which we have data analyzed in this way. It was 56.5 percent in the 1890s, the heyday of the Industrial Revolution, and 77.3 percent in the 1960s. The ratio for the colonies in the early seventeenth century likely approached that of the 1890s, and we suspect that the colonies in the eighteenth century imported an even higher percentage of finished goods than the United States of the 1820s or the 1960s. Given the progress of domestic manufacturing during the early national period, we think that the percentage for the 1820s represents a decrease from some earlier, higher figure.[8]

If more than 80 percent of total imports into the colonies in the late colonial period were manufactured or semimanufactured goods, then the percentage of such goods from England alone must have been even higher. That was so, since by law the colonists could not import manufactured goods from outside the empire and only the mother country produced such goods within the empire. Indeed nothing in table 13.2—although it is by no means a complete accounting—could be classed as raw food or raw material, except possibly the coal. North America and the West Indies, as a group of colonies, were largely self-sufficient in both raw food and materials, even if that self-sufficiency did depend on interregional coastwise trading. The colonies were also largely self-sufficient in processed foods, with some exceptions. One exception was the West Indian demand for Irish butter and Irish beef. Another was salt; in 1770 British America imported about one-quarter of the roughly three million bushels of salt that England exported. Still another was refined sugar, of which nearly one-third of England's exports went to its New World colonies. Work to date permits little more than guesses based on these data, but of the total value of English exports to British America in 1770, perhaps as little as 5 to 10 percent was in raw materials or food products.[9]

8. North, *Economic Growth*, 288; U.S. Bureau of the Census, *Historical Statistics*, II, 889–890 (Ser. U 219–224).

9. For the Irish beef trade, see Léon Vignols, "L'importation en France, au XVIIIe siècle, du boeuf salé d'Irlande: Ses emplois—les tentatives pour s'en passer," *Revue Historique*, CLIX (1928), 79–95. Compare Francis G. James, "Irish Colonial Trade in the Eighteenth Century," *WMQ*, 3d Ser., XX (1963), 574–584—which, inexplicably, fails to use the CUST 15 ledgers—and L. M. Cullen, *Anglo-Irish Trade, 1660–1800* (Manchester, 1968). For salt, see Francis Carroll Huntley, "Salt: A Study in Colonial Economy" (M.A. thesis, University of California, Berkeley, 1948), and Robert P. Multhauf, *Neptune's Gift: A History of Common Salt* (Baltimore, 1978). For sugar, see McCusker, "Rum Trade."

Thus it was that perhaps as much as 90 percent of the goods from the mother country consumed by the colonists were semimanufactured or manufactured commodities. The general impact of this on the British economy has been dealt with elsewhere. While we are here more interested in what this meant for the colonial consumer, the effect in part was clearly transatlantic. Colonial markets meant a great deal to some British producers. Since one-third of their overseas customers lived in the colonies, British sugar refiners went to extraordinary lengths to protect that market. The heavy export subsidies that Parliament granted them not only allowed their sugar to be price competitive in North America but also helped to win new customers. Around half of all English exports of copperware, ironware, glassware, earthenware, silk goods, printed cotton and linen goods, and flannels were shipped to colonial consumers. Between two-thirds and three-quarters of all exported English cordage, iron nails, beaver hats, linen, and Spanish woolen goods went to British America. Franklin knew whereof he spoke when he threatened the loss of such markets. One wonders if Englishmen involved with these commodities reacted to the Revolution differently from those who were not.[10]

What of Franklin's related point, that the colonists could either produce many of these goods themselves or easily forgo them altogether. Certainly the demand was there; it had intensified steadily during the century before 1770. So were the raw materials. A good number of the finished manufactured goods imported into America from Great Britain—cordage, iron goods, earthenware, salt, sugar, beaver hats, linen goods, and woolen goods—were made from raw materials that either had come from the colonies or might have. Franklin could confidently claim that they might be made in the colonies because a considerable and in fact flourishing domestic manufacturing sector was already producing most of these items and others as well. To put it differently, the demand among colonial consumers for finished manufactured goods was strong enough not only to have maintained, even increased, high levels of imports but also to have encouraged the establishment of some local manufacturing industries. Colonial demand absorbed the production of both

---

10. In addition to subsidies for the sugar refiners—for which see McCusker, "Rum Trade," *passim*—Parliament interested itself in other forms of colonial manufacturing. One thinks of the Woolen Act (10 William III, c. 16; 1698), the Hat Act (5 George II, c. 22; 1731), and the Iron Act (23 George II, c. 29; 1749). There are no modern studies of the passage and subsequent history of any of these laws. While one can still rely for many particulars on the traditional studies, they are clearly out-of-date. See especially Lord, *Industrial Experiments*. See also Dickerson, *Navigation Acts*, 31–57. More important, from the perspective of this book, there are no modern studies of the effects of these acts on colonial industry.

British and domestic suppliers. It grew even faster, on a real basis, than importation data alone indicate.[11]

At least initially, colonial producers catered to "down market" demand, to those who consumed goods of lower quality. During the century before the Revolution, preference among the colonists seems to have shifted to goods of higher quality. Just one example of this was the demand for earthenware. Evidence is accumulating from studies of probate records and from archaeology that, over time, the colonists set their tables with steadily finer dinnerware. Among the poor, pottery replaced handmade wooden plates. Among the better-off colonists, crude pottery was replaced by finer pottery, much of which was imported. Even though per capita importation of English earthenware declined somewhat in the eighteenth century, the quality of this imported ware went up materially. The demand for cheaper earthenware remained constant, but it was supplied increasingly by the proliferating colonial production of such goods. Per capita consumption of all earthenware increased. In other words, again as Franklin pointed out, by 1770 taste and fashion had as much to do with colonial imports from Great Britain as absolute need. British Americans preferred some British manufactures to cruder colonial goods, and they could afford to indulge that preference.[12]

The high ratio of finished to unfinished goods among colonial imports from Great Britain was not the pattern in the colonists' trade with the rest of the world. Other transatlantic imports included wine and fruit from the Wine Islands; black slaves from the coasts of Africa; and white indentured servants from the Continent. Within the categories used here, the first would be classed as foods, processed and raw respectively; the second and third as raw materials, similar in nature to coal (the output of both being measured in terms of horsepower). These trades continued to be brisk and indeed expanded during the colonial period, since colonial demand for labor and luxuries increased over the years and the quantity and quality of locally produced substitutes were inadequate. All but an insignificant portion of the trade in both servants and slaves remained in the control of British merchants, but colonists made major inroads into the wine trade.[13]

11. For domestic manufacturing, see chap. 15, below.

12. See C. Malcolm Watkins and Ivor Noël Hume, *The "Poor Potter" of Yorktown* (Washington, D.C., 1967); Barbara Carson and Cary Carson, "Styles and Standards of Living in Southern Maryland, 1670–1752" (paper presented at the annual meeting of the Southern Historical Association, New Orleans, La., Nov. 1977); and Carr and Walsh, "Changing Life Styles." See also Tate, "From Survival to Prosperity."

13. On the origins of the Wine Islands trade, see Bailyn, *New England Merchants, passim.* See also Edward Delos Beechert, Jr., "The Wine Trade of the Thirteen Colonies" (M.A. the-

Raw materials and raw foods also made up a large part of the goods that the colonists imported from each other and from the colonists of other nations on their own side of the Atlantic. Nevertheless, a growing proportion of the commodities traded were processed foods (sugar, molasses, and rum; fish and meat; flour), and many West Indian imports from North America were semimanufactured goods (lumber and lumber products). Some finished manufactures entered North America from the West Indies, but these were contraband European goods that were shipped to the British colonies illegally via the non-British islands. Such trade was insignificant except for one or two specific minor items such as sailcloth and brandy. Increasingly, too, the West Indians turned to those who were already supplying them with foods and semimanufactured goods to provide them with manufactured items. Some items were European products reexported from North America, but others were the product of colonial industry. The North American–West Indian trade acted to stimulate manufacturing on the continent. By the 1770s West Indians were import-

---

sis, University of California, Berkeley, 1949); Dickerson, *Navigation Acts*, 175–179; and David Joel Mishkin, *The American Colonial Wine Industry: An Economic Interpretation* (New York, 1975 [Ph.D. diss., University of Illinois, 1966]). Recent work by George F. Steckley suggests the possibilities for research on the wine trade with the Canaries: "The Wine Economy of Tenerife in the Seventeenth Century: Anglo-Spanish Partnership in a Luxury Trade," *Econ. Hist. Rev.*, 2d Ser., XXXIII (1980), 335–350. Also helpful is T. Duncan, *Atlantic Islands*. On the trade in indentured servants, see A. E. Smith, *Colonists in Bondage*, and Galenson, *White Servitude*. On the colonial slave trade, see Rawley, *Transatlantic Slave Trade*, which demonstrates the low level of colonial participation in the trade itself. Compare McCusker, "Rum Trade," 492–497. Coughtry, *Notorious Triangle*, tries to mount an argument for the importance of the slave trade to Rhode Island commerce. But see Frederick H. Bretz, "The African Slave Trade of Colonial Rhode Island, 1700–1777" (unpubl. seminar paper [Hist. 272B], University of California, Berkeley, 1960), who is more convincing than Coughtry for having used the colonial naval officer shipping lists as well as newspapers and manuscripts. Bretz concluded that "the trade was only a minor adjunct of the colony's total trading activities" (p. 55). The "triangular trade" idea, to which Coughtry alludes, has also been attacked recently as irrelevant. See the summary of the literature in Omi, "Juhasseiki Amerika shokuminchi." In addition see Platt, "'And Don't Forget the Guinea Voyage,'" 601–618; Tommy Todd Hamm, "The American Slave Trade with Africa, 1620–1807" (Ph.D. diss., Indiana University, 1975); and Elaine F. Crane, "'The First Wheel of Commerce': Newport, Rhode Island, and the Slave Trade, 1760–1776," *Slavery and Abolition*, I (1980). There is no adequate account of the British slave trade, although K. Davies, *Royal African Company*, is very good on early development. Some attempts have been made to describe or account for part of it (these are discussed in chap. 10, above, and in the chapters on the several regions in Part II of this book). For a quite useful collection of materials, see Donnan, ed., *Documents of the Slave Trade*. Also useful is Peter C. Hogg, *The African Slave Trade and Its Suppression: A Classified and Annotated Bibliography of Books, Pamphlets, and Periodical Articles* (London, 1973).

ing a variety of manufactured goods from the continental colonies, from cheap earthenware to furniture and vehicles. The implications of this trade for the economic development of the colonists on the continent were immense.[14]

For the West Indians, having an alternative source of some manufactured goods near at hand was also important. The advantages went beyond simple matters of cost saving. Take as an example the ubiquitous wooden cask, the universal container of the Atlantic world until the twentieth century. Wooden casks were manufactured from trees, obviously, but there were not enough trees in the West Indies to supply the need of the export industries there. Casks had to be imported, usually "shaken," or broken down, into their constituent parts (staves, headings, and hoops), to be reassembled by a cooper as required. Casks came in two basic styles, "tight," or "wet" (watertight), and "slack" (not watertight). The difference had less to do with the shape of the staves than with the porousness of the wood from which the staves were made and the care with which the parts were fitted together. Casks came in a multitude of sizes and shapes. While nearly anything could be shipped in almost any cask, considerations of efficiency quickly settled on very specific casks for particular commodities. Tightness or slackness and regularity of size and shape were critical for shipboard loading and stowing. Europe as a source of supply for casks was simply too remote, its wood supplies already too much in demand, and suppliers there too committed to fabricating casks in traditional ways of their own to serve the West Indies well. North American manufacturers of casks had the right woods easily accessible, were knowledgeable about West Indian markets, and were willing to tailor casks to their customers' requirements. North American casks not only cost West Indian consumers less to purchase but, being of a consistent size and quality, were also more easily assembled and less expensively shipped. In general, North American manufacturers could more efficiently, more quickly, less expensively, and more satisfactorily supply West Indian customers than could European suppliers of similar goods. And they did so for an increasing range of commodities over time.[15]

Another reason why West Indian consumers did progressively more of their shopping in North American markets was that North Americans accepted a wider range of West Indian commodities in payment. Both Europeans and North Americans were willing to trade for sugar, but only

14. For the trade, see Pares, *Yankees and Creoles*, and chap. 7, above.

15. McCusker, "Rum Trade," 768–787, discusses casks. For a similar accommodation to West Indian needs, this time by North American iron fabricators, see chap. 15, n. 23, below.

the North Americans also took molasses and rum in return. Molasses could be used as a kind of poor man's sugar, or it could be distilled into rum. There was no European market for molasses worth mentioning; the European market for rum developed only slowly and, significantly, only after the middle of the eighteenth century. The beauty for both partners in the North American–West Indian trade was their nearly perfect symbiotic relationship as producers and consumers.

The entrepreneurs who organized this North American–West Indian trade—as well as the Wine Island trade, the coastwise trade, and the colonial portion of the trade to the British Isles—were almost exclusively North Americans. Some of them, as particularly good entrepreneurs, recognized in these trades related opportunities for profit. One possibility was the establishment of manufacturing facilities to process at home the crude materials imported from abroad. Chief among these were sugar and molasses, for which large and varied markets existed. An intriguing aspect of these activities stems from the direct challenge they mounted to traditional mercantilist thinking about the function of colonies. Access to raw materials and the manufacturing of finished goods should have been the province of the metropolis alone. By turning imported materials into finished products, the colonists were competing with metropolitan interests twice over.

The best known of this type of colonial manufacturing was the North American distillation of West Indian molasses. Colonial merchants had quickly recognized the inherent opportunities in their processing of this foodstuff. From as early as the 1640s and 1650s, some of the molasses that colonial ships brought back to North America from Barbados and elsewhere was converted into a distilled rum. The industry grew steadily from these beginnings over the next century and a half. It supplied an inexpensive alternative—a "mere convenience"—to the more costly West Indian rums and the even more expensive imported brandy. By 1770 some 140 rum distilleries were operating on the continent, the majority of them located in the northern port towns (see figure 13.1). In that year the colonists on the continent imported over 6.5 million gallons of molasses, from the bulk of which the distillers produced nearly 5 million gallons of rum, roughly 60 percent of the 8.5 million annually consumed there. Where we can trace their history, colonial distilleries were all organized by merchants as adjuncts to their import businesses.

In the same year, 26 sugar refineries were at work in colonial cities, all of them again organized by colonial merchants as extensions of import businesses. They too were located mostly in the northern ports (see figure 13.2). Colonial merchants had recognized an opportunity in refining imported muscovado sugar into the finished white sugar that colonial con-

FIGURE 13.1.
Rum Distilleries in the
Continental Colonies, 1770

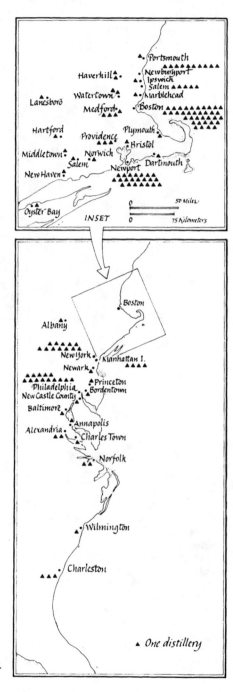

Sources: John J. McCusker, "The Rum
Trade and the Balance of Payments of the
Thirteen Continental Colonies, 1650–
1775" (Ph.D. diss., University of Pitts-
burgh, 1970), 431–447, and as supple-
mented by later research. Compare John J.
McCusker and Barbara Bartz Petchenik,
"Economic Activity," in *Atlas of Early*
American History: The Revolutionary Era,
1760–1790, ed. Lester J. Cappon *et al.*
(Princeton, N.J., 1976), 26–27, 103–104.
Adapted from the *Atlas of Early American*
History, p. 26. Drawn by Richard J. Stinely.

FIGURE 13.2.
Sugar Refineries in the
Continental Colonies, 1770

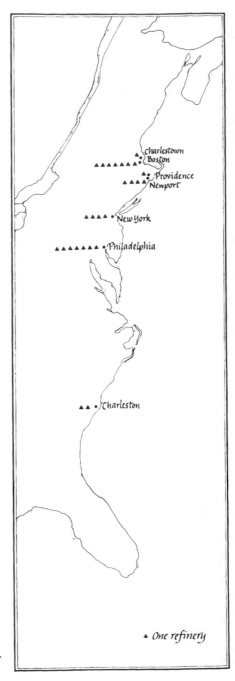

Sources: John J. McCusker, "The Rum
Trade and the Balance of Payments of the
Thirteen Continental Colonies, 1650–
1775" (Ph.D. diss., University of Pitts-
burgh, 1970), 50–55. Compare John J.
McCusker and Barbara Bartz Petchenik,
"Economic Activity," in *Atlas of Early*
American History: The Revolutionary Era,
1760–1790, ed. Lester J. Cappon *et al.*
(Princeton, N.J., 1976), 26–27, 103–104.
Adapted from the *Atlas of Early American*
History, p. 26. Drawn by Richard J. Stinely.

sumers were coming increasingly to prefer. British America's taste in sugar had altered quite markedly during the years, shifting away from the cheaper muscovado sugar and toward the more expensive refined white sugar. Over the same period of time their consumption of sugar increased as they used more and more of it to sweeten their imported chocolate, tea, and coffee. Colonial refining developed to meet a taste preference linked obviously to a rising standard of living. Refined sugar was clearly a "superfluity." Colonial refining survived despite the success that the sugar refiners in the mother country had in winning Parliament's payment of a subsidy for the export of its product to the colonies. The annual produce of colonial sugar refineries, some 23,000 hundredweight in the 1770s, supplied about three-quarters of colonial demand. The rest was imported from Great Britain.[16]

The impact of the changing patterns of consumer demand in the colonies was considerable. Initially, colonial demand created a strong transatlantic and intercolonial trading nexus that supplied a broad range of raw materials and finished products. Merchant-entrepreneurs in this network eventually responded to increases in the volume of the trade and to changes in consumer taste by organizing local sources of supply for some of the commodities they had been importing. Colonial manufacturing grew up in part as an exercise in import substitution.[17] In turning both domestic materials and imported materials into finished goods, colonial manufacturing not only diminished the sales of such commodities by metropolitan and other producers but also imposed on metropolitan interests in other ways. Export subsidies and the like came out of the coffers of the crown. Proportionately smaller quantities of goods shipped from Great Britain to the colonies increased the expenses of the round trip, which had to be paid for by raising freight rates for the return voyage and, therefore, by raising also the final price to the metropolitan consumer of colonial produce such as tobacco and sugar.[18] The benefits to

16. For colonial rum distilling and sugar refining, see John J. McCusker and Barbara Bartz Petchenik, "Economic Activity," in *Atlas of Early American History: The Revolutionary Era, 1760–1790*, ed. Lester J. Cappon *et al.* (Princeton, N.J., 1976), 26–27, 103–104.

17. As Albert O. Hirschman has pointed out, this is a familiar process because imports often make a positive contribution to development. Imports "provide the safest, most incontrovertible proof that the market is there. Moreover, they condition the consumer to the product, breaking down his initial resistance. Imports thus reconnoiter and map out the country's demand; they remove uncertainty and reduce selling costs at the same time, thereby bringing perceptibly closer the point at which domestic production can economically be started" (*Strategy of Economic Development*, 121).

18. For the interrelationship between freight rates east and west, see Harper, *English Navigation Laws*, 268.

the colonists of domestic manufacturing came at a cost to the mother country, which shared less than it would have otherwise in the fruits of the economic development of the colonies.

The impact of imports on the colonial economy was, then, both significant and varied. The demand for a range of consumer products was satisfied, while colonial labor, capital, and management were employed profitably in the commerce that carried such commodities to market. Imports stimulated colonial interest in manufacturing similar goods for sale as their replacement. And, in some cases, imported materials even provided the raw materials for the manufacture of those replacement goods. The result was economic growth and development for the colonies.

CHAPTER 14

EARLY AMERICAN

AGRICULTURE

This chapter and the next address the production and processing of domestic commodities in early British America. The bulk of these were agricultural and were consumed on the spot. The study of the production of agricultural commodities provides an opportunity to examine both the technical and the behavioral aspects of colonial farming. We have much to learn about farm organization, farming techniques, and farm output. In addition we seek to understand what motivated farmers—that is, the ways in which attitudes toward risk, security, and profit interacted with factor supplies and market possibilities to shape their behavior.

Associated with agricultural pursuits were such activities as fishing, fur trapping, and timbering. All these activities may be classified as "extractive industries" and, in the beginning at least, all frequently employed the same labor force working at different times of the year. Although at first farmers processed and manufactured most extractive products during their off-season, increasingly over the colonial period specialized firms were organized to take advantage of the growing economies of scale. Almost all of these firms were tied to the export sector: they provided processing and transport for goods destined for foreign markets. But by the end of the colonial period there were signs of a major reorientation as domestic markets gained in size and importance. While such activities were as yet of minimal quantitative significance, they represented a notable qualitative shift, pointing to a time when the American economy would no longer be export led and would shed its "colonial" character.

A considerable need exists for at least crude estimates of the total production of all colonial goods, extractive or otherwise. How much wheat was grown? How much tobacco, sugar, and rice? How many thousand shingles were fashioned? How many hundredweight of fish caught? And so forth. The amount of each commodity that the colonists exported, for which the records are available, obviously constituted only a part of total output. Domestic consumption is the other addend in our simple equation. It can best be estimated through studies of diet (for foods) and life-style (for items like clothing and household goods). Much of the work already under way is based on probate records. Estimates of per capita domestic consumption, when multiplied by population figures and added to quantities exported, will yield estimates of total production. Such informed guesses will have to be supplemented, for instance, by studies of available production facilities and techniques. Still, these initial efforts will provide a starting point for the refinement of studies of consumption and production at both the family and the aggregate level. In turn they will become the basis of any attempt to understand and to measure all of colonial agriculture and, ultimately, the grand dimensions of the entire colonial economy.[1]

1. Several existing studies will contribute to the construction of such estimates, though only one has in focus the view discussed here. Most common are the attempts to measure diet or levels of consumption among free white colonists. See Carl Bridenbaugh, "The High Cost of Living in Boston, 1728," *NEQ*, V (1932), 800–811; Herbert Renando Cederburg, Jr., "Wages and Prices in Eighteenth-Century England and the Thirteen Colonies" (M.A. thesis, University of California, Berkeley, 1962); Cederburg, *An Economic Analysis of English Settlement in North America, 1583 to 1633* (New York, 1977 [Ph.D. diss., University of California, Berkeley, 1968]); U.S. Bureau of the Census, *Historical Statistics*, II, 1175 (Ser. Z 195–212); James T. Lemon, "Household Consumption in Eighteenth-Century America and Its Relationship to Production and Trade: The Situation among Farmers in Southeastern Pennsylvania," *Agric. Hist.*, XLI (1967), 59–70; Billy G. Smith, "'The Best Poor Man's Country': Living Standards of the 'Lower Sort' in Late Eighteenth-Century Philadelphia," Regional Econ. Hist. Research Center, *Working Papers*, II, no. 4 (1979), 1–70; Carson and Carson, "Styles and Standards of Living in Southern Maryland"; McMahon, "Provisions Laid Up for the Family"; G. Main, *Tobacco Colony*, 140–236; and Shammas, "How Self-sufficient Was Early America?" Less available is information about the diet and living standards of black slaves. See Gisela Eisner, *Jamaica, 1830–1930: A Study in Economic Growth* (Manchester, 1961), 912; R. A. J. Van Lier, *Frontier Society: A Social Analysis of the History of Surinam*, trans. M. J. L. van Yperen (The Hague, 1971), 163–168; and Richard N. Bean, "Food Imports into the British West Indies, 1680–1845," in *Comparative Perspectives on Slavery*, ed. Rubin and Tuden, 581–590. Useful as points of reference are studies of contemporary consumption patterns, such as Poul Thestrup, *The Standard of Living in Copenhagen, 1730–1800: Some Methods of Measurements* (Copenhagen, 1971), and Derek Oddy and Derek Miller, eds., *The Making of the Modern British Diet* (London, 1976). Also useful are studies of later consumption patterns, such as Funk, *Value to Farm Families*, or those discussed and described in Faith M. Williams and Carle C. Zimmerman, *Studies of Family Living in the United States and Other Countries: An Analysis of Material and Method* (Washington, D.C., 1935). Funk's effort is instructive because it also addresses the rather more complex problems of estimating the value of items produced and consumed within the family. See also chap. 3, n. 2, above. For an attempt to employ this kind of analysis in order to estimate the amounts of sugar, molasses, and rum produced in the West Indies, see McCusker, "Rum Trade." One as yet untapped source in efforts to estimate the annual consumption (and production) of all goods is the contemporary tracts

Outside of a few areas—the sugar islands, perhaps the rice district of the Lower South, and the shadow of the major colonial cities—farm units in early British America were not fully commercialized. They did not specialize in a narrow range of crops nor did they purchase on the market most necessary goods and services. Rather, marketed crops and purchased commodities accounted for only a small part of total income and expenditure. The majority of each farm's productive resources was devoted to self-sufficient activities. As Gregory Stiverson has noted, "If early American farmers are placed on a spectrum ranging from bare subsistence at one end to completely commercialized agriculture at the other, most would cluster nearer to the former than to the latter."[2]

Despite an absence of detailed analysis, the reasons for this central structural characteristic of agriculture in early British America seem clear. Farms operated within a set of constraints that restricted the possibilities for specialized market agriculture and encouraged a diversity of output and a high degree of relatively self-contained subsistence production. Some constraints stemmed from shortages of certain factor supplies and from production techniques on the farm. Scarce labor and capital joined with primitive agricultural technology to limit output. Further, since it was rarely possible to hire temporary workers, most farms depended on family labor, which was inelastic in supply. The result was a diversification into crops, livestock, and handicrafts that spread work requirements throughout the year in contrast to a concentration on a single marketable crop with its highly seasonal demands for labor.

Other constraints on the farmer stemmed from small markets and in-

---

aimed at prospective emigrants from England to the colonies early in the 17th century. Many of these tracts included detailed lists of what one needed to get through the first year. See, e.g., [Virginia Company of London], *The Inconveniencies That Have Happened to Some Persons Which Have Transported Themselves from England to Virginia, without Provisions Necessary to Sustaine Themselves* . . . (London, 1622); copy in the John Carter Brown Library, Brown University, Providence, R.I.

2. Stiverson, "Early American Farming: A Comment," *Agric. Hist.*, L (1976), 38. For a similar image, see Bruchey, *Roots of American Economic Growth*, 29. We are fortunate in having two valuable older works on early American agriculture, Lewis C. Gray's classic *History of Agriculture in the Southern United States*, and Bidwell and Falconer, *History of Agriculture in the Northern United States*. For bibliographies, see Everett E. Edwards, *A Bibliography of the History of Agriculture in the United States* (Washington, D.C., 1930); Edwards, *References on American Colonial Agriculture* (Washington, D.C., 1938); John T. Schlebecker, comp., *Bibliography of Books and Pamphlets on the History of Agriculture in the United States, 1607–1967* (Santa Barbara, Calif., 1969); G. Terry Sharrer, comp., *1001 References for the History of American Food Technology* (Davis, Calif., 1978); and T. R. Liao, comp., *The History of American Agriculture* (Washington, D.C., 1981).

adequate transportation. Even when he managed to produce a substantial surplus, getting it to market proved difficult, and once there, prices were uncertain. Although the outline seems clear, the details are not. Historians must examine the interactions among factor supplies, farming techniques, unit size, access to markets, commodity prices, crop mix, and the relative importance of commercial versus subsistence production. Such studies, based chiefly on probate records and sensitive to temporal and regional variations, are a necessity if we are to understand the dynamics of agriculture in early British America.[3]

While there is general agreement, if little detailed understanding, on the existence of the high subsistence component in early American agriculture, its causes and consequences are under debate. Some historians—representing the dominant position from the mid-1940s to the later 1970s—argue that farmers were latent entrepreneurs, willing to take risks and accept innovation, who found their drive for profits frustrated by high factor prices, primitive technologies, poor transportation networks, and weak markets.[4] This has been called the "market model" of colonial agriculture. More recently, other historians have claimed that farmers were not much concerned with profit, that their principal interests were subsistence and the long-term security of the farm, that they did not try to maximize production of cash crops and marketed only their surplus, that they avoided risk and were suspicious of innovations. This has been called the "subsistence model." The complex of attitudes generated by subsistence farming are thought to have constrained responsiveness to market incentives and served as a significant barrier to economic development.[5] Some of this recent work implies a dual economy in the

3. Max George Schumacher, *The Northern Farmer and His Markets during the Late Colonial Period* (New York, 1975 [Ph.D. diss., University of California, Berkeley, 1948]), remains the best analysis of the constraints faced by early American farmers. Gavin Wright, *The Political Economy of the Cotton South: Households, Markets, and Wealth in the Nineteenth Century* (New York, 1978), suggests a useful theoretical approach to the issues; see especially chap. 3, "The Microeconomics of Plantation and Farm." Farmers in the early national period contended with similar restraints. The literature is large and beyond the scope of this book, but historians of colonial agriculture ought to be familiar with it. Darwin P. Kelsey, ed., *Farming in the New Nation: Interpreting American Agriculture, 1790–1840* (Washington, D.C., 1972), is a good introduction.

4. Lemon, *Best Poor Man's Country*; Bushman, *From Puritan to Yankee*; Grant, *Democracy in Kent*; Rodney C. Loehr, "Self-sufficiency on the Farm," *Agric. Hist.*, XXVI (1952), 37–41; R. Mitchell, *Commercialism and Frontier*.

5. Henretta, "Families and Farms," builds the most persuasive case for this position and offers a penetrating critique of the entrepreneurial school. In a sense Henretta is reviving a position taken much earlier by Bidwell—the worlds they describe show some striking similarities—but Bidwell worked out a set of economic assumptions that Henretta explicitly

colonies. In this view, British America consisted of two self-contained "worlds." One was "a hard-driving commercial society composed of plantations and seaport towns" deeply involved in markets and overseas trade. It coexisted alongside an inland pastoral society "of sleepy villages inhabited by farmers devoid of a profit orientation and almost entirely dependent upon their own households and neighborhood reciprocity for goods and services."[6]

Unfortunately, the debate so far has centered more on the collection of literary descriptions of attitudes than on testing the behavioral implications of the two models. This is not to argue that the values of farm families in early British America were unimportant to its economic history. Indeed, the attitudes of the rural population toward risk and profit, work and consumption—its *mentalité*, in the currently fashionable phrase— were critical to the workings of the economy. Economic development re-

rejects. See Percy W. Bidwell, "Rural Economy in New England at the Beginning of the Nineteenth Century," Connecticut Academy of the Arts and Sciences, *Transactions*, XX (1916), 241–399, and "The Agricultural Revolution in New England," *AHR*, XXVI (1921), 683–702. For positions similar to that taken by Henretta, see John J. Waters, "The Traditional World of the New England Peasants: A View from Seventeenth-Century Barnstable," *NEHGR*, CXXX (1976), 3–21; Robert E. Mutch, "Yeoman and Merchant in Preindustrial America: Eighteenth-Century Massachusetts as a Case Study," *Societas*, VII (1977), 279–302; Michael Merrill, "Cash Is Good to Eat: Self-sufficiency and Exchange in the Rural Economy of the United States," *Radical History Review*, IV (1977), 42–72; and Christopher Clark, "Household Economy, Market Exchange, and the Rise of Capitalism in the Connecticut Valley, 1800–1860," *Jour. Soc. Hist.*, XIII (1979), 169–189. James Lemon has responded to Henretta's critique, rather ineffectively we fear, in several pieces: "The Weakness of Place and Community in Early Pennsylvania," in *European Settlement and Development*, ed. Gibson, 190–207; "Early Americans and Their Social Environment," *Jour. Hist. Geography*, VI (1980), 115–131; and a comment on James A. Henretta's "Families and Farms: *Mentalité* in Pre-industrial America," *WMQ*, 3d Ser., XXXVII (1980), 688–700 (with a reply by Henretta). Work in progress by Lucy Simler on Chester County, Pennsylvania, promises to illuminate these issues by exploring the behavioral implications of the positions taken by Lemon and his critics. Simler, "The Township," is a preliminary statement. In this context we find suggestive the insight of an Anglican clergyman, who in 1678 complained that Virginians were interested in little more than "who can at the Fall of the Leaf produce the largest crop of Corn and Tobacco" ([Paul Williams], *The Vain Prodigal Life, and Tragical Penitent Death of Thomas Hellier . . .* [London, 1680], as printed in T. H. Breen, James H. Lewis, and Keith Schlesinger, "Motive for Murder: A Servant's Life in Virginia, 1678," *WMQ*, 3d Ser., XL [1983], 118).

6. The quotations are from Shammas, "Consumer Behavior," 67, which offers a sharp critique of the dual economy hypothesis. That hypothesis receives its most explicit defense in studies of conflict between the "two worlds." See, for example, Paul Boyer and Stephen Nissenbaum, *Salem Possessed: The Social Origins of Witchcraft* (Cambridge, Mass., 1974), and David P. Szatmary, *Shays' Rebellion: The Making of an Agrarian Insurrection* (Amherst, Mass., 1980).

quires a population willing to take advantage of its circumstances, to accept risks in anticipation of increased rewards, to try new techniques and new crops in order to capture higher profits, to work harder in hope of raising standards of consumption, to migrate in pursuit of fairer fields, and to display many other "entrepreneurial" traits. Our point is only that we will gain greater insight into those values if we pay more attention to what farm families did than to what observers say farmers thought or felt.

In this regard, the principal message of recent work seems unexceptional: most farmers placed the subsistence needs of their families and the long-term security of their farms ahead of short-run income maximization. To have done otherwise would have been to invite disaster. But the consequences of such priorities are not self-evident, and they will remain unclear until debate shifts away from its current focus on attitudes and toward the quantitative analysis of behavior. Several matters are of particular interest: the proportion of farm output that reached the market; the constraints imposed by high transport costs; the size of local markets; the responsiveness of farmers to price incentives; the dynamics of internal migration; and the diffusion of innovations.

The notion of a commercial-subsistence continuum is clearly a useful device, but we need to fill in the details. It is not enough to say that most farms clustered near the subsistence end of the spectrum, for there were variations across space and time. One major need in colonial American agricultural history is to map those variations, to classify farming regions by focusing on the proportion of total output that entered the market and by describing how that proportion changed over time. Nor can it be assumed that time and place were the only variables. There were also differences within regions by unit size and by tenure, that is, between small and large farms, between freeholders and tenants. The task is difficult because the evidence is limited, but recent work suggests that a combination of probate records, farm account books and diaries, tax lists, data on imports and exports, and travelers' accounts will permit an approximation of the pattern. As is so often the case in early American history, the map will have to be constructed from the bottom up, from intense studies of small areas, because we seldom encounter readily aggregated data covering large regions.[7]

7. J. Main, *Social Structure*, remains the best survey of regional patterns in early American agriculture, although it clearly needs refinement. Useful ideas for studying such patterns appear in Andrew Hill Clark, "Suggestions for the Geographical Study of Agricultural Change in the United States, 1790–1840," in *Farming in the New Nation*, ed. Kelsey, 155–172. For the impact of farm size and tenure on specialization, see Wright, *Political Economy of the*

One useful approach to the subject is to examine the potential for self-sufficiency among farmers. Farm families, if they were to achieve independence from the market, required a wide variety of equipment and a wide range of skills. The degree to which they possessed the skills is perhaps impossible to determine, but it is a simple matter to discover whether they owned the equipment since it was regularly listed in probate inventories. Much work remains before the issue will be settled, but available studies suggest that the self-sufficiency of colonial farm families—even those living in relatively remote interior regions—has been greatly exaggerated: most lacked the means for complete independence.[8] Of course, the question is not one of absolutes, but of degree. Moreover, we must ask it not just of families but also of communities.

Few historians would now argue that many families achieved total self-sufficiency, but some still maintain that farmers could grow much of what they needed and acquire the rest from friends and neighbors through mutual exchange. Price considerations played little role, it is claimed, and farmers were isolated from larger markets. This more subtle and more compelling version of the case for self-sufficiency is difficult to evaluate. Again, it probably exaggerates the isolation of colonial American farmers from the Atlantic economy. According to one estimate, at the end of the colonial period British Americans spent on average more than one-quarter of their total incomes on imported goods, most of them consumables. Such a proportion leaves little room for self-contained communities of subsistence farmers.[9]

Averages, as usual, are potentially misleading. It is likely that farmers in some regions spent a much greater share of their incomes on imported goods than farmers did in other areas. The issue has to be pursued at the local level. One approach would be to construct family budgets with careful attention to variations by region, time, and wealth. The needed data will be difficult to come by and the results will have to rely on some

---

Cotton South, 62–74; Kim, *Landlord and Tenant*, 157–158, 269–270; and Beverly McAnear, ed., "Mr. Robert R. Livingston's Reasons against a Land Tax," *Jour. Pol. Econ.*, XLVIII (1940), 63–90, especially pp. 88–89.

8. For evidence on the potential for self-sufficiency drawn from probate records, see Shammas, "How Self-sufficient Was Early America?"; Earle, *Evolution of a Tidewater Settlement System*, 101–142; Carr and Walsh, "Inventories and Analysis of Wealth"; and Ulrich, "'Friendly Neighbor.'" Obviously, the issue of self-sufficiency has important implications for women's history, particularly for the division of labor by sex and for the contribution to welfare of work usually done by women. Once again we have reference to Boserup, *Woman's Role*.

9. Shammas, "How Self-sufficient Was Early America?" 263–266.

educated guesswork, but probate documents—in this case the records of estate administrators—again contain much useful information, as do the account books kept by farmers and shopkeepers. Family budgets will permit more-detailed description of the sources of income and its expenditures and provide a more accurate assessment of where on the subsistence-commercial spectrum most farmers should be placed. Furthermore, such budgets would yield insight into questions of wealth and welfare and help to overcome the inadequacies of measures rooted largely in aggregate data.[10]

Close study of the markets for farm commodities is also necessary. We know a good deal about the export of agricultural products, and the data to extend the analysis are available.[11] Nevertheless, despite the importance of the foreign sector to the colonial economy, not all the farmer's customers lived overseas. Town dwellers had to be fed, as did families pursuing non-farm occupations in the countryside, even those who owned some livestock and a vegetable patch. We need to know much more about the size and organization of the domestic market for farm products. There is evidence that it was larger than we have been led to believe, especially in the northern colonies.[12]

We should also determine how far marketing networks extended into the interior. Internal transportation, about which surprisingly little is known, is central to the issue. Conventional wisdom suggests that high transport costs severely limited farmers' access to markets and that the "tyranny of distance" kept many farmers isolated, forcing them into a subsistence mode of production. Again, there is evidence that such a formulation is misleading, that it overestimates the costs and underestimates the sophistication of interior transport, and that it thus misjudges the dis-

10. For an example of the data sometimes found in administration accounts, see Menard, Carr, and Walsh, "Small Planter's Profits." See also Shammas, "Consumer Behavior," for a demonstration of how inventories can be used to study patterns of consumption among farmers and others. Billy G. Smith has had some success in estimating household budgets for workers in Philadelphia ("Material Lives"). See also Bridenbaugh, "High Cost of Living in Boston." While of little help on the issue of rural self-sufficiency, these works do suggest what might be done. See also n. 1, above.

11. See especially Schumacher, *Northern Farmer and His Markets*, 122–134, 148–173; Shepherd and Walton, *Shipping*, 91–113, 204–236; and the naval officer shipping lists discussed in chap. 4, above.

12. The best discussion of the home market remains Schumacher, *Northern Farmer and His Markets*, 105–121. See also Klingaman, "Food Surpluses and Deficits." The urban market for food merits close study. See Karen J. Friedmann, "Victualling Colonial Boston," *Agric. Hist.*, XLVII (1973), 189–205, and Elinor F. Oakes, "A Ticklish Business: Dairying in New England and Pennsylvania, 1750–1812," *Pa. Hist.*, XLVII (1980), 195–212.

tance across which farmers were willing and able to haul their products.[13]

Whether and to what extent particular regions became integrated into a larger marketing system can be determined by studying prices. "Economists understand by the term *Market*, . . . the whole of any region in which buyers and sellers are in such free intercourse with one another that the prices of the same goods tend to equality easily and quickly."[14] Augustin Cournot's classic definition implies a method of analysis. If the price of grain grown in the Pennsylvania backcountry or the interior regions of New England fluctuated with prices in Philadelphia, Boston, and New York, then the grain presumably was traded in the larger market. If that was not the case, if price fluctuations showed little relationship to movements in the major cities, one could conclude that grain produced in a particular community was intended only for local consumption.

The point may be extended to include business cycles generally. Farmers isolated from the market, locked into a subsistence mode of production, would be relatively immune to the periodic shocks, the cycles of boom and bust, the metropolitan recessions, and the disruptive impact of war that buffeted the more commercial sectors of the colonial economy. Thus, a study of the effects of colonial business cycles on particular rural regions will assess how thoroughly such regions were isolated from the larger Atlantic world. So far the few such studies that have been done offer evidence that the isolation of farmers has been much exaggerated.[15]

Some interpretations of the importance of subsistence activities in early American farming identify a distinct pattern in the production of marketable crops. Given the uncertainties of agriculture, prudent farmers concerned with providing food for their families and enough cash to purchase the necessities that could not be produced on the farm would consistently overplant to allow for normal variations in yields. Thus, in

13. On the sophistication of internal transport networks in early America, see Walzer, "Transportation in Philadelphia," and Dauer, "Colonial Philadelphia's Transportation System." On transport costs and the distances farmers traveled to market, see Winifred B. Rothenberg, "The Market and Massachusetts Farmers, 1750–1855," *Jour. Econ. Hist.*, XLI (1981), 295–300. See also chap. 16, below, and Roger N. Parks's study of transportation, which concludes "that the isolation of even some of the more remote parts of northern New England was by no means complete" ("The Roads of New England, 1790–1840" [Ph.D. diss., Michigan State University, 1966], 29).

14. Alfred Marshall, *Principles of Economics: An Introductory Volume* (1890), 9th ed. (New York, 1961), I, 324, quoting Augustin Cournot, *Recherches sur les principes mathématiques de la théorie des richesses* (Paris, 1838), chap. 4.

15. For a comparative study of urban and rural prices, see Rothenberg, "Price Index." See also William S. Sachs, "Agricultural Conditions in the Northern Colonies before the Revolution," *Jour. Econ. Hist.*, XIII (1953), 274–290.

most years farmers would produce a surplus beyond subsistence requirements. But the size of that surplus would be random with regard to price,
responsive to the vagaries of climate rather than to the incentives of the
market. Market-oriented farmers, on the other hand, would increase or
diminish output, change their product mix, and introduce new crops in
response to shifting prices.[16]

While these alternative models of farm behavior have not been tested
thoroughly, it has been argued that the "striking expansion of the wheat
belt" into the plantation South after 1750 supports this "subsistence surplus" interpretation. It is clear that production on individual farms in the
North "was not elastic enough to cope with the rising wheat market." It
is not clear, however, that the inelasticity stemmed from the "cultural
preferences" of farmers "unwilling to bid for wage labor," who avoided
"innovative, risk-taking behavior" and "chose the security of diversified
production" over the uncertainties of the market.[17] Rather, it could be
argued, the high price of labor, the inefficiencies of "sickle technology,"
and the absence of major scale economies in wheat meant that increased
demand was most efficiently met by adding new family farms and by beginning production on plantations where slavery removed the labor constraint that restricted the size of operations dependent on free workers. In
this light the extension of the wheat-growing area southward in the middle
of the eighteenth century can be seen as a rational response to market
pressures by commercially oriented farmers.[18]

The attitude of colonial American farmers toward the market also has
implications for the process of internal migration. In the subsistence
model, "push" factors dominated migration decisions: migrants moved
away from overcrowded settlements with their poor prospects for economic independence rather than *toward* better market possibilities; and
movement was financed out of family resources. In the market model, the
"pull" of better prospects predominated: migrants moved *toward* chances
for commercial agriculture rather than *away* from depressed conditions;
and it was merchants and land developers who provided much of the

16. Stiverson, "Early American Farming," 38; Henretta, "Families and Farms," 12. In a direct test of supply elasticity, Rothenberg found a different pattern, concluding "that feed
[corn] and meat [pork] prices played a statistically significant role in farmers' decisions re-
specting the weight at which to slaughter hogs" ("The Market and Massachusetts Farmers," 288).

17. Schumacher, *Northern Farmer and His Markets*, 142; Henretta, "Families and Farms,"
17–19.

18. For the notion that slavery removed the labor constraint facing individual farmers and
some of its implications, see Heywood Fleisig, "Slavery, the Supply of Agricultural Labor,
and the Industrialization of the South," *Jour. Econ. Hist.*, XXXVI (1976), 572–597.

needed capital. In practice, push and pull are of course difficult to separate—migration flows are best understood as responses to differences in
anticipated income—and, in fact, both family and outside sources financed the spread of settlement in early British America. Still, the two
models do have different and testable behavioral implications for the volume, composition, finance, organization, timing, and direction of internal migration. Close study of the process of geographic expansion will
yield useful insight into the behavior and motivation of farm families in
the colonies.[19]

The agricultural practices of early American farmers often earned the
scorn of contemporary observers, and their reputation has not fared
much better at the hands of historians.[20] In contrast to the image of the
improving British farmer, colonials appeared wasteful and slovenly: they
abused the land and cared poorly for livestock; they accepted small yields
and low incomes; they used primitive tools; and they resisted useful innovations. "The common husbandmen in the country," Jedediah Morse observed in 1789, "generally choose to continue in the old track of their
forefathers." Samuel Deane echoed Morse one year later. "Farmers do
many things for which they can assign no other reason than custom.
They usually give themselves little or no trouble in thinking, or in exam-

19. D. S. Smith, "Malthusian-Frontier Interpretation," explores some of these implications.
See also D. Jones, *Village and Seaport*, 103–121. Wilbur Zelinsky, "The Hypothesis of the
Mobility Transition," *Geographical Rev.*, LXI (1971), 219–249, is full of interesting
suggestions.

20. See, for example, Land, "Tobacco Staple." For reforming farmers in early America, see
Lucius F. Ellsworth, "The Philadelphia Society for the Promotion of Agriculture and Agri-
cultural Reform, 1785–1793," *Agric. Hist.*, XLII (1968), 189–199; Rodney C. Loehr,
"Arthur Young and American Agriculture," *ibid.*, XLIII (1969), 43–56; Chester McArthur
Destler, "The Gentleman Farmer and the New Agriculture: Jeremiah Wadsworth," *ibid.*,
XLVI (1972), 135–153; and Donald B. Marti, "Early Agricultural Societies in New York:
The Foundations of Improvement," *N.Y. Hist.*, XLVIII (1967), 313–331. Equally harsh,
unfairly so we believe, are some of the criticisms of West Indian practices in Ragatz, *Fall of
the Planter Class*, 57–60. The literature on early American agriculture is large, but useful
information is often found also in books and articles primarily concerned with other issues.
For work focused on the subject, in addition to material cited elsewhere in this chapter, see
Bonner, *History of Georgia Agriculture*; Lyman Carrier, *The Beginnings of Agriculture in
America* (New York, 1923); Stevenson Whitcomb Fletcher, *Pennsylvania Agriculture and
Country Life, 1640–1840* (Harrisburg, Pa., 1950); Albert Laverne Olson, *Agricultural
Economy and the Population in Eighteenth-Century Connecticut* (New Haven, Conn.,
1935); Howard S. Russell, *A Long, Deep Furrow: Three Centuries of Farming in New En-
gland* (Hanover, N.H., 1976); Rutman, *Husbandmen of Plymouth*; Robert R. Walcott,
"Husbandry in Colonial New England," *NEQ*, IX (1936), 218–252; and Carl Raymond
Woodward, *The Development of Agriculture in New Jersey, 1640–1880: A Monographic
Study in Agricultural History* (New Brunswick, N.J., 1927).

ining their methods of agriculture, which have been handed down from father to son, from time immemorial."[21]

Such behavior is consistent with a subsistence mode of production in which limited aspirations and the dead hand of tradition guided farming practices. But it is also consistent with an economy in which labor and capital were expensive but land was cheap, where it made little sense to follow the "best" British practices. Different factor prices call for different modes of production. George Washington's explanation of American farming methods, while distinguished by its forcefulness, is a typical defense: "The aim of the farmers in this country . . . is not to make the most they can from the land, which is, or has been cheap, but the most of the labour, which is dear, the consequence of which has been, much ground has been *scratched* over and none cultivated or improved as it ought to have been." Thomas Jefferson added, "We can buy an acre of new land cheaper than we can manure an old acre."[22]

The issues demand close quantitative analysis within a sophisticated theoretical framework. While we suspect that colonial farmers were not notably "wasteful" or "slovenly" given the constraints within which they worked, we do not yet have enough evidence to support such a conclusion. Our understanding of techniques rests too heavily on the reports of travelers, usually Englishmen accustomed to agricultural practices born

21. Morse, *The American Geography; or, A View of the Present Situation of the United States of America* . . . (Elizabeth Town, [N.J.], 1789), 182; Deane, *The New-England Farmer; or, Georgical Dictionary* . . . (Worcester, Mass., 1790), 66.

22. Washington to Arthur Young, 5 Dec. 1791, in *The Writings of George Washington from the Original Manuscript Sources, 1745–1799*, ed. John C. Fitzpatrick (Washington, D.C., 1931–1944), XXXI, 440 (emphasis in the original). In a manner typical of his time, Edward Gibbon Wakefield sought to improve on the original text and "quoted" Washington as saying that "where land is cheap and labour dear, men are fonder of cultivating much than cultivating well" (*England and America: A Comparison of the Social and Political State of Both Nations* [New York, 1834], 226n). Jefferson to Washington, 28 June 1793, in *The Writings of Thomas Jefferson*, ed. Andrew A. Lipscomb and Albert Ellery Bergh (Washington, D.C., 1903–1904), IX, 141. For Washington as an "improving" farmer, see Raymond George Peterson, Jr., "George Washington, Capitalistic Farmer: A Documentary Study of Washington's Business Activities and the Sources of His Wealth" (Ph.D. diss., Ohio State University, 1970), and Terry Sharrer, " 'An Undebauched Mind': Farmer Washington at Mt. Vernon" (paper presented at the annual meeting of the Society for Eighteenth-Century Studies, Washington, D.C., Apr. 1981). See also David O. Percy, "An Embarrassment of Richness: Colonial Soil Cultivation Practices," *Associates N[ational] A[gricultural] L[ibrary] Today*, N.S., II (1977), 4–11. Ester Boserup's discussion of the relationship between "sparse population and primitive techniques" in agriculture is helpful here; she calls it a "vicious circle" (see *Conditions of Agricultural Growth*, chap. 8, 70–76). See also Warren C. Scoville, "Did Colonial Farmers 'Waste' Our Land?" *So. Econ. Jour.*, XX (1953), 178–181, and Roger W. Weiss, "Mr. Scoville on Colonial Land Wastage," *ibid.*, XXI (1954), 87–90.

of a different situation. Our information on yields is thin, inconsistent, and often inappropriately presented, reflecting European concerns in terms of output per acre and weight per animal. More helpful would be estimates of total factor productivity or at least output per worker, since this would reflect the particular difficulties facing American farmers.[23]

We also need to know more about the available options. Why were "improvements" rejected? Were they deemed inappropriate because they demanded substitution away from cheap factors of production or because ignorance and the weight of tradition retarded innovation? And we need close study of the diffusion of those innovations that were suited to the colonial environment. Since relative factor prices changed over time and differed by region, and since slavery had a profound impact on the choice of technique, such studies must be sensitive to temporal and regional variations.[24] Again, probate records are our best source. Properly exploited and supplemented with other materials, they will yield a more detailed, precise, and sophisticated history of agricultural practice on farm and plantation than is currently available.[25]

We suspect that the recent emphasis on the subsistence component of colonial American agriculture underestimates the responsiveness of farmers to market incentives and overstates the importance of "attitudinal" or "cultural" factors as opposed to "environmental" constraints on produc-

23. Probate records can provide useful information on yields. See Mark Overton, "Estimating Crop Yields from Probate Inventories: An Example from East Anglia, 1585–1735," *Jour. Econ. Hist.*, XXXIX (1979), 363–378. See also E. L. Jones, "Agriculture, 1700–80," in *Economic History of Britain*, ed. Floud and McCloskey, I, 66–86. For efforts to measure total factor productivity in agriculture, see chap. 12, n. 11, above. The contemporary literature containing useful information on early American farming is large. Fairly full bibliographies appear in the works by Gray and Bidwell and Falconer cited in n. 2, above. Two classics are Harry J. Carman, ed., *American Husbandry* (1775) (New York, 1939), and Jared Eliot, *Essays upon Field Husbandry in New England, and Other Papers, 1748–1762*, ed. Harry J. Carman and Rexford G. Tugwell (New York, 1934). Almanacs are a useful and relatively neglected source. For a guide to available copies, see Milton Drake, comp., *Almanacs of the United States* (New York, 1962). Important collections of almanacs are owned by the American Antiquarian Society, Worcester, Mass., and by the Library of Congress. See also Robert Tolbert Sidwell, "The Colonial American Almanacs: A Study in Noninstitutional Education" (Ed.D. diss., Rutgers University, 1965). Much of importance concerning early American agriculture has been learned also by those involved in re-creating practices of the period. See John T. Schlebecker and Gale E. Peterson, *Living Historical Farms Handbook* (Washington, D.C., 1972). See especially the Research Reports of the National Colonial Farm at Accokeek, Maryland, many of them written by the farm's director, David O. Percy.

24. Again, R. Anderson and Gallman, "Slaves as Fixed Capital," provides a helpful perspective on the impact of slavery on agricultural practices.

25. Lemon, "Household Consumption," suggests some of the possibilities given the limitations of evidence.

tivity. Still, that emphasis has improved our understanding of the behavior of farmers and has suggested promising strategies for future inquiry. For one thing, it has served as an important corrective to the view that colonial farms were organized business enterprises. They were that, in part, but they were also family enterprises, consuming much of what they produced and producing much of what they consumed. Not only is this a reminder of the diversity of farm output, but it implies as well an aversion to risk and a unique set of priorities that shaped behavior and conditioned responses to markets. Small farmers had to ensure that short-term subsistence needs were met, that the long-term security of the enterprise was protected, that sufficient income was maintained over their lifetimes, and that adequate inheritance was provided for their children. The behavioral implications of such requirements are not clear, but they do suggest an interaction between market conditions, decisions to marry or to move, patterns of inheritance, and family size. The intersection of family history and economic history is a major opportunity for study.[26]

26. Henretta, "Families and Farms," is suggestive on these matters. The recent literature in New England social history, although it has tended to pay too little attention to the business side of farm life, is most helpful. See chap. 5, above, and especially Greven, *Four Generations*; Gross, *Minutemen and Their World*; Jedrey, *World of John Cleaveland*; Richard L. Bushman, "Family Security in the Transition from Farm to City," *Jour. Family Hist.*, VI (1981), 238–256; and Waters, "Family, Inheritance, and Migration." The extensive literature on fertility decline among farm families in the 19th-century United States contains much of interest to early American historians. For an introduction, see Richard A. Easterlin, "Factors in the Decline of Farm Family Fertility in the United States: Some Preliminary Research Results," *JAH*, LXIII (1976), 600–614.

CHAPTER 15

COLONIAL

MANUFACTURING

AND EXTRACTIVE

INDUSTRIES

Only a few historians have given any attention to the manufacturing industries of early British America. And rightly so, it could be argued, for they were of little consequence at the time and of real importance only for what they portended for the future. Certainly the obstacles to manufacturing in early British America were formidable. As factors of production, labor and capital were scarcer and more expensive than land. The comparative advantage of the colonies was in agriculture, or at least in businesses that were relatively more resource-intensive than manufacturing. Markets were limited, not only because of the small size and low density of colonial populations but also because of the self-sufficient bent to early American farming. Furthermore, even the small markets for manufactured goods that did exist could not be protected. Colonists were seldom successful in passing protective taxes on imports; moreover, the exportation of bulky colonial exports, in effect, subsidized the importation of manufactures from abroad by minimizing the cost of backhaul voyages, thus preventing distance from serving as a natural tariff barrier. Small unprotected markets kept colonial manufacturers from competing effectively with their British counterparts, who catered to the whole empire, produced on a larger scale, and succeeded in keeping costs down.

Various mercantilist devices—restrictions on colonial manufacturing and bounties for British manufactures—also inhibited industrial development in the colonies. Such devices were much less significant than factor prices, market size, and alternative prospects, however. At least in the short run, colonists found "it more [to] their interest to cultivate their lands and attend the fisheries than to manufacture." [1] Mercantilist restrictions were perhaps the "impertinent badges of slavery" that Adam Smith called them, but even on the eve of the Revolutionary War they were not "very hurtful to the colonies. Land is still so cheap, and, consequently, labour so dear among them, that they can import from the mother country, almost all the more refined or more advanced manufactures cheaper than they could make them for themselves." [2]

The obstacles to manufacturing became less weighty as the colonial period drew to a close. In fact, certain features of the colonial economy stimulated specific types of industry. Three elements were particularly noteworthy. First, in addition to encouraging agriculture, abundant colonial resources also offered the possibility of other extractive activities and served as the raw materials for processing industries. Second, since agriculture seldom demanded year-round work, during slack times farmers could pursue a wide range of industrial or extractive tasks. Third, the colonial foreign sector supplied materials for processing, provided fabricating and processing equipment, generated demand, and furnished transportation. When these three features combined to encourage a single industry—for example, shipbuilding—the results were most impressive.

The occasions for exploiting the colonial resource base were not restricted to agriculture. From the very beginning of settlement it was clear that income and wealth could be extracted from the wilderness more directly and immediately than by planting and harvesting crops. Indeed, fishing, fur trapping, and timbering not only preceded agriculture as major extractive industries but also remained important throughout the colonial period.

The good fishing in North American waters attracted Englishmen to the New World even before the voyages of Columbus. Fishing continued to enter into the calculations of those who settled New England in particular. At first, settlers fished simply to help feed themselves. However, they

---

1. [William Knox], *The Interest of the Merchants and Manufacturers of Great Britain, in the Present Contest with the Colonies, Stated and Considered* (London, 1774), 20, and as quoted in V. Clark, *History of Manufactures*, I, 29. For the disallowance of colonial laws that attempted to confer discriminatory economic advantage on the colonists, see E. Russell, *Review of American Colonial Legislation*.

2. A. Smith, *Wealth of Nations*, II, 582. Even though Benjamin Franklin was not the only champion of manufacturing as a way to improve the material condition of the people, his advocacy of that position has earned for him in the eyes of at least one historian the title of father of the Industrial Revolution in the United States. See Piero Bairati, "Per il bene dell'umanità: Benjamin Franklin e il problema delle manifatture," *Rivista Storica Italiana*, XC (1978), 262–293.

soon emulated other fishermen who appeared off their coasts and on their shores to profit from the harvest of the seas. The colonists learned more than one lesson from the men who organized the annual migration from the West Country English ports. Not only did New Englanders discover where to fish and how to preserve their catch, but also how and where to market the surplus. In the 1640s and after, New Englanders, especially those based in the seacoast towns north of Boston, provided the colony with its first large-scale marketable export commodity: fish. Shipped to the tables of Catholic Europeans, New England's fish proved a major earner of credits in the colony's balance of payments from a very early date—and, indeed, introduced the colonists to the ways of international trade. Later, as the slave population of the West Indies increased, they too became major consumers of fish from New England.[3]

We have only the barest understanding of the history of New England's fisheries. Some recent research has been helpful, but little systematic work, either narrative or analytical, has been done. Historians must still rely heavily on antiquarian and anecdotal studies for the most basic information. What we know best are, again, some of the international aspects of the business, but even this is much less than one might expect. For instance, the exportation of fish from New England to Portugal and to the Portuguese islands in the Atlantic established a network of commercial and human relationships that persists today. Nothing to speak of has been written about this Portuguese connection or its impact on either country, yet it served a variety of purposes, including providing a way for colonists to establish credits in London.[4]

If we know only the minimum about the "foreign" aspects of fish-

3. The standard works on early British American fishing are still useful: McFarland, *History of the New England Fisheries*; Judah, *North American Fisheries*; and Lounsbury, *British Fishery at Newfoundland*. The most valuable of such works is, of course, Innis, *Cod Fisheries*. A recent and impressive study that includes a survey of the fishing industry itself is Vickers, "Maritime Labor." See also Michell, "European Fisheries." For the interaction between the early colonists, the fisheries, and international trade, see Bailyn, *New England Merchants, passim.*

4. H. Fisher, *Portugal Trade*, only just touches on the role of the English colonies in this trade, but it does reveal something of the sources available and the context within which one can view them. Again one needs to refer to Bailyn, *New England Merchants*. For the continuation of the Portuguese connection, one can turn to works such as Leo Pap, *The Portuguese-Americans* (Boston, 1981). See also O. Louis Mazzatenta, "New England's 'Little Portugal,'" *National Geographic*, CXLVII (1975), 90–109. Some of the impact of this regional economic development is discussed in chap. 5, above. In this regard, see also Lounsbury, "Yankee Trade at Newfoundland," and Lounsbury, *British Fishery at Newfoundland*. Even more useful, for its greater span of time and more-analytical orientation as well as for its greater range of sources, is Head, *Eighteenth Century Newfoundland*. See also Matthews, "West Country–Newfoundland Fisheries." Ignored here but of consider-

ing, we know even less about its domestic side. How did the colonists organize their fishing industry? Where did the work force come from? Were most fishermen also farmers or artisans or was following the cod their only occupation? What of their wages and standard of living? And how, if at all, did any of this change over time? We get just a glimpse of something intriguing in the efforts of the government of Massachusetts in the 1640s to promote fishing. The colony encouraged fishermen-turned-farmers to return to their boats by offering to take care of minding their fields, at public expense. Later in the colonial period it appears that, during the off-season, some fishermen converted their fishing boats into coastal trading ships and themselves into merchants. The result was increased returns both to their own expertise as seamen and to the capital invested in their vessels, thus providing another example of the export sector acting as agent for the development of the colonial economy.

Cod may have been king for the fisherman, but whaling was the prince of professions. The colonists followed an old tradition in their harvesting of the world's largest mammal, less the native American tradition (the Eskimos, if not the Indians, hunted the whale) than the English tradition. That is, the colonists pursued the whale not so much to supplement food supplies as to obtain raw materials for a variety of manufacturing purposes. Ambergris for perfumes, whalebone for stays and stiffeners, whale oil for lamps, and spermaceti for candles—all, except ambergris, required some processing in the colonies before being sold to domestic and overseas customers. Centered in southern New England and the eastern end of Long Island, the whaling industry promoted the development of the region by providing the stimulus for a variety of linked enterprises, thus directly employing the capital, labor, and talent of the area. It was a very big business indeed, about which we know far too little.[5]

Early European fishermen, while drying their catch on shore, traded

---

able importance for colonial history was the French fishery off Newfoundland. See La Morandière, *Histoire de la pêche française.*

5. The best account for the early British American period is still Starbuck, *History of the American Whale Fishery.* See also Walter S. Tower, *A History of the American Whale Fishery* (Philadelphia, 1907), and Edouard A. Stackpole, *The Sea-Hunters: The New England Whalemen during Two Centuries, 1635–1835* (Philadelphia, 1953). Local studies of value include William R. Palmer, "The Whaling Port of Sag Harbor" (Ph.D. diss., Columbia University, 1959), and Douglass C. Fonda, Jr., *Eighteenth Century Nantucket Whaling, as Compiled from the Original Logs and Journals of the Nantucket Atheneum and the Nantucket Whaling Museum* (Nantucket, Mass., 1969). For the larger picture, see J. T. Jenkins, *A History of the Whale Fisheries, from the Basque Fisheries of the Tenth Century to the Hunting of the Finner Whale at the Present Date* (London, 1921), and Gordon Jackson, *The British Whaling Trade* (London, 1978). The buying and selling of whale oil is the subject of discussions in Baxter, *House of Hancock*; Hedges, *Browns of Providence Plantations*;

with the Indians for furs. Even though they may initially have bought them only for their own use, by carrying the pelts home at the end of the season they became the first to alert Europe to the possibilities of the North American fur trade. The trade quickly became a major enterprise in which the English. colonists occupied the enviable role, individually and collectively, of middlemen. Indeed, they can be viewed as standing between two "foreign" trading partners, the Indian fur trappers on the one hand and European suppliers of trade goods on the other. Enterprises such as the Hudson's Bay Company, the world's oldest extant company, were formed to manage the trade. Governments intervened. Great Britain and France contended for the best territories. Massachusetts, Virginia, and the other colonies worked to organize and license the trade within their boundaries and to extend those boundaries, the better to increase their shares of the trade. Colonial merchants, armed with colonial licenses, centered significant portions of their business on the fur trade.

Over time two things happened. The trade with the Indians moved progressively westward as the Indians and the furbearers were pushed in that direction by the advancing line of white settlement. Coincidentally, the relative weight of fur exports to the colonial balance of payments decreased. With the shift westward of the focus of the fur trade, its early commercial centers took on other roles. New Amsterdam was replaced by Albany, which a century later was itself eclipsed, initially by the French at Fort Niagara, and after the French and Indian War by the British at Detroit. Well before the 1740s the merchants at Albany had begun to take advantage of their geographic position to trade with Quebec. Comparative urban history linked to the locus of specific trades is a theme worth exploring within the context of the fur trade. Equally of interest, and equally little known, are a wide range of issues connected with how the fur trade worked. Of particular concern are the ways in which the cultures of various Indian groups shaped the organization of the trade and the ways in which those groups were, in turn, affected by participation in the international economy.[6]

Joseph Lawrence McDevitt, Jr., "The House of Rotch: Whaling Merchants of Massachusetts, 1734–1828" (Ph.D. diss., American University, 1978); Richard C. Kugler, "The Whale Oil Trade, 1750–1775," in *Seafaring in Colonial Massachusetts*, [ed. Philip Chadwick Foster Smith] (Boston, 1980), 153–173; and Vickers, "Maritime Labor." On Indians as hunters of whales, see Kugler, "Whale Oil Trade," 156n; Bruce G. Trigger, ed., *Northeast*, vol. XV of *Handbook of North American Indians*, ed. William C. Sturtevant (Washington, D.C., 1978), 162, 184; and Vickers, "Maritime Labor," *passim*.

6. There is no comprehensive treatment, even just a descriptive one, of the "fur trade in the colonial period," though several studies cover a part of the picture. See Murray G. Lawson, *Fur: A Study in English Mercantilism, 1700–1775* (Toronto, 1943); Innis, *Fur Trade in*

Some colonial farmers, as we have suggested, could have supplemented their incomes from agriculture by catching cod and trapping furs, particularly in the early years of settlement. There was yet another extractive enterprise that was even more immediate than fishing and fur trapping, one that farmers could take up and leave off as easily as they could reach for their axes. The trees of nearby forests and, indeed, of the farmers' own woodlots offered a continuing supply of timber to be converted into everything from firewood to furniture. A surprising variety of products were extracted from the vast stands of American timber. Demand for these goods was personal and commercial, domestic and foreign. Available studies touch few of the many possible topics and develop adequate analyses of almost none; they rarely do more than describe a very small portion of what was an immensely important colonial economic activity.[7]

The provision of firewood alone, in an economy that used wood as the chief source of fuel in both homes and industries, required a tremendous amount of labor and timber. We have no idea how much of either factor was involved or how much was organized individually rather than on a commercial basis. There are intriguing hints: the colonial distillery that was advertised for sale with its contract for firewood; the regular wintertime complaints in colonial towns and cities over the short supplies and high price of firewood; the importation of coal from London to fire a sugar refinery in Antigua; and the attempt by John Paul Jones during the American Revolution to cut off the supply of coal to British-held New York City by capturing colliers on their way from Nova Scotia coal mines.

Canada; and Paul Chrisler Phillips, *The Fur Trade* (Norman, Okla., 1961). Each, because it sets out to do other things, only touches on the colonial fur trade. Useful as a discussion of the interactions between Indian and European fur traders is D. W. Moodie, "Agriculture and the Fur Trade," in *Old Trails and New Directions: Papers of the Third North American Fur Trade Conference*, ed. Carol M. Judd and Arthur J. Ray (Toronto, 1980), 272–290. E. E. Rich, *The History of the Hudson's Bay Company, 1670–1870* (London, 1958–1959), approaches being the definitive treatment of the company as a company, but leaves unanswered many of the questions that interest us here. There are some studies of the fur trade in particular colonies, though they suffer from a similar defect. Especially useful, nonetheless, are Moloney, *Fur Trade in New England*; Roberts, "Fur Trade of New England"; and T. Norton, *Fur Trade in Colonial New York*. See also chap. 5, n. 3, above. The diminishing role of the fur trade in the economy of Albany is the theme of Armour, "Merchants of Albany." See also Stephen Earl Sale, "Colonial Albany: Outpost of Empire" (Ph.D. diss., University of Southern California, 1973). The continuing importance of the fur trade at the frontier is a theme of Walter Scott Dunn, Jr., "Western Commerce, 1760–1774" (Ph.D. diss., University of Wisconsin, 1971).

7. Some of the issues touched on here are treated in the essays in Brooke Hindle, ed., *America's Wooden Age: Aspects of Its Early Technology* (Tarrytown, N.Y., 1975), and Hindle, ed., *Material Culture in the Wooden Age* (Tarrytown, N.Y., 1981). See also Herndon, "Forest Products of Colonial Georgia."

We need all this tied together in a comprehensive analytical study of the supply of fuel in the colonial period.[8]

Almost any farmer could profitably spend some time turning his timber into shingles for houses or into the component parts for casks—and apparently many did. Each year shingles were exported from the colonies in considerable numbers and many more, we presume, were used by the colonists themselves. Probably most were fashioned by individual farmers working in the off-season, but some shingles were made by slaves and by specialized commercial operations. Economic historians should consult the historians of early American architecture to help calculate annual domestic construction of shingled buildings and the number of shingles each building required. Domestic consumption added to the amount exported will provide an estimate of the size and significance of yet another extractive enterprise.[9]

Almost everything shipped or stored anywhere in the colonies was packed in wooden casks. Coopers assembled the casks, but while some coopers preferred to finish their own component parts, most bought them already cut and shaped. Again, the North American colonists who cut and fashioned staves, headings, and hoops served both a domestic and a foreign market. Large quantities of "shaken" casks were exported each year, chiefly to the West Indies, there to be "knocked-up" and packed with sugar, molasses, rum, and the other Caribbean commodities. The fabrication and exportation of these timber products were considered im-

---

8. The distillery, at Alexandria, Virginia, was scheduled to consume 300 cords of ash a year; that, at least, was the amount in the contract (Pinkney's *Virginia Gazette* [Williamsburg], 1 Dec. 1774). See John J. McCusker, "The Distillation of Rum and Colonial America," in *The History of American Food Technology*, ed. G. Terry Sharrer (Washington, D.C., forthcoming). Problems with urban fuel supplies are one of the many subjects in Bridenbaugh's *Cities in the Wilderness* and *Cities in Revolt*. The mention of coal for Antigua is in Col. Samuel Martin, Sr., to Messrs. Codrington and Miller (of London), 30 July 1761, Letterbook of Samuel Martin, 1756–1762, Martin Papers, Add. MS 41349, fol. 113, BL. See also John J. McCusker, "The Tonnage of Ships Engaged in British Colonial Trade during the Eighteenth Century," *Research Econ. Hist.*, VI (1981), 87, 89. Sea coal from Nova Scotia (and from London) is mentioned regularly in Bridenbaugh's books, cited above. For the reference here, see Samuel Eliot Morison, *John Paul Jones: A Sailor's Biography* (Boston, 1959), 76–86, and John J. McCusker, *Alfred: The First Continental Flagship, 1775–1778* (Washington, D.C., 1973), 8. A most useful work for comparative purposes is William J. Hausman, *Public Policy and the Supply of Coal to London* (New York, 1981 [Ph.D. diss., University of Illinois, 1976]).

9. Merrens, *Colonial North Carolina*, 93–107 *passim*, discusses the production and export of shingles in that colony. He speculates that the large-scale production of shingles in North Carolina late in the colonial period was the result of two factors: an increasing overseas demand that older, more northerly areas could no longer supply; and the availability of the desired species of trees. His hypothesis awaits an adequate test.

portant enough to attract the attention of colonial governments, which sought to regulate their quality. Nevertheless, the colonial container industry is largely a mystery to economic historians.[10]

Perhaps the historians of early American architecture will be willing to help us out a second time, to estimate the extent of the colonial construction industry. We would like to know how many buildings were constructed annually and the quantity of materials each required. Presumably the number of houses built was a function of several variables: the growing population; the life span of such structures; changing tastes in domestic architecture; and the general state of the economy. In urban areas carpenters worked as builders; in rural areas we presume that house- and barn-raising bees involved neighbors in the construction process. However and wherever they were erected, colonial frame houses required sawn board lumber, the product of the numerous lumber mills that dotted the landscape. We know little about any of this in an organized, systematic fashion. What we do know, for certain years, is the quantity of building materials exported, most of which went to the West Indies to be fashioned into sugar mills, slave huts, and the like. The implications of this activity for the colonial economy have scarcely been addressed.[11]

10. Again Merrens, *Colonial North Carolina*, 93–107 *passim*, provides an intelligent discussion of the production and export of staves, headings, and hoops in that colony. For coopers and their craft, see George Elkington, *The Coopers: Company and Craft* (London, [1933]); Franklin E. Coyne, *The Development of the Cooperage Industry in the United States, 1620–1940* (Chicago, [1940]); and Fred Putnam Hankerson, *The Cooperage Handbook* (Brooklyn, N.Y., 1947). Such works as Klopfer, "Statistics of the Foreign Trade of Philadelphia," *passim*, and McCusker, "Rum Trade," 768–878, attempt to come to terms with colonial casks. Both demonstrate that one cannot accept as an accurate indication of the capacity of colonial casks the limits imposed by law, either colonial or imperial. Neither treats coopering itself as a business. For discussions of early British American regulation of wood products, see Arthur L. Jensen, "The Inspection of Exports in Colonial Pennsylvania," *PMHB*, LXXVIII (1954), 275–297; Newton B. Jones, "Weights, Measures, and Mercantilism: The Inspection of Exports in Virginia, 1742–1820," in *The Old Dominion: Essays for Thomas Perkins Abernethy*, ed. Darrett B. Rutman (Charlottesville, Va., 1964), 122–134; and Merrens, *Colonial North Carolina*, 101, 231, n. 31.

11. We have seen few books on colonial architecture that might be useful in this effort. Two are Abbott Lowell Cummings, *Massachusetts and Its First Period Houses: An Essay with Appendices on Architecture in Colonial Massachusetts* (Boston, 1979), and Russell F. Whitehead and Frank C. Brown, *Colonial Homes in the Southern States: From Material Originally Published as the White Pine Series of Architectural Monographs* (New York, 1977). Roger William Moss, "Master Builders: A History of the Colonial Philadelphia Building Trades" (Ph.D. diss., University of Delaware, 1972), contains much useful data. See also Richard McAlpin Candee, "Wooden Buildings in Early Maine and New Hampshire: A Technological and Cultural History, 1600–1720" (Ph.D. diss., University of Pennsylvania, 1976), and John Anthony Eisterhold, "Lumber and Trade in the Seaboard Cities

Colonial wooden buildings were outfitted with colonial-made wooden furniture, some of it very beautiful but most of it, we suspect, quite forgettable. Some pieces that were especially treasured then have been preserved to be treasured by us today, thereby coloring our view of how our forebears lived. Crude or magnificent, made in the home or in the artisan's shop, this furniture was yet another product fabricated from the forest whose economic value is unknown. As with other goods, the market for furniture was both domestic and overseas, the exported chairs and chests, tables and bedsteads going largely to the West Indies.[12]

The vehicles in which the colonists transported themselves and their goods were also made of wood, and the great numbers manufactured had a marked impact on the colonial economy. Wagons in a stunning variety hauled commodities from farm to market and from city to farm. Handsome carriages and rough wagons moved Americans long distances and short. When the weather turned cold, sledges and sleighs replaced wagons and carriages in the more northerly colonies. As with furniture, some of the fancier carriages were imported, but all of the wagons and carts, all of the sledges and sleighs, and most of the coaches and carriages were made in the colonies. Some vehicles were exported, but most were constructed to supply local demand. We have no study of the craft of the wagonwright and of his products beyond the merely descriptive. The business of providing vehicles for land transportation in the colonial period is largely an unknown subject.[13]

---

of the Old South: 1607–1860" (Ph.D. diss., University of Mississippi, 1970). Dell Upton, "Traditional Timber Framing," in *Material Culture in the Wooden Age*, ed. Hindle, 35–93, is very useful. Cary Carson et al., "Impermanent Architecture in the Southern American Colonies," *Winterthur Portfolio*, XVI (1981), 135–196, addresses several issues of interest to economic historians. We are indebted to A. J. Looyenga of Haarlem, the Netherlands, for letting us read his unpublished paper "Colonial Architecture in Africa, Asia, and the Americas: An Historical and Anthropological Approach," which links architectural styles around the world. Merrens, *Colonial North Carolina*, discusses the production and exportation of sawn lumber in that colony (pp. 93–107).

12. Not only are no studies of colonial furniture oriented in the way we require, but almost none deal with anything other than the finest of surviving pieces. Two of interest are E. Milby Burton, *Charleston Furniture, 1700–1825* (Charleston, S.C., 1955), and Edward Deming Andrews and Faith Andrews, *Shaker Furniture: The Craftsmanship of an American Communal Sect* (New Haven, Conn., 1937). We suspect that the simple, functional, sturdy furniture made by the Shakers resembles closely what most people used in the colonial period. We expect that studies of colonial probate records will help advance the kind of work we suggest here. In this regard one should consult Abbott Lowell Cummings, ed., *Rural Household Inventories: Establishing the Names, Uses, and Furnishings of Rooms in the Colonial New England Home, 1675–1775* (Boston, 1964).

13. Again, there is no comprehensive history of vehicles used in the colonial period and no attempt whatsoever to treat the business of wagon and carriage building. Two works that

Waterborne modes of transportation also depended on forest products. For its own strategic purposes, the British government intervened to promote the colonial manufacture of naval stores. Put simply, the crown wanted alternative sources of the necessities of naval warfare available within the empire. In short supply or simply unobtainable in the British Isles, it made the best of sense to have them produced in the colonies. Naval stores included masts and spars, pitch, tar, and turpentine, which the forests of North America could yield in abundance. The "Broad Arrow" policy, the Naval Stores Act of 1705, and colonial reactions to them have been the subject of numerous narratives. We know less about the nature, the extent, and the fabrication of these materials in the colonies— and the impact of all this on the colonial economy. It is clear, however, that naval stores production is a case in which local resources, the ability of farmers and plantation workers to pursue other extractive tasks when crops did not require attention, and the demands of foreign markets joined to foster a sizable colonial industry.[14]

The colonists did not produce the components of waterborne vessels only for export, however. In an age that depends on land-based transportation, we tend to think of water as a barrier, whereas the colonists viewed their rivers, bays, and lakes as highways. They constructed craft in the colonies both for their inland waterways and for the high seas. The

---

will be helpful when such an attempt is made are Don H. Berkebile, *Conestoga Wagons in Braddock's Campaign, 1755* (Washington, D.C., 1959), and George Shumway and Howard C. Frey, *Conestoga Wagon, 1750–1850: Freight Carrier for One Hundred Years of America's Westward Expansion,* 3d ed. (York, Pa., 1968). See also Museums at Stony Brook, *Catalogue of Vehicles: The Carriage House of the Suffolk Museum at Stony Brook, Long Island* (Stony Brook, N.Y., 1954). Some useful points of comparison can be gleaned from J. Geraint Jenkins, *The English Farm Wagon: Origins and Structure* (Lingfield, Surrey, 1961). On the market for the more expensive carriages, see Robert F. Oaks, "Big Wheels in Philadelphia: Du Simitière's List of Carriage Owners [1772]," *PMHB,* XCV (1971), 351–362, and Alan D. Watson, "Luxury Vehicles and Elitism in Colonial North Carolina," *So. Studies,* XIX (1980), 147–156.

14. There are several standard works on the subject: Lord, *Industrial Experiments;* Robert Greenhalgh Albion, *Forests and Sea Power: The Timber Problem of the Royal Navy, 1652–1862* (Cambridge, Mass., 1926); Curtis Nettels, "The Menace of Colonial Manufacturing, 1690–1720," *NEQ,* IV (1931), 230–269; Knittle, *Early Eighteenth Century Palatine Emigration;* Malone, *Pine Trees and Politics;* and S. F. Manning, *New England Masts and the King's Broad Arrow* ([London], 1979). The results of these policies in the Carolinas are discussed in chap. 8, above, and in Merrens, *Colonial North Carolina;* Clowse, *Economic Beginnings;* and Virginia S. Wood, *Live Oaking: Southern Timber for Tall Ships* (Boston, 1981). Usually mentioned in this context, though perhaps better relegated to a section on the early chemical industry, is the production of potash and pearl ash, a source of alkali. See William I. Roberts III, "American Potash Manufacture before the American Revolution," *Am. Phil. Soc., Procs.,* CXVI (1972), 383–395.

colonists built boats, all fabricated from wood, of every description for service in every body of water available to them. They ranged in size from the tiniest of boats to vessels capable of conveying several people as well as several tons of cargo. Propelled by pole, oar, or sail, they moved up and down the waterways of every colony. Although we are learning about the business of transporting goods, we know almost nothing about the business of building such craft.[15]

We are better off in our knowledge of the nature and extent of colonial shipbuilding. As the carriers of colonial imports and exports, large ocean-going craft were subject to imperial regulations and are therefore comparatively well documented. Shipbuilding was also a major colonial industry, the subject of contemporary investigation and government intervention. In treating it, we move the discussion from the simpler extractive enterprises to large-scale colonial manufacturing. Yet that shift parallels the progress of the colonial economy. Induced by demands from the overseas sector, the colonists slowly developed their extractive enterprises into manufacturing industries.[16]

15. One is hard put to find anything, even of a descriptive character, written about early British American boats. The business of boatbuilding, for example, has been largely ignored. Some information can be found in J. A. Anderson, *Navigation of the Upper Delaware* (Trenton, N.J., 1913). An excellent suggestion about how to research the topic can be inferred from a distinction, itself of some importance, made by William Avery Baker: "A boat can be carried on a vessel but not the reverse" ("Vessel Types of Colonial Massachusetts," in *Seafaring in Colonial Massachusetts*, [ed. P. Smith], 5). In other words, a good bit can be found about boatbuilding in the records of early British American shipbuilding because the construction of each ship usually involved the supplying of one or more boats. See, for instance, the detailed account presented in 1750 by Thomas Williams, boatbuilder, to James Burd for "a new long boat" and "a new yoall" for Burd's snow *Sally* (receipt dated 16 Feb. 1749/50 in Receipts, 1746–1756, Burd-Shippen Papers, American Philosophical Society, Philadelphia). Two recent studies of regional transportation in the Delaware River valley have considerable incidental information on the rivercraft of the area. See Walzer, "Transportation in Philadelphia," and Dauer, "Colonial Philadelphia's Transportation System," 1–10. See also Maynard Bray, *Mystic Seaport Museum Watercraft* (Mystic, Conn., 1979), which is useful for its authoritative distinctions and definitions, for its illustrations, for its discussion of the industry that produced the boats, and for its bibliographies—even if there are no 18th-century watercraft therein. That boats seem not to have altered essentially over the last century and a half suggests that they may have been somewhat similar in design in the 18th century also. As with other topics in this chapter, archaeologists are offering interesting evidence on the subject. See Basil Greenhill, *Archaeology of the Boat: A New Introductory Study* (London, 1976). At least two 18th-century North American boats have recently been discovered, raised, and analyzed. See Philip K. Lundeberg, *The Continental Gunboat* Philadelphia *and the Northern Campaign of 1776* (Washington, D.C., 1966), and Alan B. Albright, "The Brown's Ferry Vessel," N. Am. Soc. Oceanic Hist., *Procs.*, I (1977).

16. The only full study of the industry during the colonial period is neither as thorough nor as analytical as we would like. Moreover, many of the data series that the author presents are suspect, for he seems frequently to be counting ships registered as ships built, an error

Shipbuilding played a critical role in the colonial economy, both by providing most of the vessels used by the colonists themselves in their coastal and West Indian trades and by providing the colonies with a major export. On the eve of independence, ships ranked fifth in value among exports from the continental colonies, behind fish but ahead of indigo. When combined with earnings from freight carried on board colonial-owned vessels, the contributions of shipping to the balance of payments rivaled that of tobacco, the principal commodity export.

The colonists built ships both for local use and for the West Indian trade almost from the start of settlement. The industry received a major boost in the 1680s and after when war-induced increases in demand for ships permitted penetration of the English market. Shipbuilding apparently slumped in the immediate postwar decade—as did the economy in general—but grew fairly steadily from about 1730, with a significant quickening again in the period of the French and Indian War. Jacob Price provides a succinct, if tentative, account of the dimensions of the industry

---

that causes him to overstate considerably the number of vessels actually constructed. Still, there is nothing comparable to Joseph A. Goldenberg, *Shipbuilding in Colonial America* (Charlottesville, Va., 1976). Much more sensitive in its use of data, but of only a regional character is Crowther, "Shipbuilding Output." Cf. John J. McCusker, "The Pennsylvania Shipping Industry in the Eighteenth Century" (1972; typescript in Historical Society of Pennsylvania, Philadelphia). See also Bailyn and Bailyn, *Massachusetts Shipping*; William M. Kelso, "Shipbuilding in Virginia, 1763–1774," Columbia Historical Society, *Records*, XLVIII (1971), 1–13; Edward Charles Lesnick, Jr., "A Quantitative Analysis of the Supply and Demand for Ships: A Case Study of Colonial New York and South Carolina" (Ph.D. diss., University of Notre Dame, 1973); and Arthur Pierce Middleton, "Ships and Shipbuilding in the Chesapeake Bay and Tributaries," in *Chesapeake Bay in the American Revolution*, ed. Ernest M. Eller (Centerville, Md., 1981), 98–132. We have yet to begin to address many of the questions posed by Ralph Davis, "Untapped Sources and Research Opportunities in the Field of American Maritime History from the Beginning to about 1815," in *Untapped Sources and Research Opportunities in the Field of American Maritime History: A Symposium* (Mystic, Conn., 1967), 11–26. Any analysis of existing data on shipping and shipbuilding must overcome some inherent problems, two of which are addressed in Daniel Scott Smith, "A Note on the Longevity of Colonial Ships," *Am. Neptune*, XXXIV (1974), 68–69, and McCusker, "Tonnage of Ships." It should also be noted that considerable shipbuilding took place in early British America outside the continental colonies, notably in Bermuda. Bermuda sloops, recognized for their speed and grace, were that colony's prime export. Little is known about them or the industry that built them, but see Howard I. Chapelle, *The National Watercraft Collection* (Washington, D.C., 1960), 16–19. Finally, no study of early British American shipping or shipbuilding can afford to ignore Chapelle's other works or those of another fine naval architect turned maritime historian, William A. Baker. See Chapelle, *The History of American Sailing Ships* (New York, 1935), and *The Search for Speed under Sail, 1700–1855* (New York, 1967); and Baker, *Colonial Vessels: Some Seventeenth-Century Sailing Craft* (Barre, Mass., 1962), *Sloops and Shallops* (Barre, Mass., 1966), and "Vessel Types."

in continental British America at the end of the colonial period: "Ca. 1763–1775 shipbuilding in the Thirteen Colonies totalled about 40,000 measured tons annually and was worth £300,000 sterling, of which at least 18,600 tons worth £140,000 sterling were sold abroad."[17]

Shipbuilding provides a major example of how the focusing devices of the export sector initiated an elaborate and effective linkage-building process. In this case the need for transport of commodities to markets not supplied by British merchants provoked several interrelated developments. Ship construction made a substantial contribution to the diversification of the colonial economy, became a central element in the balance of payments, and laid a foundation upon which further industrial expansion could build. Given its importance, it is surprising that the industry has not attracted more attention. A thorough study of the business of shipbuilding is a major opportunity in early American economic history. Such a study should improve estimates of costs and productivity, describe volume over time and by region with greater precision, investigate the extent to which local entrepreneurs engaged in related pursuits, and explore the organization of the industry, its sources of capital, and its marketing arrangements.[18]

Except for those few at the farthest fringes of settlement, colonists had constant and considerable potential for interaction with the market economy. They had adequate information on which to base conscious choices in market matters. They knew about or could easily find out about alternative ways to employ their labor, even if it was just in the production of surplus farm goods. And they had regular access to markets at which to sell those goods. The colonists' knowledge might have been far from perfect and their scope often less extensive than they might have wished, but they had in their midst—in the person of the operator of the local gristmill—both market information and a conduit to such markets.

The miller made it his business to keep aware of the basic facts of the market economy—to whom and for how much he could sell grains, meal, and flour—because the local farmers for whom he ran his mill usu-

17. Price, "Note on Colonial Exports" (quotation on p. 722). As an essential component in his calculations, Price used figures for the cost per measured ton of shipping presented in McCusker, "Sources of Investment Capital," 150. These price data have recently been faulted as being too low, perhaps by half, thus suggesting that Price's estimates may need to be increased. See Doerflinger, "Enterprise on the Delaware," 525.

18. McCusker, "Sources of Investment Capital," tries, not completely successfully, to estimate the changing proportion of foreign to domestic capital invested in the shipping registered at the port of Philadelphia. See Omi and Sakakibara, "Economic Development," 122–123n.

ally paid him in kind. He might keep enough for his own needs, but he then hoped to trade the balance for other items. Gristmills appeared in every colonial community almost as soon as the first harvest, they remained necessary as long as farmers were in the area, and they spread everywhere settlement did, bringing with them the lines of communication that linked every colonial farmer with the wider world. We need to know much more about the business affairs of these mill operators.[19]

What we do know suggests that several noteworthy developments resulted from the activities of the gristmill operators. Many millers became the proprietors of small country stores because of their own need to exchange surplus grain, meal, and flour for other goods and because of the potential for profit inherent in the service they provided to their milling customers. Furthermore, their stores became the focal point of local information networks, places to exchange news as well as goods.[20] Neighborhood farmers, learning at the gristmill–country store of a chance to sell farm produce, could use the trading connections of the miller-storekeeper to send produce directly to market. Some millers offered to serve the farmer as agent in selling surplus grain; others purchased it outright, perhaps in exchange for store goods, and in turn sold it. In this way the miller-storekeeper became the most immediate link for colonial farmers in a commercial chain that stretched all the way to Great Britain or the West Indies and back again.

Some gristmill operators—country-store keepers eventually expanded the scale and scope of their operations. Seizing the occasion for eliminating town merchants as middlemen, they began trading overseas directly, exporting grain and importing foreign goods. To better service their overseas customers, they began to grind grain for farmers even farther afield. Still further expansion involved setting up more and larger mills, purchasing grain on yet an even wider geographical basis, broadening their network of suppliers and customers, and perhaps relocating to a swifter stream with a more reliable water supply and a better fall of water. Thus from country milling came merchant milling. In the 1740s this sequence

19. The standard work—Charles Byron Kuhlmann, *The Development of the Flour-Milling Industry in the United States* (Boston, 1929)—touches only inadequately on the colonial period. See also V. Clark, *History of Manufactures*, I, 177–180, and *passim*, and Curtis P. Nettels, *The Roots of American Civilization: A History of American Colonial Life*, 2d ed. (New York, 1963), 248–249. Compare Louis C. Hunter, *A History of Industrial Power in the United States, 1780–1930* (Charlottesville, Va., 1979), 51, and S. Innes, *Labor in a New Land*, chap. 4.

20. Laurence A. Johnson, *Over the Counter and on the Shelf: Country Store Keeping in America, 1620–1920*, ed. Marcia Ray (Rutland, Vt., 1961), is barely a beginning in our understanding of a very important topic. The entire subject of retail sales remains completely unexplored.

of developments gave rise to Wilmington, Delaware—as they did to similar settlements before and afterward. One of the spread effects of colonial trade was, therefore, the encouragement of colonial milling, a process that drew farmers into international markets. Almost nothing has been written on the subject.[21]

The further results of the expansion of colonial milling were of even greater moment for the development of the economy of early British America. Water mills were the most sophisticated source of mechanical power and one of the most advanced technologies of the eighteenth-century world. The establishment and operation of mills attracted creative talent, both entrepreneurial (as we have just suggested) and technical. To increase the returns on their capital investment, some millowners investigated ways to keep their mills in operation beyond the limited season during which they ground grain. Some were successful in that search. In the eighteenth century, even in the smaller centers, it was not unusual to find a gristmill and a sawmill on the same site. By the 1790s, in the vicinity of Wilmington, businessmen had set up along the Brandywine more than sixty gristmills, several fulling mills, a half-dozen sawmills, four paper mills, two snuff mills, a barley mill, a cotton mill, an iron-slitting mill, and a bolting cloth "manufactory."[22]

To improve the efficiency of their operations, millowners looked for ways to increase productivity and to reduce the need for that always costly factor of production, labor. The result, according to Victor S. Clark, was that "technically colonial mills were abreast of the English, and probably in advance of them." The work of Oliver Evans, "one of the world's most important inventors," epitomizes the innovative technology that appeared in this sector of the colonial economy. By 1787 Evans had

---

21. Some studies of local milling are useful, nevertheless. See Arthur G. Peterson, "Flour and Grist Milling in Virginia: A Brief History," *VMHB*, XLIII (1935), 97–108; Peter C. Welsh, "The Brandywine Mills: A Chronicle of an Industry, 1762–1816," *Delaware History*, VII (1956), 17–36; Welsh, "Merchants, Millers, and Ocean Ships: The Components of an Early American Industrial Town," *ibid.* (1957), 319–336; Harry B. Weiss and Robert J. Sim, *The Early Grist and Flouring Mills of New Jersey* (Trenton, N.J., 1956); Sharrer, "Flour Milling in the Growth of Baltimore, 1750–1830"; and G. Terry Sharrer, "The Merchant-Millers: Baltimore's Flour Milling Industry, 1783–1860," *Agric. Hist.*, LVI (1982), 138–150, based on his "Flour Milling and the Growth of Baltimore, 1783–1830" (Ph.D. diss., University of Maryland, 1975).

22. Welsh, "Merchants, Millers, and Ocean Ships," 323. Compare Carlton O. Wittlinger, "Early Manufacturing in Lancaster County, Pennsylvania, 1710–1840" (Ph.D. diss., University of Pennsylvania, 1953), and Thomas Patrick Vadasz, "The History of an Industrial Community: Bethlehem, Pennsylvania, 1741–1920" (Ph.D. diss., College of William and Mary, 1975). There is much useful information in the recent work of two historical geographers. See Lemon, *Best Poor Man's Country*, 200–207, and R. Mitchell, *Commercialism and Frontier*, 144–147.

fully automated the flour-milling process, the first instance in history of a completely automated production facility. Colonial inventors also increased the productivity of lumber mills, iron mills, and in the West Indies, sugar mills.[23]

Characteristically, inventive minds do not stop with perfecting existing technologies, but continue to search for the new. In seeking to improve sugar milling, some men tried to employ the most advanced technology then being developed, steam power. Although not fully successful, these attempts did result in the first solution to the problem of converting the lateral push-pull mechanical motion of the steam engine into the circular motion necessary to turn the crushing rollers of sugar mills, the grindstones of flour mills, the paddle wheels of steamboats, or the drive wheels of locomotives. John Stewart of Jamaica published his book on the subject at London in 1767.[24]

23. We know little about changes in early British American milling except through the occasional references to patents and prizes that were awarded for new developments. See V. Clark, _History of Manufactures_, I, 174–181 (quotation on p. 180). Very useful is Charles Howell, "Colonial Watermills in the Wooden Age," in _America's Wooden Age_, ed. Hindle, 120–159. See also Howell and Allan Keller, _The Mill at Philipsburg Manor Upper Mills and a Brief History of Milling_ (Tarrytown, N.Y., 1977). The evaluation of Evans is that by Thomas C. Cochran, _Frontiers of Change: Early Industrialism in America_ (New York, 1981), 67. See also Greville Bathe and Dorothy Bathe, _Oliver Evans: A Chronicle of Early American Engineering_ (Philadelphia, 1935), which paints an unnecessarily bleak picture of all that preceded Evans the better to enhance his image, and Eugene S. Ferguson, _Oliver Evans: Inventive Genius of the American Industrial Revolution_ (Greenville, Del., 1980). A working model of Evans's flour mill is in the Hagley Museum in Wilmington, Delaware. The mill is illustrated, its importance described, and its context explored in Eli Ginzberg, "The Mechanization of Work," _Sci. Am._, CCXLVII (Sept. 1982), 68. For improvements in sugar milling, see Ragatz, _Fall of the Planter Class_, 61–64. Very little is known about such improvements (though enough plantation records are available that a good bit could be found out), but at least one, the introduction of metal parts at key points in the mill to strengthen it and to reduce friction, involved cooperation between sugar planters and North American manufacturers. A New Jersey ironworks, the Batsto Furnace, advertised in a Philadelphia newspaper that it made "sugar mill gudgeons, neatly rounded and polished at the ends" (_Pennsylvania Journal_, 8 May 1776, as quoted in V. Clark, _History of Manufactures_, I, 176). We suspect that there were other, similar instances.

24. For the steam engine in the West Indies, see Ragatz, _Fall of the Planter Class_, 63, and John Stewart [alias Robert Rainey], _A Description of a Machine or Invention to Work Mills, by the Power of a Fire-Engine, but Particularly Useful and Profitable in Grinding Sugar-Canes_ ([London, 1767]). For Stewart see also the correspondence in the Committee of Colonies and Trade, Guard Books, Vol. B, nos. 29, 31, Royal Society of the Arts, London. For steam engines in North America, see Carroll W. Purcell, Jr., _Early Stationary Steam Engines in America: A Study in the Migration of Technology_ (Washington, D.C., 1969). Oliver Evans had developed an improved design for a steam engine by 1772, and his interest in the subject continued in later years. See Ferguson, _Oliver Evans, passim._ For a discussion of sources of power in the early American economy, see Hunter, _History of Industrial_

Colonial milling, its expansion tied directly to the enlarged overseas markets for colonial agricultural commodities such as flour and sugar, became the basis of early industrialization in British America. We know very little about the individual components of the story and less about the relationship between business and technology in the colonial period. What is available is largely descriptive, seldom analytical, and rarely concerned with the relationships outlined here.

As is suggested by the contrast between the farmer who felled trees and shaped shingles in the off-season and the great merchant mills along the Brandywine, producers in the colonial manufacturing and extractive industries varied greatly in size and degree of specialization. At one end of the spectrum, the limited commercial possibilities in colonial agriculture promoted household manufactures. Farm families without the means to purchase many manufactures on the market but with ample supplies of labor, particularly in slack times, made coarse clothing and crude implements that required few special skills. We know relatively little about such activities. They were carried on outside the market and thus seldom generated records that can be analyzed quantitatively, although once again probate inventories constitute a valuable source of information.[25]

One question is of distinct interest: to what extent did household manufacturing produce a marketable surplus and, more significantly, develop into cottage industries, perhaps organized under a "putting-out" system? There is some evidence of such developments after 1750 in the making of nails, footware, and particularly, textiles. "Many thousands" in the older and more densely settled rural areas, William Pollard observed in 1773, "rather than go farther back into the country where lands are cheap or undertake the arduous task of clearing new lands, turn to manufacturing, and live upon a small farm, as in many parts of England." This process of

---

Power. The close connection between innovative technologies and the export sector was not limited to sugar and wheat. See McCusker, "Distillation of Rum." For this entire subject see Brooke Hindle, *Technology in Early America: Needs and Opportunities for Study* (Chapel Hill, N.C., 1966).

25. We risk seriously underestimating the extent of manufacturing activity in the colonies if we accept at face value contemporary statements on the subject. Colonial authorities were very unwilling to report to imperial authorities any industrial activity (or even economic data, including population data). For instances of deliberate distortion, see C. Watkins and Noël Hume, "Poor Potter" of Yorktown; Daniels, *Connecticut Town*; and Margit Mayer, *Die Entstehung des Nationalstaates in Nordamerika* (Frankfurt am Main, 1979), as mentioned in Dirk Hoerder's review of the Daniels book, *WMQ*, 3d Ser., XXXVIII (1981), 134–136. V. Clark, *History of Manufactures*, remains the basic work on the subject of manufacturing in the colonies, while J. Leander Bishop, *A History of American Manufactures from 1608 to 1860 . . .*, 3d ed., rev. (Philadelphia, 1868), is still useful.

proto-industrialization merits intense study because of its consequence for the eventual emergence of the factory system and because it probably led to gains in income. The seeming decline in farm productivity reported in some recent work may actually reflect the diversion of family resources away from agriculture and into various manufacturing enterprises.[26]

At the other end of the spectrum from home-manufactured handicrafts were the market-oriented "mill and furnace industries" or "staple manufactures," as Clark called them, organized to exploit the abundant colonial resource base or to process agricultural goods.[27] The most studied of these is the iron industry, which had reached impressive dimensions by the eve of independence. Building upon the advantages of cheap fuel and easily mined surface ores and encouraged by the imperial government, the colonial iron industry grew rapidly during the eighteenth century. In 1775 at least 82 charcoal-fueled furnaces were in operation, each capable of producing an annual average of 300 tons of pig iron. There were also 175 forges that produced the more ductile bar iron either by refining pig iron or—in the uncommon bloomeries—by refining iron ore itself. The industry, whether measured by number of forges and furnaces or by total output, was larger than that of England and Wales. Indeed, according to one estimate, continental British America accounted for almost one-seventh of total world production in the 1770s.

Although certain aspects of the iron industry have been thoroughly studied, several questions remain. We need to know more about the processing of bar iron and the marketing of finished products. For instance, the domestic market apparently was dominant since only a small portion of total output was exported. We also need to pursue the implications of Paul Paskoff's recent finding of substantial gains in labor productivity despite a static technology. These gains and a more efficient use of fuel reflected "not augmentation or modification of the physical plant, but rather the prosaic yet very effective process of learning by doing."[28]

---

26. William Pollard to Benjamin and John Bower, 6 Apr. 1773, William Pollard Letter Book, 1772–1774, Hist. Soc. Pa., as quoted in Egnal, "Economic Development," 219. Rolla Milton Tryon, *Household Manufactures in the United States, 1640–1860: A Study in Industrial History* (Chicago, [1917]), the "standard" work, is much in need of revision. Compare John Philip Hall, "The Gentle Craft: A Narrative of Yankee Shoemakers" (Ph.D. diss., Columbia University, 1953). There is a large and growing literature on proto-industrialization, but see especially Franklin F. Mendels, "Proto-industrialization: The First Phase of the Industrialization Process," *Jour. Econ. Hist.*, XXXII (1972), 241–261.

27. V. Clark, *History of Manufactures*, I, 164, 100.

28. Arthur Cecil Bining, *British Regulation of the Colonial Iron Industry* (Philadelphia, 1933); Bining, *Pennsylvania Iron Manufacture*; Irene D. Neu, "The Iron Plantations of Co-

We know much less about the various milling industries in the colonies than we do about the iron industry. This is surprising since milling industries contributed much more in total value to the economy and were technically more progressive, chiefly in the development and diffusion of laborsaving devices. If some of the same factors were at work in the mill industries that Paskoff pointed to for the iron industry, then we can expect to find even greater productivity gains for milling over the eighteenth century than he found for iron making. As was suggested above, a thorough study of milling, particularly of the large commercial flour mills in the Middle Atlantic region and of the sawmills in the principal lumber-exporting areas, is a major opportunity in early American economic history.

Somewhere in between the handicraft activities of individual colonial farmers and the mill and furnace industries were the vast majority of manufacturing enterprises undertaken by the colonists (which we attempt to catalog in table 15.1). During the whole period, as Clark has observed, "power machinery was used to prepare raw materials for manufacturing rather than to produce finished goods—to saw lumber, forge iron, grind grain and bark, break hemp, rather than to perform the final operations which fitted these commodities for direct consumption." Craftsmen, "the true manufacturers" of the preindustrial age, were the critical intermediaries who transformed the products of mill, furnace, and tannery into consumer goods. We know little about colonial craftsmen, and the scholarship that is available has focused more on their political concerns and their world view than on their businesses.[29]

---

lonial New York," *N.Y. Hist.*, XXXIII (1952), 3–24; Allen Sheldon Marber, "The New York Iron Merchant and Manufacturer: A Study of Eighteenth-Century Entrepreneurship" (Ph.D. diss., New York University, 1974); and Paul F. Paskoff, "Labor Productivity and Managerial Efficiency against a Static Technology: The Pennsylvania Iron Industry, 1750–1800," *Jour. Econ. Hist.*, XL (1980), 129–135 (quotation on p. 135), based on his study "Colonial Merchant-Manufactures and Iron: A Study in Capital Transformation, 1725–1775" (Ph.D. diss., Johns Hopkins University, 1976). For an early ironworks, see Hartley, *Ironworks on the Saugus.* See also chap. 6, n. 20, above.

29. V. Clark, *History of Manufactures*, I, 161. We could append a long list here of books and articles that have touched on one or more aspects of each of the industries listed in table 15.1, but it would simply duplicate the standard bibliographies. While many of these studies are useful in a narrative or descriptive way, they regularly fail to address the questions of greatest interest to us here. Some of the ones we find more useful, for the detail they offer if not always for their analysis, include Blanche Evans Hazard, *The Organization of the Boot and Shoe Industry in Massachusetts before 1875* (Cambridge, Mass., 1921); Arthur Harrison Cole, *The American Wool Manufacture* (Cambridge, Mass., 1926); and William R. Bagnall, *The Textile Industries of the United States*, vol. I: *1639–1810* (Cambridge, Mass., 1893). The colonial distilling and sugar refining industries are discussed in chap. 13, above,

TABLE 15.1.
Categories of Colonial Manufactured and
Processed Goods

Food and related products
  wheat flour
  tobacco products
  animal products
    meatpacking
    leather goods
      shoes
    whale products
      lighting oil
      candles
  fermented and distilled beverages
  refined sugar
  other food products
Textiles and textile products
  woolen textiles
  cotton textiles
  linen goods
  other textile goods
Forest products
  sawmill products
  casks and other wooden containers
  masts, spars, and other ship timbers
  pitch, tar, and turpentine
  furniture
  other forest products
Paper and printed materials
  paper
  newspapers and other periodicals
  books
  other paper products
Chemicals and allied substances
  industrial chemicals
  consumer chemicals
    salt
  other chemical products

Table 15.1 continued

Stone, clay, and glass products
   construction materials
   domestic utensils
   other stone, clay, and glass products
Metals
   precious metals
   iron and steel products
   other metal products
Equipment and apparatus
   machinery, agricultural and nonagricultural
   tools
   guns
   waterborne vessels
   land vehicles
   other equipment

What we do know about colonial artisans is that few worked in a factory setting. Instead, the family was the unit of production, the workshop was attached to the home, and the master craftsman provided the labor with the help of his wife, children, and an occasional apprentice. Work was performed with simple hand tools, unassisted by power or elaborate machinery and without an extensive division of labor. Most shops were what could be called "neighborhood manufactures," dispersed rather than concentrated, producing a wide range of goods in small quantities, often made to order, for a few customers. The size of such establishments was constrained by the high price of labor, primitive technology, and small markets; their inefficiencies were protected by the high cost of transportation.[30]

---

in relation to the import of molasses and sugar. The most useful bibliography on the subject is Jack Goodwin's on-going "Current Bibliography in the History of Technology," which has appeared annually in *Technology and Culture* since 1964.

30. V. Clark, *History of Manufactures*, I, 161–164. See also Carl Bridenbaugh, *The Colonial Craftsman* (New York, 1950). Also useful are Marion N. Rawson, *Handwrought Ancestors: The Story of Early American Shops and Those Who Worked Therein* (New York, [1936]), and Paul Zankowich, "The Craftsmen of Colonial New York City" (Ed.D. diss., New York University, 1956). Compare Peter Nicholas Moogk, "The Craftsmen of New France" (Ph.D. diss., University of Toronto, 1973), and Edward Opper, "Dutch East India

Over time, some artisans began to operate differently. Able to overcome the usual limitations, they became "employing manufacturers," who produced standardized goods for domestic sale and for export, rather than individualized items made to order. They were able "to bring together in one establishment a number of special operations and to knit them into a continuous and reciprocally adjusted process." Such transformations of mechanic into manufacturer and workshop into factory merit our close study, for they led to remarkable advances in productivity and pointed to a profound and far-reaching set of changes that eventually helped the American economy shed its "colonial" structure.[31]

Company Artisans in the Early Eighteenth Century" (Ph.D. diss., Indiana University, 1975). The significance of what some call "the household mode of production" is perhaps most clearly revealed in work on its decline in the early 19th century. See two fine recent studies of Lynn, Massachusetts: Alan Dawley, *Class and Community: The Industrial Revolution in Lynn* (Cambridge, Mass., 1976); and Paul G. Faler, *Mechanics and Manufacturers in the Early Industrial Revolution: Lynn, Massachusetts, 1780–1860* (Albany, N.Y., 1981). Compare Carlton O. Wittlinger, "The Small Arms Industry of Lancaster County, 1710–1840," *Pa. Hist.*, XXIV (1957), 121–136, and Kulik, "Beginnings of the Industrial Revolution in America." See also the classic article by John R. Commons, "American Shoemakers, 1648–1895: A Sketch of Industrial Evolution," *Qtly. Jour. Econ.*, XXIV (1909), 39–84.

31. V. Clark, *History of Manufactures*, I, 193. See also Sharon V. Salinger, "Artisans, Journeymen, and the Transformation of Labor in Late Eighteenth-Century Philadelphia," *WMQ*, 3d Ser., XL (1983), 62–84. Perhaps one example of such a development will be revealed when someone has done a proper job of analyzing the early British American pottery industry. Historians who have worked with the probate inventories tell us that over time the colonists gave up wooden trenchers and pewter plates and tankards for the products of the kiln. Some pottery was imported from Great Britain and Germany (by way of Britain one presumes). Increasingly, however, the colonists' needs seem to have been met by colonial potters, whose wares included everything from the crudest goods to, eventually, fine porcelain. Colonial pottery factories were well enough established by the eve of independence that Josiah Wedgewood could worry, in 1771, that colonial potters would "in time . . . serve North America and prevent the exportation of our English China" (Graham Hood, *Bonnin and Morris of Philadelphia: The First American Porcelain Factory, 1770–1772* [Chapel Hill, N.C., 1972], 72, n. 20). The best studies to date of early American potters have been those by curators and archaeologists. See Lura Woodside Watkins, *Early New England Potters and Their Wares* (Cambridge, Mass., 1950); C. Watkins and Noël Hume, *"Poor Potter" of Yorktown*; and Hood, *Bonnin and Morris*, which contains a general discussion of pre-Revolutionary pottery factories.

CHAPTER 16

GOVERNMENT,

BUSINESS, AND

THE COLONIAL

ECONOMY

A critical characteristic of the developing economy in early British America was the declining relative cost of one of the four factors of production: management. The decline in managerial costs benefited the colonial entrepreneur directly because it tended to increase his profits, but it also worked to help the economy as a whole. Higher profits attracted more capital and induced other entrepreneurs to invest and produce. Increased local business employed more people, expanded domestic markets, and further stimulated the economy. Reduced costs in doing business resulted in large part from the greater provision of commercial services to merchants and to the entire economy by government offices and private firms. Service agencies like these, able to specialize in one function and thus to benefit from economies of scale, performed these jobs at a lower unit cost than could a general merchant.[1]

That government actively supported business during the colonial period should surprise no one. It was universally acknowledged that government's primary responsibility was the security of the state and its citizens. There were few limits in theory or in practice to what government might do in carrying out its responsibilities. The economy, as simply an-

---

1. Despite numerous studies of businesses in early British America, we are still without any broad analysis of colonial entrepreneurship. Bernard Bailyn came closest in his *New England Merchants*, but it is, at best, merely one case study and it does not address directly the issues raised in this chapter. See also Robert A. East, "The Business Entrepreneur in a Changing Colonial Economy, 1763–1795," *Jour. Econ. Hist.*, VI (Supplement, 1946), 16–27, and Bruchey, "Success and Failure Factors."

other element of national life, had to be subservient to the common good. (Contemporary thinking extended this principle to other aspects of national life, including religion.) Government had the right to ensure that the economy contribute to the interests of the state. It was this philosophy that motivated the English government to found colonies in the first place, that is, to strengthen the economy and thereby support the state.

Colonial governments shared these ideas. Americans displayed a "sturdy tradition of public responsibility for economic growth," in the words of Robert A. Lively. Certainly if the actions of colonial governments are any measure of the nature and extent of this philosophy, few areas of private economic behavior were outside government's province. When private enterprise needed help, public promotive schemes were developed. When private enterprise seemed threatened, government intervened. And when private enterprise endangered the public good, government responded by regulating economic behavior.[2]

Promotion, protection, and regulation all served to diminish the costs of doing business. Maintaining the "just price," guaranteeing the right of parties to contract, and ensuring other correct modes of economic behavior were accepted as within the proper regulatory role of colonial government. Colonial forts, militia, naval vessels, police officials, and related facilities and undertakings certainly offered the business community protection. And both government regulation and government military expenditure could clearly be seen to aid others besides merchants. This is not to suggest that either regulation or protection was insignificant, but merely to highlight the relative importance contemporaries apparently attached to them.[3] More interesting were the promotive activities of colo-

2. The point implicit in this discussion is that many of the ideas and attitudes identified by Robert A. Lively, "The American System: A Review Article," *Bus. Hist. Rev.*, XXIX (1955), 81–96, as applicable to the 19th century are equally applicable to the 17th and 18th centuries (quotation on p. 81). For all of this see also chap. 2, above, and the sources cited there, especially E. A. J. Johnson, *American Economic Thought.* See also Johnson, *The Foundations of American Economic Freedom: Government and Enterprise in the Age of Washington* (Minneapolis, Minn., 1973). Some of the work that has been done concerning the postcolonial era suggests useful modes of analysis. Warren M. Persons's rather too one-sided view in *Government Experimentation in Business* (New York, 1934), has been offset by such studies as Oscar and Mary Flug Handlin, *Commonwealth—A Study of the Role of Government in the American Economy: Massachusetts, 1774–1861* (New York, 1947), and Louis Hartz, *Economic Policy and Democratic Thought: Pennsylvania, 1776–1860* (Cambridge, Mass., 1948). See also chap. 17, below.

3. The literature on such topics as colonial business regulation and military expenditures is much more extensive than that on promotion, but those works rarely do more than describe the activity. We suggest here that it would be appropriate to attempt an assessment of the economic impact of these measures. On the subject of price and wage regulations, see,

nial legislatures, which were perceived as eventually, although perhaps indirectly, working to the common good.[4]

Colonial governmental programs that promoted private enterprise
came in two varieties. We adopt a distinction between "public enterprise," where government undertook an economic function by itself, and
"mixed enterprise," where government became, in effect, a partner with
private enterprise. Both types of government activity lowered expenses
for businessmen by socializing private costs.[5]

The public enterprise activities of government assumed a variety of
forms. Governments arranged land sales; licensed traders; built and maintained roads, harbors, and wharves; ran schools; operated loan offices
(essentially public lending institutions or banks, in the modern sense);

---

among others, Richard B. Morris and Jonathan Grossman, "The Regulation of Wages in
Early Massachusetts," *NEQ*, XI (1938), 470–500. Compare Morris, *Government and
Labor*. The pursuit of the "just price" by the General Court of Massachusetts must constitute the best-known instance of a colonial government's attempt to punish incorrect economic behavior. See Bernard Bailyn, "The *Apologia* of Robert Keayne," *WMQ*, 3d Ser., VII
(1950), 568–587. On the subject of local control of the quality of goods offered for sale, see
A. Jensen, "Inspection of Exports," 275–297; N. Jones, "Weights, Measures, and Mercantilism"; Frederick Kahler Henrich, "A Role for Regulation: Early American Legislation
to Protect the Public Interest" (Ph.D. diss., State University of New York, Buffalo, 1978);
Bruce C. Daniels, "The Political Structure of Local Government in Colonial Connecticut,"
in *Town and Country: Essays on the Structure of Local Government in the American Colonies*, ed. Daniels (Middletown, Conn., 1978), 67; and Schweitzer, "Economic Regulation."

4. The notion that government promotion of private businesses would serve the common
good was perhaps more acceptable to colonial legislatures that were controlled by colonial
business interests, agricultural as well as commercial and industrial. As Jack P. Greene has
noted, "politics everywhere was primarily elitist in nature" and that elite maintained its
business connections ("Changing Interpretations of Early American Politics," in *The Reinterpretation of Early American History: Essays in Honor of John Edwin Pomfret*, ed. Ray
Allen Billington [San Marino, Calif., 1966], 171). The colonial era much more readily than
our own would have accepted as appropriate and proper the attitude evinced in 1953 by
Charles Wilson, newly appointed secretary of defense in the cabinet of President Dwight D.
Eisenhower. When asked if there would be any conflict of interest between his position and
the job he had just left as head of General Motors, he replied: "I cannot conceive of one
because for years I thought that what was good for our country was good for General
Motors and vice versa" (*New York Times*, 24 Jan. 1953, p. 8, col. 8).

5. The literature on government involvement in the economy is considerable, but as suggested above, it is concerned almost exclusively with the 19th and 20th centuries. Still,
there is a great deal that will help those undertaking studies of the colonial period. See
Lively, "American System." For a good introduction to the subject and a useful, short bibliography, see Carter Goodrich, ed., *The Government and the Economy, 1783–1861* (Indianapolis, Ind., 1967). See also Handlin and Handlin, *Commonwealth*, and Hartz, *Economic Policy*. J. R. T. Hughes, *Social Control in the Colonial Economy* (Charlottesville,
Va., 1976), surveys many of the important issues.

and minted and printed money. These are economic functions, unrelated to governing, that provided a good or a service that might otherwise have been produced by private entrepreneurs—and sometimes were. For example, a private company could have built and operated a road, collecting tolls for its use. A government-built road, paid for out of the public treasury, diminished the transportation expenses for the individual businessman.[6]

The best example of the socializing of private costs through public enterprise with the purpose of serving the public good—and, in the process, enriching proprietors and officials—was the organization of land distribution. To promote development by stimulating settlement, colonial governments undertook to appropriate, explore, survey, and sell the rights to land. A variety of methods were employed, each tailored to local circumstances and interests. Although historians have only a poor understanding of the whole system, it seems to have worked, despite a good deal of corruption. Land was quickly transferred to private hands—too quickly for the public good, some have argued—and thus made available for productive use.[7]

Another example of public enterprise was the public loan office, frequently called the land bank. We know little about the mechanisms or the extent of public and private finance. When the story is told, we think that it will record a three-tier system. The would-be borrower, depending on the extent of his need, the time in which he lived, and whether he resided in town or in the country, could turn to friends, to business acquaintances, or to a land bank.[8]

6. While each of these activities has its historian, they have rarely been treated in the manner suggested in this chapter. See, however, Edward G. Roberts, "The Roads of Virginia, 1607–1840" (Ph.D. diss., University of Virginia, 1950).

7. The standard work is Marshall Harris, *Origin of the Land Tenure System in the United States* (Ames, Iowa, 1953). One aspect of the land distribution system that is often misunderstood is the headright system. See chap. 10, n. 12, above. Another is "speculation," for which see the classic article by Paul Wallace Gates, "The Role of the Land Speculator in Western Development," *PMHB*, LXVI (1942), 314–333. We may wish to think of land "speculation" as a form of investment, promoted by colonial governments to provoke the opening and settlement of western lands and the concomitant economic development. William Chazanof, "Land Speculation in Eighteenth-Century New York," in *Business Enterprise in Early New York*, ed. Joseph R. Frese and Jacob Judd (Tarrytown, N.Y., 1979), 55–76, deals with the reasons for land speculation and establishes the periods of such activity. For a very good study of surveying in one colony, see Sarah S. Hughes, *Surveyors and Statesmen: Land Measuring in Colonial Virginia* (Richmond, Va., 1979). For exploration, Henry Savage, Jr., *Discovering America, 1700–1875* (New York, 1979), provides an introduction to the literature.

8. There are some general studies, such as Wilbur C. Plummer, "Consumer Credit in Colonial Philadelphia," *PMHB*, LXVI (1942), 385–409. On the subject of international credit

Private individuals lent money, friend to friend, neighbor to neighbor. This type of personal borrowing was the least efficient of the three modes and therefore the most costly, to individuals and to the economy as a whole. The informality of such arrangements meant that they were poorly documented and thus difficult for historians to evaluate, although once again, probate records are useful in this regard. Whatever their inefficiencies and however hard they may be to trace, private loans were very important to the colonial economy and critical to those who needed help to start a farm, expand a small business, or ride out an unanticipated financial crisis. Despite indications that in some communities—among the Pennsylvania Germans, for instance—such loans carried no explicit interest, borrowing in this way did come at a cost: living in a community where one borrowed at no interest created an obligation to charge no interest when lending money. The result was a tendency to limit the amount lent. Personal loans were inefficient, therefore, because the larger the sum required, the more lenders a borrower needed to contact. An economy that operated under these constraints would develop more slowly than one in which it was easier to borrow on a large scale. It is likely that personal loans made up a majority of the number negotiated in the colonies, but a declining proportion over time of the total amount borrowed as colonial finance gained sophistication.[9]

Loans by merchants, planters, and other wealthy local people, made to their clients in the normal course of affairs, were probably the second-largest number negotiated. Eventually, some colonial businessmen became more involved in moneylending than in the production or sale of goods and services; they came to resemble contemporary London merchant-bankers. John Hull, seventeenth-century Boston merchant and treasurer of the Massachusetts Bay Colony, frequently styled himself

---

linked to trade, the best work is Price, *Capital and Credit*. See also Arthur Shelburn Williamson, "Credit Relations between Colonial and English Merchants in the Eighteenth Century" (Ph.D. diss., University of Iowa, 1927). William I. Roberts III, "Ralph Carr: A Newcastle Merchant and the American Colonial Trade," *Bus. Hist. Rev.*, XLII (1968), 271–287, argues that this credit linkage kept American merchants on a rather short string, restricting their ability to take risks. One might turn this around and detect in the increasingly innovative attitudes of the late colonial period another indication of the larger proportion of investment capital that was colonial in origin. This coincides with the argument in McCusker, "Sources of Investment Capital."

9. The reference is to the description by Benjamin Rush, *An Account of the Manners of the German Inhabitants of Pennsylvania* (1789), ed. Theodore E. Schmauk (Lancaster, Pa., 1910), 86–87. Compare David Sabean, "Aspects of Kinship Behaviour and Property in Rural Western Europe before 1800," in *Family and Inheritance: Rural Society in Western Europe, 1200–1800*, ed. Jack Goody, Joan Thirsk, and E. P. Thompson (Cambridge, 1976), 101. We wish to thank Dr. Elizabeth Kessell for these citations.

"goldsmith" at a time when London goldsmiths were transforming themselves into deposit and exchange bankers. Some of the larger planters behaved in similar ways. Credit on this basis was more attractive than loans from friends or relatives because it offered the possibility of larger loans at lower real rates. Nevertheless, it was still necessary to be acquainted with the person in order to effect the loan.[10]

Banks, public land banks or any other kind, still further diminished the personal element in loans and enlarged the amount one could borrow. Loans from land banks were secured with the borrower's real estate holdings. The loans were made using paper money (bills of credit) for which the land bank was itself the issuing agency under colonial charter. (Thus, along with the colonial governments, land banks became one of the two sources of paper money in early British America.) Where banks were in operation, they served to lower the costs of all borrowing, especially interest rates, for two reasons. First, land banks increased the supply of funds to be loaned, presumably to a greater degree than they stimulated demand for money to borrow. Second, the facilities of the land bank probably resulted in a more efficient mobilization of all domestic credit. In addition to lowering interest rates, land banks had the added advantage of returning their surpluses to the colonial treasury, thereby decreasing the need for direct taxes.[11] Where land banks were established, they

10. Despite his role as one of the largest planters of colonial Maryland, Charles Carroll of Annapolis in a 1764 accounting of his assets listed more than half of them as being in the form of money owed to him. See his letter to his son, Charles Carroll of Carrollton, 9 Jan. 1764, Carroll Papers, Maryland Historical Society, and as printed in Hoffman, ed., *Dear Papa, Dear Charley.* We are indebted to Professor Hoffman and to Ms. Sally Mason of his staff for help with this reference. For the operations of another individual who lent large sums, see Julian Gwyn, *The Enterprising Admiral: The Personal Fortune of Admiral Sir Peter Warren* (Montreal, 1974). For Hull, see the John Hull Papers, *passim* (e.g., bill of sale dated 26 Nov. 1672), American Antiquarian Society, Worcester, Mass., and Hermann Frederick Clarke, *John Hull: A Builder of the Bay Colony* (Portland, Maine, 1940). For English banking, see *The Mystery of the New Fashioned Goldsmiths or Bankers. Their Rise, Growth, State, and Decay, Discovered in a Merchant's Letter to a Country Gent. . . .* ([London], 1676), as reprinted in John Biddulph Martin, *"The Grasshopper" in Lombard Street* (London, 1892), and R. D. Richards, *The Early History of Banking in England* (London, 1929).

11. Concerning land banks, see Donald L. Kemmerer, "The Colonial Loan-Office System in New Jersey," *Jour. Pol. Econ.,* XLVII (1939), 867–874; Theodore Thayer, "The Land-Bank System in the American Colonies," *Jour. Econ. Hist.,* XIII (1953), 145–159; E. J. Ferguson, "Currency Finance," 168–170; and George Athan Billias, *The Massachusetts Land Bankers of 1740* (Orono, Maine, 1959). When colonial public finance is studied, it is almost exclusively in the context of crisis, either crises surrounding debates over paper money or the crisis of the American Revolution (see chap. 17, below). It is also frequently made to seem primitive when, in fact, some very modern ideas were at work. For instance, the whole notion of indexing to diminish the impact of any devaluation of the currency was enacted

tended to be very successful and very popular. John Adams afterward claimed that the British government's efforts in 1741 "to destroy the [Massachusetts] Land Bank scheme raised a greater ferment in this province, than the Stamp-Act did." [12]

Another public enterprise function served by colonial governments was as keepers of the currency. Everything they did to regularize and stabilize the currency of the colonies made it easier to exchange money for goods and services and thereby lowered the costs of doing business. By issuing paper currency—either directly or through a land bank—and by otherwise working to expand the colonial money supply, each colonial government further supported and stimulated economic development. The success of those efforts was threatened by the British government's attempts to undermine the authority of colonial governments over their local currencies. The colonists feared in measures such as the Currency Acts of 1751 and 1764 the likelihood of a diminished supply of local currency and a return to a heavier reliance on the more burdensome, less flexible alternatives: barter, commodity money (e.g., tobacco or sugar), and foreign gold and silver coin. The memory of that kind of parliamentary interference in colonial internal economic affairs influenced considerably subsequent attitudes among Americans toward the proper role of the central government. [13]

Economic historians have been busier describing how colonial governments attempted to deal with currency problems than trying to answer the question of how well they did. In part this is because of the vast historiographical tangle created by nineteenth- and early twentieth-century polemists who attempted to find lessons for their contemporaries in the experiences of the colonists. In part it is also because such questions are not subject to easy answers.

---

into legislation in the colonies. See *A Table Shewing the Value of Old Tenor Bills, in Lawful Money* . . . ([Boston, 1750]), copy at the American Antiquarian Society, and Willard C. Fisher, "The Tabular Standard in Massachusetts History," *Qtly. Jour. Econ.*, XXVII (1913), 417–454. The first of these two references provokes us to suggest the usefulness of specifying the location of copies of rare and unique printed materials, that is, treating them for purposes of citation as we do letters and manuscripts.

12. *Boston-Gazette, and Country Journal*, 13 Feb. 1775.

13. The basic treatises on currency in early British America are Leslie V. Brock, *The Currency of the American Colonies, 1700–1764: A Study in Colonial Finance and Imperial Relations* (New York, 1975 [Ph.D. diss., University of Michigan, 1941]), and Ernst, *Money and Politics*. See also Nettels, *Money Supply*; Baxter, *House of Hancock*; John J. McCusker, "Colonial Paper Money," in *Studies on Money in Early America*, ed. Eric P. Newman and Richard G. Doty (New York, 1976), 94–104; and McCusker, *Money and Exchange*.

A central question is whether the money supply of the colonists was "adequate." To be adequate for the purposes of an economy, money must be both available in sufficient quantities and of a recognized standard to facilitate rather than inhibit its use in the exchange of goods and services. The total quantity of money available to the colonists is unknown since contemporary or modern estimates are few and never include all forms of money. Some speak of the supply of coin, some of public paper, some of both; all omit commodity money and private paper.

On the eve of the War of Independence, according to Alexander Hamilton, the money stock (specie and paper money [M1]) in the thirteen colonies was worth about 30,000,000 Spanish silver dollars, the equivalent to £6,750,000 sterling, or about £2.70 per person. That compares with figures of £3.25 per person for the money stock of England and Wales in 1750 and £3.50 in 1775. Recalling our estimate of colonial per capita income for the same period, £10.70 to £12.50, and using the classic formula where velocity equals income divided by money stock, we can calculate the velocity at which money circulated in early British America. The resulting velocities, 4.0 and 4.6, fall well within the range that prevailed in England and Wales during the eighteenth century. It appears on this basis that the colonists' stock of money was adequate, at least insofar as quantity was concerned.[14]

However adequate the quantity of money in the colonies, it may have had qualitative defects that hindered its use in normal business. One-

14. For Hamilton's estimate, see McCusker, *Money and Exchange*, 7, n. 9, and Hamilton to Robert Morris, 30 Apr. 1781, in *The Papers of Robert Morris, 1781–1784*, ed. E. James Ferguson *et al.* (Pittsburgh, Pa., 1973–), I, 35. For modern estimates (that do not take Hamilton into account), see Roger W. Weiss, "The Issue of Paper Money in the American Colonies, 1720–1774," *Jour. Econ. Hist.*, XXX (1970), 779, and A. Jones, *Wealth of a Nation to Be*, 128. Both of these estimates are in the range £1.10 to £1.20; both being based on probate records, it does not at all surprise us that they are considerably less than Hamilton's estimate. Cash would have been one of the things most likely to have been distributed outside of the usual probate proceedings either as gifts before death or by the surreptitious actions of relatives after death. A. Jones, *Wealth of a Nation to Be*, 63, is the source of our estimate of per capita income (see also chap. 3, above). Rondo Cameron, "England, 1750–1844," in *Banking in the Early Stages of Industrialization: A Study in Comparative Economic History*, ed. Cameron *et al.* (New York, 1967), 42, provides our points of comparison. The specie portion of his money supply estimate is about £2.15. Compare the calculation, dated 1775, in Edward Long's "Notebook," fol. 40r, Add. MS 12413, BL: "The whole of the Gold Coin in Great Britain . . . is computed at 15 million, the silver, 3, Total 18." This is roughly £2.07 per person. See also William Letwin, "Monetary Practice and Theory of the North American Colonies during the Seventeenth and Eighteenth Centuries," in *La moneta nell'economica europea secoli XIII–XVIII*, ed. Vera Barbagli Bagnoli (Prato, 1981), 439–469. According to another estimate, the specie portion of the French per capita money stock in 1774 equaled £2.88. See Riley and McCusker, "Money Supply," 277.

quarter of the colonial money stock, according to Hamilton, was in spe-cie. The gold and silver coins that circulated in the colonies were Spanish and Portuguese. Since they were neither denominated in terms of the vari-ous colonial currencies nor always of full weight, the coins did not circu-late as freely and easily as they might have. To a certain extent these very real problems were offset by the large proportion of specie—perhaps as much as half, though that is only a guess—constituted by the Spanish silver piece of eight (the dollar), a milled coin that passed easily by tale, that is, by count rather than by weight. Nevertheless, between 10 and 15 percent of the money stock had to be weighed and its fineness proved before it could change hands. These difficulties were compounded by the efforts of counterfeiters, who seem always to have been at work in the colonies. Still, the very high value of gold minimized the impact of these problems on everyday affairs. Because of their great value, gold coins were useful only in large-scale transactions and in overseas trade, where businessmen had the expertise and the equipment to weigh and test them.[15]

At the other end of the spectrum, some colonists complained about the scarcity of small change in much the same way that we experience periodic shortages of pennies in the United States today. If inadequate supplies of small-denomination coins offset an otherwise adequate money stock, business may have been obstructed. Yet the use of some British copper pieces, local tokens, and small-denomination paper currency must have alleviated this problem at least a bit. About all of these issues we have slight evidence and almost no careful analysis. It does little to advance our understanding simply to repeat the contentions of contemporaries.[16]

15. The guess about the composition of colonial coinage is McCusker's (*Money and Exchange*, 7). A systematic analysis of contemporary coin hoards would provide the basis for a better guess, but no one has yet accomplished this work. Whoever tries it will find a particu-larly rich source in the reports of undersea archaeologists. See, for example, Jeremy N. Green, "The Wreck of the Dutch East Indiaman the *Vergulde Draeck*, 1656," *International Journal of Nautical Archaeology and Underwater Exploration*, II (1973), 267–289, and Bjørn R. Rønning, "Et funn av mynter blant vrakrestene etter den hollandske ostindia-fareren *Akerendam*, forlist ved Runde i 1725," *Nordisk Numismatisk Årsskrift (1973–1974)* (Stockholm), 68–115. Colonial statutes defined (and redefined) legal values for spe-cific coins based on their full weight. See McCusker, *Money and Exchange, passim*. One needed to have access to money scales to weigh coins, however. See Michael A. Crawforth, *Weighing Coins: English Folding Gold Balances of the Eighteenth and Nineteenth Cen-turies* (London, 1979). The extent and the economic impact of counterfeiting are not easily ascertained. See Kenneth Scott, *Counterfeiting in Colonial America* (New York, 1957). Concerning counterfeiting, see the works of Carl Bridenbaugh, especially *Cities in the Wil-derness*, 222, and *Cities in Revolt*, 111–112.

16. For instances of shortages of small change, see Bridenbaugh, *Cities in the Wilderness*, 361, and Kenneth Scott, *Counterfeiting in Colonial New York* (New York, 1953), 102–

The colonists' money supply problems were even greater with paper currency than with specie, according to the conventional wisdom over the last century. They supposedly feared and distrusted paper currency because of the potential loss of purchasing power inherent in a medium of exchange that had no intrinsic worth. Such contentions seem more relevant to the circumstances of the 1890s and the 1930s than to those of the 1690s or the 1730s. We know that all the colonies issued paper currency and that the populace accepted and used it. Paper currency had one clear advantage over specie: it was denominated in each colony's money of account. Many colonial currencies circulated not only in the colonies that issued them, where the bearer had the protection of the legal tender statutes, but also outside their official borders. Indeed, paper monies continued to be issued and accepted in some colonies even after the Currency Acts of 1751 and 1764 destroyed the guarantees afforded by legal tender status. One recent study has even suggested that it is possible to determine the extent of regional trading networks by discovering the area within which the several paper currencies circulated. It seems likely that paper money in the colonial period suffered from fewer disabilities than we have been led to believe.[17]

More to the central point in this discussion, however, is the appreciation that, whatever difficulties may have plagued an otherwise satisfac-

---

109. See also John R. Hanson II, "Small Notes in the American Colonies," *Explorations Econ. Hist.*, XVII (1980), 411–420. We are indebted to Dr. Philip L. Mossman of Hampden, Maine, who assisted us with several technical points.

17. Much of this is addressed in McCusker, *Money and Exchange, passim.* See also Letwin, "Monetary Practice and Theory"; West, "Money in the Colonial American Economy"; and John R. Hanson II, "Money in the Colonial American Economy: An Extension," *Econ. Inquiry*, XVII (1979), 281–286. Compare Cameron, "England," 46–47. For colonial paper money in general, see the works cited in n. 13, above. See also Eric P. Newman, *The Early Paper Money of America*, [2d ed.] (Racine, Wis., 1976).

There is a great need for caution in dealing with money values and comparisons of money values in and among the colonies of early British America. Each colony had its own currency, even though all used the same units for counting purposes (pounds, shillings, and pence; abbreviated £, s., d.); 1 pound equaled 20 shillings and 1 shilling equaled 12 pence. Thus it is necessary to reduce money values from different colonies to a common denominator for purposes of any comparison. McCusker, *Money and Exchange*, provides tables for reducing all colonial currencies to pounds sterling. A certain caution is required in using data from older works where such a reduction has not been made. In addition, for some of the colonies in particular—Massachusetts, Rhode Island, South Carolina—and for all of early British America generally, we must be aware of the effects of monetary depreciation on any comparisons over time. Thus it is frequently necessary to reduce current values to a constant value using a commodity price index, preferably a commodity price index specific to the individual colony. A more general colonial price index can be found in McCusker, "Historical Price Indexes." See also n. 11, above.

tory stock of specie and paper, the colonists probably still had an adequate quantity of money. That was so, we would argue, because their own calculation of the money stock included other items, among them commodity money—tobacco, sugar, and other commodities that circulated as legal tender at an officially assigned value. We need estimates of the total value of such supplements to the colonial money stock, which when added to the value of coin and paper had the healthy effect of decreasing still further the ratio of per capita income to money stock. In keeping the currency, the efforts of colonial governments, patterned on those of the mother country, were at least as satisfactory as the actions of Parliament.[18]

The imperial government engaged in a variety of similar public enterprises to the direct benefit of merchants—both at home and in the colonies. An important example of this is the operation of the imperial postal service. In 1835 William, Lord Lowther, the president of the Board of Trade, stated succinctly the raison d'être of the postal service: "The principle of the Post-office at its establishment, as distinctly laid down in [the Act of] 12 Charles II. [c. 35 (1660)], was to afford advantage to trade and commerce. The direct revenue to be derived from the Post-office was not the primary consideration." Until the middle of the eighteenth century colonial merchants benefited most directly from the postal service only in times of war, when the Post Office and the Treasury induced individuals to set up transatlantic packet services. The packets supplemented the usual method of mailing a letter from the colonies to Great Britain, that is, entrusting it to the care of a ship captain. Only in 1751, with the appointment of Benjamin Franklin as postmaster general of the colonies, did the full advantages of domestic postal service become available there. Franklin set up official mail routes and regular deliveries from Boston to Charleston. Mail moved more surely and more quickly; as Franklin himself noted, "time is money"—in this instance money in the pockets of businessmen who profited from a public post.[19]

18. On the subject of commodity money, see McCusker, *Money and Exchange*, 117–118 (especially the references cited in n. 4), and *passim*. While barter certainly existed—and had become institutionalized as an important supplement to the money supply by way of bookkeeping barter—the colonial economy still required currency to operate. As Thomas Willing, merchant of Philadelphia, explained to Codrington Carrington of Barbados, 26 May 1755: "We never barter for the Country produce because the Farmer & Miller will have money on delivery & frequently before they deliver their articles" (Willing and Morris Letter Book, 1754–1761, p. 97, Hist. Soc. Pa.). For bookkeeping barter, see Baxter, *House of Hancock*, 17–21.

19. The Lowther quote is from Great Britain, Commission Appointed to Inquire into the Management of the Post-Office Department, *The Fifth Report of the Commissioners Appointed to Inquire into the Management of the Post-Office Department* (London, 1836), 6.

However much governments might have been willing to organize nec-
essary services and to pay for them with public funds, they were less eagerto become directly involved in the production of commodities. If no
one person could be persuaded to step forward, the colonists occasionally
organized governmental production of necessary commodities.[20] But to
produce either services or goods, colonial governments preferred joint
ventures with the private sector. An example of such mixed enterprise is
that of the early transatlantic packets mentioned above.

Mixed enterprise had a venerable history, beginning with the settlement of the colonies themselves. Private investors put up the capital and
planted the settlements; the English government offered them trading
monopolies and land grants as inducements. Companies organized to
found colonies were, of course, patterned after the much older joint-stock
companies, which were granted monopoly rights to trade between England and a specified place or region, for example, the East India Company. Colonial governments later followed English precedents and promoted individual entrepreneurs, partnerships, and even locally chartered
joint-stock companies to establish everything from river ferries to iron
manufacturing. Local grain mills and blacksmith shops were the kind of
facility most frequently established in this manner. The need was patent
and its application universal. The same approach was used by governments—local, state, and federal—to promote canal and railroad building
in the nineteenth century and "private" electrical power in the twentieth.[21]

The public promotion of mixed enterprise during the colonial period
was nowhere more extensive or more concentrated than in Massachusetts
after 1640. Faced with a sharp depression that many feared would de-

---

On the postal service in general, see William Smith, *The History of the Post Office in British North America, 1639–1870* (Cambridge, 1920); Wesley Everett Rich, *The History of the United States Post Office to the Year 1829* (Cambridge, Mass., 1924); and Kay Horowicz and Robson Lowe, *The Colonial Posts in the United States of America, 1606–1738* (London, 1967). See also Bridenbaugh, *Cities in the Wilderness*, 53, 204–205, 361–362, and *Cities in Revolt*, 96–97, 290–291. On the packet services, see [J. T. Dixon], "The Problem of Imperial Communications during the Eighteenth Century, with Special Reference to the Post Office" (M.A. thesis, University of Leeds, 1964); Frank Staff, *The Transatlantic Mail* (London, 1956); and John J. McCusker, "New York City and the Bristol Packet: A Chapter in Eighteenth Century Postal History," *Postal History Journal*, XX (1968), 15–24. See also Ruth Lapham Butler, *Doctor Franklin, Postmaster General* (Garden City, N.Y., 1928).

20. Daniels, "Economic Development," 438–440.

21. On the history of joint-stock companies, see W. Scott, *Constitution and Finance of Joint-Stock Companies*. For the 19th century, see such studies as Carter Goodrich, *Government Promotion of American Canals and Railroads, 1800–1890* (New York, 1960). Earlier references in this chapter will lead interested readers to similar developments during the colonial era, but there is no systematic treatment of the subject for the period.

stroy them, the members of the General Court made every effort to save the economy and, thereby, the colony. One element of their program involved encouraging the domestic production of a variety of goods that had, until then, been imported from the mother country. The promotive measures they adopted included grants of land and exemption from taxes and military service. In time the economy improved, and though we can only speculate how important these measures were in effecting the improvement, the lesson was not lost.[22]

Perhaps the most intriguing attempts by colonial governments to promote private enterprise concern those businesses that were clearly in competition with British interests. In the 1720s New York granted a monopoly to the first sugar refinery founded there. Later, Jamaicans went still further and passed an import duty on refined sugar, which they collected on North American as well as on British refined sugars. Needless to say, British sugar refiners wondered about the propriety of colonial governments promoting and protecting local manufacturing.[23]

For similar reasons English merchants trading to Virginia complained to the Board of Trade about a law that discriminated against their ships in favor of locally owned vessels by collecting differential duties depending on where each ship's owners resided. The Privy Council disallowed the law, but the House of Burgesses passed it again in a slightly modified form and the new one stayed on the books. In 1771 one Virginian appreciated that the law saved resident merchants who traded to and from the colony in their own ships about £50 currency per voyage "in Impost[s,] Tunnage [duties,] &c."[24]

This was precisely the purpose. With this inducement Virginians became ship owners and operators, placed orders for locally built vessels, hired Virginians as masters and seamen to sail their ships, and carried freight to and from the colony that would otherwise have been carried by non-Virginians. Had it not been for government promotion of shipping, these men might have found a better return by investing their capital in

22. Some of this is discussed in chap. 5, above. The most accessible treatment of one example of this activity is Hartley, *Ironworks on the Saugus*. Compare Ceci, "First Fiscal Crisis."

23. On colonial sugar refining and the British reaction to it, see McCusker, "Rum Trade," 47–55.

24. Concerning the Virginia tonnage duty, see McCusker, "Tonnage of Ships." The quotation is from Middleton, *Tobacco Coast*, 259, citing [Thomas Adams?] to John Morton Jordan & Co., 24 Jan. 1771, Carter Papers, I, 121, Virginia Historical Society, Richmond. Other colonies passed similar laws. See, for example, the law of 1703 in Thomas Cooper and David J. McCord, eds., *The Statutes at Large of South Carolina* (Columbia, S.C., 1836–1841), II, 203.

tobacco lands or slaves or by sending it abroad to buy shares in the East
India Company. By socializing the costs of the shipping business, the government of Virginia fostered local economic growth, stimulated economic development, and helped the balance of payments.

The increased efficiency with which colonial businessmen conducted
their affairs was not solely the result of partial government socialization
of costs. Private efforts to lower expenses and increase returns followed
two paths, one toward improving the internal operations, the other toward organizing commercial mercantile services. Individual firms concentrated on upgrading office staff, changing accounting procedures, and
modernizing communications.

We know little about the internal structure of colonial businesses and
even less about how it changed over time. Yet anyone who has looked at
merchants' letters and accounts has quickly concluded that business was
more adroitly run in the eighteenth century than in the seventeenth century. Better-trained staff in the countinghouse and on the plantation must
have improved the efficiency with which such businesses were conducted.
Fewer of the letter books and account books were kept by the merchant
himself; increasingly, trained clerks penned the letters, recorded the drafts,
and maintained the books. The same was true on West Indian sugar plantations. Absentee planters were concerned to hire proper plantation
managers, accountants, and attorneys, each of whom was expected to report on his own performance and on those of his fellow employees. Scots
seem to have been prized employees because of the quality of their education. None of this has ever been sorted through.[25]

The one accountant who has studied business practices in early British
America, W. T. Baxter, concluded that colonial bookkeeping methods
were "dilatory," something he blamed on the "tiny scale of business."
Stuart Bruchey has taken issue with Baxter, arguing that while small colonial traders often did keep poor books, many merchants operated on
a large scale and most of them kept very good books in strict accor-

25. For a general discussion of some of these points, see Bernard Bailyn, "Communications
and Trade: The Atlantic in the Seventeenth Century," *Jour. Econ. Hist.*, XIII (1953), 378–
387, and Bruchey, "Success and Failure Factors." Concerning the availability of trained
clerks and accountants, one would do well to follow up the leads in Bridenbaugh, *Cities in
the Wilderness*, 359. For a very useful if much too short introduction to the surviving records, see Robert J. Wilson, *Early American Account Books: Interpretation, Cataloguing,
and Use* (Nashville, Tenn., 1981). Wilson's bibliography lists everything written on the subject. For the West Indies, see the works of Richard Pares, especially *West-India Fortune*, and
of Richard B. Sheridan, especially *Sugar and Slavery*, and "The Role of the Scots in the
Economy and Society of the West Indies," in *Comparative Perspectives on Slavery*, ed.
Rubin and Tuden, 94–106.

dance with the best contemporary standards. We tend to agree more with Bruchey and would further argue that as the scale of business expanded over the colonial period there was a commensurate improvement in bookkeeping. Again, since very little has been written on the subject, all we can do is invite the reader into the archives to have a look. We very much stand in need of studies of colonial business procedures.[26]

Such a history will have to deal with what kinds of information were available to the businessman in the colonies and with how the gathering and disseminating of economic intelligence changed over the period. "Intelligence," according to an aphorism current among colonial merchants, "is the life of business."[27] Sources of information on business matters existed in several genres, all of which the colonists were aware of and sought out with increasing vigor.

Published books of two types were especially important to the colonial merchant intent on improving his operations: the merchant's handbook, a guide to standard business practices around the world, usually arranged alphabetically by city name; and bookkeeping manuals, or how-to treatises. Publishers in Europe turned out both types regularly, in several languages and in many editions. Not only were they popular, but businessmen quite literally used them up. Few are extant in modern libraries, some only in unique copies. Among those in North American collections many bear a bookplate or inscription that identifies them as having been owned by colonial merchants. In a few the date of the inscription shows that they were purchased soon after publication, suggesting that the purchaser wanted to obtain the latest treatise as quickly as possible. Other contemporary references indicate familiarity with the standard works on all mercantile matters. The market for European publications in North America is evident from their inclusion of increasing amounts of information on how to conduct business in the colonies. By the mid-1750s one such book, John Mair's classic, *Book-keeping Methodiz'd*, had introduced a whole section tailored to colonial needs. At the same time, publishers in the colonies reacted to this hunger for information by turning out similar treatises, though they, too, are now so rare that historians of the colonial economy have not generally noted them.

26. W. T. Baxter, "Accounting in Colonial America," in *Studies in the History of Accounting*, ed. A. C. Littleton and B. S. Yamey (Homewood, Ill., 1956), 272–287 (quotation on p. 280); Bruchey, "Success and Failure Factors," 276–279. The numerous studies of early British American merchants contain little comparative analysis of business practices. Most of these studies concentrate on describing a particular firm's operations, with little or no attention paid to other firms.

27. Robert Anderson to Cuthbert Jones, 14 Oct. 1713, Robert Anderson Letter Book, 1698–1715, Alderman Library, University of Virginia, Charlottesville.

There is a grand opportunity in all of this for some economic historian of a bibliographical bent.[28]

The general colonial newspaper also conveyed economic information with increasing frequency during the eighteenth century, presumably because of a demand for such news on the part of the business community. In the earliest colonial newspapers the economy was reported on like the rest of the news: there were only generalized descriptions of events and developments from abroad. This changed rather quickly, again we presume because of pressure from local merchants, and local shipping information, local trade statistics, and ultimately local commodity prices came to be published. Merchants seem to have sought the publication of this information as a way of advertising the facilities of their market to the readers of the paper, both nearby and distant. Finally, in imitation of what they received from their European correspondents, merchants in the colonies supported the publication of two types of specialized business newspapers: the marine list and the price current. Extant copies of

28. For European handbooks, see Franco Borlandi, ed., *El libro di mercatantie et usanze de' paesi* (Turin, 1936), xiii-xx, and R. A. De Roover, "The Organization of Trade," in *Economic Organization and Policies in the Middle Ages*, vol. III of *The Cambridge Economic History of Europe*, ed. M. M. Postan, E. E. Rich, and Edward Miller (Cambridge, 1963), 94. For an example of a colonial merchant owning one such handbook, see Obadiah Brown's copy of Charles Snell, *A Guide to Book-keepers, According to the Italian Manner* (London, 1709), in the library of the Rhode Island Historical Society, Providence. Compare Hedges, *Browns of Providence Plantations*, 6–7. For Snell, see M. F. Bywater and B. S. Yamey, *Historic Accounting Literature: A Companion Guide* (London, 1982), 137–141. John Mair's *Book-keeping Methodiz'd; or, A Methodical Treatise of Merchant-Accompts, According to the Italian Form* (Edinburgh, 1736), and its revision, *Book-keeping Moderniz'd; or, Merchant-Accounts by Double Entry, According to the Italian Form* (Edinburgh, 1773), went through at least sixteen Scottish and eight (pirated) Irish editions by 1800. There are modern reprints of the 1st edition of the first title (London and Tokyo, 1982), and of the 6th edition of the second title (New York, 1978). See M. J. Mepham and W. E. Stone, "John Mair, M.A.: Author of the First Classical Book-keeping Series," *Accounting and Business Research*, VII (1977), 128–134, and Bywater and Yamey, *Historic Accounting Literature*, 164–167. See also William Weston, *The Complete Merchant's Clerk: or, British and American Compting House* (London, 1754). We know of only two similar treatises published in North America, but since each is unique to one library and neither is listed in the standard bibliographies, it is possible that others have also escaped notice. See Pieter Venema, *Arithmetica of Cyffer-Konst, Volgens de Munten Maten en Gewigten, te Nieu-York* (New York, 1730); this was printed by John Peter Zenger and the only known copy is in the New-York Historical Society. See also Robert Biscoe, *The Merchant's Magazine; or, Factor's Guide. Containing, Great Variety of Plain and Easy Tables* . . . (Williamsburg, Va., 1743); this was printed by William Parks and the only known copy is in the Library of Congress. Thus neither of these two works appears in the otherwise extremely valuable microfilm edition of economic materials being collected and published as the "Goldsmiths'-Kress Library of Economic Literature" by Research Publications, Inc.

such publications are so rare that we cannot be certain if any appeared before the American Revolution, though both were in existence shortly thereafter.[29]

The individual efforts of colonial merchants to improve their own situations were paralleled by the appearance of specialized firms offering services. The growing size and energy of the colonial mercantile community created a demand for specialized middlemen. Most of these activities were things that merchants could have done for themselves. Nevertheless, by doing them regularly and frequently, one businessman could develop superior expertise and take advantage of scale economies. Other businessmen recognized that it had become more efficient for them to pay someone else than to do it themselves.

The most prominent of these middlemen were brokers. Someone has defined a broker as a person whose job was to bring together a buyer and a seller and thereby to diminish the competitive disadvantage that would have been created had either tried to initiate the transaction. Brokers took fees for their services, which businessmen were willing to pay because they recognized that such fees were only a fraction of what a competitive disadvantage might have cost. We know little or nothing about colonial brokers, except that they were engaged in a variety of transactions: real estate, insurance, commodities, shipping, exchange, and more. Often these agencies originated in a particular port in the office of one merchant who simply started to spend larger portions of time helping clients buy and sell insurance or ships or whatever. Some offered several brokerage functions; in time a few began to specialize in a particular brokerage service. In some cities brokers met regularly at a set place—an "Exchange Alley" or a public inn—making it easier for customers to find and employ them. Of all the business intermediaries, the insurance brokers were probably the most important in the colonial period. Marine insurance especially illustrates the point of this chapter, in that the greater

29. The only history of business publishing that covers the colonial period is extremely unsatisfactory for that era since the author did not look at the ordinary newspapers to see if they, in the absence of business periodicals, published any business news. See David P. Forsyth, *The Business Press in America, 1750–1865* (Philadelphia, 1964). He also failed to distinguish between printed merchants' price lists and published commercial commodity price currents, thus mistakenly locating the "birthplace" of the New World price current at Halifax (*ibid.*, 21). Postwar Philadelphia is much more likely (*ibid.*, 23*ff.*). For this whole subject, see McCusker and Gravesteijn, *Commodity Price Currents*, and McCusker, *European Marine Lists*. The only guide to early North American newspapers is still Clarence S. Brigham's fine *History and Bibliography of American Newspapers, 1690–1820* (Worcester, Mass., 1947). The annotated copy in the American Antiquarian Society is extremely useful.

availability of locally negotiated insurance for ships and cargoes represented a considerable savings for colonial merchants.[30]

Private brokers and public highways both served parallel purposes:
they made business in the colonies more productive and spread the costs
of doing business among the community in general. The result was a saving of money for colonial businessmen, increased profitability, more businesses, more jobs, and economic development.

30. For all of this, see Bridenbaugh, *Cities in the Wilderness*, 185–188, 340, 359–360,
367–368, and *Cities in Revolt*, 93–94, 103–104, 286–288. For marine insurance, see
Sachs, "Business Outlook," 94–95. See also [Edward Rochic Hardy], *An Account of the
Early Insurance Offices in Massachusetts from 1724 to 1801* (Boston, 1901); Solomon
Huebner, "The Development and Present Status of Marine Insurance in the United States,"
American Academy of Political and Social Science, *Annals*, XXVI (1905), 421–452; and
Harrold E. Gillingham, *Marine Insurance in Philadelphia, 1721–1800: With a List of Bro-
kers and Underwriters as Shown by Old Policies and Books of Record . . .* (Philadelphia,
1933). For fire insurance, see F. C. Oviatt, "Historical Study of Fire Insurance in the United
States," Am. Acad. Pol. and Soc. Sci., *Annals*, XXVI (1905), 335–358. See also H. A. L.
Cockerell and Edwin Green, *The British Insurance Business, 1547–1970: An Introduction
and Guide to Historical Records in the United Kingdom* (London, 1976). For exchange
brokers, see McCusker, *Money and Exchange*, 122, and Edwin Wolf II and Maxwell
Whiteman, *The History of the Jews of Philadelphia from Colonial Times to the Age of Jackson* (Philadelphia, 1957), 98–113. Compare Soltow, *Economic Role of Williamsburg*, 163–
164. The legal profession also served as facilitators for the business community, but again,
we know almost nothing about this aspect of their work. We need many more studies like
Herbert Alan Johnson, *The Law Merchant and Negotiable Instruments in Colonial New
York, 1664 to 1730* (Chicago, 1963). We also need to know much more about the impact of
the law in general on colonial economic activity. Recent work on legal change after the
Revolution argues that in the 18th century "precommercial and antidevelopmental common law values" prevailed and helped to limit development. Perhaps, but we remain uncon-
vinced given the paucity of detailed empirical work on the specific ways in which the law
constrained economic growth. See Morton J. Horwitz, *The Transformation of American
Law, 1780–1860* (Cambridge, Mass., 1977), quotation on p. 253, and William E. Nelson,
*Americanization of the Common Law: The Impact of Legal Change on Massachusetts So-
ciety, 1760–1830* (Cambridge, Mass., 1975).

PART IV

CRISIS AND CHANGE

CHAPTER 17

ECONOMIC GROWTH,

REVOLUTION, AND

THE CONSEQUENCES

OF INDEPENDENCE

We do not propose to offer an economic interpretation of the American Revolution, at least not in any narrow, deterministic way. Such interpretations have been too quick to argue for motivations rooted in private, short-term, pocketbook concerns. Men on both sides of the dispute doubtless consulted their purses, but in few cases was that the exclusive or even the primary consideration. This is not to say, as some scholars have recently argued, that economic matters were unimportant to the independence movement. Quite the contrary. Economic developments were central to the Revolution, in several ways.[1]

If men engage in revolutionary action only when success seems pos-

---

1. For a recent dismissal of economic concerns as contributors to the Revolution, see Bernard Bailyn, "The Central Themes of the American Revolution: An Interpretation," in *Essays on the American Revolution*, ed. Stephen G. Kurtz and James H. Hutson (Chapel Hill, N.C., 1973), 3–31, esp. 12–13. Compare Bailyn, "Lines of Force in Recent Writings on the American Revolution," in [International Congress of the Historical Sciences, 14th, San Francisco], *Reports [of the] XIV International Congress of the Historical Sciences* (New York, 1977), I, 172–219. There are several good surveys of the historiography of the Revolutionary era. Robert E. Shalhope discusses recent work in "Republicanism and Early American Historiography," *WMQ*, 3d Ser., XXXIX (1982), 334–356, which updates his "Toward a Republican Synthesis: The Emergence of an Understanding of Republicanism in American Historiography," *ibid.*, XXIX (1972), 49–80. Also helpful are Edmund S. Morgan, "The American Revolution: Revisions in Need of Revising," *ibid.*, XIV (1957), 3–15; Merrill Jensen, "Historians and the Nature of the American Revolution," in *Reinterpretation of Early American History*, ed. Billington, 101–127; and, especially, Jack P. Greene, ed., *The Reinterpretation of the American Revolution, 1763–1789* (New York, 1968).

sible, the economic condition of the colonies obviously was an essential element in the American Revolution. The progress of the early British American economy over the colonial period had been sufficient to make independence thinkable by the 1770s. It provided the wherewithal in another way as well. The social changes that some see as a critical component in any explanation of independence—principally "the growth of a self-conscious, powerful colonial elite" and the active "involvement of the 'lower orders' in the Revolutionary movement"—were clearly rooted in the development of the economy.[2]

The economy contributed more than just the means to independence, however. The specific grievances that Americans held against the metropolis reflected economic concerns. Several of the "reforms" introduced by Parliament after mid-century seemed to many colonists designed to reduce current profits and to limit future prospects. Nor was it only Parliament that appeared determined to undermine American prosperity. The rapacious behavior of metropolitan merchants in the 1760s and 1770s threatened the abilities of Americans to engage in new or, in some cases, even traditional pursuits. Parliamentary restrictions and predatory British merchants fueled fears of a conspiracy to subvert American liberties and to turn American resources entirely to the benefit of corrupt politicians and metropolitan freebooters. Americans were particularly alienated by what they saw as the efforts of imperial authorities to subvert colonial attempts to counter the credit crises and commercial slumps that troubled the Atlantic economy in the early 1760s and again in the early 1770s. These frustrations convinced many colonists that they would be better off on their own.[3]

Economic considerations entered the independence movement also in more positive and more important ways than as reactions to perceived threats. In the years after 1750, many colonials, particularly the major merchants and the great planters, evidently developed a "profound and growing commitment . . . to the achievement of sovereignty" and to "economic autonomy," a commitment rooted in an awareness of their

2. Marc Egnal and Joseph A. Ernst, "An Economic Interpretation of the American Revolution," *WMQ*, 3d Ser., XXIX (1972), 3–32 (quotations on pp. 9, 10). This essay remains the best starting point for historians interested in the role of the economy in the Revolution. It has been translated into Italian: "Un'interpretazione economica della rivoluzione americana," [trans. Gabriella Feruggia], in *La rivoluzione americana*, ed. Tiziano Bonazzi (Bologna, 1977), 221–237. For the role of social changes, see the essays in A. F. Young, ed., *American Revolution*. See also G. Nash, *Urban Crucible*.

3. Egnal and Ernst, "Economic Interpretation"; Ernst, *Money and Politics*; and Sheridan, "British Credit Crisis."

achievements and a vision of their prospects. The successes of the colonial economy nurtured that vision. Americans could look around and see great increases in output and settled area, large and busy port cities dispatching ships throughout the Atlantic world, substantial accumulations of wealth by those at the top, prosperous farms and great plantations, and, especially, a stunning enlargement of the population. Americans perceived this as evidence of their rapid rise to "wealth and greatness," which they extrapolated into the future according to Franklin's familiar "rule of progression." Such a perception shaped the hopes and aspirations of many Americans, particularly among the elite, persuading them that they had a bountiful future, that theirs was "a rising empire." That bounty could be captured faster, the rise to greatness could be more rapid, some Americans thought, if they were freed of the constraints of the Old Empire and took firm control of their destiny.[4]

Economic historians can contribute in several ways to an understanding of these themes. One opportunity that already has been explored in some detail is the task of estimating how much of a burden the Navigation Acts placed on the colonial economy. Whig historians such as George Bancroft and Progressives such as Charles Beard argued that the burden was considerable. According to the Progressive historians, the central theme was indebtedness. Because the colonies as a whole were unable to pay for their imports they were continually in debt to Great Britain. Colonial trade was perpetually unbalanced, a consequence of the restrictions of mercantilism in general and of the Navigation Acts in particular. Colonial indebtedness was itself a function of personal indebtedness. Even the prosperity of such seemingly successful colonies as Maryland and Virginia actually masked huge debts owed by the largest planters to British factors. Lesser planters were caught in the same web of debt through their obligations to the greater planters. Thus, both individually and corporately the colonies were entailed to the metropolis. It is "generally known," Beard asserted, that "the debts due to British merchants

---

4. The quotations are from Egnal and Ernst, "Economic Interpretation," 23; [Samuel Johnson], *Taxation No Tyranny: An Answer to the Resolutions and Address of the American Congress* (London, 1775), 26; A. Smith, *Wealth of Nations*, II, 564; and George Washington, as quoted in Richard W. Van Alstyne, *The Rising American Empire* (Oxford, 1960), 1. Compare the advice offered by Col. Samuel Martin, the doyen of Antigua sugar planters, to his son: "As it is highly probable that N[orth] America will be the seat of [the] British Empire in half a century, so I think it would be prudent in your eldest brother [Samuel], yourself, and me to make our [homes(?)] there" (Col. Samuel Martin to Capt. Henry Martin, 22 Sept. 1767, Letter Book of Samuel Martin, 1765–1774, fol. 56, Martin Papers, Add. MS 41350, BL).

and other private citizens constituted one of the powerful causes leading to the Revolution."[5]

The thrust of this book—that the colonial economy was successful, grew rapidly by eighteenth-century standards, and generated a fairly widespread prosperity—clearly contradicts the Progressives' argument. Recent efforts to describe the colonial balance of payments, discussed above in chapter 4, confirm our position, as do attempts to measure more precisely the impact of the Navigation Acts. We need not review those arguments here. The issues seem largely settled and the participants in the debate agree on the central point: the cost imposed on the colonies by the restrictions on trade were small, certainly less than 3 percent of colonial income, perhaps less than 1 percent. Furthermore, whatever the costs of membership in the British Empire, they were largely offset by the benefits: naval protection; access to a large free-trading area; easy credit and cheap manufactures; and restricted foreign competition. To the extent that colonial prosperity was linked to the export sector, it is difficult to see how the Old Empire significantly restrained colonial economic development, at least before the 1760s.[6]

A focus on the burdens of membership in the Old Empire has diverted attention from the longer-term issues in colonial history that were of greater importance to the Revolutionary movement. One such issue is how the London-based imperial system worked on a day-to-day basis, how decisions were taken, who could shape policy, who could further or at least protect the colonists' fundamental interests. Another is whether the basic aims of policymakers shifted around the middle of the eighteenth century, either from a commercial to an imperial system or from an empire in which mercantilist concerns with trade predominated to one

5. Charles A. Beard, *Economic Origins of Jeffersonian Democracy* (New York, 1915), 270. For a critique, see Emory G. Evans, "Planter Indebtedness and the Coming of the Revolution in Virginia," *WMQ*, 3d Ser., XIX (1962), 511–533. While most historians now accept Evans's position that indebtedness had little to do with Revolutionary protest, Jacob M. Price has recently suggested that the question is still open (*Capital and Credit*, 135–139). Certainly the vast documentation for studying the issue, available in T 79, PRO, merits more-careful, detailed analysis than it has yet received.

6. There is a large literature on this issue, full of rebuttals, rejoinders, responses, and replies. We list only the most important contributions: Lawrence A. Harper, "The Effects of the Navigation Acts on the Thirteen Colonies," in *The Era of the American Revolution*, ed. Richard B. Morris (New York, 1939), 3–39; Robert Paul Thomas, "A Quantitative Approach to the Study of the Effects of British Imperial Policy upon Colonial Welfare: Some Preliminary Findings," *Jour. Econ. Hist.*, XXV (1965), 615–638; Peter D. McClelland, "The Cost to America of British Imperial Policy," *Am. Econ. Rev.*, LIX (1969), 370–381; and Gary M. Walton, "The New Economic History and the Burdens of the Navigation Acts," *Econ. Hist. Rev.*, 2d Ser., XXIV (1971), 533–542.

in which fiscal considerations of government revenue controlled decisions.[7] To most politically active colonials such questions were of greater importance than short-term costs, and the answers seemed clear. After 1760 colonists faced policymakers in Great Britain who were determined to change the loose-and unrestrictive commercial empire within which the colonial economy had prospered, by increasing and enforcing regulations and by tightening connections between business and politics. At the same time, American ability to influence policy was in sharp decline.[8]

The combination of a more active interference in colonial life from Whitehall and a decline of American influence provoked a constitutional crisis. The colonists insisted that Parliament could not legislate for them in such essential matters as taxation since they were not represented in that body. For Parliament to do so would have been to deprive the colonists of their property and thus to threaten their liberty and their very lives. British governmental leaders failed to recognize either the sincerity or the validity of the colonial complaints. Instead, they saw a smoke screen behind which some colonists were attempting to dilute the authority of Parliament, to weaken the Navigation Acts and the mercantile system, and thereby to destroy the empire. As these positions hardened, each side became increasingly convinced of the other's perfidy. Conflict became inevitable.

While the dispute took a constitutional form, it is clear that economic issues played a central role. The argument over Parliament's right to tax the colonies first revealed the constitutional differences that were later to be found irreconcilable. But the aims of Parliament and the interests that controlled it went beyond the taxation provisions in the Sugar Act, the Stamp Act, and the Townshend Duty Act. The Sugar Act, for instance,

---

7. On how the empire worked, three recent articles by Alison Gilbert Olson are helpful: "Parliament, the London Lobbies, and Provincial Interests in England and America," *Hist. Reflections,* VI (1979), 367–386; "The Board of Trade and London-American Interest Groups in the Eighteenth Century," *Jour. Imperial and Commonwealth Hist.,* VIII (1980), 33–50; and "The London Mercantile Lobby and the Coming of the American Revolution," *JAH,* LXIX (1982), 21–41. Michael Kammen provides a good survey and a useful bibliography in *Empire and Interest: The American Colonies and the Politics of Mercantilism* (Philadelphia, 1970). Lawrence H. Gipson's monumental study, *British Empire before the American Revolution,* is both comprehensive and detailed and contains a grand bibliography of primary and secondary materials. The classic argument for a shift in emphasis is Charles M. Andrews, *The Colonial Background of the American Revolution* (New Haven, Conn., 1924). Andrews has been challenged recently by Stephen Saunders Webb, *Governors-General.* See also chap. 2, n. 20, above.

8. Kammen, *Empire and Interest,* 116–137, is an able summary. See also Olson, "London Mercantile Lobby."

contained a number of requirements that simply made colonial trade more complicated, more difficult, and therefore more costly and less profitable. It was objectionable not only because it levied a tax, but also because it threatened to damage seriously the North American–West Indian trade. The establishment of the American Board of Customs at Boston in 1767, which was intended to enforce both the new regulations and some old ones, also encouraged, however inadvertently, the "customs racketeering" that radicalized such key figures as Henry Laurens and John Hancock.[9] The Currency Act of 1764 portended a limitation of the colonial money supply as well as the disruption of domestic commerce. Other acts assailed the western extension of colonial agriculture, attacked colonial industry, and assaulted colonial commerce. There were even rumors of outright parliamentary restrictions on the direction and extent of colonial overseas trade. From the perspective of some colonists, Parliament seemed determined to destroy their economy.[10]

The strenuous reactions of colonial merchants, colonial governments, and colonial allies in London led to the repeal or at least the relaxation of these laws, but only as a gesture to placate the colonists and not in recognition of their rights. Nonetheless, it is often argued that most colonial merchants, frightened by mob violence and the political aspirations of the popular classes at home, rested content with the redress of their immediate economic grievances after 1770. All except the most radical withdrew from the protest movement with the repeal of the bulk of the duties that were part of the Townshend measures. The economic phase of

9. See Dickerson, *Navigation Acts*, and Barrow, *Trade and Empire*. See also John L. Bullion, *A Great and Necessary Measure: George Grenville and the Genesis of the Stamp Act, 1763–1765* (Columbia, Mo., 1982). Despite the repeated claim that the "colonists duly complied" with the Sugar Act, this simply was not the case. Contrast such claims by Edmund S. Morgan, "Colonial Ideas of Parliamentary Power, 1764–1766," *WMQ*, 3d Ser., V (1948), 311–341, and Egnal and Ernst, "Economic Interpretation," 8, with Beer, *British Colonial Policy*, 294–295, and O. M. Dickerson, Letter to the Editor, *WMQ*, 3d Ser., VI (1949), 351–355. We are reminded in this context of the line from Thucydides, "Every colony that is well treated honors its parent state, but becomes estranged from it by injustice" (*Historiae*, I.34.1). For the perspectives of the colonists in the sugar islands, see Donna J. Spindel, "The Stamp Act Crisis in the British West Indies," *Jour. Am. Studies*, XI (1977), 203–221. See also Carl Anthony Lane, "The Roots of Jamaican Loyalism, 1760–1766" (Ph.D. diss., City University of New York, 1978).

10. How serious the threats to limit trade actually were is less important than the willingness of the colonists of early British America to believe that they were serious. See McCusker, "Sources of Investment Capital," 152–153n. Compare the contemporary perception in a writer such as Charles Whitworth of the need "to turn . . . this new people from . . . trade . . . into channels more advantageous to the [British] public" (*State of the Trade of Great Britain*, lv). While writing immediately of the reasons for the settlement of Georgia, he was obviously voicing larger concerns.

the Revolutionary protest, this argument runs, ended with the return of colonial prosperity.[11]

We are not persuaded that economic issues receded so quickly. Nor do we think that the behavior of merchants and other interested parties can be best understood in such a limited context. The dispute between Britain and the colonies was not over Parliament's right to regulate this or that trade, to tax a particular activity, or to pursue a specific policy. The conflict centered on the issue of power over the long haul, on the shape of things to come, on who would determine the future of the British Empire in the Americas. In the years after 1750, the men who would lead the colonists into declaring their independence and founding a new nation became increasingly captivated by a vision of an American empire, of a republican polity responsive to the common good that would protect American commerce, encourage American agriculture, develop American industry, promote the settlement of western lands, and, eventually, take Great Britain's place at the center of the Atlantic economy. That vision was at first vague, sufficiently so to conceal sharp differences among the elite that would later lead to intense conflict. However vague, that vision was firmly rooted in the reality of colonial accomplishments, particularly in the prosperity achieved by the mid-eighteenth century.[12]

It is here that the major opportunities for economic historians of the

11. See, for example, Schlesinger, *Colonial Merchants*, and Charles M. Andrews, "The Boston Merchants and the Non-importation Movement," Col. Soc. Mass., *Pubs.*, XIX: *Trans.*, 1916–1917 (1918), 159–259. Ronald Hoffman provides a detailed, insightful investigation of this question in *Spirit of Dissension*. The debate over whether or not merchants continued to participate in the Revolutionary movement once their immediate concerns were satisfied seems beside the point. Like most other people, merchants perceived the world in more-complex terms. For arguments that the merchants acted out of class motives that assumed economic considerations to be of primary importance, see Schlesinger, *Colonial Merchants, passim*; A. Jensen, *Maritime Commerce, passim*; and Egnal and Ernst, "Economic Interpretation." For arguments that merchants were a heterogeneous group with varied interests and motivations, see Robert F. Oaks, "Philadelphia Merchants and the Origins of American Independence," Am. Phil. Soc., *Procs.*, CXXI (1977), 407–436, and Doerflinger, "Enterprise on the Delaware."

12. Franklin, of course, was the key figure in articulating this vision. The literature on him is large, but see particularly Gerald Stourzh, *Benjamin Franklin and American Foreign Policy* (Chicago, 1954); Walter LaFeber, "Foreign Policies of a New Nation: Franklin, Madison, and the 'Dream of a New Land to Fulfill with People in Self-Control,' 1750–1804," in *From Colony to Empire: Essays in the History of American Foreign Relations*, ed. William Appleman Williams (New York, 1972), 9–37; Marc Egnal, "The Politics of Ambition: A New Look at Benjamin Franklin's Career," *Can. Rev. Am. Studies*, VI (1975), 151–164; and Drew R. McCoy, "Benjamin Franklin's Vision of a Republican Political Economy for America," *WMQ*, 3d Ser., XXXV (1978), 605–628. For evidence of an early convert to Franklin's ideas, see John Adams to Nathan Webb, 12 Oct. 1755, *Adams Papers*, I, 4–6.

Revolution are to be found, in what is usually called political economy, the ways in which people understood their circumstances, drew inspiration from them, and acted accordingly. Despite some valuable recent work, we still know too little about the complex relationships between economy and ideology in the late eighteenth century. Nevertheless, it seems likely that future investigations will place the development of the colonial economy at the center of the Revolutionary movement. The successes of the colonial period nurtured a vision of greatness and prosperity. After inspiring some of the colonial elite to risk independence, that vision of a bountiful future sustained the colonies through a long and costly war and informed their efforts to create an effective national government, a tool to be used in building a new American empire.[13]

The War of Independence, and more broadly the entire Revolutionary era, is often seen as a watershed in American history, for the economy as well as for the organization of politics and the structure of society. It is therefore ironic, although perhaps not surprising, that economic historians have neglected the years of the war and its immediate aftermath. Indeed, apart from its military, diplomatic, and political aspects, the period from 1776 to 1789 is among the least studied in American history. One source of this neglect is the notion of a watershed itself. The concept has invited contrasts between the late colonial and early national economies, but has done little to promote interest in the actual period of transition. Since the most striking and far-reaching change in this period was the creation of a national government for the United States, attention has focused on politics to the neglect of economic, social, and demographic issues.[14]

13. See especially Joyce Appleby's recent commentaries on Jefferson, "Commercial Farming and the 'Agrarian Myth' in the Early Republic," *JAH*, LXVIII (1982), 833–849, and "What Is Still American in the Political Philosophy of Thomas Jefferson?" *WMQ*, 3d Ser., XXXIX (1982), 287–309. See also two suggestive essays by Marc Egnal, "The Origins of the Revolution in Virginia: A Reinterpretation," *ibid.*, XXXVII (1980), 401–428, and "The Pattern of Factional Development in New York, Pennsylvania, and Massachusetts, 1682–1776," in *Parties and Political Opposition in Revolutionary America*, ed. Patricia U. Bonomi (Tarrytown, N.Y., 1980), 43–60.

14. The best introduction to the period remains Curtis Putnam Nettels, *The Emergence of a National Economy, 1775–1815* (New York, 1962), which contains a valuable bibliography. See also Jackson Turner Main, *The Sovereign States, 1775–1783* (New York, 1973), chap. 7, "Economic Changes during the War" (pp. 222–268), and the bibliography for that chapter. Other very useful bibliographies are: Shy, comp., *American Revolution*; E. J. Ferguson, comp., *Confederation, Constitution, and Early National Period*; and, notably, the monumental guide by Ronald M. Gephart, comp., *Revolutionary America, 1763–1789: A Bibliography* (Washington, D.C., 1984).

A second and perhaps more enduring reason for the neglect lies in the quality of the evidence. The war disrupted many aspects of early American life, not the least of which was record keeping. The imperial bureaucracy resident in the colonies, a fairly efficient data-gathering agency by the 1770s, was thrown into disarray and turned its attention away from commerce and toward military and political affairs. Trade was forced into new, sometimes clandestine, usually less well documented channels. The transatlantic flow of letters between men of business was interrupted, newspapers stopped publication, and local government operated with less regularity, less efficiency, and less attention to the recording of detail. Compounding all of this was a disruption of the paper currency and an inflation so rapid that it crippled the price system, with severe consequences for both the operation of the economy and the writing of economic history. Almost as quickly as old sources of evidence disappeared, new ones began to emerge, but they were initially less detailed and the continuity essential for close analysis of change over time was permanently lost.[15]

One could take a rather sanguine view of the relative neglect of the Revolutionary years by historians of the American economy. In the first place, there is some evidence of a new interest in the period; at least efforts have been made recently to identify continuities and to specify changes from the late colonial to the early national periods. If such efforts continue, students of the American economy will be confronted less often with a story that ends abruptly in the mid-1770s and begins anew circa 1787.[16] In the second place, it could be argued that the conceptualization

15. On currency, finance, and inflation during the war, the premier work is E. James Ferguson, *The Power of the Purse: A History of American Public Finance, 1776–1790* (Chapel Hill, N.C., 1961). See also Ralph Volney Harlow, "Aspects of Revolutionary Finance, 1775–1783," *AHR*, XXXV (1929), 46–68; G. Taylor, "Wholesale Commodity Prices"; Adelaide L. Fries, "North Carolina Certificates of the Revolutionary War Period," *N.C. Hist. Rev.*, IX (1932), 229–241; William B. Norton, "Paper Currency in Massachusetts during the Revolution," *NEQ*, VII (1934), 43–69; Edward A. Fuhlbruegge, "New Jersey Finances during the American Revolution," New Jersey Historical Society, *Proceedings*, N.S., LV (1937), 167–190; E. M. Coleman, "New England Convention, December 25, 1776, to January 2, 1777: An Illustration of Early American Particularism," *Historian*, IV (1941–1942), 43–55; Kenneth Scott, "Price Control in New England during the Revolution," *NEQ*, XIX (1946), 453–473; Bezanson *et al.*, *Prices and Inflation*; Elizabeth Cometti, "Inflation in Revolutionary Maryland," *WMQ*, 3d Ser., VIII (1951), 228–234; Eric P. Newman, "Counterfeit Continental Currency Goes to War," *Numismatist*, LXX (1957), 5–16, 137–147; and Kenneth Scott, "Counterfeiting in New York during the Revolution," *N.-Y. Hist. Soc. Qtly.*, XLII (1958), 221–259. For other works on finance, see n. 32, below.

16. See, for example, James F. Shepherd and Gary M. Walton, "Economic Change after the American Revolution: Pre- and Post-war Comparisons of Maritime Shipping and Trade,"

is not deficient, that apart from its political consequences the War of Independence did have only a temporary, if severely disruptive, impact on the economy. In this view, the central story for economic historians, as well as for those concerned with other aspects of early American life, ought to be that of the creation of a national government with its vast implications for the future development of the economy of the United States.[17]

Perhaps, but we are not fully persuaded—for three reasons. First, some recent scholarship, notably by John Shy and Ronald Hoffman, has demonstrated that detailed attention to the war years can yield fresh insights, in this case that the feasibility of radical change was much greater than the majority of accounts indicate. Such work has focused on political, social, and military issues, but it at least suggests that students of the economy could uncover similar surprises.[18]

Second, as Curtis Nettels emphasized, important issues of economic policy were confronted during the war. Those years witnessed the beginnings of a national commercial policy; a great increase in government intervention in economic affairs, chiefly on the state level; and a variety of reforms in taxation, land law, the regulation of business, the rights of labor, the position of debtors, and the like. All had great potential significance for the economy. Such policy matters merit further study, both to gauge their impact and to explore their continuities with the American colonial experience.[19]

Third, and most important, close study of the wartime economy provides an opportunity to assess the success of the colonial economy and to explore the consequences of the export-led process of growth and development that we have stressed in this book. If our analysis is correct, the results should be apparent in the colonies' ability to adjust to the de-

---

Explorations Econ. Hist., XIII (1976), 397–422; Geoffrey Gilbert, "The Role of Breadstuffs in American Trade, 1770–1790," *ibid.*, XIV (1977), 378–387; and for a fine regional study of the wartime economy, Papenfuse, *In Pursuit of Profit.* See also the essays in Ronald Hoffman, John J. McCusker, and Russell R. Menard, eds., *The Economy of Early America: The Revolutionary Period, 1763–1789* (Charlottesville, Va., forthcoming).

17. Such an argument is explicit in Bruchey, *Roots of American Economic Growth.*

18. Shy, *A People Numerous and Armed: Reflections on the Military Struggle for American Independence* (New York, 1976); Hoffman, "The 'Disaffected' in the Revolutionary South," in *American Revolution*, ed. Young, 273–316.

19. Nettels, *Emergence of a National Economy*, 1–6. Jackson Turner Main provides an excellent survey of the various reforms in *Sovereign States*, while Oscar and Mary F. Handlin, "Revolutionary Economic Policy in Massachusetts," *WMQ*, 3d Ser., IV (1947), 3–26, remains helpful. Compare such studies as Jonathan Grossman, "Wage and Price Controls during the American Revolution," *Monthly Labor Review*, XCVI (Sept. 1973), 3–10.

mands of war, to supply necessary goods and services despite severe disruption in the foreign sector, to develop new prospects for profit, and to use the political power that came with revolt to intervene wisely and effectively in the economy. We would not expect all of this to have been achieved without difficulty or even without a considerable decline in income, but the functioning of the American economy during the war does offer a measure of the development process across a century and a half of colonial history.

While we might argue that much is to be gained by viewing 1775 through 1790 as one long period of transition, some obvious distinctions suggest themselves. Certainly, the developments associated with the war effort itself must be sorted out from independent developments that transcended the war years. Thus the provisioning of troops, the building of warships, and the impact of privateering belong exclusively in one part of our discussion, while the problems of public finance should be treated differently.

The most obvious, and most thoroughly documented, impact of the war itself was on the foreign sector, particularly on exports. Nettels suggested a four-stage periodization. During the first stage, lasting from the nonimportation agreement of late 1774 to April 1776, prohibitions on trade by the British government and by Congress and the closing of old markets effectively curtailed foreign commerce and led to acute shortages of imported goods. In late 1774 and early 1775, Congress tried to stop all trade by employing the weapons of boycott and embargo, but once the fighting started, it sanctioned a limited exchange with foreign nations. The second stage began in April 1776, when Congress removed all restrictions on foreign trade; it lasted until mid-1778. This stage was marked by a flourishing commerce with France and with the foreign West Indies but also by a fairly successful British naval blockade of the principal northern ports, which limited volume and kept risks and costs high. Wartime trade peaked in the third period, from mid-1778 to early 1782, as increasing demands on the Royal Navy limited its ability to maintain a tight blockade and as the French, the Spanish, and the Dutch entered the war. During 1782, however, the last of Nettels's four periods, this flourishing trade with Europe and the islands declined sharply as the British concentrated an increasing share of their naval operations on attacks against American merchant shipping.[20]

In general, the war curtailed colonial exports more sharply than it did imports. Military operations slowed production in many states, frontier warfare destroyed the Indian trade, and the naval conflict crippled the

20. Nettels, *Emergence of a National Economy*, 13–18.

New England fishery. Moreover, troop movements through settled areas interfered with farming, workers being called into service diminished the supply of labor, and capital goods and resources once devoted to the export sector (such as sailing ships) were converted to meet the demands of war. Traditional markets in Great Britain and the British West Indies were closed and long-established trading partnerships suspended, with singularly severe consequences for the trade in foodstuffs and for the shipbuilding industry, while British bounties on indigo and naval stores came to an abrupt end.

Furthermore, the dramatic rise in freight charges and the decrease in tonnage available for commerce hit the relatively bulky exports with particular force. Impressive quantities of a few products were exported during the war—tobacco to France and flour and other foodstuffs to the foreign sugar islands, for example—but even these remained well below the levels achieved in the early 1770s. The net effect was a steep decline in earnings from the export sector. Imports too were affected, although much less drastically than exports. Americans had to accept smaller quantities of foreign manufactures at higher prices throughout the war years. However, there were major temporal and regional variations in this overall pattern, and by the late 1770s even British goods, obtained chiefly from Dutch middlemen or privateers, were available in significant quantities.[21]

One major consequence of the excess of imports over exports was, of course, a severe imbalance in commodity trade, an imbalance that tended to be offset in three ways: through privateering; through loans and subsidies from European cobelligerents; and through British and French military expenditures in the former colonies. Privateering emerged as a major American enterprise during the war; over the entire conflict, Great Britain lost 2,000 vessels and 12,000 sailors. The lost vessels, with their cargoes, were worth an estimated £18,000,000 sterling. At such levels, privateering gave an enormous boost to an economy staggering under the impact of war and also made major contributions to the war effort. By diverting the British naval fleet away from military action and toward the protection of commerce and by capturing military stores, privateering had a destructive effect on British shipping. In addition, privateering supplied consumers with a variety of goods, provided employment for ships

21. On the tobacco trade, see Price, *France and the Chesapeake*, 681–727. Almost all aspects of wartime commerce would benefit from further study. It should be noted that the classic article by J. Franklin Jameson, "St. Eustatius in the American Revolution," *AHR*, VIII (1903), 683–708, while still useful for the information it does contain, was constructed on a limited evidential base that included almost no North American archival materials. It deserves to be redone.

and seamen, expanded the size of the American fleet, and earned impressive fortunes for enterprising merchants and ship captains.[22] Loans and subsidies from the French, the Dutch, and the Spanish, which totaled nearly $10,000,000 between 1777 and 1783, also helped right the imbalance in commodity trade, as did the substantial military expenditures of the French ($6,000,000 by one estimate) and the British in the United Colonies—worth, together, nearly $100,000,000 in 1980 terms.[23]

A second major consequence of the disruption of foreign trade during the war years was a diversion of resources into the indigenous production of goods and services that had previously been purchased abroad. Much of this was achieved through relatively inefficient household manufacturing and led to only a temporary increase in the self-sufficiency of the economy. With peace came renewed opportunities to produce commercial crops for export, new and abundant supplies of European manufactures, and a decline in American industry. But some industries—paper, pottery, shoes, gunpowder, certain textiles, and particularly iron and steel—adopted more-advanced, efficient technologies and organizational forms, with more permanent results. The former colonies left the war

22. On privateers, see Gardner Weld Allen, *Massachusetts Privateers of the Revolution* (Boston, 1927); Octavius T. Howe, "Beverly Privateers in the American Revolution," Col. Soc. Mass., *Pubs.*, XXIV: *Trans.*, 1920–1922 (1923), 318–435; John Dewar Faibisy, "Privateering and Piracy: The Effects of New England Raiding upon Nova Scotia during the American Revolution, 1775–1783" (Ph.D. diss., University of Massachusetts, 1972); Bernard C. Steiner, "Maryland Privateers in the American Revolution," *Md. Hist. Mag.*, III (1908), 99–103; Richard K. Hart, "Maryland's Maritime Enterprise during the Revolution" (M.A. thesis, University of Maryland, 1947); William S. Dudley, "Maryland at War on the Chesapeake, 1776–1783" (paper presented to the Washington Area Seminar in Early American History, College Park, Md., Oct. 1980); Osmo Kiiskinen, "Yhdysvaltain kaapparit Euroopan vesillä, 1776–1783" (American privateers in European waters, 1776–1783) (licentiate thesis, University of Helsinki, 1982). Americans suffered as well as benefited from privateering. For a compilation of accounts based on the records of the Vice-Admiralty Court of Jamaica, see E. Arnot Robertson, *The Spanish Town Papers: Some Sidelights on the American War of Independence* (London, 1959). For the records themselves, see Bell, Parker, et al., *Guide to British West Indian Archive Materials*, 373–377. See also David Syrett, *Shipping and the American War, 1775–83: A Study of British Transport Organization* (London, 1970). Compare Syrett, "American Provincials and the Havana Campaign of 1762," *N.Y. Hist.*, XLIX (1968), 375–390; Patrick Crowhurst, *The Defence of British Trade, 1689–1815* (Folkestone, Kent, 1977); Carl E. Swanson, "The Profitability of Privateering: Reflections on British Colonial Privateers during the Wars of 1739–1748," *Am. Neptune*, XLII (1982), 36–56; Stuyvesant Fish, *The New York Privateers, 1756–1763: King George's Private Ships of War Which Cruized against the King's Enemies* (New York, 1945); and Jerome R. Garitee, *The Republic's Private Navy: The American Privateering Business as Practiced by Baltimore during the War of 1812* (Middletown, Conn., 1977).

23. Nettels, *Emergence of a National Economy*, 20–21. Compare R. Harlow, "Aspects of Revolutionary Finance." See also the works cited in n. 32, below.

years with a larger and more diversified domestic sector, although how much larger it was and how enduring the gains were have yet to be determined.[24]

The war effort itself directly encouraged much of this advance in native industry by creating a variety of new prospects for merchants, manufacturing artisans, and farmers. Military demands stimulated the munitions industry and thereby the demand for iron and steel and also provided a market for locally produced shoes, clothing, tents, and other military supplies. Congress and the several state governments supported such manufactures in a number of ways, through loans and subsidies, guaranteed markets at set prices, land grants, monopoly privileges, and the like. The British and American armies both needed to be fed, and farmers were thus presented with new markets for food products. In addition, food and equipment had to move along the supply lines, which created openings for wagon makers, blacksmiths, harness makers, teamsters, and producers of livestock and led to some permanent improvements in the inland road network. All of these activities required entrepreneurial skill—to organize industrial production, to purchase food, to ensure deliveries, to provide capital, and to take risks. American merchants, drawing on abilities honed in colonial trade, were both crucial to the success of the war effort and the principal material beneficiaries of armed conflict.[25]

24. V. Clark, *History of Manufactures*, I, 215–232; Tryon, *Household Manufactures*, 104–122. See also such studies as Eugenie Andruss Leonard, "Paper as a Critical Commodity during the American Revolution," *PMHB*, LXXIV (1950), 488–499; R. L. Hilldrup, "The Salt Supply of North Carolina during the American Revolution," *N.C. Hist. Rev.*, XXII (1945), 393–417; and Larry G. Bowman, "The Scarcity of Salt in Virginia during the American Revolution," *VMHB*, LXXVII (1969), 464–472.

25. On merchants during the Revolutionary War, see especially Robert A. East, *Business Enterprise in the American Revolutionary Era* (New York, 1938), and Clarence L. Ver Steeg, *Robert Morris: Revolutionary Financier* (Philadelphia, 1954). See also Elizabeth Miles Nuxoll, "Congress and the Munitions Merchants: The Secret Committee of Trade during the American Revolution, 1775–1777" (Ph.D. diss., City University of New York, 1979). On agriculture, see John T. Schlebecker, "Agricultural Markets and Marketing in the North, 1774–1777," *Agric. Hist.*, L (1976), 21–36; Robert D. Mitchell, "Agricultural Change and the American Revolution: A Virginia Case Study," *ibid.*, XLVII (1973), 119–131; Merrill Jensen, "The American Revolution and American Agriculture," *ibid.*, XLIII (1969), 107–124; Albert E. Van Dusen, "Connecticut, the 'Provisions State' of the American Revolution," *New England Social Studies Bulletin*, X (1952), 16–23; Harold T. Pinkett, "Maryland as a Source of Food Supplies during the American Revolution," *Md. Hist. Mag.*, XLVI (1951), 157–172; G. Melvin Herndon, "A War-Inspired Industry: The Manufacture of Hemp in Virginia during the Revolution," *VMHB*, LXXIV (1966), 301–311; and Lawrence H. Leder, "Military Victualing in Colonial New York," in *Business Enterprise in Early New York*, ed. Frese and Judd, 16–54. See also David Lewis Salay, "Arm-

While some benefited from the American Revolution, the net result of wartime disruptions and wartime opportunities for colonial merchants is an open question. A nineteenth-century historian, Richard Hildreth, concluded that the war's impact had been devastating: "One large portion of the wealthy men of colonial times had been expatriated, and another part had been impoverished." "In their place," he wrote, "a new moneyed class had sprung up, especially in the eastern states, men who had grown rich in the course of the war as sutlers, by privateering, by speculations in the fluctuating paper money, and by other operations not always of the most honorable kind." Robert East, in his book *Business Enterprise in the American Revolutionary Era*, argued just the opposite position. Colonial merchants as a class not only survived the war, but some did very nicely during it. Recent studies of individual merchants, such as Jacob E. Cooke's biography of Tench Coxe of Philadelphia and James B. Hedges's investigation of the Browns of Providence would seem to support East. Yet Hedges's own analysis of the Browns' correspondence with merchants in Boston, New York, and Philadelphia led him to quite a different conclusion: "A comparison of the names of their correspondents in the three cities before 1775 and after 1783 tends to support the view of Hildreth rather than that of East. The familiar names of the pre-Revolutionary period are conspicuous by their absence in the 1780's." One has the impression that earlier colonial wars presented more chances of success and fewer chances of ruin for the community of merchants.[26]

---

ing for War: The Production of War Material [*sic*] in Pennsylvania for the American Armies during the Revolution" (Ph.D. diss., University of Delaware, 1977); Norman Baker, *Government and Contractors: The British Treasury and War Supplies, 1775–1783* (London, 1971); and Neil Longley York, "Technology in Revolutionary America, 1760–1790" (Ph.D. diss., University of California, Santa Barbara, 1978). A different perspective is offered in William Fowler, "The Business of War: Boston as a Navy Base, 1776–1783," *Am. Neptune*, XLII (1982), 25–35.

26. Richard Hildreth, *The History of the United States of America* (New York, 1849–1852), III, 465–466, quoted in James B. Hedges, "The Brown Papers: The Record of a Rhode Island Business Family," Am. Antiq. Soc., *Procs.*, N.S., LI (1941), 21–36. See Jacob E. Cooke, *Tench Coxe and the Early Republic* (Chapel Hill, N.C., 1978); Hedges, *Browns of Providence Plantations*; and Franklin Stuart Coyle, "Welcome Arnold (1745–1798), Providence Merchant: The Founding of an Enterprise" (Ph.D. diss., Brown University, 1972). For the Hedges quote, see "Brown Papers." For studies of merchants in various communities, see Ralph V. Harlow, "Economic Conditions in Massachusetts during the American Revolution," Col. Soc. Mass., *Pubs.*, XX: *Trans.*, 1917–1919 (1920), 163–190; Richard Henry Rudolph, "The Merchants of Newport, Rhode Island, 1763–1786" (Ph.D. diss., University of Connecticut, 1975); Bernard Mason, "Entrepreneurial Activity in New York during the American Revolution," *Bus. Hist. Rev.*, XL (1966), 190–212; Willard O. Mishoff, "Business in Philadelphia during the British Occupation, 1777–1778," *PMHB*,

Perhaps the best perspective from which to view the question of the economic impact of the American Revolution is as a part of what some historians have begun to call the Second Hundred Years' War between England and France (1689–1815). While the Revolutionary War was the fifth phase of the longer struggle, it was the first in which the British Americans fought as allies of the French, with important economic consequences, predominantly for the overseas sector. During the first four phases—King William's War, or the War of the League of Augsburg, 1689–1697; Queen Anne's War, or the War of the Spanish Succession, 1702–1713; King George's War, or the War of the Austrian Succession, 1739–1748; and the French and Indian War, or the Seven Years' War, 1754–1763—the continental colonists had been, perforce, on the side of Great Britain. Because of the switch, we suspect that the Revolution disrupted the American economy more severely than had the earlier conflicts: changing sides meant the destruction of long-standing commercial networks; the Royal Navy had greater success at both protecting and interdicting trade than the French; and military action more often occurred in densely settled areas than had previously been the case. Testing these suspicions will require more thorough investigations than have so far been carried out. Indeed, a close study of the relationships between warfare and the performance of the American economy during the colonial and Revolutionary periods is a way not only of placing the Revolution in a better comparative context but also of integrating military and economic history.

The War of Independence enriched some men, made others poor, created some new chances for success, and led to some lasting structural changes in the economy. In particular, the war increased the relative importance of the domestic sector, encouraged industrial development, and promoted internal improvements. Nevertheless, despite the captures by privateers, the loans and subsidies provided by foreign governments, the military expenditures of the British and the French, and the extension of local markets, the net effect of war was a sharp decline in individual in-

---

LXI (1937), 165–181; Doerflinger, "Enterprise on the Delaware"; Papenfuse, *In Pursuit of Profit*; Todd Cooper, "Trial and Triumph: The Impact of the Revolutionary War on the Baltimore Merchants," in *Chesapeake Bay in the American Revolution*, ed. Eller, 282–309; and Joseph A. Goldenberg, "Virginia Ports in the American Revolution," *ibid.*, 310–340. See also Middleton, "Ships and Shipbuilding." Stuart M. Butler, "The Glasgow Tobacco Merchants and the American Revolution, 1770–1800" (Ph.D. thesis, University of St. Andrews, 1978), found that at least some of those whom Hildreth would have called "expatriated" returned to British America to resume business after the war had ended. The question of motive is posed directly by Fred Gerard Flegal, "Silas Deane: Revolutionary or Profiteer?" (M.A. thesis, Western Michigan University, 1976).

come. The foreign sector was simply too central to the performance of the entire economy for its disruption to be suffered lightly. Revolution carried a high price. Recovery, furthermore, was painfully slow: precise measures are as yet unavailable, but it seems unlikely that the levels of income and wealth achieved in the early 1770s were attained again before the beginning of the nineteenth century. The material returns to independence were but gradually captured.

The economic consequences of the changed situation in British America after the Treaty of 1783 were not half so radical as the political changes. Only very slowly did the United States advance out of its colonial economy; the British West Indies have yet to do so. Thus the decade immediately following the end of the war looked, economically, much the same as the decade preceding it, in basic structure if not in detail. Nonetheless, the period has not been well described or well analyzed. It was a time of major political turmoil in the United States, during which the newly established state governments learned to live with the equally new national government. Since many of the issues involved in this sorting-out process were economic ones, discussions of the economic history of the period have almost always been part of the political debate. While we cannot realistically separate them completely, we do feel that the cart has too frequently dragged the horse. A critical description and analysis of the economic history of the years 1783–1790 is still sorely needed. This will probably best be accomplished initially on a state-by-state or region-by-region basis, with a national synthesis possible only after the narrower studies have been completed.[27]

27. The standard works on the subject are Nettels, *Emergence of a National Economy*; Gordon Carl Bjork, "Stagnation and Growth in the American Economy, 1784–1792" (Ph.D. diss., University of Washington, 1963); and Bjork, "The Weaning of the American Economy: Independence, Market Changes, and Economic Development," *Jour. Econ. Hist.*, XXIV (1964), 541–560. See also Shepherd and Walton, "Economic Change." A number of state and local studies already exist: John H. Flannagan, Jr., "Trying Times: Economic Depression in New Hampshire, 1781–1789" (Ph.D. diss., Georgetown University, 1972); Withey, "Population Change"; Harvey Milton Wachtell, "The Conflict between Localism and Nationalism in Connecticut, 1783–1788" (Ph.D. diss., University of Missouri, Columbia, 1971); Robert Michael Dructor, "The New York Commercial Community: The Revolutionary Experience" (Ph.D. diss., University of Pittsburgh, 1975); George Winthrop Geib, "A History of Philadelphia, 1776–1789" (Ph.D. diss., University of Wisconsin, 1969); Lemuel David Molovinsky, "Pennsylvania's Legislative Efforts to Finance the War for Independence: A Study of the Continuity of Colonial Finance, 1775–83" (Ph.D. diss., Temple University, 1975); Robert James Gough, "Towards a Theory of Class and Social Conflict: A Social History of Wealthy Philadelphians, 1775 and 1800" (Ph.D. diss., University of Pennsylvania, 1977); Mary Jane Dowd, "The State in the Maryland Economy, 1776–1807," *Md. Hist. Mag.*, LVII (1962), 90–132, 229–258; Rhoda M. Dorsey, "The

The same kind of economic history "cooked" in aid of political history has clouded our understanding of what happened in the British sugar islands. During the war the British island colonies remained "loyal" if only because the Royal Navy made any other option impossible. Such loyalty came at a considerable cost, however. The West Indies suffered greatly during the war, both the planters, who lost their income, and their slaves, who lost their lives. The West Indian planters and their North American suppliers all expected the end of the war to bring a resumption of the old trading links between the two. Yet there was to be no resumption of trade.

Just as the trade with the British colonies became an issue in state and national politics in the United States, trade with the United States was also an issue for the British West Indies. Despite continued, vehement protests and much politicking, the West Indians failed to convince Parliament to remove the restrictions on trade with the United States. Part of these protests involved petitions and pamphlets arguing the islanders' case and describing the present and future problems for their economies if the orders-in-council of July 1783 and after were not rescinded. Many of these partisan complaints have entered the history books as objective assessments of the issues, which has tremendously confused matters. We do not think that the "fall of the planter class" in the British West Indies began in 1763. We suggest a Scotch verdict on whether it began in 1783: not proven.[28]

Pattern of Baltimore Commerce during the Confederation Period," *ibid.*, LXII (1967), 119–134; Paul Kent Walker, "The Baltimore Community and the American Revolution: A Study in Urban Development, 1763–1783" (Ph.D. diss., University of North Carolina, 1973); Louis Maganzin, "Economic Depression in Maryland and Virginia, 1783–1787" (Ph.D. diss., Georgetown University, 1967); C. H. Laub, "Revolutionary Virginia and the Crown Lands (1775–1783)," *WMQ*, 2d Ser., XI (1931), 304–314; W. A. Low, "The Farmer in Post-Revolutionary Virginia, 1783–1789," *Agric. Hist.*, XXV (1951), 122–127; Low, "Merchant and Planter Relations in Post-Revolutionary Virginia, 1783–1789," *VMHB*, LXI (1953), 308–318; Myra L. Rich, "Speculations on the Significance of Debt: Virginia, 1781–1789," *ibid.*, LXXVI (1968), 301–317; Charles Christopher Crittenden, "Ships and Shipping in North Carolina, 1763–1789," *N.C. Hist. Rev.*, VIII (1931), 1–13; Crittenden, "Overland Travel and Transportation in North Carolina, 1763–1789," *ibid.*, 239–257; James Roy Morrill III, "North Carolina Public Finance, 1783–1789: The Problems of Minimal Government in an Underdeveloped Land" (Ph.D. diss., University of North Carolina, 1967); W. Robert Higgins, "A Financial History of the American Revolution in South Carolina" (Ph.D. diss., Duke University, 1970); and Dorothy Elaine Fennell, "From Rebelliousness to Insurrection: Class, Culture, and Ideology in Western Pennsylvania, 1765–1802" (Ph.D. diss., University of Pittsburgh, 1981).

28. The classic in the field is, of course, Ragatz, *Fall of the Planter Class*. See also Herbert C. Bell's two articles, "West India Trade," and "British Commercial Policy in the West In-

Those who write the economic histories of the states and the islands have one other major problem with which to contend. Data for this period, especially compiled data, are sparse and unusually difficult to interpret. As merely one example, in the late 1780s both the United States and Great Britain revised their legal formulas for measuring the size of ships and other vessels. This change affected data on total tonnage entering and clearing ports, often (and, of course, not strictly accurately) used as a surrogate for the volume of trade. Not only are the two nations' shipping data no longer comparable as a result of the altered formulas, but also figures from before and after the change cannot validly be compared without some adjustment. Similar problems plague other data, such as prices and currencies.[29]

We need to know about the general directions of the economy over the decade. As is the case with almost everything one can say about the period, we are forced to be extremely tentative even in something as rudimentary as this. Our own data show a contraction that lasted from 1782 to 1789 (see table 3.4). Other evidence suggests a somewhat less bleak picture. After a brief boom at the end of the war, reflecting pent-up de-

---

dies, 1783–93," *Eng. Hist. Rev.*, XXXI (1916), 429–441. Compare S. H. H. Carrington, "Economic and Political Developments in the British West Indies during the Period of the American Revolution [1770–1782]" (Ph.D. thesis, University of London, 1975); and John J. McCusker, "Growth, Stagnation, or Decline? The Economy of the British West Indies, 1763–1790," in *Economy of Early America*, ed. Hoffman, McCusker, and Menard. Particularly useful is Richard B. Sheridan, "The Crisis of Slave Subsistence in the British West Indies during and after the American Revolution," *WMQ*, 3d Ser., XXXIII (1976), 615–641. See also K. Watson, "Civilised Island."

29. For the problem with tonnage, see Shepherd and Walton, "Economic Change," 414–419, and McCusker, "Tonnage of Ships." It should be emphasized that, prior to these laws, tonnage computation also differed a bit from colony to colony (and state to state). One can trace the progress toward a uniform system in the more commercially oriented newspapers. See, for example, *Pennsylvania Mercury and Universal Advertiser* (Philadelphia), 1 July 1785, 7 July 1786, 17 Aug. 1787, 11 May 1790. Mistakes made as a result of this pitfall are common. See, for instance, the otherwise quite perceptive article by Simon Rottenberg, "The Business of Slave Trading," *So. Atlantic Qtly.*, LXVI (1967), 413, where the supposed growth in the size of Liverpool vessels engaged in the slave trade is overstated by one-third.

Any who choose to investigate the economy of this period will turn with considerable profit to the reports sent home to their European governments by consular agents stationed in U.S. ports. They wrote in great detail not only about the current situation but also, frequently by way of contrast, about the past. Reports of British consuls are in the Foreign Office Records (FO 5), PRO. Reports from the French consuls are in the Fonds des Affaires Étrangères, Série BI and Série BIII, Archives Nationales, Paris, and in the Fonds de la Correspondance Politique and the Fonds de la Correspondance Consulaire et Commerciale, Archives du Ministère des Affaires Étrangères, Paris. We expect that there are similar collections in the archives of other European nations.

mand for imported goods and fueled by the heavy extension of British commercial credit, the economy followed a downward course from the fall of 1783 until mid-1785. Then things turned around and the expansion, although weak, continued into 1788. It was followed by a short contraction. The earlier of the two periods of decline seems to have been little more than the usual postwar depression, though in this instance it may have been a peculiarly aggravated one. The later decline lasted only the one year and seems not to have been nearly as sharp or severe as the first.

The various sectors of the economy participated differently in these several periods. What the United States economy did best was to produce extractive agricultural commodities and to carry them to market. Yet in the 1780s both the agricultural and the commercial sector experienced some problems, stemming largely from the closing of overseas markets for the goods produced. Outside the nation itself, the major market for its foodstuffs, draft animals, and timber products had been the West Indies. During the war, as we have noted, the direct trade with the British West Indies had been cut off. This diminished the quantity of such goods exported there and lowered the price at which the farmer or the lumberman could sell them. In addition, the British began to create some difficulties about American rights to fish in their traditional waters. Offsetting all of this somewhat was the opening to the United States of trade with both the French islands and some of the Spanish colonies. The ending of the war was expected to help still more by bringing a resumption of the old Yankee-Creole connection. Such hopes were doubly disappointed when, after the war was over, both the British and the Spanish government closed their colonies to United States ships and to some or all United States goods.[30]

Much effort went into finding new customers for United States products and shipping services in the 1780s. Trade with France had been opened by the Treaty of 1778. For the first time large-scale trade was established between the United States and northern Europe, notably Germany, the Netherlands, and Scandinavia. The 1780s also saw the open-

30. On the trade with the West Indies, see Bell, "British Commercial Policy," and Rezin Fenton Duvall, "Philadelphia's Maritime Commerce with the British Empire, 1783–1789" (Ph.D. diss., University of Pennsylvania, 1960). With regard to fishing rights, see Gordon O. Rothney, "British Policy in the North American Cod-Fisheries, with Special Reference to Foreign Competition, 1775–1819" (Ph.D. thesis, University of London, 1939). On the trade with the Spanish colonies, see Peggy Liss, *Atlantic Empires: The Network of Trade and Revolution, 1713–1826* (Baltimore, 1982), and the essays in Jacques A. Barbier and Allan J. Kuethe, eds., *The North American Role in the Spanish Imperial Economy, 1760–1819* (Manchester, 1984).

ing of trade with China and the great expansion of American involvement in the direct trade for African slaves. And, slowly, the volume of exports to the West Indies seems to have strengthened as United States produce found its way, indirectly and less profitably, back to its old customers. By the end of the decade commodity exports were at levels at least as good and perhaps a bit better than they were before the beginning of the American Revolution.[31]

31. For the trade with France, see such studies as John F. Stover, "French-American Trade during the Confederation, 1781–1789," *N.C. Hist. Rev.*, XXXV (1958), 399–414, and Edward C. Papenfuse, "An Uncertain Connection: Maryland's Trade with France during the American Revolution, 1778–1783," in *La révolution américaine et l'Europe*, [ed. Fohlen and Godechot], 243–264. See also Jean Meyer, "Les difficultés du commerce franco-américain vues de Nantes (1776–1790)," *French Historical Studies*, XI (1979), 159–183. For trade with Spain, see Fernando Barreda, *Comercio marítimo entre los Estados Unidos y Santander (1778–1829)* (Santander, Spain, 1950), and Liss, *Atlantic Empires*. See also Light Townsend Cummins, "Spanish Agents in North America during the Revolution, 1775–1779" (Ph.D. diss., Tulane University, 1977). For the trade with northern Europe, see such studies as Hedges, *Browns of Providence Plantations*; Coyle, "Welcome Arnold"; and Stuart Weems Bruchey, *Robert Oliver, Merchant of Baltimore, 1783–1819* (Baltimore, 1956). The standard bibliographies are replete with studies of trade between the United States and this or that country during and after the American Revolution (see n. 14, above). However, only works in English are included, which is unfortunate because there are many relevant books and articles in other languages. See, for example, Ernst Baasch, "Beiträge zur Geschichte der Handelsbeziehungen zwischen Hamburg und Amerika," in [Hamburg, Komité für die Amerika-Feier, Wissenschaftlichen ausschuss], *Hamburgische Festschrift zur Erinnerung an die Entdeckung Amerika's* (Hamburg, 1892); Walter Kresse, *Materialien zur Entwicklungsgeschichte der hamburger Handelsflotte, 1765–1823* (Hamburg, 1966); and Aa[ge] Rasch, *Niels Ryberg, 1725–1824: Fra bondedreng til handelsfyrste* (Aarhus, Denmark, 1964). Ryberg traded with the Browns, among others; see Brown Papers, John Carter Brown Library, Brown University, Providence, R.I. Also useful—and completely unexploited—are the numerous contemporary descriptions of international trade in merchants' manuals such as Johann Christian Hermann, *Allgemeiner Contorist welcher von allen und jeden Gegenständen der Handlung aller in und ausser Europa . . .* (Leipzig, 1788–1792), I, 31–45. And, of course, European archives are rich with materials awaiting discovery and utilization. See, e.g., the letters of Antwerp merchant J. A. J. De Lince, Brievenkopij, 1784–1791, Insolvente Boedelskammer, 2028, Stadsarchief, Antwerp, Belgium. In this regard see McCusker, "New Guides to Primary Sources." For the trade with the Orient, see Foster Rhea Dulles, *The Old China Trade* (Boston, 1930); Clarence L. Ver Steeg, "Financing and Outfitting the First United States Ship to China," *Pacific Historical Review*, XXII (1953), 1–12; Magdalen Coughlin, "The Entrance of the Massachusetts Merchant into the Pacific [in the 1780s]," *Southern Historical Quarterly*, XLVIII (1966), 327–352; Mary Veronica Kuebel, "Merchants and Mandarins: The Genesis of American Relations with China" (Ph.D. diss., University of Virginia, 1974); and Jonathan Goldstein, *Philadelphia and the China Trade, 1682–1846: Commercial, Cultural, and Attitudinal Effects* (University Park, Pa., 1978). Compare Thomas Paul Slaughter, "The American Vision of China, 1784–1806: European and Merchant-Consul Influences" (honors thesis, University of Maryland, 1976). Lawrence A. Harper makes the

The history of the manufacturing and financial sectors of the domestic economy of the United States during the 1780s is even less clear than that of the agricultural sector and the foreign sector. On the one hand, much of the small-scale manufacturing that grew up during the Revolutionary War apparently failed to survive the peace. Such enterprises produced goods that the colonists had earlier purchased from British sources, but the return to the market of the better-made, lower-priced British goods drove their erstwhile competition out of business. Also in some trouble were industrial enterprises of an older vintage. Rum distilling and sugar refining seem to have suffered because the prices for their imported raw materials were raised by the confusions in the West Indian trade. Shipbuilding had problems because of the overall decline in the commerce carried on by United States merchants and because of the loss of overseas markets. On the other hand, commercial banking had its beginnings in this era, local chambers of commerce blossomed, and brokerage of all sorts seems to have expanded considerably.

The citizens of the new republic were subjected not only to a generally poor performance from their national economy but also to very high taxes. The debts incurred in attaining their independence forced Americans both to tax their own economy and to mortgage the future in order to service a tremendous bonded debt. The need to raise revenues to meet the interest and principal payments created havoc in government at all levels. Traditional methods of public finance in the colonies were entirely inadequate to a task of this magnitude, and they would have been so even had domestic and foreign trade not been disrupted. Import duties and land taxes, the traditional methods of raising revenue, simply did not yield enough. The nation had accepted the resort to the printing press as a wartime way of "papering over" the problem. Depreciating paper money as a form of taxation at least had the redeeming grace of taxing each proportionately to his or her means. Franklin made the point best.

---

point that prior to the Revolutionary War some 60% of the goods shipped to the continental colonies from England as reexports were East India goods, while after 1783 the quantity was insignificant (*English Navigation Laws*, 266n, 267n). For the slave trade, see Rawley, *Transatlantic Slave Trade*. For trade with Great Britain, see M. L. Robertson, "Scottish Commerce and the American War of Independence," *Econ. Hist. Rev.*, 2d Ser., IX (1956), 123–131, and Jim Potter, "The Effects of the American Revolution on the Economic Relations between the Former Colonies and the Mother Country," in *La révolution américaine et l'Europe*, [ed. Fohlen and Godechot], 265–277. Compare Raymond L. Sickinger, "The Eighteenth Century Textile Trade, 1772–1792: Commercial Tensions, Colonial Turmoil, and Cotton Trends" (paper presented at the New England Conference on British Studies, Nov. 1981). See also Merrill D. Peterson, "Thomas Jefferson and Commercial Policy, 1783–1793," *WMQ*, 3d Ser., XXII (1965), 584–610.

The general effect of the depreciation among the inhabitants of the States has been this, that it has operated as a *gradual tax* upon them, . . . and every man has paid his share of the tax according to the time he retained any of the money in his hands, and to the depreciation within that time. Thus it has proved a tax on money, a kind of property very difficult to be taxed in any other mode; and it has fallen more equally than many other taxes, as those people paid most, who, being richest, had most money passing through their hands.

Yet it was not a solution acceptable in peacetime because of the disruptions it caused to trade. The resulting tensions over public debts and paper money led to the political crises of the Confederation period and, directly, to the new national government under the Constitution.[32]

The extent of the costs to the nation of the war and of an experiment or two in new modes of governing is not easily measured. Nonetheless, one of the most intriguing issues raised for us in this whole study has been the assessment of these costs. Recent work has permitted us to estimate them directly even if the tentativeness of the data sounds an even louder than usual call to caution.

Clearly, if the results of current research stand future scrutiny, something "truly disastrous" happened to the American economy between 1775 and 1790. According to one estimate presented earlier (see table 3.2), per capita gross national product in 1774 amounted in 1980 dollars to $804. By another estimate the figure for 1790 equaled $437. Neither is much more than a guess, but accepting them as being in the right order

32. "Of the Paper Money of the United States," in Jared Sparks, ed., *The Works of Benjamin Franklin . . . with Notes and a Life of the Author* (Boston, 1836–1840), II, 424 (the emphasis is Franklin's). Obviously, one begins any list of works on public finance during this era with Ferguson, *Power of the Purse*. See also Edward Forbes Robinson, "Continental Treasury Administration, 1775–1781: A Study in the Financial History of the American Revolution" (Ph.D. diss., University of Wisconsin, 1969); Higgins, "Financial History"; LeGrand Liston Baker, "The Board of Treasury, 1784–1789: Responsibility without Power" (Ph.D. diss., University of Wisconsin, 1972); John Paul Kaminski, "Paper Politics: The Northern State Loan-Offices during the Confederation, 1783–1790" (Ph.D. diss., University of Wisconsin, 1972); and Molovinsky, "Pennsylvania's Legislative Efforts." See also Robert Francis Jones, "The Public Career of William Duer: Rebel, Federalist Politician, Entrepreneur, and Speculator, 1775–1792" (Ph.D. diss., University of Notre Dame, 1967). For the perspective of the lenders, see James C. Riley, "Foreign Credit and Fiscal Stability: Dutch Investment in the United States, 1781–1794," *JAH*, LXV (1978), 654–678. Compare Donald G. Tailby, "Foreign Interest Remittances by the United States, 1785–1787: A Story of Malfeasance," *Bus. Hist. Rev.*, XLI (1967), 161–176. See, too, Benjamin J. Klebaner, "State-Chartered American Commercial Banks, 1781–1801," *ibid.*, LIII (1979), 529–538.

of magnitude, the level of performance of the economy of the United States over that decade and a half fell by 46 percent. The figure for 1790 most surely represents the culmination of several years of improvement over an even lower figure from somewhat earlier in the decade. As a point of reference, during the Great Depression, between 1929 and 1933, real per capita gross national product declined by 48 percent. The colonists paid a high cost for their freedom.[33]

So sharp a decline in the performance of the economy raises several issues. The first of these must concern the data. Perhaps the estimate for 1774 is too high, thus exaggerating the reduction. This seems less likely than the parallel objection to the estimate for 1790, about which we will say more in a moment. Our estimate for 1774 is from the work of Alice Hanson Jones, which despite the objections leveled against its design and execution, more probably resulted in a figure too low rather than too high. It is an estimate in which we can place a fair degree of confidence for present purposes.

One cannot reach the same conclusion about the estimate for 1790, which comes from the work of Thomas S. Berry. The thrust of the most perceptive criticisms of Berry's calculations is that his figures tend to overstate the rate of growth during the first decade of the new national economy because they understate gross national product at the beginning of the 1790s. If this is correct, a higher figure for 1790 will obviously have the effect on our calculations of diminishing the decrease from 1774 to that year. It will leave open the question of the extent of the fall to the nadir of the economy's performance earlier in the 1780s.

While the Jones and Berry estimates together surely exaggerate the fall in income during the Revolutionary era, other evidence reinforces the impression that the contraction was nevertheless severe. One such bit of evidence also rests on Jones's figures, this time through a comparison with a wealth estimate for the United States in 1805 assembled by Samuel Blodget. According to these figures, wealth per capita was about 14 per-

33. The descriptive phrase is Stanley L. Engerman and Robert E. Gallman's, though they are careful to use it in a conditional context, dependent upon current estimates remaining unchallenged. See "U.S. Economic Growth" (quotation on p. 19), where they also analyze these estimates. For our discussion of the first estimate, see chap. 3, above. The figure for 1790 comes from T. Berry, *Revised Annual Estimates*. The data for the Great Depression are from U.S. Bureau of the Census, *Historical Statistics*, I, 224 (Ser. F 2), but reduced to 1980 dollars as in chap. 3, above. See also Goldin and Lewis, "Role of Exports," who find an "average annual decline in per capita income of −0.34% from 1774 to 1793." In our analysis, any figure for 1793 represents a considerable improvement over the nadir of some years earlier. For an argument that the decline was less severe and the recovery more rapid, see Merrill Jensen, *The New Nation: A History of the United States during the Confederation, 1781–1789* (New York, 1950).

cent lower in 1805 than in 1774. Although the quality of Blodget's estimate is difficult to evaluate and the price index used to reduce the two figures to constant values leaves much to be desired, the comparison does suggest a considerable erosion of wealth. Indeed, if the estimates are reliable, they actually understate the collapse during and immediately after the Revolution, for there is persuasive evidence of much expansion during the period 1790 to 1805.[34]

Work on exports reported by James Shepherd and Gary Walton also indicates a significant shrinkage in the performance of the economy over the years 1775 to 1790. Exports per capita were about 25 percent lower in 1791–1792 than in 1768–1772, according to their calculations. Of course, one cannot assume that the foreign sector contributed a constant share to incomes over the period. Indeed, the importance of farm self-sufficiency, the rapid rise of population, the westward spread of settlement, and the increase of indigenous industry all suggest that exports contributed a dwindling share to total output. However, Shepherd and Walton's figures do imply a substantial fall in incomes, particularly for those individuals, sectors, and regions most closely tied to trade.

There were considerable regional differences in the severity of the setback. In 1791–1792, per capita exports were actually slightly higher in the Middle Atlantic region than they had been in 1768–1772, and roughly the same for New England. All of the decrease occurred in the South, where exports per capita were roughly twice as high around 1770 as they were in the early 1790s. This resulted in a marked change in export shares contributed by the several regions. About 1770, 64 percent of all exports from the thirteen continental colonies originated in the South; by 1790, that share had dropped to 48 percent. The pattern is also reflected in wealth figures: in 1774, 46 percent of private wealth (net of slaves) in the thirteen colonies was held in the South; by 1799, the South's share was only 32 percent. Obviously some southerners suffered significantly in the name of independence.[35]

While the extent of the reduction in gross national product remains un-

34. A. Jones, *Wealth of a Nation to Be*, 81; Samuel Blodget, *Economica: A Statistical Manual for the United States of America* (Washington, D.C., 1806), 196. There is a useful commentary on Blodget in Raymond W. Goldsmith, "The Growth of Reproducible Wealth in the United States of America, 1805–1950," in *Income and Wealth of the United States: Trends and Structure*, ed. Simon Kuznets (Cambridge, 1952), 315–316.

35. For exports, see Shepherd and Walton, "Economic Change," 413. For wealth shares, see A. Jones, *Wealth of a Nation to Be*, 51. Compare Timothy Pitkin, *A Statistical View of the Commerce of the United States of America . . .* , rev. ed. (New Haven, Conn., 1835), 313, and Stanley L. Engerman, "A Reconsideration of Southern Economic Growth, 1770–1860," *Agric. Hist.*, XLIX (1975), 343–361.

certain, it is clear that per capita product fell and that it fell enough to affect all levels of society. Considerable, if random, supplemental evidence suggests that the period did witness a reduction in individual income, especially among the lower classes, and a subsequent rise in pauperism and indebtedness. All this would have meant a weakening of domestic demand for goods, especially manufactured goods. A model of export-led economic growth becomes, in reverse, a model of decline as well.[36]

The situation in the West Indies is even less clear. Some older islands experienced an absolute reduction in population during the war, chiefly among the slaves. The resulting loss of workers, as well as of labor diverted from sugar planting to the production of food crops, helps account not only for the wartime diminution in sugar production but also for an average production during the 1780s no higher than the level for 1770–1775. (This seems to have been more of a supply-side phenomenon. Because wartime prices were high, when they fell off during the postwar period the drop was to a level still somewhat higher than before the war.) In other words, the considerable intensification in sugar production that had characterized the pre–Revolutionary War era ended during the war and was not revived until the mid-1790s. The British sugar colonies appear to have grown only slowly, if at all, during the 1780s.

The sugar planters, naturally enough, blamed this unhappy episode on the restrictions placed on their trade by the 1783 orders-in-council. These regulations kept out all United States ships and some produce. However, the bulk of United States produce could be imported and all West Indian goods exported back to the United States provided the trade was carried on in British vessels. More of the same goods from the United States arrived by way of the Dutch and French West Indies. It is not that the British West Indies were without provisions. They just cost more, considerably more, at a time when the price of sugar in London stayed rather flat. The sugar planters responded by adopting the newly introduced Otaheite cane, which yielded more sugarcane juice, and by producing more rum themselves for sale abroad. These innovations were of greater importance for suggesting the shape of the nineteenth-century

36. On the subject of increased numbers of urban poor, compare Geib, "History of Philadelphia," and Withey, "Population Change." For related demographic changes, see K. Watson, "Civilised Island," and Robert V. Wells, "Population and the American Revolution," in *The American Revolution: Changing Perspectives*, ed. William M. Fowler, Jr., and Wallace Coyle (Boston, 1979), 103–122. One of the chief developments, as Wells points out, was the expansion of western settlement. While a great deal has been written on this subject, it is largely legal and political in perspective. See, for example, Roy M. Robbins, *Our Landed Heritage: The Public Domain, 1776–1936* (Princeton, N.J., 1942).

West Indian sugar economy than for helping the planters with their plight in the 1780s.[37]

All of early British America—the United States, the West Indies, and Canada—can best be viewed, economically speaking, as being "on hold" during the decade after 1783. Even though they were to advance far during the century following 1775, little of that journey had been accomplished by 1790. Nonetheless, the pause of the 1780s was pregnant with potential for the future.

37. For developments in the "loyal" parts of British America, besides the works cited in n. 28, above, see W. B. Kerr, "The Merchants of Nova Scotia and the American Revolution," *Canadian Historical Review*, XIII (1932), 20–36, and S. Basdeo and H. Robertson, "The Nova Scotia–British West Indies Commercial Experiment in the Aftermath of the American Revolution, 1783–1802," *Dalhousie Review*, LXI (1981), 53–69.

THE PARTICIPANTS

AT THE CONFERENCE

AT WILLIAMSBURG

9 – 10 OCTOBER 1980

John J. McCusker, University of Maryland, College Park (History)

Russell R. Menard, University of Minnesota (History)

Bernard Bailyn, Harvard University (History)

Stuart Bruchey, Columbia University (History)

Lois G. Carr, St. Mary's City Commission (History)

K. G. Davies, Trinity College, Dublin (History)

Thomas Doerflinger, Paine, Webber, Mitchell, Hutchins, Inc. (History)

Richard S. Dunn, University of Pennsylvania (History)

Carville Earle, University of Maryland, Baltimore County (Geography)

Stanley Engerman, University of Rochester (Economics)

Joseph Ernst, York University, Ontario (History)

Robert Fogel, University of Chicago (Economics)

David Galenson, University of Chicago (Economics)

Robert Gallman, University of North Carolina, Chapel Hill (Economics)

P. M. G. Harris, Temple University (History and Sociology)

James Henretta, Boston University (History)

Jonathan R. T. Hughes, Northwestern University (Economics)

Alice H. Jones, Washington University, St. Louis (Economics)

Gloria L. Main, University of Colorado at Boulder (History)

Jackson T. Main, University of Colorado at Boulder (History)

Edmund S. Morgan, Yale University (History)

Jacob Price, University of Michigan (History)

James Shepherd, Whitman College (Economics)

Richard Sheridan, University of Kansas (Economics)

Daniel Scott Smith, University of Illinois, Chicago Circle (History)

APPENDIX 2

THE ORGANIZATION

OF THE CONFERENCE

AT WILLIAMSBURG

9 – 10 OCTOBER 1980

First Morning
- A. Colonial Economic Development in General
  Hughes (chair), Fogel, Gallman
- B. Regional Economic Development: The Northern Colonies
  Bailyn (chair), Ernst, Henretta

First Afternoon
- A. Regional Economic Development: The Southern Colonies
  Morgan (chair), Carr, G. Main, Earle
- B. Regional Economic Development: The West Indies
  Davies (chair), Sheridan, Dunn

Second Morning
- A. Income, Wealth, and Consumption in the British Colonies
  Bruchey (chair), Jones, Smith, Galenson
- B. American Economy in the Revolutionary Years, 1775 – 1790
  J. Main (chair), Ferguson, Shepherd, Doerflinger

Second Afternoon—Conclusions
  Harris (chair), Price, Engerman

BIBLIOGRAPHY

This bibliography is simply a record of the items cited in the book. With only minor exceptions, additions were last made in July 1983. Because the materials in the several chapters are arranged topically, the bibliography is presented alphabetically.

UNPUBLISHED MATERIALS

Domestic Repositories

District of Columbia
  Washington
    Library of Congress
      Amory Family Papers, 1697–1823
Maryland
  Baltimore
    Maryland Historical Society
      Carroll Papers
Massachusetts
  Boston
    Massachusetts Historical Society
      Amory Family Manuscripts
  Worcester
    American Antiquarian Society
      John Hull Papers
New York
  New York City
    New York Public Library
      George Chalmers Papers, 1606–1812
        Maryland, 1619–1812
Pennsylvania
  Philadelphia
    American Philosophical Society
      Burd-Shippen Papers
    Historical Society of Pennsylvania
      Coates and Reynell Papers, 1702–1843
      John Reynell Letter Books, 1729–1784
      William Pollard Letter Book, 1772–1774
      Willing and Morris Letter Book, 1754–1761
Rhode Island
  Providence
    John Carter Brown Library, Brown University
      Brown Papers

Virginia
  Charlottesville
    Alderman Library, University of Virginia
      Robert Anderson Letter Book, 1698–1715
  Richmond
    Virginia Historical Society
      Carter Papers, 1705–1785

Foreign Repositories

Belgium
  Antwerp
    Stadsarchief
      Insolvente Boedelskammer
        IB 2028: J. A. J. De Lince, Brievenkopij, 1784–1791
France
  Paris
    Archives Nationales
      Fonds des Affaires Étrangères
    Archives du Ministère des Affaires Étrangères
      Fonds de la Correspondance Politique (jusquà 1896)
      Fonds de la Correspondance Consulaire et Commerciale
        (1793–1901)
Great Britain
  London
    British Library
      Additional Manuscripts (Add. MSS)
    House of Lords Record Office
      Parchment Collection
    Public Record Office
      Board of Customs and Excise Records (CUST)
      Board of Trade Papers (BT)
      Colonial Office Records (CO)
      Foreign Office Records (FO)
      Records of the Court of Chancery (C)
      Records of the Exchequer (E)
      Treasury Office Papers (T)
    Royal Society of the Arts
      Committee of Colonies and Trade, Guard Books
  Edinburgh
    Scottish Record Office
      Hay of Haystoun Documents (Gift and Deposit No. 34)

NEWSPAPERS

Boston-Gazette, and Country Journal
Gentlemen's Magazine and Historical Chronicle (London)
New York Times

Pennsylvania Mercury and Universal Advertiser (Philadelphia)
South Carolina Gazette (Charleston)
Virginia Gazette (Williamsburg)

PUBLISHED MATERIALS

Abramovitz, Moses, and Paul David. "Reinterpreting Economic Growth: Parables and Realities." *American Economic Review*, LXIII (1973), 428–439.

Adams, Donald R., Jr. "One Hundred Years of Prices and Wages: Maryland, 1750–1850." Regional Economic History Research Center, *Working Papers*, V (1982), 90–129.

[Adams, James Truslow, ed.]. *Dictionary of American History*. [3d] ed., rev. 8 vols. New York, 1976–1978.

[Adams, John]. *Diary and Autobiography of John Adams*. Edited by L[yman] H. Butterfield *et al*. 4 vols. Cambridge, Mass., 1961.

———. *Papers of John Adams*. Edited by Robert J. Taylor *et al*. Cambridge, Mass., 1977–.

Adams, John W., and Alice B. Kasakoff. "Migration at Marriage in Colonial New England: A Comparison of Rates Derived from Genealogies with Rates from Vital Records." In *Genealogical Demography*, edited by Bennett Dyke and Warren T. Morrill, 115–138. New York, 1980.

Albion, Robert Greenhalgh. *Forests and Sea Power: The Timber Problem of the Royal Navy, 1652–1862*. Harvard Economic Studies, XXIX. Cambridge, Mass., 1926.

———. *The Rise of New York Port [1815–1860]*. New York, 1939.

Albright, Alan B. "The Brown's Ferry Vessel." North American Society for Oceanic History, *Proceedings*, I (1977).

Alden, Dauril. "The Significance of Cacao Production in the Amazon Region during the Late Colonial Period: An Essay in Comparative Economic History." American Philosophical Society, *Proceedings*, CXX (1976), 103–135.

Alexander, John K. "The Philadelphia Numbers Game: An Analysis of Philadelphia's Eighteenth-Century Population." *Pennsylvania Magazine of History and Biography*, XCVIII (1974), 314–324.

———. *Render Them Submissive: Responses to Poverty in Philadelphia, 1760–1800*. Amherst, Mass., 1980.

Allen, David Grayson. *In English Ways: The Movement of Societies and the Transferal of English Local Law and Custom to Massachusetts Bay in the Seventeenth Century*. Chapel Hill, N.C., 1981.

Allen, Gardner Weld. *Massachusetts Privateers of the Revolution*. Massachusetts Historical Society, *Collections*, LXXVII. Boston, 1927.

American Council of Learned Societies. "Report on Linguistic and National Stocks in the Population of the United States." American Historical Association, *Annual Report . . . for the Year 1931*, I, 103–441. Washington, D.C., 1932.

Ames, Susie M. *Studies of the Virginia Eastern Shore in the Seventeenth Century*. Richmond, Va., 1940.

Amin, Samir. *Accumulation on a World Scale: A Critique of the Theory of Underdevelopment*. Translated by Brian Pearce. New York, 1974.

Anderson, James Donald. "Thomas Wharton, 1730/31–1784: Merchant in Philadelphia." Ph.D. diss., University of Akron, 1977.

Anderson, J[ohn] A. *Navigation of the Upper Delaware.* Trenton, N.J., 1913.

Anderson, Ralph V. "Labor Utilization and Productivity, Diversification and Self-sufficiency: Southern Plantations, 1800–1840." Ph.D. diss., University of North Carolina, 1974.

Anderson, Ralph V., and Robert E. Gallman. "Slaves as Fixed Capital: Slave Labor and Southern Economic Development." *Journal of American History,* XLIV (1977), 24–46.

Anderson, Terry Lee. "Economic Growth in Colonial New England: 'Statistical Renaissance.'" *Journal of Economic History,* XXXIX (1979), 243–257.

———. *The Economic Growth of Seventeenth Century New England: A Measurement of Regional Income.* New York, 1975 (Ph.D. diss., University of Washington, 1972).

———. "From the Parts to the Whole: Modeling Chesapeake Population." *Explorations in Economic History,* XVIII (1981), 411–414.

———. "Wealth Estimates for the New England Colonies, 1650–1709." *Explorations in Economic History,* XII (1975), 151–176.

Anderson, Terry Lee, and Robert Paul Thomas. "Economic Growth in the Seventeenth-Century Chesapeake." *Explorations in Economic History,* XV (1978), 368–387.

———. "The Growth of Population and Labor Force in the Seventeenth-Century Chesapeake." *Explorations in Economic History,* XV (1978), 290–312.

———. "White Population, Labor Force, and Extensive Growth of the New England Economy in the Seventeenth Century." *Journal of Economic History,* XXXIII (1973), 634–667.

Andreano, Ralph L., ed. *New Views on American Economic Development: A Selective Anthology of Recent Work.* Cambridge, Mass., 1965.

Andrews, Charles M. "The Acts of Trade." In *The Old Empire: From the Beginnings to 1783.* Vol. I of *The Cambridge History of the British Empire,* edited by J. Holland Rose, A. P. Newton, and E. A. Benians, 268–299. Cambridge, 1929.

———. "The Boston Merchants and the Non-importation Movement." In Colonial Society of Massachusetts, *Publications,* XIX: *Transactions, 1916–1917,* 159–259. Boston, 1918.

———. *The Boston Merchants and the Non-importation Movement.* Reprint. New York, 1968.

———. *The Colonial Background of the American Revolution: Four Essays in American Colonial History.* New Haven, Conn., 1924.

———. "Colonial Commerce." *American Historical Review,* XX (1914), 43–63.

———. *The Colonial Period of American History.* 4 vols. New Haven, Conn., 1934–1938.

———. "The Government of the Empire, 1660–1763." In *The Old Empire: From the Beginnings to 1783.* Vol. I of *The Cambridge History of the British Empire,* edited by J. Holland Rose, A. P. Newton, and E. A. Benians, 405–436. Cambridge, 1929.

Andrews, Edward Deming, and Faith Andrews. *Shaker Furniture: The Craftsmanship of an American Communal Sect.* New Haven, Conn., 1937.

Andrews, Kenneth R. *Drake's Voyages: A Re-assessment of Their Place in Elizabethan Maritime Expansion.* New York, 1967.

———. *Elizabethan Privateering: English Privateering during the Spanish War, 1585–1603.* Cambridge, 1964.

Andrews, Kenneth R., N[icholas] P. Canny, and P[aul] E. H. Hair, eds. *The Westward Enterprise: English Activities in Ireland, the Atlantic, and America, 1480–1650.* Detroit, Mich., 1979.

Anstey, Roger T. *The Atlantic Slave Trade and British Abolition, 1760–1810.* London, 1975.

————. "*Capitalism and Slavery:* A Critique." *Economic History Review*, 2d Ser., XXI (1968), 307–320.

Anstey, Roger T., and P[aul] E. H. Hair, eds. *Liverpool, the African Slave Trade, and Abolition: Essays to Illustrate Current Knowledge and Research.* Historic Society of Lancashire and Cheshire Occasional Series, II. Liverpool, 1976.

Appleby, Joyce Oldham. "Commercial Farming and the 'Agrarian Myth' in the Early Republic." *Journal of American History*, LXVIII (1982), 833–849.

————. *Economic Thought and Ideology in Seventeenth-Century England.* Princeton, N.J., 1978.

————. "What Is Still American in the Political Philosophy of Thomas Jefferson?" *William and Mary Quarterly*, 3d Ser., XXXIX (1982), 287–309.

Archdeacon, Thomas J. *New York City, 1664–1710: Conquest and Change.* Ithaca, N.Y., 1976.

Armour, David Arthur. "The Merchants of Albany, New York: 1686–1760." Ph.D. diss., Northwestern University, 1965.

Armytage, L[ucy] Frances Horsfall. *The Free Port System in the British West Indies: A Study in Commercial Policy, 1766–1822.* Imperial Studies Series, XX. London, 1953.

————. "The Free Port System in the British West Indies, 1766–1815." Ph.D. thesis, University of London, 1939.

Ashton, T[homas] S. *Economic Fluctuations in England, 1700–1800.* Oxford, 1959.

————. *An Economic History of England: The Eighteenth Century.* London, 1961.

Atkinson, Anthony B. "On the Measurement of Inequality." *Journal of Economic Theory*, II (1970), 244–263.

Aufhauser, R. Keith. "Profitability of Slavery in the British Caribbean." *Journal of Interdisciplinary History*, V (1974), 45–67.

————. "Slavery and Technological Change." *Journal of Economic History*, XXXIV (1974), 36–50.

Auwers, Linda. "Family, Friends, and Neighbors: Social Interaction in Seventeenth-Century Windsor, Connecticut." Ph.D. diss., Brandeis University, 1973.

————. "History from the Mean—Up, Down, and Around: A Review Essay." *Historical Methods*, XII (1979), 39–45.

Axtell, James. *The School upon a Hill: Education and Society in Colonial New England.* New Haven, Conn., 1974.

Baasch, Ernst. "Beiträge zur Geschichte der Handelsbeziehungen zwischen Hamburg und Amerika." In [Hamburg. Komité für die Amerika-Feier. Wissenschaftlichen ausschuss.] *Hamburgische Festschrift zur Erinnerung an die Entdeckung Amerika's.* 2 vols. Hamburg, 1892.

Bachman, Van Cleaf. *Peltries or Plantations: The Economic Policies of the Dutch West India Company in New Netherland, 1623–1639.* Baltimore, 1969.

Bagnall, William R. *The Textile Industries of the United States. . . .* Vol. I, *1639–1810.* Cambridge, Mass., 1893.

Bailyn, Bernard. "The *Apologia* of Robert Keayne." *William and Mary Quarterly*, 3d Ser., VII (1950), 568–587.

————. "The Central Themes of the American Revolution: An Interpretation." In *Essays on the American Revolution*, edited by Stephen G. Kurtz and James H. Hutson, 3–31. Chapel Hill, N.C., 1973.

————. "Communications and Trade: The Atlantic in the Seventeenth Century." *Journal of Economic History*, XIII (1953), 378–387.

————. *Education in the Forming of American Society.* Needs and Opportunities for Study. Chapel Hill, N.C., 1960.

————. "Lines of Force in Recent Writings on the American Revolution." In [International Congress of the Historical Sciences, 14th, San Francisco], *Reports [of the] XIV International Congress of the Historical Sciences*, I, 172–219. New York, 1977.

————. *The New England Merchants in the Seventeenth Century.* Cambridge, Mass., 1955.

————. "Politics and Social Structure in Virginia." In *Seventeenth-Century America: Essays in Colonial History*, edited by James Morton Smith, 90–115. Chapel Hill, N.C., 1959.

Bailyn, Bernard, and Lotte Bailyn. *Massachusetts Shipping, 1697–1714: A Statistical Study.* Cambridge, Mass., 1959.

Bairati, Piero. "Per il bene dell'umanità: Benjamin Franklin e il problema delle manifatture." *Rivista Storica Italiana*, XC (1978), 262–293.

Bairoch, Paul. *Commerce extérieur et développement économique de l'Europe au XIXe siècle.* Paris, 1976.

————. "Europe's Gross National Product, 1800–1975." *Journal of European Economic History*, V (Fall 1976), 273–340.

Bairoch, Paul, and Maurice Lévy-Leboyer, eds. *Disparities in Economic Development since the Industrial Revolution.* New York, 1980.

Baker, E[dward] C. *A Guide to Records in the Leeward Islands.* Oxford, 1965.

————. *A Guide to Records in the Windward Islands.* Oxford, 1968.

Baker, LeGrand Liston. "The Board of Treasury, 1784–1789: Responsibility without Power." Ph.D. diss., University of Wisconsin, 1972.

Baker, Norman. *Government and Contractors: The British Treasury and War Supplies, 1775–1783.* University of London Historical Studies, XXX. London, 1971.

Baker, William Avery. *Colonial Vessels: Some Seventeenth-Century Sailing Craft.* Barre, Mass., 1962.

————. *Sloops and Shallops.* Barre, Mass., 1966.

————. "Vessel Types of Colonial Massachusetts." In *Seafaring in Colonial Massachusetts*, [edited by Philip Chadwick Foster Smith], 3–29. Colonial Society of Massachusetts, *Publications*, LII: *Collections.* Boston, 1980.

Baldwin, Robert E. "Patterns of Development in Newly Settled Regions." *Manchester School of Economic and Social Studies*, XXIV (1956), 161–179.

————, et al. *Trade, Growth, and the Balance of Payments: Essays in Honor of Gottfried Haberler.* Chicago, 1965.

Ball, Duane Eugene. "Dynamics of Population and Wealth in Eighteenth-Century Chester County, Pennsylvania." *Journal of Interdisciplinary History*, VI (1976), 621–644.

————. "The Process of Settlement in Eighteenth-Century Chester County, Pennsylvania: A Social and Economic History." Ph.D. diss., University of Pennsylvania, 1973.

Ball, Duane Eugene, and G. M. Walton. "Agricultural Productivity Change in Eighteenth-Century Pennsylvania." *Journal of Economic History*, XXXVI (1976), 102–117.

Ballagh, James Curtis. *White Servitude in the Colony of Virginia: A Study of the System of Indentured Labor in the American Colonies.* Johns Hopkins University Studies in Historical and Political Science, 13th Ser., nos. 6–7. Baltimore, 1895.

[Banister, Thomas]. *A Letter to the Right Honourable the Lords Commissioners of Trade and Plantations: or, A Short Essay on the Principal Branches of the Trade of New-England. . . .* London, 1715.

Barbagli Bagnoli, Vera, ed. *La moneta nell'economica europea secoli XIII–XVIII.* Instituto Internazionale di Storia Economica "F. Datini," Pubblicazioni, Serie II, no. 7. Prato, 1981.

Barbier, Jacques A., and Allan J. Kuethe, eds. *The North American Role in the Spanish Imperial Economy, 1760–1819.* Manchester, 1984.

Barbour, Violet. "Privateers and Pirates of the West Indies." *American Historical Review,* XVI (1911), 529–566.

Barclay, George W. *Techniques of Population Analysis.* New York, 1958.

Barker, Charles Albro. *The Background of the Revolution in Maryland.* New Haven, Conn., 1940.

Barker, T[heodore] C. "Smuggling in the Eighteenth Century: The Evidence of the Scottish Tobacco Trade." *Virginia Magazine of History and Biography,* LXII (1954), 387–399.

Barreda, Fernando. *Comercio marítimo entre los Estados Unidos y Santander (1778–1829).* Santander, Spain, 1950.

Barrow, Thomas C. *Trade and Empire: The British Customs Service in Colonial America, 1660–1775.* Cambridge, Mass., 1967.

Barton, Bonnie. "The Creation of Centrality." Association of American Geographers, *Annals,* LXVIII (1978), 34–44.

Basdeo, S., and H. Robertson. "The Nova Scotia–British West Indies Commercial Experiment in the Aftermath of the American Revolution, 1783–1802." *Dalhousie Review,* LXI (1981), 53–69.

Bassett, John Spencer. *Slavery and Servitude in the Colony of North Carolina.* Johns Hopkins University Studies in Historical and Political Science, 14th Ser., nos. 4–5. Baltimore, 1896.

Bathe, Greville, and Dorothy Bathe. *Oliver Evans: A Chronicle of Early American Engineering.* Philadelphia, 1935.

Batie, Robert Carlyle. "Why Sugar? Economic Cycles and the Changing of Staples on the English and French Antilles, 1624–54." *Journal of Caribbean History,*VIII (1976), 1–41.

Baxter, W[illiam] T. "Accounting in Colonial America." In *Studies in the History of Accounting,* edited by A. C. Littleton and B. S. Yamey, 272–287. Homewood, Ill., 1956.

———. *The House of Hancock: Business in Boston, 1724–1775.* Harvard Studies in Business History, X. Cambridge, Mass., 1945.

Bean, Richard Nelson. *The British Trans-Atlantic Slave Trade, 1650–1775.* New York, 1975 (Ph.D. diss., University of Washington, 1971).

———. "Food Imports into the British West Indies, 1680–1845." In *Comparative Perspectives on Slavery in New World Plantation Societies,* edited by Vera Rubin and Arthur Tuden, 581–590. New York Academy of Sciences, *Annals,* CCXCII. New York, 1977.

Bean, Richard Nelson, and Robert P[aul] Thomas. "The Adoption of Slave Labor in British America." In *The Uncommon Market: Essays in the Economic History of the Atlantic Slave Trade,* edited by Henry A. Gemery and Jan S. Hogendorn, 377–398. New York, 1979.

Beard, Charles A. *Economic Origins of Jeffersonian Democracy.* New York, 1915.

Beattie, J[ohn] M. *Crime and the Courts in England, 1660–1800.* Princeton, N.J., forthcoming.

Becker, Robert A. *Revolution, Reform, and the Politics of American Taxation, 1763–1783.* Baton Rouge, La., 1980.

Beckles, Hilary McD. "The Economic Origins of Black Slavery in the British West Indies, 1640–1680: A Tentative Analysis of the Barbados Model." *Journal of Caribbean History,* XVI (1982), 36–56.

———. "Land Distribution and Class Formation in Barbados, 1630–1700: The Rise of a Wage Proletariat." *Journal of the Barbados Museum and Historical Society*, XXXVI (1980), 136–143.

———. "Rebels and Reactionaries: The Political Response of White Labourers to Planter Class Hegemony in Seventeenth Century Barbados." *Journal of Caribbean History*, XV (1981), 1–19.

———. "Sugar and White Servitude: An Analysis of Indentured Labour during the Sugar Revolution of Barbados, 1643–1655." *Journal of the Barbados Museum and Historical Society*, XXXVI (1981), 236–246.

———. "The Two Hundred Year War: Slave Resistance in the British West Indies—An Overview of the Historiography." *Jamaican Historical Review*, XIII (1982), 1–10.

Beechert, Edward Delos, Jr. "The Wine Trade of the Thirteen Colonies." M.A. thesis, University of California, Berkeley, 1949.

Beeman, Richard R. "The New Social History and the Search for 'Community' in Colonial America." *American Quarterly*, XXIX (1977), 422–443.

Beer, George Louis. *British Colonial Policy, 1754–1765.* New York, 1907.

———. *The Commercial Policy of England toward the American Colonies.* Columbia University Studies in History, Economics and Public Law, III, no. 2. New York, 1893.

———. *The Old Colonial System, 1660–1754.* 2 vols. New York, 1912.

———. *The Origins of the British Colonial System, 1578–1660.* New York, 1908.

Behrens, Kathryn L. *Paper Money in Maryland, 1727–1789.* Johns Hopkins University Studies in Historical and Political Science, 41st Ser., no. 1. Baltimore, 1923.

Bell, Herbert C. "British Commercial Policy in the West Indies, 1783–93." *English Historical Review*, XXXI (1916), 429–441.

———. "The West India Trade before the American Revolution." *American Historical Review*, XXII (1917), 272–287.

Bell, Herbert C., David W. Parker, *et al. Guide to British West Indian Archive Materials, in London and in the Islands, for the History of the United States.* Washington, D.C., 1926.

Bender, Thomas. *Community and Social Change in America.* New Brunswick, N.J., 1978.

Bennett, J. Harry, Jr. *Bondsmen and Bishops: Slavery and Apprenticeship on the Codrington Plantations of Barbados, 1710–1838.* University of California Publications in History, LXII. Berkeley and Los Angeles, Calif., 1958.

———. "Cary Helyar, Merchant and Planter of Seventeenth-Century Jamaica." *William and Mary Quarterly*, 3d Ser., XXI (1964), 53–76.

———. "The English Caribbees in the Period of the Civil War, 1642–1646." *William and Mary Quarterly*, 3d Ser., XXIV (1967), 359–377.

———. "William Whaley, Planter of Seventeenth-Century Jamaica." *Agricultural History*, XL (1966), 113–123.

Bentley, William George. "Wealth Distribution in Colonial South Carolina." Ph.D. diss., Georgia State University, 1977.

Berg, Harry Dahl. "Merchants and Mercantile Life in Colonial Philadelphia: 1748–1763." Ph.D. diss., University of Iowa, 1941.

———. "The Organization of Business in Colonial Philadelphia." *Pennsylvania History*, X (1943), 157–177.

Bergstrom, Peter Victor. "Markets and Merchants: Economic Diversification in Colonial Virginia, 1700–1775." Ph.D. diss., University of New Hampshire, 1980.

Bergstrom, Peter Victor, and Kevin P. Kelly. "'Well Built Towns, Convenient Ports and Markets': The Beginnings of Yorktown, 1690–1720." Paper presented at the annual meeting of the Southern Historical Association, Atlanta, Ga., November 1980.

Berkebile, Don[ald] H. *Conestoga Wagons in Braddock's Campaign, 1755.* United States National Museum, *Bulletin,* no. 218. Washington, D.C., 1959.

Berlin, Ira. "The Development of Plantation Systems and Slave Societies: A Commentary—II." In *Comparative Perspectives on Slavery in New World Plantation Societies,* edited by Vera Rubin and Arthur Tuden, 68–71. New York Academy of Sciences, *Annals,* CCXCII. New York, 1977.

———. "Time, Space, and the Evolution of Afro-American Society on British Mainland North America." *American Historical Review,* LXXXV (1980), 44–78.

Bernard, James A., Jr. "An Analysis of British Mercantilism as It Related to Patterns of South Carolina Trade from 1717 to 1767." Ph.D. diss., University of Notre Dame, 1973.

Berry, Brian J. L. *The Geography of Market Centers and Retail Distribution.* Englewood Cliffs, N.J., 1967.

Berry, Thomas Senior. *Estimated Annual Variations in Gross National Product, 1789 to 1900.* Richmond, Va., 1968.

———. *Revised Annual Estimates of American Gross National Product, Preliminary Annual Estimates of Four Major Components of Demand, 1789–1889.* [Richmond, Va.], 1978.

Bever, Virginia Margaret. *See* Platt, Virginia Margaret Bever.

Beveridge, Sir William. *Prices and Wages in England: From the Twelfth to the Nineteenth Century.* London, 1939.

Bezanson, Anne, assisted by Blanch Daley, Marjorie C. Denison, and Miriam Hussey. *Prices and Inflation during the American Revolution: Pennsylvania, 1770–1790.* Industrial Research Department, Wharton School of Finance and Commerce, University of Pennsylvania, Research Studies, XXXV. Philadelphia, 1951.

Bezanson, Anne, Robert D. Gray, and Miriam Hussey. *Prices in Colonial Pennsylvania.* Philadelphia, 1935.

Bhagwati, Jagdish N., Ronald W. Jones, Robert A. Mundell, and Jaroslav Vanek, eds. *Trade, Balance of Payments, and Growth: Papers in International Economics in Honor of Charles P. Kindleberger.* Amsterdam, 1971.

Bickerton, B. C., comp. *Papers and Abstracts for a Symposium on Ile Royale during the French Regime.* Ottawa, 1972.

Bidwell, Percy Wells. "The Agricultural Revolution in New England." *American Historical Review,* XXVI (1921), 683–702.

———. "Rural Economy in New England at the Beginning of the Nineteenth Century." Connecticut Academy of the Arts and Sciences, *Transactions,* XX (1916), 241–399.

Bidwell, Percy Wells, and John I. Falconer. *History of Agriculture in the Northern United States, 1620–1860.* Carnegie Institution of Washington Publication no. 358. Washington, D.C., 1925.

Billias, George Athan. *The Massachusetts Land Bankers of 1740.* University of Maine Studies [in History and Government], 2d Ser., no. 74. Orono, Maine, 1959.

Billings, Warren Martin. "'Virginia's Deploured Condition,' 1660–1676: The Coming of Bacon's Rebellion." Ph.D. diss., Northern Illinois University, 1968.

Billington, Ray Allen, ed. *The Reinterpretation of Early American History: Essays in Honor of John Edwin Pomfret.* San Marino, Calif., 1966.

Bining, Arthur Cecil. *British Regulation of the Colonial Iron Industry.* Philadelphia, 1933.

———. *Pennsylvania Iron Manufacture in the Eighteenth Century.* Harrisburg, Pa., 1938.

Biraben, J. N. "Le peuplement du Canada français." *Annales de Demographie Historique,* III (1966), 105–138.

Biscoe, Robert. *The Merchant's Magazine; or, Factor's Guide. Containing, Great Variety of Plain and Easy Tables.* . . . Williamsburg, Va., 1743.

Bishop, Charles A. *The Northern Ojibwa and the Fur Trade: An Historical and Ecological Study.* Toronto, 1974.

Bishop, J[ohn] Leander. *A History of American Manufactures from 1608 to 1860.* . . . 3d ed., rev. 3 vols. Philadelphia, 1868.

Bissell, Linda Auwers. *See* Auwers, Linda.

Bjork, Gordon Carl. "Stagnation and Growth in the American Economy, 1784–1792." Ph.D. diss., University of Washington, 1963.

———. "The Weaning of the American Economy: Independence, Market Changes, and Economic Development." *Journal of Economic History*, XXIV (1964), 541–560.

Blake, John B. *Public Health in the Town of Boston, 1630–1822.* Harvard Historical Studies, LXXII. Cambridge, Mass., 1959.

Blodget, Samuel. *Economica: A Statistical Manual for the United States of America.* Washington, D.C., 1806.

Bonazzi, Tiziano, ed. *La rivoluzione americana.* Bologna, 1977.

Bonner, James C. *A History of Georgia Agriculture, 1732–1860.* Athens, Ga., 1964.

Bonomi, Patricia U., ed. *Parties and Political Opposition in Revolutionary America.* Tarrytown, N.Y., 1980.

Boogaart, Ernst van den, and Pieter C. Emmer. "The Dutch Participation in the Atlantic Slave Trade, 1596–1650." In *The Uncommon Market: Essays in the Economic History of the Atlantic Slave Trade*, edited by Henry A. Gemery and Jan S. Hogendorn, 353–375. New York, 1979.

Borah, Woodrow [W.], Jorge Hardoy, and Gilbert A. Stelter, eds. *Urbanization in the Americas: The Background in Comparative Perspective.* Ottawa, 1980.

Borlandi, Franco, ed. *El libro di mercatantie et usanze de' paesi.* Turin, 1936.

Boserup, Ester. *The Conditions of Agricultural Growth: The Economics of Agrarian Change under Population Pressure.* London, 1965.

———. *Population and Technology.* Oxford, 1981.

———. *Woman's Role in Economic Development.* London, 1970.

Boulle, Pierre H. "Marchandises de traite et développement industriel dans la France et l'Angleterre du XVIIIᵉ siècle." *Revue Française d'Histoire d'Outre-Mer*, LXII (1975), 309–330.

Bowden, William Hammond. "The Commerce of Marblehead, 1665–1775." Essex Institute, *Historical Collections*, LXVIII (1932), 117–146.

Bowman, Larry G. "The Scarcity of Salt in Virginia during the American Revolution." *Virginia Magazine of History and Biography*, LXXVII (1969), 464–472.

Boyer, Paul, and Stephen Nissenbaum. *Salem Possessed: The Social Origins of Witchcraft.* Cambridge, Mass., 1974.

Bradley, Lawrence James. "The London/Bristol Trade Rivalry: Conventional History, and the Colonial Office 5 Records for the Port of New York." Ph.D. diss., University of Notre Dame, 1971.

[Brady, Dorothy S.]. "Consumption and the Style of Life." In *American Economic Growth: An Economist's History of the United States*, edited by Lance E. Davis, Richard A. Easterlin, and William N. Parker, 61–89. New York, 1972.

Brathwaite, Edward. *The Development of Creole Society in Jamaica, 1770–1820.* Oxford, 1971.

Bray, Maynard. *Mystic Seaport Museum Watercraft.* Mystic, Conn., 1979.

Brebner, John Bartlet. *The Neutral Yankees of Nova Scotia: A Marginal Colony during the Revolutionary Years.* New York, 1937.

————. *New England's Outpost: Acadia before the Conquest of Canada.* Columbia University Studies in History, Economics and Public Law, no. 293. New York, 1927.

Breen, T[imothy] H., and Stephen Foster. "Moving to the New World: The Character of Early Massachusetts Immigration." *William and Mary Quarterly*, 3d Ser., XXX (1973), 189–222.

Breen, T[imothy] H., James H. Lewis, and Keith Schlesinger. "Motive for Murder: A Servant's Life in Virginia, 1678." *William and Mary Quarterly*, 3d Ser., XL (1983), 106–120.

Brenner, Robert Paul. "Commercial Change and Political Conflict: The Merchant Community in Civil War London." Ph.D. diss., Princeton University, 1970.

Bretz, Frederick H. "The African Slave Trade of Colonial Rhode Island, 1700–1777." Unpublished seminar paper (Hist. 272B). University of California, Berkeley, 1960.

Bridenbaugh, Carl. *Cities in Revolt: Urban Life in America, 1743–1776.* New York, 1955.

————. *Cities in the Wilderness: The First Century of Urban Life in America, 1625–1742.* New York, 1938.

————. *The Colonial Craftsman.* New York, 1950.

————. "The High Cost of Living in Boston, 1728." *New England Quarterly*, V (1932), 800–811.

Bridenbaugh, Carl, and Roberta Bridenbaugh. *No Peace beyond the Line: The English in the Caribbean, 1624–1690.* New York, 1972.

Brigham, Clarence S. *History and Bibliography of American Newspapers, 1690–1820.* 2 vols. Worcester, Mass., 1947.

Brock, Leslie V. *The Currency of the American Colonies, 1700–1764: A Study in Colonial Finance and Imperial Relations.* New York, 1975 (Ph.D. diss., University of Michigan, 1941).

Bromley, J[ohn] S., ed. *The Rise of Great Britain and Russia, 1688–1715/25.* Vol. VI of *The New Cambridge Modern History.* Cambridge, 1970.

Bronfenbrenner, Martin. *Income Distribution Theory.* Aldine Treatises in Modern Economics. Chicago, 1971.

Brown, George W., et al., eds. *Dictionary of Canadian Biography/Dictionnaire biographique du Canada.* Toronto, 1966–.

Brown, Philip M. "Early Indian Trade in the Development of South Carolina: Politics, Economics, and Social Mobility during the Proprietary Period, 1670–1719." *South Carolina Historical Magazine*, LXXVI (1975), 118–128.

Brown, Robert E. *Middle-Class Democracy and the Revolution in Massachusetts, 1691–1780.* Ithaca, N.Y., 1955.

Brown, Vera Lee. "Anglo-Spanish Relations in America in the Closing Years of the Colonial Era." *Hispanic American Historical Review*, V (1922), 325–483.

————. "Contraband Trade: A Factor in the Decline of Spain's Empire in America." *Hispanic American Historical Review*, VIII (1928), 178–189.

Browne, William Hand, et al., eds. *Archives of Maryland.* Baltimore, 1883–.

Brownell, Blaine A., and David R. Goldfield, eds. *The City in Southern History: The Growth of Urban Civilization in the South.* National University Publications, Interdisciplinary Urban Series. Port Washington, N.Y., 1977.

Bruce, Philip Alexander. *Economic History of Virginia in the Seventeenth Century: An Inquiry into the Material Condition of the People.* 2 vols. New York, 1895.

Bruchey, Stuart Weems. *Robert Oliver, Merchant of Baltimore, 1783–1819.* Johns Hopkins University Studies in Historical and Political Science, 74th Ser., no. 1. Baltimore, 1956.

————. *The Roots of American Economic Growth, 1607–1861: An Essay in Social Causation.* New York, 1965.

————. "Success and Failure Factors: American Merchants in Foreign Trade in the Eighteenth and Early Nineteenth Centuries." *Business History Review,* XXXIII (1958), 272–292.

Brunner, Karl, and Allan H. Meltzer, eds. *International Organization, National Policies, and Economic Development.* Carnegie-Rochester Conference Series on Public Policy, VI. Amsterdam, 1977.

Buck, Philip W. *The Politics of Mercantilism.* New York, 1942.

Buffinton, Arthur H. "New England and the Western Fur Trade, 1629–1675." Colonial Society of Massachusetts, *Publications,* XVIII: *Transactions, 1915–1916,* 160–192. Boston, 1917.

Bullion, John L. *A Great and Necessary Measure: George Grenville and the Genesis of the Stamp Act, 1763–1765.* Columbia, Mo., 1982.

Burghardt, A. F. "A Hypothesis about Gateway Cities." Association of American Geographers, *Annals,* LXI (1971), 269–285.

Burton, E. Milby. *Charleston Furniture, 1700–1825.* Contributions from the Charleston Museum, XII. Charleston, S.C., 1955.

Bushman, Richard L. "Family Security in the Transition from Farm to City." *Journal of Family History,* VI (1981), 238–256.

————. *From Puritan to Yankee: Character and the Social Order in Connecticut, 1690–1765.* Cambridge, Mass., 1967.

Butel, Paul. *Les Caraïbes au temps des flibustiers, XVIe–XVIIe siècles.* Paris, 1982.

Butler, Ruth Lapham. *Doctor Franklin, Postmaster General.* Garden City, N.Y., 1928.

Butler, Stuart M. "The Glasgow Tobacco Merchants and the American Revolution, 1770–1800." Ph.D. thesis, University of St. Andrews, 1978.

Byers, Edward. "Fertility Transition in a New England Commercial Center: Nantucket, Massachusetts, 1680–1840." *Journal of Interdisciplinary History,* XIII (1982), 17–40.

Bywater, M[ichael] F., and B[asil] S. Yamey. *Historic Accounting Literature: A Companion Guide.* London, 1982.

Callender, Guy Stevens. "The Early Transportation and Banking Enterprises of the States in Relation to the Growth of Corporations." *Quarterly Journal of Economics,* XVII (1902), 111–162.

————. *Selections from the Economic History of the United States, 1765–1860.* Selections and Documents in Economics. Boston, 1909.

Cameron, Rondo. "England, 1750–1844." In *Banking in the Early Stages of Industrialization: A Study in Comparative Economic History,* edited by Rondo Cameron, Olga Crisp, Hugh T. Patrick, and Richard Tilly, 15–59. New York, 1967.

Cameron, Rondo, Olga Crisp, Hugh T. Patrick, and Richard Tilly, eds. *Banking in the Early Stages of Industrialization: A Study in Comparative Economic History.* New York, 1967.

Campbell, Mildred. "English Emigration on the Eve of the American Revolution." *American Historical Review,* LXI (1955), 1–20.

————. Rebuttal to David W. Galenson, "'Middling People' or 'Common Sort'? The Social Origins of Some Early Americans Reexamined." *William and Mary Quarterly,* 3d Ser., XXXV (1978), 525–540.

————. Reply to David W. Galenson, "The Social Origins of Some Early Americans: A Rejoinder." *William and Mary Quarterly,* 3d Ser., XXXVI (1979), 277–286.

————. "Social Origins of Some Early Americans." In *Seventeenth-Century America: Essays in Colonial History,* edited by James Morton Smith, 63–89. Chapel Hill, N.C., 1959.

Canabrava, A[lice] P. "A Influência do Brasil na técnica fabrico de açucar nas Antilhas francesas e inglesas no maedo do século XVII." Faculdade de Ciéncias, Económicas e Administrativas [de Universidade de São Paulo], *Anuário, 1946–1947*, 63–76.

[Canada. Bureau of Statistics. Division of Demography]. "Chronological List of Canadian Censuses." Mimeograph. Ottawa, [1934?].

Candee, Richard McAlpin. "Wooden Buildings in Early Maine and New Hampshire: A Technological and Cultural History, 1600–1720." Ph.D. diss., University of Pennsylvania, 1976.

Candey, Charles R., III. "An Entrepreneurial History of the New York Frontier, 1739–1776." Ph.D. diss., Case Western Reserve University, 1967.

Cappon, Lester J., et al., eds. *Atlas of Early American History: The Revolutionary Era, 1760–1790*. Princeton, N.J., 1976.

Cardoso, Ciro Flamairon S., and Héctor Pérez Brignoli. *Historia económica de América Latina*. 2 vols. Barcelona, 1979.

Carman, Harry J., ed. *American Husbandry* (1775). Columbia University Studies in the History of American Agriculture, VI. New York, 1939.

Carr, Lois Green. "The Development of the Maryland Orphan's Court, 1654–1715." In *Law, Society, and Politics in Early Maryland*, edited by Aubrey C. Land, Lois Green Carr, and Edward C. Papenfuse, 41–62. Baltimore, 1977.

———. "'The Metropolis of Maryland': A Comment on Town Development along the Tobacco Coast." *Maryland Historical Magazine*, LXIX (1974), 124–145.

Carr, Lois Green, and Russell R. Menard. "Immigration and Opportunity: The Freedman in Early Colonial Maryland." In *The Chesapeake in the Seventeenth Century: Essays on Anglo-American Society*, edited by Thad W. Tate and David L. Ammerman, 206–242. Chapel Hill, N.C., 1979.

Carr, Lois Green, and Lorena S. Walsh. "Changing Life Styles in Colonial St. Mary's County." Regional Economic History Research Center, *Working Papers*, I, no. 3 (1978), 72–118.

———. "Inventories and the Analysis of Wealth and Consumption Patterns in St. Mary's County, Maryland, 1658–1777." *Historical Methods*, XIII (1980), 81–104.

———. "The Planter's Wife: The Experience of White Women in Seventeenth-Century Maryland." *William and Mary Quarterly*, 3d Ser., XXXIV (1977), 542–571.

Carrier, Lyman. *The Beginnings of Agriculture in America*. New York, 1923.

Carrington, S[elwyn] H[awthorne] H[amilton]. "Economic and Political Developments in the British West Indies during the Period of the American Revolution [1770–1782]." Ph.D. thesis, University of London, 1975.

Carroll, Charles F. *The Timber Economy of Puritan New England*. Providence, R.I., 1973.

Carroll, Lewis [Charles Lutwidge Dodgson]. *Through the Looking Glass and What Alice Found There*. London, 1872.

Carson, Barbara, and Cary Carson. "Styles and Standards of Living in Southern Maryland, 1670–1752." Paper presented at the annual meeting of the Southern Historical Association, New Orleans, La., November 1977.

Carson, Cary, et al. "Impermanent Architecture in the Southern American Colonies." *Winterthur Portfolio*, XVI (1981), 135–196.

Carson, Joseph. "The Surprising Adventures of the Brigantine *Rebecca*: Incidents in the West India Trade of 1762." American Antiquarian Society, *Proceedings*, N.S., LX (1950), 267–306.

Cassedy, James H. *Demography in Early America: Beginnings of the Statistical Mind, 1600–1800*. Cambridge, Mass., 1969.

Cates, Gerald L. "'The Seasoning': Disease and Death among the First Colonists of Georgia." *Georgia Historical Quarterly*, LXIV (1980), 146–158.

Caves, Richard E. "Export-Led Growth and the New Economic History." In *Trade, Balance of Payments, and Growth: Papers in International Economics in Honor of Charles P. Kindleberger*, edited by Jagdish N. Bhagwati, Ronald W. Jones, Robert A. Mundell, and Jaroslav Vanek, 403–442. Amsterdam, 1971.

———. "'Vent for Surplus' Models of Trade and Growth." In Robert E. Baldwin *et al.*, *Trade, Growth, and the Balance of Payments: Essays in Honor of Gottfried Haberler*, 95–115. Chicago, 1965.

Caves, Richard E., and Richard H. Holton. *The Canadian Economy: Prospect and Retrospect*. Harvard Economic Studies, CXII. Cambridge, Mass., 1959.

Caves, Richard E., and Ronald W. Jones. *World Trade and Payments: An Introduction*. 3d ed. Boston, 1981.

Ceci, Lynn. "The Effect of European Contact and Trade on the Settlement Pattern of Indians in Coastal New York, 1524–1665: The Archeological and Documentary Evidence." Ph.D. diss., City University of New York, 1977.

———. "The First Fiscal Crisis in New York." *Economic Development and Cultural Change*, XXVIII (1980), 839–847.

Cederburg, Herbert Renando, Jr. *An Economic Analysis of English Settlement in North America, 1583 to 1633*. New York, 1977 (Ph.D. diss., University of California, Berkeley, 1968).

———. "Wages and Prices in Eighteenth-Century England and the Thirteen Colonies." M.A. thesis, University of California, Berkeley, 1962.

Cell, Gillian T. *English Enterprise in Newfoundland, 1577–1660*. Toronto, 1969.

Chandler, Alfred D. "The Expansion of Barbados." *Journal of the Barbados Museum and Historical Society*, XIII (1946), 106–136.

Chandler, Julian Alvin Carroll, *et al.*, eds. *The South in the Building of the Nation*. 12 vols. Richmond, Va., 1909–1913.

Chandler, M[ichael] J[ohn]. *A Guide to Records in Barbados*. Oxford, 1965.

Chapelle, Howard I. *The History of American Sailing Ships*. New York, 1935.

———. *The National Watercraft Collection*. United States National Museum, *Bulletin*, no. 219. Washington, D.C., 1960.

———. *The Search for Speed under Sail, 1700–1855*. New York, 1967.

Charbonneau, Hubert. *Vie et mort de nos ancêtres: Étude démographique*. Montreal, 1975.

Chazanof, William. "Land Speculation in Eighteenth-Century New York." In *Business Enterprise in Early New York*, edited by Joseph R. Frese and Jacob Judd, 55–76. Tarrytown, N.Y., 1979.

Chesnutt, David Rogers. "South Carolina's Expansion into Colonial Georgia, 1720–1765." Ph.D. diss., University of Georgia, 1973.

———. "South Carolina's Impact upon East Florida, 1763–1776." In *Eighteenth-Century Florida and the Revolutionary South*, edited by Samuel Proctor, 5–14. Gainesville, Fla., 1978.

———. "South Carolina's Penetration of Georgia in the 1760's: Henry Laurens as a Case Study." *South Carolina Historical Magazine*, LXXIII (1972), 194–208.

[Child, Sir Josiah]. *A Discourse about Trade*. [London], 1690.

———. *A New Discourse of Trade*. London, 1693.

Childs, St. Julien Ravenel. "The First South Carolinians." *South Carolina Historical Magazine*, LXXI (1970), 101–108.

————. *Malaria and Colonization in the Carolina Low Country, 1526–1696.* Johns Hopkins University Studies in Historical and Political Science, 58th Ser., no. 1. Baltimore, 1940.

————. "Notes on the History of Public Health in South Carolina, 1670–1800." South Carolina Historical Association, *Proceedings*, II (1932), 13–22.

Christenson, Jack Harold. "The Administration of Land Policy in Colonial New York." Ph.D. diss., State University of New York, Albany, 1976.

Clark, Andrew Hill. *Acadia: The Geography of Early Nova Scotia to 1760.* Madison, Wis., 1968.

————. "New England's Role in the Underdevelopment of Cape Breton Island during the French Regime, 1713–1758." *Canadian Geographer*, IX (1965), 1–12.

————. "Suggestions for the Geographical Study of Agricultural Change in the United States, 1790–1840." In *Farming in the New Nation: Interpreting American Agriculture, 1790–1840*, edited by Darwin P. Kelsey, 155–172. Washington, D.C., 1972.

Clark, Christopher. "Household Economy, Market Exchange, and the Rise of Capitalism in the Connecticut Valley, 1800–1860." *Journal of Social History*, XIII (1979), 169–189.

Clark, G[eorge] N[orman]. *Guide to English Commercial Statistics, 1696–1782.* Royal Historical Society, *Guides and Handbooks*, no. 1. London, 1938.

Clark, Malcolm Cameron. "The Coastwise and Caribbean Trade of the Chesapeake Bay, 1696–1776." Ph.D. diss., Georgetown University, 1970.

Clark, Peter. "Migration in England during the Late Seventeenth and Early Eighteenth Centuries." *Past and Present*, LXXXIII (1979), 57–90.

Clark, Victor S. *History of Manufactures in the United States.* Rev. ed. 3 vols. Washington, D.C., 1929.

Clarke, Hermann Frederick. *John Hull: A Builder of the Bay Colony.* Portland, Maine, 1940.

[Claypoole, James]. *James Claypoole's Letter Book, London and Philadelphia, 1681–1684.* Edited by Marion Balderston. San Marino, Calif., 1967.

Clemens, Paul Gilbert Eli. "The Agricultural Transformation of the Northern Chesapeake, 1750–1800." Paper presented at the annual meeting of the Eighteenth-Century Studies Association, Washington, D.C., April 1981.

————. *The Atlantic Economy and Colonial Maryland's Eastern Shore: From Tobacco to Grain.* Ithaca, N.Y., 1980.

————. "Economy and Society on Maryland's Eastern Shore, 1689–1733." In *Law, Society, and Politics in Early Maryland*, edited by Aubrey C. Land, Lois Green Carr, and Edward C. Papenfuse, 153–170. Baltimore, 1977.

————. "From Tobacco to Grain: Economic Development on Maryland's Eastern Shore, 1660–1750." Ph.D. diss., University of Wisconsin, 1974.

————. "The Rise of Liverpool, 1665–1750." *Economic History Review*, 2d Ser., XXIX (1976), 211–225.

Clifton, James M. "Golden Grains of White: Rice Planting on the Lower Cape Fear." *North Carolina Historical Review*, L (1973), 365–393.

————. "The Rice Industry in Colonial America." *Agricultural History*, LV (1981), 266–283.

Clowse, Converse Dilworth. "The Charleston Export Trade, 1717–1737." Ph.D. diss., Northwestern University, 1963.

————. *Economic Beginnings in Colonial South Carolina, 1670–1730.* Tricentennial Series, III. Columbia, S.C., 1971.

————. *Measuring Charleston's Overseas Commerce, 1717–1767: Statistics from the Port's Naval Lists.* Washington, D.C., 1981.

Cochran, Thomas C. *Frontiers of Change: Early Industrialism in America.* New York, 1981.

Cockburn, J[ames] S. *A History of English Assizes, 1558–1714.* Cambridge Studies in English Legal History. Cambridge, 1972.

Cockerell, H[ugh] A. L., and Edwin Green. *The British Insurance Business, 1547–1970: An Introduction and Guide to Historical Records in the United Kingdom.* London, 1976.

Coclanis, Peter A. "Rice Prices in the 1720s and the Evolution of the South Carolina Economy." *Journal of Southern History,* XLVIII (1982), 531–544.

Codignola, Luca. *Terre d'America e burocrazia romana: Simon Stock, Propaganda Fide e la colonia di Lord Baltimore a Terranova, 1624–1649.* Venice, 1982.

Cody, Cheryll Ann. "A Note on Changing Patterns of Slave Fertility in the South Carolina Rice District, 1735–1865." *Southern Studies,* XVI (1977), 457–463.

————. "Slave Demography and Family Formation: A Community Study of the Ball Family Plantations, 1720–1896." Ph.D. diss., University of Minnesota, 1982.

Coelho, Philip R. P. "The Profitability of Imperialism: The British Experience in the West Indies, 1768–1772." *Explorations in Economic History,* X (1973), 253–280.

Cohn, Raymond L., and Richard A. Jensen. "The Determinants of Slave Mortality Rates on the Middle Passage." *Explorations in Economic History,* XIX (1982), 269–282.

————. "Mortality in the Atlantic Slave Trade." *Journal of Interdisciplinary History,* XII (1982), 317–329.

Cole, Arthur Harrison. *The American Wool Manufacture.* 2 vols. Cambridge, Mass., 1926.

————. "The Tempo of Mercantile Life in Colonial America." *Business History Review,* XXXIII (1959), 277–299.

————. *Wholesale Commodity Prices in the United States, 1700–1861.* 2 vols. Cambridge, Mass., 1938.

Cole, Thomas R. "Family, Settlement, and Migration in Southeastern Massachusetts, 1650–1805: The Case for Regional Analysis." *New England Historical and Genealogical Register,* CXXXII (1978), 171–185.

Cole, W[illiam] A. "The Arithmetic of Eighteenth-Century Smuggling." *Economic History Review,* 2d Ser., XXVIII (1975), 44–49.

————. "Trends in Eighteenth-Century Smuggling." *Economic History Review,* 2d Ser., X (1958), 395–409.

Coleman, D[onald] C. "Mercantilism Revisited." *Historical Journal,* XXIII (1980), 773–791.

————, ed. *Revisions in Mercantilism.* Debates in Economic History. London, 1969.

Coleman, D[onald] C., and A[rthur] H. John, eds. *Trade, Government, and Economy in Pre-industrial England: Essays Presented to F. J. Fisher.* London, 1976.

Coleman, E[dward] M. "New England Convention, December 25, 1776, to January 2, 1777: An Illustration of Early American Particularism." *Historian,* IV (1941–1942), 43–55.

[Colman, John]. *The Distressed State of the Town of Boston, etc. Considered.* Boston, 1720.

Colthart, James M. "Robert Ellice." *Dictionary of Canadian Biography/Dictionnaire biographique du Canada,* edited by George W. Brown et al., IV, 261–262. Toronto, 1979.

Cometti, Elizabeth. "Inflation in Revolutionary Maryland." *William and Mary Quarterly*, 3d Ser., VIII (1951), 228–234.

Comitas, Lambros. *The Complete Caribbeana, 1900–1975: A Bibliographic Guide to the Scholarly Literature*. 4 vols. Millwood, N.Y., 1977.

Commons, John R. "American Shoemakers, 1648–1895: A Sketch of Industrial Evolution." *Quarterly Journal of Economics*, XXIV (1909), 39–84.

Condon, Thomas J. *New York Beginnings: The Commercial Origins of New Netherland*. New York, 1968.

Conzen, Michael P. "A Transport Interpretation of the Growth of Urban Regions: An American Example." *Journal of Historical Geography*, I (1975), 361–382.

Cook, Edward M., Jr. *The Fathers of the Towns: Leadership and Community Structure in Eighteenth-Century New England*. Johns Hopkins University Studies in Historical and Political Science, 94th Ser., no. 2. Baltimore, 1976.

———. "Geography and History: Spatial Approaches to Early American History." *Historical Methods*, XIII (1980), 19–28.

Cook, Sherburne F., and Woodrow [W.] Borah. *Essays in Population History*. 3 vols. Berkeley and Los Angeles, Calif., 1971–1979.

Cooke, Jacob E. *Tench Coxe and the Early Republic*. Chapel Hill, N.C., 1978.

Coon, David Leroy. "The Development of Market Agriculture in South Carolina, 1670–1785." Ph.D. diss., University of Illinois, Urbana-Champaign, 1972.

———. "Eliza Lucas Pinckney and the Reintroduction of Indigo Culture in South Carolina." *Journal of Southern History*, XLII (1976), 61–76.

Cooper, Thomas, and David J. McCord, eds. *The Statutes at Large of South Carolina*. 10 vols. Columbia, S.C., 1836–1841.

Cooper, Todd. "Trial and Triumph: The Impact of the Revolutionary War on the Baltimore Merchants." In *Chesapeake Bay in the American Revolution*, edited by Ernest M. Eller, 282–309. Centerville, Md., 1981.

Cott, Nancy F. *The Bonds of Womanhood: "Woman's Sphere" in New England, 1780–1835*. New Haven, Conn., 1977.

Coughlin, Magdalen. "The Entrance of the Massachusetts Merchant into the Pacific [in the 1780s]." *Southern Historical Quarterly: The Publication of the Historical Society of Southern California*, XLVIII (1966), 327–352.

Coughtry, Jay [Alan]. *The Notorious Triangle: Rhode Island and the African Slave Trade, 1700–1807*. Philadelphia, 1981.

Coulter, Calvin Brewster, Jr. "The Virginia Merchant." Ph.D. diss., Princeton University, 1944.

Countryman, Edward. "'Out of the Bounds of the Law': Northern Land Rioters in the Eighteenth Century." In *The American Revolution: Explorations in the History of American Radicalism*, edited by Alfred F. Young, 37–69. DeKalb, Ill., 1976.

Cournot, Augustin. *Recherches sur les principes mathématiques de la théorie des richesses*. Paris, 1838.

Cowell, F[rank] A[lan]. *Measuring Inequality: Techniques for the Social Sciences*. New York, 1977.

Coyle, Franklin Stuart. "Welcome Arnold (1745–1798), Providence Merchant: The Founding of an Enterprise." Ph.D. diss., Brown University, 1972.

Coyne, Franklin E. *The Development of the Cooperage Industry in the United States, 1620–1940*. Chicago, [1940].

Crane, Elaine F. "'The First Wheel of Commerce': Newport, Rhode Island, and the Slave Trade, 1760–1776." *Slavery and Abolition*, I (1980).

Crane, Verner W. *The Southern Frontier, 1670–1732.* Durham, N.C., 1928.

Craton, Michael. "Hobbesian or Panglossian? The Two Extremes of Slave Conditions in the British Caribbean, 1783 to 1834." *William and Mary Quarterly,* 3d Ser., XXXV (1978), 324–356.

———. "Jamaican Slave Mortality: Fresh Light from Worthy Park, Longville, and the Tharp Estates." *Journal of Caribbean History,* III (1971), 1–27.

———. *Sinews of Empire: A Short History of British Slavery.* Garden City, N.Y., 1974.

Craton, Michael, and James Walvin. *A Jamaican Plantation: The History of Worthy Park, 1670–1970.* Toronto, 1970.

Craton, Michael, with the assistance of Garry Greenland. *Searching for the Invisible Man: Slaves and Plantation Life in Jamaica.* Cambridge, Mass., 1978.

Craven, Avery Odelle. *Soil Exhaustion as a Factor in the Agricultural History of Virginia and Maryland, 1606–1860.* University of Illinois Studies in the Social Sciences, XIII, no. 1. Urbana, Ill., 1926.

Craven, Wesley Frank. *The Colonies in Transition, 1660–1713.* New American Nation Series. New York, 1968.

———. *Dissolution of the Virginia Company: The Failure of a Colonial Experiment.* New York, 1932.

———. *White, Red, and Black: The Seventeenth-Century Virginian.* Charlottesville, Va., 1971.

Crawford, Walter Freeman. "The Commerce of Rhode Island with the Southern Continental Colonies in the Eighteenth Century." Rhode Island Historical Society, *Collections,* XIV (1921), 99–110, 124–130.

Crawforth, Michael A. *Weighing Coins: English Folding Gold Balances of the Eighteenth and Nineteenth Centuries.* London, 1979.

Cremin, Lawrence A. *American Education: The Colonial Experience, 1607–1783.* New York, 1970.

Crittenden, Charles Christopher. *The Commerce of North Carolina, 1763–1789.* Yale Historical Publications, *Miscellany,* XXIX. New Haven, Conn., 1936.

———. "Overland Travel and Transportation in North Carolina, 1763–1789." *North Carolina Historical Review,* VIII (1931), 239–257.

———. "Ships and Shipping in North Carolina, 1763–1789." *North Carolina Historical Review,* VIII (1931), 1–13.

Crouzet, François. "Toward an Export Economy: British Exports during the Industrial Revolution." *Explorations in Economic History,* XVII (1980), 48–93.

Crowhurst, [R.] Patrick. *The Defence of British Trade, 1689–1815.* Folkestone, Kent, 1977.

Crowley, J[ohn] E. *This Sheba, Self: The Conceptualization of Economic Life in Eighteenth-Century America.* Johns Hopkins University Studies in Historical and Political Science, 92d Ser., no. 2. Baltimore, 1974.

Crowley, Terence Allan. "Government and Interests: French Colonial Administration at Louisbourg, 1713–1758." Ph.D. diss., Duke University, 1975.

Crowther, Simeon J. "The Shipbuilding Output of the Delaware Valley, 1722–1776." American Philosophical Society, *Proceedings,* CXVII (1973), 90–104.

Cullen, L[ouis] M. *Anglo-Irish Trade, 1660–1800.* Manchester, 1968.

Cummings, Abbott Lowell. *Massachusetts and Its First Period Houses: An Essay with Appendices on Architecture in Colonial Massachusetts.* Colonial Society of Massachusetts, *Publications,* LI: *Collections.* Boston, 1979.

———, ed. *Rural Household Inventories: Establishing the Names, Uses, and Furnishings of Rooms in the Colonial New England Home, 1675–1775.* Boston, 1964.

Cummins, Light Townsend. "Spanish Agents in North America during the Revolution, 1775–1779." Ph.D. diss., Tulane University, 1977.

Curtin, Philip D. "The African Diaspora." *Historical Reflections/Reflections Historique*, VI (1979), 1–17.

———. *The Atlantic Slave Trade: A Census*. Madison, Wis., 1969.

———. "Epidemiology and the Slave Trade." *Political Science Quarterly*, LXXXIII (1968), 190–216.

———. "Slavery and Empire." In *Comparative Perspectives on Slavery in New World Plantation Societies*, edited by Vera Rubin and Arthur Tuden, 3–11. New York Academy of Sciences, *Annals*, CCXCII. New York, 1977.

Cutcliffe, Stephen Hosmer. "Indians, Furs, and Empires: The Changing Policies of New York and Pennsylvania, 1674–1768." Ph.D. diss., Lehigh University, 1976.

Daigle, Jean. "'Nos amis les ennemis': Les marchands Acadiens et le Massachusetts à la fin du 17ᵉ siècle." Société Historique Acadienne, *Cahiers*, VII (1976), 161–170.

———. "Nos amis les ennemis: Relations commerciales de l'Acadie avec le Massachusetts, 1670–1711." Ph.D. diss., University of Maine, 1975.

———. "Les relations commerciales de l'Acadie avec le Massachusetts: Le cas de Charles de Saint-Étienne de la Tour, 1695–1697." *Revue de l'Université de Moncton*, IX (1976), 53–61.

Daniels, Bruce C. *The Connecticut Town: Growth and Development, 1635–1790*. Middletown, Conn., 1979.

———. "Economic Development in Colonial and Revolutionary Connecticut: An Overview." *William and Mary Quarterly*, 3d Ser., XXXVII (1980), 429–450.

———. "Long Range Trends of Wealth Distribution in Eighteenth Century New England." *Explorations in Economic History*, XI (1973), 123–135.

———. "The Political Structure of Local Government in Colonial Connecticut." In *Town and Country: Essays on the Structure of Local Government in the American Colonies*, edited by Bruce C. Daniels, 44–71. Middletown, Conn., 1978.

———. "Probate Court Inventories and Colonial American History: Historiography, Problems, and Results." *Histoire Sociale/Social History*, IX (1976), 387–405.

———, ed. *Town and Country: Essays on the Structure of Local Government in the American Colonies*. Middletown, Conn., 1978.

Darity, William A., Jr. "A General Equilibrium Model of the Eighteenth-Century Atlantic Slave Trade: A Least-Likely Test for the Caribbean School." *Research in Economic History*, VII (1982), 287–326.

Dauer, David E. "Colonial Philadelphia's Intraregional Transportation System: An Overview." Regional Economic History Research Center, *Working Papers*, II, no. 3 (1979), 1–16.

David, Paul A. "Comment." *Journal of Economic History*, XXXIX (1979), 303–309.

———. "The Growth of Real Product in the United States before 1840: New Evidence, Controlled Conjectures." *Journal of Economic History*, XXVII (1967), 151–195.

———. "Invention and Accumulation in America's Economic Growth: A Nineteenth-Century Parable." In *International Organization, National Policies, and Economic Development*, edited by Karl Brunner and Allan H. Meltzer, 179–228. Amsterdam, 1977.

———. "New Light on a Statistical Dark Age: U.S. Real Product Growth before 1840." *American Economic Review*, LVII (1967), 294–306.

———. "Technical Appendices to U.S. Real Product Growth before 1840: New Evidence, Controlled Conjectures." Research Center in Economic Growth, Stanford University, Memorandum no. 53-A (1966). Mimeograph.

Davies, Glanville James. "England and Newfoundland, Policy and Trade, 1660–1783." Ph.D. thesis, University of Southampton, 1980.

Davies, K[enneth] G., *The North Atlantic World in the Seventeenth Century*. Minneapolis, Minn., 1974.

———. "The Origins of the Commission System in the West India Trade." Royal Historical Society, *Transactions*, 5th Ser., II (1952), 89–107.

———. *The Royal African Company*. London, 1957.

———, ed. *Documents of the American Revolution, 1770–1783 (Colonial Office Series)*. 21 vols. Shannon and Kill-o'-the-Grange, Ireland, 1972–1981.

Davis, David Brion. *The Problem of Slavery in the Age of Revolution, 1770–1823*. Ithaca, N.Y., 1975.

Davis, Kingsley. "The Urbanization of the Human Population." *Scientific American*, CCXIII (Sept. 1965), 41–53.

Davis, Lance E. "'And It Will Never Be Literature'—The New Economic History: A Critique." *Explorations in Entrepreneurial History*, 2d Ser., VI (1968), 75–92.

Davis, Lance E., Richard A. Easterlin, and William N. Parker, eds. *American Economic Growth: An Economist's History of the United States*. New York, 1972.

Davis, Ralph. *A Commercial Revolution: English Overseas Trade in the Seventeenth and Eighteenth Centuries*. Historical Association Pamphlets, General Ser., no. 64. [London], 1967.

———. "English Foreign Trade, 1660–1700." *Economic History Review*, 2d Ser., VII (1954), 150–166.

———. "English Foreign Trade, 1700–1774." *Economic History Review*, 2d Ser., XV (1962), 285–303.

———. "The European Background." In *Encyclopedia of American Economic History: Studies of the Principal Movements and Ideas*, edited by Glenn Porter, I, 19–33. New York, 1980.

———. *The Industrial Revolution and British Overseas Trade*. Leicester, 1979.

———. *The Rise of the Atlantic Economies*. London, 1973.

———. *The Rise of the English Shipping Industry in the Seventeenth and Eighteenth Centuries*. London, 1962.

———. "Untapped Sources and Research Opportunities in the Field of American Maritime History from the Beginning to about 1815." In *Untapped Sources and Research Opportunities in the Field of American Maritime History: A Symposium*, 11–26. Mystic, Conn., 1967.

Davis, Thomas Joseph. "Slavery in Colonial New York City." Ph.D. diss., Columbia University, 1974.

Davisson, William I., and Lawrence J. Bradley. "New York Maritime Trade: Ship Voyage Patterns, 1715–1765." *New-York Historical Society Quarterly*, LV (1971), 309–317.

Davisson, William I., and Dennis J. Dugan. "Commerce in Seventeenth-Century Essex County, Massachusetts." Essex Institute, *Historical Collections*, CVII (1971), 113–142.

Dawley, Alan. *Class and Community: The Industrial Revolution in Lynn*. Cambridge, Mass., 1976.

Deane, Phyllis, and W[illiam] A. Cole. *British Economic Growth, 1688–1959: Trends and Structure*. 2d ed. University of Cambridge Department of Applied Economics Monographs, VIII. Cambridge, 1967.

Deane, Samuel. *The New-England Farmer; or, Georgical Dictionary. . . .* Worcester, Mass., 1790.

Debien, Gabriel. "Les engagés pour les Antilles (1634–1715)." *Revue d'Histoire des Colonies*, XXXVIII (1951), 5–274.

————. "Les engagés pour le Canada partis de Nantes (1725–1732)." *Revue d'Histoire de l'Amérique Française*, XXXIII (1980), 583–586.

————. *Plantations et esclaves à Saint-Domingue*. Dakar, Senegal, 1962.

Decker, Robert Owen. "The New London Merchants, 1645–1909: The Rise and Decline of a Connecticut Port." Ph.D. diss., University of Connecticut, 1970.

Deerr, Noel. *The History of Sugar*. 2 vols. London, 1949–1950.

Demos, John. "Families in Colonial Bristol, Rhode Island: An Exercise in Historical Demography." *William and Mary Quarterly*, 3d Ser., XXV (1968), 40–57.

————. *A Little Commonwealth: Family Life in Plymouth Colony*. New York, 1970.

Deneven, William M., ed. *The Native Population of the Americas in 1492*. Madison, Wis., 1976.

De Roover, R[aymond] A. "The Organization of Trade." In *Economic Organization and Policies in the Middle Ages*. Vol. III of *The Cambridge Economic History of Europe*, edited by M. M. Postan, E. E. Rich, and Edward Miller, 42–118. Cambridge, 1963.

Destler, Chester McArthur. "The Gentleman Farmer and the New Agriculture: Jeremiah Wadsworth." *Agricultural History*, XLVI (1972), 135–153.

Dethlefsen, Edwin S. "Colonial Gravestones and Demography." *American Journal of Physical Anthropology*, N.S., XXXI (1969), 321–333.

Dethloff, Henry C. "The Colonial Rice Trade." *Agricultural History*, LVI (1982), 231–243.

Devèze, Michel. *Antilles, Guyanes, la mer des Caraïbes de 1492 à 1789*. Paris, 1977.

Devine, T[homas] M. "The Colonial Trades and Industrial Investment in Scotland, c. 1700–1815." *Economic History Review*, 2d Ser., XXIX (1976), 1–13.

————. *The Tobacco Lords: A Study of the Tobacco Merchants of Glasgow and Their Trading Activities, c. 1740–90*. Edinburgh, 1975.

De Vries, Jan. "Peasant Demand Patterns and Economic Development: Friesland, 1550–1750." In *European Peasants and Their Markets: Essays in Agrarian Economic History*, ed. William N. Parker and Eric L. Jones, 205–268. Princeton, N.J., 1975.

Dexter, Franklin B. "Estimates of Population in the American Colonies." American Antiquarian Society, *Proceedings*, N.S., V (1887), 22–50.

Dickerson, Oliver M. Letter to the Editor. *William and Mary Quarterly*, 3d Ser., VI (1949), 351–355.

————. "Navigation Acts." In *Dictionary of American History*, [edited by James Truslow Adams], V, 15–17. [3d] ed., rev. New York, 1976.

————. *The Navigation Acts and the American Revolution*. Philadelphia, 1951.

Dickson, R. J. *Ulster Emigration to Colonial America, 1718–1775*. Ulster-Scot Historical Series, no. 1. London, 1966.

Diffenderffer, Frank Ried. *The German Immigration into Pennsylvania through the Port of Philadelphia, 1700 to 1775*. Lancaster, Pa., 1900.

[Dixon, J. T.]. "The Problem of Imperial Communications during the Eighteenth Century, with Special Reference to the Post Office." M.A. thesis, University of Leeds, 1964.

Doar, David. *Rice and Rice Planting in the South Carolina Low Country*. Contributions from the Charleston Museum, VIII. Charleston, S.C., 1936.

Dobyns, Henry F. *Native American Historical Demography: A Critical Bibliography*. The Newberry Library Center for the History of the American Indian Bibliographical Series. Bloomington, Ind., 1976.

Dodge, Stanley D. "The Geography of the Codfishing Industry in Colonial New England." Geographical Society of Philadelphia, *Bulletin*, XXV (1927), 43–50.

Doerflinger, Thomas Main. "Enterprise on the Delaware: Merchants and Economic Development in Philadelphia, 1750–1791." Ph.D. diss., Harvard University, 1980.

402 *Bibliography*

Domar, Evsey D. "The Causes of Slavery or Serfdom: A Hypothesis." *Journal of Economic History*, XXX (1970), 18–32.

Donnan, Elizabeth, ed. *Documents Illustrative of the History of the Slave Trade to America*. 4 vols. Carnegie Institution of Washington Publication no. 409. Washington, D.C., 1930–1935.

———. "The Slave Trade into South Carolina before the Revolution." *American Historical Review*, XXXIII (1928), 804–828.

Dorfman, Joseph. *The Economic Mind in American Civilization, 1606–1933*. 3 vols. New York, 1946–1959.

Dorsey, Rhoda M. "The Pattern of Baltimore Commerce during the Confederation Period." *Maryland Historical Magazine*, LXII (1967), 119–134.

Douglas, David C., ed. *English Historical Documents*. London, 1953–.

Dowd, Mary Jane. "The State in the Maryland Economy, 1776–1807." *Maryland Historical Magazine*, LVII (1962), 90–132, 229–258.

Drake, Milton, comp. *Almanacs of the United States*. 2 vols. New York, 1962.

Drescher, Seymour. "Le 'déclin' du système esclavagiste britannique et l'abolition de la traite." Translated by C. Carlier. *Annales: Économies, Sociétés, Civilisations*, XXXI (1976), 414–435.

———. *Econocide: British Slavery in the Era of Abolition*. Pittsburgh, Pa., 1977.

Dructor, Robert Michael. "The New York Commercial Community: The Revolutionary Experience." Ph.D. diss., University of Pittsburgh, 1975.

Dudley, William S. "Maryland at War on the Chesapeake, 1776–1783." Paper presented to the Washington Area Seminar in Early American History, College Park, Md., October 1980.

Duffy, John. "Eighteenth-Century Carolina Health Conditions." *Journal of Southern History*, XVIII (1952), 289–302.

———. *Epidemics in Colonial America*. Baton Rouge, La., 1953.

———. "The Passage to the Colonies." *Mississippi Valley Historical Review*, XXXVIII (1951), 21–38.

———. "Yellow Fever in Colonial Charleston." *South Carolina Historical Magazine*, LII (1951), 189–197.

Dulles, Foster Rhea. *The Old China Trade*. Boston, 1930.

Dunaway, Wayland Fuller. "Pennsylvania as an Early Distributing Center of Population." *Pennsylvania Magazine of History and Biography*, LV (1931), 134–169.

Duncan, John Donald. "Servitude and Slavery in Colonial South Carolina, 1670–1776." Ph.D. diss., Emory University, 1972.

Duncan, T[homas] Bentley. *Atlantic Islands: Madeira, the Azores, and the Cape Verdes in Seventeenth-Century Commerce and Navigation*. Studies in the History of Discoveries. Chicago, 1972.

Dunn, Richard S. "The Barbados Census of 1680: Profile of the Richest Colony in English America." *William and Mary Quarterly*, 3d Ser., XXVI (1969), 3–30.

———. "The English Sugar Islands and the Founding of South Carolina." *South Carolina Historical Magazine*, LXXII (1971), 81–93.

———. Review of *English America and the Restoration Monarchy of Charles II: Transatlantic Politics, Commerce, and Kinship*, by J. M. Sosin. *American Historical Review*, LXXXVII (1982), 1150–1151.

———. *Sugar and Slaves: The Rise of the Planter Class in the English West Indies, 1624–1713*. Chapel Hill, N.C., 1972.

———. "A Tale of Two Plantations: Slave Life at Mesopotamia in Jamaica and Mount

Airy in Virginia, 1799 to 1828." *William and Mary Quarterly*, 3d Ser., XXXIV (1977), 32–65.

Dunn, Walter Scott, Jr. "Western Commerce, 1760–1774." Ph.D. diss., University of Wisconsin, 1971.

Duvall, Rezin Fenton. "Philadelphia's Maritime Commerce with the British Empire, 1783–1789." Ph.D. diss., University of Pennsylvania, 1960.

Dyke, Bennett, and Warren T. Morrill, eds. *Genealogical Demography*. New York, 1980.

Earle, Carville V. "Environment, Disease, and Mortality in Early Virginia." In *The Chesapeake in the Seventeenth Century: Essays on Anglo-American Society*, edited by Thad W. Tate and David L. Ammerman, 96–125. Chapel Hill, N.C., 1979.

———. *The Evolution of a Tidewater Settlement System: All Hallow's Parish, Maryland, 1650–1783*. University of Chicago Department of Geography Research Paper no. 170. Chicago, 1975.

———. "The First English Towns of North America." *Geographical Review*, LXVII (1977), 34–50.

———. "A Geographer's Observation of an Economist's Pursuit of 'Exact History.'" *Annals of Scholarship: Metastudies of the Humanities and Social Sciences*, I (1980), 107–117.

———. "A Staple Interpretation of Slavery and Free Labor." *Geographical Review*, LXVIII (1978), 51–65.

Earle, Carville V., and Ronald Hoffman. "The Foundation of the Modern Economy: Agriculture and the Costs of Labor in the United States and England, 1800–60." *American Historical Review*, LXXXV (1980), 1055–1094.

———. "Staple Crops and Urban Development in the Eighteenth-Century South." *Perspectives in American History*, X (1976), 5–78.

———. "The Urban South: The First Two Centuries." In *The City in Southern History: The Growth of Urban Civilization in the South*, edited by Blaine A. Brownell and David R. Goldfield, 23–51. National University Publications, Interdisciplinary Urban Series. Port Washington, N.Y., 1977.

East, Robert A. *Business Enterprise in the American Revolutionary Era*. Columbia University Studies in History, Economics and Public Law, no. 439. New York, 1938.

———. "The Business Entrepreneur in a Changing Colonial Economy, 1763–1795." *Journal of Economic History*, VI (Supplement, 1946), 16–27.

Easterbrook, W. T., and Hugh G. J. Aitken. *Canadian Economic History*. Toronto, 1956.

Easterlin, Richard A. "Factors in the Decline of Farm Family Fertility in the United States: Some Preliminary Research Results." *Journal of American History*, LXIII (1976), 600–614.

———. "Why Isn't the Whole World Developed?" *Journal of Economic History*, XLI (1981), 1–19.

Edel, Matthew. "The Brazilian Sugar Cycle of the Seventeenth Century and the Rise of West Indian Competition." *Caribbean Studies*, IX (1969), 24–44.

Edwards, Everett E. *A Bibliography of the History of Agriculture in the United States*. U.S. Department of Agriculture Miscellaneous Publication no. 84. Washington, D.C., 1930.

———. *References on American Colonial Agriculture*. U.S. Department of Agriculture Library Bibliographical Contributions, no. 33. Washington, D.C., 1938.

Egnal, Marc Matthew. "The Changing Structure of Philadelphia's Trade with the British West Indies, 1750–1775." *Pennsylvania Magazine of History and Biography*, XCIX (1975), 156–179.

———. "The Economic Development of the Thirteen Continental Colonies, 1720 to

1775." *William and Mary Quarterly*, 3d Ser., XXXII (1975), 191–222.

———. "The Origins of the Revolution in Virginia: A Reinterpretation." *William and Mary Quarterly*, 3d Ser., XXXVII (1980), 401–428.

———. "The Pattern of Factional Development in New York, Pennsylvania, and Massachusetts, 1682–1776." In *Parties and Political Opposition in Revolutionary America*, edited by Patricia U. Bonomi, 43–60. Tarrytown, N.Y., 1980.

———. "The Pennsylvania Economy, 1748–1762: An Analysis of Short-Run Changes in the Atlantic Trading Community." Ph.D. diss., University of Wisconsin, 1974.

———. "The Politics of Ambition: A New Look at Benjamin Franklin's Career." *Canadian Review of American Studies*, VI (1975), 151–164.

———. Reply to John R. Hanson II, "The Economic Development of the Thirteen Continental Colonies, 1720–1775: A Critique." *William and Mary Quarterly*, 3d Ser., XXXVII (1980), 172–175.

———. "Lo sviluppo economico delle tredici colonie americane, 1720–1775." [Translated by Gabriella Feruggia]. In *La rivoluzione americana*, edited by Tiziano Bonazzi, 97–118. Bologna, 1977.

Egnal, Marc Matthew, and Joseph A. Ernst. "An Economic Interpretation of the American Revolution." *William and Mary Quarterly*, 3d Ser., XXIX (1972), 3–32.

———. "Un'interpretazione economica della rivoluzione americana." [Translated by Gabriella Feruggia]. In *La rivoluzione americana*, edited by Tiziano Bonazzi, 221–237. Bologna, 1977.

Ehrlich, Jessica Kross. "A Town Study in Colonial New York: Newtown, Queens County (1642–1790)." Ph.D. diss., University of Michigan, 1974.

Eisner, Gisela. *Jamaica, 1830–1930: A Study in Economic Growth*. Manchester, 1961.

Eisterhold, John Anthony. "Lumber and Trade in the Seaboard Cities of the Old South: 1607–1860." Ph.D. diss., University of Mississippi, 1970.

Ekirch, A[rthur] Roger. *"Poor Carolina": Politics and Society in Colonial North Carolina, 1729–1776*. Chapel Hill, N.C., 1981.

Eliot, Jared. *Essays upon Field Husbandry in New England, and Other Papers, 1748–1762*. Edited by Harry J. Carman and Rexford G. Tugwell. Columbia University Studies in the History of American Agriculture. New York, 1934.

Elkington, George. *The Coopers: Company and Craft*. London, [1933].

Eller, Ernest M[cNeill], ed. *Chesapeake Bay in the American Revolution*. Centerville, Md., 1981.

Ellsworth, Lucius F. "The Philadelphia Society for the Promotion of Agriculture and Agricultural Reform, 1785–1793." *Agricultural History*, XLII (1968), 189–199.

Eltis, David, and James Walvin, eds. *The Abolition of the Atlantic Slave Trade: Origins and Effects in Europe, Africa, and the Americas*. Madison, Wis., 1981.

Engelbourg, Saul. "Guy Stevens Callender: A Founding Father of American Economic History." *Explorations in Economic History*, IX (1972), 255–267.

Engerman, Stanley L. "The Development of Plantation Systems and Slave Societies: A Commentary—I." In *Comparative Perspectives on Slavery in New World Plantation Societies*, edited by Vera Rubin and Arthur Tuden, 63–67. New York Academy of Sciences, *Annals*, CCXCII. New York, 1977.

———. "Douglass C. North's *The Economic Growth of the United States, 1790–1860* Revisited." *Social Science History*, I (1977), 248–257.

———. "Economic Adjustments to Emancipation in the United States and British West Indies." *Journal of Interdisciplinary History*, XIII (1982), 191–220.

———. "Notes on Patterns of Economic Growth in the British North American Colonies in the Seventeenth, Eighteenth, and Nineteenth Centuries." In *Disparities in Economic Development since the Industrial Revolution*, edited by Paul Bairoch and Maurice Lévy-Leboyer, 46–57. New York, 1980.

———. "The Realities of Slavery: A Review of Recent Evidence." *International Journal of Comparative Sociology*, XX (1979), 46–66.

———. "A Reconsideration of Southern Economic Growth, 1770–1860." *Agricultural History*, XLIX (1975), 343–361.

———. "The Slave Trade and British Capital Formation in the Eighteenth Century: A Comment on the Williams Thesis." *Business History Review*, XLVI (1972), 430–443.

———. "Some Considerations Relating to Property Rights in Man." *Journal of Economic History*, XXXIII (1973), 43–65.

———. "Some Economic and Demographic Comparisons of Slavery in the United States and the British West Indies." *Economic History Review*, 2d Ser., XXIX (1976), 258–275.

Engerman, Stanley L., and Robert E. Gallman. "U.S. Economic Growth, 1783–1860." *Research in Economic History*, VIII (1983), 1–46.

Engerman, Stanley L., and Eugene D. Genovese, eds. *Race and Slavery in the Western Hemisphere: Quantitative Studies*. Princeton, N.J., 1975.

Ernst, Joseph Albert. *Money and Politics in America, 1755–1775: A Study in the Currency Act of 1764 and the Political Economy of Revolution*. Chapel Hill, N.C., 1973.

Ernst, Joseph Albert, and H. Roy Merrens. "'Camden's Turrets Pierce the Skies!' The Urban Process in the Southern Colonies during the Eighteenth Century." *William and Mary Quarterly*, 3d Ser., XXX (1973), 549–574.

Essays in Colonial History Presented to Charles McLean Andrews by His Students. New Haven, Conn., 1931.

Evans, Emory G. "Planter Indebtedness and the Coming of the Revolution in Virginia." *William and Mary Quarterly*, 3d Ser., XIX (1962), 511–533.

———. "Private Indebtedness and the Revolution in Virginia, 1776 to 1796." *William and Mary Quarterly*, 3d Ser., XXVIII (1971), 349–374.

Faibisy, John Dewar. "Privateering and Piracy: The Effects of New England Raiding upon Nova Scotia during the American Revolution, 1775–1783." Ph.D. diss., University of Massachusetts, 1972.

Fairchild, Byron. *Messrs. William Pepperrell: Merchants at Piscataqua*. Ithaca, N.Y., 1954.

Faler, Paul G. *Mechanics and Manufacturers in the Early Industrial Revolution: Lynn, Massachusetts, 1780–1860*. Albany, N.Y., 1981.

Farnell, J. E. "The Navigation Act of 1651, the First Dutch War, and the London Merchant Community." *Economic History Review*, 2d Ser., XVI (1964), 439–454.

Farnie, D. A. "The Commercial Empire of the Atlantic, 1607–1783." *Economic History Review*, 2d Ser., XV (1962), 205–218.

Fei, John C. H., and Gustav Ranis. "Economic Development in Historical Perspective." *American Economic Review*, LIX (1969), 386–426.

Felt, Joseph B. "Statistics of Population in Massachusetts." American Statistical Association, *Collections*, I (1847), 121–216.

Fennell, Dorothy Elaine. "From Rebelliousness to Insurrection: Class, Culture, and Ideology in Western Pennsylvania, 1765–1802." Ph.D. diss., University of Pittsburgh, 1981.

Ferguson, E[lmer] James. "Currency Finance: An Interpretation of Colonial Monetary Practices." *William and Mary Quarterly*, 3d Ser., X (1953), 153–180.

———. *The Power of the Purse: A History of American Public Finance, 1776–1790.* Chapel Hill, N.C., 1961.

———, comp. *Confederation, Constitution, and Early National Period, 1781–1815.* Goldentree Bibliographies in American History. Northbrook, Ill., 1975.

Ferguson, Eugene S. *Oliver Evans: Inventive Genius of the American Industrial Revolution.* Greenville, Del., 1980.

Fischer, David Hackett. "Chronic Inflation: The Long View." *Journal of the Institute for Socioeconomic Studies,* V (1980), 82–103.

Fish, Stuyvesant. *The New York Privateers, 1756–1763: King George's Private Ships of War Which Cruized against the King's Enemies.* New York, 1945.

Fisher, F[rederick] J. "London's Export Trade in the Early Seventeenth Century." *Economic History Review,* 2d Ser., III (1950), 151–161.

Fisher, H[arold] E. S. *The Portugal Trade: A Study of Anglo-Portuguese Commerce, 1700–1770.* London, 1971.

Fisher, Irving. *The Making of Index Numbers: A Study of Their Varieties, Tests, and Reliability.* 3d ed., rev. Boston, 1927.

Fisher, Willard C. "The Tabular Standard in Massachusetts History." *Quarterly Journal of Economics,* XXVII (1913), 417–454.

Flannagan, John H., Jr. "Trying Times: Economic Depression in New Hampshire, 1781–1789." Ph.D. diss., Georgetown University, 1972.

Flegal, Fred Gerard. "Silas Deane: Revolutionary or Profiteer?" M.A. thesis, Western Michigan University, 1976.

Fleisig, Heywood. "Slavery, the Supply of Agricultural Labor, and the Industrialization of the South." *Journal of Economic History,* XXXVI (1976), 572–597.

Fleming, R. H[arvey]. "Phyn, Ellice and Company of Schenectady." *Contributions to Canadian Economics,* IV (1932), 7–41.

Fletcher, Stevenson Whitcomb. *Pennsylvania Agriculture and Country Life, 1640–1840.* Harrisburg, Pa., 1950.

Flick, Alexander C., ed. *History of the State of New York.* 10 vols. New York, 1933–1937.

Floud, Roderick [C.], and Donald [N.] McCloskey, eds. *The Economic History of Britain since 1700.* 2 vols. Cambridge, 1981.

Fogel, Robert William. "The Specification Problem in Economic History." *Journal of Economic History,* XXVII (1967), 283–308.

Fogel, Robert William, and Stanley L. Engerman. "Recent Findings in the Study of Slave Demography and Family Structure." *Sociology and Social Research,* LXIII (1979), 566–589.

———. *Time on the Cross: The Economics of American Negro Slavery.* 2 vols. Boston, 1974.

———, eds. *The Reinterpretation of American Economic History.* New York, 1971.

Fogel, Robert William, James Trussell, Roderick [C.] Floud, Clayne L. Pope, and Larry T. Wimmer. "The Economics of Mortality in North America, 1650–1910: A Description of a Research Project." *Historical Methods,* XI (1978), 75–108.

[Fohlen, Claude, and Jacques Godechot, eds.]. *La révolution américaine et l'Europe.* Colloques Internationaux du Centre National de la Recherche Scientifique, no. 577. Paris, 1979.

Fonda, Douglass C., Jr. *Eighteenth Century Nantucket Whaling, as Compiled from the Original Logs and Journals of the Nantucket Atheneum and the Nantucket Whaling Museum.* Nantucket, Mass., 1969.

Forsyth, David P. *The Business Press in America, 1750–1865.* Philadelphia, 1964.

Fortune, Stephen Alexander. "Merchants and Jews: The Economic and Social Relationships between the English Merchants and Jews in the British West Indian Colonies, 1650–1740." Ph.D. diss., University of California, San Diego, 1976.

Fowler, William M., Jr. "The Business of War: Boston as a Navy Base, 1776–1783." *American Neptune*, XLII (1982), 25–35.

Fowler, William M., Jr., and Wallace Coyle, eds. *The American Revolution: Changing Perspectives*. Boston, 1979.

Frank, Andre Gunder. *Dependent Accumulation and Underdevelopment*. London, 1978.

———. *World Accumulation, 1492–1789*. London, 1978.

[Franklin, Benjamin]. *The Papers of Benjamin Franklin*. Edited by Leonard W. Labaree *et al*. New Haven, Conn., 1959–.

Freidel, Frank, ed. *Harvard Guide to American History*. Rev. ed. 2 vols. Cambridge, Mass., 1974.

Frese, Joseph R., and Jacob Judd, eds. *Business Enterprise in Early New York*. Tarrytown, N.Y., 1979.

Friedlander, Amy Ellen. "Carolina Huguenots: A Study in Cultural Pluralism in the Low Country, 1679–1768." Ph.D. diss., Emory University, 1979.

Friedmann, Karen J. "Victualling Colonial Boston." *Agricultural History*, XLVII (1973), 189–205.

Fries, Adelaide L. "North Carolina Certificates of the Revolutionary War Period." *North Carolina Historical Review*, IX (1932), 229–241.

Friis, Herman R. *A Series of Population Maps of the Colonies and the United States, 1625–1790*. American Geographical Society, Mimeographed Publication no. 3. Revised. New York, 1968.

Fuhlbruegge, Edward A. "New Jersey Finances during the American Revolution." New Jersey Historical Society, *Proceedings*, N.S., LV (1937), 167–190.

Funk, W[arren] C. *Value to Farm Families of Food, Fuel, and Use of House*. U.S. Department of Agriculture Bulletin no. 410. Washington, D.C., 1916.

Galenson, David Walter. "The Atlantic Slave Trade and the Barbados Market, 1673–1723." *Journal of Economic History*, XLII (1982), 491–511.

———. "British Servants and the Colonial Indenture System in the Eighteenth Century." *Journal of Southern History*, XLIV (1978), 41–66.

———. "Immigration and the Colonial Labor System: An Analysis of the Length of Indenture." *Explorations in Economic History*, XIV (1977), 360–377.

———. "The Indenture System and the Colonial Labor Market: An Economic History of White Servitude in British America." Ph.D. diss., Harvard University, 1979.

———. "Literacy and the Social Origins of Some Early Americans." *Historical Journal*, XXII (1979), 75–91.

———. "Measuring Colonial Wealth." *Reviews in American History*, IX (1981), 49–54.

———. "'Middling People' or 'Common Sort'? The Social Origins of Some Early Americans Reexamined." *William and Mary Quarterly*, 3d Ser., XXXV (1978), 499–524.

———. "The Slave Trade to the English West Indies, 1673–1724." *Economic History Review*, 2d Ser., XXXII (1979), 241–249.

———. "The Social Origins of Some Early Americans: Rejoinder." *William and Mary Quarterly*, 3d Ser., XXXVI (1979), 264–277.

———. "White Servitude and the Growth of Black Slavery in Colonial America." *Journal of Economic History*, LXI (1981), 39–47.

———. *White Servitude in Colonial America: An Economic Analysis*. Cambridge, 1981.

Galenson, David Walter, and Russell R. Menard. "Approaches to the Analysis of Economic Growth in Colonial British America." *Historical Methods*, XIII (1980), 3–18.

Gallman, James M. "Determinants of Age at Marriage in Colonial Perquimans County,

North Carolina." *William and Mary Quarterly*, 3d Ser., XXXIX (1982), 176–191.

———. "Mortality among White Males: Colonial North Carolina." *Social Science History*, IV (1980), 295–316.

Gallman, Robert E. "The Agricultural Sector and the Pace of Economic Growth: U.S. Experience in the Nineteenth Century." In *Essays in Nineteenth Century Economic History: The Old Northwest*, edited by David C. Klingaman and Richard K. Vedder, 35–76. Athens, Ohio, 1975.

———. "Changes in Total U.S. Agricultural Factor Productivity in the Nineteenth Century." *Agricultural History*, XLVI (1972), 191–210.

———. "Comment." *Journal of Economic History*, XXXIX (1979), 311–312.

———. *Developing the American Colonies, 1607–1783*. Economic Forces in American History. Chicago, 1964.

———. "Influences on the Distribution of Landholdings in Early Colonial North Carolina." *Journal of Economic History*, XLII (1982), 549–575.

———. "The Pace and Pattern of American Economic Growth." In *American Economic Growth: An Economist's History of the United States*, edited by Lance E. Davis, Richard A. Easterlin, and William N. Parker, 15–60. New York, 1972.

———. "Slavery and Southern Economic Growth." *Southern Economic Journal*, XLV (1979), 1007–1022.

———. "The Statistical Approach: Fundamental Concepts as Applied to History." In *Approaches to American Economic History*, edited by George Rogers Taylor and Lucius F. Ellsworth, 63–86. Charlottesville, Va., 1971.

Garitee, Jerome R. *The Republic's Private Navy: The American Privateering Business as Practiced by Baltimore during the War of 1812*. Middletown, Conn., 1977.

Gates, Paul Wallace. "The Role of the Land Speculator in Western Development." *Pennsylvania Magazine of History and Biography*, LXVI (1942), 314–333.

Gay, Edwin F., ed. "Letters from a Sugar Plantation in Nevis, 1723–1732." *Journal of Economic and Business History*, I (1928), 149–173.

Gayle, Charles Joseph. "The Nature and Volume of Exports from Charleston, 1724–1774." South Carolina Historical Association, *Proceedings*, VII (1937), 25–33.

Geib, George Winthrop. "A History of Philadelphia, 1776–1789." Ph.D. diss., University of Wisconsin, 1969.

Geiser, Karl Frederick. *Redemptioners and Indentured Servants in the Colony and Commonwealth of Pennsylvania*. New Haven, Conn., [1901].

Gemery, Henry A. "Emigration from the British Isles to the New World, 1630–1700: Inferences from Colonial Populations." *Research in Economic History*, V (1980), 179–231.

Gemery, Henry A., and Jan S. Hogendorn. "The Atlantic Slave Trade: A Tentative Economic Model." *Journal of African History*, XV (1974), 223–246.

———. "Elasticity of Slave Labor Supply and the Development of Slave Economies in the British Caribbean: The Seventeenth Century Experience." In *Comparative Perspectives on Slavery in New World Plantation Societies*, edited by Vera Rubin and Arthur Tuden, 72–83. New York Academy of Sciences, *Annals*, CCXCII. New York, 1977.

———, eds. *The Uncommon Market: Essays in the Economic History of the Atlantic Slave Trade*. Studies in Social Discontinuity. New York, 1979.

Genovese, Eugene D., and Elizabeth Fox-Genovese. "The Slave Economies in Political Perspective." *Journal of American History*, LXVI (1979), 7–23.

Gephart, Ronald M., comp. *Revolutionary America, 1763–1789: A Bibliography*. 2 vols. Washington, D.C., 1984.

Gibson, James R., ed. *European Settlement and Development in North America: Essays* on *Geographical Change in Honour and Memory of Andrew Hill Clark*. Toronto, 1978.

Giddens, Paul H. "Trade and Industry in Colonial Maryland, 1753–1769." *Journal of Economic and Business History*, IV (1932), 512–538.

Gilbert, Geoffrey Neal. "Baltimore's Flour Trade to the Caribbean, 1750–1815." Ph.D. diss., Johns Hopkins University, 1975.

———. "The Role of Breadstuffs in American Trade, 1770–1790." *Explorations in Economic History*, XIV (1977), 378–387.

Gilchrist, David T., ed. *The Growth of the Seaport Cities, 1790–1825: Proceedings of a Conference Sponsored by the Eleutherian Mills–Hagley Foundation, March 17–19, 1966*. Charlottesville, Va., 1967.

Gildrie, Richard P. *Salem, Massachusetts, 1626–1683: A Covenant Community*. Charlottesville, Va., 1975.

Gill, Harold B., Jr. "Cereal Grains in Colonial Virginia." Research report, Colonial Williamsburg Foundation, Inc., 1974.

———. "Wheat Culture in Colonial Virginia." *Agricultural History*, LII (1978), 380–393.

Gill, Harold B., Jr., and George M. Curtis III. "Virginia's Colonial Probate Policies and the Preconditions for Economic History." *Virginia Magazine of History and Biography*, LXXXVII (1979), 68–73.

Gille, Bertrand. *Les sources statistiques de l'histoire de France des enquêtes du XVIIᵉ siècle à 1870*. Travaux de Droit, d'Économie, de Sociologie et de Sciences Politiques, no. 122. 2d ed. Geneva, 1980.

Gillingham, Harrold E. *Marine Insurance in Philadelphia, 1721–1800: With a List of Brokers and Underwriters as Shown by Old Policies and Books of Record. . . .* Philadelphia, 1933.

Ginzberg, Eli. "The Mechanization of Work." *Scientific American*, CCXLVII (Sept. 1982), 66–75.

Gipson, Lawrence Henry. *The British Empire before the American Revolution*. 15 vols. Caldwell, Idaho, and New York, 1936–1970.

Glass, D[avid] V., and D[avid] E. C. Eversley, eds. *Population in History: Essays in Historical Demography*. London, 1965.

Goebel, Dorothy Burne. "The 'New England Trade' and the French West Indies, 1763–1774: A Study in Trade Policies." *William and Mary Quarterly*, 3d Ser., XX (1963), 331–372.

Goldenberg, Joseph A. *Shipbuilding in Colonial America*. Charlottesville, Va., 1976.

———. "Virginia Ports in the American Revolution." In *Chesapeake Bay in the American Revolution*, edited by Ernest M. Eller, 310–340. Centerville, Md., 1981.

Goldin, Claudia D., and Frank D. Lewis. "The Role of Exports in American Economic Growth during the Napoleonic Wars, 1793 to 1807." *Explorations in Economic History*, XVII (1980), 6–25.

Goldsmith, Raymond W. "The Growth of Reproducible Wealth in the United States of America, 1809–1950." In *Income and Wealth of the United States: Trends and Structure*, edited by Simon Kuznets, 254–328. International Association for Research in Income and Wealth, Income and Wealth Series, II. Cambridge, 1952.

———. "Long Period Growth in Income and Product, 1839–1960." In United States, Congress, Joint Economic Committee, Eighty-sixth Congress, First Session, *Employment, Growth, and Price Levels: Hearings . . . Part 2—Historical and Comparative Rates of Production, Productivity, and Prices*, 229–279. Washington, D.C., 1959. Reprinted in *New Views on American Economic Development: A Selective Anthology of*

Recent Work, edited by Ralph L. Andreano, 337–361. Cambridge, Mass., 1965.

Goldsmiths'-Kress Library of Economic Literature: A Consolidated Guide to . . . the Microfilm Collection. Woodbridge, Conn., 1976–.

Goldstein, Jonathan. *Philadelphia and the China Trade, 1682–1846: Commercial, Cultural, and Attitudinal Effects.* University Park, Pa., 1978.

Goodfriend, Joyce Diane. "Burghers and Blacks: The Evolution of a Slave Society at New Amsterdam." *New York History*, LIX (1978), 125–144.

———. "'Too Great a Mixture of Nations': The Development of New York City Society in the Seventeenth Century." Ph.D. diss., University of California, Los Angeles, 1975.

Goodrich, Carter, ed. *The Government and the Economy, 1783–1861.* The American Heritage Series. Indianapolis, Ind., 1967.

———. *Government Promotion of American Canals and Railroads, 1800–1890.* New York, 1960.

Goodwin, Jack. "Current Bibliography in the History of Technology." *Technology and Culture*, volumes since 1964.

Goody, Jack, Joan Thirsk, and E[dward] P. Thompson, eds. *Family and Inheritance: Rural Society in Western Europe, 1200–1800.* Cambridge, 1976.

Gottfried, Marion H. "The First Depression in Massachusetts." *New England Quarterly*, IX (1936), 655–678.

Gouger, James Blaine, III. "Agricultural Change in the Northern Neck of Virginia, 1700–1860: An Historical Geography." Ph.D. diss., University of Florida, 1976.

Gough, Robert James. "Towards a Theory of Class and Social Conflict: A Social History of Wealthy Philadelphians, 1775 and 1800." Ph.D. diss., University of Pennsylvania, 1977.

Gould, Clarence P. "The Economic Causes of the Rise of Baltimore." In *Essays in Colonial History Presented to Charles McLean Andrews by His Students*, 225–251. New Haven, Conn., 1931.

———. *The Land System in Maryland, 1720–1765.* Johns Hopkins University Studies in Historical and Political Science, 31st Ser., no. 1. Baltimore, 1913.

———. *Money and Transportation in Maryland, 1720–1765.* Johns Hopkins University Studies in Historical and Political Science, 33d Ser., no. 1. Baltimore, 1915.

Goveia, Elsa V. *Slave Society in the British Leeward Islands at the End of the Eighteenth Century.* Caribbean Series, no. 8. New Haven, Conn., 1965.

———. *A Study on the Historiography of the British West Indies to the End of the Nineteenth Century.* Instituto Panamericano de Geografía e Historia, no. 186. Mexico City, 1956.

———. "The West Indian Slave Laws of the Eighteenth Century." *Revista de Ciencias Sociales*, IV (1960), 75–105.

Gragg, Larry Dale. *Migration in Early America: The Virginia Quaker Experience.* Studies in American History and Culture, no. 13. Ann Arbor, Mich., 1980.

Graham, Ian Charles Cargill. *Colonists from Scotland: Emigration to North America, 1707–1783.* Ithaca, N.Y., 1956.

Grant, Charles S. *Democracy in the Connecticut Frontier Town of Kent.* Columbia Studies in the Social Sciences, DCI. New York, 1961.

Grassby, Richard. "The Rate of Profit in Seventeenth-Century England." *English Historical Review*, LXXXIV (1969), 721–751.

Gray, Lewis Cecil. *History of Agriculture in the Southern United States to 1860.* Carnegie Institution of Washington Publication no. 430. 2 vols. Washington, D.C., 1933.

Gray, Ralph, and Betty Wood. "The Transition from Indentured to Involuntary Servitude in Colonial Georgia." *Explorations in Economic History*, XIII (1976), 353–370.

Gray, Stanley, and V[ertrees] J. Wyckoff. "The International Tobacco Trade in the Seventeenth Century." *Southern Economic Journal*, VII (1940), 1–26.

Great Britain. Commission Appointed to Inquire into the Management of the Post-Office Department. *The Fifth Report of the Commissioners Appointed to Inquire into the Management of the Post-Office Department*. London, 1836.

———. Parliament. House of Commons. *The Examination of Doctor Benjamin Franklin, Relative to the Repeal of the American Stamp Act, in MDCCLXVI*. London, 1767.

Green, Jeremy N. "The Wreck of the Dutch East Indiaman the *Vergulde Draeck*, 1656." *International Journal of Nautical Archaeology and Underwater Exploration*, II (1973), 267–289.

Green, William A. "Caribbean Historiography, 1600–1900: The Recent Tide." *Journal of Interdisciplinary History*, VII (1977), 509–530.

Greenberg, Douglas. "The Middle Colonies in Recent American Historiography." *William and Mary Quarterly*, 3d Ser., XXXVI (1979), 396–427.

Greene, Evarts B., and Virginia D. Harrington. *American Population before the Federal Census of 1790*. New York, 1937.

Greene, Jack P. "Autonomy and Stability: New England and the British Colonial Experience in Early Modern America." *Journal of Social History*, VII (1974), 171–194.

———. "Changing Interpretations of Early American Politics." In *The Reinterpretation of Early American History: Essays in Honor of John Edwin Pomfret*, edited by Ray Allen Billington, 151–184. San Marino, Calif., 1966.

———. "Society and Economy in the British Caribbean during the Seventeenth and Eighteenth Centuries." *American Historical Review*, LXXIX (1974), 1499–1517.

———, ed. *The Reinterpretation of the American Revolution, 1763–1789*. New York, 1968.

———, comp. *The American Colonies in the Eighteenth Century, 1689–1763*. Goldentree Bibliographies in American History. New York, 1969.

Greenhill, Basil. *Archaeology of the Boat: A New Introductory Study*. London, 1976.

Greven, Philip J., Jr. *Four Generations: Population, Land, and Family in Colonial Andover, Massachusetts*. Ithaca, N.Y., 1970.

Grim, Ronald Eugene. "The Absence of Towns in Seventeenth-Century Virginia: The Emergence of Service Centers in York County." Ph.D. diss., University of Maryland, 1977.

Gross, Robert A. *The Minutemen and Their World*. New York, 1976.

Grossman, Jonathan. "Wage and Price Controls during the American Revolution." *Monthly Labor Review*, XCVI (Sept. 1973), 3–10.

Grundfest, Jerry. "George Clymer, Philadelphia Revolutionary, 1739–1813." Ph.D. diss., Columbia University, 1973.

Gutman, Herbert G. *The Black Family in Slavery and Freedom, 1750–1925*. New York, 1976.

———. "Work, Culture, and Society in Industrializing America, 1815–1919." *American Historical Review*, LXXVIII (1973), 531–588.

Gwyn, Julian. "British Government Spending and the North American Colonies, 1740–1775." *Journal of Imperial and Commonwealth History*, VIII (1980), 74–84.

———. *The Enterprising Admiral: The Personal Fortune of Admiral Sir Peter Warren*. Montreal, 1974.

———. "The Impact of British Military Spending on Colonial American Money Markets, 1760–1783." Canadian Historical Association, *Historical Papers/Communications Historiques*, LVIII (1980), 77–99.

———. "The Impact of Louisbourg upon the Economy of Massachusetts, 1745–1749."

In *Papers and Abstracts for a Symposium on Ile Royale during the French Regime*, compiled by B. C. Bickerton, 84–106. Ottawa, 1972.

———. "War and Economic Change: Louisbourg and the New England Economy in the 1740s." In *Mélanges d'histoire du Canada français offerts au professeur Marcel Trudel*, 114–131. Ottawa, 1978.

Habakkuk, H. J. *American and British Technology in the Nineteenth Century: The Search for Labour-saving Inventions*. Cambridge, 1962.

———. "The Long-Term Rate of Interest and the Price of Land in the Seventeenth Century." *Economic History Review*, 2d Ser., V (1952), 26–45.

Hall, Douglas [G.]. "Absentee-Proprietorship in the British West Indies, to about 1850." *Jamaican Historical Review*, IV (1964), 15–35.

———. "Incalculability as a Feature of Sugar Production during the Eighteenth Century." *Social and Economic Studies*, X (1961), 340–352.

Hall, John Philip. "The Gentle Craft: A Narrative of Yankee Shoemakers." Ph.D. diss., Columbia University, 1953.

Hall, Michael Garibaldi. *Edward Randolph and the American Colonies, 1676–1703*. Chapel Hill, N.C., 1960.

Hall, Neville. "Slaves Use of Their 'Free' Time in the Danish Virgin Islands in the Later Eighteenth and Early Nineteenth Century." *Journal of Caribbean History*, XII (1980), 21–43.

Hall, Van Beck. *Politics without Parties: Massachusetts, 1780–1791*. Pittsburgh, Pa., 1972.

[Hamburg. Komité für die Amerika-Feier. Wissenschaftlichen ausschuss]. *Hamburgische Festschrift zur Erinnerung an die Entdeckung Amerika's*. 2 vols. Hamburg, 1892.

Hamilton, Earl J. "Use and Misuse of Price History." In *The Tasks of Economic History: Papers Presented at the Fourth Annual Meeting of the Economic History Association*, 47–60. *Journal of Economic History*, Supplement 4. New York, 1945.

Hamilton, Milton Wheaton. *Sir William Johnson, Colonial American, 1715–1763*. Port Washington, N.Y., 1976.

Hamm, Tommy Todd. "The American Slave Trade with Africa, 1620–1807." Ph.D. diss., Indiana University, 1975.

Handler, Jerome S. *A Guide to Source Materials for the Study of Barbados History, 1627–1834*. Carbondale, Ill., 1971.

Handler, Jerome S., and Frederick W. Lange. *Plantation Slavery in Barbados: An Archaeological and Historical Investigation*. Cambridge, Mass., 1978.

Handlin, Oscar, and Mary Flug Handlin. *Commonwealth—A Study of the Role of Government in the American Economy: Massachusetts, 1774–1861*. Studies in Economic History. New York, 1947.

———. "Origins of the Southern Labor System." *William and Mary Quarterly*, 3d Ser., VII (1950), 199–222.

———. "Revolutionary Economic Policy in Massachusetts." *William and Mary Quarterly*, 3d Ser., IV (1947), 3–26.

Hankerson, Fred Putnam. *The Cooperage Handbook*. Brooklyn, N.Y., 1947.

Hanna, Mary Alice. *Trade of the Delaware District before the Revolution*. Smith College Studies in History, II, no. 4. Northampton, Mass., 1917.

Hansen, Marcus Lee. *The Atlantic Migration, 1607–1860: A History of the Continuing Settlement of the United States*. Cambridge, Mass., 1940.

Hanson, John R., II. "The Economic Development of the Thirteen Continental Colonies, 1720–1775: A Critique." *William and Mary Quarterly*, 3d Ser., XXXVII (1980), 165–172.

————. "Money in the Colonial American Economy: An Extension." *Economic Inquiry*, XVII (1979), 281–286.

————. "Small Notes in the American Colonies." *Explorations in Economic History*, XVII (1980), 411–420.

[Hardy, Edward Rochic]. *An Account of the Early Insurance Offices in Massachusetts from 1724 to 1801*. Boston, 1901.

Harlow, Ralph Volney. "Aspects of Revolutionary Finance, 1775–1783." *American Historical Review*, XXXV (1929), 46–68.

————. "Economic Conditions in Massachusetts during the American Revolution." Colonial Society of Massachusetts, *Publications*, XX: *Transactions, 1917–1919*, 163–190. Boston, 1920.

Harlow, Vincent T. *A History of Barbados, 1625–1685*. Oxford, 1926.

————, ed. *Colonising Expeditions to the West Indies and Guiana, 1623–1667*. Hakluyt Society, 2d Ser., LVI. London, 1925.

"Harold Innis, 1894–1952: Twenty-five Years On." *Journal of Canadian Studies*, XII (Winter 1977).

Harper, Lawrence A. "The Effects of the Navigation Acts on the Thirteen Colonies." In *The Era of the American Revolution*, edited by Richard B. Morris, 3–39. New York, 1939.

————. *The English Navigation Laws: A Seventeenth-Century Experiment in Social Engineering*. New York, 1939.

Harrington, Virginia D. *The New York Merchant on the Eve of the Revolution*. New York, 1935.

Harris, Marshall [D.]. *Origin of the Land Tenure System in the United States*. Ames, Iowa, 1953.

Harris, P. M. G. "Integrating Interpretations of Local and Regionwide Change in the Study of Economic Development and Demographic Growth in the Colonial Chesapeake, 1630–1775." Regional Economic History Research Center, *Working Papers*, I, no. 3 (1978), 35–71.

————. "The Social Origins of American Leaders: The Demographic Foundations." *Perspectives in American History*, III (1969), 159–344.

Harris, Richard Colebrook. *The Seigneurial System in Early Canada: A Geographical Study*. Madison, Wis., 1966.

Harris, Richard Colebrook, and Leonard Guelke. "Land and Society in Early Canada and South Africa." *Journal of Historical Geography*, III (1977), 135–153.

Hart, Richard K. "Maryland's Maritime Enterprises during the Revolution." M.A. thesis, University of Maryland, 1947.

Hartley, E[dward] N[eal]. *Ironworks on the Saugus: The Lynn and Braintree Ventures of the Company of Undertakers of the Ironworks in New England*. Norman, Okla., 1957.

Hartman, Raymond S., and David R. Wheeler. "Schumpeterian Waves of Innovation and Infrastructure Development in Great Britain and the United States: The Kondratieff Cycle Revisited." *Research in Economic History*, IV (1979), 37–85.

Hartz, Louis. *Economic Policy and Democratic Thought: Pennsylvania, 1776–1860*. Studies in Economic History. Cambridge, Mass., 1948.

Hausman, William J. *Public Policy and the Supply of Coal to London*. New York, 1981 (Ph.D. diss., University of Illinois, 1976).

Haw, James Alfred. "Politics in Revolutionary Maryland, 1753–1788." Ph.D. diss., University of Virginia, 1972.

Haywood, C. Robert. "Mercantilism and South Carolina Agriculture, 1700–1763." *South Carolina Historical Magazine*, LX (1959), 15–27.

Hazard, Blanche Evans. *The Organization of the Boot and Shoe Industry in Massachusetts before 1875.* Harvard Economic Studies, XXIII. Cambridge, Mass., 1921.

Head, C[lifford] Grant. "The Changing Geography of Newfoundland in the Eighteenth Century." Ph.D. diss., University of Wisconsin, 1971.

―――. *Eighteenth Century Newfoundland: A Geographer's Perspective.* Carleton Library, no. 99. Toronto, 1976.

Heaton, Herbert. "Heckscher on Mercantilism." *Journal of Political Economy,* XLV (1937), 370–393.

―――. "Thomas Southcliffe Ashton, 1889–1968: A Memoir." *Journal of Economic History,* XXIX (1969), 264–267.

Heavner, Robert O. "Indentured Servitude: The Philadelphia Market, 1771–1773." *Journal of Economic History,* XXXVIII (1978), 701–713.

Hecht, Irene Winchester Duckworth. "The Virginia Colony, 1607–1640: A Study in Frontier Growth." Ph.D. diss., University of Washington, 1969.

―――. "The Virginia Muster of 1624/5 as a Source for Demographic History." *William and Mary Quarterly,* 3d Ser., XXX (1973), 65–92.

Heckscher, Eli F. *Mercantilism.* Edited by E. F. Söderlund. Translated by Mendel Shapiro. 2d ed., rev. 2 vols. London, 1955.

―――. *Merkantilismen: [ett led i den ekonomiska politikens historia].* 2d ed., rev. Stockholm, [1953].

Hedges, James B. "The Brown Papers: The Record of a Rhode Island Business Family." American Antiquarian Society, *Proceedings,* N.S., LI (1941), 21–36.

―――. *The Browns of Providence Plantations.* 2 vols. Cambridge, Mass., 1952–1968.

Heidenreich, Conrad. *Huronia: A History and Geography of the Huron Indians, 1600–1650.* Toronto, 1971.

Helm, June, ed. *Subarctic.* Vol. VI of *Handbook of North American Indians,* edited by William C. Sturtevant. Washington, D.C., 1981.

Helwig, Adelaide Berta. "The Early History of Barbados and Her Influence upon the Development of South Carolina." Ph.D. diss., University of California, Berkeley, 1930.

Hemphill, John Mickle, II. "Freight Rates in the Maryland Tobacco Trade, 1705–1762." *Maryland Historical Magazine,* LIV (1959), 36–58, 153–187.

―――. "Virginia and the English Commercial System, 1689–1733: Studies in the Development and Fluctuations of a Colonial Economy under Imperial Control." Ph.D. diss., Princeton University, 1964.

Henretta, James A. "Economic Development and Social Structure in Colonial Boston." *William and Mary Quarterly,* 3d Ser., XXII (1965), 75–92.

―――. *The Evolution of American Society, 1700–1815: An Interdisciplinary Analysis.* Civilization and Society: Studies in Social, Economic, and Cultural History. Lexington, Mass., 1973.

―――. "Families and Farms: *Mentalité* in Pre-industrial America." *William and Mary Quarterly,* 3d Ser., XXXV (1978), 3–32.

―――. "The Morphology of New England Society in the Colonial Period." *Journal of Interdisciplinary History,* II (1971), 379–398.

Henrich, Frederick Kahler. "A Role for Regulation: Early American Legislation to Protect the Public Interest." Ph.D. diss., State University of New York, Buffalo, 1978.

Henripin, Jacques. *La population canadienne au début du XVIIIᵉ siècle: Nuptialité, fécondité, mortalité infantile.* [Paris], 1954.

Henry, Louis. *Population: Analysis and Models.* Translated by Étienne van de Walle and Elise F. Jones. London, 1976.

Hermann, Johann Christian. *Allgemeiner Contorist welcher von allen und jeden*

Gegenständen der Handlung aller in und ausser Europa. . . . Leipzig, 1788–1792.

Herndon, G[eorge] Melvin. "Forest Products of Colonial Georgia." *Journal of Forest History*, XXIII (1979), 130–135.

———. "Hemp in Colonial Virginia." *Agricultural History*, XXXVII (1963), 86–93.

———. "Naval Stores in Colonial Georgia." *Georgia Historical Quarterly*, LII (1968), 426–433.

———. "Timber Products of Colonial Georgia." *Georgia Historical Quarterly*, LVII (1973), 56–62.

———. "A War-Inspired Industry: The Manufacture of Hemp in Virginia during the Revolution." *Virginia Magazine of History and Biography*, LXXIV (1966), 301–311.

Herrick, Cheesman A. *White Servitude in Pennsylvania: Indentured and Redemption Labor in Colony and Commonwealth.* Philadelphia, 1926.

Heyward, Duncan Clinch. *Seed from Madagascar.* Chapel Hill, N.C., 1937.

Higgins, W. Robert. "Charleston: Terminus and Entrepôt of the Colonial Slave Trade." In *The African Diaspora: Interpretive Essays*, edited by Martin L. Kolson and Robert I. Rotberg, 114–131. Cambridge, Mass., 1976.

———. "Charles Town Merchants and Factors Dealing in the External Negro Trade, 1735–1775." *South Carolina Historical Magazine*, LXV (1964), 205–217.

———. "A Financial History of the American Revolution in South Carolina." Ph.D. diss., Duke University, 1970.

———. "The Geographical Origins of Negro Slaves in Colonial South Carolina." *South Atlantic Quarterly*, LXX (1971), 34–47.

———. "The South Carolina Negro Duty Law, 1703–1775." M.A. thesis, University of South Carolina, 1967.

Higgs, Robert, and H. Louis Stettler III. "Colonial New England Demography: A Sampling Approach." *William and Mary Quarterly*, 3d Ser., XXVII (1970), 282–294.

Higham, C[harles] S[trachan] S[anders]. *The Development of the Leeward Islands under the Restoration, 1660–1688: A Study of the Foundations of the Old Colonial System.* Cambridge, 1921.

Higman, B[arry] W. *Slave Population and Economy in Jamaica, 1807–1834.* Cambridge, 1976.

Hildreth, Richard. *The History of the United States of America.* 6 vols. New York, 1849–1852.

Hilldrup, R[obert] L. "The Salt Supply of North Carolina during the American Revolution." *North Carolina Historical Review*, XXII (1945), 393–417.

Hilliard, Sam B. "Antebellum Tidewater Rice Culture in South Carolina and Georgia." In *European Settlement and Development in North America: Essays on Geographical Change in Honour and Memory of Andrew Hill Clark*, edited by James R. Gibson, 91–115. Toronto, 1978.

Hindle, Brooke. *Technology in Early America. Needs and Opportunities for Study.* Chapel Hill, N.C., 1966.

———, ed. *America's Wooden Age: Aspects of Its Early Technology.* Tarrytown, N.Y., 1975.

———. *Material Culture in the Wooden Age.* Tarrytown, N.Y., 1981.

Hirschman, Albert O. "A Generalized Linkage Approach to Development, with Special Reference to Staples." *Economic Development and Cultural Change*, XXV (Supplement, 1977), 67–98.

———. *The Strategy of Economic Development.* New Haven, Conn., 1958.

Hite, James Cleveland. "A Statistical Analysis of Trade in the Charleston Area, 1750–1769." M.A. thesis, Emory University, 1964.

Hoerder, Dirk. Review of *The Connecticut Town: Growth and Development, 1635–1790*, by Bruce C. Daniels. *William and Mary Quarterly*, 3d Ser., XXXVIII (1981), 134–136.

Hoffman, Ronald. "The 'Disaffected' in the Revolutionary South." In *The American Revolution: Explorations in the History of American Radicalism*, edited by Alfred F. Young, 273–316. DeKalb, Ill., 1976.

———. *A Spirit of Dissension: Economics, Politics, and the Revolution in Maryland*. Baltimore, 1973.

———, ed. *Dear Papa, Dear Charley: The Letters of Charles Carroll of Carrollton and His Father, 1749–1782*. Chapel Hill, N.C., forthcoming.

Hoffman, Ronald, John J. McCusker, and Russell R. Menard, eds. *The Economy of Early America: The Revolutionary Period, 1763–1789*. Charlottesville, Va., forthcoming.

Hogg, Peter C. *The African Slave Trade and Its Suppression: A Classified and Annotated Bibliography of Books, Pamphlets, and Periodical Articles*. London, 1973.

Hollingsworth, T[homas] H[enry]. *Historical Demography*. The Sources of History: Studies in the Uses of Historical Evidence. Ithaca, N.Y., 1969.

Homer, Sidney. *A History of Interest Rates*. New Brunswick, N.J., 1963.

Hood, Graham. *Bonnin and Morris of Philadelphia: The First American Porcelain Factory, 1770–1772*. Chapel Hill, N.C., 1972.

Horn, James. "Servant Emigration to the Chesapeake in the Seventeenth Century." In *The Chesapeake in the Seventeenth Century: Essays on Anglo-American Society*, edited by Thad W. Tate and David L. Ammerman, 51–95. Chapel Hill, N.C., 1979.

Horowicz, Kay, and Robson Lowe. *The Colonial Posts in the United States of America, 1606–1783*. London, 1967.

Horsefield, J. Keith. *British Monetary Experiments, 1650–1710*. London, 1960.

———. "The 'Stop of the Exchequer' Revisited." *Economic History Review*, 2d Ser., XXXV (1982), 511–528.

Horsfall, L[ucy] Frances. *See* Armytage, L[ucy] Frances Horsfall.

Horwitz, Morton J. *The Transformation of American Law, 1780–1860*. Cambridge, Mass., 1977.

Hoselitz, Bert F., et al. *Theories of Economic Growth*. Glencoe, Ill., 1960.

Howe, Octavius T. "Beverly Privateers in the American Revolution." Colonial Society of Massachusetts, *Publications*, XXIV: *Transactions, 1920–1922* (1923), 318–435.

Howell, Charles. "Colonial Watermills in the Wooden Age." In *America's Wooden Age: Aspects of Its Early Technology*, edited by Brooke Hindle, 120–159. Tarrytown, N.Y., 1975.

Howell, Charles, and Allan Keller. *The Mill at Philipsburg Manor Upper Mills and a Brief History of Milling*. Tarrytown, N.Y., 1977.

Huebner, Solomon. "The Development and Present Status of Marine Insurance in the United States." American Academy of Political and Social Science, *Annals*, XXVI (1905), 421–452.

Hughes, J[onathan] R. T. *Social Control in the Colonial Economy*. Charlottesville, Va., 1976.

Hughes, Sarah Shaver. "Elizabeth City County, Virginia, 1782–1810: The Economic and Social Structure of a Tidewater County in the Early National Years." Ph.D. diss., College of William and Mary, 1975.

———. *Surveyors and Statesmen: Land Measuring in Colonial Virginia*. Richmond, Va., 1979.

Hunter, Louis C. *A History of Industrial Power in the United States, 1780–1930*. Charlottesville, Va., 1979.

Huntley, Francis Carroll. "Salt: A Study in Colonial Economy." M.A. thesis, University of California, Berkeley, 1948.

————. "Trade of the Thirteen Colonies with the Foreign Caribbean Area." Ph.D. diss., University of California, Berkeley, 1949.

Igartua, José Eduardo. "The Merchants and *Négociants* of Montréal, 1750–1775: A Study in Socio-economic History." Ph.D. diss., Michigan State University, 1974.

Ingram, K[enneth] E. *Manuscripts Relating to Commonwealth Caribbean Countries in United States and Canadian Repositories.* St. Lawrence, Barbados, 1975.

————. *Sources for West Indian Studies: A Supplementary Listing, with Particular Reference to Manuscript Sources.* Zug, Switzerland, 1983.

————. *Sources of Jamaican History, 1655–1838: A Bibliographical Survey with Particular Reference to Manuscript Sources.* 2 vols. Zug, Switzerland, 1976.

Innes, F[rank] G. "The Pre-Sugar Era of European Settlement in Barbados." *Journal of Caribbean History,* I (1970), 1–22.

Innes, Stephen. *Labor in a New Land: Economy and Society in Seventeenth-Century Springfield.* Princeton, N.J., 1983.

————. "Land Tenancy and Social Order in Springfield, Massachusetts, 1652 to 1702." *William and Mary Quarterly,* 3d Ser., XXXV (1978), 33–56.

Innis, Harold A. *The Cod Fisheries: The History of an International Economy.* Toronto, 1940; rev. ed., 1954.

————. *Essays in Canadian Economic History.* Toronto, 1956.

————. *The Fur Trade in Canada: An Introduction to Canadian Economic History.* New Haven, Conn., 1930; rev. ed., Toronto, 1956.

————. "The Rise and Fall of the Spanish Fishery in Newfoundland." Royal Society of Canada, *Proceedings and Transactions,* 3d Ser., XXV (1931), sec. 2, 51–70.

[International Congress of the Historical Sciences, 14th, San Francisco, 1975]. *Reports [of the] XIV International Congress of the Historical Sciences.* 3 vols. New York, 1977.

Isaac, Rhys. *The Transformation of Virginia, 1740–1790.* Chapel Hill, N.C., 1982.

Jackson, Gordon. *The British Whaling Trade.* London, 1978.

James, C[yril] L[ionel] R[obert]. *The Black Jacobins: Toussaint L'Ouverture and the San Domingo Revolution.* 2d ed., rev. New York, 1963.

James, Francis G. "Irish Colonial Trade in the Eighteenth Century." *William and Mary Quarterly,* 3d Ser., XX (1963), 574–584.

Jameson, J[ohn] Franklin. "St. Eustatius in the American Revolution." *American Historical Review,* VIII (1903), 683–708.

Jedrey, Christopher M. *The World of John Cleaveland: Family and Community in Eighteenth-Century New England.* New York, 1979.

[Jefferson, Thomas]. *The Writings of Thomas Jefferson.* Edited by Andrew A. Lipscomb and Albert Ellery Bergh. 20 vols. Washington, D.C., 1903–1904.

Jenkins, J[ames] T. *A History of the Whale Fisheries, from the Basque Fisheries of the Tenth Century to the Hunting of the Finner Whale at the Present Date.* London, 1921.

Jenkins, J[ohn] Geraint. *The English Farm Wagon: Origins and Structure.* Lingfield, Surrey, 1961.

Jennings, Francis. *The Invasion of America: Indians, Colonialism, and the Cant of Conquest.* Chapel Hill, N.C., 1975.

Jensen, Arthur L. "The Inspection of Exports in Colonial Pennsylvania." *Pennsylvania Magazine of History and Biography,* LXXVIII (1954), 275–297.

————. *The Maritime Commerce of Colonial Philadelphia.* Madison, Wis., 1963.

Jensen, Merrill. "The American Revolution and American Agriculture." *Agricultural History*, XLIII (1969), 107–124.

———. "Historians and the Nature of the American Revolution." In *The Reinterpretation of Early American History: Essays in Honor of John Edwin Pomfret*, edited by Ray Allen Billington, 101–127. San Marino, Calif., 1966.

———. *The New Nation: A History of the United States during the Confederation, 1781–1789.* New York, 1950.

———, ed. *American Colonial Documents to 1776.* Vol. IX of *English Historical Documents*, edited by David C. Douglas. London, 1955.

Jernegan, Marcus Wilson. *Laboring and Dependent Classes in Colonial America, 1607–1783.* Chicago, [1931].

John, A[rthur] H. "Agricultural Productivity and Economic Growth in England, 1700–1760." *Journal of Economic History*, XXV (1965), 19–34.

———. "English Agricultural Improvement and Grain Exports, 1660–1765." In *Trade, Government, and Economy in Pre-industrial England: Essays Presented to F. J. Fisher*, edited by D. C. Coleman and A. H. John, 45–67. London, 1976.

Johnsen, Arne O., and J. N. Tonnessen. *The History of Modern Whaling.* Berkeley and Los Angeles, Calif., 1981.

Johnson, E[dgar] A. J. *American Economic Thought in the Seventeenth Century.* London, 1932.

———. *The Foundations of American Economic Freedom: Government and Enterprise in the Age of Washington.* Minneapolis, Minn., 1973.

———. "Some Evidence of Mercantilism in the Massachusetts-Bay." *New England Quarterly*, I (1928), 371–395.

[Johnson, Edward]. *Johnson's Wonder-Working Providence, 1628–1651.* Edited by J. Franklin Jameson. New York, 1910.

Johnson, Emory R., T[hurman] W. Van Metre, G[rover] G. Huebner, and D[avid] S. Hanchett. *History of Domestic and Foreign Commerce of the United States.* Carnegie Institution of Washington Publication no. 215a. Washington, D.C., 1915.

Johnson, Harry G. *International Trade and Economic Growth: Studies in Pure Theory.* London, 1958.

Johnson, Herbert Alan. *The Law Merchant and Negotiable Instruments in Colonial New York, 1664 to 1730.* Chicago, 1963.

[Johnson, Joshua]. *Joshua Johnson's Letterbook, 1771–1774: Letters from a Merchant in London to His Partners in Maryland.* Edited by Jacob M. Price. London Record Society, *Publications*, XV. London, 1979.

Johnson, Keach. "The Baltimore Company Seeks English Markets: A Study of the Anglo-American Iron Trade, 1731–1755." *William and Mary Quarterly*, 3d Ser., XVI (1959), 37–60.

———. "The Baltimore Company Seeks English Subsidies for the Colonial Iron Industry." *Maryland Historical Magazine*, XLVI (1951), 27–43.

———. "The Genesis of the Baltimore Ironworks." *Journal of Southern History*, XIX (1953), 157–179.

Johnson, Laurence A. *Over the Counter and on the Shelf: Country Store Keeping in America, 1620–1920.* Edited by Marcia Ray. Rutland, Vt., 1961.

[Johnson, Samuel]. *Taxation No Tyranny: An Answer to the Resolutions and Address of the American Congress.* London, 1775.

Jonas, Manfred. "Wages in Early Colonial Maryland." *Maryland Historical Magazine*, LI (1956), 27–38.

Jones, Alice Hanson. *American Colonial Wealth: Documents and Methods.* 2d ed., rev. 3 vols. New York, 1978.

———. "Estimating Wealth of the Living from a Probate Sample." *Journal of Interdisciplinary History,* XIII (1982), 273–300.

———. "La fortune privée en Pennsylvanie, New Jersey, Delaware (1774)." *Annales: Économies, Sociétés, Civilisations,* XXIV (1969), 235–249.

———. "Wealth Estimates for the American Middle Colonies, 1774." *Economic Development and Cultural Change,* XVIII, no. 4, pt. 2 (1970).

———. "Wealth Estimates for the New England Colonies about 1770." *Journal of Economic History,* XXXII (1972), 98–127.

———. *Wealth of a Nation to Be: The American Colonies on the Eve of the Revolution.* New York, 1980.

Jones, Douglas Lamar. "Poverty and Vagabondage: The Process of Survival in Eighteenth-Century Massachusetts." *New England Historical and Genealogical Register,* CXXXIII (1979), 243–254.

———. "The Strolling Poor: Transiency in Eighteenth-Century Massachusetts." *Journal of Social History,* VIII (Spring 1975), 28–54.

———. *Village and Seaport: Migration and Society in Eighteenth-Century Massachusetts.* Hanover, N.H., 1981.

Jones, E[ric] L. "Agriculture, 1700–80." In *The Economic History of Britain since 1700,* edited by Roderick Floud and Donald McCloskey, I, 66–102. Cambridge, 1981.

———. *Agriculture and the Industrial Revolution.* Oxford, 1974.

———. "Creative Disruptions in American Agriculture, 1620–1820." *Agricultural History,* XLVIII (1974), 510–528.

Jones, Newton B. "Weights, Measures, and Mercantilism: The Inspection of Exports in Virginia, 1742–1820." In *The Old Dominion: Essays for Thomas Perkins Abernethy,* edited by Darrett B. Rutman, 122–134. Charlottesville, Va., 1964.

Jones, Robert Francis. "The Public Career of William Duer: Rebel, Federalist Politician, Entrepreneur, and Speculator, 1775–1792." Ph.D. diss., University of Notre Dame, 1967.

Judah, Charles Burnet, Jr. *The North American Fisheries and British Policy to 1713.* Illinois Studies in the Social Sciences, XVIII, nos. 3–4. Urbana, Ill., [1933].

Judd, Carol M., and Arthur J. Ray, eds. *Old Trails and New Directions: Papers of the Third North American Fur Trade Conference.* Toronto, 1980.

Judd, Jacob. "Frederick Philipse and the Madagascar Trade." *New-York Historical Society Quarterly,* LV (1971), 354–374.

Kaminski, John Paul. "Paper Politics: The Northern State Loan-Offices during the Confederation, 1783–1790." Ph.D. diss., University of Wisconsin, 1972.

Kammen, Michael. *Empire and Interest: The American Colonies and the Politics of Mercantilism.* Philadelphia, 1970.

Kantrow, Louise. "Philadelphia Gentry: Fertility and Family Limitation among an American Aristocracy." *Population Studies,* XXXIV (1980), 21–30.

Karinen, Arthur Eli. "Maryland Population, 1631–1730: Numerical and Distributional Aspects." *Maryland Historical Magazine,* LIV (1959), 365–407.

———. "Numerical and Distributional Aspects of Maryland Population, 1631–1840." Ph.D. diss., University of Maryland, 1958.

Keith, George, *et al.* "An Account of the State of the Church in North America." Protestant Episcopal Historical Society, *Collections,* I (1851), xv–xxi.

Kelly, Cathy. "Marriage Migration in Massachusetts, 1765–1790." Department of Geography, Syracuse University, *Discussion Paper Series*, no. 30 (March 1977).

Kelly, Kevin Peter. "Economic and Social Development of Seventeenth-Century Surry County, Virginia." Ph.D. diss., University of Washington, 1972.

Kelsey, Darwin P., ed. *Farming in the New Nation: Interpreting American Agriculture, 1790–1840.* Washington, D.C., 1972.

Kelso, William M. "Shipbuilding in Virginia, 1763–1774." Columbia Historical Society, *Records*, XLVIII (1971), 1–13.

Kemmerer, Donald L. "The Colonial Loan-Office System in New Jersey." *Journal of Political Economy*, XLVII (1939), 867–874.

Kerr, W[ilfred] B. "The Merchants of Nova Scotia and the American Revolution." *Canadian Historical Review*, XIII (1932), 20–36.

Kerridge, Eric. *The Agricultural Revolution.* London, 1967.

Kiiskinen, Osmo. "Yhdysvaltain kaapparit Euroopan vesillä, 1776–1783" (American privateers in European waters, 1776–1783). Licentiate thesis, University of Helsinki, 1982.

Killinger, Charles L[inter], III. "The Royal African Company Slave Trade to Virginia, 1689–1713." M.A. thesis, College of William and Mary, 1969.

Kim, Sung Bok. *Landlord and Tenant in Colonial New York: Manorial Society, 1664–1775.* Chapel Hill, N.C., 1978.

Kindleberger, Charles P. *Manias, Panics, and Crashes: A History of Financial Crises.* New York, 1978.

Kindleberger, Charles P., and Peter Lindert. *International Economics.* 6th ed. Homewood, Ill., 1978.

Klarman, Herbert E., ed. *Empirical Studies in Health Economics: Proceedings of the Second Conference on the Economics of Health.* Baltimore, 1970.

Klebaner, Benjamin J. "State-Chartered American Commercial Banks, 1781–1801." *Business History Review*, LIII (1979), 529–538.

Klein, Herbert S. *The Middle Passage: Comparative Studies in the Atlantic Slave Trade.* Princeton, N.J., 1978.

―――. "Slaves and Shipping in Eighteenth-Century Virginia." *Journal of Interdisciplinary History*, V (1975), 383–412.

Klein, Herbert S., and Stanley L. Engerman. "A Demografia Morte dos Escravos Americanos." In *População e Sociedade no Passado.* São Paulo, Brazil, forthcoming.

―――. "The Demographic Study of the American Slave Population: With Particular Attention Given the Comparison between the United States and the British West Indies." Unpublished manuscript, 1975.

―――. "Fertility Differentials between Slaves in the United States and the British West Indies: A Note on Lactation Practices and Their Possible Implications." *William and Mary Quarterly*, 3d Ser., XXXV (1978), 357–374.

Klepp, Susan Edith. "Five Early Pennsylvania Censuses." *Pennsylvania Magazine of History and Biography*, CVI (1982), 483–514.

―――. "Philadelphia in Transition: A Demographic History of the City and Its Occupational Groups, 1720–1830." Ph.D. diss., University of Pennsylvania, 1980.

Klingaman, David C. "The Coastwise Trade of Colonial Massachusetts." Essex Institute, *Historical Collections*, CVIII (1972), 217–234.

―――. *Colonial Virginia's Coastwise and Grain Trade.* New York, 1975 (Ph.D. diss., University of Virginia, 1967).

―――. "Food Surpluses and Deficits in the American Colonies, 1768–1772." *Journal of Economic History*, XXXI (1971), 553–569.

—. "The Significance of Grain in the Development of the Tobacco Colonies." *Journal of Economic History*, XXIX (1969), 268–278.

Klingaman, David C., and Richard K. Vedder, eds. *Essays in Nineteenth Century Economic History: The Old Northwest.* Athens, Ohio, 1975.

Klingberg, Frank J., ed. *Codrington Chronicle: An Experiment in Anglican Altruism on a Barbados Plantation, 1710–1834.* University of California Publications in History, XXXVII. Berkeley and Los Angeles, Calif., 1949.

Klopfer, Helen Louise. "Statistics of the Foreign Trade of Philadelphia, 1700–1860." Typescript, 1936. Copies in the University of Pennsylvania Library, Philadelphia, and the Hagley Museum and Library, Greenville, Delaware.

Knittle, Walter Allen. *The Early Eighteenth Century Palatine Emigration: A British Government Redemptioner Project to Manufacture Naval Stores.* Philadelphia, 1936.

[Knox, William]. *The Interest of the Merchants and Manufacturers of Great Britain, in the Present Contest with the Colonies, Stated and Considered.* London, 1774.

Koch, Donald Warner. "Income Distribution and Political Structure in Seventeenth-Century Salem, Massachusetts." Essex Institute, *Historical Collections*, CV (1969), 50–71.

Kolson, Martin L., and Robert I. Rotberg, eds. *The African Diaspora: Interpretive Essays.* Cambridge, Mass., 1976.

Kresse, Walter. *Materialien zur Entwicklungsgeschichte der hamburger Handelsflotte, 1765–1823.* Mitteilungen aus dem Museum für Hamburgische Geschichte, N.S., III. Hamburg, 1966.

Kuebel, Mary Veronica. "Merchants and Mandarins: The Genesis of American Relations with China." Ph.D. diss., University of Virginia, 1974.

Kugler, Richard C. "The Whale Oil Trade, 1750–1775." In *Seafaring in Colonial Massachusetts*, [edited by Philip Chadwick Foster Smith], 153–173. Colonial Society of Massachusetts, *Publications*, LII: *Collections*. Boston, 1980.

Kuhlmann, Charles Byron. *The Development of the Flour-Milling Industry in the United States.* Boston, 1929.

Kulik, Gary B. "The Beginnings of the Industrial Revolution in America: Pawtucket, Rhode Island, 1672–1829." Ph.D. diss., Brown University, 1980.

Kulikoff, Allan Lee. "The Colonial Chesapeake: Seedbed of Antebellum Southern Culture?" *Journal of Southern History*, XLV (1979), 513–540.

—. "The Economic Growth of the Eighteenth-Century Chesapeake Colonies." *Journal of Economic History*, XXXIX (1979), 275–288.

—. "Growth and Welfare in Early America." *William and Mary Quarterly*, 3d Ser., XXXIX (1982), 359–365.

—. "The Origins of Afro-American Society in Tidewater Maryland and Virginia, 1700–1790." *William and Mary Quarterly*, 3d Ser., XXXV (1978), 226–259.

—. "The Progress of Inequality in Revolutionary Boston." *William and Mary Quarterly*, 3d Ser., XXVIII (1971), 375–412.

—. "A 'Prolifick' People: Black Population Growth in the Chesapeake Colonies, 1700–1790." *Southern Studies*, XVI (1977), 391–428.

—. "Tobacco and Slaves: Population, Economy, and Society in Eighteenth-Century Prince George's County, Maryland." Ph.D. diss., Brandeis University, 1976.

Kupp, Jan. "Aspects of New York–Dutch Trade under the English, 1670–1674." *New-York Historical Society Quarterly*, LVIII (1974), 139–147.

Kupperman, Karen Ordahl. "Apathy and Death in Early Jamestown." *Journal of American History*, LXVI (1979), 24–40.

Kurtz, Stephen G., and James H. Hutson, eds. *Essays on the American Revolution.* Chapel Hill, N.C., 1973.

Kussmaul, Ann [Sturm]. *Servants in Husbandry in Early Modern England.* Cambridge, 1981.

Kuznets, Simon. "Demographic Aspects of the Size Distribution of Income: An Exploratory Essay." *Economic Development and Cultural Change,* XXV (1976), 1–94.

———. *National Income: A Summary of Findings.* New York, 1946.

———. "National Income Estimates for the United States prior to 1870." *Journal of Economic History,* XII (1952), 115–130.

———. "The State as a Unit in Study of Economic Growth." *Journal of Economic History,* XI (1951), 25–41.

———. *Toward a Theory of Economic Growth.* New York, 1968.

———, ed. *Income and Wealth of the United States: Trends and Structure.* International Association for Research in Income and Wealth, Income and Wealth Series, II. Cambridge, 1952.

LaFeber, Walter. "Foreign Policies of a New Nation: Franklin, Madison, and the 'Dream of a New Land to Fulfill with People in Self-Control,' 1750–1804." In *From Colony to Empire: Essays in the History of American Foreign Relations,* edited by William Appleman Williams, 9–37. New York, 1972.

La Morandière, Charles de. *Histoire de la pêche française de la morue dans l'Amérique septentrionale.* 3 vols. Paris, 1962–1966.

Land, Aubrey C. *The Dulanys of Maryland: A Biographical Study of Daniel Dulany, the Elder (1685–1753) and Daniel Dulany, the Younger (1722–1797).* Baltimore, 1955.

———. "Economic Base and Social Structure: The Northern Chesapeake in the Eighteenth Century." *Journal of Economic History,* XXV (1965), 639–654.

———. "Economic Behavior in a Planting Society: The Eighteenth-Century Chesapeake." *Journal of Southern History,* XXXIII (1967), 469–485.

———. "The Tobacco Staple and the Planter's Problems: Technology, Labor, and Crops." *Agricultural History,* XLIII (1969), 69–81.

Land, Aubrey C., Lois Green Carr, and Edward C. Papenfuse, eds. *Law, Society, and Politics in Early Maryland.* Baltimore, 1977.

Lane, Carl Anthony. "The Roots of Jamaican Loyalism, 1760–1766." Ph.D. diss., City University of New York, 1978.

LaPotin, Armand Shelby. "The Minisink Patent: A Study in Colonial Landholding and Problems of Settlement in Eighteenth-Century New York." Ph.D. diss., University of Wisconsin, 1974.

Larson, Henrietta M. *Guide to Business History: Materials for the Study of American Business History and Suggestions for Their Use.* Cambridge, Mass., 1948.

Laslett, Peter. *Family Life and Illicit Love in Earlier Generations: Essays in Historical Sociology.* Cambridge, 1977.

Latourette, Kenneth Scott. *The History of Early Relations between the United States and China, 1784–1844.* New Haven, Conn., 1917.

Laub, C. H[erbert]. "Revolutionary Virginia and the Crown Lands (1775–1783)." *William and Mary Quarterly,* 2d Ser., XI (1931), 304–314.

Lauber, Almon Wheeler. *Indian Slavery in Colonial Times within the Present Limits of the United States.* Columbia University Studies in History, Economics and Public Law, LIV, no. 3. New York, 1913.

[Laurens, Henry]. *The Papers of Henry Laurens.* Edited by Philip M. Hamer *et al.* Columbia, S.C., 1968–.

Lawson, Murray G. *Fur: A Study in English Mercantilism, 1700–1775.* University of Toronto Studies, History and Economics Series, IX. Toronto, 1943.

———. "The Routes of Boston's Trade, 1752–1765." Colonial Society of Massachusetts, *Publications,* XXXVIII: *Transactions, 1947–1951,* 81–120. Boston, 1959.

Leder, Lawrence H. "Military Victualing in Colonial New York." In *Business Enterprise in Early New York,* edited by Joseph R. Frese and Jacob Judd, 16–54. Tarrytown, N.Y., 1979.

Lee, Ronald Demos. "Estimating Series of Vital Rates and Age Structures from Baptisms and Burials: A New Technique, with Applications to Pre-industrial England." *Population Studies,* XXVIII (1974), 495–512.

———, ed. *Population Patterns in the Past.* New York, 1977.

Lee, Ronald Demos, and R. S. Schofield. "British Population in the Eighteenth Century." In *The Economic History of Britain since 1700,* edited by Roderick Floud and Donald McCloskey, I, 17–35. Cambridge, 1981.

Lee, Susan Previant, and Peter Passell. *A New Economic View of American History.* New York, 1979.

Lemon, James T. *The Best Poor Man's Country: A Geographical Study of Early Southeastern Pennsylvania.* Baltimore, 1972.

———. Comment on James A. Henretta's "Families and Farms: *Mentalité* in Pre-industrial America" (with a reply by James A. Henretta). *William and Mary Quarterly,* 3d Ser., XXXVII (1980), 688–700.

———. "Early Americans and Their Social Environment." *Journal of Historical Geography,* VI (1980), 115–131.

———. "Household Consumption in Eighteenth-Century America and Its Relationship to Production and Trade: The Situation among Farmers in Southeastern Pennsylvania." *Agricultural History,* XLI (1967), 59–70.

———. "Urbanization and the Development of Eighteenth-Century Southeastern Pennsylvania and Adjacent Delaware." *William and Mary Quarterly,* 3d Ser., XXIV (1967), 501–542.

———. "The Weakness of Place and Community in Early Pennsylvania." In *European Settlement and Development in North America: Essays on Geographical Change in Honour and Memory of Andrew Hill Clark,* edited by James R. Gibson, 190–207. Toronto, 1978.

Lemon, James T., and Gary B. Nash. "The Distribution of Wealth in Eighteenth-Century America: A Century of Change in Chester County, Pennsylvania, 1693–1802." *Journal of Social History,* II (1968), 1–24.

Leonard, Eugenie Andruss. "Paper as a Critical Commodity during the American Revolution." *Pennsylvania Magazine of History and Biography,* LXXIV (1950), 488–499.

Leonard, Joan de Lourdes. "Operation Checkmate: The Birth and Death of a Virginia Blueprint for Progress, 1600–1676." *William and Mary Quarterly,* 3d Ser., XXIV (1967), 44–74.

Lesnick, Edward Charles, Jr. "A Quantitative Analysis of the Supply and Demand for Ships: A Case Study of Colonial New York and South Carolina." Ph.D. diss., University of Notre Dame, 1973.

Letwin, William. "Monetary Practice and Theory of the North American Colonies during the Seventeenth and Eighteenth Centuries." In *La moneta nell'economica europea secoli XIII–XVIII,* edited by Vera Barbagli Bagnoli, 439–469. Instituto Internazionale di Storia Economica "F. Datini," Pubblicazioni, Serie II, no. 7. Prato, 1981.

———. *Sir Josiah Child, Merchant Economist, with a Reprint of "Brief Observations*

Concerning Trade, and Interest of Money" (1668). Kress Library of Business and Economics Publication no. 14. Boston, 1959.

Levitt, James H. *For Want of Trade: Shipping and the New Jersey Ports, 1680–1783.* New Jersey Historical Society, *Collections,* XVII. Newark, N.J., 1981.

Levy, Barry John. "The Light in the Valley: The Chester and Welsh Tract Quaker Communities and the Delaware Valley, 1681–1750." Ph.D. diss., University of Pennsylvania, 1976.

Lewis, W. Arthur. "Economic Development with Unlimited Supplies of Labour." *Manchester School of Economic and Social Studies,* XXII (1954), 139–191.

Liao, T. R., comp. *The History of American Agriculture.* Library of Congress Science Tracer Bullet 81-15. Washington, D.C., 1981.

Ligon, Richard. *A True and Exact History of the Island of Barbados.* London, 1657.

Lindert, Peter H. "An Algorithm for Probate Sampling." *Journal of Interdisciplinary History,* XI (1981), 649–668.

Lindert, Peter H., and Jeffrey G. Williamson. *American Inequality: A Macroeconomic History.* New York, 1980.

———. "Three Centuries of American Inequality." *Research in Economic History,* I (1976), 69–123.

Lindstrom, Diane. "American Economic Growth before 1840: New Evidence and New Directions." *Journal of Economic History,* XXXIX (1979), 289–301.

———. *Economic Development in the Philadelphia Region, 1810–1850.* New York, 1978.

Lippmann, Edmund O. von. *Geschichte des Zuckers seit den ältesten Zeiten bis zum Beginn der Rübenzucker-Fabrikation: Ein Beitrag zur Kulturgeschichte.* 2d ed. Berlin, 1929. Reprint. Niederwalluf bei Wiesbaden, 1970.

[Lipsey, Robert E.]. "Foreign Trade." In *American Economic Growth: An Economist's History of the United States,* edited by Lance E. Davis, Richard A. Easterlin, and William N. Parker, 548–581. New York, 1972.

Lipson, E[phraim]. *The Economic History of England.* 6th ed. 3 vols. London, 1956.

Liss, Peggy [K.]. *Atlantic Empires: The Network of Trade and Revolution, 1713–1826.* Baltimore, 1982.

Littlefield, Daniel C. "Plantations, Paternalism, and Profitability: Factors Affecting African Demography in the Old British Empire." *Journal of Southern History,* LXVII (1981), 167–182.

———. *Rice and Slaves: Ethnicity and the Slave Trade in Colonial South Carolina.* Baton Rouge, La., 1981.

Littleton, A[nanias] C., and B[asil] S. Yamey, eds. *Studies in the History of Accounting.* Homewood, Ill., 1956.

Lively, Robert A. "The American System: A Review Article." *Business History Review,* XXIX (1955), 81–96.

Lockhart, Audrey. *Some Aspects of Emigration from Ireland to the North American Colonies between 1660 and 1775.* New York, 1976.

Lockridge, Kenneth A. "Land, Population, and the Evolution of New England Society, 1630–1790." *Past and Present,* XXXIX (1968), 62–80.

———. *Literacy in Colonial New England: An Enquiry into the Social Context of Literacy in the Early Modern West.* New York, 1974.

———. "Il mutamento sociale e il significato della rivoluzione americana." [Translated by Gabriella Feruggia]. In *La rivoluzione americana,* edited by Tiziano Bonazzi, 175–200. Bologna, 1977.

———. *A New England Town, The First Hundred Years: Dedham, Massachusetts, 1636–1736.* Norton Essays in American History. New York, 1970.

————. "The Population of Dedham, Massachusetts, 1636–1736." *Economic History Review*, 2d Ser., XIX (1966), 318–344.

————. "Social Change and the Meaning of the American Revolution." *Journal of Social History*, VI (1973), 403–439.

Loehr, Rodney C. "Arthur Young and American Agriculture." *Agricultural History*, XLIII (1969), 43–56.

————. "Self-sufficiency on the Farm." *Agricultural History*, XXVI (1952), 37–41.

Looyenga, A[rjen] J. "Colonial Architecture in Africa, Asia, and the Americas: An Historical and Anthropological Approach." Unpublished manuscript.

Lord, Eleanor Louisa. *Industrial Experiments in the British Colonies of North America*. Johns Hopkins University Studies in Historical and Political Science, Extra Volumes, no. 17. Baltimore, 1898.

Lounsbury, Ralph Greenlee. *The British Fishery at Newfoundland, 1634–1763*. Yale Historical Publications, *Miscellany*, XXVII. New Haven, Conn., 1934.

————. "Yankee Trade at Newfoundland." *New England Quarterly*, III (1930), 607–626.

Lovett, Robert W. *American Economic and Business History Information Sources*. Management Information Guide no. 23. Detroit, Mich., 1971.

Low, W. A. "The Farmer in Post-Revolutionary Virginia, 1783–1789." *Agricultural History*, XXV (1951), 122–127.

————. "Merchant and Planter Relations in Post-Revolutionary Virginia, 1783–1789." *Virginia Magazine of History and Biography*, LXI (1953), 308–318.

Lowenthal, David. "The Population of Barbados." *Social and Economic Studies*, VI (1957), 445–501.

Lundeberg, Philip K. *The Continental Gunboat* Philadelphia *and the Northern Campaign of 1776*. Washington, D.C., 1966.

Lunn, [A.] Jean [E.]. "Economic Development in New France, 1713–1760." Ph.D. diss., McGill University, 1943.

————. "The Illegal Fur Trade out of New France, 1713–1760." Canadian Historical Association, *Report of the Annual Meeting*, [XVIII] (1939), 61–76.

Lydon, James G. "Fish and Flour for Gold: Southern Europe and the Colonial American Balance of Payments." *Business History Review*, XXXIX (1965), 171–183.

————. "Fish for Gold: The Massachusetts Fish Trade with Iberia, 1700–1773." *New England Quarterly*, LIV (1981), 539–582.

————. "New York and the Slave Trade, 1700 to 1774." *William and Mary Quarterly*, 3d Ser., XXXV (1978), 375–394.

————. "North Shore Trade in the Early Eighteenth Century." *American Neptune*, XXVIII (1968), 261–274.

————. "Philadelphia's Commercial Expansion, 1720–1739." *Pennsylvania Magazine of History and Biography*, XCI (1967), 401–418.

————. *Pirates, Privateers, and Profits*. Upper Saddle River, N.J., 1970.

————. "The Salem and Bilbao Fish Trade: Symbiosis in the Eighteenth Century." North American Society for Oceanic History, *Proceedings*, I (1977).

McAnear, Beverly, ed. "Mr. Robert R. Livingston's Reasons against a Land Tax." *Journal of Political Economy*, XLVIII (1940), 63–90.

McCallum, John. *Unequal Beginnings: Agricultural and Economic Development in Quebec and Ontario until 1870*. Toronto, 1980.

McClelland, Peter D. *Causal Explanation and Model Building in History, Economics, and the New Economic History*. Ithaca, N.Y., 1975.

————. "The Cost to America of British Imperial Policy." *American Economic Review*, LIX (1969), 370–381.

McCloskey, Donald N. "The Achievements of the Cliometric School." *Journal of Economic History*, XXXVIII (1978), 13–28.

McCormac, Eugene Irving. *White Servitude in Maryland, 1634–1820*. Johns Hopkins University Studies in Historical and Political Science, 22d Ser., nos. 3–4. Baltimore, 1904.

McCoy, Drew R. "Benjamin Franklin's Vision of a Republican Political Economy for America." *William and Mary Quarterly*, 3d Ser., XXXV (1978), 605–628.

———. *The Elusive Republic: Political Economy in Jeffersonian America*. Chapel Hill, N.C., 1980.

McCusker, John J. *Alfred: The First Continental Flagship, 1775–1778*. Smithsonian Studies in History and Technology, no. 20. Washington, D.C., 1973.

———. "Colonial Civil Servant and Counterrevolutionary: Thomas Irving (1738?–1800) in Boston, Charleston, and London." *Perspectives in American History*, XII (1979), 313–350.

———. "Colonial Paper Money." In *Studies on Money in Early America*, edited by Eric P. Newman and Richard G. Doty, 94–104. New York, 1976.

———. "The Current Value of English Exports, 1697 to 1800." *William and Mary Quarterly*, 3d Ser., XXVIII (1971), 607–628.

———. "The Distillation of Rum and Colonial America." In *The History of American Food Technology*, edited by G. Terry Sharrer. Washington, D.C., forthcoming.

———. *European Marine Lists and Bills of Entry: Early Commercial Publications and the Origins of the Business Press*. Cambridge, Mass., forthcoming.

———. "Growth, Stagnation, or Decline? The Economy of the British West Indies, 1763–1790." In *The Economy of Early America: The Revolutionary Period, 1763–1789*, edited by Ronald Hoffman, John J. McCusker, and Russell R. Menard. Charlottesville, Va., forthcoming.

———. "Historical Price Indexes for Use as Deflators of Money Values in Great Britain and the United States, 1600 to the Present." Forthcoming.

———. *An Introduction to the Naval Officer Shipping Lists*. In progress.

———. *Money and Exchange in Europe and America, 1600–1775: A Handbook*. Chapel Hill, N.C., 1978.

———. "New Guides to Primary Sources on the History of Early British America." *William and Mary Quarterly*, 3d Ser., XLI (1984), 277–295.

———. "New York City and the Bristol Packet: A Chapter in Eighteenth Century Postal History." *Postal History Journal*, XX (1968), 15–24.

———. "The Pennsylvania Shipping Industry in the Eighteenth Century." Typescript in the Historical Society of Pennsylvania, Philadelphia, 1972.

———. "The Rum Trade and the Balance of Payments of the Thirteen Continental Colonies, 1650–1775." Ph.D. diss., University of Pittsburgh, 1970.

———. "Ships Registered at the Port of Philadelphia before 1776: A Computerized Listing." Unpublished manuscript, Historical Society of Pennsylvania, Philadelphia.

———. "Sources of Investment Capital in the Colonial Philadelphia Shipping Industry." *Journal of Economic History*, XXXII (1972), 146–157.

———. "The Tonnage of Ships Engaged in British Colonial Trade during the Eighteenth Century." *Research in Economic History*, VI (1981), 73–105.

———. "Weights and Measures in the Colonial Sugar Trade: The Gallon and the Pound and Their International Equivalents." *William and Mary Quarterly*, 3d Ser., XXX (1973), 599–624, and "Correction," *ibid.*, XXXI (1974), 164.

McCusker, John J., and Cora Gravesteijn. *The Commodity Price Currents, Exchange Rate Currents, and Money Currents of Early Modern Europe: The Beginnings of Commer-*

cial and Financial Journalism. Harvard University Library Bibliographical Series, no. 1. Forthcoming.

McCusker, John J., and Barbara Bartz Petchenik. "Economic Activity." In *Atlas of Early American History: The Revolutionary Era, 1760–1790,* edited by Lester J. Cappon *et al.,* 26–27, 103–104. Princeton, N.J., 1976.

McDevitt, Joseph Lawrence, Jr. "The House of Rotch: Whaling Merchants of Massachusetts, 1734–1828." Ph.D. diss., American University, 1978.

McDonald, Forrest, and Ellen Shapiro McDonald. "The Ethnic Origins of the American People, 1790." *William and Mary Quarterly,* 3d Ser., XXXVII (1980), 179–199.

McDonald, Roderick Alexander. "'Goods and Chattels': The Economy of Slaves on Sugar Plantations in Jamaica and Louisiana." Ph.D. diss., University of Kansas, 1981.

McFarland, Raymond. *A History of the New England Fisheries.* [Philadelphia], 1911.

MacFarlane, Ronald Oliver. "The Massachusetts Bay Truck-Houses in Diplomacy with the Indians." *New England Quarterly,* XI (1938), 48–65.

McKay, Donald C., ed. *Essays in the History of Modern Europe.* New York, 1936.

McKee, Samuel [D.], Jr. "The Economic Pattern of Colonial New York." In *History of the State of New York,* edited by Alexander C. Flick, II, 247–282. New York, 1933.

McMahon, Sarah F. "Provisions Laid Up for the Family: Toward a History of Diet in New England, 1650–1850." *Historical Methods,* XIV (1981), 4–21.

McManis, Douglas R. *Colonial New England: A Historical Geography.* Historical Geography of North America Series. New York, 1975.

McManus, Edgar J. *Black Bondage in the North.* Syracuse, N.Y., 1973.

———. *A History of Negro Slavery in New York.* Syracuse, N.Y., 1966.

Maganzin, Louis. "Economic Depression in Maryland and Virginia, 1783–1787." Ph.D. diss., Georgetown University, 1967.

Main, Gloria Lund. "The Correction of Biases in Colonial American Probate Records." *Historical Methods Newsletter,* VIII (1974), 10–28.

———. "Inequality in Early America: The Evidence from Probate Records of Massachusetts and Maryland." *Journal of Interdisciplinary History,* VII (1977), 559–581.

———. "Maryland and the Chesapeake Economy, 1670–1720." In *Law, Society, and Politics in Early Maryland,* edited by Aubrey C. Land, Lois Green Carr, and Edward C. Papenfuse, 134–152. Baltimore, 1977.

———. "Personal Wealth in Colonial America: Explorations in the Use of Probate Records from Maryland and Massachusetts, 1650–1720." Ph.D. diss., Columbia University, 1972.

———. "Probate Records as a Source for Early American History." *William and Mary Quarterly,* 3d Ser., XXXII (1975), 89–99.

———. *Tobacco Colony: Life in Early Maryland, 1650–1720.* Princeton, N.J., 1982.

Main, Jackson Turner. "The Distribution of Property in Colonial Connecticut." In *The Human Dimensions of Nation Making: Essays on Colonial and Revolutionary America,* edited by James Kirby Martin, 54–107. Madison, Wis., 1976.

———. *The Social Structure of Revolutionary America.* Princeton, N.J., 1965.

———. *The Sovereign States, 1775–1783.* New York, 1973.

Mair, John. *Book-keeping Methodiz'd; or, A Methodical Treatise of Merchant-Accompts, according to the Italian Form.* Edinburgh, 1736.

Makinson, David H. *Barbados: A Study of North-American–West-Indian Relations, 1739–1789.* Studies in American History, III. The Hague, 1964.

Malone, Joseph J. *Pine Trees and Politics: The Naval Stores and Forest Policy in Colonial New England, 1691–1775.* Seattle, Wash., 1964.

Malthus, Thomas Robert. *An Essay on the Principle of Population, as It Affects the Future Improvement of Society.* London, 1798.

Mank, Russell Walter, Jr. "Family Structure in Northampton, Massachusetts, 1654–1729." Ph.D. diss., University of Denver, 1975.

Manning, S[amuel] F. *New England Masts and the King's Broad Arrow.* Maritime Monographs and Reports, no. 42. [London], 1979.

Marber, Allen Sheldon. "The New York Iron Merchant and Manufacturer: A Study of Eighteenth-Century Entrepreneurship." Ph.D. diss., New York University, 1974.

Marcy, Peter T. "Factors Affecting the Fecundity and Fertility of Historical Populations: A Review." *Journal of Family History,* VI (1981), 309–326.

Marr, William L., and Donald G. Paterson. *Canada: An Economic History.* Toronto, 1980.

Marsh, Julian P. "The Spring Plantation Estate: A Study of Some Aspects of a Jamaican Sugar Plantation, 1747–1801." B.A. thesis, University of Nottingham, 1969.

Marshall, Alfred. *Industry and Trade: A Study of Industrial Technique and Business Organization; and of Their Influences on the Conditions of Various Classes and Nations.* London, 1919.

———. *Principles of Economics: An Introductory Volume* (1890). 9th ed. 2 vols. New York, 1961.

Marshall, Woodville K. "A Review of Historical Writing on the Commonwealth Caribbean since c. 1940." *Social and Economic Studies,* XXIV (1975), 271–307.

Marti, Donald B. "Early Agricultural Societies in New York: The Foundations of Improvement." *New York History,* XLVIII (1967), 313–331.

Martin, Calvin. *Keepers of the Game: Indian-Animal Relationships and the Fur Trade.* Berkeley and Los Angeles, Calif., 1978.

Martin, James Kirby, ed. *The Human Dimensions of Nation Making: Essays on Colonial and Revolutionary America.* Madison, Wis., 1976.

Martin, John Biddulph. *"The Grasshopper" in Lombard Street.* London, 1892.

Martin, Margaret E[lizabeth]. *Merchants and Trade of the Connecticut River Valley, 1750–1820.* Smith College Studies in History, XXIV. Northampton, Mass., 1939.

Martin, Robert F. *National Income in the United States, 1799–1938.* National Industrial Conference Board Studies, no. 241. New York, 1939.

Mason, Bernard. "Entrepreneurial Activity in New York during the American Revolution." *Business History Review,* XL (1966), 190–212.

Mathews, Lois Kimball. *The Expansion of New England: The Spread of New England Settlement and Institutions to the Mississippi River, 1620–1865.* Boston, 1909.

Matthews, Keith. "The West Country–Newfoundland Fisheries (Chiefly in the Seventeenth and Eighteenth Centuries)." Ph.D. thesis, Oxford University, 1968.

Mauro, Frédéric. *L'expansion européenne (1600–1870).* Nouvelle Clio, 27. 2d ed. Paris, 1967.

May, Louis Philippe. *Histoire économique de la Martinique (1635–1763).* Paris, 1930.

Mayer, Margit. *Die Entstehung des Nationalstaates in Nordamerika.* Frankfurt am Main, 1979.

Mazzatenta, O. Louis. "New England's 'Little Portugal.'" *National Geographic,* CXLVII (1975), 90–109.

Meade, James E. *The Balance of Payments.* Rev. ed. London, [1952].

Meier, Gerald M. *Leading Issues in Economic Development.* 3d ed. New York, 1976.

Mélanges d'histoire du Canada français offerts au professeur Marcel Trudel. Cahiers du Centre de Recherche en Civilisation Canadienne-Française, XIV. Ottawa, 1978.

Mellor, George R. "Emigration from the British Isles to the New World, 1765–1775." *History: The Journal of the Historical Association,* N.S., XL (1955), 68–83.

Menard, Russell Robert. "British Migration to the Chesapeake Colonies in the Seventeenth Century." Paper presented at the Economic History Workshop, University of Chicago, February 1980.

———. "Comment on Paper by Ball and Walton." *Journal of Economic History*, XXXVI (1976), 118–125.

———. "Economy and Society in Early Colonial Maryland." Ph.D. diss., University of Iowa, 1975.

———. "Farm Prices of Maryland Tobacco, 1659–1710." *Maryland Historical Magazine*, LXVIII (1973), 80–85.

———. "Five Maryland Censuses, 1700 to 1712: A Note on the Quality of the Quantities." *William and Mary Quarterly*, 3d Ser., XXXVII (1980), 616–626.

———. "From Servants to Slaves: The Transformation of the Chesapeake Labor System." *Southern Studies*, XVI (1977), 355–390.

———. "From Servant to Freeholder: Status Mobility and Property Accumulation in Seventeenth-Century Maryland." *William and Mary Quarterly*, 3d Ser., XXX (1973), 37–64.

———. "The Growth of Population in the Chesapeake Colonies: A Comment." *Explorations in Economic History*, XVIII (1981), 399–410.

———. "Immigrants and Their Increase: The Process of Population Growth in Early Colonial Maryland." In *Law, Society, and Politics in Early Maryland*, edited by Aubrey C. Land, Lois Green Carr, and Edward C. Papenfuse, 88–110. Baltimore, 1977.

———. "Immigration to the Chesapeake Colonies in the Seventeenth Century: A Review Essay." *Maryland Historical Magazine*, LXVIII (1973), 323–329.

———. "The Maryland Slave Population, 1658 to 1730: A Demographic Profile of Blacks in Four Counties." *William and Mary Quarterly*, 3d Ser., XXXII (1975), 29–54.

———. "A Note on Chesapeake Tobacco Prices, 1618–1660." *Virginia Magazine of History and Biography*, LXXXIV (1976), 401–410.

———. "The Tobacco Industry in the Chesapeake Colonies, 1617–1730: An Interpretation." *Research in Economic History*, V (1980), 109–177.

———. "Why African Slavery? Free Land, Plantation Agriculture, and the Supply of Labor in the Growth of British-American Slave Societies." Paper presented at the Conference on New World Slavery: Comparative Perspectives. Rutgers University, Newark, N.J., May 1980.

Menard, Russell Robert, Lois Green Carr, and Lorena S. Walsh. "A Small Planter's Profits: The Cole Estate and the Growth of the Early Chesapeake Economy." *William and Mary Quarterly*, 3d Ser., XL (1983), 171–196.

Menard, Russell Robert, P. M. G. Harris, and Lois Green Carr. "Opportunity and Inequality: The Distribution of Wealth on the Lower Western Shore of Maryland, 1638–1705." *Maryland Historical Magazine*, LXIX (1974), 169–184.

Menard, Russell Robert, and Lorena S. Walsh. "The Demography of Somerset County, Maryland: A Progress Report." *Newberry Papers in Family and Community History*, 81-2 (1981).

Mendels, Franklin F. "Proto-industrialization: The First Phase of the Industrialization Process." *Journal of Economic History*, XXXII (1972), 241–261.

Menken, Jane, James Trussell, and Susan Watkins. "The Nutrition Fertility Link: An Evaluation of the Evidence." *Journal of Interdisciplinary History*, XI (1981), 425–441.

Mepham, M. J., and W. E. Stone. "John Mair, M.A.: Author of the First Classical Bookkeeping Series." *Accounting and Business Research*, VII (1977), 128–134.

Merivale, Herman. *Lectures on Colonization and Colonies Delivered before the University of Oxford in 1839, 1840, 1841*. London, 1841–1842.

Meriwether, Robert L. *The Expansion of South Carolina, 1729–1765.* Kingsport, Tenn., 1940.

Merrens, Harry Roy. *Colonial North Carolina in the Eighteenth Century: A Study in Historical Geography.* Chapel Hill, N.C., 1964.

Merrill, Michael. "Cash Is Good to Eat: Self-sufficiency and Exchange in the Rural Economy of the United States." *Radical History Review*, IV (1977), 42–72.

Metcalf, George. *Royal Government and Political Conflict in Jamaica, 1729–1783.* Imperial Studies Series, XXVII. London, 1965.

Meyer, Jean. "Les difficultés du commerce franco-américain vues de Nantes (1776–1790)." *French Historical Studies*, XI (1979), 159–183.

Meyer, John R., and Alfred H. Conrad. "Economic Theory, Statistical Inference, and Economic History." *Journal of Economic History*, XVII (1957), 524–544.

Michell, A. R. "The European Fisheries in Early Modern History." In *The Economic Organization of Early Modern Europe*, edited by E. E. Rich and C. H. Wilson, 133–184. Vol. V of *The Cambridge Economic History of Europe.* Cambridge, 1977.

Middleton, Arthur Pierce. "Ships and Shipbuilding in the Chesapeake Bay and Tributaries." In *Chesapeake Bay in the American Revolution*, edited by Ernest M. Eller, 98–132. Centerville, Md., 1981.

———. *Tobacco Coast: A Maritime History of Chesapeake Bay in the Colonial Era.* Newport News, Va., 1953.

Mill, John Stuart. *Principles of Political Economy with Some of Their Applications to Social Philosophy* (1848). Edited by W. J. Ashley. London, [1940].

Millard, A[nnie] M. "Analyses of Port Books Recording Merchandises Imported into the Port of London by English and Alien and Denizen Merchants for Certain Years between 1588 and 1640." Typescript, 1960. Copies in the Public Record Office, Chancery Lane, London, and in Widener Library, Harvard University, Cambridge, Mass.

———. "The Import Trade of London, 1600–1640." 3 vols. Ph.D. thesis, University of London, 1956.

Miller, Joseph C. "Mortality in the Atlantic Slave Trade: Statistical Evidence on Causality." *Journal of Interdisciplinary History*, XI (1981), 385–423.

———. Reply to Raymond Cohn and Richard A. Jensen, "Mortality in the Atlantic Slave Trade." *Journal of Interdisciplinary History*, XIII (1982), 331–336.

———. *Slavery: A Comparative Teaching Bibliography.* Honolulu, Hawaii, 1977.

Miller, Perry. *The New England Mind: From Colony to Province.* Cambridge, Mass., 1953.

Miller, William. "The Effects of the American Revolution on Indentured Servitude." *Pennsylvania History*, VII (1940), 131–141.

Minchinton, W[alter] E. "The Slave Trade of Bristol with the British Mainland Colonies in North America, 1699–1770." In *Liverpool, the African Slave Trade, and Abolition: Essays to Illustrate Current Knowledge and Research*, edited by Roger Anstey and P. E. H. Hair, 39–59. Historic Society of Lancashire and Cheshire Occasional Series, II. [Liverpool], 1976.

———, ed. *The Growth of English Overseas Trade in the Seventeenth and Eighteenth Centuries.* Debates in Economic History. London, 1969.

Minchinton, W[alter] E., and C[hristopher] J. French. *Customs 3 (1696–1780) in the Public Record Office, London.* [Wakefield, Yorkshire], 1974.

Mirowski, Philip Edward. "The Birth of the Business Cycle." Ph.D. diss., University of Michigan, 1979.

Mishkin, David Joel. *The American Colonial Wine Industry: An Economic Interpretation.* New York, 1975 (Ph.D. diss., University of Illinois, 1966).

Mishoff, Willard O. "Business in Philadelphia during the British Occupation, 1777–

1778." *Pennsylvania Magazine of History and Biography*, LXI (1937), 165–181.

Mitchell, Robert D. "Agricultural Change and the American Revolution: A Virginia Case Study." *Agricultural History*, XLVII (1973), 119–132.

———. *Commercialism and Frontier: Perspectives on the Early Shenandoah Valley*. Charlottesville, Va., 1977.

Mitchell, Wesley C. *The Making and Using of Index Numbers*. U.S. Department of Labor, Bureau of Labor Statistics, Bulletin 656, pt. 1. Washington, D.C., 1938.

Molen, Patricia A. "Population and Social Patterns in Barbados in the Early Eighteenth Century." *William and Mary Quarterly*, 3d Ser., XXVIII (1971), 287–300.

Moller, Herbert. "Sex Composition and Correlated Culture Patterns of Colonial America." *William and Mary Quarterly*, 3d Ser., II (1945), 113–153.

Moloney, Francis Xavier. *The Fur Trade in New England, 1620–1676*. Cambridge, Mass., 1931.

Molovinsky, Lemuel David. "Pennsylvania's Legislative Efforts to Finance the War for Independence: A Study of the Continuity of Colonial Finance, 1775–83." Ph.D. diss., Temple University, 1975.

Moodie, D. W. "Agriculture and the Fur Trade." In *Old Trails and New Directions: Papers of the Third North American Fur Trade Conference*, edited by Carol M. Judd and Arthur J. Ray, 272–290. Toronto, 1980.

Moody, Robert Earle, ed. "Massachusetts Trade with Carolina, 1686–1709." *North Carolina Historical Review*, XX (1943), 43–53.

Moogk, Peter Nicholas. "The Craftsmen of New France." Ph.D. diss., University of Toronto, 1973.

Moore, Warner Oland, Jr. "Henry Laurens: A Charleston Merchant in the Eighteenth Century, 1747–1771." Ph.D. diss., University of Alabama, 1974.

Morgan, Edmund S. "The American Revolution: Revisions in Need of Revising." *William and Mary Quarterly*, 3d Ser., XIV (1957), 3–15.

———. *American Slavery, American Freedom: The Ordeal of Colonial Virginia*. New York, 1975.

———. "Colonial Ideas of Parliamentary Power, 1764–1766." *William and Mary Quarterly*, 3d Ser., V (1948), 311–341.

———. "Headrights and Head Counts: A Review Article." *Virginia Magazine of History and Biography*, LXXX (1972), 361–371.

———. "The Labor Problem at Jamestown, 1607–18." *American Historical Review*, LXXVI (1971), 595–611.

Morgan, Kenneth. "Bristol Merchants and the Colonial Trades, 1748–1783." Ph.D. thesis, Oxford University, forthcoming.

———. "The Organization of the Convict Trade to Maryland: Stevenson, Randolph & Cheston, 1768–1775." *William and Mary Quarterly*, 3d Ser., forthcoming.

Morgan, Philip David. "Afro-American Cultural Change: The Case of Colonial South Carolina Slaves." Paper presented at the annual meeting of the Organization of American Historians, New Orleans, La., April 1979.

———. "The Development of Slave Culture in Eighteenth Century Plantation America." Ph.D. thesis, University College, London, 1977.

———, ed. "A Profile of a Mid-Eighteenth Century South Carolina Parish: The Tax Return of St. James', Goose Creek." *South Carolina Historical Magazine*, LXXXI (1980), 51–65.

Morison, Samuel Eliot. *John Paul Jones: A Sailor's Biography*. Boston, 1959.

Mörner, Magnus. "'Comprar o Criar': Fuentes Alternativas de Suministro de Esclavos en las Sociedades Plantaciónistas del Nuevo Mundo." *Revista de Historia de América*, XCI

(1981), 37–81. Originally presented as "'Buy or Breed?' Alternative Sources of Slave Supply in the Plantation Societies of the New World" at the 15th International Congress of Historical Sciences, Bucharest, 1980.

Morrill, James Roy, III. "North Carolina Public Finance, 1783–1789: The Problems of Minimal Government in an Underdeveloped Land." Ph.D. diss., University of North Carolina, 1967.

Morris, Richard B. *Government and Labor in Early America.* New York, 1946.

———, ed. *The Era of the American Revolution.* New York, 1939.

Morris, Richard B., and Jonathan Grossman. "The Regulation of Wages in Early Massachusetts." *New England Quarterly,* XI (1938), 470–500.

Morris, Richard J. "Wealth Distribution in Salem, Massachusetts, 1759–1799: The Impact of the Revolution and Independence." Essex Institute, *Historical Collections,* CXIV (1978), 87–102.

[Morris, Robert]. *The Papers of Robert Morris, 1781–1784.* Edited by E[lmer] James Ferguson *et al.* Pittsburgh, Pa., 1973–.

Morriss, Margaret Shove. *Colonial Trade of Maryland, 1689–1715.* Johns Hopkins University Studies in Historical and Political Science, 32d Ser., no. 3. Baltimore, 1914.

Morse, Jedidiah. *The American Geography; or, A View of the Present Situation of the United States of America.* . . . Elizabeth Town, [N.J.], 1789.

Moss, C. G. Gordon. "The Virginia Plantation System: A Study of Economic Conditions in the Colony for the Years 1700–1750." Ph.D. diss., Yale University, 1932.

Moss, Roger William. "Master Builders: A History of the Colonial Philadelphia Building Trades." Ph.D. diss., University of Delaware, 1972.

Mui, Hoh-Cheung, and Lorna H. Mui. "Smuggling and the British Tea Trade before 1784." *American Historical Review,* LXXIV (1968), 44–73.

———. "'Trends in Eighteenth-Century Smuggling' Reconsidered." *Economic History Review,* 2d Ser., XXVIII (1975), 28–43.

Mullin, Gerald W. *Flight and Rebellion: Slave Resistance in Eighteenth-Century Virginia.* New York, 1972.

Multhauf, Robert P. *Neptune's Gift: A History of Common Salt.* Baltimore, 1978.

Murrin, John M. "Review Essay." *History and Theory,* XI (1972), 226–275.

Museums at Stony Brook. *Catalogue of Vehicles: The Carriage House of the Suffolk Museum at Stony Brook, Long Island.* Stony Brook, N.Y., 1954.

Mutch, Robert E. "Yeoman and Merchant in Pre-industrial America: Eighteenth-Century Massachusetts as a Case Study." *Societas,* VII (1977), 279–302.

Myint, H[yla]. "The 'Classical Theory' of International Trade and the Underdeveloped Countries." *Economic Journal,* LXVIII (1958), 317–337.

The Mystery of the New Fashioned Goldsmiths or Bankers. Their Rise, Growth, State, and Decay, Discovered in a Merchant's Letter to a Country Gent. . . . [London], 1676.

Narrett, David Evan. "Patterns of Inheritance in Colonial New York City, 1664–1775: A Study in the History of the Family." Ph.D. diss., Cornell University, 1981.

Nash, Gary Baring. "Economics and Politics in Colonial Pennsylvania, 1681–1701." Ph.D. diss., Princeton University, 1964.

———. "Maryland's Economic War with Pennsylvania." *Maryland Historical Magazine,* LX (1965), 231–244.

———. "The New York Census of 1737: A Critical Note on the Integration of Statistical and Literary Sources." *William and Mary Quarterly,* 3d Ser., XXXVI (1979), 428–435.

———. "Poverty and Poor Relief in Pre-Revolutionary Philadelphia." *William and Mary Quarterly,* 3d Ser., XXXIII (1976), 3–30.

————. *Quakers and Politics: Pennsylvania, 1681–1726.* Princeton, N.J., 1968.

————. "The Quest for the Susquehanna Valley: New York, Pennsylvania, and the Seventeenth-Century Fur Trade." *New York History*, XLVIII (1967), 3–27.

————. "Slaves and Slaveowners in Colonial Philadelphia." *William and Mary Quarterly*, 3d Ser., XXX (1973), 223–256.

————. "Up from the Bottom in Franklin's Philadelphia." *Past and Present*, LXXVII (1977), 57–83.

————. *The Urban Crucible: Social Change, Political Consciousness, and the Origins of the American Revolution.* Cambridge, Mass., 1979.

————. "Urban Wealth and Poverty in Pre-Revolutionary America." *Journal of Interdisciplinary History*, VI (1976), 545–584.

Nash, Gary Baring, and Billy G. Smith. "The Population of Eighteenth-Century Philadelphia." *Pennsylvania Magazine of History and Biography*, XCIX (1975), 362–368.

Nash, Robert C. "The English and Scottish Tobacco Trades in the Seventeenth and Eighteenth Centuries: Legal and Illegal Trade." *Economic History Review*, 2d Ser., XXXV (1982), 354–372.

Nelson, William E. *Americanization of the Common Law: The Impact of Legal Change on Massachusetts Society, 1760–1830.* Cambridge, Mass., 1975.

Nettels, Curtis Putnam. "The Economic Relations of Boston, Philadelphia, and New York, 1680–1715." *Journal of Economic and Business History*, III (1931), 185–215.

————. *The Emergence of a National Economy, 1775–1815.* New York, 1962.

————. "The Menace of Colonial Manufacturing, 1690–1720." *New England Quarterly*, IV (1931), 230–269.

————. *The Money Supply of the American Colonies before 1720.* University of Wisconsin Studies in the Social Sciences and History, no. 20. Madison, Wis., 1934.

————. *The Roots of American Civilization: A History of American Colonial Life.* 2d ed. New York, 1963.

Neu, Irene D. "The Iron Plantations of Colonial New York." *New York History*, XXXIII (1952), 3–24.

Newman, Eric P. "Counterfeit Continental Currency Goes to War." *Numismatist*, LXX (1957), 5–16, 137–147.

————. *The Early Paper Money of America.* Bicentennial ed. [2d ed.]. Racine, Wis., 1976.

Newman, Eric P., and Richard G. Doty, eds. *Studies on Money in Early America.* New York, 1976.

Newton, Arthur Percival. "The Beginnings of English Colonisation, 1569–1618." In *The Old Empire: From the Beginnings to 1783.* Vol. I of *The Cambridge History of the British Empire*, edited by J. Holland Rose, A. P. Newton, and E. A. Benians, 53–92. Cambridge, 1929.

————. *The Colonizing Activities of the English Puritans: The Last Phase of the Elizabethan Struggle with Spain.* Yale Historical Publications, *Miscellany*, I. New Haven, Conn., 1914.

————. "The Great Emigration, 1618–1648." In *The Old Empire: From the Beginnings to 1783.* Vol. I of *The Cambridge History of the British Empire*, edited by J. Holland Rose, A. P. Newton, and E. A. Benians, 136–182. Cambridge, 1929.

Nicholls, Michael L[ee]. "Origins of the Virginia Southside, 1703–1753: A Social and Economic Study." Ph.D. diss., College of William and Mary, 1972.

North, Douglass C. *The Economic Growth of the United States, 1790–1860.* Englewood Cliffs, N.J., 1961.

————. "Location Theory and Regional Economic Growth." *Journal of Political Economy*, LXIII (1955), 243–258.

————. "Sources of Productivity Change in Ocean Shipping, 1600–1850." *Journal of Political Economy*, LXXVI (1968), 953–970.

Norton, Mary Beth. *Liberty's Daughters: The Revolutionary Experience of American Women, 1750–1800.* Boston, 1980.

Norton, Susan L. "Marital Migration in Essex County, Massachusetts, in the Colonial and Early Federal Periods." *Journal of Marriage and the Family*, XXXV (1973), 406–418.

————. "Population Growth in Colonial America: A Study of Ipswich, Massachusetts." *Population Studies*, XXV (1971), 433–452.

Norton, Thomas Elliot. *The Fur Trade in Colonial New York, 1686–1776.* Madison, Wis., 1974.

Norton, William B. "Paper Currency in Massachusetts during the Revolution." *New England Quarterly*, VII (1934), 43–69.

Nuxoll, Elizabeth Miles. "Congress and the Munitions Merchants: The Secret Committee of Trade during the American Revolution, 1775–1777." Ph.D. diss., City University of New York, 1979.

Oakes, Elinor F. "A Ticklish Business: Dairying in New England and Pennsylvania, 1750–1812." *Pennsylvania History*, XLVII (1980), 195–212.

Oaks, Robert F. "Big Wheels in Philadelphia: Du Simitière's List of Carriage Owners [1772]." *Pennsylvania Magazine of History and Biography*, XCV (1971), 351–362.

————. "Philadelphia Merchants and the Origins of American Independence." American Philosophical Society, *Proceedings*, CXXI (1977), 407–436.

Oberseider, Nancy Lou. "A Socio-demographic Study of the Family as a Social Unit in Tidewater Virginia, 1660–1776." Ph.D. diss., University of Maryland, 1975.

O'Brien, Patrick. "European Economic Development: The Contribution of the Periphery." *Economic History Review*, 2d Ser., XXXV (1982), 1–18.

O'Callaghan, E[dward] B[ailey], [and Berthold Fernow], eds. *Documents Relative to the Colonial History of the State of New-York. . . .* 15 vols. Albany, N.Y., 1853–1887.

Oddy, Derek [J.], and Derek [S.]Miller, eds. *The Making of the Modern British Diet.* London, 1976.

O'Keefe, Doris. "Marriage and Migration in Colonial New England: A Study in Historical Population Geography." Department of Geography, Syracuse University, *Discussion Paper Series*, no. 16 (June 1976).

Oldham, Trevor. "The Administration of the System of Transportation of British Convicts, 1763–1793." Ph.D. thesis, University of London, 1933.

Olson, Albert Laverne. *Agricultural Economy and the Population in Eighteenth-Century Connecticut.* Connecticut Tercentenary Series, XL. New Haven, Conn., 1935.

Olson, Alison Gilbert. "The Board of Trade and London-American Interest Groups in the Eighteenth Century." *Journal of Imperial and Commonwealth History*, VIII (1980), 33–50.

————. "The London Mercantile Lobby and the Coming of the American Revolution." *Journal of American History*, LXIX (1982), 21–41.

————. "Parliament, the London Lobbies, and Provincial Interests in England and America." *Historical Reflections/Reflections Historique*, VI (1979), 367–386.

O'Mara, James J. "Urbanization in Tidewater Virginia during the Eighteenth Century: A Study in Historical Geography." Ph.D. diss., York University, 1979.

Omi, Kenkichi. "Juhasseiki Amerika shokuminchi no boeki kozo ni tsuite" (On the structure of trade in the eighteenth-century American colonies). *Doshisha Amerika Kenkyu (Doshisha [University] American Studies)*, XVIII (1982), 51–59.

Omi, Kenkichi, and Yasuo Sakakibara. "Economic Development of the American Colonies in the Eighteenth Century." *American Review* (Tokyo), XV (1981), 108–123, 169–170.

Opper, Edward. "Dutch East India Company Artisans in the Early Eighteenth Century." Ph.D. diss., Indiana University, 1975.

Osgood, Herbert L. *The American Colonies in the Seventeenth Century.* 3 vols. New York, 1904–1907.

Osterud, Nancy, and John Fulton. "Family Limitation and Age at Marriage: Fertility Decline in Sturbridge, Massachusetts, 1730–1850." *Population Studies*, XXX (1976), 481–494.

Ostrander, Gilman M. "The Colonial Molasses Trade." *Agricultural History*, XXX (1956), 77–84.

Ouellet, Fernand. *Histoire économique et sociale du Québec, 1760–1850: Structures et conjoncture.* Montreal, 1966.

Overton, Mark. "Estimating Crop Yields from Probate Inventories: An Example from East Anglia, 1585–1735." *Journal of Economic History*, XXXIX (1979), 363–378.

Oviatt, F[itzalan] C. "Historical Study of Fire Insurance in the United States." American Academy of Political and Social Sciences, *Annals*, XXVI (1905), 335–358.

Pagan, John R. "Dutch Maritime and Commercial Activity in Mid-Seventeenth-Century Virginia." *Virginia Magazine of History and Biography*, XC (1982), 485–501.

Paglin, Morton. "The Measurement and Trend of Inequality: A Basic Revision." *American Economic Review*, LXV (1975), 598–609.

Palmer, Stanley H. *Economic Arithmetic: A Guide to the Statistical Sources of English Commerce, Industry, and Finance, 1700–1850.* New York, 1977.

Palmer, William R. "The Whaling Port of Sag Harbor." Ph.D. diss., Columbia University, 1959.

Pap, Leo. *The Portuguese-Americans.* Boston, 1981.

Papenfuse, Edward C., Jr. "Economic Analysis and Loyalist Strategy during the American Revolution: Robert Alexander's Remarks on the Economy of the Peninsula or Eastern Shore of Maryland." *Maryland Historical Magazine*, LXVIII (1973), 173–195.

———. *In Pursuit of Profit: The Annapolis Merchants in the Era of the American Revolution, 1763–1805.* Maryland Bicentennial Series. Baltimore, 1975.

———. "Planter Behavior and Economic Opportunity in a Staple Economy." *Agricultural History*, XLVI (1972), 297–311.

———. "An Uncertain Connection: Maryland's Trade with France during the American Revolution, 1778–1783." In *La révolution américaine et l'Europe*, [edited by Claude Fohlen and Jacques Godechot], 243–264. Colloque Internationaux du Centre de la Recherche Scientifique, no. 577. Paris, 1979.

Papenfuse, Edward C., Jr., and Gregory A. Stiverson. "General Smallwood's Recruits: The Peacetime Career of the Revolutionary War Private." *William and Mary Quarterly*, 3d Ser., XXX (1973), 117–132.

Pares, Richard. "The London Sugar Market, 1740–1769." *Economic History Review*, 2d Ser., IX (1956), 254–270.

———. *Merchants and Planters. Economic History Review*, Supplement, no. 4. Cambridge, 1960.

———. *War and Trade in the West Indies, 1739–1763.* Oxford, 1936.

———. *A West-India Fortune.* London, [1950].

————. *Yankees and Creoles: The Trade between North America and the West Indies before the American Revolution.* Cambridge, Mass., 1956.

[Parker, William N., ed.]. *Trends in the American Economy in the Nineteenth Century.* National Bureau of Economic Research, Studies in Income and Wealth, XXIV. Princeton, N.J., 1960.

Parker, William N., and Eric L. Jones, eds. *European Peasants and Their Markets: Essays in Agrarian Economic History.* Princeton, N.J., 1975.

Parker, William N., and Franklee Whartenby. "The Growth of Output before 1840." In *Trends in the American Economy in the Nineteenth Century,* edited by William N. Parker, 191–216. National Bureau of Economic Research, Studies in Income and Wealth, XXIV. Princeton, N.J., 1960.

Parks, Roger N. "The Roads of New England, 1790–1840." Ph.D. diss., Michigan State University, 1966.

Parsons, William T. "Isaac Norris II, The Speaker." Ph.D. diss., University of Pennsylvania, 1955.

Paskoff, Paul Frederick. "Colonial Merchant-Manufactures and Iron: A Study in Capital Transformation, 1725–1775." Ph.D. diss., Johns Hopkins University, 1976.

————. "Labor Productivity and Managerial Efficiency against a Static Technology: The Pennsylvania Iron Industry, 1750–1800." *Journal of Economic History,* XL (1980), 129–135.

Patten, John. "Rural-Urban Migration in Pre-industrial England." University of Oxford, School of Geography, *Research Papers,* VI (1973).

Patterson, Orlando. *The Sociology of Slavery: An Analysis of the Origins, Development, and Structure of Negro Slave Society in Jamaica.* Studies in Society. London, 1967.

————. "The Structural Origins of Slavery: A Critique of the Nieboer-Domar Hypothesis from a Comparative Perspective." In *Comparative Perspectives on Slavery in New World Plantation Societies,* edited by Vera Rubin and Arthur Tuden, 12–34. New York Academy of Sciences, *Annals,* CCXCII. New York, 1977.

Pawson, Michael, and David Buisseret. *Port Royal, Jamaica.* Oxford, 1975.

Peet, J. Richard. "The Spatial Expansion of Commercial Agriculture in the Nineteenth Century: A Von Thünen Interpretation." *Economic Geography,* XLV (1969), 283–301.

Pelletier, A. J. "Canadian Censuses of the Seventeenth Century." Canadian Political Science Association, *Papers and Proceedings,* II (1930), 20–34.

Pencak, William. "The Social Structure of Revolutionary Boston: Evidence from the Great Fire of 1760." *Journal of Interdisciplinary History,* X (1979), 267–278.

Penson, Lillian M. *The Colonial Agents of the British West Indies: A Study in Colonial Administration, Mainly in the Eighteenth Century.* London, 1924.

————. "The London West India Interest in the Eighteenth Century." *English Historical Review,* XXXVI (1921), 373–392.

Percy, David O. "An Embarrassment of Richness: Colonial Soil Cultivation Practices." *Associates N[ational] A[gricultural] L[ibrary] Today,* N.S., II (1977), 4–11.

Perkins, Edwin J. *The Economy of Colonial America.* New York, 1980.

Perry, James Russell. "The Formation of a Society on Virginia's Eastern Shore, 1615–1655." Ph.D. diss., Johns Hopkins University, 1980.

Persons, Warren M. *Government Experimentation in Business.* New York, 1934.

Peterson, Arthur G. "Flour and Grist Milling in Virginia: A Brief History." *Virginia Magazine of History and Biography,* XLIII (1935), 97–108.

Peterson, Merrill D. "Thomas Jefferson and Commercial Policy, 1783–1793." *William and Mary Quarterly,* 3d Ser., XXII (1965), 584–610.

Peterson, Raymond George, Jr. "George Washington, Capitalistic Farmer: A Documentary

Study of Washington's Business Activities and the Sources of His Wealth." Ph.D. diss., Ohio State University, 1970.

Petty, Julian J. *The Growth and Distribution of Population in South Carolina.* South Carolina State Planning Board, *Bulletin*, XI. Charleston, S.C., 1943.

Phelps Brown, Henry, and Sheila V. Hopkins. *A Perspective of Wages and Prices.* London, 1981.

———. "Seven Centuries of the Prices of Consumables, Compared with Builders' Wage-Rates." *Economica*, N.S., XXIII (1956), 296–314.

Phillips, James Duncan. *Salem in the Eighteenth Century.* Boston, 1937.

———. *Salem in the Seventeenth Century.* Boston, 1933.

Phillips, Paul Chrisler. *The Fur Trade.* 2 vols. Norman, Okla., 1961.

Phillips, Ulrich Bonnell. "The Slave Labor Problem in the Charleston District." *Political Science Quarterly*, XXII (1907), 416–439.

Pingeon, Frances D. "'Land of Slavery': Blacks in New Jersey from 1665 to 1846." Ph.D. diss., Columbia University, 1977.

Pinkett, Harold T. "Maryland as a Source of Food Supplies during the American Revolution." *Maryland Historical Magazine*, XLVI (1951), 157–172.

Pitkin, Timothy. *A Statistical View of the Commerce of the United States of America.* Hartford, Conn., 1816.

———. *A Statistical View of the Commerce of the United States of America. . . .* Rev. ed. New Haven, Conn., 1835.

Pitman, Frank Wesley. *The Development of the British West Indies, 1700–1763.* New Haven, Conn., 1917.

———. "The Settlement and Financing of British West India Plantations in the Eighteenth Century." In *Essays in Colonial History Presented to Charles McLean Andrews by His Students*, 252–283. New Haven, Conn., 1931.

Platt, Virginia Margaret Bever. "'And Don't Forget the Guinea Voyage': The Slave Trade of Aaron Lopez of Newport." *William and Mary Quarterly*, 3d Ser., XXXII (1975), 601–618.

———. "The East India Company and the Madagascar Slave Trade." *William and Mary Quarterly*, 3d Ser., XXVI (1969), 548–577.

———. "Tar, Staves, and New England Rum: The Trade of Aaron Lopez of Newport, Rhode Island, with Colonial North Carolina." *North Carolina Historical Review*, XLVIII (1971), 1–22.

———. "The Trade in East India Commodities to the American Colonies, 1690–1775." Ph.D. diss., State University of Iowa, 1940.

Platt, Virginia Margaret Bever, and David Curtis Skaggs, eds. *Of Mother Country and Plantations: Proceedings of the Twenty-seventh Conference in Early American History.* Bowling Green, Ohio, 1971.

Plummer, Wilbur C. "Consumer Credit in Colonial Philadelphia." *Pennsylvania Magazine of History and Biography*, LXVI (1942), 385–409.

Porter, Glenn, ed. *Encyclopedia of American Economic History: Studies of the Principal Movements and Ideas.* 3 vols. New York, 1980.

Postan, M[ichael] M., E[dwin] E. Rich, and Edward Miller, eds. *Economic Organization and Policies in the Middle Ages.* Vol. III of *The Cambridge Economic History of Europe.* Cambridge, 1963.

Posthumus, N[icolaas] W. *Inquiry into the History of Prices in Holland.* 2 vols. Leiden, 1946–1964.

Postlethwayt, Malachy, ed. *The Universal Dictionary of Trade and Commerce.* 2 vols. London, 1751–1755.

Potter, Jim. "The Effects of the American Revolution on the Economic Relations between the Former Colonies and the Mother Country." In *La révolution américaine
et l'Europe*, [edited by Claude Fohlen and Jacques Godechot], 265–277. Colloques
Internationaux du Centre National de la Recherche Scientifique, no. 577. Paris,
1979.
————. "The Growth of Population in America, 1700–1860." In *Population in History:
Essays in Historical Demography*, edited by D. V. Glass and D. E. C. Eversley,
631–688. Chicago, 1965.
Poulson, Barry Warren. *Value Added in Manufacturing, Mining, and Agriculture in the
American Economy from 1809 to 1839*. New York, 1975 (Ph.D. diss., Ohio State Uni-
versity, 1965).
Powell, Sumner Chilton. *Puritan Village: The Formation of a New England Town*. Mid-
dletown, Conn., 1963.
Preisser, Thomas M. "Alexandria and the Evolution of the Northern Virginia Economy,
1749–1776." *Virginia Magazine of History and Biography*, LXXXIX (1981),
282–293.
Prest, W. R. "Stability and Change in Old and New England: Clayworth and Dedham."
Journal of Interdisciplinary History, VI (1976), 359–374.
Price, Jacob M. "Buchanan & Simson, 1759–1763: A Different Kind of Glasgow Firm
Trading to the Chesapeake." *William and Mary Quarterly*, 3d Ser., XL (1983), 3–41.
————. "Capital and Credit in the British-Chesapeake Trade, 1750–1775." In *Of Mother
Country and Plantations: Proceedings of the Twenty-seventh Conference in Early
American History*, edited by Virginia Bever Platt and David Curtis Skaggs, 7–36. Bowl-
ing Green, Ohio, 1971.
————. *Capital and Credit in British Overseas Trade: The View from the Chesapeake,
1700–1776*. Cambridge, Mass., 1980.
————. "Colonial Trade and British Economic Development, 1660–1775." In *La révolu-
tion américaine et l'Europe*, [edited by Claude Fohlen and Jacques Godechot], 221–
242. Colloques Internationaux du Centre National de la Recherche Scientifique, no.
577. Paris, 1979.
————. "Colonial Trade and British Economic Development, 1660–1775." *Lex et Scientia: The International Journal of Law and Science*, XIV (1978), 101–126.
————. "Economic Function and the Growth of American Port Towns in the Eighteenth
Century." *Perspectives in American History*, VIII (1974), 121–186.
————. "The Economic Growth of the Chesapeake and the European Market, 1697–
1775." *Journal of Economic History*, XXIV (1964), 496–511.
————. *France and the Chesapeake: A History of the French Tobacco Monopoly, 1674–
1791, and of Its Relationship to the British and American Tobacco Trades*. 2 vols. Ann
Arbor, Mich., 1973.
————. "Joshua Johnson in London, 1771–1775: Credit and Commercial Organization
in the British Chesapeake Trade." In *Statesmen, Scholars, and Merchants: Essays in
Eighteenth-Century History Presented to Dame Lucy Sutherland*, edited by Anne
Whiteman, J. S. Bromley, and P. G. M. Dickson, 153–180. Oxford, 1973.
————. "The Map of Commerce, 1683–1721." In *The Rise of Great Britain and Russia,
1688–1715/25*, edited by J. S. Bromley, 834–874. Vol. VI of *The New Cambridge
Modern History*. Cambridge, 1970.
————. "The Maryland Bank Stock Case: British-American Financial and Political Rela-
tions before and after the American Revolution." In *Law, Society, and Politics in Early
Maryland*, edited by Aubrey C. Land, Lois Green Carr, and Edward C. Papenfuse,
3–40. Baltimore, 1977.

————. "New Time Series for Scotland's and Britain's Trade with the Thirteen Colonies and States, 1740 to 1791." *William and Mary Quarterly*, 3d Ser., XXII (1975), 307–325.

————. "A Note on the Value of Colonial Exports of Shipping." *Journal of Economic History*, XXXVI (1976), 704–724.

————. "Quantifying Colonial America: A Comment on Nash and Warden." *Journal of Interdisciplinary History*, VI (1976), 701–709.

————. Review of *Trade and Empire: The British Customs Service in Colonial America, 1660–1775*, by Thomas C. Barrow. *Journal of Economic History*, XXVII (1967), 399–400.

————. "The Rise of Glasgow in the Chesapeake Tobacco Trade, 1707–1775." *William and Mary Quarterly*, 3d Ser., XI (1954), 179–199.

————. *The Tobacco Adventure to Russia: Enterprise, Politics, and Diplomacy in the Quest for a Northern Market for English Colonial Tobacco, 1676–1722*. American Philosophical Society, *Transactions*, N.S., LI, pt. 1. Philadelphia, 1961.

————. "The Tobacco Trade and the Treasury, 1685–1733: British Mercantilism in Its Fiscal Aspects." Ph.D. diss., Harvard University, 1954.

[Pringle, Robert]. *The Letterbook of Robert Pringle, 1737–1745*. Edited by Walter B. Edgar. 2 vols. Columbia, S.C., 1972.

Pritchard, James Stewart. "Ships, Men, and Commerce: A Study of Maritime Activity in New France." Ph.D. diss., University of Toronto, 1971.

Proctor, Samuel, ed. *Eighteenth-Century Florida and the Revolutionary South*. Gainesville, Fla., 1978.

Proud, Robert. *The History of Pennsylvania, in North America, from . . . 1681, till after the Year 1742. . . .* 2 vols. Philadelphia, 1797–1798.

Pruitt, Bettye Hobbs. "Agriculture and Society in the Towns of Massachusetts, 1771: A Statistical Analysis." Ph.D. diss., Boston University, 1981.

Puckrein, Gary A[lexander]. "The Acquisitive Impulse: Plantation Society, Factions, and the Origins of the Barbadian Civil War (1627–1652)." Ph.D. diss., Brown University, 1978.

————. "Climate, Health, and Black Labor in the English Americas." *Journal of American Studies*, XIII (1979), 179–193.

Purcell, Carroll W., Jr. *Early Stationary Steam Engines in America: A Study in the Migration of Technology*. Washington, D.C., 1969.

Quinn, David Beers. *England and the Discovery of America, 1481–1620*. New York, 1974.

————. *North America from Earliest Discovery to First Settlements: The Norse Voyages to 1612*. New York, 1977.

Rabb, Theodore K. *Enterprise and Empire: Merchant and Gentry Investment in the Expansion of England, 1575–1630*. Cambridge, Mass., 1967.

Ragatz, Lowell Joseph. "Absentee Landlordism in the British Caribbean, 1750–1833." *Agricultural History*, V (1931), 7–24.

————. *The Fall of the Planter Class in the British Caribbean, 1763–1833: A Study in Social and Economic History*. New York, 1928.

————. *A Guide for the Study of British Caribbean History, 1763–1834, Including the Abolition and Emancipation Movements*. American Historical Association, *Annual Report . . . for the Year 1930*, Vol. III. Washington, D.C., 1932.

————, comp. *Statistics for the Study of British Caribbean Economic History, 1763–1833*. London, [1928].

Rainbolt, John C. "The Absence of Towns in Seventeenth Century Virginia." *Journal of Southern History*, XXXV (1969), 343–360.

————. *From Prescription to Persuasion: Manipulation of Seventeenth-Century Virginia Economy.* Port Washington, N.Y., 1974.

Rainey, Robert. *See* John Stewart.

Ramsay, David. *History of South Carolina, from Its First Settlement in 1670, to the Year 1808.* 2 vols. Charleston, S.C., 1809.

Ramsey, Robert Wayne. *Carolina Cradle: Settlement of the Northwest Carolina Frontier, 1747–1762.* Chapel Hill, N.C., 1964.

Rankin, Hugh F. *The Golden Age of Piracy.* Williamsburg in America Series, VII. Williamsburg, Va., 1969.

Ransom, Roger L., and Richard Sutch. *One Kind of Freedom: The Economic Consequences of Emancipation.* Cambridge, 1977.

Ransom, Roger L., Richard Sutch, and Gary M. Walton, eds. *Explorations in the New Economic History: Essays in Honor of Douglass C. North.* New York, 1982.

Rasch, Aa[ge]. *Niels Ryberg, 1725–1804: Fra bondedreng til handelsfyrste.* Jysk Selskab for Historie, Sprog og Litteratur, no. 12. Aarhus, Denmark, 1964.

Rawley, James A. *The Transatlantic Slave Trade: A History.* New York, 1981.

Rawlyk, George A. *Nova Scotia's Massachusetts: A Study of Massachusetts–Nova Scotia Relations, 1630 to 1784.* Montreal, 1973.

Rawson, Marion N. *Handwrought Ancestors: The Story of Early American Shops and Those Who Worked Therein.* New York, [1936].

Ray, Arthur J. "Indians as Consumers in the Eighteenth Century." In *Old Trails and New Directions: Papers of the Third North American Fur Trade Conference,* edited by Carol M. Judd and Arthur J. Ray, 255–271. Toronto, 1980.

————. *Indians in the Fur Trade: Their Role as Trappers, Hunters, and Middlemen in the Lands Southwest of Hudson Bay, 1660–1870.* Toronto, 1974.

Ray, Arthur J., and Donald B. Freeman. *"Give Us Good Measure": An Economic Analysis of Relations between the Indians and the Hudson's Bay Company before 1763.* Toronto, 1978.

Ready, Milton L. *The Castle Builders: Georgia's Economy under the Trustees, 1732–1754.* New York, 1978 (Ph.D. diss., University of Georgia, 1970).

Rediker, Marcus. "'Under the Banner of King Death': The Social World of Anglo-American Pirates." *William and Mary Quarterly,* 3d Ser., XXXVIII (1981), 203–227.

Rees, J[ames] F. "Mercantilism and the Colonies." In *The Old Empire: From the Beginnings to 1783.* Vol. I of *The Cambridge History of the British Empire,* edited by J. Holland Rose, A. P. Newton, and E. A. Benians, 561–602. Cambridge, 1929.

Reeves, John. *A History of the Law of Shipping and Navigation.* Dublin, 1792.

Reid, John G. *Acadia, Maine, and New Scotland: Marginal Colonies in the Seventeenth Century.* Toronto, 1981.

Reps, John W. *Tidewater Towns: City Planning in Colonial Virginia and Maryland.* Williamsburg, Va., 1972.

Rich, E[dwin] E. *The History of the Hudson's Bay Company, 1670–1870.* Hudson's Bay Record Society, *Publications,* XXI–XXII. London, 1958–1959.

————. "The Population of Elizabethan England." *Economic History Review,* 2d Ser., II (1950), 247–264.

————. "Trade Habits and Economic Motivation among the Indians of North America." *Canadian Journal of Economics and Political Science,* XXVI (1960), 35–53.

Rich, E[dwin] E., and C[harles] H. Wilson, eds. *The Economic Organization of Early Modern Europe.* Vol. V of *The Cambridge Economic History of Europe.* Cambridge, 1977.

Rich, Myra L. "Speculations on the Significance of Debt: Virginia, 1781–1789." *Virginia Magazine of History and Biography*, LXXVI (1968), 301–317.

Rich, Wesley Everett. *The History of the United States Post Office to the Year 1829.* Harvard Economic Studies, XXVII. Cambridge, Mass., 1924.

Richards, R. D. *The Early History of Banking in England.* London, 1929.

———. "The 'Stop of the Exchequer.'" *Economic History: Supplement to the Economic Journal,* II (1930), 45–62.

Richardson, P. David. "Profitability in the Bristol-Liverpool Slave Trade." *Revue Française d'Histoire d'Outre-Mer,* LXII (1975), 301–308.

———. "Profits in the Liverpool Slave Trade: The Accounts of William Davenport, 1757–1784." In *Liverpool, the African Slave Trade, and Abolition: Essays to Illustrate Current Knowledge and Research,* edited by Roger Anstey and P. E. H. Hair, 60–90. Historic Society of Lancashire and Cheshire Occasional Series, II. Liverpool, 1976.

Riley, Edward M. "The Town Acts of Colonial Virginia." *Journal of Southern History,* XVI (1950), 306–323.

Riley, James C. "Foreign Credit and Fiscal Stability: Dutch Investment in the United States, 1781–1794." *Journal of American History,* LXV (1978), 654–678.

———. *International Government Finance and the Amsterdam Capital Market, 1740–1815.* Cambridge, 1980.

———. "Mortality on Long-Distance Voyages in the Eighteenth Century." *Journal of Economic History,* XLI (1981), 651–656.

Riley, James C., and John J. McCusker. "Money Supply, Economic Growth, and the Quantity Theory of Money: France, 1650–1788." *Explorations in Economic History,* XX (1983), 274–293.

Rink, Oliver Albert. "Merchants and Magnates: Dutch New York, 1609–1664." Ph.D. diss., University of Southern California, 1976.

Robbins, Michael Warren. "The Principio Company: Iron-Making in Colonial Maryland, 1720–1781." Ph.D. diss., George Washington University, 1972.

Robbins, Roy M. *Our Landed Heritage: The Public Domain, 1776–1936.* Princeton, N.J., 1942.

Roberts, Edward G[raham]. "The Roads of Virginia, 1607–1840." Ph.D. diss., University of Virginia, 1950.

Roberts, William I., III. "American Potash Manufacture before the American Revolution." American Philosophical Society, *Proceedings,* CXVI (1972), 383–395.

———. "The Fur Trade of New England in the Seventeenth Century." Ph.D. diss., University of Pennsylvania, 1958.

———. "Ralph Carr: A Newcastle Merchant and the American Colonial Trade." *Business History Review,* XLII (1968), 271–287.

Robertson, E[ileen] Arnot. *The Spanish Town Papers: Some Sidelights on the American War of Independence.* London, 1959.

Robertson, M. L. "Scottish Commerce and the American War of Independence." *Economic History Review,* 2d Ser., IX (1956), 123–131.

Robinson, Edward Forbes. "Continental Treasury Administration, 1775–1781: A Study in the Financial History of the American Revolution." Ph.D. diss., University of Wisconsin, 1969.

Rodney, Walter. *How Europe Underdeveloped Africa.* London, 1972.

Roemer, Michael. *Fishing for Growth: Export-Led Development in Peru, 1950–1967.* Cambridge, Mass., 1970.

Rønning, Bjørn R. "Et funn av mynter blant vrakrestene etter den hollandske ostindia-fareren *Akerendam,* forlist ved Runde i 1725." *Nordisk Numismatisk Årsskrift (1973–1974)* (Stockholm), 68–115.

Rogers, George C., Jr. *Charleston in the Age of the Pinckneys.* Norman, Okla., 1969.

Rolt, [Richard]. *A New Dictionary of Trade and Commerce. . . .* London, 1756.

Romanek, Carl Leroy. "John Reynell, Quaker Merchant of Colonial Philadelphia." Ph.D. diss., Pennsylvania State University, 1969.

Rose, J[ohn] Holland. "Sea Power: National Security and Expansion." In *The Old Empire: From the Beginnings to 1783.* Vol. I of *The Cambridge History of the British Empire,* edited by J. Holland Rose, A. P. Newton, and E. A. Benians, 114–135. Cambridge, 1929.

Rose, J[ohn] Holland, A[rthur] P. Newton, and E[rnest] A. Benians, eds. *The Old Empire: From the Beginnings to 1783.* Vol. I of *The Cambridge History of the British Empire.* Cambridge, 1929.

Rose, J[ohn] Holland, and F. R. Salter. "Sea Power: The Spirit of Adventure." In *The Old Empire: From the Beginnings to 1783.* Vol. I of *The Cambridge History of the British Empire,* edited by J. Holland Rose, A. P. Newton, and E. A. Benians, 93–114. Cambridge, 1929.

Rosenberg, Nathan. "Factors Affecting the Diffusion of Technology." *Explorations in Economic History,* X (1972), 3–33.

Rosenblatt, Samuel Michael. "The House of John Norton and Sons: A Study of the Consignment Method of Marketing Tobacco from Virginia to England." Ph.D. diss., Rutgers University, 1960.

———. "The Significance of Credit in the Tobacco Consignment Trade: A Study of John Norton and Sons, 1768–1775." *William and Mary Quarterly,* 3d Ser., XIX (1962), 383–399.

Rostow, W[alt] W. *The Stages of Economic Growth: A Non-Communist Manifesto.* Cambridge, Mass., 1960.

———. "The Terms of Trade in Theory and Practice." *Economic History Review,* 2d Ser., III (1950), 1–20.

Rothenberg, Winifred B. "The Market and Massachusetts Farmers, 1750–1855." *Journal of Economic History,* XLI (1981), 283–314.

———. "A Price Index for Rural Massachusetts, 1750–1855." *Journal of Economic History,* XXXIX (1979), 975–1001.

Rothney, Gordon O. "British Policy in the North American Cod-Fisheries, with Special Reference to Foreign Competition, 1775–1819." Ph.D. thesis, University of London, 1939.

Rotstein, Abraham. "Fur Trade and Empire: An Institutional Analysis." Ph.D. diss., University of Toronto, 1967.

Rottenberg, Simon. "The Business of Slave Trading." *South Atlantic Quarterly,* LXVI (1967), 409–423.

Rubin, Vera [D.], and Arthur Tuden, eds. *Comparative Perspectives on Slavery in New World Plantation Societies.* New York Academy of Sciences, *Annals,* CCXCII. New York, 1977.

Rudnyanszky, Leslie Imre. "The Caribbean Slave Trade: Jamaica and Barbados, 1680–1770." Ph.D. diss., University of Notre Dame, 1973.

Rudolph, Richard Henry. "The Merchants of Newport, Rhode Island, 1763–1786." Ph.D. diss., University of Connecticut, 1975.

Rush, Benjamin. *An Account of the Manners of the German Inhabitants of Pennsylvania* (1789). Edited by Theodore E. Schmauk. Pennsylvania-German Society, *Proceedings and Addresses,* XIX, pt. 21. Lancaster, Pa., 1910.

Russell, Elmer Beecher. *The Review of American Colonial Legislation by the King in Council.* Columbia University Studies in History, Economics and Public Law, LXIV, no. 2. New York, 1915.

Russell, Howard S. *A Long, Deep Furrow: Three Centuries of Farming in New England.* Hanover, N.H., 1976.

Rutman, Darrett B. "Community Study." *Historical Methods*, XIII (1980), 29–41.

————. "Governor Winthrop's Garden Crop: The Significance of Agriculture in the Early Commerce of Massachusetts Bay." *William and Mary Quarterly*, 3d Ser., XX (1963), 396–415.

————. "History Counts: Or, Numbers Have More Than Face Value." *Reviews in American History*, IV (1976), 372–378.

————. *Husbandmen of Plymouth: Farms and Villages in the Old Colony, 1620–1692.* Boston, 1967.

————. "People in Process: The New Hampshire Towns of the Eighteenth Century." *Journal of Urban History*, I (1975), 268–292.

————. *Winthrop's Boston: Portrait of a Puritan Town, 1630–1649.* Chapel Hill, N.C., 1965.

————, ed. *The Old Dominion: Essays for Thomas Perkins Abernethy.* Charlottesville, Va., 1964.

Rutman, Darrett B., and Anita H. Rutman. " 'More True and Perfect Lists': The Reconstruction of Censuses for Middlesex County, Virginia, 1668–1704." *Virginia Magazine of History and Biography*, LXXXVIII (1980), 37–74.

————. " 'Now-Wives and Sons-in-Law': Parental Death in a Seventeenth-Century Virginia County." In *The Chesapeake in the Seventeenth Century: Essays on Anglo-American Society*, edited by Thad W. Tate and David L. Ammerman, 153–182. Chapel Hill, N.C., 1979.

————. "Of Agues and Fevers: Malaria in the Early Chesapeake." *William and Mary Quarterly*, 3d Ser., XXXIII (1976), 31–60.

Rutman, Darrett B., Charles Wetherell, and Anita H. Rutman. "Rhythms of Life: Black and White Seasonality in the Early Chesapeake." *Journal of Interdisciplinary History*, XI (1980), 29–53.

Ryan, Dennis P. "Landholding, Opportunity, and Mobility in Revolutionary New Jersey." *William and Mary Quarterly*, 3d Ser., XXXVI (1979), 571–592.

————. "Six Towns: Continuity and Change in Revolutionary New Jersey, 1770–1792." Ph.D. diss., New York University, 1974.

Sabean, David. "Aspects of Kinship Behaviour and Property in Rural Western Europe before 1800." In *Family and Inheritance: Rural Society in Western Europe, 1200–1800*, ed. Jack Goody, Joan Thirsk, and E. P. Thompson, 96–101. Cambridge, 1976.

Sachs, William S. "Agricultural Conditions in the Northern Colonies before the Revolution." *Journal of Economic History*, XIII (1953), 274–290.

————. "The Business of Colonization." In *Studies on Money in Early America*, edited by Eric P. Newman and Richard G. Doty, 3–14. New York, 1976.

————. "The Business Outlook in the Northern Colonies, 1750–1775." Ph.D. diss., Columbia University, 1957.

Sahota, Gian Singh. "Theories of Personal Income Distribution: A Survey." *Journal of Economic Literature*, XVI (1978), 1–55.

Saladino, Gaspare John. "The Economic Revolution in Late Eighteenth Century Connecticut." Ph.D. diss., University of Wisconsin, 1964.

————. "The Maryland and Virginia Wheat Trade from Its Beginnings to the American Revolution." M.A. thesis, University of Wisconsin, 1960.

Salay, David Lewis. "Arming for War: The Production of War Material [sic] in Pennsylvania for the American Armies during the Revolution." Ph.D. diss., University of Delaware, 1977.

Sale, Stephen Earl. "Colonial Albany: Outpost of Empire." Ph.D. diss., University of Southern California, 1973.

Salerno, Anthony. "The Social Background of Seventeenth-Century Emigration to America." *Journal of British Studies*, XIX (1979), 31–52.

Salinger, Sharon Vineberg. "Artisans, Journeymen, and the Transformation of Labor in Late Eighteenth-Century Philadelphia." *William and Mary Quarterly*, 3d Ser., XL (1983), 62–84.

————. "Colonial Labor in Transition: The Decline of Indentured Servitude in Late Eighteenth-Century Philadelphia." *Labor History*, XXII (1981), 165–191.

————. "Labor and Indentured Servants in Colonial Pennsylvania." Ph.D. diss., University of California, Los Angeles, 1980.

Salley, A[lexander] S., Jr. *The Introduction of Rice Culture into South Carolina*. Bulletins of the Historical Commission of South Carolina, no. 6. Columbia, S.C., 1919.

Savage, Henry, Jr. *Discovering America, 1700–1875*. New York, 1979.

Scammell, G[eoffrey] V. *The World Encompassed: The First European Maritime Empire, c. 800–1650*. London, 1981.

Scharf, J[ohn] Thomas, and Thompson Westcott. *History of Philadelphia, 1609–1884*. 3 vols. Philadelphia, 1884.

Schlebecker, John T. "Agricultural Markets and Marketing in the North, 1774–1777." *Agricultural History*, L (1976), 21–36.

————, comp. *Bibliography of Books and Pamphlets on the History of Agriculture in the United States, 1607–1967*. Santa Barbara, Calif., 1969.

Schlebecker, John T., and Gale E. Peterson. *Living Historical Farms Handbook*. Smithsonian Studies in History and Technology, no. 16. Washington, D.C., 1972.

Schlesinger, Arthur Meier. *The Colonial Merchants and the American Revolution, 1763–1776*. Columbia University Studies in History, Economics and Public Law, LXXVIII, no. 182. New York, 1918.

Schlotterbeck, John Thomas. "Plantation and Farm: Social and Economic Change in Orange and Greene Counties, Virginia, 1716 to 1860." Ph.D. diss., Johns Hopkins University, 1980.

Schmidt, Frederick Hall. "British Convict Servant Labor in Colonial Virginia." Ph.D. diss., College of William and Mary, 1976.

Schmoller, Gustav F. "Das Merkantilsystem in seiner historischen Bedeutung: Städtische, territoriale und staatliche Wirtschafts-politik." Pt. 2 of "Studien über die wirtschaftsliche Politik Friedrichs der Großen und Preußens überhaupt von 1680–1786." *Jahrbuch für Gesetzgebung, Verwaltung und Volkswirtschaft im deutschen Reich*, VIII (1884), 15–61.

Schnakenbourg, Christian. "Recherches sur l'histoire de l'industrie sucrière à Marie-Galante, 1664–1964." *Bulletin de la Société d'Histoire de la Guadeloupe*, XLVIII–L (1981), 5–144.

————. "Les sucreries de la Guadeloupe dans la seconde moitié du XVIIIème siècle (1760–1790): Contribution à l'étude de la crise de l'économie coloniale à la fin de l'Ancien Régime." Ph.D. thesis, Université de Paris II, 1973.

Schnore, Leo F., and Henry Fagin, eds. *Urban Research and Policy Planning*. Beverly Hills, Calif., 1967.

Schnore, Leo F., and Eric E. Lampard. "Social Science and the City: A Survey of Research

Needs." In *Urban Research and Policy Planning*, edited by Leo F. Schnore and Henry Fagin, 21–47. Beverly Hills, Calif., 1967.

Schultz, Theodore W. *Transforming Traditional Agriculture*. Studies in Comparative Economics, no. 3. New Haven, Conn., 1964.

Schumacher, Max George. *The Northern Farmer and His Markets during the Late Colonial Period*. New York, 1975 (Ph.D. diss., University of California, Berkeley, 1948).

Schumpeter, Elizabeth Boody. *English Overseas Trade Statistics, 1697–1808*. Oxford, 1960.

Schumpeter, Joseph A. *Business Cycles: A Theoretical, Historical, and Statistical Analysis of the Capitalist Process*. 2 vols. New York, 1939.

Schutz, Robert R. "On the Measurement of Income Inequality." *American Economic Review*, XLI (1951), 107–122.

Schwartz, Stuart B. "Indian Labor and New World Plantations: European Demands and Indian Responses in Northwestern Brazil." *American Historical Review*, LXXXIII (1978), 43–79.

Schweitzer, Mary McKinney. "Economic Regulation and the Colonial Economy: The Maryland Tobacco Inspection Act of 1747." *Journal of Economic History*, XL (1980), 551–569.

Scott, Kenneth. *Counterfeiting in Colonial America*. New York, 1957.

———. *Counterfeiting in Colonial New York*. American Numismatic Society Numismatic Notes and Monographs, no. 127. New York, 1953.

———. "Counterfeiting in New York during the Revolution." *New-York Historical Society Quarterly*, XLII (1958), 221–259.

———. "Price Control in New England during the Revolution." *New England Quarterly*, XIX (1946), 453–473.

Scott, William Robert. *The Constitution and Finance of English, Scottish, and Irish Joint-Stock Companies to 1720*. 3 vols. Cambridge, 1911.

Scoville, Warren C. "Did Colonial Farmers 'Waste' Our Land?" *Southern Economic Journal*, XX (1953), 178–181.

Sellers, Leila. *Charleston Business on the Eve of the American Revolution*. Chapel Hill, N.C., 1934.

Shalhope, Robert E. "Republicanism and Early American Historiography." *William and Mary Quarterly*, 3d Ser., XXXIX (1982), 334–356.

———. "Toward a Republican Synthesis: The Emergence of an Understanding of Republicanism in American Historiography." *William and Mary Quarterly*, 3d Ser., XXIX (1972), 49–80.

Shammas, Carole. "Constructing a Wealth Distribution from Probate Records." *Journal of Interdisciplinary History*, IX (1978), 297–307.

———. "Consumer Behavior in Colonial America." *Social Science History*, VI (1982), 67–86.

———. "English Commercial Development and American Colonization, 1560–1620." In *The Westward Enterprise: English Activities in Ireland, the Atlantic, and America, 1460–1650*, edited by K. R. Andrews, N. P. Canny, and P. E. H. Hair, 151–174. Detroit, Mich., 1979.

———. "How Self-sufficient Was Early America?" *Journal of Interdisciplinary History*, XIII (1982), 247–272.

Sharlin, Allan. "Natural Decrease in Early Modern Cities: A Reconsideration." *Past and Present*, LXXIX (1978), 126–138.

Sharrer, G[eorge] Terry. "Flour Milling and the Growth of Baltimore, 1783–1830." Ph.D. diss., University of Maryland, 1975.

————. "Flour Milling in the Growth of Baltimore, 1750–1830." *Maryland Historical Magazine*, LXXI (1976), 322–333.

————. "The Indigo Bonanza in South Carolina, 1740–1790." *Technology and Culture*, XII (1971), 447–455.

————. "Indigo in Carolina, 1671–1796." *South Carolina Historical Magazine*, LXXII (1971), 94–103.

————. "The Merchant-Millers: Baltimore's Flour Milling Industry, 1783–1860." *Agricultural History*, LVI (1982) 138–150.

————. "'An Undebauched Mind': Farmer Washington at Mt. Vernon." Paper presented at the annual meeting of the Society for Eighteenth-Century Studies, Washington, D.C., April 1981.

————, comp. *1001 References for the History of American Food Technology*. Davis, Calif., 1978.

————, ed. *The History of American Food Technology*. Washington, D.C., forthcoming.

Shaw, A[lan] G. L. *Convicts and the Colonies: A Study of Penal Transportation from Great Britain and Ireland to Australia and Other Parts of the British Empire*. London, 1966.

Sheffield, John [Baker Holroyd], Lord. *Observations on the Commerce of the American States*. 6th ed. London, 1784.

Shepherd, James Floyd, Jr. "A Balance of Payments for the Thirteen Colonies, 1768–1772." Ph.D. diss., University of Washington, 1966.

————. "Commodity Exports from the British North American Colonies to Overseas Areas, 1768–1772: Magnitude and Patterns of Trade." *Explorations in Economic History*, VIII (1970), 5–76.

————. "Economy from the Revolution to 1815." In *Encyclopedia of American Economic History: Studies of the Principal Movements and Ideas*, edited by Glenn Porter, I, 51–65. New York, 1980.

————. "Staples and Eighteenth-Century Canadian Development: The Case of Newfoundland." In *Explorations in the New Economic History: Essays in Honor of Douglass C. North*, edited by Roger L. Ransom, Richard Sutch, and Gary M. Walton, 97–124. New York, 1982.

Shepherd, James Floyd, Jr., and Gary M. Walton. "Economic Change after the American Revolution: Pre- and Post-war Comparisons of Maritime Shipping and Trade." *Explorations in Economic History*, XIII (1976), 397–422.

————. *Shipping, Maritime Trade, and the Economic Development of Colonial North America*. Cambridge, 1972.

Shepherd, James Floyd, Jr., and Samuel H. Williamson. "The Coastal Trade of the British North American Colonies, 1768–1772." *Journal of Economic History*, XXXII (1972), 783–810.

Sheridan, Richard B. "Africa and the Caribbean in the Atlantic Slave Trade." *American Historical Review*, LXXVII (1972), 15–35.

————. "The British Credit Crisis of 1772 and the American Colonies." *Journal of Economic History*, XX (1960), 161–186.

————. "The Commercial and Financial Organization of the British Slave Trade, 1750–1807." *Economic History Review*, 2d Ser., XI (1958), 249–263.

————. "The Crisis of Slave Subsistence in the British West Indies during and after the American Revolution." *William and Mary Quarterly*, 3d Ser., XXXIII (1976), 615–641.

————. *The Development of the Plantations to 1750 [and] An Era of West Indian Prosperity, 1750–1775*. Barbados, 1970.

————. "The Molasses Act and the Market Strategy of the British Sugar Planters." *Journal of Economic History*, XVII (1957), 62–83.

————. "Planters and Merchants: The Oliver Family of Antigua and London, 1716–1784." *Business History*, XIII (1971), 104–113.

————. "The Rise of a Colonial Gentry: A Case Study of Antigua, 1730–1775." *Economic History Review*, 2d Ser., XIII (1960), 342–357.

————. "The Role of the Scots in the Economy and Society of the West Indies." In *Comparative Perspectives on Slavery in New World Plantation Societies*, edited by Vera Rubin and Arthur Tuden, 94–106. New York Academy of Sciences, *Annals*, CCXCII. New York, 1977.

————. "Samuel Martin, Innovating Sugar Planter of Antigua, 1750–1776." *Agricultural History*, XXXIV (1960), 126–139.

————. "Simon Taylor, Sugar Tycoon of Jamaica, 1740–1813." *Agricultural History*, XLV (1971), 285–296.

————. "Slave Demography in the British West Indies and the Abolition of the Slave Trade." In *The Abolition of the Atlantic Slave Trade: Origins and Effects in Europe, Africa, and the Americas*, edited by David Eltis and James Walvin, 259–285. Madison, Wis., 1981.

————. *Sugar and Slavery: An Economic History of the British West Indies, 1623–1775*. St. Lawrence, Barbados, 1974.

————. "The Wealth of Jamaica in the Eighteenth Century." *Economic History Review*, 2d Ser., XVIII (1965), 292–311.

————. "The Wealth of Jamaica in the Eighteenth Century: A Rejoinder." *Economic History Review*, 2d Ser., XXI (1968), 46–61.

Shipton, Clifford K. "Immigration to New England, 1680–1740." *Journal of Political Economy*, XLIV (1936), 225–239.

Shryock, Henry S., Jacob S. Siegel, *et al. The Methods and Materials of Demography*. 2d ed. Washington, D.C., 1973.

Shumway, George, and Howard C. Frey. *Conestoga Wagon, 1750–1850: Freight Carrier for One Hundred Years of America's Westward Expansion*. 3d ed. York, Pa., 1968.

Shurtleff, Nathaniel B., ed. *Records of the Governor and Company of the Massachusetts Bay in New England*. 5 vols. in 6. Boston, 1853–1854.

Shy, John. *A People Numerous and Armed: Reflections on the Military Struggle for American Independence*. New York, 1976.

————, comp. *The American Revolution*. Goldentree Bibliographies in American History. Northbrook, Ill., 1973.

Sickinger, Raymond L. "The Eighteenth Century Textile Trade, 1772–1792: Commercial Tensions, Colonial Turmoil, and Cotton Trends." Paper presented at the New England Conference on British Studies, November 1981.

Sidwell, Robert Tolbert. "The Colonial American Almanacs: A Study in Non-institutional Education." Ed.D. diss., Rutgers University, 1965.

Simler, Lucy. "The Township: The Community of the Rural Pennsylvanian." *Pennsylvania Magazine of History and Biography*, CVI (1982), 41–68.

Simon, Julian L. *The Economics of Population Growth*. Princeton, N.J., 1977.

Sirmans, M[arion] Eugene. *Colonial South Carolina: A Political History, 1663–1763*. Chapel Hill, N.C., 1966.

Slaski, Eugene R. "Thomas Willing: Moderation during the American Revolution." Ph.D. diss., Florida State University, 1971.

————. "Thomas Willing: A Study in Moderation, 1774–1778." *Pennsylvania Magazine of History and Biography*, C (1976), 491–506.

Slaughter, Thomas Paul. "The American Vision of China, 1784–1806: European and Merchant-Consul Influences." Honors thesis, University of Maryland, 1976.

Smith, Abbot Emerson. *Colonists in Bondage: White Servitude and Convict Labor in America, 1607–1776*. Chapel Hill, N.C., 1947.

———. "The Transportation of Convicts to the American Colonies in the Seventeenth Century." *American Historical Review*, XXXIX (1934), 232–249.

Smith, Adam. *An Inquiry into the Nature and Causes of the Wealth of Nations* (1776). Edited by R[oy] H. Campbell, A[ndrew] S. Skinner, and W[illiam] B. Todd. 2 vols. Oxford, 1976.

Smith, Billy G. "'The Best Poor Man's Country': Living Standards of the 'Lower Sort' in Late Eighteenth-Century Philadelphia." Regional Economic History Research Center, *Working Papers*, II, no. 4 (1979), 1–70.

———. "Death and Life in a Colonial Immigrant City: A Demographic Analysis of Philadelphia." *Journal of Economic History*, XXXVII (1977), 863–889.

———. "The Material Lives of Laboring Philadelphians, 1750 to 1800." *William and Mary Quarterly*, 3d Ser., XXXVIII (1981), 163–202.

Smith, Daniel Blake. "Mortality and Family in the Colonial Chesapeake." *Journal of Interdisciplinary History*, VIII (1978), 403–427.

———. "The Study of the Family in Early America: Trends, Problems, and Prospects." *William and Mary Quarterly*, 3d Ser., XXXIX (1982), 3–28.

Smith, Daniel Scott. "The Demographic History of Colonial New England." *Journal of Economic History*, XXXII (1972), 165–183.

———. "Early American Historiography and Social Science History." *Social Science History*, VI (1982), 267–291.

———. "The Estimates of Early American Historical Demographers: Two Steps Forward, One Step Back, What Steps in the Future?" *Historical Methods*, XII (1979), 24–38.

———. "A Homeostatic Demographic Regime: Patterns in West European Family Reconstitution Studies." In *Population Patterns in the Past*, edited by Ronald Demos Lee, 19–51. New York, 1977.

———. "A Malthusian-Frontier Interpretation of United States Demographic History before c. 1815." In *Urbanization in the Americas: The Background in Comparative Perspective*, edited by Woodrow Borah, Jorge Hardoy, and Gilbert A. Stelter, 15–24. Ottawa, 1980.

———. "A Note on the Longevity of Colonial Ships." *American Neptune*, XXXIV (1974), 68–69.

———. "Parental Power and Marriage Patterns: An Analysis of Historical Trends in Hingham, Massachusetts." *Journal of Marriage and the Family*, XXXV (1973), 419–428.

———. "A Perspective on Demographic Methods and Effects in Social History." *William and Mary Quarterly*, 3d Ser., XXXIX (1982), 442–468.

———. "Population, Family, and Society in Hingham, Massachusetts, 1635–1880." Ph.D. diss., University of California, Berkeley, 1973.

———. "Underregistration and Bias in Probate Records: An Analysis of Data from Eighteenth-Century Hingham, Massachusetts." *William and Mary Quarterly*, 3d Ser., XXXII (1975), 100–110.

Smith, George L. *Religion and Trade in New Netherland: Dutch Origins and American Development*. Ithaca, N.Y., 1973.

Smith, James Morton, ed. *Seventeenth-Century America: Essays in Colonial History*. Chapel Hill, N.C., 1959.

[Smith, Philip Chadwick Foster, ed.]. *Seafaring in Colonial Massachusetts.* Colonial Society of Massachusetts, *Publications,* LII: *Collections.* Boston, 1980.

Smith, Warren B. *White Servitude in Colonial South Carolina.* Columbia, S.C., 1961.

Smith, William. *The History of the Post Office in British North America, 1639–1870.* Cambridge, 1920.

Snell, Charles. *A Guide to Book-keepers, According to the Italian Manner.* . . . London, 1709.

Snell, William Robert. "Indian Slavery in Colonial South Carolina, 1671–1795." Ph.D. diss., University of Alabama, 1972.

Snow, Sinclair. "Naval Stores in Colonial Virginia." *Virginia Magazine of History and Biography,* LXXII (1964), 75–93.

Snydacker, Daniel. "Kinship and Community in Rural Pennsylvania, 1749–1820." *Journal of Interdisciplinary History,* XIII (1982), 41–61.

Soltow, James H. *The Economic Role of Williamsburg.* Williamsburg Research Studies. Williamsburg, Va., 1965.

———. "The Role of Williamsburg in the Virginia Economy, 1750–1775." *William and Mary Quarterly,* 3d Ser., XV (1958), 467–482.

———. "Scottish Traders in Virginia, 1750–1775." *Economic History Review,* 2d Ser., XII (1959), 83–98.

Sorensen, Charles William. "Responses to Crisis: An Analysis of New Haven, 1638–1665." Ph.D. diss., Michigan State University, 1973.

Sosin, J[ack] M. *English America and the Restoration Monarchy of Charles II: Transatlantic Politics, Commerce, and Kinship.* Lincoln, Nebr., 1980.

———. *English America and the Revolution of 1688: Royal Administration and the Structure of Provincial Government.* Lincoln, Nebr., 1982.

Souden, David. "'Rogues, whores, and vagabonds': Indentured Servant Emigrants to North America, and the Case of Mid-Seventeenth-Century Bristol." *Social History,* III (1978), 23–41.

———. "Seventeenth-Century Indentured Servants Seen within a General English Migration System." Paper presented at the annual meeting of the Organization of American Historians, New Orleans, La., April 1979.

Southwick, Albert B. "The Molasses Act—Source of Precedents." *William and Mary Quarterly,* 3d Ser., VIII (1951), 389–405.

Sparks, Jared, ed. *The Works of Benjamin Franklin . . . with Notes and a Life of the Author.* 10 vols. Boston, 1836–1840.

Spengler, Joseph J. "Mercantilist and Physiocratic Growth Theory." In Bert F. Hoselitz *et al., Theories of Economic Growth,* 3–64. Glencoe, Ill., 1960.

Spindel, Donna J. "The Stamp Act Crisis in the British West Indies." *Journal of American Studies,* XI (1977), 203–221.

Spruill, Julia Cherry. *Women's Life and Work in the Southern Colonies.* Chapel Hill, N.C., 1938.

Spry, Irene M. "Innis, the Fur Trade, and Modern Economic Problems." In *Old Trails and New Directions: Papers of the Third North American Fur Trade Conference,* edited by Carol M. Judd and Arthur J. Ray, 291–307. Toronto, 1980.

Stackpole, Edouard A. *The Sea-Hunters: The New England Whalemen during Two Centuries, 1635–1835.* Philadelphia, 1953.

Staff, Frank. *The Transatlantic Mail.* London, 1956.

Starbuck, Alexander. *History of the American Whale Fishery from Its Earliest Inception to the Year 1876.* Washington, D.C., 1878.

Starkey, Otis Paul. *The Economic Geography of Barbados: A Study of the Relationships between Environmental Variations and Economic Development.* New York, 1939.

Stearns, Raymond Phineas. *Science in the British Colonies of America.* Urbana, Ill., 1970.

Steckley, George F. "The Wine Economy of Tenerife in the Seventeenth Century: Anglo-Spanish Partnership in a Luxury Trade." *Economic History Review,* 2d Ser., XXXIII (1980), 335–350.

Stedman, J[ohn] G. *Narrative of a Five Years' Expedition, against the Revolted Negroes of Surinam in Guiana, on the Wild Coast of South America, from the Year 1772, to 1777.* 2 vols. London, 1796.

Steele, Ian K. "Another Early America: Getting and Begetting in the Chesapeake." *Canadian Review of American Studies,* XII (1981), 313–322.

Steiner, Bernard C. "Maryland Privateers in the American Revolution." *Maryland Historical Magazine,* III (1908), 99–103.

Stetson, Kenneth Winslow. "A Quantitative Approach to Britain's American Slave Trade, 1700–1773." M.S. thesis, University of Wisconsin, 1967.

Stettler, H. Louis, III. "The New England Throat Distemper and Family Size." In *Empirical Studies in Health Economics: Proceedings of the Second Conference on the Economics of Health,* edited by Herbert E. Klarman, 17–27. Baltimore, 1970.

Stewart, John [alias Robert Rainey]. *A Description of a Machine or Invention to Work Mills, by the Power of a Fire-Engine, but Particularly Useful and Profitable in Grinding Sugar-Canes.* [London, 1767].

Stiverson, Gregory A. "Early American Farming: A Comment." *Agricultural History,* L (1976), 37–44.

———. *Poverty in a Land of Plenty: Tenancy in Eighteenth-Century Maryland.* Maryland Bicentennial Series. Baltimore, 1977.

Stone, Lawrence. "Family History in the 1980s." *Journal of Interdisciplinary History,* XII (1981), 51–87.

Stourzh, Gerald. *Benjamin Franklin and American Foreign Policy.* Chicago, 1954.

Stover, John F. "French-American Trade during the Confederation, 1781–1789." *North Carolina Historical Review,* XXXV (1958), 399–414.

Stumpf, Stuart Owen. "Implications of King George's War for the Charleston Mercantile Community." *South Carolina Historical Magazine,* LXXVII (1976), 161–188.

———. "The Merchants of Colonial Charleston, 1680–1756." Ph.D. diss., Michigan State University, 1971.

Sturtevant, William C., ed. *Handbook of North American Indians.* Washington, D.C., 1978–.

Supple, B[arry] E. *Commercial Crisis and Change in England, 1600–1642: A Study in the Instability of a Mercantile Economy.* Cambridge, 1959.

Sutch, Richard. "The Breeding of Slaves for Sale and the Westward Expansion of Slavery, 1850–1860." In *Race and Slavery in the Western Hemisphere: Quantitative Studies,* edited by Stanley L. Engerman and Eugene D. Genovese, 173–210. Princeton, N.J., 1975.

Sutherland, Stella H. "Colonial Statistics." *Explorations in Entrepreneurial History,* 2d Ser., V (1967), 58–107.

———. *Population Distribution in Colonial America.* New York, 1936.

Suttell, Elizabeth [Louise]. "The British Slave Trade to Virginia, 1698–1728." M.A. thesis, College of William and Mary, 1965.

Swanson, Carl E. "The Profitability of Privateering: Reflections on British Colonial Privateers during the Wars of 1739–1748." *American Neptune,* XLII (1982), 36–56.

Swedlund, Alan C. "The Genetic Structure of an Historical Population: A Study of Marriage and Fertility in Old Deerfield, Massachusetts." Department of Anthropology, University of Massachusetts, Amherst, *Research Reports*, no. 7 (May 1971).

Swedlund, Alan C., Helena Temkin, and Richard Meindl. "Population Studies in the Connecticut Valley: Prospectus." *Journal of Human Evolution*, V (1976), 75–93.

Sydnor, Charles S. *Gentlemen Freeholders: Political Practices in Washington's Virginia*. Chapel Hill, N.C., 1952.

Syrett, David. "American Provincials and the Havana Campaign of 1762." *New York History*, XLIX (1968), 375–390.

———. *Shipping and the American War, 1775–83: A Study of British Transport Organization*. University of London Historical Studies, no. 27. London, 1970.

Szatmary, David P. *Shays' Rebellion: The Making of an Agrarian Insurrection*. Amherst, Mass., 1980.

A Table Shewing the Value of Old Tenor Bills, in Lawful Money. . . . [Boston, 1750].

Tailby, Donald G. "Foreign Interest Remittances by the United States, 1785–1787: A Story of Malfeasance." *Business History Review*, XLI (1967), 161–176.

Tate, Thad W. "From Survival to Prosperity: The Artistic Greening of Eighteenth-Century America." *Key Reporter*, XLIV (Autumn 1978), 1–3, 8.

———. "The Seventeenth-Century Chesapeake and Its Modern Historians." In *The Chesapeake in the Seventeenth Century: Essays on Anglo-American Society*, edited by Thad W. Tate and David L. Ammerman, 3–50. Chapel Hill, N.C., 1979.

Tate, Thad W., and David L. Ammerman, eds. *The Chesapeake in the Seventeenth Century: Essays on Anglo-American Society*. Original Essay Series. Chapel Hill, N.C., 1979.

Taylor, Clifton James. "John Watts in Colonial and Revolutionary New York." Ph.D. diss., University of Tennessee, 1981.

Taylor, George Rogers. "American Economic Growth before 1840: An Exploratory Essay." *Journal of Economic History*, XXIV (1964), 427–444.

———. "Wholesale Commodity Prices at Charleston, South Carolina, 1732–1791." *Journal of Economic and Business History*, IV (1932), 356–377.

———, comp. *American Economic History before 1860*. Goldentree Bibliographies in American History. New York, 1969.

Taylor, George Rogers, and Lucius F. Ellsworth, eds. *Approaches to American Economic History*. Charlottesville, Va., 1971.

Temkin-Greener, H., and A[lan] C. Swedlund. "Fertility Transition in the Connecticut Valley: 1740–1850." *Population Studies*, XXXII (1978), 27–41.

Terry, George David. "'Champaign Country': A Social History of an Eighteenth Century Lowcountry Parish in South Carolina, St. Johns Berkeley County." Ph.D. diss., University of South Carolina, 1981.

Thayer, Theodore [G.]. "The Land-Bank System in the American Colonies." *Journal of Economic History*, XIII (1953), 145–159.

Thestrup, Poul. *The Standard of Living in Copenhagen, 1730–1800: Some Methods of Measurements*. Københavns Universitet Institut for Økonomisk Historie Publikation Nr. 5. Copenhagen, 1971.

Thieme, Otto Charles. *By Inch of Candle: A Sale at East-India-House, 21 September 1675*. James Ford Bell Lectures, no. 19. Minneapolis, Minn., 1982.

Thirsk, Joan. *Economic Policy and Projects: The Development of a Consumer Society in Early Modern England*. Oxford, 1978.

Thoburn, John T. *Primary Commodity Exports and Economic Development: Theory, Evidence, and a Study of Malaysia*. London, 1977.

Thomas, Brinley. "The Rhythm of Growth in the Atlantic Economy of the Eighteenth Century." *Research in Economic History*, III (1978), 1–46.

Thomas, Keith. "Work and Leisure in Pre-industrial Society." *Past and Present*, XXIX (1964), 50–66.

Thomas, Robert Paul. "A Quantitative Approach to the Study of the Effects of British Imperial Policy upon Colonial Welfare: Some Preliminary Findings." *Journal of Economic History*, XXV (1965), 615–638.

———. "The Sugar Colonies of the Old Empire: Profit or Loss for Great Britain." *Economic History Review*, 2d Ser., XXI (1968), 30–45.

Thomas, Robert Paul, and Richard Nelson Bean. "The Fishers of Men: The Profits of the Slave Trade." *Journal of Economic History*, XXXIV (1974), 885–914.

Thompson, E[dward] P. "Time, Work-Discipline, and Industrial Capitalism." *Past and Present*, XXXVIII (1967), 56–97.

Thompson, R. "Seventeenth-Century English and Colonial Sex Ratios: A Postscript." *Population Studies*, XXVIII (1974), 153–165.

Thoms, D[avid] W. "The Mills Family: London Sugar Merchants of the Eighteenth Century." *Business History*, XI (1969), 3–10.

Thomson, Robert Polk. "The Merchant in Virginia, 1700–1775." Ph.D. diss., University of Wisconsin, 1955.

———. "The Tobacco Export of the Upper James River Naval District, 1773–75." *William and Mary Quarterly*, 3d Ser., XVIII (1961), 393–401.

Thornton, A[rchibald] P. "The Organization of the Slave Trade in the English West Indies, 1660–1685." *William and Mary Quarterly*, 3d Ser., XII (1955), 399–409.

———. "Some Statistics of West Indian Produce, Shipping, and Revenue, 1660–1685." *Caribbean Historical Review*, IV (1954), 251–280.

Thucydides. *Historiae*. Edited by John Enoch Powell. Rev. ed. 2 vols. Oxford, 1942.

Tolles, Frederick B. *Meeting House and Counting House: The Quaker Merchants of Colonial Philadelphia, 1682–1763*. Chapel Hill, N.C., 1948.

Tower, Walter S. *A History of the American Whale Fishery*. Philadelphia, 1907.

Towne, Marvin W., and Wayne D. Rasmussen. "Farm Gross Product and Gross Investment in the Nineteenth Century." In *Trends in the American Economy in the Nineteenth Century*, edited by William N. Parker, 255–315. National Bureau of Economic Research, Studies in Income and Wealth, XXIV. Princeton, N.J., 1960.

Towner, Lawrence William. "A Good Master Well Served: A Social History of Servitude in Massachusetts, 1620–1750." Ph.D. diss., Northwestern University, 1955.

Tracy, Patricia J. *Jonathan Edwards, Pastor: Religion and Society in Eighteenth-Century Northampton*. American Century Series. New York, 1980.

Trigger, Bruce G., ed. *Northeast*. Vol. XV of *Handbook of North American Indians*, edited by William C. Sturtevant. Washington, D.C., 1978.

Truxes, Thomas M. "Connecticut in the Irish-American Flaxseed Trade, 1750–1775." *Eire-Ireland*, XII (Summer 1977), 34–62.

Tryon, Rolla Milton. *Household Manufactures in the United States, 1640–1860: A Study in Industrial History*. Chicago, [1917].

Tully, Alan. "Patterns of Slaveholding in Colonial Pennsylvania: Chester and Lancaster Counties, 1729–1758." *Journal of Social History*, VI (1973), 284–305.

Turner, Edward Raymond. *The Negro in Pennsylvania, Slavery—Servitude—Freedom, 1639–1861*. Washington, D.C., 1911.

Turner, Frederick Jackson. "The Significance of the Frontier in American History." In *American Historical Association, Annual Report . . . for the Year 1893*, 197–227. Reprinted in *Frontier and Section: Selected Essays of Frederick Jackson Turner*, 37–62. Englewood Cliffs, N.J., 1961.

Tutino, John. "Slavery in a Peasant Society: Indians and Africans in Colonial Mexico." Unpublished paper, St. Olaf's College, 1979.

Tyack, N[orman] C. P. "Migration from East Anglia to New England before 1660." Ph.D. diss., University of London, 1951.

Tyler, John W. "Foster Cunliffe and Sons: Liverpool Merchants in the Maryland Tobacco Trade, 1738–1765." *Maryland Historical Magazine*, LXXIII (1978), 246–277.

———. "The Long Shadow of Benjamin Barons: The Politics of Illicit Trade at Boston, 1760–1762." *American Neptune*, XL (1980), 245–279.

Ulrich, Laurel Thatcher. "'A Friendly Neighbor': Social Dimensions of Daily Work in Northern Colonial New England." *Feminist Studies*, VI (1980), 392–405.

United Nations. Statistical Office. *Statistical Yearbook/Annuaire statistique, 1978*. 30th ed. New York, 1979.

U.S. Bureau of the Census. *A Century of Population Growth: From the First Census of the United States to the Twelfth, 1790–1900*. Washington, D.C., 1909.

———. *Historical Statistics of the United States, Colonial Times to 1970*. 2 vols. Bicentennial ed. Washington, D.C., 1975. Reprinted as *The Statistical History of the United States, from Colonial Times to the Present*, ed. Ben J. Wattenberg. New York, 1976.

———. *Statistical Abstract of the United States, 1981*. 102d ed. Washington, D.C., 1981.

U.S. Congress. Joint Economic Committee, Eighty-sixth Congress, First Session. *Employment, Growth, and Price Levels: Hearings . . . Part 2—Historical and Comparative Rates of Production, Productivity, and Prices*. Washington, D.C., 1959.

Untapped Sources and Research Opportunities in the Field of American Maritime History: A Symposium. Mystic, Conn., 1967.

Upton, Dell. "Traditional Timber Framing." In *Material Culture in the Wooden Age*, edited by Brooke Hindle, 35–93. Tarrytown, N.Y., 1981.

Vadasz, Thomas Patrick. "The History of an Industrial Community: Bethlehem, Pennsylvania, 1741–1920." Ph.D. diss., College of William and Mary, 1975.

Van Alstyne, Richard W. *Empire and Independence: The International History of the American Revolution*. America in Crisis. New York, 1965.

———. *The Rising American Empire*. Oxford, 1960.

Vance, James E., Jr. *The Merchant's World: The Geography of Wholesaling*. Englewood Cliffs, N.J., 1970.

Van Deventer, David E. *The Emergence of Provincial New Hampshire, 1623–1741*. Baltimore, 1976.

Van Dusen, Albert E. "Connecticut, the 'Provisions State' of the American Revolution." *New England Social Studies Bulletin*, X (1952), 16–23.

Van Lier, R[udolph] A. J. *Frontier Society: A Social Analysis of the History of Surinam*. Translated by M. J. L. van Yperen. Koninklijk Instituut voor Taal-, Land- en Volkenkunde, Translation Series 14. The Hague, 1971.

Van Metre, T[hurman] W. "American Coastwise Trade before 1789." In Emory R. Johnson, T. W. Van Metre, G. G. Huebner, and D. S. Hanchett, *History of Domestic and Foreign Commerce of the United States*, I, 162–174. Carnegie Institution of Washington Publication no. 215a. Washington, D.C., 1915.

Vaughan, Alden T., comp. *The American Colonies in the Seventeenth Century*. Goldentree Bibliographies in American History. New York, 1971.

Venema, Pieter. *Arithmetica of Cyffer-Konst, Volgens de Munten Maten en Gewigten, te Nieu-York*. New York, 1730.

Ver Steeg, Clarence L. "Financing and Outfitting the First United States Ship to China."
    Pacific Historical Review, XXII (1953), 1–12.
———. *Origins of a Southern Mosaic: Studies of Early Carolina and Georgia.* Athens,
    Ga., 1975.
———. *Robert Morris: Revolutionary Financier.* Philadelphia, 1954.
Vickers, Daniel F. "Maritime Labor in Colonial Massachusetts: A Case Study of the Essex
    County Cod Fishery and the Whaling Industry of Nantucket, 1630–1775." Ph.D. diss.,
    Princeton University, 1981.
Vignols, Léon. "L'importation en France, au XVIIIᵉ siècle, du boeuf salé d'Irlande: Ses
    emplois—les tentatives pour s'en passer." *Revue Historique*, CLIX (1928), 79–95.
Villiers, Patrick. *Le commerce colonial atlantique et la guerre d'indépendence des États-
    Unis d'Amérique, 1778–1783.* New York, 1977 (Ph.D. diss., Université de Paris,
    1975).
Viner, Jacob. *Studies in Theory of International Trade.* London, 1937.
Vinovskis, Maris A. "American Historical Demography: A Review Essay." *Historical
    Methods Newsletter*, IV (1971), 141–148.
———. "Estimating the Wealth of Americans on the Eve of the Revolution." *Journal of
    Economic History*, XLI (1981), 415–420.
———. *Fertility in Massachusetts from the Revolution to the Civil War.* New York, 1981.
———. "Mortality Rates and Trends in Massachusetts before 1860." *Journal of Eco-
    nomic History*, XXXII (1972), 184–213.
———. "Recent Trends in American Historical Demography: Some Methodological and
    Conceptual Considerations." *Annual Review of Sociology*, IV (1978), 603–627.
———. "The 1789 Life Table of Edward Wigglesworth." *Journal of Economic History*,
    XXXI (1971), 570–590.
———, ed. *Studies in American Historical Demography.* New York, 1979.
[Virginia Company of London]. *The Inconveniencies That Have Happened to Some Per-
    sons Which Have Transported Themselves from England to Virginia, without Provi-
    sions Necessary to Sustaine Themselves. . . .* London, 1622.
Wachtell, Harvey Milton. "The Conflict between Localism and Nationalism in Connecti-
    cut, 1783–1788." Ph.D. diss., University of Missouri, Columbia, 1971.
[Wakefield, Edward Gibbon]. *England and America: A Comparison of the Social and
    Political State of Both Nations.* New York, 1834.
Walcott, Robert R. "Husbandry in Colonial New England." *New England Quarterly*, IX
    (1936), 218–252.
Walker, Paul Kent. "The Baltimore Community and the American Revolution: A Study in
    Urban Development, 1763–1783." Ph.D. diss., University of North Carolina, 1973.
———. "Business and Commerce in Baltimore on the Eve of Independence." *Maryland
    Historical Magazine*, LXXI (1976), 296–309.
Wallace, D[avid] D. "Indigo Culture in the South." In *The South in the Building of the
    Nation*, edited by Julian A. C. Chandler *et al.*, V, 178–183. Richmond, Va., 1909.
Waller, G[eorge] M. *Samuel Vetch: Colonial Enterpriser.* Chapel Hill, N.C., 1960.
Wallerstein, Immanuel. *The Modern World-System.* 2 vols. New York, 1974–1980.
Walne, Peter, ed. *A Guide to Manuscript Sources for the History of Latin America and the
    Caribbean in the British Isles.* London, 1973.
Walsh, Lorena Seebach. "Charles County, Maryland, 1658–1705: A Study of Chesapeake
    Social and Political Structure." Ph.D. diss., Michigan State University, 1977.
———. "The Historian as Census Taker: Individual Reconstitution and the Reconstruc-
    tion of Censuses for a Colonial Chesapeake County." *William and Mary Quarterly*, 3d
    Ser., XXXVIII (1981), 242–260.

———. "Servitude and Opportunity in Charles County, Maryland, 1658–1705." In *Law, Society, and Politics in Early Maryland,* edited by Aubrey C. Land, Lois Green Carr, and Edward C. Papenfuse, 111–133. Baltimore, 1977.

Walsh, Lorena Seebach, and Russell R. Menard. "Death in the Chesapeake: Two Life Tables for Men in Early Colonial Maryland." *Maryland Historical Magazine,* LXIX (1974), 211–227.

Walsh, Margaret. "Another New Look? The Encyclopedia of American Economic History—A Review Article." *Business History Review,* LV (1981), 403–418.

Walton, Gary M. "The Colonial Economy." In *Encyclopedia of American Economic History: Studies of the Principal Movements and Ideas,* edited by Glenn Porter, I, 34–50. New York, 1980.

———. "A Measure of Productivity Change in American Colonial Shipping." *Economic History Review,* 2d Ser., XXI (1968), 268–282.

———. "The New Economic History and the Burdens of the Navigation Acts." *Economic History Review,* 2d Ser., XXIV (1971), 533–542.

———. "Sources of Productivity Change in American Colonial Shipping, 1675–1775." *Economic History Review,* 2d Ser., XX (1967), 67–78.

Walton, Gary M., and James F. Shepherd. *The Economic Rise of Early America.* Cambridge, 1979.

Walzer, John Flexer. "Transportation in the Philadelphia Trading Area, 1740–1775." Ph.D. diss., University of Wisconsin, 1968.

Ward, J. R. "The Profitability of Sugar Planting in the British West Indies, 1650–1834." *Economic History Review,* 2d Ser., XXXI (1978), 197–213.

Ward, Jane, comp. "The Published Works of H. A. Innis." *Canadian Journal of Economics and Political Science,* XIX (1953), 233–244.

Warden, G[erard] B. "The Distribution of Property in Boston, 1692–1775." *Perspectives in American History,* X (1976), 79–129.

———. "Inequality and Instability in Eighteenth-Century Boston: A Reappraisal." *Journal of Interdisciplinary History,* VI (1976), 585–620.

Wareing, John. "Migration to London and Transatlantic Emigration of Indentured Servants, 1683–1775." *Journal of Historical Geography,* VII (1981), 356–378.

Waring, Joseph I. *A History of Medicine in South Carolina, 1670–1825.* [Charleston, S.C.], 1964.

Warner, Sam Bass, Jr. *The Private City: Philadelphia in Three Periods of Its Growth.* Philadelphia, 1968.

[Washington, George]. *The Writings of George Washington from the Original Manuscript Sources, 1745–1799.* Edited by John C. Fitzpatrick. 39 vols. Washington, D.C., 1931–1944.

Waterhouse, Richard. "England, the Caribbean, and the Settlement of Carolina." *Journal of American Studies,* IX (1975), 259–281.

———. "South Carolina's Colonial Elite: A Study in the Social Structure and Political Culture of a Southern Colony, 1670–1760." Ph.D. diss., Johns Hopkins University, 1973.

Waters, John J., Jr. "Family, Inheritance, and Migration in Colonial New England: The Evidence from Guilford, Connecticut." *William and Mary Quarterly,* 3d Ser., XXXIX (1982), 64–86.

———. *The Otis Family in Provincial and Revolutionary Massachusetts.* Chapel Hill, N.C., 1968.

———. "Patrimony, Succession, and Social Stability: Guilford, Connecticut, in the Eighteenth Century." *Perspectives in American History,* X (1976), 129–160.

———. "The Traditional World of the New England Peasants: A View from Seventeenth-Century Barnstable." *New England Historical and Genealogical Register*, CXXX (1976), 3–21.

Watkins, C. Malcolm, and Ivor Noël Hume. *The "Poor Potter" of Yorktown*. United States National Museum, *Bulletin*, no. 249: Contributions from the Museum of History and Technology, Paper 54. Washington, D.C., 1967.

Watkins, Lura Woodside. *Early New England Potters and Their Wares*. Cambridge, Mass., 1950.

Watkins, Melville H. "A Staple Theory of Economic Growth." *Canadian Journal of Economics and Political Science*, XXIX (1963), 141–158.

Watson, Alan D. "Household Size and Composition in Pre-Revolutionary North Carolina." *Mississippi Quarterly*, XXXI (1978), 551–569.

———. "Luxury Vehicles and Elitism in Colonial North Carolina." *Southern Studies*, XIX (1980), 147–156.

Watson, Karl Stewart. "The Civilised Island: Barbados, a Social History, 1750–1816." Ph.D. diss., University of Florida, 1975.

Wax, Darold D. "Black Immigrants: The Slave Trade in Colonial Maryland." *Maryland Historical Magazine*, LXXIII (1978), 30–45.

———. "The Demand for Slave Labor in Colonial Pennsylvania." *Pennsylvania History*, XXXIV (1967), 331–345.

———. "Negro Import Duties in Colonial Virginia: A Study in British Commercial Policy and Local Public Policy." *Virginia Magazine of History and Biography*, LXXIX (1971), 29–44.

———. "Negro Imports into Pennsylvania, 1720–1766." *Pennsylvania History*, XXXII (1965), 254–287.

———. "Quaker Merchants and the Slave Trade in Colonial Pennsylvania." *Pennsylvania Magazine of History and Biography*, LXXXVI (1962), 143–159.

———. "Robert Ellis, Philadelphia Merchant and Slave Trader." *Pennsylvania Magazine of History and Biography*, LXXXVIII (1964), 52–69.

Weaver, Glenn. *Jonathan Trumbull, Connecticut's Merchant Magistrate (1710–1785)*. Hartford, Conn., 1956.

Webb, Stephen Saunders. *The Governors-General: The English Army and the Definition of the Empire, 1569–1681*. Chapel Hill, N.C., 1979.

Weeden, William B. *Economic and Social History of New England, 1620–1789*. 2 vols. Boston, 1891.

Weidman, John McI. "The Economic Development of Pennsylvania until 1723." Ph.D. diss., University of Wisconsin, 1935.

Weiss, Harry B., and Robert J. Sim. *The Early Grist and Flouring Mills of New Jersey*. Trenton, N.J., 1956.

Weiss, Roger W. "The Issue of Paper Money in the American Colonies, 1720–1774." *Journal of Economic History*, XXX (1970), 770–784.

———. "Mr. Scoville on Colonial Land Wastage." *Southern Economic Journal*, XXI (1954), 87–90.

Wells, Robert V. "A Demographic Analysis of Some Middle Colony Quaker Families of the Eighteenth Century." Ph.D. diss., Princeton University, 1969.

———. "Family Size and Fertility Control in Eighteenth-Century America: A Study of Quaker Families." *Population Studies*, XXV (1971), 73–82.

———. "The New York Census of 1731." *New-York Historical Society Quarterly*, LVII (1973), 255–259.

———. "Population and the American Revolution." In *The American Revolution: Chang-*

ing Perspectives, edited by William M. Fowler, Jr., and Wallace Coyle, 103–122. Boston, 1979.

———. *The Population of the British Colonies in America before 1776: A Survey of Census Data*. Princeton, N.J., 1975.

———. "Quaker Marriage Patterns in a Colonial Perspective." *William and Mary Quarterly*, 3d Ser., XXIX (1972), 415–442.

Welsh, Peter C. "The Brandywine Mills: A Chronicle of an Industry, 1762–1816." *Delaware History*, VII (1956), 17–36.

———. "Merchants, Millers, and Ocean Ships: The Components of an Early American Industrial Town." *Delaware History*, VII (1957), 319–336.

Wertenbaker, Thomas J. *The Planters of Colonial Virginia*. Princeton, N.J., 1922.

West, Robert Craig. "Money in the Colonial American Economy." *Economic Inquiry*, XVI (1978), 1–15.

Westbury, Susan Alice. "Colonial Virginia and the Atlantic Slave Trade." Ph.D. diss., University of Illinois, 1981.

Weston, William. *The Complete Merchant's Clerk: or, British and American Compting House*. London, 1754.

Wetherell, Charles. "A Note on Hierarchical Clustering." *Historical Methods Newsletter*, X (1977), 109–116.

White, Philip L. *The Beekmans of New York in Politics and Commerce, 1647–1877*. New York, 1956.

Whitehead, Russell F., and Frank C. Brown. *Colonial Homes in the Southern States: From Material Originally Published as the White Pine Series of Architectural Monographs*. New York, 1977.

Whiteman, Anne, J[ohn] S. Bromley, and P[eter] G. M. Dickson, eds. *Statesmen, Scholars, and Merchants: Essays in Eighteenth-Century History Presented to Dame Lucy Sutherland*. Oxford, 1973.

Whitney, Herbert A. "Estimating Precensus Populations: A Method Suggested and Applied to the Towns of Rhode Island and Plymouth Colonies in 1689." Association of American Geographers, *Annals*, LV (1965), 179–189.

Whitworth, Charles. *State of the Trade of Great Britain in Its Imports and Exports Progressively from the Year 1697 [to 1773]. . . .* London, 1776.

Wiecek, William M. "The Statutory Law of Slavery and Race in the Thirteen Mainland Colonies of British America." *William and Mary Quarterly*, 3d Ser., XXXIV (1977), 258–280.

Wilkenfeld, Bruce Martin. "The Social and Economic Structure of the City of New York, 1695–1796." Ph.D. diss., Columbia University, 1973.

Williams, Carlton Rowe. "Sir Thomas Modyford, 1620–1679: 'That Grand Propagator of English Honour and Power in the West Indies.'" Ph.D. diss., University of Kentucky, 1979.

Williams, Eric Eustace. *Capitalism and Slavery*. Chapel Hill, N.C., [1944].

———. *From Columbus to Castro: The History of the Caribbean, 1492–1969*. London, 1970.

Williams, Faith M., and Carle C. Zimmerman. *Studies of Family Living in the United States and Other Countries: An Analysis of Material and Method*. U.S. Department of Agriculture Miscellaneous Publication no. 233. Washington, D.C., 1935.

Williams, Justin. "English Mercantilism and Carolina Naval Stores, 1705–1776." *Journal of Southern History*, I (1935), 169–185.

Williams, Neville. "England's Tobacco Trade in the Reign of Charles I." *Virginia Magazine of History and Biography*, LXV (1957), 403–449.

[Williams, Paul]. *The Vain Prodigal Life, and Tragical Penitent Death of Thomas Hellier.* . . . London, 1680.

Williams, William Appleman, ed. *From Colony to Empire: Essays in the History of American Foreign Relations.* New York, 1972.

Williamson, Arthur Shelburn. "Credit Relations between Colonial and English Merchants in the Eighteenth Century." Ph.D. diss., University of Iowa, 1927.

Williamson, J[ames] A. "The Beginnings of an Imperial Policy, 1649–1660." In *The Old Empire: From the Beginnings to 1783.* Vol. I of *The Cambridge History of the British Empire,* edited by J. Holland Rose, A. P. Newton, and E. A. Benians, 207–238. Cambridge, 1929.

———. "England and the Opening of the Atlantic." In *The Old Empire: From the Beginnings to 1783.* Vol. I of *The Cambridge History of the British Empire,* edited by J. Holland Rose, A. P. Newton, and E. A. Benians, 22–52. Cambridge, 1929.

Williamson, Jeffrey G., and Peter H. Lindert. "Long-Term Trends in American Wealth Inequality." Institute for Research on Poverty, *Discussion Papers,* nos. 472–477 (1977).

Willis, Jean Louise. "The Trade between North America and the Danish West Indies, 1756–1807, with Special Reference to St. Croix." Ph.D. diss., Columbia University, 1963.

Wilms, Douglas C. "The Development of Rice Culture in Eighteenth Century Georgia." *Southeastern Geographer,* XII (1972), 45–57.

Wilson, Arthur M. "The Logwood Trade in the Seventeenth and Eighteenth Centuries." In *Essays in the History of Modern Europe,* edited by Donald C. McKay, 1–15. New York, 1936.

Wilson, Charles [Henry]. *Anglo-Dutch Commerce and Finance in the Eighteenth Century.* Cambridge, 1941.

———. *Mercantilism.* Historical Association Pamphlets, General Series, no. 37. [London], 1958.

———. *Profit and Power: A Study of England and the Dutch Wars.* London, 1957.

Wilson, Robert J. *Early American Account Books: Interpretation, Cataloguing, and Use.* American Association for State and Local History Technical Leaflet 140. Nashville, Tenn., 1981.

Winberry, John J. "Reputation of Carolina Indigo." *South Carolina Historical Magazine,* LXXX (1979), 242–250.

[Winthrop, John]. *Winthrop's Journal: "History of New England," 1630–1649.* Edited by James Kendall Hosmer. 2 vols. New York, 1908.

Winthrop Papers, 1498–1649. 5 vols. Boston, 1929–1947.

Withey, Lynne Elizabeth. "Population Change, Economic Development, and the Revolution: Newport, Rhode Island, as a Case Study, 1760–1800." Ph.D. diss., University of California, Berkeley, 1976.

———. *Urban Growth in Colonial Rhode Island: Newport and Providence in the Eighteenth Century.* Albany, N.Y., 1984.

Wittlinger, Carlton O. "Early Manufacturing in Lancaster County, Pennsylvania, 1710–1840." Ph.D. diss., University of Pennsylvania, 1953.

———. "The Small Arms Industry of Lancaster County, 1710–1840." *Pennsylvania History,* XXIV (1957), 121–136.

Wokeck, Maria (Marianne) Sophia. "The Flow and the Composition of German Immigration to Philadelphia, 1727–1775." *Pennsylvania Magazine of History and Biography,* CV (1981), 249–278.

———. "A Tide of Alien Tongues: The Flow and Ebb of German Immigration to Pennsylvania, 1683–1776." Ph.D. diss., Temple University, 1983.

Wolf, Edwin, II, and Maxwell Whiteman. *The History of the Jews of Philadelphia from Colonial Times to the Age of Jackson.* Philadelphia, 1957.

Wolf, Stephanie Grauman. *Urban Village: Population, Community, and Family Structure in Germantown, Pennsylvania, 1683–1800.* Princeton, N.J., 1976.

Wood, Jerome H., Jr. *Conestoga Crossroads: Lancaster, Pennsylvania, 1730–1790.* Harrisburg, Pa., 1979.

Wood, Peter H. *Black Majority: Negroes in Colonial South Carolina from 1670 through the Stono Rebellion.* New York, 1974.

————. "'I Did the Best I Could for My Day': The Study of Early Black History during the Second Reconstruction, 1960 to 1976." *William and Mary Quarterly,* 3d Ser., XXXV (1978), 185–225.

————. "'More Like a Negro Country': Demographic Patterns in Colonial South Carolina, 1700–1740." In *Race and Slavery in the Western Hemisphere: Quantitative Studies,* edited by Stanley L. Engerman and Eugene D. Genovese, 131–171. Princeton, N.J., 1975.

Wood, Virginia S[teele]. *Live Oaking: Southern Timber for Tall Ships.* Boston, 1981.

Woodward, C. Vann. "The Southern Ethic in a Puritan World." *William and Mary Quarterly,* 3d Ser., XXV (1968), 343–370.

Woodward, Carl Raymond. *The Development of Agriculture in New Jersey, 1640–1880: A Monographic Study in Agricultural History.* New Brunswick, N.J., 1927.

Wright, Gavin. *The Political Economy of the Cotton South: Households, Markets, and Wealth in the Nineteenth Century.* New York, 1978.

Wrigley, E[dward] A. "Population History in the 1980s." *Journal of Interdisciplinary History,* XII (1981), 207–226.

————, ed. *An Introduction to English Historical Demography: From the Sixteenth to the Nineteenth Century.* New York, 1966.

Wrigley, E[dward] A., and R. S. Schofield. *The Population History of England, 1541–1871: A Reconstruction.* Cambridge, Mass., 1981.

Wyckoff, Vertrees J. "Land Prices in Seventeenth-Century Maryland." *American Economic Review,* XXVIII (1938), 82–88.

————. "Seventeenth-Century Maryland Prices." *Agricultural History,* XII (1938), 299–310.

————. "Ships and Shipping of Seventeenth Century Maryland." *Maryland Historical Magazine,* XXXIII (1938), 334–342.

————. *Tobacco Regulation in Colonial Maryland.* Johns Hopkins University Studies in Historical and Political Science, Extra Volumes, N.S., no. 22. Baltimore, 1936.

York, Neil Longley. "Technology in Revolutionary America, 1760–1790." Ph.D. diss., University of California, Santa Barbara, 1978.

Young, Alfred F., ed. *The American Revolution: Explorations in the History of American Radicalism.* DeKalb, Ill., 1976.

Young, Arthur. ["An Inquiry into the Situation of the Kingdom on the Conclusion of the Late Treaty"]. *Annals of Agriculture and Other Useful Arts,* I (1784), 1–88.

Zankowich, Paul. "The Craftsmen of Colonial New York City." Ed.D. diss., New York University, 1956.

Zelinsky, Wilbur. "The Hypothesis of the Mobility Transition." *Geographical Review,* LXI (1971), 219–249.

Zook, George Frederick. *The Company of Royal Adventurers Trading into Africa.* Lancaster, Pa., 1919.

Zuckerman, Michael. *Peaceable Kingdoms: New England Towns in the Eighteenth Century.* New York, 1970.

SUPPLEMENTARY BIBLIOGRAPHY

This supplement extends the bibliography of *The Economy of British America, 1607–1789* to works published since mid-1983. We have also listed a few items published earlier that were overlooked in our survey of the literature. As with the initial bibliography, we have been inclusive rather than exclusive. Our guiding principle has been to ask whether, were we rewriting the text, a particular essay or book would inform our understanding of the field of British American economic history broadly understood. Doubtless there are occasional omissions and oversights, but we are confident that readers will find here a reasonably comprehensive listing of work on the early American economy over the past seven years. The length of the bibliography suggests that the field has not lost its liveliness. We hope our efforts, both in the first printing of *The Economy of British America* and in preparing this supplementary bibliography, have contributed a bit to the energy the scholars in the field continue to display.

We would like to thank all those readers who called omissions in the initial bibliography to our attention, and hope that others will let us know of oversights in this supplement. We would also like to thank Edward Tebbenhoff and Susan Cahn, who helped assemble the references, and the Graduate School of the University of Minnesota, which provided research support.

Adams, Donald R., Jr. "Prices and Wages in Maryland, 1750–1850." *Journal of Economic History*, XLVI (1986), 625–645.

Adams, John W., and Alice Bee Kasakoff. "Anthropology, Genealogy, and History: A Research Log." In *Generations and Change: Genealogical Perspectives in Social History*, edited by Robert M. Taylor, Jr., and Ralph J. Crandall, 53–78. Macon, Ga., 1986.

———. "Migration and the Family in Colonial New England: The View from Genealogies." *Journal of Family History*, IX (1984), 24–43.

———. "Wealth and Migration in Massachusetts and Maine, 1771–1798." *Journal of Economic History*, XLV (1985), 363–368.

Allen, David Grayson. "The Matrix of Motivation" (in "On English Migration to Early New England"). *New England Quarterly*, LIX (1986), 408–418.

Alston, Lee J., and Morton Owen Schapiro. "Inheritance Laws across Colonies: Causes and Consequences." *Journal of Economic History*, XLIV (1984), 277–287.

Altman, Morris. "Economic Growth in Canada, 1695–1739: Estimates and Analysis." *William and Mary Quarterly*, 3d Ser., XLV (1988), 684–711.

Anderson, Robert Charles. "A Note on the Changing Pace of the Great Migration" (in "On English Migration to Early New England"). *New England Quarterly*, LIX (1986), 406–407.

Anderson, Virginia DeJohn. "Migration, Kinship, and the Integration of Colonial New England Society: Three Generations of the Danforth Family." In *Generations and Change: Genealogical Perspectives in Social History*, edited by Robert M. Taylor, Jr., and Ralph J. Crandall, 269–287. Macon, Ga., 1986.

———. "Religion, the Common Thread" (in "On English Migration to Early New England"). *New England Quarterly*, LIX (1986), 418–424.

———. "To Pass beyond the Seas: The Great Migration and the Settlement of New England, 1630–1670." Ph.D. diss., Harvard University, 1984.

Anderson, William G. *The Price of Liberty: The Public Debt of the American Revolution*. Charlottesville, Va., 1983.

Andresen, Karen Elizabeth. "The Layered Society: Material Life in Portsmouth, N.H., 1680 to 1740." Ph.D. diss., University of New Hampshire, 1982.

Andrews, Kenneth R. *Trade, Plunder, and Settlement: Maritime Enterprise and the Genesis of the British Empire, 1480–1630*. New York, 1985.

Arndt, John Christopher. " 'The Solid Men of Bangor': Economic, Business, and Political Growth on Maine's Urban Frontier, 1769–1845." Ph.D. diss., Florida State University, 1987.

Bailey, Ronald W. "Africa, the Slave Trade, and the Rise of Industrial Capitalism in Europe and the United States: A Historiographic Review." *American History*, II (1986), 1–91.

Bailyn, Bernard. *The Peopling of British North America: An Introduction*. New York, 1986.

———— *Voyagers to the West: A Passage in the Peopling of America on the Eve of the Revolution*. New York, 1986.

Baker, Emerson W. " 'A Scratch with a Bear's Paw': Anglo-Indian Land Deeds in Early Maine." *Ethnohistory*, XXXVI (1989), 235–256.

Balcom, B. A. *The Cod Fishery of Isle Royale, 1713–58*. Studies in Archaeology, Architecture, and History. Ottawa, 1984.

Barbier, Jacques A., and Allan J. Kuethe, eds. *The North American Role in the Spanish Imperial Economy, 1760–1819*. Manchester, England, 1984.

Beales, Ross W., Jr. "The Reverend Ebenezer Parkman's Farm Workers, Westborough, Massachusetts, 1726–82." American Antiquarian Society, *Proceedings*, XCIX (1989), 121–149.

Becker, Marshall Joseph. "Lenape Population at the Time of European Contact: Estimating Native Numbers in the Lower Delaware Valley." American Philosophical Society, *Proceedings*, CXXXIII (1989), 112–125.

Beckles, Hilary McD. *Black Rebellion in Barbados: The Struggle against Slavery, 1627–1838*. Bridgetown, Barbados, 1984.

———— . *The History of Barbados: From Amerindian Society to Nation-State*. New York, 1989.

———— . "Plantation Production and White 'Proto-Slavery': White Indentured Servants and the Colonisation of the English West Indies, 1624–1645." *Americas*, XLI (1985), 21–45.

———— . "Rebels without Heroes: Slave Politics in Seventeenth Century Barbados." *Journal of Caribbean History*, XVIII (1983), 1–21.

———— . *White Servitude and Black Slavery in Barbados, 1627–1715*. Knoxville, Tenn., 1989.

Beckles, Hilary McD., and Andrew Downes. "The Economics of Transition to the Black Labor System in Barbados, 1630–1680." *Journal of Interdisciplinary History*, XVIII (1987–1988), 225–247.

Beeman, Richard R. *The Evolution of the Southern Backcountry: A Case Study of Lunenburg County, Virginia, 1746–1832*. Philadelphia, 1984.

Bergstrom, Peter V. *Markets and Merchants: Economic Diversification in Colonial Virginia, 1700–1775*. New York, 1985 (Ph.D. diss., University of New Hampshire, 1980).

Berleant-Schiller, Riva. "Free Labor and the Economy in Seventeenth-Century Montserrat." *William and Mary Quarterly*, 3d Ser., XLVI (1989), 539–564.

———— . Letter [on Berleant-Schiller, "Free Labor"]. *William and Mary Quarterly*, 3d Ser., XLVII (1990), 323.

Berlin, Ira, and Ronald Hoffman, eds. *Slavery and Freedom in the Age of the American Revolution*. Charlottesville, Va., 1983.

Bernhard, Virginia. "Bermuda and Virginia in the Seventeenth Century: A Comparative View." *Journal of Social History*, XIX (1985), 57–70.

————. "Beyond the Chesapeake: The Contrasting Status of Blacks in Bermuda, 1616–1663." *Journal of Southern History*, LIV (1988), 545–564.

Bernstein, Michael A., and Sean Wilentz. "Marketing, Commerce, and Capitalism in Rural Massachusetts." *Journal of Economic History*, XLIV (1984), 171–173.

Bhagat, G. "Americans and American Trade in India, 1784–1814." *American Neptune*, XLVI (1986), 6–15.

Biemer, Linda Briggs. *Women and Property in Colonial New York: The Transition from Dutch to English Law, 1643–1727*. Ann Arbor, Mich., 1983.

Bodenstein, William G. "St. Michaels, Maryland: An Eighteenth Century Speculative Development." *Maryland Historical Magazine*, LXXX (1985), 228–239.

Bodle, Wayne. "The 'Myth of the Middle Colonies' Reconsidered: The Process of Regionalization in Early America." *Pennsylvania Magazine of History and Biography*, CXIII (1989), 527–548.

Bogin, Ruth. "Petitioning and the New Moral Economy of Post-Revolutionary America." *William and Mary Quarterly*, 3d Ser., XLV (1988), 391–425.

Bordo, Michael D., and Ivan A. Marcotte. "Purchasing Power Parity in Colonial America: Some Evidence for South Carolina, 1732–1774." *Carnegie-Rochester Conference Series on Public Policy*, XXVII (1987), 311–324.

Bosher, J. F. *The Canada Merchants, 1713–1763*. New York, 1987.

Boydston, Jeanne. "Home and Work: The Industrialization of Housework in the Northeastern United States from the Colonial Period to the Civil War." Ph.D. diss., Yale University, 1984.

Breen, T. H. " 'Baubles of Britain': The American and Consumer Revolutions of the Eighteenth Century." *Past and Present*, no. 119 (May 1988), 73–104.

————. "An Empire of Goods: The Anglicization of Colonial America, 1690–1776." *Journal of British Studies*, XXV (1986), 467–499.

————. *Tobacco Culture: The Mentality of the Great Tidewater Planters on the Eve of Revolution*. Princeton, N.J., 1985.

Brenner, Elise Melanie. "Strategies for Autonomy: An Analysis of Ethnic Mobilization in Seventeenth-Century Southern New England." Ph.D. diss., University of Massachusetts, 1984.

Brody, David. "Time and Work during Early American Industrialism." *Labor History*, XXX (1989), 5–46.

Brown, Richard D. "Farm Labor in Southern New England during the Agricultural-Industrial Transition: Introduction." American Antiquarian Society, *Proceedings*, XCIX (1989), 113–119.

————. *Knowledge Is Power: The Diffusion of Information in Early America, 1700–1865*. New York, 1989.

Bruchey, Stuart. "Economy and Society in an Earlier America." *Journal of Economic History*, XLVII (1987), 299–319.

————. *The Wealth of the Nation: An Economic History of the United States*. New York, 1988.

Buisseret, David J. "Slaves Arriving in Jamaica, 1684–1692." *Revue Française d'Histoire d'Outre-Mer*, LXVI (1977), 85–88.

Bullion, John L. "Security and Economy: The Bute Administration's Plans for the American Army and Revenue, 1762–1763." *William and Mary Quarterly*, 3d Ser., LXV (1988), 499–509.

Bumsted, J. M. *Land, Settlement, and Politics on Eighteenth-Century Prince Edward Island*. Kingston, Ont., 1987.

————. *The People's Clearance: Highland Emigration to British North America, 1770–1815*. Edinburgh, 1982.

Burnard, Trevor Graeme. "A Colonial Elite: Wealthy Marylanders, 1691–1776." Ph.D. diss., Johns Hopkins University, 1988.

Bushman, Richard L. *King and People in Provincial Massachusetts*. Chapel Hill, N.C., 1985.

Byers, Edward. *The Nation of Nantucket: Society and Politics in an Early American Commercial Center, 1660–1820*. Boston, 1986.

————. "Putting History Back in Historical Demography: Nantucket Re-Reexamined." *Journal of Interdisciplinary History*, XVI (1985–1986), 683–690.

Calabro, David Joseph. "Consensus for Empire: American Expansionist Thought and Policy, 1763–1789." Ph.D. diss., University of Virginia, 1982.

Calhoun, Jeanne A., Martha A. Zierden, and Elizabeth A. Paysinger. "The Geographic Spread of Charleston's Mercantile Community, 1732–1767." *South Carolina Historical Magazine*, LXXXVI (1985), 182–220.

Calomiris, Charles W. "The Depreciation of the Continental: A Reply." *Journal of Economic History*, XLVIII (1988), 693–698.

————. "Institutional Failure, Monetary Scarcity, and the Depreciation of the Continental." *Journal of Economic History*, XLVIII (1988), 47–68.

Carll-White, Mary Allison. "The Role of the Black Artisan in the Building Trades and the Decorative Arts in South Carolina's Charleston District, 1760–1800." Ph.D. diss., University of Tennessee, 1982.

Carp, E. Wayne. *To Starve the Army at Pleasure: Continental Army Administration and American Political Culture, 1775–1783*. Chapel Hill, N.C., 1984.

Carr, Lois Green. "Diversification in the Colonial Chesapeake: Somerset County, Maryland, in Comparative Perspective." In *Colonial Chesapeake Society*, edited by Lois Green Carr, Philip D. Morgan, and Jean B. Russo, 342–388. Chapel Hill, N.C., 1988.

————. "Inheritance in the Colonial Chesapeake." In *Women in the Age of the American Revolution*, edited by Ronald Hoffman and Peter J. Albert, 155–208. Charlottesville, Va., 1989.

Carr, Lois Green, and Russell R. Menard. "Land, Labor, and Economies of Scale in Early Maryland: Some Limits to Growth in the Chesapeake System of Husbandry." *Journal of Economic History*, XLIX (1989), 407–418.

Carr, Lois Green, Philip D. Morgan, and Jean B. Russo, eds. *Colonial Chesapeake Society*. Chapel Hill, N.C., 1988.

Carr, Lois Green, and Lorena S. Walsh. "Economic Diversification and Labor Organization in the Chesapeake, 1650–1820." In *Work and Labor in Early America*, edited by Stephen Innes, 144–188. Chapel Hill, N.C., 1988.

————. "The Standard of Living in the Colonial Chesapeake" (in "Toward a History of the Standard of Living in British North America"). *William and Mary Quarterly*, 3d Ser., XLV (1988), 135–159.

Carrington, Selwyn H. H. "The American Revolution and the British West Indies' Economy." *Journal of Interdisciplinary History*, XVII (1986–1987), 823–850.

————. *The British West Indies during the American Revolution*. Koninklijk Instituut voor Taal-, Land- en Volkenkunde, Caribbean Series, No. 8. Dordrecht, 1988 (Ph.D. diss., University of London, 1975).

Chase, Jeanne, ed. *Géographie du Capital Marchand aux Amériques, 1760–1860*. Paris, 1987.

Chevignard, Bernard. "Les voyageurs européens et la pratique du 'bondelage' (bundling) en Nouvelle-Angleterre à la fin du XVIIIe siècle." *Amérique et Europe*, II (1986), 75–87.

Chu, Jonathan M. "Nursing a Poisonous Tree: Litigation and Property Law in Seventeenth-Century Essex County, Massachusetts: The Case of Bishop's Farm." *American Journal of Legal History*, XXXI (1987), 221–252.

Churchill, E. A. "A Most Ordinary Lot of Men: The Fishermen at Richmond Island, Maine, in the Early Seventeenth Century." *New England Quarterly*, LVII (1984), 184–204.

Claypoole, W. "The Merchants of Port Royal, 1655–1700." Ph.D. diss., University of the West Indies, 1974.

Clemens, Paul G. E., and Lucy Simler. "Rural Labor and the Farm Household in Chester County, Pennsylvania, 1750–1820." In *Work and Labor in Early America*, edited by Stephen Innes, 106–143. Chapel Hill, N.C., 1988.

Clowse, Converse D. "Shipowning and Shipbuilding in Colonial South Carolina: An Overview." *American Neptune*, XLIV (1984), 91–107.

Coakley, Robert Walter. "Virginia Commerce during the American Revolution." Ph.D. diss., University of Virginia, 1949.

Coclanis, Peter A. "Bitter Harvest: The South Carolina Low Country in Historical Perspective." *Journal of Economic History*, XLV (1985), 251–259.

———. "Death in Early Charleston: An Estimate of the Crude Death Rate for the White Population of Charleston, 1722–1732." *South Carolina Historical Magazine*, LXXXV (1984), 280–291.

———. "The Rise and Fall of the South Carolina Low Country: An Essay in Economic Interpretation." *Southern Studies*, XXIV (1985), 143–166.

———. *The Shadow of a Dream: Economic Life and Death in the South Carolina Low Country, 1670–1920*. New York, 1989.

Coclanis, Peter A., and Lacy K. Ford. "The South Carolina Economy Reconstructed and Reconsidered: Structure, Output, and Performance." In *Developing Dixie: Modernization in a Traditional Society*, edited by Winfred B. Moore, Jr., Joseph F. Tripp, and Lyon G. Tyler, Jr., 93–110. Westport, Conn., 1988.

Cohen, David Steven. "How Dutch Were the Dutch of New Netherland?" *New York History*, LXII (1981), 43–60.

Cohen, Robert. "Early Caribbean Jewry: A Demographic Perspective." *Jewish Social Studies*, XLV (1983), 123–134.

Cohn, Raymond L. "Deaths of Slaves in the Middle Passage." *Journal of Economic History*, XLV (1985), 685–692.

Coker, William S., and Thomas D. Watson. *Indian Traders of the Southeastern Spanish Borderlands: Panton, Leslie & Company and John Forbes & Company, 1783–1847*. Pensacola, Fla., 1986.

Cook, Peter W. "Domestic Livestock of Massachusetts Bay, 1625–1725." In *The Farm: Dublin Seminar for New England Folklife*, XI (1986), edited by Peter Benes, 109–125. Boston, 1988.

———. "To Graze the Common: The Cattle and Sheep of Seventeenth-Century Massachusetts." Essex Institute, *Historical Collections*, CXXI (1985), 91–106.

Cooke, Edward Strong, Jr. "Rural Artisanal Culture: The Preindustrial Joiners of Newtown and Woodbury, Connecticut, 1760–1820." Ph.D. diss., Boston University, 1984.

Coons, Martha, ed. *All Sorts of Good Sufficient Cloth: Linen-Making in New England, 1640–1860*. North Andover, Mass., 1980.

Countryman, Edward. "Of Republicanism, Capitalism, and the 'American Mind.'" *William and Mary Quarterly*, 3d Ser., XLIV (1987), 556–562.

———. "Stability and Class, Theory and History: The South in the Eighteenth Century." *Journal of American Studies*, XVII (1983), 243–250.

Cowan, Thomas. "William Hill and the Aera Ironworks." *Journal of Early Southern Decorative Arts*, XIII (1987), 1–31.

Crane, Elaine Forman. *A Dependent People: Newport, Rhode Island, in the Revolutionary Era.* New York, 1985.

Crapster, Basil L. "Hampton Furnace in Colonial Frederick County." *Maryland Historical Magazine*, LXXX (1985), 1–8.

Craton, Michael. "The Passion to Exist: Slave Rebellions in the British West Indies, 1650–1832." *Journal of Caribbean History*, XIII (1980), 1–20.

———. *Testing the Chains: Resistance to Slavery in the British West Indies.* Ithaca, N.Y., 1982.

Cray, Robert E., Jr. *Paupers and Poor Relief in New York City and Its Rural Environs, 1700–1830.* Philadelphia, 1988.

Cressy, David. *Coming Over: Migration and Communication between England and New England in the Seventeenth Century.* New York, 1987.

———. "The Seasonality of Marriage in Old and New England." *Journal of Interdisciplinary History*, XVI (1985–1986), 1–21.

Cronon, William. *Changes in the Land: Indians, Colonists, and the Ecology of New England.* New York, 1983.

Crowley, John E. "Family Relations and Inheritance in Early South Carolina." *Histoire Sociale / Social History*, XVII (1984), 35–57.

———. "The Importance of Kinship: Testamentary Evidence from South Carolina." *Journal of Interdisciplinary History*, XVI (1985–1986), 559–577.

Crowther, Simeon John. "The Shipbuilding Industry and the Economic Development of the Delaware Valley, 1681–1776." Ph.D. diss., University of Pennsylvania, 1970.

Culbert, Sheila Anne. "Sturdy Beggars and the Worthy Poor: Poverty in Massachusetts, 1750–1820." Ph.D. diss., Indiana University, 1985.

Daniels, Bruce C. "The Colonial Background of New England's Secondary Urban Centers." *Historical Journal of Massachusetts*, XIV (1986), 11–24.

———. *Dissent and Conformity on Narragansett Bay: The Colonial Rhode Island Town.* Middletown, Conn., 1983.

Davidson, Thomas E. "Free Blacks in Old Somerset County, 1745–1755." *Maryland Historical Magazine*, LXXX (1985), 151–156.

Davis, David Brion. "The Significance of Excluding Slavery from the Old Northwest in 1787." *Indiana Magazine of History*, LXXXIV (1988), 75–89.

Davis, Thomas J. "These Enemies of Their Own Household: A Note on the Troublesome Slave Population in Eighteenth-Century New York City." *Journal of the Afro-American Historical and Genealogical Society*, V (1984), 133–147.

Day, Alan F. *A Social Study of Lawyers in Maryland, 1660–1775.* New York, 1985 (Ph.D. diss., Johns Hopkins University, 1976).

Deal, Douglas. "A Constricted World: Free Blacks on Virginia's Eastern Shore, 1680–1750." In *Colonial Chesapeake Society*, edited by Lois Green Carr, Philip D. Morgan, and Jean B. Russo, 275–305. Chapel Hill, N.C., 1988.

———. "Race and Class in Colonial Virginia: Indians, Englishmen, and Africans on the Eastern Shore during the Seventeenth Century." Ph.D. diss., University of Rochester, 1981.

Dell, Richard F. "The Operational Record of the Clyde Tobacco Fleet, 1747–1775." *Scottish Economic and Social History*, II (1982).

Deutsch, Sarah. "The Elusive Guineamen: Newport Slavers, 1735–1774." *New England Quarterly*, LV (1982), 229–253.

Devine, T. M. "Glasgow Merchants and the Collapse of the Tobacco Trade, 1775–1783." *Scottish Historical Review*, LII (1973), 50–74.

Dickinson, John A. "Old Routes and New Wares: The Advent of European Goods in the St. Lawrence Valley." In *"Le Castor Fait Tout": Selected Papers of the Fifth North American*

Fur Trade Conference, 1985, edited by Bruce G. Trigger, Toby Morantz, and Louise Dechêne, 25–41. Montreal, 1987.

Ditz, Toby L. *Property and Kinship: Inheritance in Early Connecticut, 1750–1820.* Princeton, N.J., 1986.

Dobyns, Henry F. "More Methodological Perspectives on Historical Demography." *Ethnohistory*, XXXVI (1989), 285–299.

———. *Their Number Become Thinned: Native American Population Dynamics in Eastern North America.* Knoxville, Tenn., 1983.

Doerflinger, Thomas M. "Commercial Specialization in Philadelphia's Merchant Community, 1750–1791." *Business History Review*, LVII (1983), 20–49.

———. "Farmers and Dry Goods in the Philadelphia Market Area, 1750–1800." In *The Economy of Early America: The Revolutionary Period, 1763–1790*, edited by Ronald Hoffman, John J. McCusker, Russell R. Menard, and Peter J. Albert, 166–195. Charlottesville, Va., 1988.

———. "Hibernia Furnace during the Revolution." *New Jersey History*, XC (1972), 97–114.

———. "Philadelphia Merchants and the Logic of Moderation, 1760–1775." *William and Mary Quarterly*, 3d Ser., XL (1983), 197–226.

———. *A Vigorous Spirit of Enterprise: Merchants and Economic Development in Revolutionary Philadelphia.* Chapel Hill, N.C., 1986.

Doty, Richard G. "New York Money: A Problem for Constitutional Solution." *Bronx County Historical Society Journal*, XXIV (1987), 109–126.

Doutrich, Paul Erb. "The Evolution of an Early American Town: Yorktown, Pennsylvania, 1740–1790." Ph.D. diss., University of Kentucky, 1985.

Ducoff-Barone, Deborah. "Marketing and Manufacturing: A Study of Domestic Cast Iron Articles Produced at Colebrookdale Furnace, Berks County, Pennsylvania, 1735–1751." *Pennsylvania History*, L (1983), 20–37.

Dufour, Ronald Paul. "Modernization in Colonial Massachusetts, 1630–1763." Ph.D. diss., College of William and Mary, 1982.

Dunn, Richard S. "Black Society in the Chesapeake, 1776–1810." In *Slavery and Freedom in the Age of the American Revolution*, edited by Ira Berlin and Ronald Hoffman, 49–82. Charlottesville, Va., 1983.

———. "'Dreadful Idlers' in the Cane Fields: The Slave Labor Pattern on a Jamaican Sugar Estate, 1762–1831." *Journal of Interdisciplinary History*, XVII (1986–1987), 795–822.

———. "Servants and Slaves: The Recruitment and Employment of Labor." In *Colonial British America: Essays in the New History of the Early Modern Era*, edited by Jack P. Greene and J. R. Pole, 157–194. Baltimore, 1984.

Durel, John Walter. "From Strawbery Banke to Puddle Dock: The Evolution of a Neighborhood, 1630–1850." Ph.D. diss., University of New Hampshire, 1984.

Eccles, W. J. "The Fur Trade and Eighteenth-Century Imperialism." *William and Mary Quarterly*, 3d Ser., XL (1983), 341–362.

Egnal, Marc. *A Mighty Empire: The Origins of the American Revolution.* Ithaca, N.Y., 1988.

Ekirch, A. Roger. "Bound for America: A Profile of British Convicts Transported to the Colonies, 1718–1775." *William and Mary Quarterly*, 3d Ser., XLII (1985), 184–200.

———. *Bound for America: The Transportation of British Convicts to the Colonies, 1718–1775.* Oxford, 1987.

———. "Poverty, Class, and Dependence in Early America." *Historical Journal*, XXVII (1984), 493–502.

Eltis, David, and Lawrence C. Jennings. "Trade between Western Africa and the Atlantic

World in the Pre-Colonial Era." *American Historical Review*, XCIII (1988), 936–959.

Ens, Gerhard. "The Political Economy of the 'Private Trade' on the Hudson Bay: The Example of Moose Factory, 1741–1744." In *"Le Castor Fait Tout": Selected Papers of the Fifth North American Fur Trade Conference, 1985*, edited by Bruce G. Trigger, Toby Morantz, and Louise Dechêne, 382–410. Montreal, 1987.

Ernst, Joseph A. "The Political Economy of the Chesapeake Colonies, 1760–1775: A Study in Comparative History." In *The Economy of Early America: The Revolutionary Period, 1763–1790*, edited by Ronald Hoffman, John J. McCusker, Russell R. Menard, and Peter J. Albert, 196–243. Charlottesville, Va., 1988.

Fabel, Robin F. A. *The Economy of British West Florida, 1763–1783*. Tuscaloosa, Ala., 1987.

Fabend, Firth Haring. "The Yeoman Ideal: A Dutch Family in the Middle Colonies, 1660–1800." Ph.D. diss., New York University, 1988.

Farmer, Charles James. "Country Stores and Frontier Exchange Systems in Southside Virginia during the Eighteenth Century." Ph.D. diss., University of Maryland, 1984.

Fausz, J. Frederick. "Profits, Pelts, and Power: English Culture in the Early Chesapeake, 1620–1652." *Maryland History*, XIV (1983), 14–30.

———. " 'To Draw Thither the Trade of Beavers': The Strategic Significance of the English Fur Trade in the Chesapeake, 1620–1660." In *"Le Castor Fait Tout": Selected Papers of the Fifth North American Fur Trade Conference, 1985*, edited by Bruce G. Trigger, Toby Morantz, and Louise Dechêne, 42–71. Montreal, 1987.

Fenstermaker, J. Van, John E. Filer, and Robert Stanley Herren. "Money Statistics of New England, 1785–1837." *Journal of Economic History*, XLIV (1984), 441–453.

Ferguson, E. James. "Political Economy, Public Liberty, and the Formation of the Constitution." *William and Mary Quarterly*, 3d Ser., XL (1983), 389–412.

Fischer, David Hackett. *Albion's Seed: Four British Folkways in America*. New York, 1989.

Fischer, Lewis R. "Revolution without Independence: The Canadian Colonies, 1749–1775." In *The Economy of Early America: The Revolutionary Period, 1763–1790*, edited by Ronald Hoffman, John J. McCusker, Russell R. Menard, and Peter J. Albert, 88–125. Charlottesville, Va., 1988.

Fogel, Robert William. "Nutrition and the Decline of Mortality since 1700: Some Preliminary Findings." In *Long-Term Factors in American Economic Growth*, edited by Stanley L. Engerman and Robert E. Gallman, 439–555. Studies in Income and Wealth, LI. Chicago, 1986.

———. *Without Consent or Contract: The Rise and Fall of American Slavery*. New York, 1989.

Folbre, Nancy R. "The Wealth of Patriarchs: Deerfield, Massachusetts, 1760–1840." *Journal of Interdisciplinary History*, XVI (1985–1986), 199–220.

Fortune, Stephen Alexander. *Merchants and Jews: The Struggle for British West Indian Commerce, 1650–1750*. Gainesville, Fla., 1984.

Fowler, David J. "Egregious Villains, Wood Rangers, and London Traders: The Pine Robber Phenomenon in New Jersey during the Revolutionary War." Ph.D. diss., Rutgers University, 1987.

Francis, Daniel, and Toby Morantz. *Partners in Furs: A History of the Fur Trade in Eastern James Bay, 1600–1870*. Kingston, Ont., 1983.

Franz, George William. "Paxton: A Study of Community Structure and Mobility in the Colonial Pennsylvania Backcountry." Ph.D. diss., Rutgers University, 1974.

Fraser, Walter J., Jr. "The City Elite, 'Disorder,' and the Poor Children of Pre-Revolutionary Charleston." *South Carolina Historical Magazine*, LXXXIV (1983), 167–179.

French, Christopher J. "Productivity in the Atlantic Shipping Industry: A Quantitative

Study." *Journal of Interdisciplinary History*, XVII (1986–1987), 613–638.

———. "The Trade and Shipping of the Port of London, 1700–1776." Ph.D. diss., University of Exeter, 1980.

Frey, Sylvia R. "In Search of Roots: The Colonial Antecedents of Slavery in the Plantation Colonies." *Georgia Historical Quarterly*, LXVIII (1984), 244–259.

Galenson, David W. "The Market Evaluation of Human Capital: The Case of Indentured Servitude." *Journal of Political Economy*, LXXXIX (1981), 446–467.

———. "Population Turnover in the English West Indies in the Late Seventeenth Century: A Comparative Perspective." *Journal of Economic History*, XLV (1985), 227–235.

———. "The Rise and Fall of Indentured Servitude in the Americas: An Economic Analysis." *Journal of Economic History*, XLIV (1984), 1–26.

———. *Traders, Planters, and Slaves: Market Behavior in Early English America.* New York, 1986.

Gallay, Alan. *The Formation of a Planter Elite: Jonathan Bryan and the Southern Colonial Frontier.* Athens, Ga., 1989.

———. "Jonathan Bryan's Plantation Empire: Land, Politics, and the Formation of a Ruling Class in Colonial Georgia." *William and Mary Quarterly*, 3d Ser., XLV (1988), 253–279.

———. "The Origins of Slaveholders' Paternalism: George Whitefield, the Bryan Family, and the Great Awakening in the South." *Journal of Southern History*, LIII (1987), 369–394.

———. "The Search for an Alternate Source of Trade: The Creek Indians and Jonathan Bryan." *Georgia Historical Quarterly*, LXXIII (1989), 209–230.

Gallman, James Matthew. "Relative Ages of Colonial Marriages." *Journal of Interdisciplinary History*, XIV (1983–1984), 609–617.

Gallman, Robert E. "Changes in the Level of Literacy in a New Community of Early America." *Journal of Economic History*, XLVIII (1988), 567–582.

———. "Two Problems in the Measurement of American Colonial Signature-Mark Literacy." *Historical Methods*, XX (1987), 137–141.

Galloway, J. H. *The Sugar Cane Industry: An Historical Geography from Its Origins to 1914.* New York, 1989.

Garland, Charles, and Herbert S. Klein. "The Allotment of Space for Slaves aboard Eighteenth-Century British Slave Ships." *William and Mary Quarterly*, 3d Ser., XLII (1985), 238–248.

Garrison, J. Ritchie, and Joseph H. Hall IV. "Market Regulations and Agricultural Change in Suffolk County, Massachusetts, 1675–1725." *Pioneer America*, XIII, no. 2 (September 1981), 29–42.

Garvin, James Leo. "Academic Architecture and the Building Trades in the Piscataqua Region of New Hampshire and Maine, 1715–1815." Ph.D. diss., Boston University, 1983.

Gaspar, David Barry. *Bondmen and Rebels: A Study of Master-Slave Relations in Antigua, with Implications for Colonial British America.* Baltimore, 1985.

Gemery, Henry A. "Disarray in the Historical Record: Estimates of Immigration to the United States, 1700–1860." American Philosophical Society, *Proceedings*, CXXXIII (1989), 123–127.

———. "European Emigration to North America, 1700–1820: Numbers and Quasi-Numbers." *Perspectives in American History*, N.S., I (1984), 283–342.

———. "The Uses of Quantitative Analysis" (in "*Voyagers to the West*: A Review Colloquium"). *Business History Review*, LXII (1988), 687–691.

Gough, Robert J. "The Significance of the Demographic Characteristics of Wealthy Philadelphians at the End of the Eighteenth Century." American Philosophical Society,

Proceedings, CXXXIII (1989), 305–311.

Grabbe, Hans-Jürgen. "European Immigration to the United States in the Early National Period, 1783–1820." American Philosophical Society, *Proceedings,* CXXXIII (1989), 190–214.

Gragg, Larry D. "The Barbados Connection: John Parris and the Early New England Trade with the West Indies." *New England Historical and Genealogical Register,* CXL (1986), 99–113.

———. "Puritans in Paradise: The New England Migration to Barbados, 1640–1660." *Journal of Caribbean History,* XXI (1988), 154–167.

Green, William A. "Race and Slavery: Considerations on the Williams Thesis." In *British Capitalism and Caribbean Slavery: The Legacy of Eric Williams,* edited by Barbara L. Solow and Stanley L. Engerman, 25–49. New York, 1987.

———. "Supply versus Demand in the Barbadian Sugar Revolution." *Journal of Interdisciplinary History,* XVIII (1987–1988), 403–418.

Greene, Jack P. "Colonial South Carolina and the Caribbean Connection." *South Carolina Historical Magazine,* LXXXVIII (1987), 192–210.

———. *Pursuits of Happiness: The Social Development of Early Modern British Colonies and the Formation of American Culture.* Chapel Hill, N.C., 1988.

Greene, Jack P., and J. R. Pole, eds. *Colonial British America: Essays in the New History of the Early Modern Era.* Baltimore, 1984.

Greer, Allan. *Peasant, Lord, and Merchant: Rural Society in Three Quebec Parishes, 1740–1840.* Toronto, 1985.

Grubb, Farley. "The Auction of Redemptioner Servants, Philadelphia, 1771–1804: An Economic Analysis." *Journal of Economic History,* XLVIII (1988), 583–603.

———. "Colonial Immigrant Literacy: An Economic Analysis of Pennsylvania-German Evidence, 1727–1775." *Explorations in Economic History,* 2d Ser., XXIV (1987), 63–76.

———. "Colonial Labor Markets and the Length of Indenture: Further Evidence." *Explorations in Economic History,* 2d Ser., XXIV (1987), 101–106.

———. "Immigrant Servant Labor: Their Occupational and Geographic Distribution in the Late Eighteenth-Century Mid-Atlantic Economy." *Social Science History,* IX (1985), 249–275.

———. "Immigration and Servitude in the Colony and Commonwealth of Pennsylvania: A Quantitative and Economic Analysis." Ph.D. diss., University of Chicago, 1984.

———. "The Incidence of Servitude in Trans-Atlantic Migration, 1771–1804." *Explorations in Economic History,* 2d Ser., XXII (1985), 316–339.

———. "The Market for Indentured Immigrants: Evidence on the Efficiency of Forward-Labor Contracting in Philadelphia, 1745–1773." *Journal of Economic History,* XLV (1985), 855–868.

———. "The Market Structure of Shipping German Immigrants to Colonial America." *Pennsylvania Magazine of History and Biography,* CXI (1987), 27–48.

———. "Morbidity and Mortality on the North Atlantic Passage: Eighteenth-Century German Immigration." *Journal of Interdisciplinary History,* XVII (1986–1987), 565–585.

———. "Redemptioner Immigration to Philadelphia: Evidence on Contract Choice and Profitability." *Journal of Economic History,* XLVI (1986), 407–418.

———. "Servant Auction Records and Immigration into the Delaware Valley, 1745–1831: The Proportion of Females among Immigrant Servants." American Philosophical Society, *Proceedings,* CXXXIII (1989), 154–169.

Gundersen, Joan Rezner. "The Double Bonds of Race and Sex: Black and White Women in a Colonial Virginia Parish." *Journal of Southern History,* LII (1986), 351–372.

Gwyn, Julian. "British Government Spending and the North American Colonies, 1740–

1775." In *The British Atlantic Empire before the American Revolution*, edited by Peter Marshall and Glyn Williams, 74–84. London, 1980.

———. "Financial Revolution in Massachusetts: Public Credit and Taxation, 1692–1774." *Histoire Sociale / Social History*, XVII (1984), 59–77.

———. "Shipbuilding for the Royal Navy in Colonial New England." *American Neptune*, XLVIII (1988), 22–30.

Haan, Richard L. "The 'Trade Do's Not Flourish as Formerly': The Ecological Origins of the Yamassee War of 1715." *Ethnohistory*, XXVIII (1982), 341–358.

Hammon, Neal O. "Settlers, Land Jobbers, and Outlyers: A Quantitative Analysis of Land Acquisition on the Kentucky Frontier." *Kentucky Historical Society Register*, LXXXIV (1986), 241–262.

Handler, Jerome S., and Robert S. Corruccini. "Plantation Slave Life in Barbados: A Physical Anthropological Analysis." *Journal of Interdisciplinary History*, XIV (1983–1984), 65–90.

———. "Weaning among West Indian Slaves: Historical and Bioanthropological Evidence from Barbados." *William and Mary Quarterly*, 3d Ser., XLIII (1986), 111–117.

Harley, C. Knick. "Ocean Freight Rates and Productivity, 1740–1913: The Primacy of Mechanical Invention Reaffirmed." *Journal of Economic History*, XLVIII (1988), 851–876.

Harrington, Faith. "The Emergent Elite in Early Eighteenth Century Portsmouth Society: The Archaeology of the Joseph Sherburne Houselot." *Historical Archaeology*, XXIII (1989), 2–18.

———. "Sea Tenure in Seventeenth-Century New Hampshire: Native Americans and Englishmen in the Sphere of Coastal Resources." *Historical New Hampshire*, XL (1985), 18–33.

Harris, P. M. G. "The Demographic Development of Colonial Philadelphia in Some Comparative Perspective." American Philosophical Society, *Proceedings*, CXXXIII (1989), 262–304.

Harris, R. Cole, ed. *Historical Atlas of Canada*. Vol. I: *From the Beginning to 1800*. Toronto, 1987.

Heintzelman, Andrea J. "Colonial Wharf Construction: Uncovering the Untold Past." *Log of Mystic Seaport*, XXXVII (1986), 124–135.

Hemphill, John Mickle, II. *Virginia and the English Commercial System, 1689–1733: Studies in the Development and Fluctuations of a Colonial Economy under Imperial Control*. New York, 1985 (Ph.D. diss., Princeton University, 1964).

Henige, David. "On the Current Devaluation of the Notion of Evidence: A Rejoinder to Dobyns." *Ethnohistory*, XXXVI (1989), 304–307.

———. "Primary Source by Primary Source? On the Role of Epidemics in New World Depopulation." *Ethnography*, XXXIII (1986), 293–312.

Henretta, James A. "The War for Independence and American Economic Development." In *The Economy of Early America: The Revolutionary Period, 1763–1790*, edited by Ronald Hoffman, John J. McCusker, Russell R. Menard, and Peter J. Albert, 45–87. Charlottesville, Va., 1988.

———. "Wealth and Social Structure." In *Colonial British America: Essays in The New History of the Early Modern Era*, edited by Jack P. Greene and J. R. Pole, 262–289. Baltimore, 1984.

Heyrman, Christine Leigh. *Commerce and Culture: The Maritime Communities of Colonial Massachusetts, 1690–1750*. New York, 1984.

———. "The Fashion among More Superior People: Charity and Social Change in Provincial New England, 1700–1740." *American Quarterly*, XXXIV (1982), 107–124.

Hodges, Graham Russell. *New York City Cartmen, 1667–1850*. New York, 1986.

Hoffman, Ronald, and Peter J. Albert, eds. *Women in the Age of the American Revolution.* Charlottesville, Va., 1989.

Hoffman, Ronald, John J. McCusker, Russell R. Menard, and Peter J. Albert, eds. *The Economy of Early America: The Revolutionary Period, 1763–1790.* Charlottesville, Va., 1988.

Hogendorn, Jan S. "The Economics of the African Slave Trade." *Journal of American History,* LXX (1983–1984), 854–861.

Holmes, Jack D. "Benjamin Hawkins and United States Attempts to Teach Farming to Southeastern Indians." *Agricultural History,* LX (1986), 216–232.

Hood, Adrienne Dora. "Organization and Extent of Textile Manufacture in Eighteenth-Century, Rural Pennsylvania: A Case Study of Chester County." Ph.D. diss., University of California, San Diego, 1988.

Horn, James. "Adapting to a New World: A Comparative Study of Local Society in England and Maryland, 1650–1700." In *Colonial Chesapeake Society,* edited by Lois Green Carr, Philip D. Morgan, and Jean B. Russo, 133–175. Chapel Hill, N.C., 1988.

Innes, Stephen, ed. *Work and Labor in Early America.* Chapel Hill, N.C., 1988.

Jensen, Joan M. "Butter Making and Economic Development in Mid-Atlantic America from 1750 to 1850." *Signs,* XIII (1988), 813–829.

―――. *Loosening the Bonds: Mid-Atlantic Farm Women, 1750–1850.* New Haven, Conn., 1986.

Johnson, G. D. "Capitalism, Protestantism, and the Private Family: Comparisons among England, France, and the American Colonies." *Journal of Sociological Inquiry,* LIX (1989), 144–164.

Jones, Alice Hanson. "Wealth and Growth of the Thirteen Colonies: Some Implications." *Journal of Economic History,* XLIV (1984), 239–254.

Jones, Robert F. "Economic Opportunism and the Constitution in New York State: The Example of William Duer." *New York History,* LXVIII (1987), 357–372.

Jordan, Winthrop D., and Sheila L. Skemp, eds. *Race and Family in the Colonial South.* Jackson, Miss., 1987.

Kantrow, Louise. "Life Expectancy of the Gentry in Eighteenth and Nineteenth-Century Philadelphia." American Philosophical Society, *Proceedings,* CXXXIII (1989), 312–327.

Karsky, Barbara. "Sustenance and Sociability: Eating Habits in Eighteenth-Century America." *Revue Française d'Études Américaines,* XI (1986), 51–66.

Kay, Marvin L. Michael, and Lorin Lee Cary. "A Demographic Analysis of Colonial North Carolina with Special Emphasis upon the Slave and Black Populations." In *Black Americans in North Carolina and the South,* edited by Jeffrey J. Crow and Flora J. Hatley, 71–121. Chapel Hill, N.C., 1984.

―――. "'They Are Indeed the Constant Plague of Their Tyrants': Slave Defence of a Moral Economy in Colonial North Carolina, 1748–1772." *Slavery and Abolition,* VI (1985), 37–56.

Kellow, Margaret M. R. "Indentured Servitude in Eighteenth-Century Maryland." *Histoire Sociale / Social History,* XVII (1984), 229–255.

Kelly, Kevin. *Economic and Social Development of Seventeenth-Century Surry County, Virginia.* New York, 1989 (Ph.D. diss., University of Washington, 1972).

Kierner, Cynthia Anne. "Traders and Gentlefolk: The Livingstons of Colonial New York, 1675–1790." Ph.D. diss., University of Virginia, 1986.

Kilbourne, Lawrence J. "The Fertility Transition in New England: The Case of Hampton, New Hampshire, 1655–1840." In *Generations and Change: Genealogical Perspectives in Social History,* edited by Robert M. Taylor, Jr., and Ralph J. Crandall, 203–214. Macon, Ga., 1986.

Kiple, Kenneth F. *The Caribbean Slave: A Biological History.* New York, 1984.

Kiple, Kenneth F., and Virginia H. Kiple. "Deficiency Diseases in the Caribbean." *Journal of Interdisciplinary History*, XI (1980–1981), 197–215.

Klepp, Susan E. "Demography in Early Philadelphia, 1690–1860." American Philosophical Society, *Proceedings*, CXXXIII (1989), 85–111.

———. "Fragmented Knowledge: Questions in Regional Demographic History." American Philosophical Society, *Proceedings*, CXXXIII (1989), 223–233.

Knight, R. J. B. "New England Forests and British Seapower: Albion Revisited." *American Neptune*, XLVI (1986), 221–229.

Kross, Jessica. *The Evolution of an American Town: Newtown, New York, 1642–1775*. Philadelphia, 1983.

———. "Taxation and the Seven Years' War: A New York Test Case." *Canadian Review of American Studies*, XVIII (1987), 351–366.

Kruger, Vivienne L. "Born to Run: The Slave Family in Early New York, 1626 to 1827." Ph.D. diss., Columbia University, 1985.

Kukla, Jon. "Kentish Agues and American Distempers: The Transmission of Malaria from England to Virginia in the Seventeenth Century." *Southern Studies*, XXV (1986), 135–147.

Kulik, Gary. "Dams, Fish, and Farmers: Defense of Public Rights in Eighteenth-Century Rhode Island." In *The Countryside in the Age of Capitalist Transformation*, edited by Steven Hahn and Jonathan Prude, 25–50. Chapel Hill, N.C., 1985.

Kulikoff, Allan. "Migration and Cultural Diffusion in Early America, 1600–1860: A Review Essay." *Historical Methods*, XIX (1986), 153–169.

———. *Tobacco and Slaves: The Development of Southern Cultures in the Chesapeake, 1680–1800*. Chapel Hill, N.C., 1986.

———. "The Transition to Capitalism in Rural America." *William and Mary Quarterly*, 3d Ser., XLVI (1989), 120–144.

Landsman, Ned C. "Ethnicity and National Origin among British Settlers in the Philadelphia Region: Pennsylvania Immigration in the Wake of *Voyagers to the West*." American Philosophical Society, *Proceedings*, CXXXIII (1989), 170–174.

———. *Scotland and Its First American Colony, 1683–1760*. Princeton, N.J., 1985.

Lane, Raymond M. "The Henrietta Marie: Slave Ship." *American Visions*, I (1986), 14–20.

Larkin, Jack. " 'Labor Is the Great Thing in Farming': The Farm Laborers of the Ward Family of Shrewsbury, Massachusetts, 1787–1860." American Antiquarian Society, *Proceedings*, XCIX (1989), 189–226.

Larsen, Grace Hutchison. "Profile of a Colonial Merchant: Thomas Clifford of Pre-Revolutionary Philadelphia." Ph.D. diss., Columbia University, 1955.

Lee, Charles R. "Public Poor Relief and the Massachusetts Community, 1620–1715." *New England Quarterly*, LV (1982), 564–585.

Lee, Jean Butenhoff. "Land and Labor: Parental Bequest Practices in Charles County, Maryland, 1732–1783." In *Colonial Chesapeake Society*, edited by Lois Green Carr, Philip D. Morgan, and Jean B. Russo, 342–388. Chapel Hill, N.C., 1988.

———. "The Problem of Slave Community in the Eighteenth-Century Chesapeake." *William and Mary Quarterly*, 3d Ser., XLIII (1986), 333–361.

Lemon, James T. "Agriculture and Society in Early America." *Agricultural History Review*, XXXV (1987), 76–94.

———. "A Geographer's Perspective" (in "*Voyagers to the West*: A Review Colloquium"). *Business History Review*, LXII (1988), 691–696.

———. Letter [on Pruitt, "Self-Sufficiency"]. *William and Mary Quarterly*, 3d Ser., XLII (1985), 555–559.

Levy, Daniel S. "The Life Expectancies of Colonial Maryland Legislators." *Historical Methods*, XX (1987), 17–27.

Lewis, James Hoffman. "Farmers, Craftsmen, and Merchants: Changing Economic Organization in Massachusetts, 1730 to 1775." Ph.D. diss., Northwestern University, 1984.

Littlefield, Daniel C. "Charleston and Internal Slave Redistribution." *South Carolina Historical Magazine*, LXXXVII (1986), 93–105.

Littlefield, Douglas R. "Eighteenth-Century Plans to Clear the Potomac River: Technology, Expertise, and Labor in a Developing Nation." *Virginia Magazine of History and Biography*, XCIII (1985), 291–322.

Logue, Barbara. "The Case for Birth Control before 1850: Nantucket Reexamined." *Journal of Interdisciplinary History*, XV (1984–1985), 371–391.

———. "Demographic Change in a Maritime Community: Nantucket, Massachusetts, 1660 to 1850." Ph.D. diss., University of Pennsylvania, 1983.

———. "The Whaling Industry and Fertility Decline: Nantucket, Massachusetts, 1660–1850." *Social Science History*, VII (1983), 427–456.

Looney, Jefferson. "Social Mobility and Capital Accumulation on Proprietary Long Island." Part 1, *de Halve Maen*, LVI, no. 3 (Winter 1982), 4–6, 18; part 2, *de Halve Maen*, LVII, no. 2 (February 1983), 12–13, 18.

Lyman, Richard B., Jr. " 'What Is Done in My Absence?': Levi Lincoln's Oakham, Massachusetts, Farm Workers, 1807–1820." American Antiquarian Society, *Proceedings*, XCIX (1989), 151–187.

McAllister, J. "Colonial America, 1607–1776." *Economic History Review*, XLII (1989), 245–259.

McCarthy, Ronald Michael. "The Political Economy of Commercial Resistance in Massachusetts, 1765–1775." Ph.D. diss., Brandeis University, 1983.

McColley, Robert. "Slavery in Virginia, 1619–1660: A Reexamination." In *New Perspectives on Race and Slavery in America: Essays in Honor of Kenneth M. Stampp*, edited by Robert H. Abzug and Stephen E. Maizlish, 11–24. Lexington, Ky., 1986.

McCurdy, Linda. "The Potts Family Iron Industry in the Schuylkill Valley." Ph.D. diss., Pennsylvania State University, 1974.

McCusker, John J. "Comment" (in "Toward a History of the Standard of Living in British North America"). *William and Mary Quarterly*, 3d Ser., XLV (1988), 167–170.

———. "Growth, Stagnation, or Decline? The Economy of the British West Indies, 1763–1790." In *The Economy of Early America: The Revolutionary Period, 1763–1790*, edited by Ronald Hoffman, John J. McCusker, Russell R. Menard, and Peter J. Albert, 275–302. Charlottesville, Va., 1988.

———. Letter [on Berleant-Schiller, "Free Labor"]. *William and Mary Quarterly*, 3d Ser., XLVII (1990), 322.

———. *Rum and the American Revolution: The Rum Trade and the Balance of Payments of the Thirteen Continental Colonies*. 2 vols. New York, 1989 (Ph.D. diss., University of Pittsburgh, 1970).

———. "The View from British North America" (in "*Voyagers to the West*: A Review Colloquium"). *Business History Review*, LXII (1988), 691–696.

McCusker, John J., and Cora Gravesteijn. *The Beginnings of Commercial and Financial Journalism: The Commodity Price Currents, Exchange Rate Currents, and Money Currents of Early Modern Europe*. Nederlandsch Economisch-Historisch Archief, Series III, no. 11. Amsterdam, 1991.

McGuire, Robert A., and Robert L. Ohsfeldt. "Economic Interests and the American Constitution: A Quantitative Rehabilitation of Charles A. Beard." *Journal of Economic History*, XLIV (1984), 509–519.

———. "An Economic Model of Voting Behavior over Specific Issues at the Constitutional Convention of 1787." *Journal of Economic History*, XLVI (1986), 79–111.

Mackiewicz, Susan. "Philadelphia Flourishing: The Material World of Philadelphians, 1682–1760." Ph.D. diss., University of Delaware, 1988.

McMahon, Sarah F. "A Comfortable Subsistence: The Changing Composition of Diet in Rural New England, 1620–1840." *William and Mary Quarterly*, 3d Ser., XLII (1985), 26–65.

———. " 'A Comfortable Subsistence': A History of Diet in New England, 1630–1850." Ph.D. diss., Brandeis University, 1982.

Magnaghi, Russell M. "Red Slavery in the Great Lakes Country during the French and British Regimes." *Old Northwest*, XII (1986), 201–217.

Main, Gloria L. "American Colonial Economic History: A Review Essay." *Historical Methods*, XIX (1986), 27–31.

———. "The Standard of Living in Colonial Massachusetts." *Journal of Economic History*, XLIII (1983), 101–108.

———. "The Standard of Living in Southern New England, 1640–1773" (in "Toward a History of the Standard of Living in British North America"). *William and Mary Quarterly*, 3d Ser., XLV (1988), 124–134.

———. "Widows in Rural Massachusetts on the Eve of the Revolution." In *Women in the Age of the American Revolution*, edited by Ronald Hoffman and Peter J. Albert, 67–90. Charlottesville, Va., 1989.

Main, Gloria L., and Jackson T. Main. "Economic Growth and the Standard of Living in Southern New England, 1640–1774." *Journal of Economic History*, XLVIII (1988), 27–46.

Main, Jackson Turner. *Society and Economy in Colonial Connecticut*. Princeton, N.J., 1985.

———. "Standards of Living and the Life Cycle in Colonial Connecticut." *Journal of Economic History*, XLIII (1983), 159–165.

———. "Summary: The Hereafter" (in "Toward a History of the Standard of Living in British North America"). *William and Mary Quarterly*, 3d Ser., XLV (1988), 160–162.

Mancall, Peter Cooper. "Environment and Economy: The Upper-Susquehanna Valley in the Age of the American Revolution." Ph.D. diss., Harvard University, 1986.

———. "Independence and Interdependence in the Upper Susquehanna Valley after the American Revolution." *Locus: An Historical Journal of Regional Perspectives*, II, no. 1 (Fall 1989), 1–15.

Manges, Frances May. "Women Shopkeepers, Tavernkeepers, and Artisans in Colonial Philadelphia." Ph.D. diss., University of Pennsylvania, 1958.

Mansouri, Gail Fabricant. "Women as Laborers in Colonial North America: The Impact of Legal Rules and Relations on the Development of Capitalism." Ph.D. diss., New School for Social Research, 1985.

Marshall, Bernard. "Social Stratification and the Free Coloured in the Slave Society of the British Windward Islands." *Social and Economic Studies*, XXXI, no. 1 (March 1982), 1–39.

Marshall, Peter. "The Government of the Quebec Fur Trade: An Imperial Dilemma, 1761–1775." In *"Le Castor Fait Tout": Selected Papers of the Fifth North American Fur Trade Conference, 1985*, edited by Bruce G. Trigger, Toby Morantz, and Louise Dechêne, 122–143. Montreal, 1987.

Marshall, Peter, and Glyn Williams, eds. *The British Atlantic Empire before the American Revolution*. London, 1980.

Martin, Alfred Simpson. "The Port of Philadelphia, 1763–1776: A Biography." Ph.D. diss., State University of Iowa, 1941.

Martin, John Frederick. "Entrepreneurship and the Founding of New England Towns: The Seventeenth Century." Ph.D. diss., Harvard University, 1985.

Masur, Louis P. "Slavery in Eighteenth-Century Rhode Island: Evidence from the Census of 1774." *Slavery and Abolition*, VI (1985), 139–150.

Matson, Cathy. "Fair Trade, Free Trade: Economic Ideas and Opportunities in Eighteenth-Century New York City Commerce." Ph.D. diss., Columbia University, 1986.

Matthaei, Julie A. *An Economic History of Women in America: Women's Work, the Sexual Division of Labor, and the Development of Capitalism.* New York, 1982.

Matthews, Sara. " 'Set Thy House in Order': Inheritance Patterns of the Colonial Pennsylvania Germans." *Pennsylvania Folklife,* XXXIII (1983), 36–40.

Meinig, D. W. *The Shaping of America: A Geographical Perspective on Five Hundred Years of History.* Vol. I: *Atlantic America, 1492–1800.* New Haven, Conn., 1986.

Menard, Russell R. "The Africanization of the Lowcountry Labor Force, 1670–1730." In *Race and Family in the Colonial South,* edited by Winthrop D. Jordan and Sheila L. Skemp, 81–108. Jackson, Miss., 1987.

———. "British Migration to the Chesapeake Colonies in the Seventeenth Century." In *Colonial Chesapeake Society,* edited by Lois Green Carr, Philip D. Morgan, and Jean B. Russo, 99–132. Chapel Hill, N.C., 1988.

———. *Economy and Society in Early Colonial Maryland.* New York, 1985 (Ph.D. diss., University of Iowa, 1975).

———. "Slavery, Economic Growth, and Revolutionary Ideology in the South Carolina Lowcountry." In *The Economy of Early America: The Revolutionary Period, 1763–1790,* edited by Ronald Hoffman, John J. McCusker, Russell R. Menard, and Peter J. Albert, 244–274. Charlottesville, Va., 1988.

———. "Was There a 'Middle Colonies Demographic Regime'?" American Philosophical Society, *Proceedings,* CXXXIII (1989), 215–218.

Merchant, Carolyn. *Ecological Revolutions: Nature, Gender, and Science in New England.* Chapel Hill, N.C., 1989.

Merrell, James H. *The Indians' New World: Catawbas and Their Neighbors from European Contact through the Era of Removal.* Chapel Hill, N.C., 1989.

Merrens, H. Roy, and George D. Terry. "Dying in Paradise: Malaria, Mortality, and the Perceptual Environment in Colonial South Carolina." *Journal of Southern History,* L (1984), 533–550.

Merrill, Michael. "The Political Economy of Agrarian America." Ph.D. diss., Columbia University, 1985.

Michener, Ron. "Backing Theories and the Currencies of Eighteenth-Century America: A Comment." *Journal of Economic History,* XLVIII (1988), 682–692.

———. "Fixed Exchange Rates and the Quantity Theory in Colonial America." *Carnegie-Rochester Conference Series on Public Policy,* XXVII (1987), 233–308.

Miller, Christopher L., and George R. Hamell. "A New Perspective on Indian-White Contact: Cultural Symbols and Colonial Trade." *Journal of American History,* LXXIII (1986–1987), 311–328.

Miller, Henry M. "An Archaeological Perspective on the Evolution of Diet in the Colonial Chesapeake, 1620–1745." In *Colonial Chesapeake Society,* edited by Lois Green Carr, Philip D. Morgan, and Jean B. Russo, 176–199. Chapel Hill, N.C., 1988.

———. "Colonization and Subsistence Change on the Seventeenth-Century Chesapeake Frontier." Ph.D. diss., Michigan State University, 1984.

Miller, Randall M. "The Golden Isles: Rice and Slaves along the Georgia Coast." *Georgia Historical Quarterly,* LXX (1986), 81–96.

Minchinton, Walter E. "Characteristics of British Slaving Vessels, 1698–1775." *Journal of Interdisciplinary History,* XX (1989–1990), 53–81.

Minchinton, Walter, Celia King, and Peter Waite. *Virginia Slave-Trade Statistics, 1698–1775.* Richmond, Va., 1984.

Mintz, Sidney W. "Caribbean Marketplaces and Caribbean History." *Radical History Review,* XXVII (1983), 110–120.

———. *Sweetness and Power: The Place of Sugar in Modern History.* New York, 1985.
Monaghan, E. Jennifer. "Literacy Instruction and Gender in Colonial New England." *American Quarterly*, XL (1988), 18–41.
Moogk, Peter N. "Reluctant Exiles: Emigrants from France in Canada before 1760." *William and Mary Quarterly*, 3d Ser., XLVI (1989), 463–505.
Morgan, Kenneth. "Convict Runaways in Maryland, 1745–1775." *Journal of American Studies*, XXIII (1989), 253–268.
———. "English and American Attitudes towards Convict Transportation, 1718–1775." *History*, LXXII (1987), 416–431.
———. "The Organization of the Convict Trade to Maryland: Stevenson, Randolph & Cheston, 1768–1775." *William and Mary Quarterly*, 3d Ser., XLII (1985), 201–227.
———. "Shipping Patterns and the Atlantic Trade of Bristol, 1749–1770." *William and Mary Quarterly*, 3d Ser., XLVI (1989), 506–538.
Morgan, Philip D. "Black Life in Eighteenth-Century Charleston." *Perspectives in American History*, N.S., I (1984), 187–232.
———. "Black Society in the Lowcountry, 1760–1810." In *Slavery and Freedom in the Age of the American Revolution*, edited by Ira Berlin and Ronald Hoffman, 83–141. Charlottesville, Va., 1983.
———. "Colonial South Carolina Runaways: Their Significance for Slave Culture." *Slavery and Abolition*, VI (1985), 57–78.
———. "Slave Life in Piedmont Virginia, 1720–1800." In *Colonial Chesapeake Society*, edited by Lois Green Carr, Philip D. Morgan, and Jean B. Russo, 433–484. Chapel Hill, N.C., 1988.
———. "Task and Gang Systems: The Organization of Labor on New World Plantations." In *Work and Labor in Early America*, edited by Stephen Innes, 189–220. Chapel Hill, N.C., 1988.
———. "Three Planters and Their Slaves: Perspectives on Slavery in Virginia, South Carolina, and Jamaica, 1750–1790." In *Race and Family in the Colonial South*, edited by Winthrop D. Jordan and Sheila L. Skemp, 37–79. Jackson, Miss., 1987.
———. "Work and Culture: The Task System and the World of Lowcountry Blacks, 1700 to 1880." *William and Mary Quarterly*, 3d Ser., XXXIX (1982), 563–599.
Morgan, Philip D., and Michael L. Nicholls. "Slaves in Piedmont Virginia, 1720–1790." *William and Mary Quarterly*, 3d Ser., XLVI (1989), 211–251.
Morgan, Philip D., and George D. Terry. "Slavery in Microcosm: A Conspiracy Scare in Colonial South Carolina." *Southern Studies*, XXI (1982), 121–145.
Morgan, William S. "The Commerce of a Southern Port: New Bern, North Carolina, 1783 to 1812." *Southern History*, V (1984), 11–22.
Morris, Richard J. "Urban Population Migration in Revolutionary America: The Case of Salem, Massachusetts, 1759–1799." *Journal of Urban History*, IX (1982), 3–30.
Morrissey, Marietta. "Women's Work, Family Formation, and Reproduction among Caribbean Slaves." *Review*, IX (1985–1986), 339–367.
Moss, Richard Shannon. "Slavery on Long Island: Its Rise and Decline during the Seventeenth through Nineteenth Centuries." Ph.D. diss., St. John's University, 1985.
Munson, James Donald. "From Empire to Commonwealth: Alexandria, Virginia, 1749–1780." Ph.D. diss., University of Maryland, 1984.
Murdoch, D. H. "Land Policy in the Eighteenth-Century British Empire: The Sale of Crown Lands in the Ceded Islands, 1763–1783." *Historical Journal*, XXVII (1984), 549–574.
Narrett, David E. "Dutch Customs of Inheritance, Women, and the Law in Colonial New York City." In *Authority and Resistance in Early New York*, edited by William Pencak and Conrad Edick Wright, 27–55. New York, 1988.

———. "Men's Wills and Women's Property Rights in Colonial New York." In *Women in the Age of the American Revolution*, edited by Ronald Hoffman and Peter J. Albert, 91–133. Charlottesville, Va., 1989.

Nash, Gary B. "Artisans and Politics in Eighteenth-Century Philadelphia." In *Race, Class, and Politics: Essays on American Colonial and Revolutionary Society*, by Gary B. Nash, 243–267. Urbana, Ill., 1986.

———. "The Failure of Female Factory Labor in Colonial Boston." In *Race, Class, and Politics: Essays on American Colonial and Revolutionary Society*, by Gary B. Nash, 119–140. Urbana, Ill., 1986.

———. *Forging Freedom: The Formation of Philadelphia's Black Community, 1720–1840.* Cambridge, Mass., 1988.

Nash, Gary B., Billy G. Smith, and Dirk Hoerder. "Laboring Americans and the American Revolution" (in "Labor in the Era of the American Revolution: An Exchange"). *Labor History*, XXIV (1983), 414–439.

Nash, R. C. "English Transatlantic Trade, 1660–1730: A Quantitative Study." Ph.D. diss., University of Cambridge, 1982.

———. "Irish Atlantic Trade in the Seventeenth and Eighteenth Centuries." *William and Mary Quarterly*, 3d Ser., XLII (1985), 329–356.

Nellis, Eric G. "Misreading the Signs: Industrial Imitation, Poverty, and the Social Order in Colonial Boston." *New England Quarterly*, LIX (1986), 486–507.

———. "Work and Social Stability in Pre-Revolutionary Massachusetts." *Historical Papers / Communications Historiques*, 1981, 81–100.

———. "The Working Poor of Pre-Revolutionary Boston." *Historical Journal of Massachusetts*, XVII (1989), 137–159.

Nicholls, Michael L. "Passing through This Troublesome World: Free Blacks in the Early Southside." *Virginia Magazine of History and Biography*, XCII (1984), 50–70.

Oaks, Robert Francis. "Philadelphia Merchants and the American Revolution, 1765–1776." Ph.D. diss., University of Southern California, 1970.

Oblinger, Carl Douglas. "New Freedoms, Old Miseries: The Emergence and Disruption of Black Communities in Southeastern Pennsylvania, 1780–1860." Ph.D. diss., Lehigh University, 1988.

Olson, Alison G. "The Virginia Merchants of London: A Study in Eighteenth-Century Interest-Group Politics." *William and Mary Quarterly*, 3d Ser., XL (1983), 363–388.

O'Malley, Patricia Trainor. " 'Belovid Wife' and 'Inveigled Affections': Marriage Patterns in Early Rowley, Massachusetts." In *Generations and Change: Genealogical Perspectives in Social History*, edited by Robert M. Taylor, Jr., and Ralph J. Crandall, 181–201. Macon, Ga., 1986.

O'Mara, James. *An Historical Geography of Urban System Development: Tidewater Virginia in the Eighteenth Century.* Atkinson College, York University, Geographical Monographs, no. 13. Downsview, Ont., 1983.

Omi, Kenkichi. "Paper Money in the American Mainland Colonies" [in Japanese; English summary]. *American Review* [Japan], XX (1986), 204–219, 240–242.

Onuf, Peter S. "Liberty, Development, and Union: Visions of the West in the 1780s." *William and Mary Quarterly*, 3d Ser., XLIII (1986), 179–213.

Orser, Charles E., Jr. "The Archaeological Analysis of Plantation Society: Replacing Status and Caste with Economics and Power." *American Antiquity*, LIII (1988), 735–751.

Oshimo, Shoichi, Kozo Ikemoto, Minoru Kawakita, and Torao Tomita. "The Shaping of Anglo-America: A Symposium on Early American History." *Japanese Journal of American Studies*, II (1985), 157–172.

Otto, John Solomon. "Livestock-Raising in Early South Carolina, 1670–1700: Prelude to the Rice Plantation Economy." *Agricultural History,* LXI (1987), 13–24.

———. "The Origins of Cattle-Ranching in Colonial South Carolina, 1670–1715." *South Carolina Historical Magazine,* LXXXVII (1986), 117–124.

———. *The Southern Frontiers, 1607–1860: The Agricultural Evolution of the Colonial and Antebellum South.* New York, 1989.

Pagan, John R. "Growth of the Tobacco Trade between London and Virginia, 1614–40." *Guildhall Studies in London History,* III (1979), 248–262.

Page, Willie F. "The African Slave during the Early English Period, 1664 to 1700." *Journal of the Afro-American Historical and Genealogical Society,* V (1984), 123–132.

Palmer, Colin. *Human Cargoes: The British Slave Trade to Spanish America, 1700–1739.* Urbana, Ill., 1981.

Parent, Anthony S., Jr. "'Either a Fool or a Fury': The Emergence of Paternalism in Colonial Virginia Slave Society." Ph.D. diss., University of California, Los Angeles, 1982.

Paskoff, Paul F. *Industrial Evolution: Organization, Structure, and Growth of the Pennsylvania Iron Industry, 1750–1860.* Baltimore, 1983.

Pencak, William. "Warfare and Political Change in Mid-Eighteenth-Century Massachusetts." In *The British Atlantic Empire before the American Revolution,* edited by Peter Marshall and Glyn Williams, 51–73. London, 1980.

Piccarello, Louis J. "Social Structure and Public Welfare Policy in Danvers, Massachusetts: 1750–1850." Essex Institute, *Historical Collections,* CXVIII (1982), 248–263.

Porcher, Richard D. "Rice Culture in South Carolina: A Brief History, the Role of the Huguenots, and the Preservation of Its Legacy." Huguenot Society of South Carolina, *Transactions,* XCII (1987), 1–22.

Postma, Johannes M. *The Dutch in the Atlantic Slave Trade, 1600–1815.* New York, 1989.

Potter, Jim. "Demographic Development and Family Structure." In *Colonial British America: Essays in the New History of the Early Modern Era,* edited by Jack P. Greene and J. R. Pole, 123–156. Baltimore, 1984.

Presley, Justine A. "The Establishing of the Indian Trade in Colonial Georgia." *Richmond County History,* XVI (1984), 22–29.

Price, Jacob M. "Glasgow, the Tobacco Trade, and the Scottish Customs, 1707–1730." *Scottish Historical Review,* LXIII (1984), 1–36.

———. "The Last Phase of the Virginia-London Consignment Trade: James Buchanan & Co., 1758–1768." *William and Mary Quarterly,* 3d Ser., XLIII (1986), 64–98.

———. "One Family's Empire: The Russell-Lee-Clerk Connection in Maryland, Britain, and India, 1707–1857." *Maryland Historical Magazine,* LXXII (1977), 165–225.

———. "Reflections on the Economy of Revolutionary America." In *The Economy of Early America: The Revolutionary Period, 1763–1790,* edited by Ronald Hoffman, John J. McCusker, Russell R. Menard, and Peter J. Albert, 303–322. Charlottesville, Va., 1988.

———. "Sheffeild v. Starke: Institutional Experimentation in the London-Maryland Trade c. 1696–1706." *Business History,* XXVIII, no. 3 (July 1986), 19–39.

———. "The Transatlantic Economy." In *Colonial British America: Essays in the New History of the Early Modern Era,* edited by Jack P. Greene and J. R. Pole, 18–42. Baltimore, 1984.

———. "What Did Merchants Do? Reflections on British Overseas Trade, 1660–1790." *Journal of Economic History,* XLIX (1989), 267–284.

———, ed. *Joshua Johnson's Letterbook, 1771–1774: Letters from a Merchant in London to His Partners in Maryland.* London Record Society Publications, XV. London, 1979.

Price, Jacob M., and Paul G. E. Clemens. "A Revolution of Scale in Overseas Trade: British Firms in the Chesapeake Trade, 1675–1775." *Journal of Economic History,* XLVII (1987), 1–43.

Pruitt, Bettye Hobbs. Letter [on Pruitt, "Self-Sufficiency"]. *William and Mary Quarterly*, 3d Ser., XLII (1985), 559–562.

———. "Self-Sufficiency and the Agricultural Economy of Eighteenth-Century Massachusetts." *William and Mary Quarterly*, 3d Ser., XLI (1984), 333–364.

Puckrein, Gary A. *Little England: Plantation Society and Anglo-Barbadian Politics, 1627–1700*. New York, 1984.

Puglisi, Michael J. "'An Insupportable Burden': Paying for King Philip's War on the Massachusetts Frontier." *Historical Journal of Massachusetts*, XVI (1988), 187–203.

Purvis, Thomas L. "Disaffection along the Millstone: The Petition of Dollens Hegeman and Anti-Proprietary Sentiment in Eighteenth-Century New Jersey." *New Jersey History*, CI, no. 3/4 (Fall/Winter 1983), 60–82.

———. "Economic Diversification and Labour Utilization among the Rural Elite of the British Mid-Atlantic Colonies: A Case Study from the Delaware Valley." *Histoire Sociale / Social History*, XIX (1986), 57–71.

———. "The National Origins of New Yorkers in 1790." *New York History*, LXVII (1986), 133–153.

———. "Origins and Patterns of Agrarian Unrest in New Jersey, 1735 to 1754." *William and Mary Quarterly*, 3d Ser., XXXIX (1982), 600–627.

———. *Proprietors, Patronage, and Paper Money: Legislative Politics in New Jersey, 1703–1776*. New Brunswick, N.J., 1986.

Ragsdale, Bruce A. "George Washington, the British Tobacco Trade, and Economic Opportunity in Prerevolutionary Virginia." *Virginia Magazine of History and Biography*, XCVII (1989), 133–162.

Rea, Robert R. "British West Florida Trade and Commerce in the Customs Records." *Alabama Review*, XXXVII (1984), 124–159.

Reddock, Rhoda E. "Women and Slavery in the Caribbean: A Feminist Perspective." *Latin American Perspectives*, XII, no. 1 (Winter 1985), 63–80.

Rediker, Marcus. "The Anglo-American Seaman as Collective Worker, 1700–1750." In *Work and Labor in Early America*, edited by Stephen Innes, 252–286. Chapel Hill, N.C., 1988.

———. *Between the Devil and the Deep Blue Sea: Merchant Seamen, Pirates, and the Anglo-American Maritime World, 1700–1750*. New York, 1987.

———. "'Good Hands, Stout Hearts, and Fast Feet': The History and Culture of Working People in Early America." *Labour / Le Travailleur*, X (1982), 123–144.

Reid, Gerald Frank. "Dependence to Development: A World Systems Analysis of Elite Formation in Greenfield, Massachusetts: 1770s to 1840s." Ph.D. diss., University of Massachusets, 1987.

Reynolds, Edward. *Stand the Storm: A History of the Atlantic Slave Trade*. London, 1985.

Richardson, David. "The Costs of Survival: The Transport of Slaves in the Middle Passage and the Profitability of the Eighteenth-Century British Slave Trade." *Explorations in Economic History*, 2d Ser., XXIV (1987), 178–196.

———. "The Slave Trade, Sugar, and British Economic Growth, 1748–1776." *Journal of Interdisciplinary History*, XVII (1986–1987), 739–769.

Riesman, Janet Ann. "The Origins of American Political Economy, 1690–1781." Ph.D. diss., Brown University, 1983.

Rink, Oliver A. *Holland on the Hudson: An Economic and Social History of Dutch New York*. Ithaca, N.Y., 1986.

———. "The People of New Netherland: Notes on Non-English Immigration to New York in the Seventeenth Century." *New York History*, LXII (1981), 5–42.

Robinson, W. Stitt. "Conflicting Views on Landholding: Lord Baltimore and the Experiences of Colonial Maryland with Native Americans." *Maryland Historical Magazine*, LXXXIII (1988), 85–97.

Roeber, A. G. "The Origins and Transfer of German-American Concepts of Property and Inheritance." *Perspectives in American History*, N.S., III (1987), 115–171.

Rossano, Geoffrey L. "Down to the Bay: New York Shippers and the Central American Logwood Trade, 1748–1761." *New York History*, LXX (1989), 229–250.

——— . "Launching Prosperity: Samuel Townsend and the Maritime Trade of Colonial Long Island, 1747–1773." *American Neptune*, XLVIII (1988), 31–43.

Rothenberg, Winifred B. "The Emergence of a Capital Market in Rural Massachusetts, 1730–1838." *Journal of Economic History*, XLV (1985), 781–808.

——— . "Farm Account Books: Problems and Possibilities." *Agricultural History*, LVIII (1984), 106–112.

——— . "The Market and Massachusetts Farmers: Reply." *Journal of Economic History*, XLIII (1983), 479–480.

——— . "Markets and Massachusetts Farmers: A Paradigm of Economic Growth in Rural New England, 1750–1855." Ph.D. diss., Brandeis University, 1985.

——— . "Markets, Values, and Capitalism: A Discourse on Method." *Journal of Economic History*, XLIV (1984), 174–178.

Rozbicki, Michal J. "Tobacco Economy and Cultural Change in Seventeenth-Century America." *American Studies* [Poland], V (1985), 33–49.

Russo, Jean Burrell. "Free Workers in a Plantation Economy: Talbot County, Maryland, 1690–1759." Ph.D. diss., Johns Hopkins University, 1983.

——— . "Self-sufficiency and Local Exchange: Free Craftsmen in the Rural Chesapeake Economy." In *Colonial Chesapeake Society*, edited by Lois Green Carr, Philip D. Morgan, and Jean B. Russo, 389–432. Chapel Hill, N.C., 1988.

Rutman, Anita H. "Still Planting the Seeds of Hope: The Recent Literature of the Early Chesapeake Region." *Virginia Magazine of History and Biography*, XCV (1987), 3–24.

Rutman, Darrett B. "Assessing the Little Communities of Early America." *William and Mary Quarterly*, 3d Ser., XLIII (1986), 163–178.

Rutman, Darrett B., and Anita H. Rutman. *A Place in Time*. Vol. I: *Middlesex County, Virginia, 1650–1750*; vol. II: *Explicatus*. New York, 1984.

Salinger, Sharon V. " 'Send No More Women': Female Servants in Eighteenth-Century Philadelphia." *Pennsylvania Magazine of History and Biography*, CVII (1983), 29–48.

——— . *"To Serve Well and Faithfully": Labor and Indentured Servants in Pennsylvania, 1682–1800*. New York, 1987.

Salinger, Sharon V., and Charles Wetherell. "A Note on the Population of Pre-Revolutionary Philadelphia." *Pennsylvania Magazine of History and Biography*, CIX (1985), 369–386.

——— . "Wealth and Renting in Prerevolutionary Philadelphia." *Journal of American History*, LXXI (1984–1985), 826–840.

Salisbury, Neal. *Manitou and Providence: Indians, Europeans, and the Making of New England, 1500–1643*. New York, 1982.

Salmon, John S. "Ironworks on the Frontier: Virginia's Iron Industry, 1607–1783." *Virginia Cavalcade*, XXXV (1986), 184–191.

——— . *The Washington Iron Works of Franklin County, Virginia, 1733–1850*. Richmond, Va., 1986.

Salmon, Marylynn. "The Legal Status of Women in Early America: A Reappraisal." *Law and History Review*, I (1983), 129–151.

——— . "Republican Sentiment, Economic Change, and the Property Rights of Women in American Law." In *Women in the Age of the American Revolution*, edited by Ronald

Hoffman and Peter J. Albert, 447–475. Charlottesville, Va., 1989.

——— . *Women and the Law of Property in Early America*. Chapel Hill, N.C., 1986.

Schaeffer, Robert Keith. "The Chains of Bondage Broke: The Proletarianization of Sea-faring Labor, 1600–1800." Ph.D. diss., State University of New York, Binghamton, 1984.

Schafer, Daniel L. "Early Plantation Development in British East Florida." *Escribano*, XIX (1982), 37–53.

——— . "Plantation Development in British East Florida: A Case Study of the Earl of Egmont." *Florida Historical Quarterly*, LXIII (1984), 172–183.

Schweitzer, Mary M. *Custom and Contract: Household, Government, and the Economy in Colonial Pennsylvania*. New York, 1987.

——— . "A New Look at Economic Causes of the Constitution: Monetary and Trade Policy in Maryland, Pennsylvania, and Virginia." *Social Science Journal*, XXVI (1989), 15–26.

——— . "State-Issued Currency and the Ratification of the U.S. Constitution." *Journal of Economic History*, XLIX (1989), 311–322.

Shammas, Carole. "Black Women's Work and the Evolution of Plantation Society in Virginia." *Labor History*, XXVI (1985), 5–28.

——— . "Early American Women and Control over Capital." In *Women in the Age of the American Revolution*, edited by Ronald Hoffman and Peter J. Albert, 134–154. Charlottesville, Va., 1989.

——— . "English Inheritance Law and Its Transfer to the Colonies." *American Journal of Legal History*, XXXI (1987), 145–163.

Shammas, Carole, Marylynn Salmon, and Michel Dahlin. *Inheritance in America: From Colonial Times to the Present*. New Brunswick, N.J., 1987.

Shatzman, Aaron Mark. "Servants into Planters, the Origins of an American Image: Land Acquisition and Status Mobility in Seventeenth Century South Carolina." Ph.D. diss., Stanford University, 1981.

Sheller, Tina H. "Artisans, Manufacturing, and the Rise of a Manufacturing Interest in Revolutionary Baltimore Town." *Maryland Historical Magazine*, LXXXIII (1988), 3–17.

Shepherd, James A. "British America and the Atlantic Economy." In *The Economy of Early America: The Revolutionary Period, 1763–1790*, edited by Ronald Hoffman, John J. McCusker, Russell R. Menard, and Peter J. Albert, 3–44. Charlottesville, Va., 1988.

Sheridan, Richard B. *Doctors and Slaves: A Medical and Demographic History of Slavery in the British West Indies, 1680–1834*. New York, 1985.

——— . "The Domestic Economy." In *Colonial British America: Essays in the New History of the Early Modern Era*, edited by Jack P. Greene and J. R. Pole, 43–85. Baltimore, 1984.

Shirai, Yoko. "The Indian Trade in Colonial Pennsylvania, 1730–1768: Traders and Land Speculation." Ph.D. diss., University of Pennsylvania, 1985.

Shomette, Donald G. *Pirates on the Chesapeake: Being a True History of Pirates, Picaroons, and Sea Raiders on Chesapeake Bay, 1610–1807*. Centerville, Va., 1985.

Siener, William H. "Charles Yates, the Grain Trade, and Economic Development in Fred-ericksburg, Virginia, 1750–1810." *Virginia Magazine of History and Biography*, XCIII (1985), 409–426.

——— . "Economic Development in Revolutionary Virginia: Fredericksburg, 1750–1810." Ph.D. diss., College of William and Mary, 1982.

Simler, Lucy. "Tenancy in Colonial Pennsylvania: The Case of Chester County." *William and Mary Quarterly*, 3d Ser., XLIII (1986), 542–569.

Simler, Lucy, and Paul G. E. Clemens. "The 'Best Poor Man's Country' in 1783: The Popu-lation Structure of Rural Society in Late-Eighteenth-Century Southeastern Pennsylvania." *American Philosophical Society, Proceedings*, CXXXIII (1989), 234–261.

Skaggs, David Curtis. "John Semple and the Development of the Potomac Valley, 1750–1773." *Virginia Magazine of History and Biography*, XCII (1984), 282–308.

Slaughter, Thomas P. "The Tax Man Cometh: Ideological Opposition to Internal Taxes, 1760–1790." *William and Mary Quarterly*, 3d Ser., XLI (1984), 566–591.

Sloan, William Neville. "A New Direction for the Anthropological Study of Social Change and Economic Development: A Case Study of Vermont, 1535–1870." Ph.D. diss., McGill University, 1982.

Smith, Barbara Clark. "The Politics of Price Control in Revolutionary Massachusetts, 1774–1780." Ph.D. diss., Yale University, 1983.

Smith, Billy G. "Comment" (in "Toward a History of the Standard of Living in British North America"). *William and Mary Quarterly*, 3d Ser., XLV (1988), 163–166.

―――. "The Family Lives of Laboring Philadelphians during the Late Eighteenth Century." American Philosophical Society, *Proceedings*, CXXXIII (1989), 328–332.

―――. "Inequality in Late Colonial Philadelphia: A Note on Its Nature and Growth." *William and Mary Quarterly*, 3d Ser., XLI (1984), 629–645.

―――. "Poverty and Economic Marginality in Eighteenth-Century America." American Philosophical Society, *Proceedings*, CXXXII (1988), 85–118.

―――. "The Vicissitudes of Fortune: The Careers of Laboring Men in Philadelphia, 1750–1800." In *Work and Labor in Early America*, edited by Stephen Innes, 221–251. Chapel Hill, N.C., 1988.

Smith, Bruce D. "American Colonial Monetary Regimes: The Failure of the Quantity Theory and Some Evidence in Favour of an Alternative View." *Canadian Journal of Economics*, XVIII (1985), 531–565.

―――. "Money and Inflation in Colonial Massachusetts." Federal Reserve Bank of Minneapolis, *Quarterly Review*, VIII, no. 1 (Winter 1984), 1–14.

―――. "Some Colonial Evidence on Two Theories of Money: Maryland and the Carolinas." *Journal of Political Economy*, XCIII (1985), 1178–1211.

Smith, Daniel Blake. "In Search of the Family in the Colonial South." In *Race and Family in the Colonial South*, edited by Winthrop D. Jordan and Sheila L. Skemp, 21–36. Jackson, Miss., 1987.

Smith, Daniel Scott. "Child-Naming Practices, Kinship Ties, and Change in Family Attitudes in Hingham, Massachusetts, 1641 to 1880." *Journal of Social History*, XVIII (1985), 541–566.

―――. "Inheritance and the Social History of Early American Women." In *Women in the Age of the American Revolution*, edited by Ronald Hoffman and Peter J. Albert, 45–66. Charlottesville, Va., 1989.

―――. "Notes on the Measurement of Values." *Journal of Economic History*, XLV (1985), 213–218.

Smith, David A. "Dependent Urbanization in Colonial America: The Case of Charleston, South Carolina." *Social Forces*, LXVI (1987), 1–27.

Smith, Julia Floyd. *Slavery and Rice Culture in Low Country Georgia, 1750–1860.* Knoxville, Tenn., 1985.

Smith, Philip Chadwick Foster. "The Privateering Impulse of the American Revolution." Essex Institute, *Historical Collections*, CXIX (1983), 49–62.

Snapp, James Russell. "Exploitation and Control: The Southern Frontier in Anglo-American Politics in the Era of the American Revolution." Ph.D. diss., Harvard University, 1988.

Snow, Dean R., and Kim M. Lanphear. "European Contact and Indian Depopulation in the Northeast: The Timing of the First Epidemics." *Ethnohistory*, XXXV (1988), 15–33.

———. " 'More Methodological Perspectives': A Rejoinder to Dobyns." *Ethnohistory*, XXXVI (1989), 299–304.

Snow, Dean R., and William A. Starna. "Sixteenth-Century Depopulation: A View from the Mohawk Valley." *American Anthropologist*, XCI (1989), 142–149.

Snydacker, Daniel. "Traders in Exile: Quakers and Jews of New York and Newport in the New World Economy, 1650–1776." Ph.D. diss., Johns Hopkins University, 1982.

Soderlund, Jean R. "Black Importation and Migration into Southeastern Pennsylvania, 1682–1810." American Philosophical Society, *Proceedings*, CXXXIII (1989), 144–153.

———. *Quakers and Slavery: A Divided Spirit*. Princeton, N.J., 1985.

Solow, Barbara L., and Stanley L. Engerman, eds. *British Capitalism and Caribbean Slavery: The Legacy of Eric Williams*. New York, 1987.

Soltow, James H. "Thomas Riche's 'Adventure' in French Guiana, 1764–1766." *Pennsylvania Magazine of History and Biography*, LXXXIII (1959), 409–419.

Speth, Linda E. "More Than Her 'Thirds': Wives and Widows in Colonial Virginia." *Women and History*, IV (1982), 5–41.

Springer, James Warren. "American Indians and the Law of Real Property in Colonial New England." *American Journal of Legal History*, XXX (1986), 25–58.

Stakeman, Randolph. "Slavery in Colonial Maine." *Maine Historical Society Quarterly*, XXVII (1987), 58–81.

Statom, Thomas Ralph, Jr. "Negro Slavery in Eighteenth-Century Georgia." Ph.D. diss., University of Alabama, 1982.

Steckel, Richard H., and Richard A. Jensen. "New Evidence on the Causes of Slave and Crew Mortality in the Atlantic Slave Trade." *Journal of Economic History*, XLVI (1986), 57–77.

Steele, Ian K. *The English Atlantic, 1675–1740: An Exploration of Communication and Community*. New York, 1986.

Steffen, Charles. "Gentry and Bourgeois: Patterns of Merchant Investment in Baltimore County, Maryland, 1658 to 1776." *Journal of Social History*, XX (1987), 531–548.

———. *The Mechanics of Baltimore: Workers and Politics in the Age of Revolution, 1763–1812*. Urbana, Ill., 1984.

———. "The Rise of the Independent Merchant in the Chesapeake: Baltimore County, 1660–1769." *Journal of American History*, LXXVI (1989–1990), 9–33.

Stewart, Larry. "The Edge of Utility: Slaves and Smallpox in the Early Eighteenth Century." *Medical History*, XXIX (1985), 54–70.

Stiverson, Cynthia Z., and Gregory A. Stiverson. "The Colonial Retail Book Trade: Availability and Affordability of Reading Material in Mid-Eighteenth-Century Virginia." In *Printing and Society in Early America*, edited by William L. Joyce, David D. Hall, Richard D. Brown, and John B. Hench, 132–173. Worcester, Mass., 1983.

Stone, Garry Wheeler. "Manorial Maryland." *Maryland Historical Magazine*, LXXXII (1987), 3–36.

Stumpf, Stuart O. "A Case of Arrested Development: Charles Town's Commercial Life, 1670–1690." *Southern Studies*, XX (1981), 361–377.

———. "South Carolina Importers of General Merchandise, 1735–1765." *South Carolina Historical Magazine*, LXXXIV (1983), 1–10.

Stumpf, Stuart, and Jennings B. Marshall. "Trends in Charleston's Inter-Regional Import Trade, 1735–1764." *Southern Studies*, XXIII (1984), 243–265.

Swanson, Carl E. "American Privateering and Imperial Warfare, 1739–1748." *William and Mary Quarterly*, 3d Ser., XLII (1985), 357–382.

———. "The Competition for American Seamen during the War of 1739–1748." In *Man and Nature: Proceedings of the Canadian Society for Eighteenth-Century Studies,* 119–129. London, Ont., 1982.

———. "Predators and Prizes: Privateering in the British Colonies during the War of 1739–1748." Ph.D. diss., University of Western Ontario, 1979.

Sweig, Donald M. "The Importation of African Slaves to the Potomac River, 1732–1772." *William and Mary Quarterly,* 3d Ser., XLII (1985), 507–524.

———. "Northern Virginia Slavery: A Statistical and Demographic Investigation." Ph.D. diss., College of William and Mary, 1982.

Syrett, David. "The Navy Board and Merchant Shipowners during the American War, 1776–1783." *American Neptune,* XLVII (1987), 5–13.

Tanner, Helen Hornbeck, *et al.,* eds. *Atlas of Great Lakes Indian History.* Norman, Okla., 1987.

Taylor, Robert M., Jr., and Ralph J. Crandall. *Generations and Change: Genealogical Perspectives in Social History.* Macon, Ga., 1986.

Tebbenhoff, Edward H. "Tacit Rules and Hidden Structures: Naming Practices and God-parentage in Schenectady, New York, 1680–1800." *Journal of Social History,* XVIII (1985), 567–585.

Thistlethwaite, Frank. *Dorset Pilgrims: The Story of West Country Pilgrims Who Went to New England in the Seventeenth Century.* London, 1989.

Thomas, Peter A. "The Fur Trade, Indian Land, and the Need to Define Adequate 'Environmental' Parameters." *Ethnohistory,* XXVIII (1981), 359–379.

Thomas, Peter D. G. "The Cost of the British Army in North America, 1763–1775." *William and Mary Quarterly,* 3d Ser., XLV (1988), 510–516.

Thompson, Thomas C. "The Life Course and Labor of a Colonial Farmer." *Historical New Hampshire,* XL (1985), 135–155.

Thompson, Tommy R. "Marylanders, Personal Indebtedness, and the American Revolution." Ph.D. diss., University of Maryland, 1972.

Thornton, Russell. *American Indian Holocaust and Survival: A Population History since 1492.* Norman, Okla., 1987.

Tracy, Patricia J. "Re-Considering Migration within Colonial New England." *Journal of Social History,* XXIII (1989), 93–113.

Treckel, Paula A. "Breastfeeding and Maternal Sexuality in Colonial America." *Journal of Interdisciplinary History,* XX (1989–1990), 25–51.

Trigger, Bruce G., Toby Morantz, and Louise Dechêne, eds. *"Le Castor Fait Tout": Selected Papers of the Fifth North American Fur Trade Conference, 1985.* Montreal, 1987.

Truxes, Thomas M. *Irish-American Trade, 1660–1783.* New York, 1988.

Turgeon, Laurier, and Evelyne Picot-Bermond. "Pêcheurs basques et la traite de la fourrure dans le Saint-Laurent au XVIe siècle." In *"Le Castor Fait Tout": Selected Papers of the Fifth North American Fur Trade Conference, 1985,* edited by Bruce G. Trigger, Toby Morantz, and Louise Dechêne, 14–24. Montreal, 1987.

Tyack, Norman C. P. "English Exports to New England, 1632–1640: Some Records in the Port Books." *New England Historical and Genealogical Register,* CXXXV (1981), 213–238.

Tyler, John W. *Smugglers and Patriots: Boston Merchants and the Advent of the American Revolution.* Boston, 1986.

Ulrich, Laurel Thatcher. "Housewife and Gadder: Themes of Self-sufficiency and Community in Eighteenth-Century New England." In *"To Toil the Livelong Day": America's Women at Work, 1780–1980,* edited by Carol Groneman and Mary Beth Norton, 21–34. Ithaca, N.Y., 1987.

———. "Martha Ballard and Her Girls: Women's Work in Eighteenth-Century Maine."

In *Work and Labor in Early America*, edited by Stephen Innes, 70–105. Chapel Hill, N.C., 1988.

Usner, Daniel H., Jr. "Food Marketing and Interethnic Exchange in the Eighteenth-Century Lower Mississippi Valley." *Food and Foodways*, I (1986), 279–310.

———. "The Frontier Exchange Economy of the Lower Mississippi Valley in the Eighteenth Century." *William and Mary Quarterly*, 3d Ser., XLIV (1987), 165–192.

Vickers, Daniel. "The First Whalemen of Nantucket." *William and Mary Quarterly*, 3d Ser., XL (1983), 560–583.

———. "'A Knowen and Staple Commoditie': Codfish Prices in Essex County, Massachusetts, 1640–1775." Essex Institute, *Historical Collections*, CXXIV (1988), 186–203.

———. Letter [on Pruitt, "Self-Sufficiency"]. *William and Mary Quarterly*, 3d Ser., XLII (1985), 553–555.

———. "Nantucket Whalemen in the Deep-Sea Fishery: The Changing Anatomy of an Early American Labor Force." *Journal of American History*, LXII (1985–1986), 277–296.

———. "Work and Life on the Fishing Periphery of Essex County, Massachusetts, 1630–1675." In *Seventeenth-Century New England*, edited by David D. Hall and David Grayson Allen, 83–117. Publications of the Colonial Society of Massachusetts, Collections, LXIII. Boston, 1984.

———. "Working the Fields in a Developing Economy: Essex County, Massachusetts, 1630–1675." In *Work and Labor in Early America*, edited by Stephen Innes, 49–69. Chapel Hill, N.C., 1988.

Villaflor, Georgia C., and Kenneth L. Sokoloff. "Migration in Colonial America: Evidence from the Militia Muster Rolls." *Social Science History*, VI (1982), 539–570.

Waciega, Lisa Wilson. "A 'Man of Business': The Widow of Means in Southeastern Pennsylvania, 1750–1850." *William and Mary Quarterly*, 3d Ser., XLIV (1987), 40–64.

Walsh, Lorena S. "Community Networks in the Early Chesapeake." In *Colonial Chesapeake Society*, edited by Lois Green Carr, Philip D. Morgan, and Jean B. Russo, 200–241. Chapel Hill, N.C., 1988.

———. "Land, Landlord, and Leaseholder: Estate Management and Tenant Fortunes in Southern Maryland, 1642–1820." *Agricultural History*, LIX (1985), 373–396.

———. "Plantation Management in the Chesapeake, 1620–1820." *Journal of Economic History*, XLIX (1989), 393–406.

———. "Questions and Sources for Exploring the Standard of Living" (in "Toward a History of the Standard of Living in British North America"). *William and Mary Quarterly*, 3d Ser., XLV (1988), 116–123.

———. "Staying Put or Getting Out: Findings for Charles County, Maryland, 1650–1720." *William and Mary Quarterly*, 3d Ser., XLIV (1987), 89–103.

———. "Urban Amenities and Rural Sufficiency: Living Standards and Consumer Behavior in the Colonial Chesapeake, 1643–1777." *Journal of Economic History*, XLIII (1983), 109–117.

Ward, Barbara McLean. "The Craftsman in a Changing Society: Boston Goldsmiths, 1690–1730." Ph.D. diss., Boston University, 1983.

Ward, Gerald W. R. "Silver and Society in Salem, Massachusetts, 1630–1820: A Case Study of the Consumer and the Craft." Ph.D. diss., Boston University, 1984.

Waterhouse, Richard. "The Development of Elite Culture in the Colonial American South: A Study of Charles Town, 1679–1770." *Australian Journal of Politics and History*, XXVIII (1982), 391–404.

Waters, John J. "Naming and Kinship in New England: Guilford Patterns and Usage, 1693–1759." *New England Historical and Genealogical Register*, CXXXVIII (1984), 161–181.

Watson, Alan D. "North Carolina Slave Courts, 1715–1785." *North Carolina Historical Review*, LX (1983), 24–36.

Wax, Darold D. "Africans on the Delaware: The Pennsylvania Slave Trade, 1759–1765." *Pennsylvania History*, L (1983), 38–49.

———. " 'New Negroes Are Always in Demand': The Slave Trade in Eighteenth-Century Georgia." *Georgia Historical Quarterly*, LXVIII (1984), 193–220.

Weiss, Rona Stephanie. "The Development of the Market Economy in Colonial Massachusetts." Ph.D. diss., University of Massachusetts, 1981.

———. "The Market and Massachusetts Farmers, 1750–1850: Comment." *Journal of Economic History*, XLIII (1983), 475–478.

———. "Primitive Accumulation in the United States: The Interaction between Capitalist and Noncapitalist Class Relations in Seventeenth-Century Massachusetts." *Journal of Economic History*, XLII (1982), 77–82.

Welch, William L. "The Massachusetts Land Lottery of 1786–87." *Historical Journal of Massachusetts*, XIV (1986), 103–113.

Wellenreuther, Hermann. "Rejoinder [to Gary B. Nash, Billy G. Smith, and Dirk Hoerder]" (in "Labor in the Era of the American Revolution: An Exchange"). *Labor History*, XXIV (1983), 440–454.

Wells, Robert V. "The Demography of a Region: Historical Reality or Historian's Creation?" American Philosophical Society, *Proceedings*, CXXXIII (1989), 219–222.

———. "Marriage Seasonals in Early America: Comparisons and Comments." *Journal of Interdisciplinary History*, XVIII (1987–1988), 299–307.

———. *Uncle Sam's Family: Issues in and Perspectives on American Demographic History.* Albany, N.Y., 1985.

Weslager, C. A. "The City of Amsterdam's Colony on the Delaware, 1656–1664; With Unpublished Dutch Notarial Abstracts." Translations by Sytha Hart. *Delaware History*, XX (1982), 1–26.

Westbury, Susan. "Slaves of Colonial Virginia: Where They Came From." *William and Mary Quarterly*, 3d Ser., XLII (1985), 228–237.

Wetherell, Charles. " 'Boom and Bust' in the Colonial Chesapeake Economy." *Journal of Interdisciplinary History*, XV (1984–1985), 185–210.

Wicker, Elmus. "Colonial Monetary Standards Contrasted: Evidence from the Seven Years' War." *Journal of Economic History*, XLV (1985), 869–884.

Wilkinson, Norman B. "Land Policy and Speculation in Pennsylvania, 1779–1800." Ph.D. diss., University of Pennsylvania, 1958.

Williams-Meyers, A. J. "The African Presence in the Hudson River Valley: The Defining of Relationships between the Masters and the Slaves." *Afro-Americans in New York Life and History*, XII (1988), 81–98.

Wilson, Bruce. *The Enterprises of Robert Hamilton: A Study of Wealth and Influence in Early Upper Canada, 1776–1812.* Ottawa, 1983.

Windley, Lathan A., comp. *Runaway Slave Advertisements: A Documentary History from the 1730s to 1790.* Vol. I: *Virginia and North Carolina*; vol. II: *Maryland*; vol. III: *South Carolina*; vol. IV: *Georgia*. Westport, Conn., 1983.

Withey, Lynne. *Urban Growth in Colonial Rhode Island: Newport and Providence in the Eighteenth Century.* Albany, N.Y., 1984.

Witkowski, Terrence H. "Colonial Consumers in Revolt: Buyer Values and Behavior during the Nonimportation Movement, 1764–1776." *Journal of Consumer Research*, XVI (1989–1990), 216–226.

Wokeck, Marianne S. "German and Irish Immigration to Colonial Philadelphia." American Philosophical Society, *Proceedings*, CXXXIII (1989), 128–143.

————. "Promoters and Passengers: The German Immigrant Trade, 1683–1775." In *The World of William Penn*, edited by Richard S. Dunn and Mary Maples Dunn, 259–278. Philadelphia, 1986.

Wood, Betty. *Slavery in Colonial Georgia, 1730–1775*. Athens, Ga., 1984.

Wood, J. S. "Elaboration of a Settlement System: The New England Village in the Federal Period." *Journal of Historical Geography*, X (1984), 331–356.

Wood, Peter H. "The Changing Population of the Colonial South: An Overview by Race and Region, 1685–1790." In *Powhatan's Mantle: Indians in the Colonial Southeast*, edited by Peter H. Wood, Gregory A. Waselkov, and M. Thomas Hatley, 35–103. Lincoln, Nebr., 1989.

Worcester, Donald E., and Thomas F. Schilz. "The Spread of Firearms among the Indians on the Anglo-French Frontiers." *American Indian Quarterly*, VIII (1984), 103–115.

Wright, Gavin. "Capitalism and Slavery on the Islands: A Lesson from the Mainland." *Journal of Interdisciplinary History*, XVII (1986–1987), 851–870.

Wrigley, E. A. "The British Scene" (in "*Voyagers to the West*: A Review Colloquium"). *Business History Review*, LXII (1988), 678–683.

York, Neil Longley. *Mechanical Metamorphosis: Technological Change in Revolutionary America*. Westport, Conn., 1985.

Yosihmasta, Asaba. "Public Land Bank in Massachusetts" [in Japanese]. *Keizai Kenkyu*, XXXI (1986), 103–148.

Youings, Joyce, ed. *Raleigh in Exeter, 1985: Privateering and Colonization in the Reign of Elizabeth I*. Exeter Studies in History, No. 10. Exeter, 1985.

Zahedieh, Nuala. "The Merchants of Port Royal, Jamaica, and the Spanish Contraband Trade, 1655–1692." *William and Mary Quarterly*, 3d Ser., XLIII (1986), 570–593.

————. "Trade, Plunder, and Economic Development in Early English Jamaica, 1655–89." *Economic History Review*, 2d Ser., XXXIX (1986), 205–222.

INDEX

Absenteeism: in British West Indies, 154–
155, 162, 167, 344; in Lower South,
183–184, 186
Acadia, 111, 113
Account books, 302
Accounting, 344–346
Adams, John, 337
Africa, 7, 8, 42, 134, 241; and slave trade,
41n, 79, 137, 166, 232, 233, 240; trade
of, with British America, 82, with Lower
South, 174, 180, with Middle Colonies,
199, with New England, 107, 108. See
also Slave trade
Afro-Americans: in Barbados, 153; in British America, 53–54, 219, 221–222, 235;
in Lower South, 172, 181–182, 219,
221–222, 230, 282; in Middle Colonies,
203, 219, 221–222, 229; in New England, 103, 219, 221–222, 226; in Philadelphia, 206–207; in Upper South, 136,
219, 221–222, 228, 282; in West Indies,
146, 154, 219, 221–222, 230–231. See
also Africa; Slavery; Slaves; Slave trade
Age: and wealth levels, 263, 272, 274–275
Agriculture, 12, 32, 33, 34, 69, 295, 296,
297–308, 309, 310, 314; and American
Revolution, 357, 362; and British economic growth, 43; in colonies, 22–23;
investment in, 257n; in Lower South,
184, 187, 188; in metropolis, 21; in
Middle Colonies, 189, 201, 206–207;
and migration, 254; in New England,
92, 93, 96, 104–106, 110, 246; in New
York, 192n; productivity gains in, 43,
178, 249, 266–267, 269, 270, 326; seasonal labor in, 238, 239, 297; in 1780s,
370; threatened by British policy, 356;
wages in, 247; and wealth distribution,
274–275; work force in, 248. See also
Farmers; Farms; Plantations; Planters
Albany, N.Y., 313

Albemarle Sound, 87, 170. See also North
Carolina
Alexandria, Va., 197
Almanacs, 307n
America, 7, 8, 42, 241. See also British
America; British North America; Latin
America
American Revolution, 12–13, 49; and cit-
ies, 250; and economy, 51, 351–358,
360–367; and English manufacturers,
286; historiography of, 351n, 353–354;
in Lower South, 184; and merchants,
190, 198, 251; and Navigation Acts,
353–354; neglected by economic histori-
ans, 358–360; in New England, 93; in
Upper South, 139; as watershed in
American history, 358
Amin, Samir, 42
Amsterdam, 77, 191
Anderson, Terry, 216, 265, 266
Anglo-Dutch wars, 46, 65
Annapolis, Md., 131
Antigua, 165, 314. See also West Indies,
British
Apprenticeship, 244, 329. See also Labor
Archaeology: and boatbuilding, 319n; and
coins, 339n; and pottery industry, 330n;
and standard of living, 287
Architecture, 315, 316
Artisans: and fishing industry, 312; as
manufacturers, 327, 329–330; and
Revolutionary War, 364. See also By-
employments; Labor
Ashley River, 171
Ashton, Thomas S., 61, 62, 63
Asia, 40, 42
Atlantic Canada: defined, 111; exports of,
115; and New England economy, 114;
population in, 111–112, 113n, 217, 218.
See also British America; Canada; New-
foundland; Nova Scotia; Quebec

Printed in the United States
73853LV00003B/17